The
SCHOMBURG CENTER
Guide to
Black
Literature

The
SCHOMBURG CENTER
Guide to
Black
Literature

From the
Eighteenth
Century to
the Present

Roger M. Valade III,
Editor
with Denise Kasinec

Gale Research

An ITP Information/Reference Group Company

I(T)P

Changing the Way the World Learns

NEW YORK • LONDON • BONN • BOSTON • DETROIT
MADRID • MELBOURNE • MEXICO CITY • PARIS
SINGAPORE • TOKYO • TORONTO • WASHINGTON
ALBANY NY • BELMONT CA • CINCINNATI OH

STAFF

Roger M. Valade III, *Editor*, with Denise Kasinec
Daniel G. Marowski, *Senior Editor*
Dana Ramel Barnes, Catherine C. Dominic, and Mary L. Onorato, *Associate Editors*
Matthew C. Altman, Gerald R. Barterian, and Ondine LeBlanc, *Assistant Editors*
James E. Person Jr., *Contributing Editor*

Susan M. Trosky, *Managing Editor*

Cynthia Baldwin, *Product Design Manager*; Pamela A. E. Galbreath, *Art Director*

Pamela A. Hayes, *Photography Coordinator*; Willie Mathis, *Camera Operator*

Marlene S. Hurst, *Permissions Manager*
Arlene Johnson and Kimberly F. Smilay, *Permissions Associates*

Victoria B. Cariappa, *Research Manager*
Barbara McNeil, *Research Specialist*
Maria Bryson, Tamara C. Nott, and Michele P. Pica, *Research Associates*
Alicia Noel Biggers, Julia C. Daniel, and Amy Beth Wieczorek, *Research Assistants*

Mary Beth Trimper, *Production Director*; Shanna Philpott Heilveil, *Production Assistant*

Library of Congress Cataloging-in-Publication Data will be found on page 545

 This book is printed on acid-free paper that meets the minimum requirements of American National Standard for Information Sciences—Permanence Paper for Printed Library Materials, ANSI Z39.48-1984.

The name "The Schomburg Center" and any related logo are marks and the property of The New York Public Library, Astor, Lenox and Tilden Foundations.

Library of Congress Catalog Card Number 95-36733
ISBN 0-7876-0289-2

I(T)P™   Gale Research Inc., an International Thomson Publishing Company.
ITP logo is a trademark under license.

10 9 8 7 6 5 4 3 2 1

Advisory Board

Emily M. Belcher
General and Humanities Reference Librarian of the Firestone Library at Princeton University

Doris Hargrett Clack
Professor of Library and Information Studies at Florida State University, Tallahassee

Henry Louis Gates Jr.
Chair of the African American Studies Department at Harvard University

Barbara Hull
Library Media Specialist at Jamaica High School, New York

Barbara Osborne
Department Head, Language Arts, at Nova High School, Seattle, Washington

Katie Weiblen
Assistant Department Head, Language and Literature, at the Minneapolis Public Library

John Edgar Wideman
Author and Professor of English at the University of Massachusetts at Amherst

Hear my cry, O God the Reader;
vouchsafe that this my book fall
not still-born into the world
wilderness.... Let the ears of a
guilty people tingle with truth,
and seventy millions sigh for the
righteousness which exalteth
nations, in this drear day when
human brotherhood is mockery
and a snare. Thus in Thy good
time may infinite reason turn
the tangle straight, and these
crooked marks on a fragile leaf
be not indeed
The End.

The Souls of Black Folk,
W. E. B. Du Bois, 1903

Table of Contents

Preface

The Schomburg Center Guide to Black Literature from the Eighteenth Century to the Present has been designed to serve as a ready reference source on the authors, works, characters, general themes and topics, and literary theories relating to black literature. Developed in response to strong demand by students, librarians, teachers, and other readers for a one-stop, authoritative guide to black literature, *The Schomburg Center Guide to Black Literature* spans the eighteenth century to the present and offers an introduction to fiction and nonfiction black writing from United States authors and from international authors whose works have been translated into English.

Inclusion Criteria

Authors, works of literature, and topics and terms were selected for inclusion based on the recommendations of a specially formed advisory panel made up of university, high school, and public librarians and university and high school teachers. The final entry list was reviewed by The Schomburg Center for Research in Black Culture.

Organization

Entries in *The Schomburg Center Guide to Black Literature* are arranged alphabetically in word-by-word order. Included are

- **Biographical Essays** which provide concise summaries of the lives of more than 500 novelists, poets, critics, short story writers, dramatists, journalists, essayists, editors, screenwriters, children's writers, and historians and other nonfiction writers relevant to black literature. **Entry heads** contain name, nationality, occupation, and birth/death dates. **Further Readings** sections point readers to further study of specific authors or black literature in general. Listed are other Gale series as well as additional bibliographical sources. Biographical entries are alphabetized according to surname.

- **Literary Work Synopses** which provide brief plot summaries and explain the relevance of approximately 460 major works. **Entry heads** contain title of work, author, genre, and date of publication. Foreign-language works that have been translated into English are listed by their English-language title with the foreign-language title following in parentheses. Page references to these foreign-language titles are included in the index.

- **Themes, Topics, and Literary Movements Essays** which describe and define themes, movements, and subjects relating to black literature. Each essay summarizes the historical and literary significance of its topic and highlights the major writers and works associated with the subject of the essay. Entries include the Harlem Renaissance, black power, and the civil rights movement.

- **Terms and Genres Essays** which define and explain literary terms and genres within the specific framework of black literature. These essays also point out major writers and works within each genre. Topics include trickster tale, autobiography, slave narrative, and the novel.

Additional Features

The Schomburg Center Guide to Black Literature also includes a

- **Master Chronology** listing the birth and death dates of major authors, the publication dates of major works covered in the text, the dates of major literary awards won by black authors covered in the text, and major events relevant to black literature in general.

- **Comprehensive Subject Index** listing all titles, names, and subjects covered in the text. Page numbers of main entries appear in bold.

- **Descriptive Essay** which recounts the history of The Schomburg Center for Research in Black Culture and explains its current status.

- **Photos** of nearly 100 authors and reproductions of approximately 50 dustjackets, manuscript pages, title pages, and book covers. Each photo is accompanied by a descriptive caption.

- **Character Listings** which provide cross-references to the works in which characters appear. Entries on these works are included within *The Schomburg Center Guide to Black Literature.*

In addition, bold-faced names, titles, and terms in entries direct readers to full-length entries also found in *The Schomburg Center Guide to Black Literature.*

Acknowledgments

Special Thanks are offered to *The Schomburg Center Guide to Black Literature*'s advisory board members, whose names are listed opposite the staff page. Special thanks are also extended to the contributors to *The Schomburg Center Guide to Black Literature:* Diane Andreassi, John Beckman, John Benci, Michael Broder, Melissa Clark, Jane Stewart Cook, Simon Dixon, Rose Estioco, Jason Gallman, Tracie Gardner, Anne Janette Johnson, J. Sydney Jones, Elizabeth Judd, Jim Kamp, Jennifer Swift Kramer, Jeanne Lesinski, John Little, Doris Maxfield, Philip McKinney, Emily J. McMurray, Margaret Monforton, Paula Morin, Jay Pederson, Marijke Rijsberman, Jean Ross, Maria Sheler-Edwards, Pamela L. Shelton, Kenneth R. Shepherd, Douglas Smith, Linda Wasmer Smith, Patricia Walsh, Giselle Weiss, and Michaela Swart Wilson.

Comments Are Welcome

The editors hope that readers will find *The Schomburg Center Guide to Black Literature* to be a useful reference tool, and we welcome comments about the work. Send comments and suggestions to: Editors, *The Schomburg Center Guide to Black Literature,* Gale Research Inc., 835 Penobscot Bldg., Detroit, MI 48226-4094; call toll-free at 1-800-347-GALE; or fax to 1-313-961-6599.

by Howard Dodson
Chief of The Schomburg Center for Research in Black Culture

About The Schomburg Center for Research in Black Culture

The flurry of activity by artists and scholars known as the Harlem Renaissance gave impetus to at least two significant cultural events in 1925. The first significant examination of contemporary culture, *The New Negro: An Interpretation,* was published; its editor, Alain Locke, wrote that "Whoever wishes to see the Negro in his essential traits, in the full perspective of his achievement and possibilities, must seek the enlightenment of that self-portraiture which the present developments of Negro culture are offering." The other event was the opening of the Division of Negro Literature, History, and Prints in the 135th Street branch of the New York Public Library. A repository for materials on black life that documented past achievements and served as a foundation for the solicitation of future contributions, this special library was the forerunner of the Schomburg Center for Research in Black Culture, which stands today as one of the world's foremost facilities dedicated to the preservation and interpretation of black cultural artifacts.

From its inception the Schomburg Center has served both as a repository and as a center for black intellectual and artistic activities. Its location in Harlem has given added significance to those roles, for by the early 1920s Harlem had become the "black capital," home to an amalgam of blacks from various parts of the United States, the Caribbean, and Africa. Economic expansion, especially during World War I, increased opportunities for black home ownership; simultaneously, literacy and race consciousness were expanding within the black community. Political consciousness and race pride were heightened by the activities of the National Association for the Advancement of Colored People (NAACP), the National Urban League, and the preachments of Marcus Garvey. More outlets for literature were becoming available through black newspapers and magazines such as the *Crisis,* edited by W. E. B. Du Bois of the NAACP; the Urban League's *Opportunity,* edited by Charles Johnson; and the *Messenger,* edited by A. Philip Randolph of the Brotherhood of Sleeping Car Porters. Critic Sterling Brown, writing about poets from 1914 to 1936, also captured the concerns of other black literary figures when he noted their five major concerns were "(1) a discovery of Africa as a source of race pride, (2) a use of Negro heroes and heroic episodes from American history, (3) propaganda of protest, (4) a treatment of the Negro masses with more understanding and less apology, and (5) franker and deeper self revelation." Black writing during the period sprang from social concerns as well as literary interests; and early anthologies of black writings covered a broad spectrum ranging from poetry to prose to social and political criticism.

As Harlem became the focal point for black artistic and intellectual activities, the 135th Street branch library took on a new dimension. The New York Public Library had opened the branch in 1905 in a neighborhood that was predominantly Jewish. Within fifteen years it was half black. Ernestine Rose, who had developed services in other ethnic neighborhoods, was assigned to adapt the library's resources to meet the needs of the changing community. In 1921 the branch began to sponsor annual art exhibitions which were planned by committees including cultural leaders such as W. E. B. Du Bois, James Weldon Johnson, and Arthur Schomburg. It also sponsored lectures and book discussions. By 1924, however, the library was facing a serious dilemma. The community's heightened interest in materials by and about black people had begun to strain its limited resources. To meet this challenge Rose called a community meeting in December 1924, during which a citizen's committee was created which elected Schomburg, Johnson, Hubert H. Harrison, and John Nail as officers. The group recommended that the rarest books be set aside as a Negro reference library. Gifts and loans for the special collection came from the private libraries of noted black collectors, including John Bruce, Louise Latimer, Harrison, George Young, Charles D. Martin, and Schomburg.

At the formal opening of the Division of Negro Literature, History, and Prints on 8 May 1925, Rose noted the existence of similar collections in the Library of Congress, in the libraries of institutions such as Tuskegee Institute and Howard University, in certain large city reference libraries, and in a few private libraries. She predicted, however, that the collection at the 135th Street library would become one of the largest and most valuable in the world because of its location in Harlem, "the greatest negro city in the world"; and because it would make materials "available equally to scholars, to the man in the street, and to school children of all races." As a result of the publicity surrounding the opening of the Negro division and the efforts of Charles S. Johnson, L. Hollingsworth Wood, and Eugene Knickle Jones of the Urban League, the Carnegie Corporation provided a grant of ten thousand dollars for the New York Public Library to purchase Schomburg's personal collection. This acquisition brought the division immediate international stature.

Schomburg continued to augment the collection and also served as an unpaid consultant to the library, addressing staff meetings and assisting young scholars. A second Carnegie grant in 1932 made it possible for him to be hired as curator of the Negro division, a position he held until his death in 1938. In 1940 the library was renamed the Schomburg Collection of Negro Literature, History, and Prints in his honor.

The 1940s were a time of increasing use for the collection. In 1942 the collection moved into the entire top floor of the new 135th Street branch library building. The American Negro Theater staged productions in the basement auditorium, serving as training ground for performers such as Frederick O'Neal, Hilda Simms, Hilda Haynes, Rosetta LeNoire, Earle Hyman, Sidney Poitier, and Harry Belafonte, and for playwrights such as Alice Childress and Abram Hill. The collection was a primary resource for writers such as Richard Wright and Langston Hughes. Discussions drew the participation of African and Caribbean visitors to the United States who were involved in struggles for self-government, such as Ja Ja Wachuku, former ambassador from Nigeria; George Westermann, former ambassador from Panama; and Kwame Nkrumah, who became the first president of Ghana. The collection was a center for black scholars involved in WPA projects; and later, during the 1950s, provided resources for research done for Kenneth Clark's report on the effect of segregated education on black and white children, which was cited in the U.S. Supreme Court's historic *Brown v. Board of Education* decision in 1954.

From 1948 through the 1970s the collection continued to expand under the guidance of Jean Blackwell Hutson. By 1966, however, it was in serious jeopardy. Materials were deteriorating from overuse by readers, air pollution, and unsatisfactory climatic conditions. Although the collection had been moved back into the entire space in the 135th Street building in 1954, it was overcrowded. Hutson launched a successful campaign to rally support within the New York Public Library and in the black community. In a reorganization the Schomburg Collection was designated as part of the research libraries of the New York Public Library in 1972, and its name was changed to the Schomburg Center for Research in Black Culture.

Today, the Schomburg Center is looking toward the twenty-first century as it expands its services, facilities, and technology to meet the contemporary needs of writers, scholars, artists, and others who are studying and making contributions to black culture. In the tradition established by Schomburg, the center continues to be a repository for materials documenting black life and a participant in the evolution of black culture.

Chronology

1701-1799

1700s Portuguese, British, and French trade with prosperous African kingdoms in West Africa. Kingdoms and city-states in East Africa trade with Turkish, Arab, and European traders.

1731 November 9. American Benjamin Banneker is born.

1753(?) West-African born American Phillis Wheatley is born.

1773 Phillis Wheatley's collection *Poems on Various Subjects* is published.

1775-1783 American Revolutionary War.

1776 The United States declares its independence from Britain.

1777 July 2. The Republic of Vermont passes the first constitution in America to prohibit slavery, in Windsor, Vermont.

December 31. U.S. President George Washington reverses previous policy and allows the recruitment of black soldiers. Approximately 5000 participate in the Revolutionary War.

1784 December 5. West African-born American Phillis Wheatley dies.

1786 Quakers in Pennsylvania begin to organize the Underground Railroad, a covert network of safe havens that helps fugitive slaves escape to freedom.

1788 The Constitution of the United States is ratified.

1793 February 12. Congress passes the first Fugitive Slave Act.

1795 British occupy Cape Town in southern Africa.

Late 1700s European explorers begin to penetrate the African interior.

1800-1849

1801 Slaves led by Toussaint L'Ouverture revolt and seize power in Haiti.

1806 October 9. American Benjamin Banneker dies.

1808 January 1. The importation of African slaves is forbidden by the U.S. government. This law is largely circumvented.

1813 American William Wells Brown is born.

1817(?) February. American Frederick Douglass is born.

1822 African American settlers found Monrovia, capital of modern-day Liberia.

1825 September 24. American Frances Ellen Watkins Harper is born.

1827(?) American Harriet Wilson is born.

1830s The growing abolitionist movement—among both blacks and whites—becomes a potent force.

In southern Africa, Dutch settlers move into lands northeast of Cape Town, seizing land from Xhosa, Sotho, and Zulu farmers.

1831 August 21-22. An American slave, Nat Turner, leads a short-lived uprising against white slaveowners in Virginia, killing over 60 whites. Turner is captured and hanged.

1832 The anti-slavery Abolitionist Party is founded in Boston.

1833 Slaves are freed in all British possessions.

1837(?) August 17. American Charlotte L. Forten is born.

1845 Frederick Douglass's autobiography *Narrative of the Life of Frederick Douglass* is published.

1847 July 26. Liberia becomes an independent republic.

1849 July. Harriet Tubman escapes from slavery. She returns to the South at least twenty times, leading hundreds of slaves to freedom.

1850-1899

1850 Slave trade is forbidden in the District of Columbia.

1853 William Wells Brown's novel *Clotel; or, The President's Daughter* is published.

1856 April 5. American Booker T. Washington is born.

1857 March 6. In the case of *Dred Scott vs. Sandford,* the Supreme Court denies blacks U.S. citizenship and denies the power of Congress to restrict slavery in any federal territory.

1858 June 20. American Charles W. Chesnutt is born.

1859 Militantly anti-slavery, John Brown is found guilty of treason after raiding a federal arsenal at Harpers Ferry, Virginia. Brown is subsequently hanged.

Harriet Wilson's novel *Our Nig* is published.

1861-1865 American Civil War.

1862 July 16. American Ida B. Wells is born.

July 17. Congress allows the enlistment of blacks in the Union Army. More than 186,000 blacks serve in the army during the Civil War; 38,000 die in service.

The first southern school for freed slaves is established in Frogmore, South Carolina.

1863 January 1. U.S. President Abraham Lincoln issues the Emancipation Proclamation, freeing slaves living in the Confederate states.

The Kansas First Colored Volunteers becomes the first black unit in the U.S. Civil War, at Fort Scott, Kansas.

1864 The Ku Klux Klan is organized in Pulaski, Tennessee.

1865 December 18. The Thirteenth Amendment, which outlaws slavery in the U.S., is ratified.

U.S. President Abraham Lincoln is assassinated by John Wilkes Booth.

1868 February 23. American-born Ghanaian W. E. B. Du Bois is born.

July 28. The Fourteenth Amendment, validating citizenship rights for all persons born or naturalized in the U.S., is ratified. The amendment also provides for equal protection under the law.

1870 March 30. The ratification of the Fifteenth Amendment secures voting rights for all male U.S. citizens.

1871 June 17. American James Weldon Johnson is born.

1872 June 27. American Paul Laurence Dunbar is born.

1875 December 19. American Carter G. Woodson is born.

Tennessee adopts the first "Jim Crow" segregation laws.

1880 February 27. American Angelina Weld Grimké is born.

1880-1914 European countries vie for African colonies, bringing all of Africa south of the Sahara except Ethiopia and Liberia under European colonial rule.

1881 Booker T. Washington establishes the Tuskegee Institute, an industrial school for blacks, in Alabama.

1884 November 6. American William Wells Brown dies.

1886 September 10. American Georgia Douglas Johnson is born.

September 13. American Alain Locke is born.

1887 August 17. Jamaican Marcus Garvey is born.

1889 September 15. Jamaican-born American Claude McKay is born.

1891 January 7. American Zora Neale Hurston is born.

April 13. American Nella Larsen is born.

1891(?) October 20. Kenyan Jomo Kenyatta is born.

1893 July 1. American Walter White is born.

1894 December 26. American Jean Toomer is born.

1895 February 20. American Frederick Douglass dies.

Paul Laurence Dunbar's poetry collection *Majors and Minors* is published.

1896 March 1. Ethiopian forces defeat Italian invaders at the Battle of Adowa.

Paul Laurence Dunbar's poetry collection *Lyrics of Lowly Life* is published.

The U.S. Supreme Court decides in *Plessy v. Ferguson* that "separate but equal" public facilities do not violate the Constitution.

1897 June 20. American Charlemae Hill Rollins is born.

1898(?) February 6. American Melvin B. Tolson is born.

1898 April 9. American Paul Robeson is born.

1899 December 19. American Martin Luther King Sr. is born.

1899-1902 The Boer War in South Africa between Britain and Dutch settlers extends British control in South Africa.

1900-1920

1900 The first Pan-African Congress convenes in London.

1901 May 1. American Sterling A. Brown is born.

August 30. American Roy Wilkins is born.

Booker T. Washington's autobiography *Up from Slavery* is published.

1902 February 1. American Langston Hughes is born.

October 13. American Arna Bontemps is born.

1903 May 30. American Countee Cullen is born.

W. E. B. Du Bois's collection *The Souls of Black Folk: Essays and Sketches* is published.

1904 August 7. American Ralph Bunche is born.

1905 July 11-13. The Niagara Movement, the forerunner of the National Association for the Advancement of Colored People (NAACP), is established. Among its leaders is W. E. B. Du Bois.

1906 February 9. American Paul Laurence Dunbar dies.

1907 June 2. American Dorothy West is born.

1908 January 1. American children's author Jesse Jackson is born.

September 4. American Richard Wright is born.

October 12. American Ann Petry is born.

1909 July 29. American Chester Himes is born.

September 21. Ghanaian Kwame Nkrumah is born.

The National Association for the Advancement of Colored People (NAACP) is founded in New York. The signers of the original charter include W. E. B. Du Bois.

1910(?) March 17. American Bayard Rustin is born.

1910 June 22. American Katherine Dunham is born.

1910-1934 W. E. B. Du Bois publishes and edits the magazine *Crisis.*

1911 February 22. American Frances Ellen Watkins Harper dies.

April 1. American Augusta Baker is born.

1912 November 30. American Gordon Parks is born.

James Weldon Johnson's novel *The Autobiography of an Ex-Coloured Man* is published.

1913 August 4. American Robert Hayden is born.

1914 March 1. American Ralph Ellison is born.

July 23. American Charlotte L. Forten dies.

July 24. American Kenneth B. Clark is born.

November 28. American Owen Dodson is born.

Marcus Garvey founds the Universal Negro Improvement Association under the slogan "One God! One Aim! One Destiny!"

1914-1918 World War I. Between 300,000 and 400,000 African Americans serve in the U.S. armed forces; only 10 percent are assigned to combat duty.

1915 January 1. American John Henrik Clarke is born.

January 2. American John Hope Franklin is born.

July 7. American Margaret Walker is born.

November 14. American Booker T. Washington dies.

1915(?) The Great Migration of southern blacks to the North begins, sparked by the demand for unskilled labor in northern industrial cities.

1916 January 14. American John Oliver Killens is born.

September 5. American Frank Yerby is born.

1917 June 7. American Gwendolyn Brooks is born.

November 1. American Margaret Taylor Burroughs is born.

December 18. American Ossie Davis is born.

1918 March 29. American Pearl Bailey is born.

South African Nelson Mandela is born.

1920 October 12. American Alice Childress is born.

1921-1940

1921 July 31. American Whitney M. Young Jr. is born.

August 11. American Alex Haley is born.

1922 Claude McKay's poetry collection *Harlem Shadows* is published.

1923 July 16. American Mari Evans is born.

Jean Toomer's *Cane,* a miscellany of fiction, prose, poetry, and drama, is published.

1923-1925 Marcus Garvey's *The Philosophy and Opinions of Marcus Garvey,* a two-volume collection of his essays and manifestos, is published.

1924 August 2. American James Baldwin is born.

November 30. American Shirley Chisholm is born.

1925 May 19. American Malcolm X is born.

July 20. French Frantz Fanon is born.

August 11. American Carl Thomas Rowan is born.

December 5. American John A. Williams is born.

The Harlem Renaissance, a golden age of black literature and art in the U.S., is formally recognized as a movement with the publication of the anthology *The New Negro: An Interpretation,* edited by Alain Locke.

1927 February 20. American Sidney Poitier is born.

April 27. American Coretta Scott King is born.

The poetry collection *Caroling Dusk,* edited by Countee Cullen, is published.

Langston Hughes's poetry collection *Fine Clothes to the Jew* is published.

James Weldon Johnson's poetry collection *God's Trombones: Seven Negro Sermons in Verse* is published.

1928 April 4. American Maya Angelou is born.

October 17. American Lerone Bennett Jr. is born.

1929 January 15. American Martin Luther King Jr. is born.

April 9. American Paule Marshall is born.

1930 January 23. West Indian Derek Walcott is born.

May 11. Barbadian Edward Kamau Brathwaite is born.

May 19. American Lorraine Hansberry is born.

November 16. Nigerian Chinua Achebe is born.

1931 February 18. American Toni Morrison is born.

March 25. American Ida B. Wells dies.

September 12. American Kristin Hunter is born.

September 13. American Adrienne Kennedy is born.

October 7. South African Desmond Tutu is born.

1932 March 4. South African Miriam Makeba is born.

October 12. American Dick Gregory is born.

November 15. American Charles W. Chesnutt dies.

1933 January 15. American Ernest J. Gaines is born.

The publication of the journal *L'étudiant noir* marks the official birth of the negritude movement.

1934 February 18. American Audre Lorde is born.

July 13. Nigerian Wole Soyinka is born.

September 9. American Sonia Sanchez is born.

October 7. American Amiri Baraka is born.

1935 July 2. American Ed Bullins is born.

August 31. American Eldridge Cleaver is born.

October 3. Italy invades Ethiopia; Italian occupation continues until 1941.

October 12. American William J. Raspberry is born.

Zora Neale Hurston's collection *Mules and Men* is published.

1936 February 21. American Barbara Jordan is born.

March 12. American Virginia Hamilton is born.

June 27. American Lucille Clifton is born.

July 9. American June Jordan is born.

September. South African Winnie Mandela is born.

October 22. American Bobby Seale is born.

December 31. American Clarence Major is born.

Arna Bontemps's novel *Black Thunder* is published.

1937 February 23. American Claude Brown is born.

July 12. American Bill Cosby is born.

Zora Neale Hurston's novel *Their Eyes Were Watching God* is published.

1938 February 22. American Ishmael Reed is born.

June 26. American James Weldon Johnson dies.

1939 January 27. American Julius Lester is born.

March 25. American Toni Cade Bambara is born.

June 6. American Marian Wright Edelman is born.

1939-1945 World War II.

1940 January 14. American Julian Bond is born.

June 10. Jamaican Marcus Garvey dies.

Richard Wright's novel *Native Son* is published.

1941-1960

1941 June 29. Trinidadian-born American Stokely Carmichael is born.

1942 February 23. American Haki R. Madhubuti is born.

February 27. American Charlayne Hunter-Gault is born.

April 1. American Samuel R. Delany is born.

Zora Neale Hurston's autobiography *Dust Tracks on a Road* is published.

1943 June 7. American Nikki Giovanni is born.

July 10. American Arthur Ashe is born.

September 16. American James Alan McPherson is born.

October 4. American H. Rap Brown is born.

1943-1965 Langston Hughes's "Simple" Stories are published.

1944 January 26. American Angela Davis is born.

February 9. American Alice Walker is born.

The Supreme Court rules that an American cannot be denied the right to vote because of skin color.

1945 Gwendolyn Brooks's poetry collection *A Street in Bronzeville* is published.

Gabriela Mistral receives the Nobel Prize for literature.

Adam Clayton Powell Jr. becomes the first black congressperson from the northeastern U.S. (New York).

American August Wilson is born.

Richard Wright's autobiography *Black Boy: A Record of Childhood and Youth* is published.

The League of Arab States is founded.

1946 January 9. American Countee Cullen dies.

1947 June 22. American Octavia E. Butler is born.

John Hope Franklin's *From Slavery to Freedom,* a history of African Americans, is published.

Présence Africaine, Africa's leading literary journal, is founded by Léopold Senghor, Aimé Césaire, and Léon Damas.

1948 April 23. American Charles Johnson is born.

May 22. Jamaican-born American Claude McKay dies.

October 18. American Ntozake Shange is born.

Apartheid is instituted in South Africa. The white minority government in South Africa, the Afrikaner Nationalist party, is led by Daniel F. Malan. The party platform calls for strict racial segregation and the supremacy of whites.

U.S. President Harry Truman bans segregation in the armed forces.

1949 May 25. West Indian-born American Jamaica Kincaid is born.

November 23. American Gayl Jones is born.

Gwendolyn Brooks's poetry collection *Annie Allen* is published.

1950 January 25. American Gloria Naylor is born.

April 3. American Carter G. Woodson dies.

September 14. American John Steptoe is born.

September 16. American Henry Louis Gates Jr. is born.

September 22. Ralph Bunche receives the Nobel Peace Prize for his work as a mediator in Palestine.

Poet Gwendolyn Brooks receives the Pulitzer Prize for her collection *Annie Allen.* Brooks is the first African American to be awarded the prize.

1950-1953 Korean War.

1951 October 18. American Terry McMillan is born.

1952 August 28. American Rita Dove is born.

Ralph Ellison's novel *Invisible Man* is published.

1952-1956 Black Africans in Kenya rebel against British rule in the "Mau-Mau" uprising.

1953 James Baldwin's novel *Go Tell It on the Mountain* is published.

Ralph Ellison receives the National Book Award for fiction for his novel *Invisible Man.*

1954 May 17. In *Brown v. Board of Education of Topeka, Kansas,* the U.S. Supreme Court rules unanimously that racial segregation in public schools is unconstitutional, overruling *Plessy v. Ferguson.*

June 9. American Alain Locke dies.

1954-1962 Algerian uprising against French rule.

1955 March 21. American Walter White dies.

December 1. Rosa Parks refuses to give up her seat to a white man on a Montgomery, Alabama, bus. On December 5, blacks begin a boycott of the bus system.

James Baldwin's essay collection *Notes of a Native Son* is published.

1956 December. The U.S. Supreme Court outlaws segregated seating on buses.

James Baldwin's novel *Giovanni's Room* is published.

The First Congress of African Writers is held in Paris.

1957 February 14. The Southern Christian Leadership Conference, the first organization devoted to coordinating the efforts of groups working to end racial segregation, is formed. Martin Luther King Jr. is the group's first president.

March 6. Kwame Nkrumah leads Ghana to independence.

March 20. American Spike Lee is born.

August 29. Congress passes the Voting Rights Act of 1957, the first major civil rights legislation in more than 75 years. The Act expands the role of the federal government in civil rights matters and establishes the U.S. Commission on Civil Rights to monitor the protection of black rights.

Black Orpheus, a journal of African writing in English, is founded in Nigeria.

1958 June 10. American Angelina Weld Grimké dies.

Chinua Achebe's novel *Things Fall Apart* is published.

The Book of Negro Folklore, a collection edited by Arna Bontemps and Langston Hughes, is published.

Paul Robeson's autobiography *Here I Stand* is published.

1959 Nigerian Ben Okri is born.

Lorraine Hansberry's play *A Raisin in the Sun* is produced and published.

1960 January 28. American Zora Neale Hurston dies.

1960 March. South African police fire on black demonstrators at Sharpeville, killing 67. Thousands of black South Africans are arrested in ensuing protests.

April 15-17. Marion Barry founds the Student Nonviolent Coordinating Committee (SNCC) in Raleigh, North Carolina.

October 1. Nigeria achieves independence from Britain.

November 28. American Richard Wright dies.

Chinua Achebe's novel *No Longer at Ease* is published.

French colonies in West and West Central Africa achieve independence.

1961-1970

1961-1975 U.S. military involvement in the Vietnam War.

1961 December 6. French writer Frantz Fanon dies.

December 9. Led by Julius Nyerere, Tanganyika (later united with Zanzibar to form Tanzania) achieves independence from Britain.

James Baldwin's essay collection *Nobody Knows My Name* is published.

Ossie Davis's play *Purlie Victorious* is produced and published.

1962 July 3. Algeria wins independence from France.

1963 May 25. The Organization of African Unity is founded by 30 heads of African states and governments meeting in Addis Ababa, Ethiopia.

August 27. American-born Ghanaian W. E. B. Du Bois dies.

August 28. The March on Washington is the largest civil rights demonstration to date. Martin Luther King Jr. delivers his famous "I Have a Dream" speech at the Lincoln Memorial.

December 12. Under the leadership of Jomo Kenyatta, Kenya achieves independence from Britain.

James Baldwin's essay collection *The Fire Next Time* is published.

Martin Luther King Jr.'s *Letter from Birmingham City Jail* is published.

Gordon Parks's novel *The Learning Tree* is published.

Wole Soyinka's play *The Lion and the Jewel* is published (first produced in 1959).

Wole Soyinka's play *A Dance of the Forests* is published (first produced in 1960).

The Organization of African Unity is founded.

1964 March 30. American Nella Larsen dies.

Chinua Achebe's novel *Arrow of God* is published.

Amiri Baraka's play *Dutchman* is produced and published.

Martin Luther King Jr. is awarded the Nobel Prize for Peace.

The Civil Rights Act abolishes segregation in public accommodations throughout the South. The Act leads to the establishment of the Equal Employment Opportunity Commission and the institution of affirmative action programs to redress past discrimination against African Americans.

Eight South African anti-apartheid leaders, including Nelson Mandela, are sentenced to life imprisonment.

1965 January 12. American Lorraine Hansberry dies.

February 21. Malcolm X is assassinated in New York City, eleven months after his split from Elijah Muhammad's Nation of Islam.

August 11-21. Race riots in the Watts district of Los Angeles, California, result in 34 deaths, more than 3,500 arrests, and approximately 225 million dollars in property damage.

November 11. A white minority regime declares Rhodesia (now Zimbabwe) independent of Britain, touching off a civil war that lasts until 1979.

James Baldwin's short story collection *Going to Meet the Man* is published.

Claude Brown's novel *Manchild in the Promised Land* is published.

Lorraine Hansberry's play *The Sign in Sidney Brustein's Window* is published (first produced in 1964).

The Autobiography of Malcolm X is published. The book was dictated by Malcolm X and written by Alex Haley.

Nelson Mandela's *No Easy Walk to Freedom,* a collection of his articles, speeches, and trial addresses, is published.

Wole Soyinka's novel *The Interpreters* is published.

The Voting Rights Act provides guarantees for black voting in the South.

1966 May 14. American Georgia Douglas Johnson dies.

August 29. American Melvin B. Tolson dies.

October. Bobby Seale and Huey Newton found the Black Panther Party in Oakland, California.

Chinua Achebe's novel *A Man of the People* is published.

Samuel R. Delany wins a Nebula Award for his novel *Babel-17.*

Margaret Walker's novel *Jubilee* is published.

1967 March 30. American Jean Toomer dies.

May 22. American Langston Hughes dies.

Samuel R. Delany wins Nebula awards for his novel *The Einstein Intersection* and for his short story "Aye and Gomorrah."

1967-1970 Civil war in Nigeria as the region of Biafra seeks independence.

1968 April 4. Martin Luther King Jr. is assassinated in Memphis, Tennessee. In the fol-

lowing week, riots occur in at least 125 places throughout the country.

Eldridge Cleaver's essay collection *Soul on Ice* is published.

The anthology *Black Fire,* edited by Larry Neal and Amiri Baraka (under the name LeRoi Jones), is published.

1969 October 29. The Supreme Court rules that school districts must end racial segregation at once and must operate only unitary school systems.

Samuel R. Delany wins a Nebula Award for his novelette *Time Considered as a Helix of Semi-Precious Stones.*

Toni Morrison's novel *The Bluest Eye* is published.

1970 Maya Angelou's first autobiography, *I Know Why the Caged Bird Sings,* is published.

Charles Gordone wins a Pulitzer Prize for drama for his play *No Place to Be Somebody.*

1971-1980

1971 March 11. American Whitney M. Young Jr. dies.

December 9. American Ralph Bunche dies.

Ernest J. Gaines's novel *The Autobiography of Miss Jane Pittman* is published.

Virginia Hamilton's novel *M. C. Higgins, the Great* is published.

1972 April 27. Ghanaian Kwame Nkrumah dies.

Lorraine Hansberry's play *Les Blancs* is published (first produced in 1970).

Ishmael Reed's novel *Mumbo Jumbo* is published.

Wole Soyinka's autobiography *The Man Died: Prison Notes of Wole Soyinka* is published.

1973 June 4. American Arna Bontemps dies.

The nonfiction *A Dialogue* is published. The volume contains a transcription of a

1971 conversation between James Baldwin and Nikki Giovanni.

Alice Childress's novel *A Hero Ain't Nothin' but a Sandwich* is published.

Toni Morrison's novel *Sula* is published.

Sonia Sanchez's poetry collection *A Blues Book for Blue Black Magical Women* is published.

Wole Soyinka's novel *Season of Anomy* is published.

1974 September 2. Emperor Haile Selassie of Ethiopia is deposed by a military junta known as the Derg.

1975 The last remaining Portuguese colonies in Africa achieve independence.

Virginia Hamilton receives both a Newbery Medal and a National Book Award for her novel *M. C. Higgins, the Great.*

Wole Soyinka's play *Death and the King's Horseman* is published (first produced in 1976).

1976 January 23. American Paul Robeson dies.

June. Police fire on demonstrating students and school children in the South African township of Soweto, sparking a wave of protests throughout the country.

Alex Haley's novel *Roots: The Saga of an American Family* is published.

Ishmael Reed's novel *Flight to Canada* is published.

Ntozake Shange's play *for colored girls who have considered suicide* is produced and published.

1977 James Alan McPherson's short story collection *Elbow Room* is published.

Toni Morrison's novel Song of Solomon is published.

Mildred D. Taylor wins a Newbery Medal for her novel *Roll of Thunder, Hear My Cry.*

1978 August 21. Kenyan Jomo Kenyatta dies.

Audre Lorde's poetry collection *The Black Unicorn* is published.

James Alan McPherson receives a Pulitzer Prize for his short story collection *Elbow Room.*

1979 February 3. American Charlemae Hill Rollins dies.

James Baldwin's novel *Just Above My Head* is published.

1980 February 25. American Robert Hayden dies.

Toni Cade Bambara's novel *The Salt Eaters* is published.

April 18. The Republic of Zimbabwe is formed.

1981-1990

1981 September 8. American Roy Wilkins dies.

Toni Morrison's novel *Tar Baby* is published.

Ntozake Shange's play collection *Three Pieces* is published.

Wole Soyinka's memoir *Aké: The Years of Childhood* is published.

1982 Toni Cade Bambara wins an American Book Award for her short story collection *Gorilla, My Love.*

Charles Fuller receives a Pulitzer Prize for drama for *A Soldier's Play.*

Gloria Naylor's novel *The Women of Brewster Place* is published.

Alice Walker's novel *The Color Purple* is published.

John A. Williams wins an American Book Award for his novel *!Click Song.*

1983 April 14. American children's author Jesse Jackson dies.

June 21. American Owen Dodson dies.

Ernest J. Gaines's novel *A Gathering of Old Men* is published.

Gloria Naylor wins an American Book Award for best first fiction for *The Women of Brewster Place.*

Alice Walker wins both an American Book Award and a Pulitzer Prize for her novel *The Color Purple.*

1984 November 11. American Martin Luther King Sr. dies.

November 12. American Chester Himes dies.

Amiri Baraka's *The Autobiography of LeRoi Jones* is published.

Octavia E. Butler wins a Hugo Award for her short story "Speech Sounds."

The essay collection *Black Women Writers (1950-1980),* edited by Mari Evans, is published.

Sonia Sanchez's poetry collection *homegirls & handgrenades* is published.

Archbishop Desmond Tutu of South Africa receives the Nobel Peace Prize for his efforts to end apartheid.

Civil rights activist Jesse Jackson becomes the first African American to mount a serious bid for the U.S. presidency.

1985 Octavia E. Butler wins a Hugo Award, Nebula Award, and Locus Award for her novelette "Bloodchild."

Jamaica Kincaid's novel *Annie John* is published.

Sonia Sanchez receives an American Book Award for her poetry collection *homegirls & handgrenades.*

August Wilson's play *Fences* is produced and published.

1986 January. The first national Martin Luther King Jr. holiday is celebrated.

Rita Dove's poetry collection *Thomas and Beulah* is published.

Wole Soyinka is awarded the Nobel Prize for literature.

1987 August 24. American Bayard Rustin dies.

October 27. American John Oliver Killens dies.

December 1. American James Baldwin dies.

Chinua Achebe's novel *Anthills of the Savannah* is published.

Rita Dove receives a Pulitzer Prize for her poetry collection *Thomas and Beulah.*

Terry McMillan's novel *Mama* is published.

Toni Morrison's novel *Beloved* is published.

August Wilson receives a Pulitzer Prize for his play *Fences.*

1988 Terry McMillan wins an American Book Award for her novel *Mama.*

Toni Morrison receives a Pulitzer Prize for her novel *Beloved.*

1989 January 13. American Sterling A. Brown dies.

August 28. American John Steptoe dies.

Spike Lee's film *Do the Right Thing* is released.

Terry McMillan's novel *Disappearing Acts* is published.

The Civil Rights Memorial is dedicated in Montgomery, Alabama.

1990 February. South African president F. W. de Klerk pledges to eliminate apartheid and releases Nelson Mandela, who has been held prisoner for more than 25 years.

March 21. Namibia becomes independent following a long struggle to end South African occupation.

August 17. American Pearl Bailey dies.

Charles Johnson's novel *Middle Passage* is published and receives a National Book Award.

Jamaica Kincaid's novel *Lucy* is published.

Itabari Njeri receives an American Book Award for her memoir *Every Good-bye Ain't Gone.*

Arnold Rampersad wins an American Book Award for his biography *I Dream a World.*

Derek Walcott's poem *Omeros* is published.

August Wilson's play *The Piano Lesson* is published (first produced in 1987) and wins a Pulitzer Prize.

1991—

1991 November 29. American Frank Yerby dies.

Ben Okri's novel *The Famished Road* wins a Booker Prize.

1992 February 10. American Alex Haley dies.

Late April to early May. A race riot sweeps across Los Angeles, California, following the acquittal of four police officers charged with excessive force in the arrest of Rodney King.

November 17. American Audre Lorde dies.

Henry Louis Gates Jr.'s essay collection *Loose Canons: Notes on the Culture Wars* is published.

Spike Lee's film *Malcolm X* is released.

Terry McMillan's novel *Waiting to Exhale* is published.

Toni Morrison's novel *Jazz* is published.

Derek Walcott is awarded the Nobel Prize for literature.

1993 January. Maya Angelou reads her poem "On the Pulse of Morning" at Bill Clinton's presidential inauguration.

February 6. American Arthur Ashe dies.

October 7. Toni Morrison becomes the first African American woman to win the Nobel Prize for literature.

Arthur Ashe's autobiography *Days of Grace: A Memoir* is published.

Rita Dove is named poet laureate of the United States. Dove is the first African American to hold that title.

Ernest J. Gaines's novel *A Lesson before Dying* is published.

Nelson Mandela shares the Nobel Peace Prize with F. W. de Klerk for their efforts at establishing a multi-racial government in South Africa.

1994 April 16. American Ralph Ellison dies.

May 10. Nelson Mandela takes office as South Africa's first black president, following the country's first free legislative elections (April 26-29).

August. American Alice Childress dies.

The
SCHOMBURG CENTER
Guide to
Black
Literature

. . . forever impelled by the restlessness for change and new realms to conquer that is the essence of the creative artist, and of exemplary American lives, white and black.

Lynn Z. Bloom on Maya Angelou, *Dictionary of Literary Biography*, Vol. 38, 1985.

Aaor

Series character in "Xenogenesis" Trilogy

Abdulla

Character in *Petals of Blood*

Abeba Torch

Character in *Let the Lion Eat Straw*

Abioseh

Character in *Les Blancs*

Abolitionism

Abolitionism was an international reform movement of the eighteenth and nineteenth centuries dedicated to the elimination of **slavery**, especially in English-speaking countries. It was the prime motivator behind an influential body of nineteenth-century literature. In the United States, abolitionist literature in the form of novels, **poetry**, **essays**, **speeches**, sermons, **slave narratives**, and **folk tales** proliferated after 1831, when the South intensified its system of slave controls in the aftermath of the bloody slave revolt led by Nat Turner. That was also the year in which William Lloyd Garrison founded *The Liberator,* a Boston newspaper that soon became a leading voice in American abolitionism.

The abolitionist movement produced numerous organizations concerned with issues of importance to African Americans, including the American Colonization Society (founded in 1816), the New England Anti-Slavery Society (founded in 1832), and the American Anti-Slavery Society (founded by Garrison in 1833). Although most of these organizations were dominated by whites, black leaders such as Paul Cuffe and **Frederick Douglass** played prominent roles as well. Douglass was among the many fugitive slaves who recounted their experiences in political orations and autobiographical narratives. His *Narrative of the Life of Frederick Douglass, an American Slave, Written by Himself* (1845) is considered one of the era's most compelling antislavery documents and is valued as an eloquent argument for human rights.

Another black lecturer for the cause who wrote an autobiographical account of his life as a slave and his escape to freedom was **William Wells Brown**, who went on to author the first **novel** and first drama published by an African American. Poets also were well represented among the crusaders. For example, **Frances Ellen Watkins Harper**, who wrote the first **short story** published by a black woman in the United States, also penned popular verse that dealt with abolitionist issues.

The passage of the Fugitive Slave Act of 1850, which required that runaway slaves be returned to their owners, added fuel to the fire of abolitionism. The publication of Harriet Beecher Stowe's influential antislavery novel *Uncle Tom's Cabin; or, Life among the Lowly* (1852) soon followed. Tensions were further heightened in 1859, when a white abolitionist named John Brown led the seizure of a federal arsenal at Harper's Ferry, Virginia, an act that many Southerners interpreted as showing the willingness of Northerners to use force in their attack on slavery. Brown was hanged, which prompted Henry David Thoreau to compose three antislavery essays.

In 1860, Abraham Lincoln, a northern Republican, was elected president, which led to a further heightening of tensions. Soon afterward, the Civil War commenced. This, in turn, led Lincoln to issue a key work of abolitionist literature, his *Proclamation of Emancipation by the President of the United States, January 1st, 1863,* in which he freed the slaves in those states that had seceded from the Union. Among black writers of the time, one notable figure was **James Madison Bell**, who commemorated significant antislavery events in writings such as *A Poem Entitled "The Day and the War," Delivered January 1, 1864, at Platt's Hall at the Celebration of the First Anniversary of President Lincoln's Emancipation Proclamation.*

Peter Abrahams

South African novelist
Born March 19, 1919.

Abrahams is regarded as a pivotal figure in the literary heritage of South Africa. The examination of South African political development unifies his work. In fiction and **autobiography**, Abrahams discusses such topics as political power, racial prejudice, mixed-race relationships, and the history of black emancipation. The basis of Abrahams's solid literary reputation remains his early **novels.**

Abrahams was born into poverty in Johannesburg's slum suburb, Vrededorp, on March 19, 1919. Following his schooling, Abrahams spent several years writing **short stories** and poems and working with political activists. He joined the crew of an English freighter in 1939 and lived in England for several years. In 1956, he emigrated to Jamaica.

Abrahams's first **novel**, *Song of the City* (1945), takes place during World War II and deals with the political conflicts within black and white communities. *Mine Boy* (1946) depicts the poverty and political oppression experienced by blacks in South Africa. These and later novels received praise for their study of South African politics and history. Abrahams's next two books, the autobiographical *Return to Goli* (1953) and *Tell Freedom* (1954), state Abrahams's political ideology.

After writing several other political novels, including *A Wreath for Udomo* (1956), *A Night of Their Own* (1965), *This Island Now* (1966), and *The View from Coyaba* (1985), Abrahams produced *Hard Rain* (1988), a mystery/political thriller about murder and political deception in the 1960s; *Revolution #9* (1992); and *Lights Out* (1994).

Further Readings

Black Writers, first edition, Gale, 1989.

Dictionary of Literary Biography, Volume 117: *Twentieth-Century Caribbean and Black African Writers,* First Series, Gale, 1992.

Ogungbesan, Kolawole, *The Writing of Peter Abrahams,* Africana Publishing, 1979.

Wade, Michael, *Peter Abrahams,* Evans Brothers, 1971.

Absolutely Nothing to Get Alarmed About

Charles Stevenson Wright
Essays, 1973

This collection of **essays** is based on a series of columns (called "Wright's World") that **Charles Stevenson Wright** wrote for the *Village Voice.* They are loosely autobiographical, and form a novel-like assembly that is thematically related to Wright's earlier **novels** *The Messenger* (1963) and *The Wig* (1966). Wright's initial optimism and subsequent skepticism have been replaced with a thoroughly pessimistic view. He writes of his personal experience with New York's junkies, prostitutes, and criminals; of ineffective police and detectives; of the desolated urban landscape; of pervasive **racism**. He includes reflections on the assassinations of the Kennedys, **Martin Luther King Jr.**, and **George Jackson**. Wright also comments on the Vietnam War and the failure of government social programs.

Chinua Achebe

Nigerian fiction writer, essayist, and poet
Born November 16, 1930.

Achebe is a leading figure in contemporary African literature. His **novels** depict the colonization and independence of Nigeria and are considered among the first works in English to portray an authentic view of African culture. His vivid language, characters, and craftsmanship have contributed to his established literary reputation.

The son of Ibo missionary teachers, Albert Chinualumogu Achebe was born in the village of Ogidi in eastern Nigeria. He was educated in Church Mission Society in Ogidi and Government College in Umahia, and received his Bachelor of Arts degree in 1953 from Ibadan University. Achebe then became a producer for the Nigerian Broadcasting Corporation. He resigned in 1966 and moved to Eastern Nigeria, where he wrote **poetry, short stories,** and children's literature. His poems of this time are col-

Chinua Achebe often depicts his native Nigeria in his works.

Like his novels, many of his stories illustrate the struggle between traditional and modern values in African culture. His **essays**, written on various literary and political subjects, are published in *Morning Yet on Creation Day* (1975) and *Hopes and Impediments* (1988).

Achebe is recognized as a teacher as well as a writer. In the early 1970s, he served as visiting professor at the University of Massachusetts—Amherst, and later at the University of Connecticut. He was the founding editor of "African Writers Series" as well as the literary journal *Okike: A Nigerian Journal of New Writing.* Achebe returned to Nigeria in 1976 to teach at the University of Nigeria—Nsukka. As a result of a car accident, he has been confined to a wheelchair since 1990. That year, he joined the faculty at Bard College. In 1994, he declared himself an exile, after the Nigerian government made it clear he would be arrested if he returned to Nigeria.

Further Readings

Black Writers, second edition, Gale, 1994.

Carroll, David, *Chinua Achebe,* Macmillan, 1990.

Dictionary of Literary Biography, Volume 117: *Twentieth-Century Caribbean and Black African Writers,* First Series, Gale, 1992.

Achille

Character in *Omeros*

Adam Johnson

Character in *Possessing the Secret of Joy*

Adam Miller

Character in *The Marrow of Tradition*

An Address to the Negroes

Jupiter Hammon
Essay, 1787

The earliest published black American writer, **Jupiter Hammon** wrote his most popular

lected in *Beware Soul Brother, and Other Poems* (1971), and were later published as *Christmas in Biafra and Other Poems* (1973).

In his first novel, ***Things Fall Apart*** (1958), Achebe combines traditional Ibo language and rhythms with a Western novelistic approach in the tale of Okonkwo and his life in Umuofia before colonization in the late 1880s. This novel is considered a classic of contemporary African fiction and has been adapted for stage, television, and radio. His second novel, ***No Longer at Ease*** (1960), chronicles the life of Okonkwo's grandson, Obi Okonkwo. Other critically acclaimed novels include ***Arrow of God*** (1964), ***A Man of the People*** (1966) and ***Anthills of the Savannah*** (1987), which was nominated for the Booker Prize.

Achebe's stories are collected in *The Sacrificial Egg, and Other Short Stories* (1962), *Girls at War* (1972), and *The Heinemann Book of Contemporary African Short Stories* (1992).

piece, *An Address to the Negroes in the State of New York,* at age seventy-six, after being freed by the family he served for three generations. In the *Address,* Hammon preaches that slaves are capable of accepting Christ, and that those who do not are morally enslaved by their masters. By accepting Christ, slaves guarantee themselves freedom after death, the only freedom Hammon believed was imminently possible. Drawing heavily on biblical theology, Hammon encouraged blacks to have high moral standards precisely because their enslavement on earth had already secured their place in heaven, where the color veil would be lifted. He also advocated a plan of gradual emancipation as a compromise to ending **slavery** immediately, and thought a pension should be established by slave owners for slaves emancipated after they were no longer able to work. However, Hammon was criticized for his insistence that older slaves should be cared for by their masters if they were incapable of caring for themselves. Hammon's **essay** was published by the New York Quakers twice during his lifetime, and once after his death by members of the Pennsylvania Society for Promoting the Abolition of Slavery.

Adele Parker

Character in *Ceremonies in Dark Old Men*

Adenebi

Character in *A Dance of the Forests*

Adulthood Rites

Please see "Xenogenesis" Trilogy

Africa, My Africa

Margaret Taylor Burroughs
Poems, 1970

Africa, My Africa is **Margaret Taylor Burroughs**'s second volume of **poetry**. Inspired largely by her 1968 trip to Ghana, it chronicles an African American's journey to Africa through a series of eighteen interrelated poems. Throughout the volume, Burroughs merges personal history with the larger social and cultural history of the African American community. Some of the poems address the social transformation and economic stratification of an Africa increasingly influenced by American and European music, television, automobiles, and other consumer products. Other poems in the series reflect on the slave trade, whose history is enshrined in the slave castles built to hold African captives for transport to the Americas. Overall, the poems explore the African American experience as both a continuation of and a break with African roots, and evoke the ambiguities of Africa in the consciousness of African Americans.

African Civilizationism

African Civilizationism is a scholarly movement that ascribes to black Africans a larger role in the origin of human civilization than has generally been recognized. It is often a central component of Afrocentric education, which attempts to place the black student at the center of world history. Some critics charge that, in practice, this worthy goal has sometimes been pursued at the expense of historical and scientific accuracy. Both African Civilizationism and **Afrocentrism** have as one aim the restoration of black people's pride in their African heritage.

A leading proponent of African Civilizationism was Senegalese historian **Cheikh Anta Diop**, who was honored by the World Festival of Negro Arts as the black intellectual who had most influenced the twentieth century. Diop contended that the first signs of civilization appeared in sub-Saharan Africa. He further argued that the ancient Egyptians, with their technologically and culturally advanced civilization, were black. His book *Nations negres et culture (The African Origin of Civilization: Myth or Reality,* 1974) appeared in 1955. Another historian who has argued for the

African origins of civilization is **Yosef ben-Jochannan**. His works include *African Origins of the Major "Western Religions"* (1970), *Africa: Mother of "Western Civilization"* (1971), and *We the Black Jews: Witness to the "White Jewish Race" Myth* (1983).

African Notebook: Views on Returning 'Home'

Charles E. Cobb Jr.
Nonfiction, 1971

In *African Notebook,* **Charles E. Cobb Jr.** examines the relationship between African Americans and Africans. Sent to Tanzania by the Drum and Spear Press, Cobb investigated the social and political issues related to the "separation and fragmentation that exists" between blacks in America and in Africa. He maintains that while black Americans have a romanticized view of their connection to Africa, Africans have ambivalent feelings toward American blacks.

An African-American in South Africa

Ralph Bunche
Travelogue, 1992

As a recipient of a Social Science Research Council grant, then-Howard University political science professor **Ralph Bunche** visited South Africa in the last quarter of 1937 to gain field experience in anthropological methods. His nationality as an African American allowed him entrees otherwise denied to non-native South Africans. *An African-American in South Africa: The Travel Notes of Ralph J. Bunche, 28 September 1937-1 January 1938* describes his experiences. He toured numerous sites and spoke with many inhabitants. Among his experiences were attendance at political meetings or annual gatherings of the All-African Convention, the Native Representative Council,

and the African National Congress. Bunche observed racial issues first-hand, and his posthumously published travel **diary** documents many of the attitudes and biases of both white and black South Africans.

Africans at the Crossroads

John Henrik Clarke
Essays, 1991

John Henrik Clarke's *Africans at the Crossroads: Notes for an African World Revolution* explores the black struggle for freedom in the context of: the nineteenth-century roots of black resistance; the "uncompleted revolutions" of **Kwame Nkrumah**, Patrice Lumumba, **Marcus Garvey**, **Malcolm X**, and Tom Mboya; the viability of working within established political structures; the tenuousness of Africa's relationship with the Middle East; and the effects of **colonialism**. Clarke's **essays** focus on Africa rather than blacks in America because, according to Clarke, the plight of African Americans can succeed only when rooted in the struggle to regain their African homeland.

The Africans: A Triple Heritage

Ali A. Mazrui
Nonfiction, 1986

Ali A. Mazrui's *The Africans* is a photographically illustrated companion volume to a nine part television series broadcast by the British Broadcasting Corporation in October, 1986. In this controversial work, the author focuses on how Africans have historically dealt with Western and Islamic influences. Mazrui treats a number of topics, among them **religion**, politics, economics, militarism, the slave trade, language, technology, cultural change, and sports. He attributes many of Africa's problems to Western imperialism, citing an "informal pact" between African and Western leaders, which has resulted in the subordination of African nations. Mazrui also faults Africa's climate and natural resources, as well as short-sighted decisions by African leaders as sources of the problems that Africa and its people face.

Afrocentrism

Afrocentrism is an educational philosophy that emphasizes the importance of African people as agents of history and culture. It arose in the United States around 1980 in response to perceived inadequacies in the education of African American students. In contrast to the nation's Eurocentric model of education, Afrocentrism places the black student at the center of history. Proponents claim that this instills a sense of dignity and pride in African heritage. They further suggest that the integration of an Afrocentric perspective into the American consciousness will ultimately benefit students of all colors in a racially diverse society. In addition, advocates believe that black students who are empowered in this way will be better equipped to succeed in an increasingly complex world.

A leading figure in the Afrocentric movement is activist, scholar, and poet **Molefi Kete Asante**. In his book *The Afrocentric Idea* (1987), Asante contends that aspects of culture originating in Africa directly affect speech and behavior in black communities in the West. For example, he claims that African heritage is manifest in black achievements in music and sports. Asante is also author of *Malcolm X as Cultural Hero and Other Afrocentric Essays* (1993). Another spokesperson for this position is historian **Yosef ben-Jochannan,** whose books include *Africa: Mother of "Western Civilization"* (1971) and *From Afrikan Captives to Insane Slaves: The Need for Afrikan History in Solving the "Black" Mental Health Crisis in "America" and the World* (1992). In practice, adherents of Afrocentrism often adopt the theory of **African Civilizationism**, which argues for the African origins of civilization.

Agatha Cramp

Character in *The Walls of Jericho*

Agbale

Character in *The Dahomean*

Ama Ata Aidoo

Ghanaian dramatist and
short story writer
Born March 23, 1942.

Aidoo is a versatile writer who has combined western literary forms with those of African **oral tradition**. Her works have dealt with cultural conflict and oppression and incorporate a strong feminist stance.

Born to the chief of the Fanti town of Abeadzi Kyiakor, Ghana, Christina Ama Ata Aidoo was raised in a royal household but was educated in a Western manner. While she was attending the University of Ghana, Legon, her first **play**, *The Dilemma of a Ghost* (1964), was performed. The play deals with the conflict in values between Western individualism and African communalism. *Anowa* (1970), Aidoo's second play, is loosely based on a **folk tale** and displays Aidoo's strong feminist inclination.

The collection of eleven **short stories** *No Sweetness Here* (1970) is considered Aidoo's most successful synthesis of Western and African forms. In her **novel** *Our Sister Killjoy; or, Reflections from a Black-Eyed Squint* (1976), Aidoo utilizes several genres to condemn all forms of oppression. *Someone Talking to Sometime* (1985) is a collection of forty-four poems in which pain and tragedy are blended with affirmation and humor, while the novel *Changes: A Love Story* (1991) examines alternatives to love and marriage for women in contemporary Africa.

Further Readings

Black Writers, first edition, Gale, 1989.

Dictionary of Literary Biography, Volume 117: *Twentieth-Century Caribbean and Black African Writers,* First Series, Gale, 1992.

John J. Akar

Sierra Leonean dramatist
Born May 20, 1927.
Died June 23, 1975.

John Joseph Akar's *Valley Without Echo* (1949) became one of the first African plays to be produced in Europe when the British Council mounted a production in 1954. His second **play**, *Cry Tamba* (1954), was awarded the 1961 Independence Competition prize by the Congress for Cultural Freedom. Born in Rotifunk, Sierra Leone, in 1927, Akar enjoyed a diverse career as a writer, actor, and diplomat. Following his graduation from the University of California in 1950, he became a broadcaster for the Voice of America and the Sierra Leone Broadcasting System. An actor on Broadway and London stages, Akar later served as his country's ambassador to the United States and high commissioner to Canada. He died of a heart ailment in 1975 in Jamaica, his home for the last years of his life.

Further Readings

Black Writers, second edition, Gale, 1994.

Aké: The Years of Childhood

Wole Soyinka
Memoir, 1981

Wole Soyinka, the first black African to be awarded the Nobel Prize in literature, gained a loyal readership in the United Kingdom and in the United States with *Aké: The Years of Childhood,* his memoir of life through age eleven. Raised in the Nigerian village of Aké, Soyinka describes the people of his village, many of whom belonged to the Yoruba tribe. He also recounts memories that helped shape his artistic vision in later years. Soyinka grew up in the compound of a parsonage. His mother was a teacher and a Christian convert, and his father, whom Soyinka calls "Essay," was principal at St. Peter's Primary School, a village school established by the British. Although both of his parents were deeply influenced by European beliefs and colonial culture, Soyinka's paternal grandfather made

sure that he was educated in Yoruba **folklore** traditions. Specifically, Soyinka's grandfather taught him about the egungun, or the spirits of the dead who return to this world when special masks are worn and dances are performed in festive processions. In his memoir, Soyinka looks for balance both to Yoruba beliefs and to **Christianity**. Unity in three realms—that of one's ancestors, the living, and the as-of-yet unborn—is an important hallmark of African belief. Throughout his youth, Soyinka was aware of symbolic and spiritual incidents. When Soyinka's younger sister died on her first birthday, he believed that a universal disaster would soon follow.

Soyinka's memoir is a loosely structured collection of anecdotes. The sounds, scents, and flavors of the West Africa of his childhood give Soyinka's memoir a shape, as does his emerging consciousness. As the young Soyinka matures, his observations become more sophisticated. He gradually becomes aware of the serious conflicts that his community faces. *Aké* concludes with a tax revolt organized by Soyinka's mother; this event points to the beginnings of Nigerian independence. In 1989, Soyinka published a sequel to *Aké* called *Isara: A Voyage around Essay.*

Akin

Series character in "Xenogenesis" Trilogy

Nanina Alba

American poet and short story writer
Born November 21, 1915(?).
Died June 24, 1968.

Nannie Williemenia ("Nanina") Champney Alba was a teacher and a versatile poet of many themes and styles whose writings were often inspired by her life experiences. The subject matter of her work ranges from **religion** and spirituality to modern technology and music. Alba was born in 1915 (some sources say 1917) in Montgomery, Alabama, to a Presbyterian minister and his wife. Alba's first collection, *The Parchments: A Book of Verse* (1962), contains many poems that pay homage to her heroes, including musicians, writers, and scientists. In her second volume, *The Parchments II: A Book of Verse* (1967), Alba departed from the more traditional form of her earlier work to incorporate free verse and haiku. In other works, Alba created memorable prose **satire** in a series featuring a character named Miss Lucy.

Further Readings
Black Writers, second edition, Gale, 1994.
Dictionary of Literary Biography, Volume 41: *Afro-American Poets since 1955,* Gale, 1985.

Albert Wilkes
Character in *Sent for You Yesterday*

Delores P. Aldridge
American nonfiction writer and editor

A respected educator and sociologist, Delores Patricia Aldridge is the author of *Focusing: Black Male-Female Relationships* (1991). Her scholarship has been recognized with several honors, including the 1989 Presidential Award from the National Council for Black Studies and the 1990 Oni Award from the International Black Women's Congress.

Aldridge was born in Tampa, Florida. After receiving her Ph.D. from Purdue University in 1971, she began teaching sociology in Atlanta at Emory University, where she was founding director of the Afro-American and African studies department. Aldridge is the editor of *Black Male-Female Relationships: A Resource Book of Selected Materials* (1989) and *River of Tears: The Politics of Black Women's Health* (1993).

Further Readings
Black Writers, second edition, Gale, 1994.

Alec Lee
Character in *Compromise*

Estella Conwill Alexander
American poet
Born January 19, 1949.

After attending the University of Louisville, Alexander taught black **poetry** at the University of Iowa, where she also earned her doctorate. Having received grants in 1986 from the Kentucky Arts Council and the Kentucky Foundation for Women, Alexander published a collection of her poetry, *Jiva Telling Rites: An Initiation* (1989). She currently teaches English at Kentucky State University and Hunter College of the City University of New York.

Further Readings
Black Writers, second edition, Gale, 1994.

Ali
Character in *The Golden Serpent*

Alice Manfred
Character in *Jazz*

All God's Children Need Traveling Shoes
Maya Angelou
Autobiography, 1986

The fifth volume of **Maya Angelou**'s **autobiography** takes her through the early 1960s. It chronicles her four-year stay in Ghana, which was undertaken as part of her search for self and community. As the book begins, Angelou, who was accompanied to Ghana by her son Guy, is trying to establish herself in her adopted homeland. Resistance from native Ghanaians, however, in the form of disrespect and low pay, reminds her at times of the behavior of racist white Americans. After an assassination attempt on the life of Ghanaian president **Kwame Nkrumah** sours Ghanaian attitudes toward the expatriate American community, Angelou realizes that her search for a home outside the country of her birth is futile. Angelou contends that in order to feel at home, she must establish her own home within herself.

ogy of African poetry and has published **essays** on themes similar to those in his verse.

See also **Poetry of Samuel W. Allen**

Further Readings

Black Writers, first edition, Gale, 1989.

Dictionary of Literary Biography, Volume 41: *Afro-American Poets since 1955,* Gale, 1985.

Samuel W. Allen
American poet and critic
Born December 9, 1917.

A noted poet and critic, Samuel Washington Allen has emphasized the importance of African American heritage as a resource from which blacks can draw strength and understanding. His verse combines African traditions with aspects of black culture in America, particularly the black church, which Allen considers one of the most important influences on his poetry.

Born the son of a minister in Columbus, Ohio, Allen attended Fisk University, where he studied creative writing with the author and civil rights leader **James Weldon Johnson**. He graduated from Harvard Law School in 1941 and served as civil attorney for the United States Armed Forces in Europe between 1951 and 1955. During this period Allen was influenced by the **negritude** poets, a group of African and West Indian poets who wrote in French. He also became extensively involved in a magazine called *Presence Africaine,* in which his verse was first published in 1949.

Allen's first volume of **poetry,** *Elfenbein Zahne* (1968; title means "Ivory Tusks") was published in Germany under the pseudonym Paul Vesey. This bilingual edition, which contains English poems and their German translations, was not widely read in America. *Ivory Tusks and Other Poems* (1968) was published in the United States; despite the similarity of its title to Allen's first book, it was a collection of mostly new poetry. The poems in *Paul Vesey's Ledger* (1975) trace the history of racial oppression in America. Allen has also edited an anthol-

All-Night Visitors
Clarence Major
Novel, 1969

All-Night Visitors, **Clarence Major**'s first **novel,** is the story of Eli Bolton, an orphan, college dropout, Vietnam veteran, and sexual adventurer who seeks a sense of manhood through his relationships with women. In the course of this quest, several themes central to Major's fiction emerge: the mystery of women, the psychosexual nature of taboos, and the problem of self-identity in a chaotic and bigoted world. The publication of this novel by Maurice Girodias's Olympia Press did not go smoothly, as Girodias insisted on excising about half of the original manuscript. Wanting to publish and needing the money, Major reluctantly agreed to the terms.

Alphonse
Character in *Eva's Man*

Alton Scales
Character in *The Sign in Sidney Brustein's Window*

T. M. Aluko
Nigerian novelist
Born June 14, 1918(?).

Timothy Mofolorunso Aluko's **novels** offer a unique glimpse into Nigerian politics and society. His satiric portrayal of his compatriots has at times provoked scathing criticism. Yet the skill with which he develops his tragicomic vision has also brought appreciation for novels such as *One Man, One Matchet* (1964), *Kinsman and Foreman* (1966), and *Chief the Honourable Minister* (1970).

Born in Ilesha, West Nigeria, in 1918 (one source says 1920), Aluko is married and the father of six children. He is a municipal engineer who drew heavily upon his civil service experience for his early fiction. His later works, which afford closer examinations of Nigerian affairs, include *His Worshipful Majesty* (1972), *Wrong Ones in the Dock* (1982), and *A State of Our Own* (1986).

Further Readings

Black Writers, first edition, Gale, 1989.

Dictionary of Literary Biography, Volume 117: *Twentieth-Century Caribbean and Black African Writers,* First Series, Gale, 1992.

Elechi Amadi

Nigerian novelist, dramatist, and nonfiction writer
Born May 12, 1934.

Elechi Emmanuel Amadi is considered one of the foremost chroniclers of African village life in English literature. His **novels** have garnered acclaim for their style of narration and dialogue. Amadi was born in the Nigerian village of Aluu, the setting for his first three novels: *The Concubine* (1966), *The Great Ponds* (1969), and *The Slave* (1979). Unlike these works, Amadi's fourth **novel**, *Estrangement* (1985), takes place in an urban, postcolonial setting. Amadi has also written **plays** and a nonfiction book, *Ethics in Nigerian Culture* (1982).

Further Readings

Black Writers, first edition, Gale, 1989.

Dictionary of Literary Biography, Volume 117: *Twentieth-Century Caribbean and Black African Writers,* First Series, Gale, 1992.

Eko, Ebele, *Elechi Amadi: The Man and His Work,* Kraft, 1991.

Amamu

Character in *This Earth, My Brother*

Amy Taylor

Character in *Dhalgren*

And Then We Heard the Thunder

John Oliver Killens
Novel, 1962

John Oliver Killens's experience during World War II while stationed in the South Pacific inspired his second **novel**. *And Then We Heard the Thunder* depicts a group of soldiers who are subject to the institutional **racism** of a segregated military. Solly Saunders gave up law school for the officer's training program, but soon realizes its limitations. His wife, Millie Bedford Saunders, wants him to further his military career as much as he can during the conflict. Solly complains about the policies to Lt. Robert Samuels, a sympathetic Jewish northern liberal. While the war is characterized as a simple attack on fascism, a bitter twist ensues when Solly must lead his own men to fight white Americans in Australian territory.

Henry L. Anderson

American nonfiction writer
Born May 23, 1934.

Henry Lee Norman Anderson has had a multifaceted career as an academic administrator, nonfiction writer, lecturer, and radio and television host. In addition, he has published a **novel**, *No Use Cryin'* (1961). Born in Ogeechee, Georgia, in 1934, Anderson is married and the father of three children. After completing his Ed.D. degree from the University of California at Los Angeles in 1972, he went on to write *Revolutionary Urban Teaching* (1973) and to serve as chancellor of City University, also in Los Angeles. A licensed counsellor and host of a weekly television series on health, Anderson has also written

Helping Hand: Eight-Day Diet Programs for People Who Care About Wellness (1986) and *Organic Wellness Fasting Technique* (1992).

Further Readings
Black Writers, second edition, Gale, 1994.

Jervis Anderson

Jamaican nonfiction writer and journalist
Born October 1, 1936.

Jervis B. Anderson worked as a journalist in Kingston, Jamaica, before coming to the United States to study literature at New York University. He has continued to live in New York City while pursuing a writing career. He has been a staff writer at the *New Yorker* magazine since 1968. His first book, *A. Philip Randolph: A Biographical Portrait* (1973), which examines the life of the black labor leader, won the Sidney Hillman Foundation Award. Anderson is also the author of the well-received books *This Was Harlem: A Cultural Portrait, 1900-1950* (1982) and *Guns in American Life* (1984).

Further Readings
Black Writers, second edition, Gale, 1994.

Angela Davis: An Autobiography

Angela Davis
Autobiography, 1974

Angela Davis: An Autobiography was written and published following a highly publicized conspiracy trial. **Angela Davis** uses episodes in her life to dramatize her experiences with **racism** and political activism. The book is divided into six sections, beginning with Davis' incarceration in 1970. Davis also discusses her childhood, her college years and study abroad, and her commitment to commu-

nism while a teacher in California. She also describes her extradition and pre-trial negotiations between officials and her defense team. The narrative ends with an account of her trial and acquittal.

Angela Murray

Character in *Plum Bun: A Novel Without a Moral*

Angela Williams Lavoisier

Character in *Let the Lion Eat Straw*

Angelina Green

Character in *Who Is Angelina?*

Maya Angelou

American novelist, poet, and dramatist
Born April 4, 1928.

Angelou is best known as a poet and the author of a series of autobiographical **novels.** She has been praised for confronting both the racial and sexual pressures on black women and her work combines her perspective as an individual with her involvement in larger social and political movements, including civil rights.

Angelou was born Marguerita Johnson in St. Louis, Missouri, to Bailey and Vivien Baxter Johnson. Her parents soon divorced and she was sent to live with her grandmother in rural Arkansas, where she spent most of her early childhood. During a visit to St. Louis when she was eight years old, Angelou was raped by her mother's boyfriend, whom her uncles subsequently killed. Angelou did not speak for some years afterwards.

In 1940, Angelou moved to San Francisco with her mother. While attending high school, she became pregnant and gave birth to a son in 1945, just after receiving her diploma. To support her child and herself, she worked several odd jobs, and was also a madam and a prostitute. While appearing as a dancer in a cabaret, she changed her name to Maya Angelou. Her experience there led to an acting and singing career and she joined a cast performing *Porgy and Bess* throughout Europe.

When she was thirty, Angelou moved to New York and joined the Harlem Writers Guild, where she met **James Baldwin**. She became involved in the **civil rights movement**, serving as northern coordinator for **Martin Luther King Jr.**'s Southern Christian Leadership Conference from 1959 to 1960. She later moved to Egypt, where she edited an English-language newspaper, and then to Ghana, working as a writer and editor.

In 1970, Angelou published **I *Know Why the Caged Bird Sings,*** written with the encouragement of Baldwin. An account of her childhood up to the birth of her son, it is her most critically acclaimed work and was nominated for a National Book Award. *Gather Together in My Name* (1974) describes her search for identity and her struggle for survival as a young, unwed mother. In *Singin' and Swingin' and Gettin' Merry Like Christmas* (1976), Angelou chronicles her show business career, and in *The Heart of a Woman* (1981) she describes her emergence as a writer and a political activist. Based on her experience in Ghana, *All God's Children Need Traveling Shoes* (1986) examines the relationship between Africa and black culture in America. Angelou has written several **plays** for the stage and television, as well as several volumes of **poetry**, including the Pulitzer-Prize nominated *Just Give Me a Cool Drink of Water 'fore I Diiie* (1971), *And Still I Rise* (1976), and *Shaker, Why Don't You Sing?* (1983).

In January, 1993, Angelou became the first woman and the first African American to read her work at a presidential inauguration; her inaugural poem, **"On the Pulse of Morning"** (1993), celebrates the diversity of the American and world communities and calls on them to work together to create a better future. That same year she collected several of her

Angelou in 1971 with her best-selling autobiography.

essays in *Wouldn't Take Nothing For My Journey Now,* in which she offers autobiographical pieces along with meditations on her philosophy of life. Many of her writings have been anthologized in *The Complete Collected Works of Maya Angelou* (1994).

See also **Poetry of Maya Angelou**

Further Readings

Black Literature Criticism, Gale, 1992.

Black Writers, second edition, Gale, 1994.

Contemporary Literary Criticism, Gale, Volume 35, 1985.

Dictionary of Literary Biography, Volume 38: *Afro-American Writers after 1955: Dramatists and Prose Writers,* Gale, 1985.

Angie Tucci

Character in *Jungle Fever*

Annie

Character in *Annie Allen* and *The Conjure Woman*

Annie Allen
Gwendolyn Brooks
Poetry, 1949

Gwendolyn Brooks's *Annie Allen* won the 1950 Pulitzer Prize for poetry. The **poetry** combines romance and **realism** and includes a more symbolic and mythic dimension than her earlier collection, *A Street in Bronzeville* (1945). A young woman's dreams of romance, marriage, and family are influenced by European American lore, while the discouraging realities of married life are identified with difficulties of life in the black community. Annie is at once a black mythic heroine and a black woman caught in realistic situations that bring the mythic down to earth. The voice of the narrator, which combines realism and romance, reflects the natural human tendency to include the language and forms of **myth** in its descriptions of Annie's struggle to reach maturity.

The book's sections form an **epic** cycle. The first poem, "The Birth in a Narrow Room," uses imagery from both fairy tales and the "real" world. The title "Anniad" plays on titles of epics in general and on the title of Virgil's epic *Aeneid* in particular. "Anniad," "Notes from the Childhood and the Girlhood," "Appendix to the Anniad," and "The Womanhood" form the main part of the epic cycle. These sections deal with Annie's growth to maturity as they warn against the dangers of trying to prolong one's youth with romantic dreams. In *Annie Allen,* a young woman experiences the emergence of her own whole psyche as she grows into the community of adult black women.

Other poems in *Annie Allen* include "Beverly Hills, Chicago," in which a poor couple comes to terms with the luxuries possessed by the rich. The book also contains a sonnet sequence titled "The Children of the Poor." "The Parents: People Like Our Marriage, Maxie and Andrew" illustrates Brooks's habit of combining established poetic conventions with unconventional language and forms to express her own unique poetic voice.

Annie Henderson
Character in *I Know Why the Caged Bird Sings*

Annie John
Character in *Annie John*

Annie John
Jamaica Kincaid
Novel, 1985

The structure of **Jamaica Kincaid**'s first **novel** is much like her short story collection *At the Bottom of the River*. Sections are episodic, though all eight form a complete narrative trajectory. Annie John is a young black girl in Antigua who must experience the basic initiation rites of puberty, both physical and social. In "Figures at a Distance," Annie comes to terms with her father's occupation and the implications it has for her future. Since he makes coffins, she becomes occupied by thoughts of his reaction to her imaginary death. "The Circling Hand" refers to the confines of marriage. Annie's mother encourages the child's freedom of choice, but only in terms of certain implied expectations of her future involving domesticity. This foreshadows the later entrance of Annie's grandmother, against whom Annie's mother rebelled by following a more Westernized path of homemaking and childrearing. Two following chapters regard Annie's school friends. The section "Gwen" introduces Gweneth Joseph on the first day of the school year. Gwen is left behind when Annie reaches menarche and begins to feel like a woman. In "The Red Girl" Annie and another friend, known as "the Red Girl," sneak off together and hide to play marbles. Annie's mother reacts so strongly against the girls' activities that mother and daughter are still estranged when the Red Girl relocates to another school. "The Long Rain" depicts a crisis point in Annie's internal drama. When Annie develops a mysterious illness, a conventional doctor and a local healer both fail to make her better. However, Annie's maternal grandmother nurses the girl through the rainy season. By the time she is cured, Annie has experienced a growth spurt. The last chapter is symbolically titled "A Walk to the Jetty." Annie has been recognized as a promising talent and is off to nursing school, yet she remains on deck waving good-bye to her mother until the shoreline is no longer visible.

Another Life
Derek Walcott
Poem, 1972

The book-length poem *Another Life* is **Derek Walcott**'s autobiographical portrait of the West Indian artist. The work is divided into four parts. Part one, "The Divided Child," deals with Walcott's childhood education and the provincialism of Castries, St. Lucia. In part two, "Homage to Gregorias" Walcott remembers his teenage years and his friendship with the painter Dunstan St. Omer, who comes to symbolize all struggling artists of his generation. In the third part, "A Simple Flame," the poet remembers his first love, and considers the fire in 1948 that destroyed much of Castries, changing the town permanently except in memory. In the fourth and final part, "The Estranging Sea," Walcott recalls with bitterness the suicides and attempted suicides of his artist friends, but he finally rejects his anger and hopes instead to forget, and start afresh.

Sunday O. Anozie
Nigerian literary critic and writer
Born 1942.

Trained as a sociologist in Nigeria and at the Sorbonne, Paris, Sunday Ogbonna Anozie has devoted his career to **literary criticism**. While in Paris in 1969 he founded the African culture and literary journal *Conch,* which is now published at the University of Texas at Austin, where Anozie

serves as the journal's managing editor. He was born in Owerri, eastern Nigeria, in 1942. His first book, *Sociologie du roman africaine* (1970), examines the social and political background of a vast array of African **novels** in French and English from a structuralist perspective. His subsequent writings, including *Christopher Okigbo: Creative Rhetoric* (1972) and *Structural Models and African Poetics: Towards a Pragmatic Theory of Literature* (1981), are similarly characterized by a highly theoretical approach to African literature. In 1982 Anozie edited *Phenomenology in Modern African Studies,* a selection of contributions to *Conch.*

Further Readings
Black Writers, second edition, Gale, 1994.

Tina McElroy Ansa
American novelist and journalist
Born November 18, 1949.

A recipient of the American Library Association Best Fiction for Young Adults Award, Ansa is known for her **novels** focusing on African American family life. Her widely praised *Baby of the Family* (1989) is a coming-of-age novel about a teenaged girl who possesses mystical powers, whereas *Ugly Ways* (1993) focuses on three sisters reminiscing about their very unusual upbringing. Both novels are set in the author's home state of Georgia.

Ansa received a B.A. degree in English from Spelman College in 1971. She has worked as a newspaper editor, feature writer, and reporter for the *Atlanta Constitution* and the *Charlotte (NC) Observer.* In addition, she has written book reviews for various periodicals, including *New York Newsday* and the *Los Angeles Times Book Review.*

Further Readings
Black Writers, second edition, Gale, 1994.

Dust jacket for Achebe's novel of political corruption and societal reform.

Anthills of the Savannah
Chinua Achebe
Novel, 1987

In *Anthills of the Savannah* **Chinua Achebe** examines themes similar to those of his earlier work *A Man of the People:* integrity, honesty, sacrifice, and political corruption. The **novel** takes place in Kangan, a fictional West African country modelled on Nigeria, and reflects many of Achebe's opinions and criticisms about his homeland. *Anthills of the Savannah* tells the story of three friends who grew up together: Sam, the president of Kangan, who seeks to become president for life; Ikem Osodi, editor of the *National Gazette,* who assisted Sam in his bid for the presidency; and Chris Oriko, who serves in Sam's cabinet as minister for information.

Sam's government begins honestly, but he soon begins to listen to advisors who attempt to manipulate Sam for their own reward. At a meeting of African heads of state Sam is influenced by several characters—whom Achebe based on historical African figures—including Haile Selassie, the former emperor of Ethiopia, who advises him on how to increase his personal power, and Ngongo, who counsels him to discard his boyhood friends because they pose a potential threat to him. Accordingly, on his return Sam begins the process of eliminating both Ikem and Chris.

Ikem falls victim to a trumped-up conspiracy charge after he is overheard commenting sarcastically on Sam's plan to mint coins in his own likeness. The state police arrest him, accuse him of plotting Sam's death, and kill him. Chris reacts to his friend's murder by using his contacts in the information industry to spread the true story. Government opposition forces him into hiding, however, and he is finally tracked down by soldiers and shot. Sam's regime falls to a military coup on the same day that Chris dies. Its collapse is chronicled by Beatrice, a writer who makes Sam realize the consequences of his actions.

Anthony Cross

Character in *Plum Bun: A Novel Without a Moral*

A Apartheid

Apartheid is a policy of institutionalized racial **segregation** long practiced by the government of South Africa. The stated aim of this system was the separate development of the races, but critics charged that it was actually a means of maintaining white European domination over nonwhites. **Racism** and **discrimination** had been part of the South African social, political, and economic scene ever since the first European settlers arrived in the seventeenth century; by the early part of the twentieth century, segregation had fallen under formal regulations. Separate land areas were designated for European and non-European ownership and residence, and blacks working in white areas were subjected to severe restrictions. This policy of government-imposed segregation was expanded through later legislation, especially after World War II. It was perpetuated, in part, by the fact that nonwhites were granted very limited political rights.

Over the years, some black South Africans managed to speak out against the injustices of apartheid. For example, **Dennis Brutus** published his *Letters to Martha, and Other Poems from a South African Prison* (1968) after beginning a period of forced exile. A later book of poems about exile and alienation, published under a pseudonym, circulated in South Africa until the true identity of the author was discovered and all copies were con-

fiscated. In the memoir *Kaffir Boy: The True Story of a Black Youth's Coming of Age in Apartheid South Africa* (1986; *Kaffir Boy: Growing Out of Apartheid,* 1987), **Mark Mathabane** describes the oppression he endured growing up in a black township near Johannesburg, where he lived until receiving a tennis scholarship to an American college. Black writers from other countries added their voices to the protest. For instance, after black Guyanese writer E. R. Braithwaite was named an "honorary white" by the South African government so that he could visit that country and enjoy white privileges there, he chronicled the experience in *"Honorary White": A Visit to South Africa* (1975).

Apartheid laws were relaxed slightly during the late 1970s and 1980s. In 1984, the Nobel Peace Prize was awarded to **Desmond Tutu**, a black Anglican clergyman in South Africa who promoted the use of nonviolent resistance against apartheid. Many of Tutu's most important **speeches** and sermons have been collected in books such as *Crying in the Wilderness: The Struggle for Justice in South Africa* (1982). In 1990, President F. W. De Klerk resolved to eliminate apartheid. Over the next few years, the government dismantled much of the legal structure supporting the apartheid system. However, racism and inequality remained volatile issues in South African society.

One longtime leader in the struggle against apartheid had been **Nelson Mandela**, who was sentenced to life imprisonment for political offenses in 1964. Although possession of his writings became a crime after his conviction, collections of Mandela's speeches and **essays** such as **No Easy Walk to Freedom** (1965) and **The Struggle Is My Life** (1978) were published abroad and widely circulated among anti-apartheid activists within South Africa. Mandela was finally released from prison in 1990. Four years later, he was elected the first black president of that country, signaling the beginning of a new political era there.

Anthony Appiah

English-Nigerian philosopher and writer
Born May 8, 1954.

Kwame Anthony Appiah was born in London, England, to a Nigerian father and English mother and brought up in both cultures. He examines his own complex African identity in *In My Father's House: Africa in the Philosophy of Culture* (1992), finding it an evolving concept based on far more than race.

Appiah was trained in philosophy at Cambridge University and has taught at Yale, Cornell, Duke, and Harvard. His scholarly books include *Assertion and Conditionals* (1985), *For Truth in Semantics* (1986), *Necessary Questions: An Introduction to Philosophy* (1989), and several edited works. He has also written a mystery **novel,** *Avenging Angel* (1990). Appiah is a founding member and past president of the Society for African Philosophy in North America.

Further Readings
Black Writers, Gale, second edition, 1994.

Arcella Jefferson

Character in *The Learning Tree*

Ayi Kwei Armah

Ghanaian novelist and essayist
Born October 28, 1939.

Considered an innovative and controversial writer, Armah combines Western and African influences in a variety of literary genres. His works communicate the forces—both foreign and domestic—that impact upon Africa.

Armah was born in Takoradi, Gold Coast (now Ghana), to Fante-speaking parents. Educated in Ghana and the United States, Armah has been influenced by revolutionary movements in Africa and civil rights struggles in America.

Armah's first three **novels,** *The Beautyful Ones Are Not Yet Born* (1968), *Fragments* (1970), and *Why Are We So Blest?* (1972), each present an alienated, western-educated protagonist for whom there is no escape from the corruption in contemporary Africa. Although reviews of these novels were generally positive, some critics considered the books too European in viewpoint.

In his next two novels, *Two Thousand Seasons* (1973) and *The Healers* (1978), Armah drastically changed his stance and focus. In these works, Armah examines the struggles and successes of African communities within a historical context.

Since the publication of *The Healers,* Armah has primarily written nonfiction to expound upon concerns in modern Africa.

Further Readings
Black Literature Criticism, Gale, 1992.
Black Writers, first edition, Gale, 1989.
Fraser, Robert, *The Novels of Ayi Kwei Armah: A Study in Polemical Fiction,* Heinemann, 1979.

Armenta

Character in *Corner Boy*

The Arrivants: A New World Trilogy

Edward Kamau Brathwaite
Poetry, 1973

The Arrivants, a trilogy of autobiographical poems, established **Edward Kamau Brathwaite**'s international reputation as a poet. The poems of these separately published volumes are organized into a single narrative. The recurring character in *Rights of Passage* is Tom, who survives the passage to America and attempts to discover his identity as both an African and a black man in a new land. In *Masks* Brathwaite searches for his ancestry in Africa, while *Islands* celebrates African culture, now transplanted to the Caribbean. The central issue that links the volumes involves African-American displacement and identity.

Arrow of God

Chinua Achebe
Novel, 1964

Chinua Achebe's *Arrow of God* examines the abuse of power and the impact of **colonialism** in early twentieth-century Nigeria. The story takes place in the village of Umuaro, an Ibo settlement. The chief political and religious figure of the village is Ezeulu, chief priest of the god Ulu. Ezeulu has to defend his power against threats from both Nwaka, a rich rival chief, and Ezidemili, chief priest of another god named Idemili, as well as from the British colonial authorities. The **novel** centers on the conflict between Ezeulu's desire to expand his personal power and his sense of duty to his people and his god.

Ezeulu's downfall begins when colonial authorities arrest and imprison him for political reasons. Until then Ezeulu had been exploiting the British, using the information he had gained to enhance his personal power. The two months that Ezeulu is locked up, however, force the delay of yam-eating ceremonies that mark the passing of the calendar year and determine the planting season. On his return he discovers that some of the villagers have turned away from the worship of Ulu. In order to assert his own authority over both the British who imprisoned him and his fellow villagers, Ezeulu delays the yam harvest by two months. As a result, the unharvested yams rot and the village faces starvation.

Ezeulu's decision destroys his personal power and damages his family. Many worshipers desert Ulu, turning instead to the **Christianity** of the British colonists, which allows them to gather the yams they need to survive. In an effort to repair his father's reputation, Ezeulu's son Obika runs a memorial race while sick with a fever and dies soon after. Forced to face the consequences of his actions and no longer certain of his faith, Ezeulu goes mad.

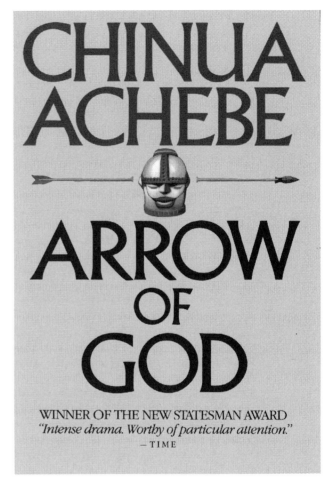

Achebe's novel examines politics and colonialism in Nigeria early in the twentieth century.

Arthur Montana

Character in *Just Above My Head*

Arveyda

Character in *The Temple of My Familiar*

Molefi Kete Asante

American scholar and poet
Born August 14, 1942.

Asante is a scholar of intercultural communication and a leading proponent of Afrocentric thought, which promotes the importance of African people as agents of history and culture.

Many critics believe his work in this area has helped make the Afrocentric perspective crucial to any noteworthy analysis of black society in America.

Born Arthur Lee Smith Jr. in Valdosta, Georgia, Asante legally changed his name in 1975. He received his degree from Oklahoma Christian College in 1964 and his doctorate from the University of California, Los Angeles, in 1968. He is currently chair of African American Studies at Temple University in Philadelphia.

In *The Afrocentric Idea* (1987), Asante argues that cultural ethics originating in Africa have had a direct effect on speech and behavior in black communities in the Western Hemisphere. He emphasizes the prominence in black culture of oral dialogue over the written word and suggests that African American heritage is manifest in achievements in music and sports. Asante concludes by insisting on the critical role played by the balance between African and European experiences in developing the African American identity. *Historical and Cultural Atlas of African Americans* (1991) is a chronological history presenting African American experiences from their African origins to the present day. The book provides several resources for the reader, including charts, maps, lists of important dates, statistical data, highlights of selected events, and brief biographies of important individuals. Asante has also published *Malcolm X as Cultural Hero and Other Afrocentric Essays* (1993) and *Fury in the Wilderness* (1994).

Further Readings
Black Writers, second edition, Gale, 1994.

Arthur Ashe

American tennis player, sportswriter, and autobiographer
Born July 10, 1943.
Died February 6, 1993.

The first black man to be inducted into the International Tennis Hall of Fame, Ashe attained worldwide acclaim for his 1975 Wimbledon singles triumph over Jimmy Connors. Although a heart condition forced his retirement from the sport only a few years later, Ashe continued to encourage young black players through his writings and lectures. In 1992, he revealed that he had contracted AIDS through a blood transfusion after surgery.

The son of a playground superintendent in then-segregated Richmond, Virginia, Arthur Robert Ashe Jr. demonstrated potential as a tennis player as early as age seven. However, he often encountered racial **discrimination**; as a member of the University of California—Los Angeles tennis team, for instance, he was excluded from a tournament held at an exclusive country club. Ashe discussed the **racism** he encountered before the days of the **civil rights movement** in the co-written autobiographies *Advantage Ashe* (1967), *Arthur Ashe: Portrait in Motion* (1975), *Off the Court* (1981), and the posthumously published **Days of Grace: A Memoir** (1993).

In 1979 Ashe was a member of the Davis Cup team and ranked as one of America's leading players when he suffered a heart attack. During his recovery he began *A Hard Road to Glory: A History of the African-American Athlete* (1988), a three-volume history that focuses on black athletes and their attempts to overcome prejudice from 1619 to 1986. Ashe also wrote how-to books for would-be tennis players, including *Getting Started in Tennis* (1977), *Mastering Your Tennis Strokes* (1978), and *Arthur Ashe's Tennis Clinic* (1981). He died in 1993.

Further Readings
Black Writers, second edition, Gale, 1994.

Contemporary Black Biography: Profiles from the International Black Community, Volume 1, Gale, 1992.

Robinson, Louie Jr., *Arthur Ashe: Tennis Champion,* Doubleday, 1970.

Assimilation

Assimilation occurs when one group of people is absorbed into the culture of another group, acquiring new customs and attitudes as a result. Full assimilation of an immigrant group, for instance, occurs when members of the new group become indistinguishable from longer-term members of the society. This concept is closely related to acculturation, which involves the cultural change that takes place when two or more different societies are in continual contact. Although this can be an equitable merging of customs and beliefs, more often it involves one society completely absorbing the cultural patterns of another. Such acculturation is often imposed by military or political domination—for example, through a system of **colonialism**. The **negritude** movement of the mid-twentieth century was, in part, designed to help blacks resist assimilation in the face of European colonialism and reclaim their African culture.

Many African American writers have, in one way or another, touched upon the basic theme of what it means to be black in America. *The Shaping of Black America* (1975), by **Lerone Bennett Jr.**, comprises a study of African Americans in the contexts of **slavery**, emancipation, and work. *The Black Woman* (1970), an anthology edited by **Toni Cade Bambara**, explores the African American female experience through the writings of such well-known black women writers as **Nikki Giovanni** and **Alice Walker**. *Black Is the Color of the Cosmos: Essays on Afro-American Literature and Culture, 1942-1981* (1982), by **Charles T. Davis**, examines the development of a black American literature.

Ashe in 1981, after the release of his third autobiography.

At the Bottom of the River

Jamaica Kincaid
Short stories, 1983

Jamaica Kincaid's collection of lyrical and impressionistic set pieces portrays the narrator, a black girl, and her relationships with her mother and father. A secondary character, the Red Woman, may or may not really exist. The first story is called "Girl" but takes the form of a monologue uttered by the narrator's mother. "In the Night" and "Wingless" both feature the Red Woman, a heroic but dangerous figure. Some episodes are presented as nightmares or the musings of someone in a state of depression, like "What I Have Been Doing Lately," "Blackness," and "In the Dark." "My Mother" also uses **fantasy** and imaginary figures symbolic of separation. Other episodes depict the real separations common in childhood: "Holidays" and "The Letter from Home." The last story, "At the Bottom of the River," describes a separation that is psychological rather than physical. The narrator's father appears in this section, and reveals a sensibility radically different from his daughter's. In the end, the girl undergoes a transformative experience that allows her to come to terms with her identity. The fantastic and poetic elements of this odyssey are subtly influenced by Afro-Caribbean religious themes of conjuring, herbal medicine, and the spirit realm. The narrator's initiation ritual at the end of the work has its roots in African tradition.

At the Rendezvous of Victory

C. L. R. James
Nonfiction, 1984

C. L. R. James's collection *At the Rendezvous of Victory* contains twenty-one literary, political, and historical pieces written over the fifty-year period between 1931 and 1981. The first two **essays**, "Revolution" and "The Star That Would Not Shine," originally appeared in *The Beacon,* a prominent West Indian periodical during the early 1930s. In "Revolution," the narrator relates a conversation with a Venezuelan living in Port-of-Spain who shares information about ousted Venezuelan president Castro. In "The Star That Would Not Shine," again involving an apparently innocuous discussion with a stranger, the narrator learns about the somewhat peculiar opportunity of the stranger's son to have a Hollywood film career. Other pieces in the collection include book reviews, portions of lectures, interviews, essays, and articles for periodicals.

Russell Atkins

American poet, dramatist, and essayist
Born February 25, 1926.

Advocating an experimental approach to literature and music, Atkins cofounded the influential *Free Lance,* one of the oldest black-owned literary magazines in the United States. He was, moreover, an early proponent of concrete **poetry,** in which the arrangement of the words creates a visual impact that takes precedence over their meaning, and he contributed significantly to **avant-garde** musical thought with his theory of psychovisualism, which emphasizes the importance of the brain, rather than the ear, in understanding music.

With the publication of his controversial dramas *The Abortionist* (1954) and *The Corpse* (1954), Atkins began experimenting with poems as **plays.** In the 1960s, Atkins published some of his best-known poetry collections, including *A Podium Presentation* (1960), *Phenomena* (1961), *Objects* (1963), *Objects 2* (1963), and *Heretofore* (1968).

See also **Poetry of Russell Atkins**

Further Readings

Black Writers, first edition, Gale, 1989.

Dictionary of Literary Biography, Volume 41: *Afro-American Poets since 1955,* Gale, 1985.

The Atonists

Characters in **Mumbo Jumbo**

William Attaway

American novelist and screenwriter
Born November 19, 1911.
Died June 17, 1986.

William Alexander Attaway's **novels** chronicle the migration of black Americans from the South to the North. Born in Mississippi on November 19, 1911, he moved with his family to Chicago while he was still young in order to escape the caste system of the South. Attaway is chiefly remembered for two novels: *Let Me Breathe Thunder* (1939), the story of two white hoboes and their attachment to a nine-year-old Mexican boy, and ***Blood on the Forge*** (1941), which details the experiences of three brothers at a steel mill in Pennsylvania. Attaway lived in Barbados for eleven years and spent the last part of his life in California writing screenplays. He died on June 17, 1986.

Further Readings

Black Literature Criticism, Gale, 1992.

Dictionary of Literary Biography, Volume 76: *Afro-American Writers, 1940-1955,* Gale, 1988.

Alvin Aubert

American poet
Born March 12, 1930.

Alvin Bernard Aubert's **poetry** is notable for its skill and the extent to which its rather aloof style ran counter to the prevailing currents in African American literature of the 1960s and 1970s. Beginning in 1975, Aubert's role as publisher and editor of *Obsidian: Black Literature in Review* allowed him to foster the scholarship and creativity of other black writers.

A high school dropout at fourteen, Aubert entered college after a stint in the army and eventually earned a master's degree from the University of Michigan in 1960. His first volume of poetry, *Against the Blues* (1972), drew its themes from his native Louisiana. His subsequent poetry collections have included *Feeling Through* (1976), *A Noisesome Music* (1979), and *South Louisiana: New and Selected Poems* (1985).

Further Readings

Black Writers, first edition, Gale, 1989.

Dictionary of Literary Biography, Volume 41: *Afro-American Poets since 1955,* Gale, 1985.

Aunt Carrie

Character in *Through the Ivory Gate*

Autobiography

An autobiography is a narrative in which an individual recounts his or her life story. The autobiography has been particularly important in the history of African American literature, because many of the first works by African American writers to be published and popularly accepted were **slave narratives**, in which African Americans described their experiences in **slavery** and often their escapes to freedom. More recent autobiographical works of note include E. R. Braithwaite's *To Sir, with Love* (1959), **Claude Brown**'s *Manchild in the Promised Land* (1965), **Maya Angelou**'s series of autobiographies that begins with *I Know Why the Caged Bird Sings* (1970), and **Mark Math-**

abane's *Kaffir Boy: The True Story of a Black Youth's Coming of Age in Apartheid South Africa* (1986; *Kaffir Boy: Growing Out of Apartheid,* 1987). Many prominent public figures have recorded their life experiences in autobiographies, including **Malcolm X**, **Coretta Scott King**, **Nelson Mandela**, and **Barbara Jordan**. Frequently, works of fiction will contain autobiographical elements. In addition, several well-known **novels** adopt the form of the autobiography in that their fictitious protagonists give first-person accounts of their life stories. These include **Ralph Ellison**'s *Invisible Man* (1952) and *The Autobiography of Miss Jane Pittman* (1971), by **Ernest J. Gaines**.

The Autobiography of an Ex-Coloured Man

James Weldon Johnson
Novel, 1912.

This **novel** posing as an **autobiography** was published anonymously in Boston, while **James Weldon Johnson** was in Nicaragua. The narrative, a critique of race relations, recounts how a light-skinned black woman and her son move north to Connecticut and into a middle-class existence. Their income is made up of subsidy checks sent by the absent white father to his ex-mistress and the mother's wages for seamstress work. The young boy grows up to be a musical prodigy, but children at school will not accept him as white. The father comes to visit when his son reaches the age of twelve, but later he drifts away, abandoning the family of two even when the woman becomes deathly ill. When the child finally graduates from high school, he is already an orphan. He becomes a drifter and returns to Georgia, ostensibly to continue his education; however, all his money is stolen the day after his arrival. He secures work but is laid off and must move on. In New York, he falls in with the ragtime crowd, finding a wealthy and perhaps homosexual patron, who takes him on a tour of Europe. When he returns to the United States his consciousness

This novel was originally published anonymously in 1912.

book to be truly autobiographical that Johnson eventually wrote his real life story, *Along This Way* (1933), to avoid confusion.

The Autobiography of LeRoi Jones
Amiri Baraka
Autobiography, 1984

The Autobiography of LeRoi Jones focuses primarily on **Amiri Baraka**'s early life and his rise to distinction as poet, playwright, and essayist LeRoi Jones. The son of lower-middle-class parents, Baraka provides an account of his childhood in Newark, New Jersey, during the Depression, emphasizing the influence of his loving grandmother and bebop music. He recalls his education at Rutgers and Howard Universities, whose middle-class hypocrisy he rejected, and discusses his stint in the Air Force, which discharged him for submitting poems to purportedly communist journals. Overwhelmed by feelings of alienation and **racism**, Baraka moved to New York's Greenwich Village, where he took refuge in the Beat movement's social rebelliousness, intellectual seriousness, and aesthetic freedom. While developing an interest in the new black music, white women, and surrealist art, he rose to become one of the movement's most recognizable figures, publishing numerous poems and **essays** on black music and culture. Following the death of **Malcolm X**, however, Baraka rejected his Bohemian past and his white wife.

Characterizing his cultural nationalist phase as "petty bourgeois fanaticism," Baraka writes of his move to Harlem and his founding role in the **black arts movement**, outlining its objectives both in political terms—as the African American fight for civil rights and the African struggle against imperialism and **colonialism**—and aesthetic terms—as a forum for creating accessible forms of cultural and artistic expression. While Baraka concedes that the movement's young, middle-class leadership once may have spoken for the African American

has been raised, and he travels among blacks from Boston down to Macon. However, a lynching makes him quail, so he returns to the North and his former existence as a white man. Almost desperately he throws himself into the New York business world. He is successful at last, though realizing it has been at the expense of his birthright. Later, he tries to salve his conscience by telling the secret of his racial identity to the woman he is about to marry. *The Autobiography* attracted little attention until it was reissued under Johnson's own name more than a decade after its original publication. So many readers believed the masses, he argues that its ideals were corrupted by the influence of mass media and opportunistic individuals within the movement. After condemning his critics for dwelling on his "white wife and white life," he praises his second wife, Amina, for keeping his bourgeois habits and male supremacist attitudes in check and for facilitating his conversion to Marxism.

The Autobiography of Malcolm X

Malcolm X, with Alex Haley
Autobiography, 1965

The **autobiography** of the charismatic African American leader **Malcolm X**, published shortly after he was assassinated in February, 1965, is widely viewed as one of the most influential works of African American literature to be produced in this century. Based on material dictated by Malcolm X, the book itself was written by Haley; although some critics initially questioned its authenticity, it is generally accepted as a valid expression of Malcolm's views. The book recounts the many transformations Malcolm underwent during his lifetime. Starting with his childhood in Nebraska and Michigan, it describes his drift into life as a hustler, drug dealer, pimp, and eventually, convict, his subsequent conversion to Islam, and his rise through the ranks of the **Nation of Islam**, an African American organization headed by Elijah Muhammad that preached black pride and typified whites as inherently evil. Malcolm's eloquent and biting denunciations of white culture, **Christianity**, integration, nonviolence, and the **civil rights movement** made him a prominent and controversial national figure. In the early 1960s, Malcolm became increasingly critical of Elijah Muhammad's worldly lifestyle; he broke with the Nation of Islam and made a pilgrimage to Mecca, where the apparent absence of racial **discrimination** among Muslims of many races caused him to revise some of his earlier ideas,

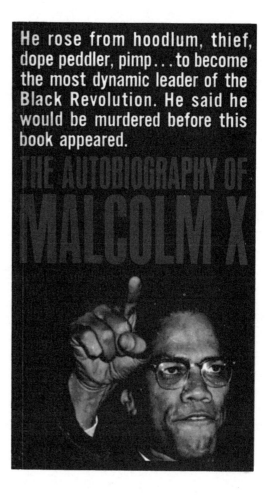

B-146 **$1.25**

He rose from hoodlum, thief, dope peddler, pimp... to become the most dynamic leader of the Black Revolution. He said he would be murdered before this book appeared.

One of the most influential works of contemporary African American literature.

including his blanket condemnation of whites. Taking the name El-Hajj Malik El-Shabazz, he began to expound worldwide black unity based on Marxist-Leninist principles. His disagreements with the Nation of Islam had led to his being targeted for retribution by that organization, and the end of the book portrays him enduring the harassment and threats that would soon culminate in his assassination.

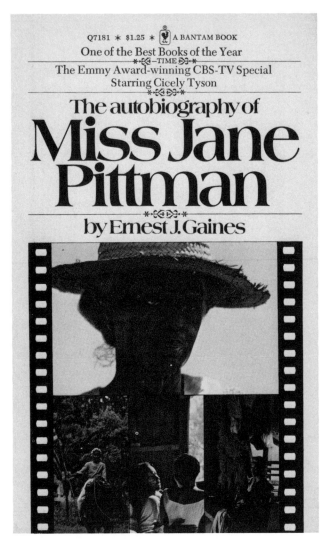

Q7181 ✳ $1.25 ✳ 🐰 A BANTAM BOOK
One of the Best Books of the Year
✳⊰ —TIME ⊱✳
The Emmy Award-winning CBS-TV Special
Starring Cicely Tyson
✳⊰⊱✳
The autobiography of
Miss Jane Pittman
✳⊰⊱✳
by Ernest J. Gaines

A television movie adapted from Gaines's book won nine Emmy Awards.

rights movement. **Ernest J. Gaines**'s **novel** offers the life history of Jane Pittman, who begins her tale by describing her life as a slave girl named Ticey. Incited by a Union soldier to assert her rights, Ticey is beaten severely. She decides to leave Louisiana for Ohio and joins a group led by an ex-slave named Big Laura. Retreating Confederate soldiers assault the group and kill the adults. Ticey—who has renamed herself Jane—survives, as does Big Laura's son, Ned. After facing the fact that Ohio is simply too far to reach on foot, the pair settle in rural Louisiana and endure the **racism** of the **Reconstruction** era.

The heart of the novel concerns the fate of the men in Jane's life. Ned, who takes the name Ned Douglass, becomes a teacher and orator who is eventually lynched by southern racists when he tries to run a school in his hometown. Joe Pittman, Jane's common-law husband, works as a horsebreaker, and is eventually killed. When Jane has become elderly, her deep love for the martyred civil rights worker Jimmy Aaron leads her into his struggle even though she is more than one hundred years old. Jimmy's death compels Jane to defy her white employer, plantation owner Robert Samson, for the first time in her life. Belatedly she assumes the courage of her departed friends—Big Laura, Ned, and Jimmy.

First published in 1971, *The Autobiography of Miss Jane Pittman* received both popular and critical recognition and solidified its author's reputation. The book was adapted for a television movie, which won nine Emmy Awards. Gaines was a consultant on the script.

A The Autobiography of Miss Jane Pittman

Ernest J. Gaines
Novel, 1971

Told in the singular voice of a 108-year-old former slave, *The Autobiography of Miss Jane Pittman* covers events from the end of the Civil War until the tense years of the **civil**

A Avant-garde

Avant-garde, a French term meaning "vanguard," is used in **literary criticism** to describe writing that rejects traditional approaches to literature in favor of innovations in style or content. *Free Lance,* one of the oldest black-owned literary magazines in the United

States, was established in 1950 as an avant-garde periodical. An example of avant-garde **poetry** is the work of *Free Lance* co-founder **Russell Atkins**. His subject matter covers such unconventional topics as sexual aberration, drug addiction, and abortion, and his stylistic innovations include unusual contractions and grammatical constructions. Examples of avant-garde fiction can be found in the short stories of **Eric Walrond**. His stories collected in *Tropic Death* (1926) are written in an impressionistic style that shifts quickly from image to image.

Avatar "Avey" Johnson

Character in *Praisesong for the Widow*

Obafemi Awo Awolowo

Nigerian sociopolitical writer and autobiographer
Born March 6, 1909.
Died May 10, 1987.

Awolowo first became politically active while attending the University of London and writing *Path to Nigerian Freedom* (1947). Growing increasingly liberal, Awolowo further immersed himself in politics, becoming a union organizer, a cabinet minister, and premier of Nigeria's Western Region. During a period of upheaval in his political party, Awolowo was found guilty of treason and imprisoned in 1962. When he was pardoned four years later, Awolowo resumed his political activities. Awolowo's *Thoughts on Nigerian Constitution* (1966), *The People's Republic* (1968) and *The Strategy and Tactics of the People's Republic of Nigeria* (1970) examine the challenges facing postwar Nigeria. Awolowo died in Western Nigeria in 1987.

Further Readings
Black Writers, second edition, Gale, 1994.

Kofi Awoonor

Ghanaian poet and essayist
Born March 13, 1935.

Formerly known as George Awoonor-Williams, Kofi Nyidevu Awoonor grew up in Ghana listening to Ewe oral poetry. Educated in Ghana, England, and the United States, Awoonor is best known for his **poetry.** His collections **Night of My Blood** (1971) and *Until the Morning After: Selected Poems, 1963-85* (1987) include work from his first collection, *Rediscovery, and Other Poems* (1964), as well as subsequent writings. His most recent poetry includes *Comes the Voyager at Last: A Tale of Return to Africa* (1992) and *The Latin American and Caribbean Notebook* (1993). Awoonor also wrote **This Earth, My Brother... An Allegorical Tale of Africa** (1971) and **The Breast of the Earth: A Survey of the History, Culture, and Literature of Africa South of the Sahara** (1975), a collection of essays. In 1983, Awoonor became Ghana's ambassador to Brazil.

Further Readings
Black Writers, second edition, Gale, 1994.

Dictionary of Literary Biography, Volume 117:- *Twentieth-Century Caribbean and Black African Writers,* First Series, Gale, 1992.

B

There is never time in the

future in which we will

work out our salvation. The

challenge is in the moment,

the time is always now.

Nobody Knows My Name:
More Notes of a Native Son,
James Baldwin, 1961

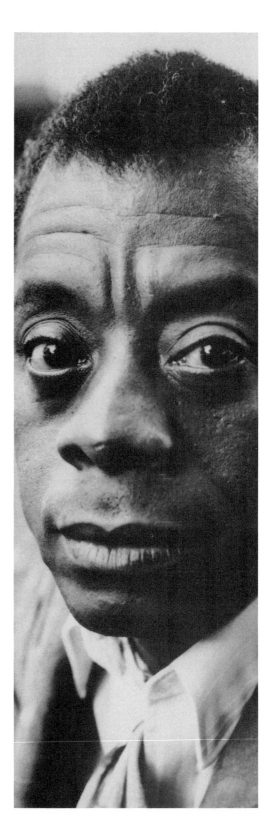

Mariama Ba

Senegalese novelist
Born in 1929.
Died in 1981.

Although her literary career was short, Ba won critical acclaim for her two **novels,** which focus on women's struggles under oppression. Ba was born in Senegal, where she worked as a secretary and a primary school teacher. Her first novel, *Une si longue lettre* (1980; *So Long a Letter,* 1981), earned Ba the first Noma Award for Publishing in Africa. In *Une si longue lettre,* a Senegalese woman named Ramatoulaye is abandoned by her husband, who marries a younger woman. *Une si longue lettre* chronicles her reacting to the betrayal and regaining her emotional stability. Ba's second, posthumous novel, *Un chant écarlate* (1981; *Scarlet Song,* 1986), portrays a tumultuous mixed marriage that disintegrates due to cultural differences.

Further Readings
Black Writers, second edition, Gale, 1994.

Babel-17

Samuel R. Delany
Novel, 1966

Samuel R. Delany's *Babel-17,* a **science fiction novel**, is divided into five parts, each introduced by a Marilyn Hacker poem. According to the author, words have an imagistic nature. This poetic function collapses any distinction between content and style. Such a subliminal impact is embodied by Babel-17, reputedly an alien code used by the Invaders. Rydra Wong is an Asian poetess of intergalactic repute. Her military assignment is to crack Babel-17. Through cryptographic analysis, Wong discovers that Babel-17 is actually an insidious mind-controlling language. She calls upon a friend, African psychologist Dr. Makus T'mwarba, who aids her resistance to this sabotage, preventing a takeover of the Earth-based Alliance. Wong responds to the challenge by inventing a counter-language, Babel-18. *Babel-17* won Delany his first Nebula Award.

Baby Girl

Character in *Clara's Old Man*

Baby Suggs

Character in *Beloved*

Back-to-Africa Movement

The back-to-Africa philosophy espoused by **Marcus Garvey** in the early twentieth century spurred the first mass movement with **black nationalism** as its central theme. In persuasive **essays**, poems, and **speeches**, Garvey urged people of African heritage to form an independent nation in Africa. At one point, he had more than a million followers, making him the leader of the largest and most powerful black movement in American history. Many of his most influential writings are collected in *The Philosophy and Opinions of Marcus Garvey; or, Africa for the Africans* (1923). Historian **Tony Martin** has published a number of books on Garvey, including *Race First: The Ideological and Organizational Struggles of Marcus Garvey and the Universal Negro Improvement Association* (1976).

In 1914, Garvey founded the Universal Negro Improvement Association, which aimed to unite blacks under the slogan "One God! One Aim! One Destiny!" Four years later, he launched a weekly newspaper, *Negro World,* which helped spread his message. Soon thereafter, he established the Black Star Shipping Line to create new economic opportunities for blacks, who bought stock in the line. Garvey wrote extensively about his movement and race philosophy. His ideas, in turn, shaped such prominent African American thinkers as **Adam Clayton Powell Jr.**, who went on to serve in the U.S. House of Representatives and write *Marching Blacks: An Interpretive History of the Rise of the Black Common Man* (1945). Another Garvey disciple was a Baptist minister whose son later took the name **Malcolm X** and became leader of the **Nation of Islam**, a group also known for its black nationalist views.

Tony Award-winning entertainer Pearl Bailey.

Bad Man

Please see **Six Plays for a Negro Theatre**

Bailey Johnson

Character in *Gather Together in My Name* and *I Know Why the Caged Bird Sings*

Pearl Bailey

American entertainer and autobiographer
Born March 29, 1918.
Died August 17, 1990.

Pearl Mae Bailey was a vocalist with musicians such as Count Basie, a performer in a number of Broadway productions, and the star of several movies and television shows, including *Porgy and Bess* (1959) and *All the Fine Young Cannibals* (1960). Born in Newport News, Virginia, in 1918, Bailey grew up in Philadelphia. Her entertainment career began when she won

first prize in an amateur night contest in 1933. She continued in vaudeville and then moved on to cabarets, eventually becoming one of the most popular nightclub performers in the United States. Her starring role in the long-running Broadway musical *Hello, Dolly* (1967-69) earned her a special Tony Award and widespread critical acclaim.

In 1968, Bailey published an autobiographical account of her life, *The Raw Pearl,* and subsequently wrote the memoir *Talking to Myself* (1971). In 1979, Bailey enrolled as an undergraduate at Georgetown University and received her bachelor's degree in theology in 1985. This event prompted her third autobiographical volume, *Between You and Me: A Heartfelt Memoir on Learning, Loving and Living* (1989), in which she encourages senior citizens to pursue their lifelong dreams. The first section of the book describes Bailey's experiences as a college student, the second comments on the breakdown of the American family, and the third recalls memorable experiences and people she encountered during her long and varied career. Bailey was visiting her sisters in Philadelphia when she suffered a heart attack and died in 1990.

Further Readings

Black Writers, second edition, Gale, 1994.

Augusta Baker

American librarian, storyteller, and writer
Born April 1, 1911.

Baker has combined her love of young people with her skills as a librarian and storyteller to broaden the experiences of children across the United States. Through her story compilations *The Talking Tree* (1955) and *The Golden Lynx* (1960), as well as the many reading lists she has compiled, Baker presents treasured old stories in formats that speak to a new generation of young readers.

Baker was born in 1911 in Baltimore, Maryland, and graduated from the New York College for Teachers in 1934. In her thirty-five years at the New York Public Library, she founded the **James Weldon Johnson** Memorial

Collection of books, which centers on the African American experience. In 1971, under her editorship, the library published the most comprehensive bibliographic sources then available on African American-based children's literature. *The Black Experience in Children's Books* (1971) guided writers, teachers, and students to over seven hundred titles reflecting black cultural traditions emanating not only from the United States but from Central and South America, Africa, England, and the Caribbean as well.

Baker's interest in exposing young audiences to a diversity of cultures also resulted in two collections of **short stories** designed to be read aloud: *The Talking Tree* includes fairy stories from fifteen different countries, many of which Baker rescued from obscurity. *The Golden Lynx* continues the tradition, with stories from seven lands told in a simple, direct style that combines humor with an Old World sensibility. In 1980 Baker became storyteller-in-residence at the University of South Carolina.

Further Readings
Black Writers, first edition, Gale, 1989.

Augusta Baker, a storyteller and librarian.

Houston A. Baker Jr.
American essayist and literary critic
Born March 22, 1943.

Baker is a literary critic whose work has been devoted to defining the African American literary tradition. He has argued that this literary tradition is a cultural phenomenon that only members of the culture are qualified to evaluate, and he has developed linguistic and sociohistorical methods that can be used in the study of other cultures that exist in the shadow of a dominant one.

Baker was born in 1943 in Louisville, Kentucky, and earned his B.A. in English from Howard University in 1965. After receiving his Ph.D. from the University of California, Los Angeles, he began teaching at Yale University. He taught at the University of Virginia in the early 1970s before accepting an appointment at the University of Pennsylvania in 1974.

Baker's first book-length study of black literature, *Long Black Song,* examines the works of **Frederick Douglass**, **W. E. B. Du Bois**, and others, and argues for the existence of an African American literary tradition. He continued to explore these themes in *Singers of Daybreak* (1974). He began his detailed treatment of poetic and narrative language in *The Journey Back: Issues in Black Literature and Criticism* (1980). In *Blues, Ideology, and Afro-American Literature* (1984), Baker studied the role of **the blues** in black culture, extending his theoretical work into both semiotic theory and economic history. Baker continued his examination of black culture and music in *Black Studies, Rap, and the Academy* (1993).

Further Readings
Black Writers, second edition, Gale, 1994.
Dictionary of Literary Biography, Volume 67: *Modern American Critics Since 1955,* Gale, 1988.

Baldwin explored the psychological implications of racism for both the oppressed and the oppressor.

James Baldwin

American novelist, essayist, and dramatist
Born August 2, 1924.
Died December 1, 1987.

James Arthur Baldwin is recognized as one of the most important twentieth-century American writers. In his works, he exposed racial and sexual polarization in American society and challenged readers to confront and resolve these differences. Baldwin's influence and popularity peaked during the 1960s, when he was regarded as the leading literary spokesperson of the **civil rights movement**.

Baldwin was born in Harlem, New York, on August 2, 1924. His stepfather, a Pentecostal preacher, struggled to support his large family. As a youth, Baldwin was an excellent student who sought to escape his impoverished environment by reading, writing, and attending movies and plays. He served as a junior minister at the Fireside Pentecostal Assembly as a teenager. After graduating from high school in 1942, Baldwin took a job in Belle Meade, New Jersey, to help support his brothers and sisters. Following his stepfather's death in 1943, Baldwin, determined to make writing his profession, moved to Greenwich Village and began a **novel.** Five years later, he moved to Paris; he remained in France for most of his life.

In Paris, Baldwin accepted his heritage and admitted his bisexuality. He also completed his first novel, *Go Tell It on the Mountain* (1953), which many critics consider his most accomplished. Baldwin's next novel, *Giovanni's Room* (1956), was controversial, apparently because of its openly homosexual content. *Another Country* (1962) provoked more debate and received largely negative reviews due to its candid depiction of sexual relations.

Baldwin's nonfiction works have also received substantial critical attention. The **essay** "Everybody's Protest Novel" (1949) generated controversy for its attack on authors of **protest fiction**. Critics praised this essay and those collected in *Notes of a Native Son* (1955), *Nobody Knows My Name: More Notes of a Native Son* (1961), and *The Price of the Ticket: Collected Nonfiction, 1948-1985* (1985). The book *The Fire Next Time* (1963) is considered both a passionate plea for reconciliation between the races and a manifesto for black liberation.

Baldwin was one of the few black authors to have had more than one **play** produced on Broadway. Both *The Amen Corner* (1955) and *Blues for Mister Charlie* (1964) had successful Broadway runs and numerous revivals. In the late 1960s and 1970s, much of Baldwin's fiction was influenced by his involvement in the civil rights movement. He saw his writing as an attempt to alter the daily environment of American blacks. The **short stories** collected in *Going to Meet the Man* (1965) center on the problems of black protagonists living amid racial strife in the United States. The novel *Tell Me How Long the Train's Been Gone* (1968) centers on two brothers' attempts to escape the ghetto, and *If Beale Street Could Talk* (1974) examines the plight of a young man unjustly caught in the American judicial system. *Just Above My Head* (1979) returns to the themes of **religion** and sexuality with a complex story of a homosexual gospel singer. In 1973 Baldwin published *A Dialogue* with **Nikki Giovanni,** a transcription of a 1971 conversation between the two writers about the status of blacks in the United States and abroad.

Baldwin died from stomach cancer in St. Paul de Vence, France, on December 1, 1987. At the time, he had been at work on two projects: a play, *The Welcome Table,* and a **biography** of **Martin Luther King Jr.** Baldwin's death prompted generally laudatory reassessments of his career and literary legacy.

Further Readings

Black Literature Criticism, Gale, 1992.

Black Writers, first edition, Gale, 1989.

Campbell, James, *Talking at the Gates: A Life of James Baldwin,* Viking, 1991.

Leeming, David, *James Baldwin: A Biography,* Knopf, 1994.

Porter, Horace A., *Stealing the Fire: The Art and Protest of James Baldwin,* Wesleyan University Press, 1989.

Standley, Fred L., and Nancy V. Burt, editors, *Critical Essays on James Baldwin,* G. K. Hall, 1988.

Bale Baroka

Character in *The Lion and the Jewel*

Toni Cade Bambara

American fiction writer, scriptwriter, and essayist
Born March 25, 1939.

Bambara is known as a writer, teacher, social activist, and community leader. Born Toni Cade in New York City, she acquired the name Bambara from a sketchbook she found in her great-grandmother's trunk and had her name legally changed in 1970.

In 1959, Bambara graduated from Queens College and published her first **short story,** "Sweet Town," in *Vendome* magazine. After studying abroad, she received her Master's degree in 1965 from City College of New York and continued to teach there until 1969. During this time she was involved in community activities, working as a social investigator for the New York State Department of Welfare and as the director of recreation in the psychiatry department of New York City's Metropolitan Hospital. She taught in the English department at Livingston College from 1969 until 1974 and remains active as an educator and with various community and arts organizations.

Bambara edited and published an anthology called *The Black Woman* (1970), which includes works by **Nikki Giovanni, Alice Walker**, and Bambara herself. This anthology was an attempt to explore the black female experience from the perspective of black women. In another anthology, *Tales and Stories for Black Folks* (1971), Bambara combined the work of well-known authors with writings from students in her composition class.

Gorilla, My Love (1972) is Bambara's first collection of short stories. A majority of the stories revolve around children and adolescents as they learn about themselves through their urban environments. This compilation was published to enthusiastic reviews and earned Bambara the American Book Award in 1981. Her second compilation of stories, *The Sea Birds are Still Alive* (1977) was inspired by her travels to Cuba and Vietnam.

Primarily a short story writer, Bambara wrote her first **novel, *The Salt Eaters*** (1980), in an attempt to reveal the divisions she felt were prevalent not only in the African American community but within other ethnic communities in the United States. The novel revolves around a community organizer's recovery from a suicide attempt. Her other novels include *If Blessing Comes* (1987) and *Raymond's Run* (1990).

Bambara's **essays** and articles have been included in numerous anthologies and books of **literary criticism**. Her interest in film has led her to write nine screenplays, including *Tar*

Baby, based on the novel by her friend and editor, **Toni Morrison**.

See also **Short Stories of Toni Cade Bambara**

Further Readings

Black Writers, second edition, Gale, 1994.

Dictionary of Literary Biography, Volume 38: *Afro-American Writers after 1955: Dramatists and Prose Writers*, Gale, 1985.

Bandele

Character in *The Interpreters*

Banina

Character in *M. C. Higgins, the Great*

Timothy Bankole

Sierra Leonean journalist and poet
Born in 1920(?).

Bankole, the first African journalist to work for a London newspaper, was born in Freetown, the capital of Sierra Leone, and educated at London University. He began his career as a staff member and journalist at the *London Daily Express*. In 1951 he became an assistant editor at the London *Daily Graphic*, where he has remained until the present. He has also been a correspondent from Ghana for the *London Observer* and *Ceylon Daily News*.

In addition to the book *Kwame Nkrumah—His Rise to Power* (1955), Bankole has written stories and poems, some of which have been presented on the British Broadcasting Corporation's Overseas and African "Voices" programs.

Further Readings

Black Writers, second edition, Gale, 1994.

Benjamin Banneker

American astronomer and mathematician
Born November 9, 1731.
Died October 9, 1806.

Banneker's achievements were considered unique for a black man in Colonial America. Self-taught in mathematics and astronomy, he produced an almanac that was the first scientific book published by an African American, and his accomplishments made him one of the most recognized black men of his time.

Banneker was born on November 9, 1731, in Baltimore County, Maryland. His only formal education was at a country school, which he quit after a few years in order to help his father on his tobacco farm. At the age of twenty-one, Banneker constructed a striking wooden clock solely from his observations of a pocket watch; the clock worked until his death.

Banneker's interest in astronomy was stimulated by George Ellicott, a neighboring farmer who loaned Banneker several books on astronomy along with a telescope and drafting instruments. In 1791, Banneker accompanied Major Andrew Ellicott on a survey of the territory on which the national capital was to be built, collecting data and recording astronomical observations.

Banneker returned home and compiled an ephemeris (a table identifying the location of celestial bodies) for the year of 1792. Supported by the Pennsylvania and Maryland abolition societies, it was published as *Benjamin Banneker's Pennsylvania, Delaware, Maryland and Virginia Almanack and Ephemeris, for the Year of Our Lord, 1792.* Shortly before its publication, Banneker sent a copy of it to Thomas Jefferson along with a cover letter promoting the abolition of **slavery**. Jefferson acknowledged the letter and their correspondence was published as a pamphlet. Banneker's almanacs were published through 1797 and he continued to calculate ephemerides until 1804.

Banneker died on October 9, 1806, in his house in Baltimore County. During the funeral two days later, his house caught fire and burned to the ground; his possessions, including his wooden clock and most of his writings, were destroyed. His only surviving writings are those given to George Ellicott prior to the funeral.

Further Readings

Bedini, Silvio A., *The Life of Benjamin Banneker,* 1972.

Tyson, Martha Ellicott, *Banneker: The Afric-American Astronomer,* 1884.

Amiri Baraka

American poet, dramatist, essayist, and novelist
Born October 7, 1934.

Baraka (known as LeRoi Jones until the late 1960s) is best known for his controversial **plays.** His literary career has been characterized by sharp ideological transitions, but he has long advocated the essential relationship between art and politics.

Baraka was born Everett LeRoy Jones in Newark, New Jersey. His father, Coyette LeRoy Jones, worked in the post office, and his mother, Anna Russ Jones, was a social worker. He spent a year at Rutgers University and then enrolled at Howard University in 1952, studying English and philosophy. He left in 1954 to join the Air Force. The isolation of military duty provided him with the opportunity to start writing **poetry.**

After his discharge in 1957, Baraka moved to New York City, where he became a part of the Beat movement. He wrote pieces on **jazz** and helped found a magazine for Beat poetry called *Yugen.* In 1960, he made a trip to Cuba that left him determined to address racial issues in America.

Dutchman (1964) was Baraka's first professionally produced drama; the play is about an encounter between a bourgeois black man and a white woman who taunts him about his race and eventually kills him. This was Baraka's most successful play, winning him an Obie Award as well as both notoriety and admiration. Baraka continued to attack white liberalism and question the value of integration in his next two plays, *The Slave* (1964) and *The Toilet* (1964).

Baraka in 1975.

In 1965, Baraka divorced his white wife and moved to Harlem, determined to dedicate himself solely to the needs of the black community. In 1968, he changed his name to Imamu Amiri Baraka, meaning "blessed spiritual leader." In his writings, he called for a black revolution and the establishment of a separatist state. His work during this period includes his only **novel,** *The System of Dante's Hell* (1965), based on his childhood; *A Black Mass* (1966), a play that criticizes Western technological culture; *Black Fire: An Anthology of Afro-American Writing* (1968), which he coedited with **Larry Neal**; and *Black Art* (1969), a well-known poem that addresses the creation of a black aesthetic. Baraka is also known as an essayist, having published several books on the history of black music, including *The Music: Reflections on Jazz and Blues* (1987). He has also published several volumes of poetry, including *Preface to a Twenty Volume Suicide*

Note (1961) and *The Dead Lecturer* (1964), as well as *The Autobiography of LeRoi Jones* (1984), which focuses on Baraka's childhood and early career.

During the 1970s, Baraka abandoned **black nationalism** for a Marxist analysis of oppression based on economic rather than racial divisions. In 1979, he accepted a faculty position at State University of New York at Stony Brook as professor of African Studies. In the early 1990s he published such works as *Thornton Dial: Images of the Tiger* (1994) and *Jesse Jackson and Black People* (1994).

See also **Poetry of Amiri Baraka**

Further Readings
Black Literature Criticism, Gale, 1992.

Black Writers, second edition, Gale, 1994.

Sollors, Werner, *Amiri Baraka/LeRoi Jones: The Quest for a "Populist Modernism,"* Columbia University Press, 1978.

"Barbados" (novella)

Please see *Soul Clap Hands and Sing*

Gerald William Barrax
American poet
Born June 21, 1933.

Born in Alabama, Barrax earned a B.A. from Duquesne University and an M.A. from the University of Pittsburgh. He worked as a U.S. postal carrier before publishing *Another Kind of Rain* (1970), *An Audience of One* (1980), *The Deaths of Animals and Lesser Gods* (1984), and *Leaning Against the Sun* (1992). Barrax's **poetry** typically focuses on the black experience and issues of death; he has also written tribute poems to **Malcolm X** and **Martin Luther King Jr.** Barrax has won several awards for his work, including the Gold Medal Award from the Catholic Poetry Society of America. Barrax has taught English at North Carolina State University since 1970.

Further Readings
Black Writers, second edition, Gale, 1994.

Dictionary of Literary Biography, Volume 41: *Afro-American Poets since 1955,* Gale, 1985.

Lindsay Barrett
Jamaican journalist, novelist, poet, and playwright
Born in 1941.

Eseoghene Lindsay Barrett began his career as news editor for the Jamaican Broadcasting Company, then wrote for the *Daily Gleaner* and *Jamaica Star.* He also freelanced for the British Broadcasting Company, taught in Sierra Leone and Ghana, and worked for Nigerian television and radio. He has contributed to *Frontline, West Indian World,* and other periodicals.

Born in 1941 in Lucea, Jamaica, Barrett examines themes involving black identity and history in his writings. Among his works are the **novel** *Song for Mumu* (1967); the **poetry** volume *The Conflicting Eye* (1973), which he wrote under the pseudonym Eseoghene; and *Agbada to Khaki* (1985), an account of political changes in Nigeria from 1979 through 1983. His **play** *Sighs of a Slave Dream* was produced in England in the early 1970s.

Further Readings
Black Writers, second edition, Gale, 1994.

Bart Judson
Character in *The Living Is Easy*

Gaston Bart-Williams
Sierra Leonean playwright, poet, and short story writer
Born in 1938.

Bart-Williams's **poetry** was widely anthologized in the 1960s, appearing in such volumes as *Black Orpheus, Commonwealth Poems of Today, Pergamon Poets-2,* and *New*

Voices of the Commonwealth. His radio **plays** have been internationally broadcast, including *A Bouquet of Carnations,* on BBC radio in England and *Uhuru* on West German Radio. His work has also garnered him the All African Short Story Award and the French Karolyi International Award. Despite such recognition, little of his work has been independently published, although some of his poems and plays are circulated in mimeographed form, including *Poems* and the play *Curse Your God and Die.*

Further Readings
Black Writers, second edition, Gale, 1994.

Bea
Character in *The Hippodrome*

Beast Girl
Character in *A Beast's Story*

Beast Man
Character in *A Beast's Story*

A Beast's Story
Adrienne Kennedy
Play, first produced 1966, published 1969

Adrienne Kennedy's *A Beast's Story* utilizes a dream-like setting and plot to depict the destructive relationships within an African American family. Beast Girl is continually victimized by other members of her family. Her father, a minister called Beast Man, forces his daughter to marry Dead Human against her will after lusting after her himself. Dead Human rapes her after she refuses to submit to sexual relations with him. Later, Beast Girl's parents force her to murder the child conceived from that union. In a self-destructive fit of despair at her loss of innocence, Beast Girl murders her husband as her parents look on.

Beatrice
Character in *Anthills of the Savannah*

Beau Boutan
Character in *A Gathering of Old Men*

Beau Willie
Character in *for colored girls who have considered suicide*

The Beautyful Ones Are Not Yet Born
Ayi Kwei Armah
Novel, 1968

Ayi Kwei Armah's *The Beautyful Ones Are Not Yet Born* deals with Ghana's struggle for independence and the corruption engendered during its genesis as a nation. The author describes the outward grime and squalor of the landscape as a symbol of the inner immorality of the inhabitants. In Armah's **novel**, its protagonist, "the man," encounters dishonesty throughout every part of his day, including a partnership in a deceptive business deal proposed by his relative, government minister Koomson. When the Nkrumah regime is overthrown in 1966, Koomson's escape through the latrine hole and sewers serves as a metaphor for the purging of the filth permeating Ghana's government. Yet Armah suggests that corruption and cleansing follow in a continuous cycle in both life and bureaucracy.

Francis Bebey
Cameroonian novelist and nonfiction writer
Born July 15, 1929.

Bebey began his career as a radio journalist and has enjoyed an international reputation as a musician as well as an author. Bebey has written extensively about music and in several other genres. He is probably best known for his **novel** *Le Fils d'Agatha Moudio* (1967; *Agatha Moudio's Son,* 1971), for which he received the Grand Prix Littéraire de l'Afrique Noire. His *Musique de l'Afrique* (1969; *African Music: A People's Art,* 1975) and *La Musique africaine moderne* (1975; title means "Modern African Music") focus primarily on the culture of Bebey's native West Africa. Bebey works as a freelance writer, composer, and concert guitarist.

Further Readings

Black Writers, first edition, Gale, 1989.

Barry Beckham

American novelist
Born March 19, 1944.

Beckham is recognized as a leading writer of African American fiction. Born in Philadelphia on March 19, 1944, he moved at age nine with his mother to Atlantic City, New Jersey, and, in 1962, he was one of only eight black freshmen at Brown University. The struggle of being black in America is a chief concern in Beckham's works. His two most acclaimed **novels,** *My Main Mother* (1969) and *Runner Mack* (1972), portray black male protagonists whose search for identity is shaped by a relationship with a fellow black struggler. His third novel, *Double Dunk* (1980), is a fictional **biography** of basketball player Earl "The Goat" Manigault.

Further Readings

Black Writers, first edition, Gale, 1989.

Dictionary of Literary Biography, Volume 33: *Afro-American Fiction Writers after 1955,* Gale, 1984.

Becky

Character in *Cane*

Beetlecreek

William Demby
Novel, 1950

William Demby's first **novel,** *Beetlecreek* describes how loneliness and gang violence affect three people living in a small American town. The first character is a teenage boy named Johnny Johnson. Johnny's mother, widowed and ailing, sends him to live with his aunt and uncle in Beetlecreek. Initially a loner, Johnny soon joins a gang of youths and meets Bill Trapp, a reclusive white man living in the black section of Beetlecreek. When Bill Trapp breaks the social code of Beetlecreek, Johnny, motivated by the need for acceptance, acts as an enforcer, with nightmarish results. The third main character is Johnny's uncle, David. Trapped in a bad marriage, David searches for happiness, which leads him away from Beetlecreek into a relationship that is no better than the one he abandons.

Before the Mayflower

Lerone Bennett Jr.
Nonfiction, 1962

Lerone Bennett Jr.'s *Before the Mayflower: A History of the Negro in America, 1619-1966* began as a series of articles appearing in ***Ebony*** magazine, which was edited by Bennett. The title refers to the arrival of twenty blacks in Jamestown, Virginia, in 1619, a year before the landing of the Mayflower. Bennett traces the history of African Americans from slave trading in the Nile Valley to the **civil rights movement** of the 1950s and 1960s and provides sketches of African American leaders such as **Frederick Douglass, W. E. B. Du Bois**, and Coleman Young. *Before the Mayflower* also includes a chronology of African American history and "Black Firsts." A revised edition of the work was published in 1982.

Bell

Character in *Roots: The Saga of an American Family*

Derrick Albert Bell Jr.

American essayist and novelist
Born November 6, 1930.

Bell is a lawyer who worked for the **National Association for the Advancement of Colored People** (NAACP) and justice and civil rights departments before teaching law at the University of Oregon, New York University, and Harvard University. At Harvard Law School, Bell became the first black instructor to be granted tenure; however, this was revoked more than twenty years later after he refused to return from an unpaid leave until a black woman was hired for the school's tenured faculty. During his literary career, Bell has written extensively on the racial aspects of American law in such publications as *Race, Racism, and American Law* (1973) and *Shades of Brown: New Perspectives on School Desegregation* (1980). Although these books established Bell as a popular essayist, he has also been recognized for his **novels.** *And We Are Not Saved: The Elusive Quest for Racial Justice* (1987) and *Faces at the Bottom of the Well: The Permanence of Racism* (1992) use fictional parables as a forum for characters to discuss racial and legal issues.

Further Readings
Black Writers, second edition, Gale, 1994.

James Madison Bell

American poet, social activist, and orator
Born April 3, 1826.
Died in 1902.

Bell is known primarily for his writings and activism during the American Civil War. His most admired work, the poem "Modern Moses, or 'My Policy' Man," satirizes President Andrew Johnson and his management of Recon-struction. Bell's best-known writings celebrated significant events in the abolitionist movement, including *A Poem Entitled "The Day and the War," Delivered January 1, 1864, at the Celebration of the First Anniversary of President Lincoln's Emancipation Proclamation,* which moves from **slavery** to emancipation, and *An Anniversary Poem Entitled "The Progress of Liberty," Delivered January 1st, 1866...at the Celebration of the Third Anniversary of President Lincoln's Proclamation,* which chronicles the assassination of Lincoln and the beginning of **Reconstruction**. Many of his verses have been collected in *The Poetical Works of James Madison Bell* (1901).

Further Readings
Black Literature Criticism, Gale, 1992.
Black Writers, first edition, Gale, 1989.
Dictionary of Literary Biography, Volume 50: *Afro-American Writers before the Harlem Renaissance,* Gale, 1986.

Roseann P. Bell

American editor
Born May 2, 1945.

Bell has co-edited books that focus on the literary contributions of African American, African, and Caribbean women. Born in Atlanta, Georgia, Bell attended Howard and Emory universities and later taught at Spelman College and Cornell University. She co-edited *Sturdy Black Bridges: Visions of Black Women in Literature* (1979), a survey of literature by black women. Dividing the volume into three sections, Bell and her colleagues examine the theories and attitudes of black female characters and writers; record interviews with black female authors, critics, and mothers; and provide samples of female subgenres. Bell also co-edited *Erotique Noire: Black Erotica* (1992), a collection of **short stories** and **poetry** by black writers.

Further Readings
Black Writers, second edition, Gale, 1994.

Beloved

Character in *Beloved*

Beloved

Toni Morrison
Novel, 1987

Toni Morrison's Pulitzer Prize-winning fifth **novel**, *Beloved,* combines themes of familial love and the institution of **slavery**. Most of the story takes place in post-Civil War Cincinnati, where a former slave, Sethe, and her only surviving daughter, Denver, live. Sethe is obsessively devoted to Denver and tries to isolate her from other African Americans. Their house is haunted by a vindictive ghost they call Beloved, in memory of one of Sethe's other children, who died violently. Sethe is also haunted by her memories of her slave days in the 1850s at a plantation in Kentucky called Sweet Home. The master of the plantation, a man named Garner, strikes a deal with Sethe's husband, Halle Suggs, and as a result Halle's mother, Baby, is given her freedom and moves to Cincinnati. When Garner dies, a man the slaves call Schoolteacher takes over Sweet Home and his cruel treatment causes the slaves to flee. All the men are lost during the escape, including Halle.

Sethe settles in Baby's home and begins a career as a cook. The arrival of Paul D., another former slave from Sweet Home, exorcises the ghostly presence from the house. However, Paul D. soon discovers that Sethe had killed Beloved herself to prevent the child from being carried back into slavery. Paul D., overwhelmed by this revelation, deserts the two women temporarily. Beloved herself soon returns in an older and more solid form and begins to wreck the relationships of the other three. She seduces Paul D. and tries to alienate Denver and Sethe by monopolizing Sethe's attention. When she realizes Beloved's malicious motives, Denver turns away from her and seeks entry into the black community. Paul D. and Sethe come to a similar reconciliation, realizing that they have to confront their collective as well as their individual pasts.

Ben

Character in *The Women of Brewster Place*

Ben Carter

Character in *Compromise*

Beneatha

Character in *A Raisin in the Sun*

Benja-Benja

Character in *One Man, One Machet*

Benjamin Banneker's Almanack and Ephemeris

Benjamin Banneker
Almanac, 1792

Benjamin Banneker's Pennsylvania, Delaware, Maryland and Virginia Almanack and Ephemeris, for the Year of Our Lord, 1792 was the first of five years' worth of almanacs and astronomical tables published by the Baltimore printers Goddard & Angell in collaboration with the Pennsylvania and Maryland societies for the abolition of **slavery**. Banneker worked with his neighbor, the surveyor Major Andrew Ellicott, to gather data on federal lands. Upon returning home, he used his astronomical experience to calculate the data for the *Almanack*. The significance of the *Almanack* grew when Banneker sent a manuscript copy of the work to Secretary of State Thomas Jefferson, who had made derogatory comments about the mental powers of African Americans. Confronted with the evidence of the *Almanack,* Jefferson modified his views.

Benjie Johnson

Character in *A Hero Ain't Nothin' but a Sandwich*

Yosef ben-Jochannan

Historian
Born December 31, 1918.

In his numerous books, pamphlets, and recordings, ben-Jochannan advances the theory of Afrocentricity, contending that the importance of Africans in history has been purposely overlooked in the classroom. Instead, he says, Europeans have been credited with providing the essential contributions to the history of the world. A prolific writer, ben-Jochannan's works include *African Origins of the Major "Western Religions"* (1970), *Africa: Mother of "Western Civilization"* (1971), the three-volume *The Black Man's Religion* (1974), *We the Black Jews: Witness to the "White Jewish Race" Myth* (1983), and *From Afrikan Captives to Insane Slaves: The Need for Afrikan History in Solving the "Black" Mental Health Crisis in "America" and the World* (1992). Ben-Jochannan has been adjunct professor of history and African studies at Cornell University since 1970.

Further Readings

Black Writers, second edition, Gale, 1994.

Gwendolyn B. Bennett

American poet and artist
Born July 8, 1902.
Died May 30, 1981.

Bennett was a minor figure in the **Harlem Renaissance**. Although her poetic works were favorably reviewed, few were published and a collection of her work has not been printed. Her column "The Ebony Flute," which appeared in *Opportunity: A Journal of Negro Life* from 1926 to 1928, offered news and commentary about contemporary black artists and their works. The column has proven to be a notable chronicle of African American cultural history during the early twentieth century. Aside from her writing, Bennett illustrated covers for both *Opportunity* and *Crisis*.

Further Readings

Black Writers, first edition, Gale, 1989.

Dictionary of Literary Biography, Volume 51: *Afro-American Writers from the Harlem Renaissance to 1940,* Gale, 1987.

Hal Bennett

American novelist and short story writer
Born April 21, 1930.

George Harold (Hal) Bennett's first **novel,** *A Wilderness of Vines,* introduced the fictional Burnside, Virginia, a location to which Bennett returns in much of his fiction. His novels *Lord of the Dark Places* (1970), an experimental and satirical work, and *Wait until the Evening* (1974) received more critical acclaim than his earlier fiction, and Bennett received the PEN/Faulkner Award for fiction in 1973. His **short story** collection *Insanity Runs in Our Family* (1977) includes the story "Dotson Gerber Resurrected," for which Bennett was named most promising young writer of 1970 by *Playboy* magazine.

Further Readings

Black Writers, first edition, Gale, 1989.

Dictionary of Literary Biography, Volume 33: *Afro-American Fiction Writers after 1955,* Gale, 1984.

Lerone Bennett Jr.

American journalist and historian
Born October 17, 1928.

Bennett has been an editor at *Ebony* magazine for over thirty years and has written several popular books on black history noted for both their factual accuracy and readability.

Bennett was born in Clarksdale, Mississippi, the son of Lerone and Alma Reed Bennett. He received his A.B. from Morehouse College in 1949 and began his journalistic career the same year with the *Atlanta Daily World,* where he became city editor before joining *Ebony* as an associate editor in 1954. Bennett was promoted to senior editor at the magazine in 1958 and executive editor in 1987.

In 1962, Bennett published *Before the Mayflower: A History of the Negro in America, 1619-1966,* which critics praised for his dramatic but responsible treatment of the historical record. *Confrontation: Black and White* (1965) was hailed by reviewers as an objective analysis of social problems touching black Americans in the 1960s. In the book, Bennett calls for better communication not only between black and white Americans, but also between black leaders and the masses, whom Bennett says have grown apart and need to work more closely toward meaningful change. In *Black Power U.S.A.: The Human Side of Reconstruction, 1867-1877* (1967), Bennett examines the racial power structure in Southern cities after the Civil War, charting the efforts of African Americans to preserve a working political relationship with both Southern and Northern whites. *The Shaping of Black America* (1975) is a study of black Americans in the worlds of **slavery**, emancipation, work, and business. Bennett is also the author of *Wade in the Water: Great Moments in Black History* (1979), *Succeeding against the Odds* (1989), and *Listen to the Blood: Was Abraham Lincoln a White Supremacist? and Other Essays and Stories* (1994).

Further Readings
Black Writers, second edition, Gale, 1994.

Louise Bennett

Jamaican poet, storyteller, and folklorist
Born September 7, 1919.

Bennett is considered an important contemporary Jamaican poet. Writing in Creole, she relies heavily on Jamaican myths, folktales, and songs to create her **dialect poetry**. In the 1940s and 1950s she traveled to England and the United States to perform her poetry; in 1955 she returned to Jamaica, where she continued writing and performing. *Jamaica Labrish* (1966) and *Selected Poems* (1982) are regarded as her best works, reflecting her pride in the black tradition. She has also written several books on the adventures of Brer Anancy, the African spider who is the protagonist of most Jamaican folktales, including *Anancy Stories and Poems in Dialect* (1944) and *Anancy and Miss Lou* (1979).

See also **Poetry of Louise Bennett**

Further Readings
Black African Writers, First Series, 1992.
Dictionary of Literary Biography, Volume 117: *Twentieth-Century Caribbean and Black African Writers,* First Series, Gale, 1992.

Bento Santiago
Character in *Dom Casmurro*

Bentu Moraga
Character in *Possessing the Secret of Joy*

Bernadine
Character in *Waiting to Exhale*

Berniece
Character in *The Piano Lesson*

Mary Frances Berry
American historian and government official
Born February 17, 1938.

Berry is recognized for her work as a historian, public servant, and civil rights activist. After attending segregated public schools in Tennessee, Berry enrolled at Howard University and later at the University of Michigan, from which she received both her Ph.D. and J.D. Her works, which are noted for her research and analysis, include *Black Resistance/White Law: A History of Constitutional Racism in America* (1971); *Long Memory: The Black Experience in America* (1982), which she wrote with **John W. Blassingame**; and *The Politics of Parenthood: Child Care, Women's Rights, and the Myth of the Good Mother* (1993). Berry has served on the U.S. Civil Rights Commission under Presidents Jimmy

Carter, Ronald Reagan, and Bill Clinton, and is a founder of the Free South Africa Movement.

Further Readings
Black Writers, first edition, Gale, 1989.
Epic Lives: One Hundred Black Women Who Made a Difference, Visible Ink Press, 1993.

Bertha Flowers

Character in *I Know Why the Caged Bird Sings*

Beti

Series character in *The "Guyana Quartet"*

Mongo Beti
Cameroonian novelist
Born June 30, 1932.

A francophone novelist who combines humor and social criticism, Beti is one of Africa's most recognized writers. Educated in French schools, Beti, who was born Alexandre Biyidi and has written under the pseudonym Eza Boto, studied at France's University of Aix-en-Provence and the Sorbonne. His controversial reputation began with *Le Pauvre Christ de Bomba* (1956; *The Poor Christ of Bomba,* 1971), *Mission terminée* (1957; *Mission Accomplished,* 1958*),* and *Le roi miraculé: Chronique des Essazam* (1958; *King Lazarus,* 1960*),* harsh but comic indictments of French colonial rule in Cameroon. His *Remember Ruben* (1973) and *Perpétue et l'habitude du malheur* (1974; *Perpetua and the Habit of Unhappiness,* 1978) criticize the corruption underlying Cameroon independence. Beti teaches French literature and classical Greek and Latin in France.

Further Readings
Black Writers, first edition, Gale, 1989.
Black Literature Criticism, Gale, 1992.

Beukes

Character in *In the Fog of the Seasons' End*

Beulah

Character in *Thomas and Beulah*

Beyond Racism: Building an Open Society
Whitney M. Young Jr.
Nonfiction, 1969

When **Whitney M. Young Jr.** first wrote *Beyond Racism,* he was predicting the eventual shift of white populations out to the suburbs, leaving blacks behind in the cities. This sort of insight drew respectful praise even from blacks who previously doubted his sincerity, such as publisher **Nathan Hare**. Young proposed a federal plan he called the Open Society, which granted blacks positions in controlling government agencies. Citing grim statistics on poverty, infant mortality rates, and the issue of equal pay, Young suggested the equal distribution of unequal resources. A sort of neo-New Deal was to be funded by the sale of Federal bonds to engineer job programs. Most importantly, Young argued, control of urban projects should be in the hands of community councils made up of local citizens. Tax incentives would foster business and industry involvement in cities, while the minimum wage, social security and Medicare entitlements should be made to apply to everyone. Young also proposed tax reforms to grant bonuses to every child in the country and to close corporate loopholes. The welfare system should be eliminated and military spending should be cut by a withdrawal from the Vietnam conflict. Additionally, Young asked unions to be more aggressive in recruiting blacks and endorsed boycotting and picketing as resistance tactics.

Big Girl

Character in *Clara's Old Man*

Big Laura

Character in *The Autobiography of Miss Jane Pittman*

Big Mat Moss

Character in *Blood on the Forge*

Big Walter

Character in *A Raisin in the Sun*

Bigger Thomas

Character in *Native Son*

Bill

Character in *Mules and Men*

Bill Horton

Character in *The Fabulous Miss Marie*

Bill James

Character in *A Short Walk*

Bill Trapp

Character in *Beetlecreek*

Andrew Billingsley

American nonfiction writer
Born March 20, 1926.

Billingsley has sought to provide a realistic portrayal of African Americans in both historic and contemporary terms, and is recognized for his leadership in challenging existing sociological work. In 1965, the U.S. Department of Labor released Daniel Patrick Moynihan's *The Negro Family: A Case for Action,* which contended that **discrimination** had disintegrated the African American family. Billingsley's *Black Families in White America* (1968), considered a response to Moynihan's work, illustrates the black family's adaptation to circumstances in a largely hostile social climate. Billingsley, who has served as chair of the family studies department at the University of Maryland, has also published *Children of the Storm: Black Children and American Child Welfare* (1972). Co-written with Jeanne M. Giovannoni, the volume illustrates the effect of **racism** on the youngest members of society and suggests child welfare system reforms. Billingsley's *Climbing Jacob's Ladder: The Enduring Legacy of African American Families* (1993) examines both the strengths and the difficulties of contemporary black family life.

Further Readings
Black Writers, second edition, Gale, 1994.

Biography

A biography is a narrative that tells another person's life story, typically with the aim of objectivity and an eye to the telling detail. In 1907, noted educator and writer **Booker T. Washington** published the biography of another eminent African American, *Frederick Douglass.* More recently, literary historian **Arnold Rampersad** won praise for his *Life of Langston Hughes,* published in two volumes in 1986 and 1988, and **John Hope Franklin** produced an acclaimed biography of George Washington Williams, author of one of the first historical studies of African Americans. Not all biographies focus on famous figures: **Pauli Murray**'s *Proud Shoes: The Story of an American Family* traces the life story of the author's maternal grandparents, presented as ordinary people whose experiences are representative of those of African Americans as a whole. Authors for children and young adults have written numerous books on the lives of prominent and lesser-known African Americans from many walks of life. **Louise Meriwether** has published biographies of civil rights activist Rosa Parks, heart surgeon Daniel Hale Williams, and escaped slaves Peter Mango and Robert Small. Other noted authors of biographies for children and young adults include **James S. Haskins** and **Ellen Tarry**.

Becky Birtha

American short story writer and poet
Born in 1948.

Birtha is noted for her insights into the lives of black and lesbian women. In the story collection *Lovers' Choice* (1987) and the verse collection *The Forbidden Poems* (1991), Birtha's characters must make choices that promise to result in significant change. Capturing the rhythms of everyday conversation, Birtha explores such topics as interracial relationships, loss, white women viewed from a black perspective, the breakup of a long-term love relationship, and black lesbians. Birtha is also the author of *For Nights Like This One: Stories of Loving Women* (1983).

Further Readings
Black Writers, second edition, Gale, 1994.

The Bishop

Character in *Caleb, the Degenerate*

Maurice Bishop

Aruban-born Grenadine writer and
political activist
Born May 29, 1944.
Died October 19, 1983.

In 1979, Bishop led the leftist New Jewel Movement that peacefully overthrew Prime Minister Eric Gairy, ruler of the Caribbean island nation of Grenada. As the country's new prime minister, Bishop promoted moderate socialism while allowing private business to continue with little government interference. Although he was credited with stabilizing Grenada's economy and improving health and education, his Communist contacts unsettled U.S. authorities, who questioned his motives in building an airport large enough to accommodate Soviet fighter planes.

Bishop's administration encountered internal difficulties as well. The escalating turmoil ended when Bishop was arrested and executed in 1983. After his death, a selection of his **speeches** was collected in *Maurice Bishop Speaks: The Grenada Revolution, 1979-1983,* which includes Bishop's final speech, delivered four months before his death. Bishop also authored *Forward Ever!* (1982).

Further Readings
Black Writers, first edition, Gale, 1989.

Black Aesthetic (Arts) Movement

The black aesthetic movement—sometimes known as the black arts movement—was the first major African American artistic movement after the **Harlem Renaissance**. Lasting from the early 1960s through the mid-1970s, it was closely paralleled by the civil rights and **black power** movements. For the most part, African American writers during this period were supportive of separatist politics and **black nationalism**. Rebelling against mainstream society by being essentially anti-white, anti-American, and anti-middle class, these artists moved from the Harlem Renaissance view of art for art's sake into a posture of art for politics' sake.

The black aesthetic writers attempted to produce works of art that would be meaningful to the black masses. Toward this end, they looked for inspiration in such sources as popular music, including John Coltrane's **jazz** and James Brown's **rhythm and blues**, and street talk. In fact, some of the language used by these writers was considered vulgar and shocking, a conscious tactic intended to show the vitality of their position. Adherents tended to be revolutionaries rather than diplomats—**Malcolm X** was more of a role model for these artists than **Martin Luther King Jr.** In addition, they believed that artists had a responsibility to be political activists in order to advance the black nationalist agenda.

One of the founders of the black aesthetic movement was poet and playwright **Amiri Baraka,** formerly known as LeRoi Jones. His play *Dutchman* (1964), which portrays a shocking symbolic confrontation between blacks and whites, won a 1964 Obie Award. Baraka's growing militancy toward white society is evident in two subsequent plays, *The Slave* (1964) and *The Toilet* (1964). Along with playwright **Larry Neal**, Baraka later edited *Black Fire: An Anthology of Afro-American Writing* (1968), a collection of **essays**, stories, and plays by African American writers that helped define the movement. **Ishmael Reed** also was an organizer of the movement; however, he later dissented with some of the movement's doctrines and became inspired more and more by the black magic and spiritual practices of the West Indies. Another key figure in black aesthetics was poet and essayist **Haki R. Madhubuti**, formerly Don L. Lee. Madhubuti's books were quite popular, selling over one hundred thousand copies without a national distributor. He identified the chief influences on African American poets of the day as black music, lifestyles, churches, and contemporaries. His own poems in collections such as *Don't Cry, Scream* (1969) contain references to black musicians and lines that imitate the sounds of jazz.

While African American women also were drawn to the black aesthetic movement, they often protested the subordinate role in which women were cast in male-oriented nationalist politics. One leading voice in the movement who managed to combine feminism with her commitment to nationalist ideals was poet and playwright **Sonia Sanchez**. In **poetry** collections such as *We a BaddDDD People* (1970), she deals with the importance of positive role models for blacks. Yet another major figure in black aesthetics was Obie Award-winning dramatist **Ed Bullins**, who probed ghetto life and advocated cultural separatism in numerous plays. Bullins joined other young artists and activists, including Baraka and Sanchez, to establish a cultural-political group called Black House. Among the numerous other African American writers associated with the black aesthetic movement were poets **Eugene B. Redmond**, **Margaret Taylor Burroughs**, **Jayne Cortez**, and **Lucille Clifton** and playwright **Ben Caldwell**. This era in literature brought wide acclaim to many African American writers and fostered the growth of black studies departments at universities around the country.

Black Art
Amiri Baraka
Poem, 1969

"Black Art," the title of one of **Amiri Baraka**'s well-known poems, is also the title of one of three sections in the 1969 collection *Black Magic*. While the collection's first section, "Sabotage," illustrates America's social problems, and the second section, "Target Study," deals with necessary solutions to the problems, "Black Art," the third section of *Black Magic,* expresses a new ethnic spirit in which blacks separate themselves from society.

While art and political statement can be seen as distinct, Baraka's choice of the title *Black Magic* illustrates his vision of their relationship. Magic here refers to a transformational creative process. Thus a transformation of the world can be brought on by the power of the poet's magic, his chant and spell, and by individuals acting out their new-found self love. The renewed world created by this magic is the expression of the ethnic separation Baraka sought and can be seen in microcosm in the poem "Black Art." The poem deals with the creation of a black aesthetic, a subset of the concerns about the nature of the creative process in the context of revolutionary politics that are the main issues of the "Black Art" section of *Black Magic.*

Black Arts Movement
Please see Black Aesthetic (Arts) Movement

Black Banana King
Character in *The Living Is Easy*

Black Boy: A Record of Childhood and Youth

Richard Wright
Autobiography, 1945

Black Boy: A Record of Childhood and Youth describes **Richard Wright**'s life from 1912 to 1927. Although the book is an **autobiography**, Wright's biographer Michel Fabre has suggested that it may not be an entirely truthful account of Wright's early years. Regardless, the book is primarily Wright's attempt to understand those years from a mature perspective.

The young Wright often went hungry, and scenes of his starving recur in the book. His mother often sent him to beg for food from his father, who lived with his mistress. Having to belittle himself to survive stirred Wright's animosity toward the white South. He also blamed his father, a criticism that he extended to the black race generally: "I used to mull over the strange absence of real kindness in Negroes, how unstable was our tenderness, how lacking in genuine passion we were...." Abandoned by whites and blacks alike, Wright felt alone and helpless.

Black Boy met with popular and critical success, and its admirers included William Faulkner. Although some have criticized Wright's discussion of Southern black despair, *Black Boy* nonetheless records a black writer trying to understand and deal with the oppressive culture in which he was raised. A continuation of his autobiography appeared in the *Atlantic Monthly* as "I Tried to Be a Communist" (1944) and posthumously as *American Hunger* (1977).

The Black Cat Club

James D. Corrothers
Novel, 1902

In *The Black Cat Club,* his first **novel**, **James D. Corrothers** uses black dialect to tell the comic yet realistic story of Sandy Jenkins

and eight of his friends. Through the first half of the novel, Sandy and his friends share raucous stories and boisterously argue the merits of their experiences. As these tales unwind, Sandy meets a middle-class black woman and falls in love. By the end of the novel, Sandy is married and working as a caterer. Most of the other members of the club also move into respectable, middle-class lives.

Black Drama

Loften Mitchell
Essays, 1967

Based partly on **Loften Mitchell**'s own compilation of oral histories, these twelve **essays** chronicle the participation of blacks in American theatre from 1769 to 1964. *Black Drama: The Story of the American Negro in the Theatre* discusses black playwrights, producers, directors, and **plays** about blacks. Mitchell outlines the founding of black theatre groups and the success of particular artists as he showcases the pride and talent of black players who steadily developed a theatre that truly expressed the spirit of the black community. *Black Drama* also illustrates the positive effects white and black theatre have on each other. The work is considered a standard reference source for information on blacks in American theatre.

Black Fire

Larry Neal and LeRoi Jones, editors
Anthology, 1968

Edited by **Larry Neal** and LeRoi Jones (**Amiri Baraka**), *Black Fire: An Anthology of Afro-American Writing* is a collection of works in various genres by nearly seventy young black writers from 1960s America. While critics were neither unanimous nor generous in their praise, they recognized the aim of the editors to set the stage for a new African American esthetic unattached to Western cultural standards. The initial **essay** by James T. Stewart announced the paradigm of working exclusively from nonwhite literary models. Comparing wordsmiths to **jazz** musicians, Stewart championed the use of improvisation in all forms of esthetic expression. Neal's closing statement offered the new black standard of human models, instead of abstract ideals, as an antidote to **W. E. B. Du Bois**'s characterization of the double-consciousness of blacks in a white environment. Neal's embrace of black nationalist art went so far as to sacrifice older works such as *Native Son* and *Invisible Man*, in favor of rewriting **poetry** to read like James Brown songs. Many of the poems included are devoted to musicians like Sun-Ra and Sonny Rollins. Major and minor figures in the **black arts movement** contributed stories. In one, an Uncle Tom is lectured by a burglar posing as God. Co-editor **Amiri Baraka**, then still using the name LeRoi Jones, contributed "Madheart" to the collection. Other writers represented include **Stokely Carmichael** and **Charles Fuller**.

Black Is Beautiful Aesthetic

The slogan "black is beautiful" was an expression of pride associated with the black aesthetic and **black power** movements of the 1960s. African American writers who espoused these philosophies were determined to articulate what it meant to be black in a white culture. While writers of the **Harlem Renaissance** had seemed to stumble upon an identity, those of the **black aesthetic movement** were intent upon defining themselves and their era before being defined by outsiders. Other manifestations of the black is beautiful aesthetic included the Afro hairstyle and African clothing adopted by many young African Americans of the day, as well as student demands for more black studies courses and African American teachers.

Many African American writers of the period made a conscious effort to foster black pride through their work. Prominent among these was poet **Haki R. Madhubuti**, formerly known as Don L. Lee. Madhubuti believed that,

through the accurate rendering of black life and speech, a poet could reinforce people's awareness of the richness of their lives. He even titled his second volume of **poetry** *Black Pride* (1968) and coined the strung-together word "blackisbeautifulblack."

A Black Mass

Amiri Baraka
Play, first produced 1966, published 1969

One of **Amiri Baraka**'s longer plays, *A Black Mass* reverses the typical meanings of "white magic" and "black magic" in order to criticize the alienation caused by Western technological culture. The **play** dramatizes a **myth** in the Black Muslim tradition, still popular among the **Nation of Islam**, called "Yacub's History." A black scientist named Jacoub creates the first white being, which runs amuck. Like Dr. Frankenstein, Jacoub has created a thing bereft of social context, homeless, and useless. He merely pandered to the Western value system and becomes tainted by association with his barely communicative invention. The being is sterile and without a functional moral system, and it corrupts blacks into betraying their own people. Jacoub's damaged self-respect manifests itself as an obsession with clock time and its passing. Colleagues decry Jacoub, who, by making the white beast, has created a world-view governed by time and narrow definitions of progress and development. The rival scientists reveal themselves to be magicians who aim to integrate knowledge and experience instead of fostering destructive technologies. They explain to Jacoub the error of his narrow conceptions of exploration and invention, and they outline their black nationalist ideal.

Black Nationalism

Black nationalism, in the broadest sense, is a movement among African Americans emphasizing pride in their African heritage and a desire to control their own destinies. In its classic nineteenth-century form, this led to efforts to establish a national homeland with the intention of demonstrating the ability of black people to govern themselves. One leading exponent of this position in the United States was **Martin Robinson Delany**, author of the influential 1852 book *The Condition, Elevation, Emigration, and Destiny of the Colored People of the United States, Politically Considered.* Closely allied with this is a movement sometimes dubbed "black cultural nationalism," in which African Americans have sought to create a body of literary works by and for blacks. An early example of this is **William Wells Brown**'s 1863 book *The Black Man: His Antecedents, His Genius, and His Achievements.*

The roots of black nationalism lie in the need for a response to the brutal conditions of **slavery**. Documents expressing the ideology of black nationalism began to appear during the late eighteenth century. Then in 1801, slaves revolted and seized power in Haiti. According to eminent black historian **W. E. B. Du Bois**, this served as further inspiration to both slaves and free African Americans. The earliest effort to put black nationalist ideas to a practical test may have been organized by Paul Cuffe, the first black to sail as master of his own ship. In 1811, Cuffe began transporting blacks from the United States to Africa in a repatriation attempt. The 1850s brought a fresh wave of interest in the black nationalist philosophy. In his 1854 speech "Political Destiny of the Colored Race on the American Continent," Delany argued that blacks could only achieve self-reliance outside the United States.

One outgrowth of nineteenth-century black nationalism was the **back-to-Africa movement** founded by **Marcus Garvey** after 1910. This, in turn, prompted the rise of the **Nation of Islam**, which exchanged the goal of a separate nation outside the United States for that of separatism and autonomy within the country. Modern proponents of black nationalism such as poet **Sonia Sanchez** have stressed the need to create a distinct cultural identity for African Americans. Another well-known poet, **Gwendolyn Brooks**, addressed the theme of black nationalism in books such as *Riot* (1969) and *Family Pictures* (1970).

Black No More

George Samuel Schuyler
Novel, 1931

George Samuel Schuyler's *Black No More: Being an Account of the Strange and Wonderful Workings of Science in the Land of the Free* is a satirical **novel** which views **racism** as part of a wider human folly. The main story concerns a process which allows blacks to become whites. Dr. Crookman, a black scientist, turns African American Max Disher into the white Matthew Fisher. Fisher, after becoming an assistant to the Reverend Givens, the leader of a racist organization modelled on the Ku Klux Klan, marries Givens's daughter. Anthropological research suggests that Givens has black ancestry, so when his daughter gives birth to a black child, Givens, his daughter, and his son-in-law are obliged to flee to Mexico. When Dr. Crookman discovers that his method makes whites lighter than authentic Caucasians, racial **discrimination** is revived, but now dark skin is fashionable. It is not long before a method is developed for staining skins brown.

Throughout the novel, Schuyler maintains the lighthearted tone typical of Horatian **satire**, until he describes a lynching scene near the novel's conclusion. In addition to his ridicule of racism and the Ku Klux Klan, Schuyler also attacks the **National Association for the Advancement of Colored People** (NAACP), organized **religion**, and the black response to racism.

Black Power

The late 1960s was a period of growing disillusionment with the **civil rights movement** among some black Americans. In particular, there was increasing doubt in some quarters about the effectiveness of nonviolent tactics to combat **racism**. Against this backdrop, political activist and essayist **Stokely Carmichael** first popularized the slogan "black power" during a mid-1960s voter registration drive through Mississippi. In its broadest sense, black power refers to any attempts by African Americans to make the most of their political and economic power. In practice, though, the term has often been linked to black leaders advocating violence and separatism to achieve empowerment.

In 1966, Carmichael became head of the Student Nonviolent Coordinating Committee (SNCC), a group that had successfully staged peaceful sit-ins. Carmichael altered that group's orientation from nonviolent action to black liberation. In the book *Black Power: The Politics of Liberation in America* (1967), coauthored with **Charles V. Hamilton**, Carmichael argued that black Americans should reject the racist values of mainstream white society and develop their own independent, self-sufficient organizations. In 1967, Carmichael was succeeded as chair of the SNCC by **H. Rap Brown,** another influential figure in the rise of the black power movement. Two years later, Brown published his controversial **autobiography**, *Die Nigger Die!* (1969). Brown publicly urged black Americans to use deadly force in the struggle against racism. In well-publicized **speeches**, he suggested that the race riots then sweeping the country's inner cities were harbingers of a violent revolution.

Many other black activists began to adopt a militant stance around this time. **Malcolm X**, who became leader of the **Nation of Islam**, believed that total withdrawal from Western society was the only solution to the problem of racism. His story is recorded in *The Autobiography of Malcolm X* (1965), written with **Alex Haley**, while his speeches are collected in *Malcolm X Speaks* (1965). A year after Malcolm X's assassination in February of 1965, **Bobby Seale** and Huey P. Newton formed the Black Panther Party, a radical group aimed at protecting ghetto residents from police brutality and securing equal rights for blacks. Two books by Seale are *Seize the Time: The Story of the Black Panther Party and Huey P. Newton* (1970) and *A Lonely Rage: The Autobiography of Bobby Seale* (1978). He also contributed to a book edited by G. Louis Heath titled *The Black Panther Leaders Speak* (1976).

The historical trends and events associated with the black power movement have served as rich subject matter for many black nonfiction writers. For example, **James S. Haskins** and **Gordon Parks** each discussed the movement in their books, and **Calvin Hernton** wrote *Coming Together: Black Power, White Hatred, and Sexual Hang-ups* (1971). In addition, the militant tone of much of the 1960s political rhetoric has influenced the voices of countless African American writers who followed.

Black Power

Stokely Carmichael and
Charles V. Hamilton
Nonfiction, 1967

In *Black Power: The Politics of Liberation in America*, **Stokely Carmichael** and **Charles V. Hamilton** define "**Black Power**" as the principle that African Americans need to "close ranks" in order to obtain a fair share of power in American society. They criticize American middle-class values and institutions, which, they argue, perpetuate racial **discrimination**, and they reject the feasibility of a broad coalition between white and black Americans. Instead of seeking accommodation with the existing, white-dominated power structure, they contend that African Americans should build their own power structure by taking control of their local schools, businesses, and communities. The slogan "Black Power" was coined by Carmichael in the mid-1960s when he chaired the Student Nonviolent Coordinating Committee (SNCC).

Black Power U.S.A.

Lerone Bennett Jr.
Nonfiction, 1967

Black Power U.S.A.: The Human Side of Reconstruction, 1867-1877 grew out of a collection of articles that originally appeared in **Ebony** magazine, which was edited by **Lerone Bennett Jr.** In the book, Bennett examines the psychology of the South during the **Reconstruction** era following the Civil War. Discussing the political motivations of both black and white legislators, Bennett details the successes and failures of black politicians in securing "**black power**." Among the individuals he profiles are the well-liked Franklin J. Moses Jr., South Carolina's white governor, and Blanche Kelso Bruce, the first black man in Mississippi to serve a full congressional term. Bennett also points out legislative achievements, such as South Carolina's civil rights bill, which helped protect against **discrimination**, and the state's homestead law, which provided aid to destitute farmers. In addition, Bennett describes educational reforms, including programs to provide free books to needy students and policies for the establishment of scholarships.

Black Theatre Present Condition
Woodie King Jr.
Essays, 1981

Black Theatre Present Condition assembles sixteen of **Woodie King Jr.**'s influential writings on African American theater, most of which have been previously published in various periodicals in the 1960s and 1970s. The **essays** expound principles King has embraced in his own theatrical career. King calls for the formation of African American theater companies located in African American neighborhoods, both to provide opportunities for African American actors, playwrights, and directors, and to foster the development of a dramatic tradition that serves the needs of the African American community. Two essays discuss the enduring contributions of **Langston Hughes** and **Lorraine Hansberry** to the development of African American theater, and several discuss the history of African American theater.

Black Thunder
Arna Bontemps
Novel, 1936

A historical **novel** set in Virginia in 1800, *Black Thunder* is **Arna Bontemps**'s best-known

novel. A fictionalized account of a slave revolt known as the Gabriel Insurrection, the book portrays Gabriel Prosser, the young slave who plans the rebellion. His goal is to arm himself and his supporters with weapons from the Richmond arsenal, then seize control of the city. Among his fellow rebels is Mingo, a free black whose reading ability and relative mobility are great assets. Although Prosser gains widespread support from other blacks and a few whites, his scheme unravels; on the crucial night a torrential rainstorm forces a change in plans. On a literal level, the "black thunder" of the title refers to this pivotal plot event. However, it also symbolizes rebellion, the central theme in this book.

Ultimately, Gabriel's rebellion is suppressed, in part due to betrayal by a slave named Pharaoh and Old Ben Woodfolk, a domestic slave who divulges secrets out of loyalty to his master. Gabriel remains on the loose for some time after most of his supporters have given up; he surrenders only when it becomes necessary to prevent the punishment of another man who has helped him. Gabriel is eventually hanged along with some of his loyal lieutenants: Ditcher and General John. As the day of their execution draws to a close, storm clouds roll in once again.

The Black Unicorn
Audre Lorde
Poetry, 1978

A collection of sixty-seven poems that is widely recognized as **Audre Lorde**'s most successful work, *The Black Unicorn* draws extensively from African culture in affirming the poet's womanhood, blackness, and homosexuality. Written in a free verse style that resembles **the blues**, the poems in this collection evoke various figures from African mythology to address themes of motherhood, blackness, and spiritual renewal. The first set of poems, for instance, focuses on black mothers, daughters, and sisters, emphasizing the strength of black female relationships within the framework of an African consciousness. In the later sections, Lorde focuses on the redemptive power of art while addressing social and political injustice. Although she recognizes the potency of her art, Lorde concludes the volume with a cautionary statement of self-instruction ("Eulogy for Alvin Frost"): "But unless I learn to use / the difference between poetry and rhetoric / my power too will run corrupt as poisonous mold."

 ## Black Women Writers (1950-1980)

Mari Evans, editor and contributor
Essay collection, 1984

Edited by **Mari Evans**, *Black Women Writers (1950-1980): A Critical Evaluation* is a critical history of fifteen authors: **Maya Angelou, Toni Cade Bambara, Gwendolyn Brooks, Alice Childress, Lucille Clifton**, Mari Evans, **Nikki Giovanni, Gayl Jones, Audre Lorde, Paule Marshall, Toni Morrison**, Carolyn Rodgers, **Sonia Sanchez, Alice Walker**, and **Margaret Walker**. In the preface, editor Evans calls the book "an effort to meet an observed need." It was the first comprehensive study of those black women writers who came to prominence in the 1950s, 1960s, and 1970s.

Each of the authors included in *Black Women Writers* was asked to provide a statement about her life and work in response to a questionnaire; all but two complied. The writers' comments explore intentions, obstacles, and rewards. Childress, for example, discusses the distinction between writers who choose to present "winners" as exemplars of success and those, such as herself, who prefer to portray "losers" who would otherwise have no voice. Evans writes about the roles of idiom and imagery.

Each writer is also the subject of two critical essays written for the occasion by black critics, both female and male. These essays, representing differences in critical approach, vary widely in style and complexity. Among them are Ruth Elizabeth Burks's **essay** on language and **jazz** patterns in Bambara's **novels** and John McClusky Jr.'s piece on ritual and set-

ting in Marshall's work. Also included in the collection are detailed biographical and bibliographical sketches of the writers.

Les Blancs

Lorraine Hansberry
Play, first produced 1970, published 1972

A disturbing **play** that met with strong reaction, **Lorraine Hansberry**'s *Les Blancs* focuses on the struggles of African nations against **colonialism**. The play's protagonist, the English-educated intellectual Tshembe Matoseh, lives in London with his white wife, but returns to his homeland of Zatembe for his father's funeral. Once back in Africa, Tshembe becomes involved in his nation's freedom struggle and faces a series of dilemmas stemming from his divided loyalties to the colonialists—white Christian missionaries and other settlers who have helped raise him—and to the nationalist political cause. While Tshembe thinks he should take part in the struggle, his brother Abioseh has become a Catholic priest and supports the colonial government. Tshembe's vacillation over loyalties is resolved by Ntali, one of the rebels, who tells him the fable of Modingo, the wise hyena. In the story, Modingo is asked to mediate a conflict between hyenas and elephants over land, but while Modingo pauses to consider the arguments, the elephants take the land by force. The hyena's laugh, Ntali tells him, is a laugh of bitterness at having thought too much before acting. Meanwhile, a well-meaning but arrogant American journalist Charlie Morris, who has come to meet the paternalistic Reverend Torvald Neilsen, engages Tshembe in further discussions about **racism** and the political struggle in Zatembe. The play reaches its climax when the discussions finally end in action: Tshembe decides to become active in the freedom struggle. He kills first his brother, who has betrayed members of the resistance movement to the police, and then Madame Neilsen, who has been like a second mother to him. At the play's close, Tshembe's hysterical sobbing recalls the hyena's bitter laughter.

John W. Blassingame

American historian
Born March 23, 1940.

John Wesley Blassingame has chronicled black history in America in several scholarly studies and collections. Born in Georgia, he holds a Ph.D. from Yale University and in 1970 he became a professor there.

Besides coediting *The Booker T. Washington Papers,* Volume I (1972), *Antislavery Newspapers and Periodicals,* Volumes I-V (1980-84), *The Frederick Douglass Papers: Series I* (1979-92), and other historical documents and collections of **essays** on black history, he has written *The Slave Community: Plantation Life in the Antebellum South* (1972, revised and enlarged, 1979), *Black New Orleans: 1860-1880* (1973), and (with Mary F. Berry) *Long Memory: The Black Experience in America* (1982). Blassingame has also contributed widely to history journals.

Further Readings
Black Writers, Gale, first edition, 1989.
Contemporary Issues Criticism, Volume 1, Gale, 1982.

Bleeding Hearts

Please see *Six Plays for a Negro Theatre*

Bleek Gilliam

Character in *Mo' Better Blues*

"Blind" Eddie

Character in *The Soul Brothers and Sister Lou*

Charles L. Blockson

American nonfiction writer and editor
Born December 16, 1933.

Committed to the preservation of black history, Charles Leroy Blockson has written several books concerning the history of African Americans. Written with Ron Fry, *Black Geneal-*

Evans's study of contemporary black women writers.

ogy (1977) addresses the difficulties faced by blacks tracing family trees whose branches were severed by the slave trade. *The Underground Railroad: First Person Narratives of Escapes to Freedom in the North* (1987), edited by Blockson, contains first-hand accounts by blacks travelling the secret routes North to escape **slavery**. He is also the author of the *Hippocrene Guide to the Underground Railroad* (1994).

Born in 1933 in Norristown, Pennsylvania, Blockson has established a collection of African American artifacts in Philadelphia at Temple University. His collection contains books, pamphlets, drawings, sheet music, posters, and other artifacts spanning nearly four centuries of African American history.

Further Readings
Black Writers, second edition, Gale, 1994.

Blood on the Forge

William Attaway
Novel, 1941

William Attaway's *Blood on the Forge* is the tragic story of three brothers who escape Southern **racism** by migrating to Pennsylvania, only to be devastated by the harsh circumstances of Northern industrialism.

Originally Kentucky sharecroppers, each of the Moss brothers represents a distinctive aspect of the African American experience. Big Mat studies the Bible in hopes of becoming a preacher, Chinatown is a pleasure-seeker, and Melody is a blues guitarist, symbolizing the artist. After Big Mat severely beats the brothers' white overseer, they are recruited to work at a Pennsylvania steel mill.

Made to work like machines, the three brothers suffer physical, spiritual, and psychological damage. Big Mat abandons **religion**, begins drinking, and kills a striker in a fit of anger. Melody stops playing the guitar after wounding his hand in a steel mill accident, and Chinatown is blinded by an explosion. Eventually, Big Mat is killed, and his two brothers move to the slums of Pittsburgh.

The Blues

The blues is a form of African American folk music with a twelve-bar pattern that makes it adaptable to popular song writing. It is characterized by a unique harmonic quality derived from a "flattening" of the third and seventh notes of a standard major scale. While seemingly simple, this musical style lends itself to infinite variation. Blues lyrics tend to lament the trials and tribulations of living and loving. They usually take the form of a three-line stanza comprised of an initial line, its repetition, and a new third line. Each sung phrase is typically followed by an improvised instrumental section, creating a call-and-response pattern that is derived from African music.

Blues singing, which has its roots in slave **spirituals**, was common in the South by the late nineteenth century. Not long afterward, it entered the realm of popular song. In 1902, Ma Rainey became the first black person to sing the blues in a professional show. Ten years later, W. C. Handy published "Memphis Blues," the first written blues composition. By 1923 singer Bessie Smith had sold over a million copies of her recording of "Downhearted Blues / Gulf Coast Blues." Noted black poet and playwright **Amiri Baraka** discusses the sociological and historical context of this musical form's development in *Blues People: Negro Music in White America* (1963). In addition, in his nonfiction volume *Shadow and Act* (1964), **Ralph Ellison** traces the evolution of the blues and **jazz** and examines the relationship of the black artist to the growth of the musical forms.

When blues playing was adapted to solo piano, it evolved into boogie-woogie. After World War II, the blues gave rise to a commercially successful style known as **rhythm and blues**. The blues was also closely intertwined with, and sometimes almost indistinguishable from, jazz. However, its influence has not been limited to musicians. Black writers have also attempted to reproduce the blues experience. For example, **William Waring Cuney** wrote blues poems that, like their musical counterpart, take as their theme the harsh realities of life. In form, too, these poems echo the sounds of the blues, and some, such as "Bessie Smith," pay homage to blues icons. **Sterling Brown** employed mournful subject matter, typical of traditional blues tunes, contemplating themes of alienation and lost loves. **Audre Lorde**'s poems in his successful 1978 collection *The Black Unicorn* resemble the blues form, utilizing a free verse style, while **Calvin Forbes**'s poems in the collections *Blue Monday* (1974) and *From the Book of Shine* (1979) adopt the rhythm patterns of traditional blues music. **Langston Hughes** also often reproduced the themes and forms of the blues in his **poetry**.

Prose writers have attempted to imitate the structure and rhythm of the blues as well. For example, **Albert L. Murray**'s **novel** *Train Whistle Guitar* (1974) is composed of episodes

This long praise poem examines African American womanhood.

that are arranged sequentially, as in the blues, without apparent attention to their hierarchy. These episodes are linked together by brief italicized segments that serve to introduce new sections, much as riffs in the blues serve to keep the music flowing. In his choice of language, Murray depends upon linking phrases rather than subordinate or qualifying clauses. The rhythm he subsequently achieves is reminiscent of the twelve-bar, twelve-string guitar. Other writers of prose have introduced blues musicians into their works. Both **Gayl Jones**'s novel *Corregidora* (1975) and **Alice Walker**'s novel *The Color Purple* (1982) feature blues singers, while **James Baldwin**'s **short story** "Sonny's Blues" revolves around a jazz pianist.

A Blues Book for Blue Black Magical Women

Sonia Sanchez
Poetry, 1973

Sonia Sanchez's *A Blues Book for Blue Black Magical Women* is a long praise poem that examines African American womanhood and emphasizes the importance of personal freedom in attaining moral and spiritual self-affirmation. The introduction, "Queens of the Universe," serves as a call for women to abandon false roles created by **racism**, and claim their own identity. Part II, "The Past," chronicles the poet's life from childhood into an imagined old age. The next section, "The Present," focuses on her conversion and spiritual rebirth into the **Nation of Islam**. The second half of the book draws from both the Koran and the Bible, providing a celebratory vision of personal and collective rebirth.

The Bluest Eye

Toni Morrison
Novel, 1969

The Bluest Eye, **Toni Morrison**'s first **novel**, examines **racism**, sexuality, and growing up in a hostile world. Set in Morrison's hometown of Lorain, Ohio, in the early 1940s, the novel focuses on three young girls: Pecola Breedlove and Claudia and Frieda McTeer. Claudia serves as the narrator of the book and summarizes the plot: Pecola was raped by her father, became pregnant with a child that died, and went insane.

Pecola's parents, Cholly and Pauline, send their daughter to live with the McTeers because their own home has been destroyed in a fire Cholly started. Claudia and Frieda sense how much Pecola's sensibilities have been shaped by the standards of white American culture: Pecola falls in love with the McTeers's Shirley Temple mug, drinking three quarts of milk in one day in order to continue admiring it, and she confides that she prays every night that God will give her blue eyes, which she considers the epitome of beauty. Pauline thinks much like her daughter does, considering the feelings and property of her white employers more important than those of her own family. Cholly, the product of a broken home, cannot come to terms with Pauline's expectations and his own desires. Other members of the community, including Geraldine, a neighborhood black woman, and Soaphead Church, a West Indian religious leader, express similar feelings of self-hatred. While she is living with the McTeers, Pecola begins to menstruate and to explore her sexuality. After she returns home, Cholly assaults his daughter while she is doing the dishes. Pecola retreats further and further from the real world into madness, finally coming to

believe that she has attained her wish for blue eyes. Claudia concludes the book by revealing that Pecola has become a homeless beggar.

Bob Jones

Character in *If He Hollers Let Him Go*

Bobby Parker

Character in *Ceremonies in Dark Old Men*

SDiane Bogus

American poet and nonfiction writer
Born January 22, 1946.

Winner of the 1990 Lambda Literary award, SDiane Adams Bogus has been a major contributor to the growing lesbian literary movement. Her first **poetry** collection, *Women in the Moon* (1971), was in its fourth edition by 1994, and the enduring success of the volume prompted Bogus to adopt the book's title for the name of the publishing company she started. Throughout her career as a writer, teacher, and publisher, Bogus has been motivated by current issues, with interests including new age writings on spirituality, gay and lesbian literature, and the work of black writers such as **Alice Walker**, **Audre Lorde**, **Toni Morrison**, and **James Baldwin**. Her other poetry volumes include *Dyke Hands and Sutras: Erotic Lyric* (1989) and *The Chant of the Women of Magdalena* (1990). Bogus is also the editor of *The Poetry Workbook: A Poet's Workbook* (1991).

Further Readings
Black Writers, second edition, Gale, 1994.

Robert Boles

American novelist and short story writer
Born in 1943.

Robert E. Boles had his first **novel,** *The People One Knows* (1964), published when he was only twenty-one. Possibly autobiographical, it is the story of Saul Beckworth, the young son of a mixed marriage, who suffers from the effects of **racism** and attempts suicide while he is in Libya with the army. Boles's second novel, *Curling* (1968), recounts the tale of a young man whose family problems lead him to commit murder. Boles's **short stories** have appeared both in periodicals, such as *TriQuarterly,* and in collections, including *The Best Short Stories by Negro Writers: An Anthology from 1899 to the Present* (1967) and *An Introduction to Black Literature in America.*

Further Readings
Black Writers, second edition, Gale, 1994.

Julian Bond
American activist and politician
Born January 14, 1940.

Bond was well known as a civil rights activist even before he was elected to the Georgia House of Representatives in 1965. Members of the Georgia legislature prevented him from taking his seat because they objected to his statements about the Vietnam War. After Bond won a second election in 1966, a special House Committee again voted to bar him from the legislature. Bond won a third election in November, 1966, and in December the United States Supreme Court ruled unanimously that the Georgia House had erred in refusing him his seat. He officially became a member of the Georgia House of Representatives on January 7, 1967.

At the Democratic National Convention in 1968, Bond led a rival delegation from Georgia, charging that the local party leadership had deliberately kept blacks from participating in the nomination process. He argued that the officially sanctioned state delegation should not be seated. After a heated battle, his group was granted half the votes normally given to the Georgia delegation. At the same time, Bond became the first black man to have his name entered for the nomination for the vice-presidential spot on the Democratic Party ticket. Reporters acclaimed him as the political successor to **Martin Luther King Jr.** Although Bond

Morrison's first novel examines black self-hatred occasioned by white American ideals.

did not win the nomination, the increased exposure led to his first book, *The Black Man in American Politics: Three Views* (1969), which he wrote with **Kenneth B. Clark** and Richard G. Hatcher.

In keeping with his belief that blacks can best further their own interests through political activism, Bond published *A Time to Speak, A Time to Act: The Movement in Politics* (1972;

Julian Bond, a political activist, at a 1966 news conference.

with Hal Gulliver), which outlines his political strategy. In 1974, he was elected to the Georgia State Senate, and he served there throughout the 1970s and 1980s. In 1986, Bond campaigned for a Democratic seat in Congress but was defeated for the nomination.

Further Readings
Black Writers, first edition, Gale, 1989.

Arna Bontemps

American poet, novelist, author of children's literature, and anthologist
Born October 13, 1902.
Died June 4, 1973.

An important figure in the **Harlem Renaissance**, Arnauld Wendell Bontemps is noted for stressing in his **poetry, novels,** and juvenile works a sense of pride in one's color and heritage. Many, however, consider his work as a librarian and an anthologist to be as important a contribution to African American literature as his original writings.

Born in Alexandria, Louisiana, on October 13, 1902, Bontemps moved with his family to Los Angeles when he was three years old. His mother died when he was twelve, and his childhood was dominated by the conflicting influences of his father, who warned him against acting "colored," and his father's brother, Buddy, who delighted in retelling traditional African American stories.

Bontemps graduated from Pacific Union College in 1923 and moved to New York to teach at Harlem Academy. His poetry, which was later collected in *Personals* (1963), soon caught the attention of such figures as **Langston Hughes** and **W. E. B. Du Bois**. Bontemps married Alberta Johnson in 1926. His first novel, ***God Sends Sunday,*** appeared in 1931. The same year, he left Harlem with his growing family and moved first to Alabama and then to Chicago, teaching at small colleges. His best-known work, ***Black Thunder*** (1936), is a historical novel about a slave rebellion. In an effort to reach younger readers, in the 1930s Bontemps also began to write children's books.

In 1943, Bontemps earned a master's degree in library science from the University of Chicago. He became a librarian at Fisk University in Nashville, where he would remain until 1965. While at Fisk, Bontemps developed a collection of African American literature that included the papers of many important authors. He compiled several literary anthologies that were widely used in schools and wrote biographies for young readers of prominent black Americans, including George Washington Carver and **Frederick Douglass**. He also wrote critical essays on black poetry and **folklore**, and in 1958 he and Hughes published ***The Book of Negro Folklore***. Bontemps enjoyed a distinguished academic career, teaching and writing into the 1970s. He died of a heart attack in Nashville on June 4, 1973.

See also **Poetry of Arna Bontemps**

Further Readings
Black Literature Criticism, Gale, 1992.

Black Writers, first edition, Gale, 1989.

Dictionary of Literary Biography, Gale, Volume 48: *American Poets, 1880-1945,* 1986; Volume 51, *Afro-American Writers from the Harlem Renaissance to 1940,* 1987.

Boogie Woogie Landscapes (play)
Please see *Three Pieces*

The Book of Negro Folklore
Arna Bontemps and Langston Hughes, editors
Folklore and essays, 1958

Arna Bontemps and **Langston Hughes** present a collection of a wide variety of African and African American **folklore** in this anthology. The collection includes animal tales, rhymes for religious functions and for group games, **slave narratives**, ghost stories, superstitions, conjure tales, preacher stories, sermons, prayers, and lyrics to various kinds of music such as **spirituals**, gospel songs, ballads, blues, work songs, and prison songs, some never printed before.

Bontemps and Hughes connect the folk tradition represented by such material with contemporary black culture in a final section. Included are **essays** on black burial societies and **poetry** in **the blues**, anecdotal and biographical sketches by and about famous **jazz** artists, and a glossary of Harlem jive talk. The anthology also contains modern tales, songs, and stories by several writers who draw on traditional materials. Contributors include **Paul Laurence Dunbar**, **Richard Wright**, **Ralph Ellison**, and **Gwendolyn Brooks**.

In his writings, Bontemps stressed a return to one's roots.

Booker Savage
Character in *The Learning Tree*

Boris A. Max
Character in *Native Son*

Born Black
Gordon Parks
Essays, 1971

A collection of **Gordon Parks**'s articles, interviews, **essays**, and photographs commissioned by *Life* magazine, *Born Black* describes the racial climate of the 1960s. Parks writes about the Black Muslims and Black Panthers, an execution at San Quentin penitentiary, the assassination of **Martin Luther King Jr.**, and such figures as Muhammad Ali, **Eldridge Cleaver**, **Malcolm X**, **Stokely Carmichael**, and Huey Newton.

Boy Willie Charles
Character in *The Piano Lesson*

Boy at the Window
Owen Dodson
Novel, 1951

Owen Dodson's semi-autobiographical *Boy at the Window* takes place in a mixed-race Brooklyn neighborhood in the 1920s and explores the coming-of-age of a young black boy. Nine-year-old Coin Foreman is determined to find a cure for his mother's paralyzed arm and leg. He attends the church of a Baptist faith healer and participates in a baptism ceremony in the vain hope that his intense belief will persuade God to heal his mother. When his mother eventually dies, the family undergoes emotional changes, and Coin moves to Washington to stay with a blind uncle. Through his experiences there and from his eventual understanding of his mother's death, Coin gains strength and maturity, accepting his mother's fate and finding meaning in life.

Boyd
Series character in "Simple" Stories

Bra Man
Character in *Brother Man*

David Bradley
American novelist
Born September 7, 1950.

Bradley gained critical acclaim for his second **novel, *The Chaneysville Incident*** (1981), which won the 1982 PEN/Faulkner Award. This novel makes use of such historical issues as **slavery** and the **Underground Railroad** in its depiction of a contemporary rural Pennsylvania town. Bradley's first novel, **South Street** (1975), was written while he was an undergraduate at the University of Pennsylvania and focuses on life in a Philadelphia ghetto. Bradley has also worked a professor of English, a freelance magazine writer, and a reviewer for the *New York Times Book Review* and the *Washington Post Book World*.

Further Readings
Black Literature Criticism, Gale, 1992.

Dictionary of Literary Biography, Volume 33: *Afro-American Fiction Writers after 1955,* Gale, 1984.

Ed Bradley
American television journalist
Born June 22, 1941.

Edward R. Bradley is well-known for his work on the CBS-TV news magazine *60 Minutes.* Born in 1941 in Philadelphia, Pennsylvania, Bradley began his career as an elementary school teacher, leaving in 1967 to join CBS radio. He later switched to television, and by 1973 he had gained recognition for his coverage of the fall of Cambodia and Vietnam. In 1978 Bradley became a principal correspondent for *CBS Reports* and made several award-winning documentaries, including the Emmy Award-winning reports entitled "The Boat People" (1978), on the Indochinese political refugees, and "Blacks in America: With All Deliberate Speed" (1979), on the progress of blacks in public schools after the U.S. Supreme Court outlawed **segregation** in 1954 in *Brown v. Board of Education.* Bradley joined *60 Minutes* in 1981.

Further Readings
Black Writers, first edition, Gale, 1989.

E. R. Braithwaite
Guyanese autobiographer and novelist
Born June 27, 1920.

Despite his degree in physics and experience serving in the Royal Air Force, Eustace Edward Adolf Ricardo Braithwaite was denied several jobs due to racial **discrimination**. He eventually became a schoolmaster in a working-class area of London, an experience he chronicled in *To Sir, with Love* (1959), which was later adapted as a movie. Braithwaite then became a London welfare officer, which he described in *Paid Servant* (1962). His **novel** *Choice of Straws* (1965) portrays working-class London from the perspective of a white factory worker. In the late sixties, Braithwaite held diplomatic posts on behalf of Guyana. In 1973, South Africa's **apartheid** government named Braithwaite an "honorary white" so he could visit and enjoy privileges not normally granted to blacks. *"Honorary White": A Visit to South Africa* (1975) describes his trip. Braithwaite currently teaches at New York University.

Further Readings

Black Writers, first edition, Gale, 1989.

 ## William Stanley Braithwaite

American editor, poet, and critic
Born December 6, 1878.
Died June 8, 1962.

Braithwaite is best known for his *Anthology of Magazine Verse and Yearbook of American Poetry* (1913-1929), through which he promoted and reviewed the works of various American poets during an era of disinterest in the genre. As a poet, the racially mixed Braithwaite has been both reproached for ignoring racial issues and praised for holding art above sociopolitical matters.

Born in Boston, William Stanley Beaumont Braithwaite was self-educated from age twelve, when he began to work to help support his family. At age fifteen, Braithwaite's love of **poetry** was sparked after reading the John Keats poem "Ode on a Grecian Urn." By 1903, he began to contribute verse and criticism to journals. Shortly after, he published his first two books of poetry, *Lyrics of Life and Love* (1904) and *The House of Falling Leaves, with Other Poems* (1908).

Braithwaite won the NAACP's Spingarn Medal in 1918, and, in 1921, founded the B.J. Brimmer Publishing Company, serving as editor until its bankruptcy in 1927. Appointed Professor of Creative Literature at Atlanta University in 1935, Braithwaite concurrently worked on the editorial board of *Phylon*. Retiring in 1945, Braithwaite moved to Harlem, where he continued to write for periodicals and published his last poetry collection, *Selected Poems* (1948), as well as a **biography** of the Brontës entitled *The Bewitched Parsonage* (1950) and his last poetry anthology in 1959.

See also **Poetry of William Stanley Braithwaite**

Further Readings

Black Literature Criticism, Gale, 1992.

Black Writers, first edition, Gale, 1989.

Dictionary of Literary Biography, Volume 50: *Afro-American Writers before the Harlem Renaissance,* Gale, 1986.

William Branch

American playwright, screenwriter, and television writer
Born September 11, 1927.

Branch's first **play,** *A Medal for Willie* (1951), describes the funeral of a black soldier whose recognition as a hero is ironic considering the racial oppression he had endured. In his second play, **In Splendid Error** (1954), Branch recreates a meeting that took place between **Frederick Douglass** and John Brown. Although he completed other plays, Branch was discouraged by the lack of support for black theater in the 1960s and turned to radio, television, and films. His documentary *Still a Brother: Inside the Negro Middle Class* (1968) was nominated for an Emmy Award and won a blue ribbon at the American Film Festival. *Black Thunder: An Anthology of Contemporary African American Drama* (1992), which he edited, earned an American Book Award. In addition to several teaching positions, Branch has headed an independent media consulting firm.

Further Readings

Black Writers, second edition, Gale, 1994.

Dictionary of Literary Biography, Volume 76: *Afro-American Fiction Writers, 1940-1955,* Gale, 1984.

Dionne Brand

Trinidadian poet, fiction writer,
and journalist
Born January 7, 1953.

Brand is best known for her **poetry,** in which she explore issues related to racial and sexual identity. Having immigrated to Canada as a teenager, Brand demonstrates her ties to other Trinidadians both in her native country and in Canada. She holds a bachelor's degree in English from the University of Toronto and has worked with the Black Education Project and as a Caribbean counselor with the Immigrant Women's Centre.

Among Brand's poetry collections are *'Fore Day Morning* (1978), *Chronicles of the Hostile Sun* (1984), and *No Language Is Neutral* (1990). She has also written *Sans Souci, and Other Stories* (1989) and cowritten *Rivers Have Sources, Trees Have Roots: Speaking of Racism* (1986) and *No Burden to Carry: Narratives of Black Working Women in Ontario, 1920s-1950s* (1991).

Further Readings

Black Writers, Gale, second edition, 1994.

Edward Kamau Brathwaite

Barbadian poet, historian, and essayist
Born May 11, 1930.

Brathwaite is a prolific West Indian writer whose reputation rests primarily on several volumes of verse, including two trilogies. Throughout his career, Brathwaite has been concerned with exploring the Caribbean identity.

Brathwaite was born in Bridgetown, Barbados, and christened Lawson Edward Brathwaite. After attending Harrison College in Barbados, he won a scholarship to Cambridge University, where he received a bachelor's degree in history in 1953 and a certificate in education the following year. Brathwaite married Doris Monica Welcome, a teacher, in 1960.

During and just after college, Brathwaite had numerous poems published in magazines and broadcast by the British Broadcasting Corporation (BBC). However, the publication of *Rights of Passage* (1967), *Masks* (1968), and *Islands*(1969) introduced his **poetry** to a wider audience. This autobiographical series, collectively titled *The Arrivants: A New World Trilogy* (1973), examines a Caribbean man's identity quest.

Around this time, Brathwaite was at the University of Sussex in England, where he received a doctoral degree in 1968 for historical research later published as *The Development of Creole Society in Jamaica, 1770-1820* (1971). After Brathwaite returned to teaching at the University of the West Indies in Kingston, Jamaica, he continued to publish **literary criticism**, essays, and books, including *Folk Culture of the Slaves in Jamaica* (1970), *History of the Voice* (1984), and *Roots* (1986). He also released more of his own poetry in books and recordings. His second verse trilogy—comprising the volumes *Mother Poem* (1977), *Sun Poem* (1982), and *X/Self* (1987)—further investigates the issue of selfhood. Brathwaite won the Neustadt International Prize for Literature in 1994. He is currently professor of Social and Cultural History at the University of the West Indies.

Further Readings

Black Writers, second edition, Gale, 1994.

Brathwaite, Doris Monica, *A Descriptive and Chronological Bibliography (1950-1982) of the Work of Edward Kamau Brathwaite,* New Beacon, 1988.

Brathwaite, Doris Monica, *Edward Kamau Brathwaite: His Published Prose and Poetry 1948-1986,* Savacou Publications, 1986.

Dictionary of Literary Biography, Volume 125: *Twentieth-Century Caribbean and Black African Writers,* Second Series, Gale, 1993.

Benjamin Brawley

American educator, critic, and nonfiction writer
Born April 22, 1882.
Died February 1, 1939.

An educator and prolific author, Benjamin Griffith Brawley is known for his works in literary and social history. He wrote several books that are still considered standard college texts, including *The Negro in Literature and Art in the United States* (1918) and *New Survey of English Literature* (1925).

Brawley was born on April 22, 1882, in Washington, DC, to Edward and Margaret Dickerson Brawley. Brawley received his B.A. from Atlanta Baptist College (later Morehouse College) in 1901, his second B.A. from the University of Chicago in 1906, and an M.A. from Harvard University in 1908.

Brawley taught at Howard University for two years and became professor of English at Morehouse College in 1912. In 1921, he was ordained in the Baptist ministry and left teaching for a year to serve as pastor of a church in Massachusetts before accepting a position at Shaw University. In 1931, he returned to Howard University, where he published two collections of short biographies: *The Negro Genius* (1937), which focuses on black artists and literary figures, and *Negro Builders and Heroes* (1937) which surveys a wider field of notable African Americans. Brawley died of a stroke on February 1, 1939.

Further Readings
Black Writers, first edition, Gale, 1989.

Braz Cubas

Character in *Epitaph of a Small Winner*

"Brazil" (novella)

Please see *Soul Clap Hands and Sing*

Breaking Barriers: A Memoir

Carl Thomas Rowan
Autobiography, 1991

In his memoir *Breaking Barriers,* **Carl Thomas Rowan** recounts his life story as one of the first prominent black journalists in the United States. Rowan was an eyewitness to many of the major events in the **civil rights movement**, including the Montgomery, Alabama, bus boycotts and the school integration struggle in Little Rock, Arkansas. Rowan's memoir opens with his impoverished childhood in Tennessee, where he was raised in a house that had no plumbing and no electricity. After having begun classes at Tennessee State University, Rowan was offered the chance to serve in a small corps of black Navy officers during World War II. Once the war ended, Rowan finished college at Oberlin and was later hired by the *Minneapolis Tribune,* where he wrote a series of articles about **segregation** in the South. In the early 1960s Rowan served as ambassador to Finland and headed the U.S. Information Agency. He describes several presidents with whom he was personally acquainted—John F. Kennedy, Lyndon B. Johnson, and Ronald Reagan—as well as pivotal civil rights figures like **Martin Luther King Jr.** and Jesse Jackson. Rowan's personal memoir concludes around the time he turned forty, when he launched a career as a television commentator, newspaper columnist, and lecturer. However, Rowan continues to comment upon current events, especially those of consequence to African Americans.

The Breast of the Earth

Kofi Awoonor
Essay collection, 1975

In *The Breast of the Earth: A Survey of the History, Culture, and Literature of Africa South of the Sahara,* based on his doctoral dissertation, **Kofi Awoonor** explores the oral narrative as the basis for Africa's written word. He asserts that most of Africa's literature stems from a rich tradition of oral history and narration. He also examines the effect of colonial rule on the literature, suggesting that the introduction of new European languages and cultures profoundly influenced the oral and printed word. In addition, he specifically addresses the issue of African literature written in English, making particular mention of **poetry** and the dynamics of African culture and heritage expressed in English.

Breeders

Please see *Six Plays for a Negro Theatre*

The Breedlove Family

Characters in *The Bluest Eye*

Brer Dog

Character in *Mules and Men*

Brer Rabbit

Character in *Mules and Men*

A Brighter Sun

Sam Selvon
Novel, 1952

Sam Selvon's first **novel**, *A Brighter Sun,* traces the growth of Tiger, the young protagonist, from childish dependence upon his parents to adult responsibility in a colonial and pluralistic Trinidadian society. Early in the story Tiger is an innocent boy who appears rather ignorant about many issues. His conception of manhood, for example, is that men smoke. His self-assertiveness as well as his political and social sensitivity begin to develop soon after his arranged marriage to Urmilla, which uproots him from the Chaguanas cane fields and the security of his parents to a situation in which he must fend for two people. Tiger and Urmilla establish themselves in racially mixed Barataria, and though

Tiger's East Indian parents disapprove of his relationships with Trinidadian blacks, Tiger cultivates friendships with neighbors Joe and Rita. Tiger's quest for knowledge contrasts with Joe's satisfaction with physical, ephemeral pleasures. Tiger realizes maturity is accepting the consequences of his actions and decisions, and understanding and accepting his individuality.

"British Guiana" (novella)

Please see *Soul Clap Hands and Sing*

"Brooklyn" (novella)

Please see *Soul Clap Hands and Sing*

Gwendolyn Brooks

American poet and novelist
Born June 7, 1917.

The first black author to win the Pulitzer Prize, Brooks is noted for her mastery of poetic technique and her treatment of themes of black identity and the struggle for racial equality.

Born in Topeka, Kansas, on June 7, 1917, Brooks grew up in Chicago, where she began writing **poetry** while still in elementary school. As a teenager, her talent was recognized by **James Weldon Johnson** and **Langston Hughes**. After graduating from Wilson Junior College in 1936, she worked briefly as a maid and then as a secretary to a man who ran a Chicago slum building called the Mecca. In 1939, she married Henry Lowington Blakely.

Brooks's first volume of poetry, *A Street in Bronzeville* (1945), concerns the moral, racial, and economic struggles facing the inhabitants of a black district in Chicago. Her next volume, **Annie Allen** (1949), a poetic narrative chronicling the growth of a girl to adulthood in the inner city, won the Pulitzer Prize. In 1953, Brooks published *Maud Martha,* her only **novel,** based in part on her experiences as a maid.

While continuing to expand on her portrayals of life in the ghetto, in the 1960s Brooks began to shift her focus away from the inner lives of individuals toward social and political issues, particularly as she became acquainted with more militant young black writers. Her collection *In the Mecca* (1968), which was nominated for a National Book Award, is considered a transitional work, marking a turn from traditional verse forms to free verse, an increased use of black speech patterns, and a greater focus on black consciousness. Brooks continued to write poetry on **black nationalism** and racial solidarity in volumes that included *Riot* (1969) and *Family Pictures* (1970). She also began publishing her work with African American publishing houses.

Brooks has taught poetry at several colleges and universities, including City College of the City University of New York. She has also continued writing such books as *Report from Part One: An Autobiography* (1972), *Primer for Blacks* (1980), *The Near-Johannesburg Boy* (1987), and *Children Coming Home* (1991). In 1985 she was appointed poetry consultant for the Library of Congress.

See also **Poetry of Gwendolyn Brooks**

Further Readings

Black Literature Criticism, Gale, 1992.

Black Writers, second edition, Gale, 1994.

Dictionary of Literary Biography, Volume 76: *Afro-American Writers, 1940-1955,* Gale, 1988.

Kent, George, *Gwendolyn Brooks: A Life,* University Press of Kentucky, 1988.

Melhem, D. H., *Gwendolyn Brooks: Poetry and the Heroic Voice,* University Press of Kentucky, 1987.

Gwendolyn Brooks at the Library of Congress in 1986.

values of peace and love, saves the prostitute Minette from the streets, is betrayed by one of his own, and dies. Through *Brother Man,* Mais examines differences between reality and ideals of human existence.

Brother Man

Roger Mais
Novel, 1954

In *Brother Man,* **Roger Mais** parallels the life of Jesus Christ with that of his protagonist, John Power, also known as "Bra Man." This highly symbolic **novel** takes place in the slums of Kingston, where Bra Man becomes a leader of Rastafarianism, a Jamaican cultural and religious movement which focuses on the goal of blacks returning to Africa. Bra Man preaches

Brother Tate

Character in *Sent for You Yesterday*

Cecil Brown

American novelist, screenwriter, and autobiographer
Born July 3, 1943.

Cecil Morris Brown earned a B.A. in English at Columbia University and an M.A. at the University of Chicago. His first novel, *The*

Claude Brown in Harlem in 1986.

Claude Brown

American autobiographer and essayist
Born February 23, 1937.

Brown is best known for his portrayal of Harlem in **Manchild in the Promised Land** (1965), which many still consider the definitive account of life in an African American ghetto during the 1940s and 1950s.

Born in New York City on February 23, 1937, Brown grew up on the streets of Harlem. A gang member by the age of ten, he sold hard drugs and served three terms in reform school before he left Harlem for Greenwich Village at the age of seventeen. Supporting himself with various jobs, including a stint as a playwright with the American Negro Theater Guild, he completed high school. He married Helen Jones on September 9, 1961, and in 1965 he received his B.A. from Howard University.

During his first year at Howard, Brown published an article on Harlem in the magazine *Dissent*. The piece attracted the attention of a publisher, who encouraged him to write an **autobiography**. This book, *Manchild in the Promised Land,* depicts a generation Brown believed had been lost in the ghetto. Praised for its realist portrayal of ghetto conditions, as well as its fierce and dignified anger, the book was particularly important because it appeared just as the **civil rights movement** began extending its campaign to northern cities.

In the 1970s, Brown returned to Harlem to document the efforts of a group of young adults to help each other rise above the dangers of their environment, principally by avoiding drug use. He account of his findings, *The Children of Ham* (1976), received mixed reviews, with many critics finding it less moving than his first book.

Brown has contributed numerous articles to magazines, including a piece on Harlem published in *The New York Times Magazine* in 1984.

Life and Loves of Mr. Jiveass Nigger (1969), portrays George Washington, a black American stranded in Europe who becomes a gigolo but later decides to find a legitimate way to return to America. A satirical and controversial novel, the book draws on the archetype of the prodigal son and parallels **Ralph Ellison**'s *Invisible Man*. Brown published **essays** and lectured at several universities. In the late 1970s, he penned scripts for Universal Studios and Warner Brothers, an experience that informed *Days without Weather* (1982), another satirical novel. His **autobiography** *Coming Up Down Home: A Memoir of a Southern Childhood* (1993) describes his adolescence as a Southern sharecropper.

Further Readings

Black Writers, first edition, Gale, 1989.

Dictionary of Literary Biography, Volume 33: *Afro-American Fiction Writers after 1955,* Gale, 1984.

Further Readings

Black Literature Criticism, Gale, 1992.

Black Writers, first edition, Gale, 1989.

Contemporary Literary Criticism, Volume 30, Gale, 1984.

Elaine Brown

American activist and autobiographer
Born March 2, 1943.

Brown served as the militant Black Panther Party's deputy minister of information and became the only woman to ever hold the Party's chair in 1974, when she was appointed by Party cofounder Huey Newton, who was fleeing to Cuba to avoid murder charges. Brown's memoir *A Taste of Power: A Black Woman's Story* (1992) describes her childhood in Philadelphia and her rise in the Party in Oakland, California. Despite endorsing Black Panther political ideals, *A Taste of Power* criticizes the organization's sexist policies, drug-using members, and some of the leaders' violent tendencies. Brown also writes of her sexual encounters with Party members, her persistent depression, and a number of Party personalities, including **Bobby Seale** and **Eldridge Cleaver**. Brown left the Black Panther Party after Newton returned to the United States and she has since moved to France.

Further Readings

Black Writers, second edition, Gale, 1994.

Frank London Brown

American novelist, short story writer, and journalist
Born October 7, 1927.
Died March 12, 1962.

During the 1950s, Brown read his **short stories** to **jazz** accompaniment, and is the first writer to have done so. He also wrote book reviews for Chicago newspapers and vignettes that appeared in the *Chicago Review* and *Negro Digest*. In 1958, he interviewed Thelonious Monk for *Down Beat* magazine. His most noted work, the **novel Trumbull Park** (1959), describes a Chicago housing project in which black families resist harassment by the white majority. In 1960, Brown earned a master's degree from the University of Chicago. His thesis, published posthumously as *The Myth Maker*

(1969), portrays a drug addict who murders an old man. In 1961, while working on his Ph.D., Brown discovered he had leukemia. He died the following year.

Further Readings

Black Writers, second edition, Gale, 1994.
Dictionary of Literary Biography, Volume 76: *Afro-American Writers, 1940-1955,* Gale, 1988.

Brown Girl, Brownstones

Paule Marshall
Novel, 1959

Brown Girl, Brownstones, **Paule Marshall**'s autobiographical first **novel**, helped usher in a new period of black women's fiction. This story of an African American woman's search for personal identity within a black community established Marshall as a deft portrayer of character. The novel's heroine is Selina Boyce, daughter of Barbadian immigrants, whose maturation is marked by family crises. Selina's mother, Silla Boyce, a complex mixture of strength and vulnerability, harbors an intense desire to purchase the family's rented brownstone. Selina's father, Deighton Boyce, is a spendthrift and dreamer who believes that life is more than materialism. The marital conflict in the narrative stems from Deighton's refusal to sell a piece of land he owns in Barbados, where he still hopes to return, in order to buy the New York brownstone.

Sorting out her parents' conflict, Selina learns more about herself, her Barbadian American immigrant culture, and the hostile white society. As she develops into a young woman, she both affirms and expands her community's definition of womanhood. In this way, *Brown Girl, Brownstones* foreshadowed a major shift in African American fiction toward the depiction of intelligent and complex female characters.

H. Rap Brown, leader of the SNCC, at a 1967 news conference.

H. Rap Brown

American political activist
and autobiographer
Born October 4, 1943.

H. Rap Brown, who later changed his name to Jamil Abdullah Al-Amin, came to prominence in the late 1960s, after what many perceived as the failure of the **civil rights movement**. As head of the Student Nonviolent Coordinating Committee (SNCC), Brown advocated violent struggle against **racism**.

Born Hubert Gerold Brown in Baton Rouge, Louisiana, on October 4, 1943, Brown studied sociology at Southern University but left without graduating. In 1964, he became chair of the Nonviolent Action Group (NAG), an affiliate of the SNCC, and in May, 1967, he succeeded **Stokely Carmichael** as chairman of the SNCC.

Brown's statements urging black people to defend their rights with deadly force earned him national notoriety. Viewing American racism as integral to a political and economic system based on exploitation in the United States and abroad, he argued that only violent revolution could bring change. "This country was born of violence," he observed in a televised speech. "Violence is as American as cherry pie." He suggested that riots sweeping America's poor black neighborhoods heralded a political insurrection.

In 1967, police cited a speech by Brown as the "sole reason" for a riot in Cambridge, Maryland. Indicted on charges of arson and inciting to riot, Brown spent the next several years fighting these and related charges. During this period he published his **autobiography**, *Die Nigger Die!* (1969), which traces his life from childhood onwards, recounting his experience in the civil rights movement and setting forth his analysis of racial injustice. While some commentators accused Brown of fueling racial hatred, others praised his articulation of his radical viewpoint and responded positively to the poignancy and humor they perceived underlying the book's anger.

In 1970, rather than face trial for inciting the 1967 Cambridge riot, Brown went underground and was placed on the FBI's ten-most-wanted list. In October, 1971, he was shot by police officers in New York near the scene of an armed robbery. Convicted of taking part in the holdup, he spent several years in prison, where he converted to Islam and adopted the name Al-Amin. Paroled in 1976, he moved to Atlanta, Georgia, where he operates a grocery.

Further Readings

Black Literature Criticism, Gale, 1992.
Black Writers, first edition, Gale, 1989.

Lloyd L. Brown

American novelist
Born in 1913.

Since first published in the weekly *The New Masses* in the mid-1940s, writer Lloyd Louis Brown has remained an outspoken proponent of communism. Born in 1913 in St. Paul,

Minnesota, he was a strong supporter of the American actor **Paul Robeson**, and aided the outspoken actor in defending his pro-Soviet sympathies by helping Robeson write his **autobiography**, *Here I Stand,* in 1958.

Brown's most notable work in support of his political beliefs is the **novel** *Iron City* (1951). The story of a condemned black man who is aided by communists in trying to overturn his death sentence, *Iron City* demonstrates the compassion communists hold for blacks, in contrast to their capitalist counterparts. Brown has also written numerous pamphlets and has contributed to periodicals.

Further Readings
Black Writers, second edition, Gale, 1994.

Margery W. Brown
American illustrator and
author of juvenile literature

Margery Wheeler Brown began her literary career as a writer of juvenile fiction after she established herself as an illustrator. Having studied at Spelman College and Ohio State University, Brown became an art teacher at Newark Public School System, where she worked for nearly thirty years. Brown's illustrations were first published in Gordon Allred's *Old Crackfoot* (1965) and *Dori the Mallard* (1968), but she soon began writing and illustrating her own books, including *That Ruby* (1969), *Animals Made by Me* (1970), *The Second Stone* (1974), *Yesterday I Climbed a Mountain* (1976), and *No Jon, No Jon, No!* (1981). Brown has recently authored *Afro-Bets: Book of Shapes* (1991), *Afro-Bets: Book of Colors: Meet the Color Family* (1991), and *Baby Jesus, Like My Brother* (1994).

Further Readings
Black Writers, second edition, Gale, 1994.

Sterling A. Brown
American poet, folklorist, and critic
Born May 1, 1901.
Died January 13, 1989.

Considered one of the best black American poets of the early twentieth century, Sterling Allen Brown was a pioneer of the academic study of black literature. He was one of the first critics to identify **folklore** and folk music as vital to the black aesthetic.

Brown was born May 1, 1901, in Washington, D.C., where his father, Sterling N. Brown, was a professor of **religion** at Howard. After graduating from Williams College in 1922 and receiving his M.A. in literature from Harvard University in 1923, Brown spent six years teaching in the South, where he began to study African American folklore. He collected worksongs, ballads, **blues,** and **spirituals**, conducting this research at a time when most black poets had stopped using dialect in their **poetry.** In 1927, he married Daisy Turnbull. Two years later he became a professor at Howard, where he would teach for the next forty years.

In 1932, Brown published *Southern Roads,* a volume of poetry based on material he had gathered in the South. Yet, despite laudatory reviews, Brown could not find a publisher for his second book of poetry. With no new published poetry to support his reputation, Brown quickly came to be considered, even within the black community, as a poet of the past. He then turned his creative energies to critical and historical analyses of black art and culture. In 1937, he published two seminal studies of black literary history, *Negro Poetry and Drama* and *The Negro in American Fiction.* He also co-edited an anthology of black American literature, *The Negro Caravan* (1941).

Neglected as a poet and shunned by the more conservative members of the English department at Howard for his interest in folklore and **jazz,** Brown suffered periods of extreme depression, occasionally requiring hospitalization. He was rediscovered during the late 1960s; subsequently, he received several honorary doctorates and in 1984 was named poet laureate of Washington, D.C. The *Collected Poems of Sterling A. Brown* (1980) won the Lenore Marshall

Poetry Prize. Brown died of leukemia on January 13, 1989, in Takoma Park, Maryland.

See also **Poetry of Sterling A. Brown**

Further Readings
Black Literature Criticism, Gale, 1992.

Black Writers, first edition, Gale, 1989.

Dictionary of Literary Biography, Volume 51: *Afro-American Writers from the Harlem Renaissance to 1940,* Gale, 1987.

Gabbin, Joanne V., *Sterling Brown: Building the Black Aesthetic Tradition,* Greenwood Press, 1985.

Tony Brown

American television journalist and columnist
Born April 11, 1933.

After earning his master's degree at Wayne State University, William Anthony Brown worked in Detroit for the *Detroit Courier* and the public television station WTVS-TV. Beginning in 1970, Brown produced and hosted the New York-based public television series "Black Journal" (renamed "Tony Brown's Journal" in 1977), which was nominated for an Emmy Award in 1972. The show presents a positive vision of black life by publicizing black accomplishments. In order to draw more blacks into the communications field, in 1971 Brown founded and served as dean of Howard University's school of communications. Brown also owns the public relations and advertising firm Tony Brown Productions, Inc., and has written a syndicated column.

Further Readings
Black Writers, first edition, Gale, 1989.

Wesley Brown

American novelist and poet
Born May 23, 1945.

Brown, a native of New York City who holds a bachelor's degree from Oswego State University, has attracted critical attention for his sensitive depiction of black city life and the search for identity, which are themes in the **novel** *Tragic Magic* (1978). Brown has also coedited with Amy Ling *Imagining America: Stories from the Promised Land* (1991) and *Visions of America: Personal Narratives from the Promised Land* (1992). In 1994 Brown published *Darktown Strutters,* a novel about a dancing stage slave named Jim Crow.

Brown's work is also represented in anthologies, including *Poetry* and *We Be Word Sorcerers,* and his poems and short stories have been published in *Essence, Harper's, Black Creation,* and other periodicals.

Further Readings
Black Writers, second edition, Gale, 1994.

William Wells Brown

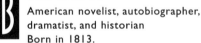

American novelist, autobiographer, dramatist, and historian
Born in 1813.
Died November 6, 1884.

Brown was a prominent abolitionist and the author of the first **novel** and first drama published by an African American writer. He was also an internationally admired historian and lecturer on the African American experience.

The son of a slaveholder and a slave, Brown was born in Kentucky and spent the first twenty years of his life in **slavery** before escaping in 1834 to Ohio, where he took the name of a Quaker, Wells Brown, who had assisted him. He taught himself to read and write, became involved in the **Underground Railroad**, and began lecturing for the abolitionist cause in 1843. His *Narrative of William W. Brown, a Fugitive Slave, Written by Himself* (1847), which recounts his life as a slave and his escape to freedom, was a great success.

After representing the American Peace Society at the Paris Peace Congress of 1849, Brown remained in Europe for five years. During this time several English friends raised the funds to buy his freedom. His novel *Clotel; or, The President's Daughter: A Narrative of Slave Life in the United States* (1853), whose protagonist is depicted as a slave daughter of former U.S. president Thomas Jefferson, was published in England, where it was well received. Several revised versions deleting references to Jefferson were published in the U.S. during the 1860s.

After returning to the U.S., Brown wrote two **plays,** *Experience; or, How to Give a Northern Man a Backbone* (1856), since lost, and *The Escape; or, A Leap for Freedom* (1858). He also published several books on African American history and culture before his death from cancer in 1884.

Further Readings

Black Literature Criticism, Gale, 1992.

Dictionary of Literary Biography, Volume 50: *Afro-American Writers before the Harlem Renaissance,* Gale, 1986.

Farrison, William Edward, *William Wells Brown: Author and Reformer,* University of Chicago Press, 1969.

William Wells Brown was a well-known advocate of abolitionism.

The Brownsville Raid

Charles Fuller
Play, first produced 1976

Charles Fuller's first major success, *The Brownsville Raid,* is based on a true story about an entire black regiment that was dishonorably discharged by Theodore Roosevelt in 1906. When a riot killed one white man in Brownsville, Texas, black soldiers were blamed for inciting it; however, no soldier would admit to the crime. Although no firm evidence was provided, and witnesses gave conflicting accounts, all one-hundred and sixty-seven black soldiers in the 25th Infantry unit were discharged. The drama unfolds as a mystery, focusing on one black sergeant major, Mingo Saunders, who questions his faith in his government as a result of the Army's betrayal.

Dennis Brutus

Zimbabwean-born South African poet
Born November 28, 1924.

A highly regarded poet, Brutus has long struggled against the injustices of **apartheid**. Although his works have been banned in South Africa, Brutus continues to oppose repression through political poems based on personal experience.

Brutus was born in Harare, Zimbabwe (then Salisbury, South Rhodesia), to South African parents who were teachers. Initially a teacher himself, Brutus began actively protesting apartheid during the late 1950s. This led to a series of arrests and escape attempts that culminated in Brutus being shot and imprisoned in 1963.

In that same year, his first volume of **poetry,** *Sirens, Knuckles, Boots,* was published and won the Mbari Prize. This work contains love poems as well as others protesting apartheid. Forbidden to write poetry while in jail, Brutus instead wrote letters from prison chronicling his experiences there. These were published as *Letters to Martha, and Other Poems from a South African Prison* (1968) following Brutus's exit from South Africa on the condition that he never return. Brutus soon moved to the United States and taught at various universities during his exile. He was granted political asylum in 1983.

Under the pseudonym John Bruin, Brutus published *Thoughts Abroad* (1970), which contains poems about exile and alienation. This book circulated in South Africa until Brutus's identity was discovered and all copies were confiscated. *A Simple Lust* (1973) prominently portrays Brutus's persona of the troubadour who fights against social injustice and hypocrisy. *Stubborn Hope* (1978) contains selections from the earlier volumes *Strains* (1975) and *China Poems* (1975), the latter revealing non-Western literary influences. Other collections of Brutus's poems include *Salutes and Censure* (1984) and *Airs and Tributes* (1989). In 1990 Brutus coedited the anthology *African Literature, 1988: New Masks.*

See also **Poetry of Dennis Brutus**

Further Readings

Black Literature Criticism, Gale, 1992.

Black Writers, second edition, Gale, 1994.

Dictionary of Literary Biography, Volume 117: *Twentieth-Century Caribbean and Black African Writers,* First Series, Gale, 1992.

Ashley F. Bryan

American folklorist and author of children's literature
Born July 13, 1923.

Bryan has compiled collections of slave **spirituals** and written books as part of a tradi-

tion that hands black culture to younger generations by teaching African spirituals and **folklore**. Born on July 13, 1923, in New York City, Bryan attended Cooper Union and Columbia universities. He published his first book, *The Ox of the Wonderful Horns and Other African Folktales* in 1971. His first volume of spirituals, *Walk Together Children* (1974), was praised for the quality of its selections.

In addition to historical spirituals, several of Bryan's collections contain stories that explain why certain animals became natural enemies. In *The Adventures of Aku* (1976), Bryan recounts the day that the enmity between dogs and cats began. The story features a magic ring, a stupid son, a heroic quest, and Ananse, the standard trickster figure in African folklore. *The Dancing Granny* (1977) continues the saga of Ananse, recounting the day when an old lady foiled his plan to eat all her food. The Nigerian folktales in *Beat the Story-Drum, Pum-Pum* (1980) also reveal the origins of hostilities between animals, such as that between the snake and the frog or the bush cow and the elephant. *Turtle Knows Your Name* (1989) is a retelling of a folktale from the West Indies, and *Sing to the Sun* (1992) is a collection of **poetry**. Bryan often illustrates his own works for children.

Further Readings

Black Writers, second edition, Gale, 1994.

Bub Johnson

Character in *The Street*

Buckingham Palace, District Six

Richard Rive
Novel, 1986

In the **novel** *Buckingham Palace, District Six,* **Richard Rive** depicts the forced resettlement of the inhabitants of the Cape Town, South Africa, slum called District Six. Rive prefaces the three parts of the book with personal memories of his childhood in the row of old houses the residents called Buckingham Palace. Through the large cast of fictional characters, including Zoot September, a gang leader, dancer, and poet and the prostitute Mary, Rive brings to life the ghetto. As the machinations of the white leaders move forward, district residents, including the Jewish landlord Katzen, band together to protest. A barber, Last-Knight, who earlier left the district, returns to tell of the miserable new townships. In the end, the residents of District Six are forced to abandon their homes and bulldozers raze the abandoned neighborhood.

Gail Lumet Buckley

American historian and journalist
Born December 21, 1937.

Gail Horne Jones Lumet Buckley graduated from Radcliffe College in 1959 and, for the next four years, worked simultaneously for *Life* magazine in New York and *Marie-Claire* in Paris. The daughter of singer-actor Lena Horne, Buckley chronicled her family's history in *The Hornes: An American Family* (1986). In the book, Buckley traces her ancestry back six generations to an eighteenth-century slave, Sinai Reynolds. The book details the Horne family's membership in the black bourgeoisie and explicates the social and economic conditions that made Lena Horne's stardom possible. Acclaimed for its discretion, the book is both a historical study of the black American middle-class and an **autobiography**.

Further Readings
Black Writers, Gale, second edition, 1994.

Buddy Clark
Character in *The Planet of Junior Brown*

Bug Eyes
Character in *The Narrows*

Buggin' Out
Character in *Do the Right Thing*

Buggy Martin
Character in *Trumbull Park*

Ed Bullins
American dramatist and novelist
Born July 2, 1935.

Bullins, who also writes under the pseudonym Kingsley B. Bass Jr., began writing **plays** as a political activist in the mid-1960s and soon emerged as a principal figure in the **black arts movement**. He has probed the conditions of ghetto life in over fifty dramatic works.

Born in Philadelphia on July 2, 1935, Bullins grew up in the tough north Philadelphia ghetto. At seventeen, he dropped out of high school and joined the Navy. He returned to Philadelphia after his discharge in 1955, but in 1958 he moved to Los Angeles, where he earned a high school degree and began writing short stories and **poetry.**

After moving to San Francisco in 1964, Bullins began writing plays. His early dramas include *Clara's Ole Man* (1965), his first play to focus on the street people and tenement dwellers central to his later work. Bullins joined with a group of other young black artists and revolutionaries, including **Amiri Baraka** (LeRoi Jones) and **Sonia Sanchez**, to create a cultural-political organization called Black House. When group members Huey Newton and **Bobby Seale** formed the Black Panther Party in 1966, Bullins served briefly as its minister of culture.

In 1967, Bullins left the Black Panthers and moved to New York to work at the New Lafayette Theater. Between 1968 and 1980, various New York theaters presented twenty-five of his plays, including *In New England Winter* (1969), *The Fabulous Miss Marie* (1971), and *The Taking of Miss Janie* (1975), each of which won an Obie Award. Many of his plays were

Ed Bullins in 1971, as associate director of the New Lafayette Theater.

highly controversial; at the height of his militancy, he advocated cultural separatism between races and outspokenly dismissed white aesthetic standards.

Although Bullins stopped producing and publishing his work after 1980, he remains at work on a projected series of twenty plays, the Twentieth-Century Cycle, which includes some of his early dramas. He has also taught at several colleges and universities, including Columbia University and Dartmouth College. A selection of his writings was collected in 1994 as *New—Lost Plays by Ed Bullins*.

Further Readings

Black Literature Criticism, Gale, 1992.

Black Writers, second edition, Gale, 1994.

Dictionary of Literary Biography, Volume 38: *Afro-American Writers after 1955: Dramatists and Prose Writers*, Gale, 1985.

Nelson, Emmanuel, editor, *Connections: Essays in Black Literatures*, 1988.

Bummie

Character in *In New England Winter*

Ralph Bunche

American diplomat and political scientist
Born August 7, 1904.
Died December 9, 1971.

Bunche is considered one of the most significant American diplomats of the twentieth century. He took a leading role in negotiating peace talks between the Arab and Israeli states in 1949 and arbitrated peace discussions in the Congo, Yemen, Cyprus, Suez, India, and Pakistan. Garnering worldwide praise for his successful peacekeeping efforts, Bunche became the first black recipient of the Nobel Peace Prize in 1950.

Born in Detroit, Michigan, in 1904, Ralph Johnson Bunche moved to Los Angeles after the death of his parents. He received his bachelor's degree from the University of California—Los Angeles in 1927, his master's degree in government at Harvard University the following year, and his doctorate in 1934. Bunche's postdoctoral work in anthropology and colonial policy led to the publication of *A World View of Race* (1936). His work in the American South with Swedish sociologist Gunnar Myrdal culminated in *An American Dilemma* (1944), a study of race relations.

Bunche came to the United Nations through the State Department. After World War II, he was recommended by Secretary-General Trygve Lie to direct the Trusteeship Division at the United Nations. In 1948, he became head of the Palestine Commission when its original appointee, Count Folke Bernadotte of Sweden, was assassinated. Bunche wrote about his experience with the organization in *Peace and the United Nations* (1952).

Bunche was particularly interested in the impact of **segregation** on black life. *The Political Status of the Negro in the Age of FDR* (1973) collects more than five hundred interviews conducted in the American South. *An African-American in South Africa: The Travel Notes of Ralph J. Bunche, 28 September 1937-1 January 1938* (1992) examines living conditions in racially polarized South Africa.

Further Readings

Black Writers, second edition, Gale, 1994.

Kugelmass, J. Alvin, *Ralph J. Bunche: Fighter for Peace,* Messner, 1962.

Mann, Peggy, *Ralph Bunche: UN Peacemaker,* Coward, McCann & Geoghegan, 1975.

Margaret Taylor Burroughs

American poet
Born November 1, 1917.

Margaret Taylor Goss Burroughs began her career primarily as an artist and art teacher but, beginning in the 1960s, she also became prominent in the Chicago **black arts movement**. Her **poetry,** which frequently reveals African influences, reflects her lifelong interest in preserving and enriching black culture.

Burroughs was born in St. Rose, Louisiana, but her family soon moved to Chicago in search of a better life. As an adult, Burroughs pursued a dual career as a painter and sculptor and an educator. In 1961, she founded the DuSable Museum of African American History, where she served as director for 24 years. In this capacity, Burroughs built a collection that includes not only African and African American art, but also manuscripts and over 10,000 books.

A few years later, Burroughs launched a literary career, when she collaborated with **Dudley Randall** to edit an anthology titled *For Malcolm: Poems on the Life and Death of Malcolm X* (1967). This book brought together the work of both established poets, such as **Gwendolyn Brooks** and **Amiri Baraka**, and unknown writers, such as Burroughs herself. The following

Bunche in 1949, one year before receiving the Nobel Peace Prize.

year, Burroughs published her first volume of poetry, *What Shall I Tell My Children Who Are Black?* (1968). She is also the author of several children's books.

In 1968, Burroughs received a travel grant to Ghana. Her experiences there provided the raw material for her next poetry volume, *Africa, My Africa* (1970), a series of 18 poems chronicling an African American's journey to Africa. In later life, Burroughs has continued to promote the heritage of blacks by both creating her own work and supporting other artists and writers.

See also **Poetry of Margaret Taylor Burroughs**

Further Readings

Black Writers, first edition, Gale, 1989.

Dictionary of Literary Biography, Volume 41: *Afro-American Poets since 1955,* Gale, 1985.

Kofi Abrefa Busia

Ghanaian prime minister
and nonfiction writer
Born July 11, 1913(?).
Died August 28, 1978.

Busia was a member of the Ghanaian royal family of Wenchi. In 1957, Ghana's government under **Kwame Nkrumah** arrested opposition leaders and charged them with conspiracy. Busia, the opposition head, was lecturing in Holland at the time and chose to remain in exile, writing *The Sociology and Culture of Africa* (1960) and *Purposeful Education for Africa* (1964). Nkrumah was overthrown by a military coup in 1966 and Busia returned to Ghana to serve as prime minister three years later. He wrote several more books on African society, including *Africa in Search of Democracy* (1967) and *The African Consciousness: Continuity and Change in Africa* (1968). In 1972, Busia was deposed by a bloodless coup while he was in England. He lectured at Oxford University until his death in 1978.

Further Readings
Black Writers, Gale, second edition, 1994.

Butch Fuller

Character in *The Women of Brewster Place*

Anna M. Butler

American poet, journalist, and teacher
Born October 7, 1901.

Anna Mabel Land Butler taught elementary school from 1922 to 1964 and was a newspaper correspondent for the *Pittsburgh Courier* from 1936 to 1965. In 1965, she became an editor and reporter for the *Philadelphia Tribune.* While pursuing these careers, Butler published three **poetry** volumes, *Album of Love Letters—Unsent. Volume 1: Morning 'til Noon* (1952), *Touchstone* (1961), and *High Noon* (1971). Her poems address a wide range of subjects, including nature, love, death, and racial equality. Butler has received a number of honors, including the 1966 National Association Sojourner Truth Award.

Further Readings
Black Writers, second edition, Gale, 1994.

Octavia E. Butler

American novelist
Born June 22, 1947.

Octavia Estelle Butler has earned acclaim from critics and readers of **science fiction.** Many of her **novels** focus on genetic engineering, advanced alien beings, and the nature and proper use of power.

Born in Pasadena, California, Butler grew up in a strict Baptist household. She received an associate's degree in 1968 from Pasadena City College and attended classes at universities in southern California. Butler received what she considers her most useful training while working with the Writers Guild of America, West, Inc.

In her work, including the five-novel **"Patternist Saga"** beginning with *Patternmaster* (1978) and the **"Xenogenesis" Trilogy** beginning with *Dawn* (1987), Butler focuses on themes of racial and sexual awareness. Critics praise Butler for her ability to create believable, independent female characters. Among these heroes is Lauren Oya, a fifteen-year-old prophet at the center of *Parable of the Sower* (1993).

In 1985, Butler won three of science fiction's top honors—the Hugo Award, Nebula Award, and Locus Award—for the novelette "Bloodchild." She received a MacArthur Foundation grant in 1995.

Further Readings
Black Writers, second edition, Gale, 1994.
Dictionary of Literary Biography, Volume 33: *Afro-American Fiction Writers after 1955,* Gale, 1984.

Byrd

Character in *A Soldier's Play*

The goal of black self-determination and black self-identity—Black Power—is full participation in the decision-making processes affecting the lives of black people, and recognition of the virtues in themselves as black people.

Black Power: The Politics of Liberation in America, Stokely Carmichael and Charles V. Hamilton, 1967

C. C. Baker

Character in *The Women of Brewster Place*

C. J. Memphis

Character in *A Soldier's Play*

George Cain

American novelist
Born October(?), 1943.

Born in Harlem, George M. Cain is known primarily for his autobiographical **novel** *Blueschild Baby* (1970), in which the protagonist bears the author's name. The book chronicles Cain's return to Harlem after his release from prison. He battles his drug addiction with the help of his family and his childhood sweetheart. During a painful three-day withdrawal, he reexamines his life. Cain recalls moving to an all-white neighborhood so he could receive a better education and a basketball scholarship; his parents wanted him to pursue the "American dream." However, Cain realizes that other peoples' expectations have made him miserable and angry, and he vows to forge his identity apart from the wishes of others. *Blueschild Baby* is Cain's only published work.

Further Readings

Black Writers, second edition, Gale, 1994.

Dictionary of Literary Biography, Volume 33: *Afro-American Fiction Writers after 1955,* Gale 1984.

Ben Caldwell

American playwright
Born September 24, 1937.

Benjamin Caldwell studied commercial and industrial design until his writing was recognized by LeRoi Jones (**Amiri Baraka**). Caldwell moved to Newark and wrote *Hypnotism* (1969), a one-act **play** in which a magician hypnotizes a black couple, making them forget the oppression they had endured and suppressing their resistance. Like much literature of the **black arts movement**, *Hypnotism* describes the white power structure, decries the pacification of blacks, and calls on blacks to assert themselves. Caldwell's most acclaimed play, ***Prayer Meeting; or, The First Militant Minister*** (1967), which premiered in 1967 at Jones's Spirit House Theatre, considers both nonviolent rebellion and justified uprising. Caldwell returned to New York in 1966, received a Guggenheim Fellowship for playwrighting in 1970, and continues to write plays, including *Moms* (1987).

Further Readings

Black Writers, Gale, first edition, 1989.

Dictionary of Literary Biography, Volume 38: *Afro-American Writers after 1955: Dramatists and Prose Writers,* Gale, 1985.

Caleb

Character in *Caleb, the Degenerate*

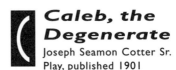

Caleb, the Degenerate

Joseph Seamon Cotter Sr.
Play, published 1901

Caleb, the Degenerate: A Study of the Types, Customs, and Needs of the American Negro, written in blank verse, is **Joseph Seamon Cotter Sr.**'s only drama and one of the earliest dramas written by an African American. Caleb is a brutal villain. His mentor, Rahab, is a disreputable minister and politician who convinces Caleb that his evil ways are the result of his mother's sinfulness. Caleb and Rahab conspire to kill Caleb's father and sell his corpse to a medical student. Rahab also indoctrinates Dude, an upright young man active in politics and the **Back-to-Africa movement**. Rahab's corrupting influence contrasts with the beneficent leadership of the Bishop and his daughter, Olivia, who run Industrial School, an institution that empowers African American boys and girls. In the end, the good leaders prevail: Olivia raises one hundred thousand dollars for her school from local philanthropists, and Dude enters the military.

Call Me Charley

Jesse Jackson
Novel, 1945

Call Me Charley, **Jesse Jackson**'s first **novel** for young adults, depicts the struggle for acceptance of the protagonist Charles Moss, a black boy who moves into Arlington Heights, an all-white suburb of Chicago. At first the school principal will not allow Charles to attend the all-white school, but he succumbs to the pressure of the prominent white doctor who employs Charles's parents. Charles gradually makes friends with some of his schoolmates and eventually wins their respect, an achievement that is marked by his initiation into a club of school boys.

Camilo Treadway

Character in *The Narrows*

Bebe Moore Campbell

American novelist and memoirist
Born in 1950.

Campbell wrote **short stories** and radio **plays** and received the Body of Work Award (1978) from the National Association of Negro Business and Professional Women before completing *Sweet Summer: Growing Up with and without My Dad* (1989), a memoir in which she describes her experiences as a child of divorce. Campbell lived with her mother during the school year and her father during the summer; *Sweet Summer* attempts to understand these two distinct spheres. Her first **novel,** *Your Blues Ain't Like Mine* (1992), which earned her the NAACP's Image Award for Outstanding Literary Work, describes the social upheaval caused by a lynching. Her novel *Brothers and Sisters* (1994) explores friendship and race relations among middle-class professionals. Campbell has contributed to numerous periodicals and often appears on radio and television talk shows.

Further Readings
Black Writers, second edition, Gale, 1994.

James Edwin Campbell

American poet
Born September 28, 1867.
Died January 26, 1896.

The first African American to publish a collection of black **dialect poems**, Campbell is considered the most important contemporary of **Paul Laurence Dunbar**. Like Dunbar, Campbell wrote both dialect poems and verse in standard English, although most critics consider the former to be his best work. Because of his early death and Dunbar's subsequent popularity, many critics believe that Campbell has not received the attention he deserves.

Campbell was born and educated in Pomeroy, Ohio. After graduating from high school, Campbell taught for two years in a nearby community before moving to West Virginia in 1887. He soon accepted a staff position on a black newspaper and began teaching at another school. In 1891 Campbell was appointed principal of the newly founded West Virginia Colored Institute. His duties involved traveling through black farming and mining communities and encouraging people to further their education. It was during these trips that he gathered the material for his **dialect poetry**. In 1894 Campbell moved to Chicago, where he began compiling the verse he had written over the last ten years. Collected in *Echoes from the Cabin and Elsewhere* (1895), these poems are arranged in dramatic sequence and describe both comic and tragic incidents. Many are suited for dramatic recitation at large dinners or other rural gatherings and reflect the emotions and experiences of southern blacks who remembered the oppression of **slavery**. In 1895 Campbell returned to Ohio to spend Christmas with his parents. He contracted pneumonia and died there in January of the following year.

Further Readings
Dictionary of Literary Biography, Volume 50: *Afro-American Writers before the Harlem Renaissance,* Gale, 1986.

Candy Marshall

Character in *A Gathering of Old Men*

Toomer's collection of poetry, drama, and fiction.

dren by a black man. She lives as a recluse, trying to deny her existence. Only when her cabin burns down is the community relieved of its guilt at having ostracized her. In "Carma" a woman is unfaithful to her husband while he is on a chain gang. "Fern," which is about the daughter of a black mother and a Jewish father, is another story of illegitimacy and miscegenation. "Esther" is the story of a young girl who falls in love with a travelling preacher King Barlo and is sustained by her infatuation for fourteen years. When Barlo finally returns, however, Esther realizes she has only deceived herself. The last story in the first section, "Blood-Burning Moon," is about Louisa, a woman with both a white lover and a black lover. The black lover, field-worker Tom Burwell, kills the white man and is himself killed by a mob of whites. The second section contains a series of imagistic sketches of urban life. In "Avey," the narrator describes a woman who has been a teacher and is now a prostitute. Other stories in this section, "Theater," "Box Seat" and "Bona and Paul," deal with the intrusions of racial **discrimination** on love relationships. The third section of *Cane* is the drama "Kabnis," in which the protagonist, Ralph Kabnis, an idealistic poet and school teacher, returns to Georgia from New York hoping to do good. However, he is rejected by the very people he has come to help, and his enthusiastic idealism soon turns to despair.

Cane

Jean Toomer
Fiction, prose, poetry, and drama, 1923

Set in Georgia, Washington, D.C., and Chicago, **Jean Toomer**'s *Cane* is a miscellany comprised of **poetry**, prose sketches, a **play** and short stories. In the first section, most of the stories are about women and deal with violent sexual relationships and their aftermath. In the first sketch, a young girl named Karintha has an illegitimate child that she murders; she later becomes a prostitute. In another vignette, a white woman named Becky has two illegitimate chil-

David Wadsworth Cannon Jr.

American poet
Born in 1911(?).
Died December 14, 1938.

Cannon, the son of a minister, is known for the collection *Black Labor Chant and Other Poems* (1940) and his contributions to anthologies including *The Poetry of the Negro: 1746-1970* and *Ebony Rhythm*.

Cannon earned a bachelor's degree at Hillside College, Michigan, in 1931 and continued his studies on a fellowship at the University of Michigan, where he took an M.A. the following year. He taught psychology at Junior State College in Cranford, New Jersey, beginning in 1937 and was a Ph.D. candidate at Columbia University and a member of the board of directors of the National Council of Religious Education at the time of his death in 1938.

Further Readings
Black Writers, Gale, second edition, 1994.

Capitu
Character in *Dom Casmurro*

Captain Falcon
Character in *Middle Passage*

Jan Carew
Guyanese novelist, poet, playwright, and author of children's literature
Born September 24, 1925.

Carew is an educator, editor, and writer whose body of work includes **novels** for both adults and children, histories, **poetry,** and **plays.** His works primarily deal with colonized peoples' search for identity, and many of his protagonists are black men estranged both from the white-dominated societies in which they were educated and from their indigenous cultures. Among Carew's books are novels such as *Black Midas* (1958) (also published as *A Touch of Midas*), for which Carew received the National Film Institute Award, and children's literature such as *The Third Gift* (1974) and *Children of the Sun* (1980). Carew taught at Northwestern University for fifteen years, becoming professor emeritus in 1987.

Further Readings
Black Writers, Gale, second edition, 1994.

Carlotta
Character in *The Temple of My Familiar*

Political activist Carmichael in 1966.

Stokely Carmichael
Trinidadian-born American political activist and essayist
Born June 29, 1941.

Carmichael became nationally famous in the late 1960s, during a period of growing frustration with the efficacy of nonviolent tactics in combatting **racism**. He coined the phrase **"black power"** and played a critical role in the creation of the Black Power Movement. His career marked a shift among some black activists from a belief in integration and peaceful protest to a conviction that black Americans must defend themselves through violence and separatism.

Born in Port-of-Spain, Trinidad, on June 29, 1941, Carmichael immigrated to the United States in 1952, settling in Harlem. After graduating from Howard University in 1964, he became involved with the **civil rights movement** as a participant in the Freedom Rides. He joined the Student Nonviolent Coordinating Committee (SNCC) in 1964 and headed its task force registering black voters in Lowndes County, Mississippi. When he assumed the chair of the SNCC in 1966, his use of the slogan "black power" led many to accuse him of reverse racism. With **Charles V. Hamilton,** Carmichael co-wrote ***Black Power: The Politics of Liberation in America*** (1967), which examines the concept of black power and its implications for the civil rights movement. Carmichael and Hamilton argued that blacks should reject the values of racist American society and devote their energies to developing their own independent, self-supportive organizations.

In 1967, Carmichael resigned from the SNCC to join the more radical Black Panther Party, serving as its prime minister from 1967 to 1969. He then resigned his membership, charging that the organization had become overly dogmatic and was being influenced by white radicals. In May, 1969, he emigrated to Guinea in West Africa.

In Africa, Carmichael became interested in **Pan-Africanism** and began advocating a homeland in Africa for oppressed black minorities throughout the world. In 1971, he published ***Stokely Speaks: Black Power Back to Pan-Africanism***, a collection of his **speeches** and **essays.**

Further Readings
Black Writers, first edition, Gale, 1989.

Caroling Dusk

Countee Cullen, editor
Poetry, 1927

First published in 1927 and republished in 1955 and 1993, *Caroling Dusk: An Anthology of Verse by Black Poets of the Twenties* is a critically acclaimed collection of black **poetry** from the 1920s. **Countee Cullen** edited the book, and published it in the same year as *Copper Sun,* his second volume of original poetry. *Caroling Dusk* contains poems by 38 important African American authors, many of whom were part of the **Harlem Renaissance** movement. Contributors to *Caroling Dusk* include Cullen himself, **Paul Laurence Dunbar, James Weldon Johnson, Angelina Weld Grimke, Georgia Douglas Johnson, Claude McKay, Jean Toomer, Sterling A. Brown, Langston Hughes,** and **Arna Bontemps**. The poetry selections are accompanied by brief biographical sketches, in most cases written by the poets themselves.

In the foreword, Cullen discusses his philosophy regarding poetry and its publication, further articulating the views he had stated in his "Dark Tower" column in *Opportunity* magazine. According to Cullen, poetry is instrumental to the cultural development of a race. However, Cullen does not consider art to be culture-specific and believes that African American poets are borne out of the English tradition: "rather is [Negro poetry] a variety within a uniformity that is trying to maintain the higher traditions of English verse."

Vinnette Carroll

American director and playwright
Born in 19(?).

Vinnette Justine Carroll has been an influential director in African American theater since the 1950s. She created and led New York City's Urban Arts Theater, in which many black actors, singers, and writers have begun their careers, and she has won several major drama awards.

Carroll began her career in the theater as an actor but was frustrated by the limitations racial prejudice imposed on her. Frequently denied the opportunity to perform roles she wanted, she began to work independently. In 1960, Carroll began to direct for the stage and among her early projects was *Trumpets of the Lord,* featuring gospel music and **poetry** by **James Weldon Johnson.**

Like other **plays** Carroll directed in the early 1960s, *Trumpets of the Lord* displayed the talents of black actors, many of whom became the nucleus of the Urban Arts Theater in 1967. In 1970, Carroll collaborated with Micki Grant on the two-art revue *Don't Bother Me, I Can't Cope* (1970), which won the Los Angeles Drama Critics Circle Award and the Drama Desk Award. Carroll's best-known work—also a collaboration with Grant—is perhaps *Your Arms Too Short to Box with God*, a musical that appeared on Broadway in 1975 and went on a successful U.S. tour. Both plays received Tony Award nominations. Carroll is the artistic director of the Vinnette Carroll Repertory Company in southern Florida.

Further Readings
Black Writers, first edition, Gale, 1989.

Martin Carter

Guyanese poet
Born June 7, 1927.

Considered one of the Caribbean's most important poets, Carter was born and spent most of his life in Guyana (formerly British Guiana). When the British occupied Guyana in 1953, Carter became involved in radical politics and denounced the British government. Carter was imprisoned, during which time he wrote *Poems of Resistance from British Guiana* (1954), his most acclaimed work. The collection reflects his country's anger and its struggle for independence. When Guyana gained its independence in 1966, the country failed to realize Carter's expectations, and his later **poetry** volumes, such as *Poems of Succession* (1977) and *Poems of Affinity, 1978-1980* (1980), reflect his disappointment. Carter has taught at the University of Guyana since 1977 and his *Selected Poems* was published in 1989.

See also **Poetry of Martin Carter**

Further Readings
Black Writers, Gale, second edition, 1994.
Dictionary of Literary Biography, Volume 117: *Twentieth-Century Caribbean and Black African Writers,* First Series, Gale, 1992.

Lorene Cary

American memoirist and journalist
Born November 29, 1956.

After attending the University of Pennsylvania and Sussex University, Cary began a career in **journalism** at *Time* and later became associate editor of *TV Guide.* In 1982, she began teaching at St. Paul's School, then lectured at Antioch University and the Philadelphia University of the Arts. In 1985, Cary resumed her career in journalism, writing freelance articles for periodicals such as *Essence* and *American Visions.* In 1991, she published *Black Ice,* a memoir about her childhood experiences as a student at St. Paul's, an exclusive New-Hampshire boarding school. *Black Ice* describes Cary's guilt at having left the black community and chronicles her attempts to fit into the rich, white world of St. Paul's. The same year *Black Ice* was published, Cary became a contributing editor at *Newsweek.*

Further Readings
Black Writers, second edition, Gale, 1994.

Cast the First Stone

Chester Himes
Novel, 1952

Cast the First Stone, while third to be published, was actually **Chester Himes**'s first **novel**. A story of life behind bars, it recounts a five-year period in the life of Jim Monroe, a brash, white Mississippian. Growing up in less than ideal circumstances and then disabled due to a broken back, Monroe makes an effort at attending a local university but is sidetracked by his parents' divorce. After a year of hard drinking and gambling, during which he is convicted of forgery, Monroe is finally arrested for armed robbery. The novel opens on the day that Monroe enters a state prison in the late 1940s to begin serving a twenty to twenty-five-year sentence for his armed robbery conviction, and follows Monroe as he becomes involved in a prison riot, and engages in gambling and other surreptitious prison activities. When Monroe begins an affair with a fellow prisoner named Dido, the two men are punished for their open homosexuality by being placed first in solitary confinement and then into a section of the prison reserved for "known perverts." Monroe denies his affair with Dido and is finally vindicated, although Dido commits suicide. The novel closes as Monroe moves from the cell block to the prison farm, the first step towards his release from incarceration.

Cat Jimmy

Character in *The Narrows*

The Catacombs

William Demby
Novel, 1965

William Demby's second **novel**, *The Catacombs* is set in Rome and tells the story of an ill-fated love triangle. Its characters include Demby himself, as well as the fictional Doris and her aristocratic lover, the Count. The chaos in their personal lives echoes in news briefs about contemporary events, including the Algerian War, the Cuban missile crisis, the launching of a Russian spaceship, and the suicide of Marilyn Monroe. The novel is organized according to the daily, monthly, and seasonal cycles of life, and is suffused with images of death and resurrection. Doris becomes pregnant on Christmas. The Pope calls for universal peace on Easter. The child Doris carries is never born; but Demby leaves the ancient ruins of Rome for the modern skyscrapers of New York, implying hope for the future and a possibility of salvation.

Cecil Green

Character in *A Short Walk*

Celie

Character in *The Color Purple* and *The Temple of My Familiar*

Cephus Miles

Character in *Home*

Ceremonies in Dark Old Men

Lonne Elder III
Play, first produced 1965, published 1969

Ceremonies in Dark Old Men, which marked **Lonne Elder III**'s debut as a professional playwright, portrays a Harlem family struggling for economic stability and self-fulfillment. Russell B. Parker, the family patriarch, is the proprietor of a failing barbershop. His sons, Theopolis and Bobby, sell bootleg corn liquor and steal from local store owners. Russell and his sons also run a numbers game from the family's barbershop. The only member of the family with a legitimate job and a weekly paycheck is Russell's daughter Adele, who works as a secretary downtown. The **play** explores the various means through which African Americans try to assure their material and spiritual survival, including **religion**, civil rights activism, memories of a happier past, schemes of easy money, and dreams of prosperity.

Aimé Césaire

West Indian poet
Born June 25, 1913.

Aimé Fernand Césaire has been acknowledged as "The Father of Negritude" for his role in creating and promoting **negritude**, a cultural movement that urges blacks to renounce Western society and instead honor their racial heritage. The first occurrence of the word is in his poem *Cahier d'un retour au pays natal* (1939; *Return to My Native Land, 1968),* in which Césaire uses surreal language to deal with the reawakening of black racial awareness; the poet's definition of his own negritude comes to symbolize all blacks' growing self-awareness of their cultural heritage. *Cahier d'un retour au* *pays natal* is considered a major work in contemporary French-language literature.

Further Readings
Black Literature Criticism, Gale, 1992.
Black Writers, second edition, Gale, 1994.

The Chaneysville Incident
David Bradley
Novel, 1981

In **David Bradley**'s *The Chaneysville Incident,* black historian John Washington becomes involved with a white psychiatrist, Judith Powell, despite his buried conflicts regarding his family history and the fate of Africans in the South. When "Old Jack" Crawley, who raised John after the boy's father Moses committed suicide, is on his deathbed, John learns that in his will, Moses asked his son to figure out why he chose a certain site at which to kill himself. After tracking down the identity of the people buried at the site, John comes to terms with his own hatred of racial injustice. *The Chaneysville Incident* was awarded the PEN/Faulkner Award for best **novel** of 1981.

Charles Moss
Character in *Call Me Charley*

Charles Taylor
Character in *The Third Generation*

Charlie Cotchipee
Character in *Purlie Victorious*

Charlie Morris
Character in *Les Blancs*

Barbara Chase-Riboud
American sculptor, novelist, and poet
Born June 26, 1939.

Chase-Riboud is an internationally known sculptor, poet, and novelist. The issues she raises in her writings are often reflected in her art; she feels there are harmonious ways for races and sexes to influence each other, much as colors and materials can, and her work emphasizes the acceptance of racial and cultural diversity.

Barbara De Wayne Chase-Riboud was born on June 26, 1939, to a middle-class family in Philadelphia, Pennsylvania. She graduated from Temple University in 1957 and received her M.F.A. from Yale in 1960. In 1961, she married Marc Riboud, a French photojournalist; her first collection of poems, *From Memphis and Peking* (1974), was based on her experiences traveling with him in China and Africa. After their divorce in 1981, she married archeologist and publisher Sergio Tosi.

Fascinated by a **biography** of Thomas Jefferson that touched on his rumored affair with a quadroon slave named Sally Hemings, Chase-Riboud decided to research their relationship. The result was her 1979 best-selling historical **novel**, *Sally Hemings*. The novel presents the relationship from various angles and explores some of its implications for blacks and whites, for men and women, and for American society. Chase-Riboud based another historical novel, *Echo of Lions* (1989), on the true story of a rebellion of Africans on the slave ship Amistad. In 1994, Chase-Riboud focused on Harriet Hemings, the purported child of Jefferson and Hemings, in the historical novel *The President's Daughter.* Spanning the years from the early 1820s to the aftermath of the Civil War, the narrative focuses on racial attitudes and examines the theme of self-identity.

Further Readings
Black Writers, second edition, Gale, 1994.
Dictionary of Literary Biography, Volume 33: *Afro-American Fiction Writers after 1955,* Gale, 1984.

Chauncey

Character in *The Learning Tree*

Charles W. Chesnutt

American short story writer, novelist, and essayist
Born June 20, 1858.
Died November 15, 1932.

Charles Waddell Chesnutt used fiction to comment on social injustice and racial **discrimination** encountered by blacks of the post-Civil War era. Although he never secured a wide audience during his lifetime, he is recognized as one of the first American writers to portray the black experience in America realistically.

Chesnutt was born in Cleveland, Ohio, to parents of mixed race. In 1866, his parents returned to their hometown of Fayetteville, North Carolina, where Chesnutt worked in the family store. Pressed to help support his family, Chesnutt ended his formal education at fourteen and took a position as pupil-teacher at the school. At sixteen he taught full time in Charlotte. He returned to Fayetteville as assistant principal of the Howard School and later became principal. Temporarily leaving his wife, whom he married in 1878, he found a job in New York City as a stenographer and journalist on Wall Street in the early 1880s.

Chesnutt and his family settled in Cleveland in 1884, where he studied law, established a court reporting business, and devoted his evenings to writing fiction. Chesnutt's first published volume, *The Conjure Woman* (1899), is a collection of dialect stories, which garnered some critical attention for its uncompromising depiction of **slavery**. A second collection of short stories, *The Wife of His Youth, and Other Stories of the Color Line* (1899), explores the racial identity of mixed-blood Americans. Also during that year, Chesnutt's **biography** *Frederick Douglass* (1899) was accepted for the series "Beacon Biographies of Eminent Americans."

Chesnutt's first two **novels,** *The House behind the Cedars* (1900) and *The Marrow of Tradition* (1901) attracted little critical acclaim and few sales due in part to their controversial themes of miscegenation and prejudice. He continued writing and published his last book-length work, the novel *The Colonel's Dream,* in 1905; this narrative netted fewer sales than his second novel. Critics still consider his earlier **short story** collections to be his most valuable contributions to American literature. In recognition of his pioneering literary work, Chesnutt was awarded the National Association for the Advancement of Colored People's Spingarn Medal in 1928.

Further Readings

Black Writers, first edition, Gale, 1989.

Dictionary of Literary Biography, Volume 50: *Afro-American Writers before the Harlem Renaissance,* Gale, 1986.

Pickens, Ernestine Williams, *Charles W. Chesnutt and the Progressive Movement,* University Press of America, 1994.

Chicken George

Character in *Roots: The Saga of an American Family*

Chicken Little

Character in *Sula*

Chief Nanga

Character in *A Man of the People*

Childhood

Bill Cosby
Nonfiction, 1991

In his fourth book, *Childhood,* **Bill Cosby** recounts growing up in North Philadelphia in the 1940s under the supervision of Mom and Dad and with brother Russell and others, including Fat Albert and Weird Harold. The book emphasizes the eternal conflict between children and their parents and provides instructive passages on animals, sex, manners, and the fine points of such "sports" as after-school fist fights. Cosby compares the independent, adventurous street antics of his childhood with the structured, dull lives of youth today. Though he thinks children were more resourceful back then, Cosby points out similarities between the generations, such as the persistent use of two-or three-word sentences and the deadly, "Mom, I'm bored."

Alice Childress

American dramatist and novelist
Born October 12, 1920.
Died August, 1994.

Childress is considered a seminal figure in African American drama, though she may be best known for a children's book, *A Hero Ain't Nothin' but a Sandwich* (1973). Although her first **novel** for adults, *A Short Walk* (1979) was nominated for a Pulitzer Prize, she has not received a great deal of critical attention despite her prolific and varied career. Childress once described herself as "one of the best known of unknown persons."

Born in Charleston, South Carolina, in 1920, Childress was raised in Harlem by her grandmother, who influenced her artistic development. They would sit together at a window, watching people pass on the street, and her grandmother would encourage her to imagine what the people were thinking. Childress left high school without receiving a degree and joined the American Negro Theater in Harlem. She was chosen for the original cast of a Broadway play but found her acting career unfulfilling, in part because her range was stifled by contemporary prejudices. She married young and subsequently divorced, working menial jobs to support herself and her young daughter, Jean.

Her first **play** was produced in 1949; set in a segregated railway station, *Florence* depicts a conversation between a white woman and a black woman whose daughter is a struggling actress in New York City. The play received high praise from many critics and effectively

Childress in 1977, receiving the first Paul Robeson Award.

launched Childress's career. *Gold through the Trees* (1952) became the first play by a black woman to be professionally produced on the American stage. Childress was also the first woman to receive an Obie Award, which was presented to her for *Trouble in Mind* (1955), a play about a cast rehearsing a fictional drama about a lynching. On July 17, 1957, Childress married Nathan Woodard.

Her success in the early years of black theater forged a path for many of the women who followed her. Childress made her pioneering role all the more important by holding fast to her principles, refusing to revise *Trouble in Mind* for Broadway and not shirking controversy in her treatment of racial issues. Her play *Wedding Band* (1966) revolves around a love affair between a white baker and a black seamstress in South Carolina. *Wine in the Wilderness* (1969) is set during a riot; a painter finds a model for his triptych of black womanhood.

Television productions of these two plays met with resistance in states as diverse as Alabama and New York. Her children's book, *A Hero Ain't Nothin' but a Sandwich,* about a boy defeating his addiction to heroin, has also been banned from some school systems.

In the 1960s Childress accepted an appointment at the Radcliffe Institute for Independent Study. She published *A Short Walk* in 1979, and another children's book, ***Rainbow Jordan***, in 1981. She died of cancer in August, 1994.

Further Readings
Black Literature Criticism, Gale, 1992.

Chinatown Moss
Character in *Blood on the Forge*

Shirley Chisholm
American autobiographer
Born November 30, 1924.

The first black female member of Congress, Chisholm became the first African American woman to run for president. She has discussed her political experiences in two autobiographies, ***Unbought and Unbossed*** (1970) and ***The Good Fight*** (1973), both of which exemplify the intense individualism of her public and private life.

Chisholm was born in Brooklyn, New York. She attended Brooklyn College, where she prepared for a career in teaching, one of the few professions open to her as a young black woman. She graduated in 1946, married Conrad Q. Chisholm in 1949, and received her graduate degree from Columbia University in 1952. Chisholm spent many years working in child care centers around New York and was appointed education consultant to the New York City Bureau of Child Welfare in 1959.

During this period, Chisholm also became involved in local politics, holding leadership positions in several groups. In 1964, after ten years of doing everything from decorating cigar boxes to helping voters get to the polls, she ran for a seat in the New York State Assembly. She encountered much opposition to her candidacy, mainly because of her sex, but won her first campaign by a wide margin. During her term Chisholm learned more about the intricacies of politics, while her constituents learned more about her political priorities. She pushed constantly for equality for ethnic minorities and women, supporting better educational opportunities and other programs for the poor and disadvantaged. Chisholm continued to further these causes following her election to Congress in 1968.

While serving in Washington Chisholm published *Unbought and Unbossed,* which was also the slogan of her first campaign for Congress. Critics considered it an absorbing account of how she had learned to put her idealism and her strong sense of purpose to work in politics. *The Good Fight* details her campaign for the 1972 Democratic presidential nomination. Although she failed in her bid, many commentators considered the attempt an important event that infused contemporary political debate with a new vitality.

Chisholm divorced her first husband and married Arthur Hardwick in 1977. She served in Congress until 1983 and soon thereafter began teaching in the department of sociology and anthropology at Mount Holyoke College. In 1993 President Bill Clinton nominated her for ambassador to Jamaica.

Further Readings
Black Writers, first edition, Gale, 1989.

Brownmiller, Susan, *Shirley Chisholm,* Doubleday, 1970.

A Choice of Weapons
Gordon Parks
Autobiography, 1966

In *A Choice of Weapons,* the first in a trio of autobiographies, **Gordon Parks** recounts his childhood and his rise to success as a photographer. He remembers his early years as the youngest of fifteen children born to Sarah and Andrew Parks in Fort Scott, Kansas. Following his mother's death, the sixteen-year-old Parks lived with his sister in St. Paul, Minnesota. Parks recounts how he worked a number of odd jobs, including busboy, janitor, pianist, basketball player, and waiter before pursuing a career in photography. Teaching himself the basics of photography, Parks captured the urban life of blacks and earned critical acclaim as an internationally recognized photographer for *Life* magazine. In 1941 he won a Julius Rosenwald Fellowship. He later worked for the Farm Security Administration and the Office of War Information.

Cholly Breedlove

Character in *The Bluest Eye*

Chris Oriko

Character in *Anthills of the Savannah*

Barbara T. Christian

American literary critic
Born December 12, 1943.

Christian, who was born in the U.S. Virgin Islands, is known for her critical works, especially *Black Women Novelists: Development of a Tradition, 1892-1976* (1980), which won the Before Columbus Foundation American Book Award in 1984. She holds a Ph.D. from Columbia University and, in 1972, began teaching African American studies at the University of California at Berkeley.

Christian's other works include *Black Feminist Criticism: Perspectives on Black Women Writers* (1985), a teaching guide for Dorthy Sterling's *Black Foremothers, Three Lives* (1980), and contributions to the periodicals *Black Scholar* and *Journal of Ethnic Studies*.

Further Readings
Black Writers, first edition, Gale, 1989.

Chisholm, the first African American female member of Congress, in 1980.

Christianity

Organized **religion** has always been a strong institution among African Americans, and the denominations with the largest black membership in the United States are Christian. The link between Christianity and black reading and writing dates back to slave days, when missionaries whose primary goal was to convert Africans to Christianity often provided general education as a secondary benefit. Today the pervasive Christian influence is evident in a great deal of black literature. To take but one small example, storefront churches situated in movie theaters or rented stores, which have historically been found in black urban ghettos, provide the setting for a large portion of **James Baldwin**'s acclaimed **novel** *Go Tell It on the Mountain* (1953) and are also prominently featured in works by **Langston**

Hughes and **Ralph Ellison**. Episcopal priest and literary critic **Nathan A. Scott Jr.** has examined the complex relationship between religion and literature in such works as *Craters of the Spirit: Studies in the Modern Novel* (1968) and *The Poetics of Belief: Studies in Coleridge, Arnold, Peter, Santayana, Stevens, and Heidegger* (1985).

As far back as the sixteenth century, white missionaries urged Africans to convert to Christianity. In eighteenth-and early nineteenth-century America, these efforts intensified. Yet **racism** was never absent from the American religious scene. Although the level of **discrimination** varied from region to region, some factors were more or less constant. For one thing, there was a relative paucity of ordained African American clergy; for another, segregated seating in churches was common in both the North and the South. To protest such discrimination, some black leaders led their followers out of white churches and set up independent African American congregations. In 1816, Richard Allen founded the African Methodist Episcopal Church. In 1841, this church established the oldest continuously published black periodical, now known as the *Christian Recorder,* which boasted as one of its earliest publishers noted writer and black nationalist **Martin Robinson Delany**.

As African American churches flourished, their ministers assumed great importance, not only as religious figures, but as social and political leaders as well. Many preachers achieved renown for their poetic and emotional speaking style, and some incorporated elaborate imagery into their sermons. **James Weldon Johnson**'s poems in *God's Trombones: Seven Negro Sermons in Verse* (1927) recreate the speech patterns heard in such preaching. **Ralph Ellison**'s novel *Invisible Man* (1952) offers the fictional character Homer Barbee as an example of a black preacher. Sermons by African American clergyman and politician **Adam Clayton Powell Jr.** are found in his collection *Keep the Faith, Baby!* (1967).

In the early twentieth century, many black ministers became advocates of Social Gospel. These clergymen highlighted the reality of collective, societal sin, such as hunger in children and the denial of human rights. They maintained that Christian repentance of such sins must be followed by concrete action to rectify the injustice. **Martin Luther King Jr.** was profoundly influenced by the Social Gospel movement, which foreshadowed the **civil rights movement** of the 1950s and 1960s. One pastor and scholar who helped lay the foundation for King's work was **Howard Thurman**, who wrote books espousing the political philosophy of nonviolent resistance developed by Mahatma Gandhi. Thurman, whose commitment to desegregation led him to cofound the interracial Church for the Fellowship of All Peoples in 1944, recorded his experiences in an **autobiography** titled *With Head and Heart* (1980). Another religious leader who helped shape King's civil rights career was educator **Benjamin E. Mays**. Among the books outlining Mays's religious views are *Seeking to Be Christian in Race Relations* (1957) and *Lord, the People Have Driven Me On* (1981).

In the years following King's assassination, proponents of a Black Theology movement attempted to critique Christianity in light of the civil rights and **black power** campaigns. Some of these theologians take the position that Jesus is a black messiah and that black liberation should be seen as situated at the very core of the Christian gospels. Among black writers who have taken an Afrocentric view of religion is historian Yosef ben-Jochannan, author of *African Origins of the Major "Western Religions"* (1970). In the 1980s, some black theorists formulated "womanist" theologies, which attempt to combat the triple oppression of race, class, and gender experienced by many black women.

Over the years, numerous African American writers have drawn on the powerful, emotion-laden symbolism provided by Christianity. For example, in his poem "Simon the Cyrenian Speaks," **Harlem Renaissance** poet **Countee Cullen** identifies blacks with Simon, the bearer of Christ's cross, who has been singled out because of his color. A number of contemporary African writers, too, have taken Christianity as a theme for their work—for example, Kenyan **Ngugi wa Thiong'o,** whose novels include

Caitaani mutharaba-ini (1980), which translates as *Devil on the Cross* (1982). One book that discusses Christianity in the context of African culture is *Death and the Hereafter in the Light of Christianity and African Religion* (1974), by Kenyan comparative religion scholar **John S. Mbiti**.

Christmas Gif'

Compiled by Charlemae Hill Rollins
Anthology, 1963

Charlemae Hill Rollins's interest in promoting black heritage and a positive portrayal of blacks in children's literature inform *Christmas Gif': An Anthology of Christmas Poems, Songs, and Stories, Written by and about Negroes*, a title that derives from a game played by slaves on Christmas Day. Illustrated by Tom O'Sullivan, the book collects poems, songs, stories, **essays**, and recipes written by noted African American authors, including Paul Lawrence Dunbar, **Langston Hughes**, and **Countee Cullen**.

Christopher Cary

Character in *Comedy, American Style*

Christopher Cary Jr.

Character in *Comedy, American Style*

Chuckie

Character in *In New England Winter*

Grace Ciee

Jamaican writer
Born August 22, 1961.

Born Grace Melecia Cornish, Ciee attended Hampshire College and became an image consultant for department stores and cosmetic companies after graduating in 1982. Her interest in female beauty has fueled her writing. Ciee has written *The Fortune of Being Yourself: You Can*

Have It All—Love, Beauty, Money, and Happiness (1991), for which she received a Certificate of Recognition for Black Women in Literature from the International Public Relations Group; *Think and Grow Beautiful: A Teenage Woman's Guide to Total Beauty* (1992); and *Radiant Women of Color: Embrace, Enhance and Enjoy the Beauty of Your Natural Coloring* (1993).

Further Readings
Black Writers, Gale, second edition, 1994.

Civil Rights Movement

Black Americans had made small dents in **racism** by the end of World War II, and in the ensuing decades—particularly in the 1950s and 1960s—civil rights for blacks became a major political issue. The driving force behind this movement was **Martin Luther King Jr.**, who emphasized nonviolence and Christian love as the means to fight social injustice. King's eloquent **oratory** and prose captured the attention of a nation. However, numerous other African American writers and speakers have made important contributions to the movement as well, among them **Maya Angelou**, **James Baldwin**, **Bayard Rustin**, and **James Weldon Johnson**, who wrote the lyrics for *Lift Every Voice and Sing,* the poem often referred to as the black national anthem.

In the mid-1950s King led a bus boycott in Montgomery, Alabama, that was prompted when Rosa Parks refused to give up her seat to a white passenger. The resulting protest handed blacks their first important victory achieved through direct nonviolent action. King recounted the story of this boycott in his book *Stride toward Freedom: The Montgomery Story* (1958). In 1957, the Civil Rights Act, the first federal civil rights law to be passed since the 1870s, was enacted. It established the Commission on Civil Rights, a federal agency whose mission was to investigate any violations of such civil rights as free speech and voting. Also in that year, the Southern Christian Leadership Conference was formed by King, Rustin, and Stanley Levinson. This was the first organization devoted to coordinating the efforts of nonviolent groups working to end racial **segregation** and improve black Americans' lives.

Peaceful sit-ins began to force desegregation at lunch counters across the South in 1960. That same year, leaders of the sit-in movement, including future Washington, D.C., mayor Marion Barry, founded the Student Nonviolent Coordinating Committee (SNCC). The following year, well-publicized "freedom rides," designed to defy segregation on interstate buses, were organized by the Congress of Racial Equality (CORE). In 1963, King was arrested while leading a civil rights drive in Birmingham, Alabama. His published statement on the experience, *Letter from Birmingham City Jail* (1963), outlined his reasons for fighting racism. The high point of these civil rights efforts came that same year in the massive March on Washington for Jobs and Freedom, which drew some 250,000 demonstrators to the nation's capital. It was during this protest that King delivered his famous "**I Have a Dream**" speech, a stirring plea for racial justice. Rustin, who helped organize the march, later published *Strategies for Freedom: The Changing Patterns of Black Protest* (1976).

In 1964, largely spurred by these actions, a new Civil Rights Act was passed, outlawing racial **discrimination** by unions, employers, and voting registrars and in public facilities. The Twenty-fourth Amendment to the Constitution, which banned poll taxes, was also ratified. King's pivotal role in these successes was recognized with the Nobel Peace Prize. The struggle was not over, though, as shown by events the next year in Selma, Alabama. Civil rights demonstrators there were attacked by police with tear gas, whips, and clubs, and many were arrested. Yet the protesters' cause—the removal of obstacles to voter registration among southern blacks—was also brought to the fore. In response, Congress passed a Voting Rights Act that eliminated discriminatory qualifying tests for voters and provided for federal registrars. King was assassinated in 1968. In the aftermath of his death, Congress prohibited racial discrimination in federally financed housing.

The historic changes brought about by the civil rights movement have since been documented by numerous nonfiction writers. For example, **Calvin C. Hernton** wrote *White Papers for White Americans* (1966) about events of the 1960s, while **James S. Haskins** authored a children's book about the civil rights movement. Several autobiographies by African Americans have dealt with this period, too, including **Gordon Parks**'s *Voices in the Mirror: An Autobiography* (1990) and **Coretta Scott King**'s *My Life with Martin Luther King Jr.* (1969). Likewise, biographies of prominent civil rights activists abound. For example, **Sara E. Wright**'s *A. Philip Randolph: Integration in the Workplace* (1990) explores the life of one civil rights pioneer. The movement has also served as the backdrop for many **novels** by black authors, such as **Ossie Davis**'s *Just Like Martin* (1992) and **Alice Walker**'s *Meridian* (1976). The civil rights struggle provided more than just subject matter, however. The battle against racism, which stood at the movement's core, remains a vital theme in black literature.

Clara

Character in *Clara's Old Man* and *No Longer at Ease*

Clara's Ole Man

Ed Bullins
Play, 1965

Clara's Ole Man was the first of **Ed Bullins**'s plays to receive wide recognition. Departing from the absurdism of his earlier work, he turned in this drama to realistic portrayals of people struggling to survive in the ghetto. The **play** depicts the lives of three women, Big Girl, Clara, and Baby Girl, and their relationship with one another as seen through the eyes of Jack, a suitor who believes he is visiting Clara while her "ole man" is at work.

The women live together as a family, though only two of them are sisters. Strong willed, articulate, and angry, Big Girl holds them together; Clara is young, attractive, and unsure of herself, while Baby Girl is Big Girl's mentally retarded sister. When Jack arrives, Big Girl is home unexpectedly from work and they all sit in the kitchen, talking to him about their lives. Though originally from the neighborhood, Jack is now a college student, an outsider who does not understand much about them. He makes the mistake of announcing that he is there because Clara told him her "ole man" would be working. But Big Girl is Clara's lover. Some neighborhood youths have joined them in the kitchen, fleeing from the police, and at the denouement of the play Big Girl has them beat Jack severely.

Clare Kendry

Character in *Passing*

Clarence

Character in *The Radiance of the King*

J. P. Clark

Nigerian poet, playwright, essayist, and filmmaker
Born April 6, 1935.

A widely known Nigerian writer, John Pepper Clark gained an interest in **poetry** while attending University College in Ibaden. His poems are collected in *The Song of a Goat* (1961), and *Casualties: Poems 1966-68* (1970). His *A Reed in the Tide* (1965) was the first collection of poems by a black writer in Africa to be published internationally. Clark studied for a year at Princeton University; upon his return to Nigeria, he wrote a satirical book about his experience entitled *America, Their America* (1964). His dramatic works include *Three Plays* (1964), *Ozidi* (1966), *The Wives' Revolt* (1984), and *The Return Home* (1985). Clark was professor of English at the University of Lagos until his retirement in 1980. His collected **plays** and poems were published in 1980.

Further Readings
Black Literature Criticism, Gale, 1992.

Dictionary of Literary Biography, Volume 117: *Twentieth-Century Caribbean and Black African Writers,* First Series, Gale, 1992.

Kenneth B. Clark

American psychologist and nonfiction writer
Born July 24, 1914.

Kenneth Bancroft Clark is an influential thinker in the field of psychology. His studies on the psychological effects of **racism** were cited by the United States Supreme Court in *Brown v. Board of Education of Topeka,* its landmark school desegregation decision of 1954. His first book on the subject, *Prejudice and Your Child* (1955), went through two enlarged editions by 1963. In 1961, Clark was awarded the Spingarn Medal by the **National Association for the Advancement of Colored People** (NAACP).

Clark began his career as an assistant professor of psychology at the Hampton Institute in Virginia in 1940. He then moved to the Office of War Information in Washington, D.C., and worked as an assistant social science analyst during the early years of World War II. In 1942, he obtained a position at City College of the City University of New York; while working there, Clark published some of his most noted studies of **segregation** and its effects on African American life. These include *The Negro Student at Integrated Colleges* (1963), written with Lawrence Plotkin, and *Social and Economic Implications of Integration in the Public Schools* (1965).

As a founder of Harlem Youth Opportunities Unlimited (HARYOU), Clark developed several concepts which became important measures in the national anti-poverty program of the 1960s. *Dark Ghetto: Dilemmas of Social Power* (1965), based on his experiences with HARYOU, has been translated into German, Spanish, and Italian and remains one of his best-known works. Clark further examined the issue of poverty in *A Relevant War against Poverty: A Study of Community Action Programs and Observable Change* (1968), written with Jean-

Kenneth B. Clark in 1986 in the state Education Building in New York.

nette Hopkins, and edited the discussions resulting from a 1971 conference on education and racism for *Racism and American Education: A Dialogue and Agenda for Action* (1970; with Elinor L. Gordon). He published *Pathos of Power* in 1974 and is currently professor emeritus of psychology at City College.

Further Readings

Black Writers, first edition, Gale, 1989.

Austin C. Clarke

Barbadian-Canadian novelist and
short story writer
Born July 26, 1934.

Considered one of Canada's foremost black writers, Austin Chesterfield Clarke emi-

grated there from Barbados in 1955 and began writing **poetry** and fiction, often using the immigrant experience as the basis for his works. Clarke set his first two **novels,** *The Survivors of the Crossing* (1964), and *Amongst Thistles and Thorns* (1965), in Barbados. He wrote a Toronto trilogy including *The Meeting Point* (1967), *Storm of Fortune* (1973), and *The Bigger Light* (1975), in which he focused on the struggle of working-class immigrants in an inhospitable white society. His short stories are compiled in *When He Was Free and Young and He Used to Wear Silks* (1971), *When Women Rule* (1985) and *Nine Men Who Laughed* (1986). He moved back to Barbados in 1975 to work for the Caribbean Broadcasting Company, but after conflict with the government, he returned to Toronto and completed two more novels about Barbadian politics, *The Prime Minister* (1977) and *Proud Empires* (1986), and the **autobiography** *Growing Up Stupid under the Union Jack: A Memoir* (1980).

Further Readings

Black Literature Criticism, Gale, 1992.

Dictionary of Literary Biography, Volume 125: *Twentieth-Century Caribbean and Black African Writers,* Second Series, Gale, 1993.

Clarke Bentancourt

Character in *Mo' Better Blues*

Cheryl Clarke

American poet
Born May 16, 1947.

Born in Washington, D.C., Clarke earned her B.A. at Howard and her M.A. and M.S.W. at Rutgers University. Her first collection, *Narratives: Poems in the Tradition of Black Women* (1983), draws on the **oral tradition** and Clarke's black lesbian-feminist perspective. Recognized by critics such as **Calvin Hernton,** *Narratives* uses a variety of voices to deal with such issues as community among women, female sexuality (especially lesbianism), male violence against women, and incest. *Living as a Lesbian* (1986) and *Humid Pitch: Narrative*

Poetry (1989) cover similar themes but are considered more lyrical due to Clarke's use of **jazz** elements. Clarke's **poetry** volume *Experimental Love* was published in 1993.

Further Readings
Black Writers, Gale, second edition, 1994.

John Henrik Clarke
American editor, essayist, and educator
Born January 1, 1915.

Clarke has written and lectured extensively about both African and African American history. He has been awarded the **Carter G. Woodson** Award for both his editing and his teaching, and he has been cited by the National Association of Television and Radio Announcers for his use of television as an educational tool.

Clarke began his career in 1956 as an educator at the New School for Social Research in New York City, where he taught African and African American history. In 1957 and 1958 he also worked as a journalist for papers in Pittsburgh and in the African nation of Ghana. The black community in New York was the subject of Clarke's first two publications as an editor, *Harlem U.S.A.: The Story of a City within a City* (1964) and *Harlem: A Community in Transition* (1965). One of Clarke's best-known works, ***Malcolm X: The Man and His Times*** (1969), won critical attention for presenting the African American religious and political leader in the context of both his personal past and the period in which he lived. The following year Clarke co-edited *Black Titan: W. E. B. Du Bois* (1970), another study of a leading African American figure.

In 1970, Clarke joined the faculty of Hunter College of the City University of New York, where he served as associate professor of African and Puerto Rican studies until he became professor emeritus in 1985. In his subsequent writings, Clarke has concentrated on African rather than African American issues.

Africans at the Crossroads: Notes for an African World Revolution (1991), *Christopher Columbus and the African Holocaust* (1992), and *African People in World History* (1993) all reflect his interest in African issues and history.

Further Readings
Authors in the News, Volume 1, Gale, 1976.
Black Writers, second edition, Gale, 1994.

Claude Bowers
Character in *South Street*

Claudia McTeer
Character in *The Bluest Eye*

Clay
Character in *Dutchman*

Pearl Cleage
American playwright and poet
Born December 7, 1948.

Pearl Michelle Cleage, some of whose work has appeared under her married name, Pearl Cleage Lomax, is a prolific playwright whose works have been produced in New York, Washington, and Atlanta. Cleage became the playwright-in-residence of the Just Us Theater Co. in 1983 and the artistic director in 1987. She also became Spelman College's playwright-in-residence in 1991. Cleage has worked in several broadcast positions, has been a columnist for Atlanta newspapers, and founded the magazine *Catalyst* in 1987.

Cleage's produced **plays,** some of which have also been published, include *Hymn for the Rebels* (1968); *Duet for Three Voices* (1969); *puppetplay* (1983), a full-length work that broke the Atlanta New Play Project's attendance records; *Hospice* (1983), which won five Audience Development Committee (AUDELCO) Recognition Awards, including Best Play and Best Playwright; *Banana Bread* (1985); *Porch*

Songs (1985); and *Late Bus to Mecca* (1992). Her **poetry** is collected in *We Don't Need No Music* (1971), *Dear Dark Faces: Portraits of a People* (1980), and *One for the Brothers* (1983). Cleage is also the author of the **essay** collection *Deals with the Devil: And Other Reasons to Riot* (1993).

Further Readings

Black Writers, second edition, Gale, 1994.

Eldridge Cleaver

American essayist
Born August 31, 1935.

A member of the Black Panther Party, Cleaver is best known for his **essay** collection *Soul on Ice* (1968). His attacks on racial injustice in America and his calls for militant action elevated him into a position of international prominence during the 1960s.

Leroy Eldridge Cleaver was born on August 31, 1935, in Wabbaseka, Arkansas. While a child, Cleaver moved with his family to Los Angeles, where his parents separated and he became increasingly involved in crime. In 1954, he was sentenced to two and a half years in California State Prison. Here he completed his high school education and read such authors as Karl Marx and **W. E. B. Du Bois**. Soon after his release, however, Cleaver was convicted of rape and assault with intent to commit murder. While serving his term at Folsom Prison, he became a follower of **Malcolm X**.

Cleaver was still in prison in 1965 when he began writing the essays that would later appear in *Soul on Ice*. One of them, an attack on **James Baldwin** entitled "Notes on a Native Son," was published in the leftist magazine *Ramparts,* attracting the attention of prominent writers and intellectuals. With their support, Cleaver won parole in November, 1966. Shortly after his release, he joined the Black Panther Party and began touring America as their Minister of Information. The publication of *Soul on Ice* in 1968 made Cleaver a national figure. His prose and frankness were widely praised, although some

critics contended that his perception of American race relations was extremely narrow.

In April, 1968, Cleaver was charged with assault and attempted murder following a gun battle between Black Panthers and the San Francisco police. Support for him came from around the world; later that year Cleaver was chosen as the presidential candidate of the Peace and Freedom Party, an organization of black and white radicals. Rather than facing the charges against him, however, Cleaver fled the country. *Post-Prison Writings and Speeches* (1969) was published while he was a fugitive in Cuba, Algeria, and France. This work offers a detailed statement of the Black Panthers' political ideology and attempts to dispel public conceptions of the Panthers as a violent hate-group.

During his exile, Cleaver became increasingly disillusioned with communism. He converted to **Christianity** and returned to America in 1975, surrendering to federal authorities. Presenting himself as a changed man, Cleaver able to strike a deal with the government and avoid a prison sentence. In 1978, he published *Soul on Fire*, in which he discusses his conversion to Christianity and explains his changed political views. Cleaver eventually joined the Republican Party and in 1986 ran unsuccessfully for the party nomination for United States Senate.

Further Readings
Black Literature Criticism, Gale, 1992.

Black Writers, first edition, Gale, 1989.

Lockwood, Lee, *Conversation with Eldridge Cleaver: Algiers,* McGraw, 1970.

Cleo Judson

Character in *The Living Is Easy*

!Click Song

John A. Williams
Novel, 1982

William Cato Douglass is a novelist and the central character of **John A. Williams**'s *!Click Song*. His career is mirrored by that of a Jewish writer, Paul Cummings, whom Douglass meets while they attend college under the G.I. Bill. The two writers become friends but grow apart as Cummings' career skyrockets. Although Douglass writes better material without getting the same financial rewards, Cummings eventually commits suicide. By facing the implications of his friend's death, Douglass realizes that he writes to exorcise his own suffering. *!Click Song* won the American Book Award in 1982.

Cliff Dawson

Character in *In New England Winter*

Michelle Cliff

Jamaican-born American novelist and poet
Born November 2, 1946.

Cliff was born in Kingston, Jamaica, and has since become a United States citizen. She obtained her master's in philosophy at the Warburg Institute in London and worked for several years in publishing in New York before embarking on a career as a writer and teacher.

Cliff's work is concerned with social and political issues and how they affect the lives of people. The **novel** *Abeng* (1984), for instance, particularizes the evils of **slavery** and **colonialism** in the relationship between a light-skinned girl and her dark-skinned friend. When a violent incident reveals the differences in their status, the girls' relationship crumbles. Cliff pursues these and other themes in the novels *No Telephone to Heaven* (1987), and *Free Enterprise* (1993), about the slave trade and resistance to it. A continuing interest of Cliff's is how history is often submerged or distorted, but can be discerned in the survival of African art forms and the persistence of African philosophical and religious principles among African American artists.

Cliff's poems are compiled in *The Land of Look Behind* (1985), and *Claiming an Identity They Taught Me to Despise* (1991). *Bodies of Water* (1990) is a **short story** collection. Cliff has lectured around the world and speaks several languages. Her work is widely anthologized.

Further Readings
Black Writers, Gale, second edition, 1994.

Cleaver at a 1969 press interview in Algiers.

Lucille Clifton

American poet and author of children's literature
Born June 27, 1936.

Clifton's **poetry** often expresses her concern for the welfare of black families. Her children's books are characterized by a positive view of black heritage. She has received a nomination for the Pulitzer Prize and two grants from the National Endowment for the Arts.

Thelma Lucille Clifton was born and raised in Depew, New York. Clifton attended Howard University and majored in drama, associating with such writers as **Amiri Baraka** (LeRoi Jones) and Sterling Brown. Clifton left Howard after two years and attended Fredonia State Teachers College, where she developed a style of poetry that reflected the spoken word.

Clifton's first poetry collection, *Good Times: Poems* (1969), was named one of the ten

Lucille Clifton, a poet and children's author.

best books of the year by *The New York Times*. In this volume, she sketches the lives of people in the ghetto, focusing on their hardships yet evoking a sense of strength and celebration that reflects her association with the **black arts movement** during the 1960s and 1970s. Clifton's second collection of verse, *Good News about the Earth: New Poems* (1972), is more overtly political than her first, containing poems dedicated to such black leaders as **Malcolm X** and **Angela Davis**.

In *An Ordinary Woman* (1974) Clifton moved toward a broader assessment of her role as an African American woman. *Generations: A Memoir* (1976) is an exploration of her ancestry, including her great-great-grandmother Caroline, who was abducted in West Africa and sold as a slave in New Orleans. Clifton's later volumes of poetry include *Quilting: Poems 1987-1990* (1991) and *The Book of Light* (1993).

In her children's books, Clifton has also worked to impart an understanding of black his-

tory. *All Us Come across the Water* (1973) describes the relationship between blacks in America and Africa, while the subject of *The Times They Used to Be* (1974) is the rural, Southern origins of many African Americans.

See also **Poetry of Lucille Clifton**

Further Readings
Black Literature Criticism, Gale, 1992.

Black Writers, second edition, Gale, 1994.

Dictionary of Literary Biography, Volume 41: *Afro-American Poets since 1955*, Gale, 1985.

Clotel
Character in *Clotel; or, The President's Daughter*

Clotel; or, The President's Daughter
William Wells Brown
Novel, 1853

The first **novel** written by a black American, **William Wells Brown**'s *Clotel; or, The President's Daughter: A Narrative of Slave Life in the United States* is a passionate and encyclopedic denunciation of the horrors of **slavery**. The heroine of the tale, Clotel, is a daughter of President Thomas Jefferson by his slave mistress. As the narrative opens, Clotel is depicted as a sensitive teenager, set upon the auction block and bid for by rude and despicable whites. The novel contains numerous sub-plots as well as authorial commentary, but the story nevertheless follows the sad plight of Clotel—who ultimately kills herself by leaping from a bridge—and her daughter, Mary.

Brown used the action in the novel to denounce those whom he felt responsible for slavery; unscrupulous masters, slave traders, and other Southern villains are depicted, but the author also censured Northern religious leaders who supported slavery through their bigoted notions of black inferiority. Brown was so angered by the prejudice of one New York clergyman, Reverend John Peck, that he used Peck's name for one of the novel's principal villains.

Illustration from *Clotel* (1853), the first novel written by an African American.

Clotel was published in England just a year and a half after Harriet Beecher Stowe's *Uncle Tom's Cabin*, though Brown's novel failed to find a similarly vast audience. During his lifetime Brown revised *Clotel* several times and published it under different titles, including *Miralda; or the Beautiful Quadroon* and *The Colored Heroine; A Tale of the Southern States.*

Charlie Cobb

American poet, journalist, and nonfiction writer
Born June 23, 1943.

Charles Earl Cobb Jr.'s literary works, cast in a writing style marked by succinct phrasing and syntactical experimentation, revolve around political and social themes, particularly injustice. His first collection of poems, *In the*

Furrows of the World (1967), explores his experiences with the Student Nonviolent Coordinating Committee (SNCC) from 1962 to 1967. *Everywhere Is Yours* (1971) reflects his views regarding oppressed peoples, while ***African Notebook: Views on Returning 'Home'*** (1971) addresses the relationship between Africa and African Americans. The son of a Methodist minister, Cobb was born in 1943 in Washington, D.C., and worked in public radio and television before joining *National Geographic* magazine, where he has been a writer since 1985.

Further Readings
Black Writers, second edition, Gale, 1994.
Dictionary of Literary Biography, Volume 41: *African American Poets since 1955,* Gale, 1985.

Coin Foreman

Character in *Boy at the Window*

Wanda Coleman

American poet and short story writer
Born November 13, 1946.

Coleman is best known for her powerful portrayal of the lives of poor urban blacks in Los Angeles, where she grew up. Her works of **poetry** and short fiction include *Mad Dog Black Lady* (1979) and *Imagoes* (1983). Many of the pieces in *Heavy Daughter Blues: Poems and Stories, 1968-1986* (1991), are based on **the blues** or **jazz** and treat such topics as **racism** and sexism. *A War of Eyes and Other Stories* (1988) focuses on the struggle for self-identity. *African Sleeping Sickness: Stories and Poems* (1990) includes autobiographical pieces and examines the theme of African American displacement. Coleman has also published the poetry collection *Hand Dance* (1993).

Coleman has also worked as a staff writer for *Days of Our Lives* and in this capacity became the first black writer to receive an Emmy Award for outstanding writing for daytime drama. She has also received a National Endowment for the Arts grant for 1981-1982 and a Guggenheim Fellowship for poetry in 1984.

Further Readings
Black Writers, second edition, Gale, 1994.

Eugenia W. Collier

American short story writer
and playwright
Born April 6, 1928.

Born in 1928 in Baltimore, Maryland, Eugenia Williams Collier is an English professor at Baltimore's Morgan State University. She has written such books as *Impressions in Asphalt: Images of Urban America* (with Ruthe T. Sheffey; 1969) and *A Bridge to Saying it Well* (with Joel I. Glasser and others; 1970). She also co-edited two volumes of *Afro-American Writing: An Anthology of Prose and Poetry* (1972). In 1976 the Kuumba Workshop in Chicago produced *Ricky,* Collier's one-act **play** based on her

short story by the same title. Her stories are collected in *Spread My Wings* (1992), and *Breeder and Other Stories* (1993).

Further Readings
Black Writers, second edition, Gale, 1994.

Colonialism

Colonialism is a system of political and economic control by a country over a dependent area outside its borders. European colonialism from the fifteenth through the nineteenth centuries usually had economic aims. The colonization of Africa had a tremendous impact on its peoples, culture, and history, which brought with it a great effect on black literature inside and outside the African continent.

In the mid-nineteenth century, the European presence in Africa was limited to Dutch and British colonists in South Africa and British and French soldiers in North Africa. However, in 1869, two pivotal events occurred: the Suez Canal opened and diamonds were discovered in South Africa. The rush was on for European powers to claim African territory, whether by reaching agreements with local leaders or by using military force. Soon Britain, France, Portugal, and Belgium all had sizable African holdings. Germany also had African colonies, but it lost them after World War I. Although styles of rule varied, in general, Africans were given little say in their own destiny, and little was done to develop the colonies, which were viewed merely as exploitable sources of raw materials and markets for manufactured goods. In many instances, Europeans settled in spots with fertile land and a temperate climate, forcing the indigenous populations to relocate to less desirable areas.

This pattern of political and economic oppression had a number of far-reaching consequences. First, the continent was carved up into numerous states whose boundaries were set with little regard for existing political divisions between ethnic groups. This has led to continuing tension and border conflicts. Second, colonialism had a devastating impact on native economic systems. It encouraged economic dependence by such means as substituting cash crops for food crop production. Third, colonialism introduced the concept of white European racial and cultural superiority over black Africans. Blacks were encouraged to relinquish their own identities and cultural heritage. Only two countries in Africa were never colonies: Ethiopia and Liberia. By the twentieth century, however, a powerful desire for independence had set in among the others, bolstered by the experience of African soldiers who fought for France and Great Britain in World Wars I and II.

Ironically, these feelings of nationalism and anticolonialism often found expression in the languages of Africa's colonial rulers. The first literary movement to protest the French policy of **assimilation** and to reassert the positive values of African culture was **negritude,** a movement founded in the 1930s. The negritude philosophy has been outlined in such French-language works as *Liberté I: Négritude et humanisme* (1964; *Freedom I: Negritude and Humanism,* 1974), by **Léopold Sédar Senghor,** who served as president of the Republic of Senegal when that country secured its independence. In the mid-twentieth century, a robust English-language African literature began to emerge as well. Two examples are Nigerian authors **Gabriel Okara**, considered the first significant black African poet to write in English, and **Wole Soyinka**, the first black African to be awarded the Nobel Prize in literature. The latter's **play** *The Lion and the Jewel* (1963) lampoons the unquestioning embrace of Western modernization, but his *A Dance of the Forests* (1963) warns against automatically attributing all of Nigeria's problems to colonialism. In East Africa, one of the most highly regarded writers is novelist and playwright **Ngugi wa Thiong'o.** His **novel** *Weep Not, Child* (1964) attacks colonialism in his native Kenya.

The first colonial area in Africa to gain its independence was Egypt in 1922, and the first in sub-Saharan Africa was Ghana in 1957. The next year, the French colony of Guinea became independent, and most of the remaining French colonies followed suit in 1960. Shortly thereafter, most British colonies became independent as well. However, it was not until the mid-1970s that Portugal relinquished control over its African colonies. In 1988, Africa's last colony, South-West Africa, finally secured independent status as Namibia. Many nonfiction writers have chronicled the human and economic costs of colonialism. Among them is French psychologist and activist **Frantz Fanon**, author of *Les damnés de la terre* (1961; *The Damned,* 1963; **The Wretched of the Earth,** 1965), in which he suggests that political independence is the prerequisite of genuine social and economic change.

Black writers in the Americas have tackled the subject of colonialism in their work as well. West Indian poet and dramatist **Derek Walcott** is well known for his work exploring the impact of colonialism in the Caribbean. His **poetry** earned the Nobel Prize for literature in 1992. The following year, American novelist **Toni Morrison** became the first African American woman to receive that prize. Her novel *Tar Baby* (1981) is an allegorical fable about colonialism that takes place on a fictitious island in the French West Indies.

The Color Purple
Alice Walker
Novel, 1982

The Color Purple, **Alice Walker**'s third **novel**, brought worldwide fame to its author and won both the American Book Award and the Pulitzer Prize. The novel's major theme is womanhood: how black women interact with—and are abused by—men and how they relate to each other. Its secondary themes include self-discovery and growth. The story is told in the form of letters exchanged between two sisters, Celie and Nettie, and in letters Celie addresses to God. Celie is a victim of incest, having been repeatedly raped by her father and threatened by him not to tell anyone. As a result of these rapes, she

This acclaimed novel was adapted for film by Steven Spielberg.

bears two children, who are taken from her. She is also stuck in an unhappy marriage to a man whom she detests so much that she won't speak his name. Celie writes about these incidents in her letters to God.

Celie's life continues unchanged until her husband's former lover, a **blues** singer named Shug Avery, shows up. Shug's sense of independence inspires Celie; they become friends and, for a time, lovers. Shug discovers a series of letters addressed to Celie from Nettie that had been intercepted by Celie's husband and convinces him to stop abusing Celie. She also encourages Celie to choose an occupation for herself so that

she feels less dependent on her husband. Celie establishes her own business, designing and making pants for men and women. Nettie, who has been working as a missionary in Africa with her husband Samuel, reveals in her letters that Celie's abuser was not her biological father and that Celie's children are with her in Africa. At the novel's end, Nettie returns home and the two sisters are reunited.

Colored People

Henry Louis Gates Jr.
Memoir, 1994

A literature theorist who has taught at Yale, Cornell, and Harvard universities, **Henry Louis Gates Jr.** tells the story of his West Virginia childhood in *Colored People*. He grew up in Piedmont—a paper mill town—in essentially segregated surroundings. In the memoir, Gates recalls his youth with fondness, while describing the changes that desegregation brought to black communities. Emphasizing that the people in his neighborhood fostered a strong sense of unity, he revealed that he took pride in his family and valued his community. He also recounted his experiences as a student after integration, pointing out the limited social interaction between blacks and whites and how he became one of the first in his town to enter into an interracial relationship. Gates, who is the recipient of a prestigious MacArthur Foundation Fellowship, stated that he wrote the memoir for his two bi-racial daughters so that they could understand his pre-Civil Rights childhood and its influence on his life.

Cyrus Colter

American novelist and short story writer
Born January 8, 1910.

In his fiction, Colter often emphasizes black individuals' humanity, portraying a wide range of African American experiences, including those of the under-represented middle class. Born in 1910 in Noblesville, Indiana, Colter has been a Chicago lawyer since the 1940s. He began teaching in 1973 at Northwestern University, where he became chair of African American studies. Inspired by the range of characters depicted by Russian authors, Colter turned to writing as a way of addressing issues in African American culture. His collection of short stories entitled *The Beach Umbrella* received the 1970 University of Iowa School of Letters Award for Short Fiction. His **novels** include *The Rivers of Eros* (1972), *The Hippodrome* (1973), *Night Studies* (1979), and *City of Light* (1993). His collection of old and new stories, *The Amoralists and Other Tales* (1989), received critical praise.

Further Readings

Black Writers, first edition, Gale, 1989.

Dictionary of Literary Biography, Volume 33: *Afro-American Fiction Writers after 1955,* Gale, 1984.

Comedy, American Style

Jessie Redmon Fauset
Novel, 1933

Jessie Redmon Fauset's *Comedy, American Style* portrays African American family life in the early twentieth century. Olivia Cary is a light-skinned black woman who wants to be white. Unable to love others because of her own self-loathing, Olivia nonetheless marries Christopher Cary. While her hatred of her own race has little effect upon her attitude towards the couple's first two children, her third child, Oliver—the handsomest and most dark-complexioned—repels her. Two of her children are eventually destroyed by Olivia's color mania: Oliver kills himself at a young age, and Teresa self-destructively enters into a loveless marriage. Olivia herself grows old, impoverished and alone. Only her husband and son Christopher Jr. overcome the destructive nature of Olivia's prejudice. Christopher Jr. eventually marries a black woman who proudly proclaims her African heritage.

Comedy

In strict literary terms, a comedy is a **play** whose aim is to amuse and which typically ends happily. Comedy can assume many forms, including farce and burlesque, and apply various techniques, including parody and **satire**. Examples of stage comedies are *Purlie Victorious* (1953), by **Ossie Davis**, which portrays a Southern black preacher who hopes to establish a racially integrated church, and **Home** (1978), by **Samm-Art Williams**, which was nominated for a Tony Award. In general usage, the comedy label is applied to nontheatrical works as well. Examples of comic writing that were very popular in their day include most of **Paul Laurence Dunbar**'s dialect poems and short stories and, more recently, **Bill Cosby**'s humor books such as *Fatherhood* (1986) and *Time Flies* (1987).

James P. Comer

American nonfiction writer
Born September 25, 1934.

A psychiatrist and author, James Pierpont Comer has received recognition for his medical and educational work, theorizing that improving the academic performance of inner-city children requires a family-like atmosphere in the classroom. Born in 1934 in East Chicago, Indiana, Comer has served as an associate dean at Yale University Medical School since 1969. His first book, *Beyond Black and White* (1972), describes his experiences as a black member of the academic elite. Recognizing a need for a black parenting book, Comer joined Alvin Poussaint in writing *Black Child Care: How to Bring up a Healthy Black Child in America; A Guide to Emotional and Psychological Development* (1975; revised edition published in 1992 as *Raising Black Children: Questions and Answers for Parents and Teachers*). Comer also wrote

School Power: Implications of an Intervention Project (1980) and *Maggie's American Dream: The Life and Times of a Black Family* (1988).

Further Readings
Black Writers, second edition, Gale, 1994.

Compromise
Willis Richardson
Play, first produced 1925, published 1925

Willis Richardson's one-act **play**, his fifth work for adults, portrays two Southern families during the 1920s. In this folk drama, the Lees, an African American family, are brought misfortune over many years by the Carters, a white family. When Joe Lee is killed by Ben Carter, Joe's father Jim is paid off by the Carter family, and uses the money to drink himself to death in despair. Several years later, Alec Lee discovers that Jack Carter has impregnated one of the Lee sisters. The two men fight and Alec breaks Jack's arm. As the play closes, Ben threatens to take legal action against Alec and Alec's mother promises to save her son.

The Concubine
Elechi Amadi
Novel, 1966

Elechi Amadi's first **novel**, *The Concubine,* explores the line between **folklore** and realistic fiction, placing realistic characters in a tribal village against the **supernatural** actions of the evil and controlling Sea King. The novel takes place in a Nigerian village and follows the adult life of the beautiful Ilhuoma, who is loved by Emenike. After Emenike dies somewhat mysteriously after unknowingly affronting the Chief Priest of Amadioha, Madume and Ekweume both pay suit to Ilhuoma. Eventually, Madume and Ekweume also die in unexpected and unusual ways. Amadi explores both the

supernatural element present in African legend as well as the acceptable rituals and conduct characteristic of tribal communities.

Maryse Condé
West Indian novelist and playwright
Born February 11, 1937.

Condé, who sometimes uses the name Maryse Boucolon, was born in Guadeloupe, West Indies, in 1937 and received her Ph.D. from the Sorbonne in 1976. In such **novels** as *Heremakhonon* (1976; English translation, 1982), *Une Saison à Rihata* (1981; *A Season in Rihata,* 1988), *Ségou: Les Murailles de terre* (1984; *Segu,* 1987), *La Vie scélérate* (1987; *Tree of Life,* 1992), she seeks to understand large-scale events on an interpersonal level. *Moi, Tituba, sorcière noire de Salem* (1976; *I, Tituba, Black Witch of Salem,* 1992) is an interpretation of the Salem witch trials. She has also written **plays,** including *Dieu nous l'a donné* (1972; *God Given*) and *Mort d'Oluwemi d'Ajumako* (1973; *Death of a King*). In 1986 Condé received both the Prix Littéraire de la Femme and the Prix Alain Boucheron for *Moi, Tituba.*

Further Readings
Black Writers, second edition, Gale, 1994.

The Conjure Man Dies

Rudolph Fisher
Novel, 1932

Rudolph Fisher's second **novel**, *The Conjure Man Dies: A Mystery Tale of Dark Harlem* is the first African American detective novel. Conjure man N'Gana Frimbo is apparently murdered during an interview with a patron, Jinx Jenkins, who is subsequently framed for the murder. Through a series of flashbacks, the novel explains what has led up to Frimbo's death, and reveals possible motives that the various characters may have had for assaulting Frimbo. Soon the body disappears and Frimbo turns up alive and well; but a murder has been witnessed nonetheless, and Jinx is not yet off the hook. Forensic doctor John Archer succeeds in unraveling the intriguing puzzle with the help of his assistant, Perry Dart.

The Conjure Woman
Charles W. Chesnutt
Short stories, 1899

Charles W. Chesnutt's first volume of short stories, *The Conjure Woman*, consists of a series of stories told in dialect by an ex-slave, Uncle Julius, to a white couple who have moved from Ohio to North Carolina to farm grapes. The couple, John and Annie, learn about the history of the plantation on which they settle by listening to Uncle Julius's stories. While Annie accepts Uncle Julius's stories and sees the underlying brutality of **slavery** in them, John sees them only as an expression of Uncle Julius's self-interest.

Each of Chesnutt's stories traces a strain of magic and how it affected the lives of slaves. For instance, in "The Goophered Grapevine," Uncle Julius describes how the master of the plantation hired a "conjure woman," or practicing witch, to place a curse, or goopher, on the plantation's grapevines to discourage slaves from stealing the fruit. When a new slave eats the grapes before learning about the curse, however, the conjure woman has to place a counter-curse on him. After this the slave's life cycle begins to mimic that of the grapes: vibrant and alive in spring, withered and weak in autumn. This cycle continues until the master of the plantation, who has used the slave's cycles to his own advantage, cuts the vines back too far. The grapes and the goophered slave die at the same time.

Consciencism
Kwame Nkrumah
Nonfiction, 1964

Kwame Nkrumah pleads the case for pan-African unity and a collective resistance to Western capitalist neo-colonialism in *Consciencism: Philosophy and Ideology of Decolonization and Development with Particular Reference to the African Revolution,* a book-length **essay**. The first portion of the book provides an account of the history of philosophy through Karl Marx. Nkrumah then associates the Marxist theory of dialectical materialism with Africa's fight against **colonialism**. Nkrumah goes on to discuss his philosophy of Consciencism, an ideology aimed at containing "the African experience of Islamic and Euro-Christian presence" as well as the "original humanist principles underlying African society." He describes how Consciencism can apply proper action towards winning independence. Nkrumah defines a three-fold heritage for Africans in the form of Islamic and Christian religious influences and traditional social organization and argues that the communalism of tribal life can be refashioned into socialist politics. Nkrumah emphasizes Consciencism's incompatibility with free enterprise and contends that capitalism is a form of refined **slavery**. The work concludes with Nkrumah's translation of his theory of Consciencism into mathematical formulae for the liberation of African territories.

Mercer Cook
American author, editor, and translator
Born March 30, 1903.
Died October 4, 1987.

Will Mercer Cook was the United States ambassador to the Republic of Niger from 1961 to 1964 and the ambassador to Senegal and Gambia from 1964 to 1966. Before and after these political appointments, Cook was a professor of romance languages at Howard University; he also served as the head of the department from 1966 to 1970. He wrote several books, including two volumes of criticism: *Five French Negro Authors* (1943) and, with Stephen Henderson, *The Militant Black Writer in Africa and the United States* (1969). Cook also worked as a translator and edited *The Haitian-American Anthology: Haitian Readings from American Authors* (1944).

Further Readings
Black Writers, first edition, Gale, 1989.

Orde M. Coombs

West Indian nonfiction writer and editor
Born circa 1939.
Died August 27, 1984.

Coombs's collection of **essays** *Do You See My Love For You Growing?* (1972) has been recognized for confronting integral black community issues. His other nonfiction works include *Drums of Life* (1974), which he wrote with Chester Higgins Jr.; *Sleep Late with Your Dreams* (1977); and *Some Time Ago: A Historical Portrait of Black Americans from 1850-1950* (1980), which he also wrote with Higgins. After working as an editor at Doubleday and Co. and McCall Publishing Co., he cohosted the television talk show "Black Conversations" on WPIX-TV in 1975. He also edited *We Speak as Liberators: Young Black Poets* (1970), and *Is Massa Day Dead? Black Moods in the Caribbean* (1974).

Further Readings
Black Writers, first edition, Gale, 1989.

J. California Cooper

American short story writer and novelist
Born in 19(?).

Cooper has been praised for her simple, direct style; her strong characterizations; and her effective use of the African American **oral tradi-**

tion. Born in Berkeley, California, she attended a technical high school and several colleges.

Cooper has published two **novels,** *Family* (1991) and *In Search of Satisfaction* (1994), and several story collections, including *A Piece of Mine* (1984), *Homemade Love* (1986), *Some Soul to Keep* (1987), and *The Matter Is Life* (1992). She has also published several **plays.** Her writings often portray rural or small-town black women struggling to survive and to maintain dignity and self-respect despite the indifference of lovers and husbands. The women in her fiction manage to sustain optimism, courage, and a sense of humor despite the many disappointments and hardships in their lives. Many of her stories are monologues in which a woman recounts a crisis in the life of a friend, relative, or acquaintance. Using dialogue that closely resembles spoken language, Cooper focuses on the bonds between women and emphasizes the importance of these bonds to women's resistance to male oppression.

Further Readings
Black Writers, first edition, Gale, 1989.
Contemporary Literary Criticism, Volume 56, Gale, 1989.

Cora

Character in *Reflex and Bone Structure*

Cora Lee

Character in *The Women of Brewster Place*

Steven Corbin

American novelist
Born October 3, 1953.

Corbin, who has taught fiction writing at the University of California, Los Angeles, since 1988, is the author of *No Easy Place to Be* (1989), which is set during the **Harlem Renaissance** and concentrates on the historical and artistic background of that era. The **novel** combines historical figures and important social issues with fictional characters. *Fragments That Remain* (1993) chronicles the history of a family divided by self-hatred and *A Hundred Days from Now* (1994) examines the relationship between two gay men as one of them struggles against the progression of AIDS.

Further Readings
Black Writers, second edition, Gale, 1994.

Cornelia Smith Fitzgerald

Character in *Proud Shoes: The Story of an American Family*

Corner Boy
Herbert A. Simmons
Novel, 1957

Corner Boy is American novelist and newspaper reporter Herbert A. Simmons's first **novel**. In the narrative a character named Jake Adams tours the streets of St. Louis selling drugs, but there is more to his life than gangs and drug deals. When he falls in love with Armenta, he tells his white gang boss Monk that he wants to go to college to be with her. Armenta's father's disapproval of Jake splits the couple apart, and Jake drops out of college. Jake is nostalgic about his former love, but fate intervenes when a car accident leads to his arrest on drug charges. Even in jail, Jake intends to go on with his life as it was once he is finally released. *Corner Boy* won Simmons a Houghton Mifflin Literary Fellowship.

Sam Cornish
American poet and author of children's literature
Born December 22, 1935.

Samuel James Cornish's reputation as a poet grew during the art revolution of the late 1960s, when he became involved in the **black**

Fiction writer Cooper often focuses on rural African American women in her work.

arts movement. His books of poems include *Generations, and Other Poems* (1964), *Angels* (1965), and *Winters* (1968). *Sam's World: Poems* (1978) is Cornish's largest collection of **poetry** and has been critically lauded. In *Folks Like Me* (1993), Cornish writes of a number of noted African American personalities, constructing a portrait of the migration of African Americans from the South to the North during the middle of the twentieth century. Cornish has also written books for children, including *Your Hand in Mine* (1970) and *My Daddy's People Were Very Black* (1976). He has taught at Highland Park Free School and Emerson College.

See also **Poetry of Sam Cornish**

Further Readings
Black Writers, first edition, Gale, 1989.
Dictionary of Literary Biography, Volume 41: *Afro-American Poets since 1955,* Gale, 1985.

Anita R. Cornwell

American nonfiction writer and author of
children's literature
Born in 1923.

Cornwell is a freelance writer and novelist who works for the Pennsylvania State
Department of Public Welfare. She has published two books: the nonfiction *Black Lesbian
in White America* (1983) and *The Girls of Summer* (1989), a **novel** targeted at juveniles.

Further Readings
Black Writers, second edition, Gale, 1994.

Corregidora

Gayl Jones
Novel, 1975

Corregidora, **Gayl Jones**'s first **novel**, is
the saga of the effects of incest, abuse, and **slavery** upon three generations of African American
women. Blues singer Ursa Corregidora is the
descendant of two generations of former female
slaves, her mother and her grandmother, who
have vowed to submit to the sexual desire of
men only to bear future generations. The sole
purpose of childbearing is to keep alive the
memory of the evils the women were forced to
endure at the hands of their former owner, the
Portuguese plantation-owner Corregidora.
Ursa's husband Mutt is responsible for thwart-
ing Ursa's need to procreate and destroying her
singing career. Jealous of the men who watch
Ursa perform, Mutt insists that Ursa quit
singing. He becomes enraged at her refusal and
throws her down a flight of stairs. She is saved
from death after doctors perform a hysterec-
tomy. Ursa's accumulated bitterness destroys
her second marriage as well. While undergoing
a lengthy recovery, Ursa recalls the stories of her
mother and grandmother about the slaveowner
that fathered both their children, about her marriages, and about the bitterness and misanthropy
that she has inherited from her mother and
grandmother. Near the end of the book, Ursa
finally separates the indoctrinations she has
received from these two women from the reality
of human relationships, accepts that tensions
between men and women are natural, and comes

to a new understanding about her feelings for
her first husband, Mutt.

James D. Corrothers

American poet
Born July 2, 1869.
Died February 12, 1917.

James David Corrothers was one of the
most widely published black poets around the
turn of the twentieth century. Born in Cass
County, Michigan, he longed to write nondialect
verse, but the need to make a living dictated the
style of poems like " 'Way in de Woods, an'
Nobody Dar" (1899) and "A Dixie Thanks-
givin'" (1899). He experimented nevertheless
with broader themes of racial prejudice, faith,
hope, and identity in "An Awful Problem
Solved" (1903), "The Negro Singer" (1912), "At
the Closed Gate of Justice" (1913), and "The
Black Man's Soul" (1915), among others. Corrothers also wrote short stories, and two books,
The Black Cat Club (1902) and *In Spite of the
Handicap* (1916), an **autobiography**. He died of
a stroke in West Chester, Pennsylvania, in 1917.

Further Readings
Black Writers, second edition, Gale, 1994.

Dictionary of Black Literature, Volume 50: *Afro-
American Writers before the Harlem Renaissance,*
Gale, 1986.

Jayne Cortez

American poet
Born May 10, 1936.

Noted as a "jazz" and a performance poet,
Cortez has published as many sound recordings
as printed volumes and has performed throughout North and South America and Europe. Her
poetry often focuses on resistance to racial
injustice and political repression.

Born May 10, 1936, in Arizona, Cortez
spent most of her childhood in Watts, California,
where in 1964 she became the artistic director of
the Watts Repertory Theater Company. She

moved to New York City in 1967 and has lived there since. Her collection *Pissstained Stairs and the Monkey Man's Wares* (1969) established her as a significant figure in the **black arts movement**. **Jazz** musicians are the subjects of many of these poems, which evoke the bleakness of ghetto life and explore themes of death and eroticism. Her poetry of the 1970s ventured more deeply into problems of African American identity and political struggle, treating such issues as the Vietnam war and **apartheid** while continuing to explore her poetry's roots in jazz and **the blues**. She also began composing longer, more complex poems.

From 1977 to 1983, Cortez was writer in residence at Livingston College of Rutgers University. In her 1982 collection *Firespitter,* she continued her concern with social and political issues within more controlled and deliberate verse forms that established her among the American surrealists. Her collection *Poetic Magnetic* was published in 1991.

See also **Poetry of Jayne Cortez**

Further Readings

Black Writers, second edition, Gale, 1994.

Dictionary of Literary Biography, Volume 41: *Afro-American Poets since 1955,* Gale, 1985.

Cory

Character in *Fences*

Bill Cosby

American comedian and actor
Born July 12, 1937.

William Henry Cosby Jr. uses his comedic talent to entertain and educate. His humor revolves around everyday occurrences, especially interactions between siblings and parents. From his early appearances in nightclubs as a stand-up comedian to his portrayal of obstetrician Cliff Huxtable on the television program *The Cosby Show,* as well as throughout his writing, Cosby has continued to uphold the dignity and universality of the black experience.

Bill Cosby, American comedic entertainer.

Cosby was raised in Philadelphia, Pennsylvania, the son of a Navy cook and a domestic worker. Although his father was often away from home for long periods of time, his mother provided a strong moral foundation for the family. Cosby himself was placed in a class for gifted students when he reached high school. However, his interest in athletics distracted him from his studies and he quit school to join the Navy. He later entered Temple University but left without receiving a degree when he began a successful career as a comedian. Cosby later worked as an actor in television and films. He also returned to school and received a doctorate in education. His thesis examines the potential of *Fat Albert and the Cosby Kids,* an animated cartoon based on characters Cosby had created, as an educational tool.

The paternal image of Cliff Huxtable led a publisher to ask Cosby for a humorous book to be called ***Fatherhood*** (1986). Following its success, Cosby wrote *Time Flies* (1987), in which he treats the subject of aging. In *Love and Marriage* (1989), Cosby draws upon his own marriage for an advice book on maintaining domestic tranquility, and he reminisces about his own youth in Philadelphia in *Childhood* (1991), comparing that period of his life with the experiences of children today.

Further Readings

Adams, Barbara Johnston, *The Picture Life of Bill Cosby,* F. Watts, 1986.

Black Writers, second edition, Gale, 1994.

Johnson, Robert E., *Bill Cosby: In Words and Pictures,* Johnson Publishing, 1987.

Smith, R. L., *Cosby,* St. Martin's, 1986.

Ellis Jonathan Cose

American journalist and nonfiction writer
Born February 20, 1951.

The political and social activities of the late 1960s helped lead Cose to a career in **journalism**, where he hoped writing could help bridge differences among people. In 1970, he became a columnist for the *Chicago Sun-Times,* writing about Chicago communities. In 1976, he was assigned to cover Jimmy Carter's presidential campaign, a post that took him out of Chicago and exposed him to new issues. His experiences are reflected in *Energy and the Urban Crisis* (1978), *The Quiet Crisis* (1987), and *The Press* (1989). His book *A Nation of Strangers* (1992) traces immigration and prejudice in United States history and *The Rage of a Privileged Class* (1994) examines middle-class African America. In 1995 he published *A Man's World: How Real Is Male Privilege—and How High Is Its Price?,* in which he suggests that males hold no real power over others. Cose has served as a contributing editor to *Newsweek.*

Further Readings

Black Writers, second edition, Gale, 1994.

The Cotillion

John Oliver Killens
Novel, 1971

Modeled after the "dozens," a game won by the worst insult, **John Oliver Killens**'s *The Cotillion; or, One Good Bull Is Half the Herd* charmed critics who went along with its high-spirited clowning. However, the **novel** is serious in intent, satirizing the white middle-class values of socially aspiring African Americans. The plot centers on the annual soiree or cotillion put on by the "Femmes Fatales," an exclusive Brooklyn women's club. The main character in the novel is named Daphne Doreen Braithwaite Lovejoy; she does not approve of her husband Matt's consorting with the guys at the barbershop. Their daughter Yoruba Evelyn has been brought up with no mention of her mother's homeland, Barbados. The denouement of the novel comes when her boyfriend returns home from Vietnam, interrupts their party, and stages a walkout.

Joseph Seamon Cotter Jr.

American poet and playwright
Born September 2, 1895.
Died February 3, 1919.

Cotter's emergence as a poet was cut short by his death from tuberculosis at the age of twenty-three. The son of **Joseph Seamon Cotter Sr.**, Cotter attended college at Fisk University. His **poetry,** which often addresses the cruel treatment of black Americans, is collected in *The Band of Gideon and Other Lyrics* (1918). His one-act **play,** *On the Fields of France* (1920), was published posthumously in *Crisis* magazine.

Further Readings

Dictionary of Literary Biography, Volume 50: *Afro-American Writers before the Harlem Renaissance,* Gale, 1986.

Joseph Seamon Cotter Sr.

American poet, dramatist, and
short story writer
Born February 2, 1861.
Died March 14, 1949.

Cotter is best known as the author of
*Caleb, the Degenerate: A Study of the Types,
Customs, and Needs of the American Negro*
(1901), one of the earliest dramas by an African
American writer. A respected educator and com-
munity leader dedicated to overcoming negative
African American stereotypes, Cotter also wrote
sonnets, folk ballads, and black dialect poems.

Cotter was born near Bardstown, Kentucky, the illegitimate son of a Scotch-Irishman
and the freeborn daughter of an American slave.
He left school at age eight and educated himself
while working at a variety of odd jobs. Returning to school as an adult, Cotter became a
teacher, and he established a black community
near Louisville known as "Little Africa" in
1891. Two years later, he founded a school
named after the black poet **Paul Laurence Dunbar**, who visited him the following year and
praised Cotter's **poetry.**

Cotter supported the work ethic as a
means of social and economic reform for black
Americans, and he expressed his conviction in
"Dr. Booker T. Washington to the National
Negro Business League," a poem published in
his collection *A White Song and a Black One*
(1909). Cotter's only drama, *Caleb, the Degenerate,* was written in blank verse and probably
never staged during his lifetime. While some
critics regard the **play** as conciliatory to a white
audience, others have evaluated it in different
terms, citing an African American literary tradition in which social protest was often disguised.
Cotter later broke from **Booker T. Washington**'s
beliefs and published poetry in support of **W. E.
B. Du Bois**, who opposed Washington's emphasis on vocational training as the key to social
advancement. Cotter published his last collection
of miscellaneous work in 1947. He died in 1949.

Further Readings
Black Literature Criticism, Gale, 1992.
Black Writers, first edition, Gale, 1989.

Dictionary of Literary Biography, Volume 50: *Afro-
American Writers before the Harlem Renaissance,*
Gale, 1986.

William Couch Jr.

American editor, poet, and essayist

Couch taught at North Carolina College
(now Carolina Central University) from
1962 to 1978. He contributed articles and poems
to periodicals, including *CLA Journal, Negro
Story,* and *Phylon,* before editing *New Black
Playwrights: An Anthology* (1968), a collection
of six plays written by **Douglas Turner Ward,
Adrienne Kennedy, Lonne Elder, Ed Bullins,**
and **William Wellington Mackey.** Couch's
introduction to the volume outlines the history
of blacks in the American theater from 1858 to
1968. Couch taught and held administrative
positions at Federal City College (now University of the District of Columbia) from 1968
through 1990. In 1980 he married Ola B. Criss,
a teacher of gerontology. Since 1991, Couch has
lived in Africa.

Further Readings
Black Writers, second edition, Gale, 1994.

The Count

Character in *The Catacombs*

Country Place

Ann Petry
Novel, 1947

Country Place, **Ann Petry**'s second
novel, tells the story of two intertwining sets of
characters residing in the quiet town of Lennox,
Connecticut. The central figure of one narrative
line is Johnnie Roane, a World War II veteran
who returns home to find his beautiful wife
involved with another man. The focus of the
second story line is Mrs. Gramby, a respectable
aristocrat who is burdened by a weak son and a
materialistic daughter-in-law. Petry presents the

novel through the voices of Doc, the town druggist who philosophizes as well as narrates, and Weasel, a cab driver and gossip who not only spreads news but also impels action.

Cousin Bee

Character in *Purlie Victorious*

Craig Butler

Character in *A Hero Ain't Nothin' but a Sandwich*

"Creole" Du Bois

Character in *The Landlord*

Crisis

W. E. B. Du Bois
Magazine, 1910-1934

One of the founding members of the **National Association for the Advancement of Colored People** (NAACP), **W. E. B. Du Bois** served as publicity director and as editor of the organization's magazine, *Crisis*. Du Bois and the leaders of the NAACP were often at odds during Du Bois's twenty-five year tenure, each vying for control of the magazine's content. By 1918 *Crisis* magazine enjoyed a readership of 18,000. The far-ranging subject matter of the magazine included politics, science, culture, education, and art.

In his early years as editor, Du Bois focused on his diatribes against **discrimination**, particularly lynchings and disenfranchisement. He advocated the use of legal means—legal challenges, political maneuvering, publicity—to lobby for equality. He also treated the issues of crimes against blacks and crimes perpetrated by blacks. A longstanding source of editorial material was **Booker T. Washington**'s accommodationist political views, which ran directly opposite those of the integrationist NAACP. Another recipient of harsh criticism by Du Bois was **Marcus Garvey,** founder of the Universal

Negro Improvement Association, another proponent of **segregation**. With the outbreak of World War I, Du Bois voiced his patriotism, urging support for the U.S. government. However, after the war, upon investigating the treatment of black servicemen, Du Bois decried the widespread **racism** black soldiers suffered at the hand of their white compatriots. This experience focused Du Bois' political interests on socialism, trade unionism, and international efforts for emancipation. But by 1930 Du Bois saw little progress made through any means and became disillusioned. During the Great Depression, through *Crisis,* Du Bois reversed his position on many issues, particularly segregation, espousing political, economic, cultural, and educational separatism. He also began to applaud such tactics as boycotting, retaliatory ostracism, and the use of threats. This new stance puzzled his friends and brought him into conflict with the NAACP. He was forced to resign as the editor of *Crisis* and from the NAACP in 1934.

Crook

Character in *Mama*

Ricardo Cortez Cruz

American novelist and short story writer
Born August 10, 1964.

Cruz writes in a fast-paced style about black life and culture. His first **novel,** *Straight Outta Compton* (1992), received the Charles H. and N. Mildred Nilon Excellence in Minority Fiction Award and is considered the first major rap novel, borrowing elements from that music genre. *Five Days of Bleeding* (1992), his second novel, acquired its title from a reggae song. Cruz has contributed **short stories** to various literary magazines and has taught English at Heartland Community College in Bloomington, Indiana, since 1992.

Further Readings
Black Writers, second edition, Gale, 1994.

Victor Hernández Cruz

Puerto Rican-born American poet
Born February 6, 1949.

Cruz helped to usher in the Neorican writer's movement, the creative effort of Puerto Rican-born writers raised in the United States who write in an English dialect inspired by Spanish and black English. In works influenced by his musical background and memories of life in the tropics, Cruz attempts to portray the reality of Spanish Harlem and, more broadly, the urban experience in America. Critics cite the wit, energy, and imagination of his poems, which are collected in *Papo Got His Gun! and Other Poems* (1966), written when Cruz was seventeen, *Snaps* (1969), *Mainland* (1973), *Tropicalization* (1976), *By Lingual Wholes* (1982), and *Red Beans* (1991).

See also **Poetry of Victor Hernández Cruz**

Further Readings

Black Writers, second edition, Gale, 1994.

Dictionary of Literary Biography, Volume 41: *Afro-American Poets since 1955,* Gale, 1985.

Crying in the Wilderness

Desmond Tutu
Nonfiction, 1982

Crying in the Wilderness: The Struggle for Justice in South Africa is a compendium of **speeches**, interviews and sermons given by **Desmond Tutu** while he served as the General Secretary of the South African Council of Churches, between 1978 and 1980. In this collection Tutu champions non-violent reform, but also predicts bloodshed and rioting will ensue if conditions in South Africa do not improve. Tutu recounts his experiences of having his passport revoked and serving time in jail. He insists that there is no Christian Scriptural defense for **apartheid**, as his opposers claim. He also counters accusations that his politics are Marxist or

Communist. Editor John Webster includes introductions to each section, to place the speeches within historical context. Events such as the Steven Biko case are also covered.

Crystal

Character in *for colored girls who have considered suicide*

Cudjoe

Character in *Philadelphia Fire*

Countee Cullen

American poet, novelist, and dramatist
Born May 30, 1903.
Died January 9, 1946.

Cullen is best remembered for the five early volumes of **poetry** that established him as a luminary in the **Harlem Renaissance**. He was committed to themes of **Pan-Africanism**, racial equality, and artistic freedom, yet he feared being categorized as a strictly "racial" poet and measured himself against the formalist standards of the nineteenth century, especially those of romantic poet John Keats.

Cullen is believed to have been born in Louisville, Kentucky, on May 30, 1903. In 1918, following the death of his guardian grandmother, he was taken in by Reverend Frederick A. Cullen, a Methodist pastor and a central figure in Harlem politics. At age nineteen Cullen entered New York University, where he received several awards, including *Poetry* magazine's John Reed Memorial Prize, for such poems as "The Ballad of the Brown Girl." Upon graduation he published *Color* (1925), his well-received first volume of poetry. In 1926, after earning a master's degree from Harvard, he became an assistant editor at *Opportunity*. There, he created "The Dark Tower," a column wherein he aired his opinions on African American art and social responsibility.

In 1927, Cullen published his second poetry volume, *Copper Sun,* and edited *Carol-*

Countee Cullen, a preeminent poet of the Harlem Renaissance.

ing Dusk: An Anthology of Verse by Negro Poets. His 1929 volume, *The Black Christ and Other Poems,* furthers his earlier themes of death, black identity, racial conflict, and **Christianity**.

In 1932, Cullen published his first and only **novel,** *One Way to Heaven.* Receiving mixed reviews, the work contains two dissimilar plotlines: a love story and a rollicking **satire** of Harlem's intellectuals. In 1934, Cullen began teaching English and French in New York. He also wrote two collections of didactic children's stories, translated a stage production of *Medea* (1935), and collaborated on the writing of several **plays.** One of these, *St. Louis Woman* (1971), was heavily criticized for its perceived focus on the seamier side of black life, but it eventually opened on Broadway shortly after Cullen's death in early 1946.

See also **Poetry of Countee Cullen**

Further Readings

Black Literature Criticism, Gale, 1992.

Dictionary of Literary Biography, Volume 51: *Afro-American Writers from the Harlem Renaissance to 1940,* Gale, 1987.

William Waring Cuney

American poet
Born May 6, 1906.
Died June 30, 1976.

Considered a largely overlooked poet of the **Harlem Renaissance**, Cuney experimented with black speech and music, especially the **Blues**. Born in Washington, D.C., Cuney attended Howard University and Lincoln University, and later studied music in New England and Italy. His first collection of **poetry,** *Chain Gang Chant,* was published in 1930. Cuney served in the U.S. Army during World War II, after which he attended Columbia University, where he continued to write. In addition to several broadside publications, Cuney published *Puzzles* (1960) and *Storefront Church* (1973), which include the widely anthologized poem "No Images." Under the name Waring Cuney, he also coedited *Lincoln University Poets: Centennial Anthology, 1854-1954* (1954) with **Langston Hughes** and Bruce M. Wright.

See also **Poetry of William Waring Cuney**

Further Readings

Black Writers, first edition, Gale, 1989.

Dictionary of Literary Biography, Volume 51: *Afro-American Writers from the Harlem Renaissance to 1940,* Gale, 1987.

Curie

Character in *A Short Walk*

Cynthia

Character in *Roots: The Saga of an American Family*

Our song, our toil, our cheer, and warning have been given to this nation in blood-brotherhood. Are not these gifts worth the giving? Is not this work and striving? Would America have been America without her Negro people?

The Souls of Black Folk,
W. E. B. Du Bois, 1903

David Dabydeen
Guyanese poet, novelist, and
nonfiction writer
Born December 9, 1955.

Dabydeen's **poetry** collection *Slave Song* (1985) earned him the Commonwealth Poetry Prize. The poems in the volume, lauded by critics, portray life on the sugar plantations in Guyana and are written in Guyanese Creole, which combines various dialects. Dabydeen, who immigrated to England in 1969, has also written *Hogarth's Blacks: Images of Blacks in Eighteenth Century English Art* (1985), which explores the nature of black characters that occur frequently in William Hogarth's works; *Caribbean Literature: A Teacher's Handbook* (1986); *Hogarth and Walpolean England* (1988); the **novels** *The Intended* (1991) and *Disappearance* (1993); and the poetry volume *Turner* (1994).

Further Readings
Black Writers, first edition, Gale, 1989.

Contemporary Literary Criticism, Volume 34, Gale, 1985.

Daddy
Character in *Mine Boy*

Daddy King: An Autobiography
Martin Luther King Sr., with Clayton Riley
Autobiography, 1980

Martin Luther King Sr.'s memoirs trace his life from his childhood in rural Georgia through his rise to prominence as minister of a large Atlanta congregation, community leader, and political activist. King provides numerous insights into the intricate workings of racial inequality in the South, Atlanta politics in the years preceding the **civil rights movement**, and the development of the civil rights movement itself in the 1950s and 1960s. While cautioning that much progress remains to be made towards eradicating **racism** and achieving world peace, King reaffirms his belief in non-violence and racial equality.

Daddy Was a Number Runner
Louise Meriwether
Novel, 1970

In **Louise Meriwether**'s *Daddy Was a Number Runner,* twelve-year-old Francie Coffin narrates a series of episodes that illustrate her coming of age in Depression-era Harlem. An avid reader and capable student, she indulges her adolescent curiosity about boys while resisting their sexual advances, as well as the sometimes violent advances of several men. She draws her own identity and strength from her disadvantaged family and community, both torn apart by social and economic forces. Her father, who can hardly support his family as janitor, piano player, and numbers runner for the mob, eventually leaves; one brother becomes a pimp and the other quits school to work; her proud mother works outside their home but strengthens Francie by her courage. The resourceful Francie survives the physical and psychological onslaughts as she is initiated into womanhood.

Bernard B. Dadie
Ivorian statesperson, novelist, poet, and
playwright
Born in 1916.

Bernard Binlin Dadie belongs to a group of noted African authors writing in French that includes **Chinua Achebe**, **Camara Laye**, and **Wole Soyinka**. Born in Assinie on the Ivory Coast, Dadie attended school in his country and in Senegal before beginning his career in government. An early activist for African independence, in 1961 Dadie became the Ivory Coast's director of Cultural Affairs for the Ministry of National Education, a post that he still holds. His numerous works include **novels, poetry,**

plays, short stories, and **essays.** Dadie's most acclaimed works are *Patron de New York* (1964), a novel that won the Lauréat du Grand Prix Littéraire de l'Afrique Noire, and *Le Pagne noir: Contes africaines* (1955; *The Black Cloth: A Collection of African Folktales,* 1987).

Further Readings
Black Writers, first edition, Gale, 1989.

The Dahomean
Frank Yerby
Novel, 1972

Frank Yerby's **novel** *The Dahomean* examines the life of a nineteenth-century prince of the African nation of Dahomey. Nyasanu, the second son of village chief Gbenu, rejects his culture's practice of polygamy and marries Agbale. Distinguishing himself in a war against a neighboring tribe in which his father is killed, Nyasanu becomes chief. Against his better judgment, he accepts other wives from his late father and from the king, Gezo. As Nyasanu rises to the position of governor, he is betrayed by one of his wives and his half-brother. In an effort to prove his good faith and humility to his constituents, Nyasanu takes up residence in an unprotected shelter in the outskirts of his village. He is soon captured by an unfriendly tribe and sold into **slavery.**

Dale
Character in *Reflex and Bone Structure*

Les Damnés de la terre
Please see *The Wretched of the Earth*

Dan
Character in *A Question of Power*

Daryl Cumber Dance
American folklorist
Born January 17, 1938.

Dance's works focus on African American and Caribbean **folklore.** Born in Richmond, Virginia, Dance earned her Ph.D. at the University of Virginia. She received a Ford Foundation fellowship in 1970 and a Fulbright grant for study in Jamaica in 1978. Her works include *Shuckin' and Jivin': Folklore from Contemporary Black Americans* (1978), *Folklore from Contemporary Jamaicans* (1985), *Fifty Caribbean Writers: A Bio-Bibliographical-Critical Sourcebook* (1986), *Long Gone: The Mecklenburg Six and the Theme of Escape in Black Folklore* (1987), and *New World Adams: Conversations with West Indian Writers* (1992). In 1993, Dance became professor of English at the University of Richmond.

Further Readings
Black Writers, second edition, Gale, 1994.

A Dance of the Forests
Wole Soyinka
Play, first produced 1960, published 1963

Commissioned as part of Nigeria's Independence Celebrations, **Wole Soyinka**'s *A Dance of the Forests* is a cautionary tale for a nation on the brink of assuming power. The **play** opens as a group of tribal leaders meet in the clearing of a forest to summon the egungun. The egungun, or the spirits of the dead honored in the Yoruba tradition, are one of many elements of Yoruba **folklore** that Soyinka incorporates into his play. Adenebi, the orator, announces that by summoning the dead, the nation is celebrating its heritage and its heroism. When the ground breaks open, however, the husband and wife who arise are pathetic; Dead Man and Dead Woman both have sorrowful histories. In the past, Kharibu, a cruel king who lashed out whenever opposed, sold Dead Man into **slavery** in exchange for a cask of rum. Kharibu symbolizes the past that is sometimes falsely revered by the living, illustrating that black leaders have been capable of barbarism, as have white leaders. Kharibu's involvement in the slave trade sends the message that some Africans shared the guilt for slavery. Meanwhile, Dead Woman is pregnant as she has been for a hundred generations. The baby she gives birth to symbolizes the future of Nigeria.

When the egungun convey the unwelcome message that slavery is a permanent feature of African history, the tribal leaders refuse to listen and mistreat the dead pair. The ungracious behavior of the tribal leaders is proof that the message the egungun have delivered is at least partially true. Because the leaders reject the past and are inhospitable to their deceased guests, it seems clear that the sad pattern of African history will continue into the future. Soyinka underscores his themes musically, with dancing, drumming, and singing. The message for a newly independent Nigeria is clear: the end of British rule alone will not solve all of Nigeria's problems.

Raymond Garfield Dandridge
American poet
Born in 1882.
Died February 24, 1930.

Known as "The Paul Laurence Dunbar of Cincinnati," Dandridge was most famous for his black dialect poems. Born near Cincinnati, Dandridge suffered a stroke in 1912 that deprived him of the use of his legs and right arm, after which he learned to write with his left hand and composed **poetry.** During his short career, Dandridge published three books—*Penciled Poems* (1917), *The Poet and Other Poems* (1920), and *Zalka Peetruza and Other Poems* (1928). His early work deals primarily with folk life and humor but his later poetry, in which Dandridge discusses issues of racial identity and rebellion, reflects the influence of the **Harlem Renaissance**.

Further Readings
Black Writers, first edition, Gale, 1989.

Dictionary of Literary Biography, Volume 51: *Afro-American Writers from the Harlem Renaissance to 1940,* Gale, 1987.

Rita B. Dandridge
American scholar and author
Born September 16, 1940.

Rita Bernice Dandridge is an authority on African American literature and women's studies. Born in Richmond, Virginia, Dandridge attended Virginia Union and Howard universities before beginning an academic career in literature. Dandridge's works include *Relevant Expository Techniques and Programmed Grammar* (1971), written under the name Rita Dandridge Simons, with DeLois M. Flemons, *Ann Allen Shockley: An Annotated Primary and Secondary Bibliography* (1987), and *Black Women's Blues: A Literary Anthology, 1934-1988* (1992). She contributed to *All the Women Are White, All the Blacks Are Men, But Some of Us Are Brave* (1982), edited by **Gloria T. Hull** and others, and has written other articles and reviews. In 1974 Dandridge was made professor of English at Norfolk State University in Virginia.

Further Readings
Black Writers, second edition, Gale, 1994.

Daniel Torch
Character in *Let the Lion Eat Straw*

Margaret Danner
American poet
Born January 12, 1915.

Margaret Essie Danner has been praised for her imagery, her messages of protest, and her celebration of African heritage. Danner was born to Caleb and Naomi Danner, in Pryorsburg, Kentucky, but subsequently moved to Chicago, where she attended high school and studied at both Loyola and Northwestern Universities. She worked with Karl Shapiro and Paul Engle, and received second prize in the Poetry Workshop of the Midwestern Writers Conference in 1945. In

1951, she published a series of four poems, "Far from Africa," in *Poetry: The Magazine of Verse.* These poems won her the John Hay Whitney fellowship, an award intended to help her travel to Africa, though she did not make the trip for many years.

In 1961, Danner accepted a position as poet-in-residence at Wayne State University in Detroit, where she helped establish Boone House, a community arts center primarily for children. This concern for the black community surfaces in her work, especially in her collaboration with **Dudley Randall** entitled *Poem Counterpoem* (1966). The book consists of poems by each author on alternating pages, in which they treat a wide variety personal and political subjects.

Danner finally traveled to Africa in 1966, an experience which heightened her commitment to the traditions of that continent. After her return, she published *Iron Lace* (1968) and in 1973 participated in the Phillis Wheatley Poetry Festival, a gathering of leading black women poets. *The Down of a Thistle* (1976), an illustrated volume, contains poems constructed around African images and symbols as well as protest poems such as "The Endangered Species."

See also **Poetry of Margaret Danner**

Further Readings
Black Writers, first edition, Gale, 1989.

Danny

Character in *Manchild in the Promised Land*

Daphne Doreen Braithwaite Lovejoy

Character in *The Cotillion*

Dark Days in Ghana

Kwame Nkrumah
Political history, 1968

Kwame Nkrumah's *Dark Days in Ghana* describes the February, 1966, military coup—masterminded by police commissioner John Harlley —that overthrew Ghana's government and led to Nkrumah's exile in Guinea. Nkrumah relates the events immediately preceding the rebellion, including his trip with the president of Ghana and other administrative officials to Hanoi to discuss ending the Vietnam conflict. Discussing the apparent lack of resistance to the revolt, Nkrumah suggests that instances of severe brutality toward government defenders intimidated the average Ghanaian citizen into accepting the usurpers. He further explains the internal government structure and how it affected public attitudes and reactions, concluding with a broader application of Ghana's experience to other African countries.

Dark Ghetto: Dilemmas of Social Power

Kenneth B. Clark
Nonfiction, 1965

Based on **Kenneth B. Clark**'s experiences as founder and chair of Harlem Youth Opportunities Unlimited (HARYOU) from 1962 to 1964, *Dark Ghetto* analyzes the dynamics of racial inequality in Harlem in the early 1960s and proposes a pragmatic approach to the struggle for racial equality. In a chapter devoted to "ghetto psychology," Clark examines the psychological and social impact of life in the ghetto on its inhabitants. Citing test scores and extensive social and economic data, Clark debunks the argument that "cultural deprivation" alone can account for the overall poor academic performance of ghetto youths. Clark blames instead the inadequacy of ghetto schools, and calls for immediate action by government, business, and industrial leaders to provide better education for inner-city youths. Clark's ideas were influential in the formation of government anti-poverty programs during the late 1960s.

Dark Symphony: Negro Literature in America

James A. Emanuel and Theodore L. Gross, editors
Anthology, 1968

Although it contains some of the authors' lesser known works, *Dark Symphony* represents a cross-section of representative African American literature from the mid-1800s through the late 1960s. In total, the book, edited by **James A. Emanuel** and Theodore L. Gross, anthologizes **poetry**, short stories, **essays**, and memoirs from thirty-four African American writers. *Dark Symphony* is divided into four sections, the first being "Early Literature," which includes the works of writers such as **Frederick Douglass** and **W. E. B. Du Bois**. "Negro Awakening" focusses on the writings of **Claude McKay** and **Countee Cullen**, among others. The works of **Langston Hughes**, **Richard Wright**, **Ralph Ellison**, and **James Baldwin**, are featured in the section "Major Authors." The section "Contemporary Literature" includes selections from a number of authors, including **Arna Bontemps**, **Gwendolyn Brooks**, and **James A. Emanuel**.

Biographies of the authors, introductory essays outlining different periods in the history of black literature, and an extensive bibliography accompany the selected texts. *Dark Symphony*'s detailed introductions to each section attempt to firmly establish a black racial identity and a distinctive race consciousness among African American writers.

Darlene

Character in *The Hippodrome*

Doris Davenport

American poet and actress
Born in 1915.
Died June 18, 1980.

Early in her career, Davenport acted in several movies, including *Kid Millions* (1934), *The Westerner* (1940), and *Behind the News*

(1940). She later began to write **poetry,** most of which was published posthumously in *It's Like This* (1980), *Eat Thunder and Drink Rain* (1982), and *Voodoo Chile, Slight Return* (1991).

Further Readings
Black Writers, second edition, Gale, 1994.

Davey Brooks

Character in *Teacup Full of Roses*

David

Character in *Beetlecreek, Giovanni's Room,* and *The View from Coyaba*

David Ragin

Character in *The Sign in Sidney Brustein's Window*

David Weldon

Character in *The Soul Brothers and Sister Lou*

Davis

Character in *Eva's Man*

Angela Davis

American essayist and autobiographer
Born January 26, 1944.

Best known as a political activist during the 1960s, Davis has worked for more than two decades against economic and racial injustice and is still actively involved in the Communist Party.

Angela Yvonne Davis was born January 26, 1944, in Birmingham, Alabama, the daughter of B. Frank and Sallye E. Davis. She received her B.A. from Brandeis University in 1965 and attended graduate school at the University of California, San Diego, where she became a member of the Communist Party in 1968.

Davis's growing radicalism damaged her academic career and the University of California dismissed her as an assistant professor in 1969. In 1970, she was associated with an escape attempt from a California courthouse. Several months later, Davis was implicated in a violent incident that led to her arrest on murder, kidnapping, and conspiracy charges. She was subsequently acquitted. Soon thereafter she took up a teaching position at San Francisco State University.

In 1971, Davis published **essays** in a collection entitled *If They Come in the Morning: Voices of Resistance,* in which she offers a Marxist analysis of racial oppression in America. In ***Angela Davis: An Autobiography*** (1974), Davis describes how her commitment found expression in communism. In 1980, she was the Communist Party candidate for vice president of the United States. Davis's communism was also the basis of her book on the feminist movement, *Women, Race and Class* (1981). In 1989, she published ***Women, Culture, and Politics***, a collection of her **speeches**. In 1991, she transferred to the University of California at Santa Cruz, where she was appointed to a President's Chair in 1995.

Further Readings
Black Writers, second edition, Gale, 1994.

Angela Davis in 1969, one year after joining the Communist Party.

Arthur P. Davis
American educator and critic
Born November 21, 1904.

Arthur Paul Davis has taught and written about African American literature during much of his career. Born in Hampton, Virginia, Davis attended Columbia University, where he earned his Ph.D. in English. From 1929 to 1944, he taught at Virginia Union University, coediting *The Negro Caravan* (1941) and writing *Isaac Watts: His Life and Works* (1943). In 1944, Davis began teaching at Howard University. During his time at Howard, Davis has coedited *Cavalcade: Negro American Writers from 1760 to the Present* (1971), *The New Negro Renaissance: An Anthology* (1975), and the two-volume *The New Cavalcade: African American Writing from 1760 to the Present* (1991), and has written *From the Dark Tower: Afro-American Writers from 1900 to 1960* (1974). Davis became professor emeritus at Howard University in 1969.

Further Readings
Black Writers, second edition, Gale, 1994.

Benjamin O. Davis Jr.
American military officer
and autobiographer
Born December 18, 1912.

Davis was the first black to graduate from the U.S. Military Academy at West Point in the twentieth century. He served in the U.S. Air Force from 1932 to 1970, during which time he commanded the first all-black fighter squadron—the Tuskegee Airmen—during World War II, served as chief of staff for the United Nations Command and U.S. Forces in Korea from 1965 to 1967, earned three distinguished service medals and numerous other military recognitions, and retired as a lieutenant general. He also served with the Pentagon and the U.S. Department of Transportation. Davis's **autobiography**, *Benjamin O. Davis Jr., American* (1991), presents an account of his struggles to succeed in the armed forces despite racial **discrimination**.

Further Readings
Black Writers, second edition, Gale, 1994.

Charles T. Davis

American critic and essayist
Born April 29, 1918.
Died in 1981.

Charles Twitchell Davis is considered an influential scholar of black and nineteenth-century American literature. Davis began his teaching career at New York University, where he and Gay Wilson Allen compiled *Walt Whitman's Poems: Selections with Critical Aids* (1955). Davis later taught at Princeton University, Pennsylvania State University, and the University of Iowa. In 1972, Davis became professor of English and chair of the Afro-American studies department at Yale University, where he and **Henry Louis Gates Jr.** coedited *The Slave's Narrative* (1985). In his posthumously published *Black Is the Color of the Cosmos: Essays on Afro-American Literature and Culture, 1942-1981* (1982), Davis explores black literature from nineteenth-century American **romanticism** to the **black arts movement** of the 1960s, focusing on authors such as **Frederick Douglass** and **Charles W. Chesnutt**.

Further Readings
Black Writers, first edition, Gale, 1989.

Frank Marshall Davis

American poet and journalist
Born December 31, 1905.
Died July 26, 1987.

Through his **poetry** in the 1930s and 1940s, Davis portrayed black life in the United States, protested racial inequalities, and promoted black pride. Many critics praised his work for its social consciousness, while others labeled it propaganda.

Davis was born in Arkansas City, Kansas, and grew up surrounded by the **racism** that would later shape much of his poetry. He attended Friends University and Kansas State Agricultural College in the 1920s. In 1927 Davis moved to Chicago and worked for several black newspapers. Encouraged by the attention his poem "Chicago's Congo (Sonata for an Orchestra)" received, Davis published his first volume of poetry, *Black Man's Verse* (1935), for which he was awarded a grant from the Julius Rosenwald Foundation. This work was followed by *I Am the American Negro* (1937) and *47th Street* (1948), the latter of which is considered by some critics to be the culmination of Davis's poetic development.

In 1948 Davis moved to Hawaii, where he operated a wholesale paper business and wrote a regular weekly column for a local newspaper. Rediscovered by literary critic Stephen Henderson and poet **Dudley Randall**, Davis toured several black colleges in 1973. As a result, a new generation learned to appreciate his social awareness and racial pride. Davis died in Honolulu, Hawaii.

See also **Poetry of Frank Marshall Davis**

Further Readings
Dictionary of Literary Biography, Volume 51: *Afro-American Writers from the Harlem Renaissance to 1940,* Gale, 1987.
King, Woodie, *The Forerunners: Black Poets in America,* Howard University Press, 1975.

George B. Davis

American novelist and nonfiction writer
Born November 29, 1939.

A writer, university professor, and businessperson, Davis is best known for his work on the status of African Americans in management positions, reported in his *Black Life in Corporate America: Swimming in the Mainstream* (1982), written with Glegg Watson.

Born in Shepherdstown, West Virginia, on November 29, 1939, Davis received his B.A. from Colgate University in 1961. After serving in the U.S. Air Force from 1961 to 1968, he worked as a journalist and earned an M.F.A from Columbia University in 1971, the same year he published his **novel** *Coming Home.* He joined the faculty of City University of New York in 1974 and became an assistant professor at Rutgers University in 1978. Davis is also cofounder and president of Black Swan Communications and president of Contemporary Communications, a marketing firm.

Further Readings
Black Writers, first edition, Gale, 1989.

Michael D. Davis
American journalist
Born January 12, 1939.

Davis was born in Washington, D.C., on January 12, 1939. The first suit challenging segregated schools in the nation's capital was brought in his name in 1943. After graduating from Morehouse College in 1963, Davis wrote for the *Atlanta Constitution* and the *Baltimore Afro-American,* winning a **National Association for the Advancement of Colored People** (NAACP) award for his coverage of black troops during the Vietnam war. Davis has also reported for the *Baltimore Sun,* the *San Diego Union,* and the *Washington Star,* and has worked as a reporter, editor, and commentator for Washington, D.C., television news programs. He has written *Black Women in Olympic Track and Field* (1992), *Our World* (in press), and, with Hunter R. Clark, *Thurgood Marshall: Warrior at the Bar, Rebel on the Bench* (1992).

Further Readings
Black Writers, second edition, Gale, 1994.

Ossie Davis
American dramatist, screenwriter, and novelist
Born December 18, 1917.

In an acting and writing career that has spanned five decades, Davis has explored contemporary racial and social issues, producing **plays** such as **Purlie Victorious** (1961) as well

Ossie Davis, a longtime actor and writer, in 1987.

as the musical adaptation *Purlie* (1970). In addition, he is recognized, along with his wife, **Ruby Dee**, for his commitment to the **civil rights movement**.

Davis was born on December 18, 1917, in Cogdell, Georgia. While attending high school, he began writing and acting in plays, an interest that was strengthened during his years at Howard University. He made his debut on Broadway in 1946, playing the title role in *Jeb* and gaining the attention of critics. In the production Davis costarred with Ruby Dee, whom he married in 1948.

Davis's first important work as a dramatist was the one-act play *Alice in Wonder* (1952), which he expanded as *The Big Deal* (1953). Although *Alice* was not generally well received, the debut on Broadway of *Purlie Victorious,* with Davis in the title role, garnered a much more favorable response. The **comedy**, about a Southern black preacher who hopes to establish a racially integrated church, was adapted by Davis for the film *Gone Are the Days* (1963). In addition, Davis collaborated with Philip Rose, Peter Udell, and Gary Geld on *Purlie,* the successful stage musical adaptation of the story.

Davis has also written two plays about notable black figures: *Escape to Freedom* (1976), adapted from **Frederick Douglass**'s **autobiography**, and *Langston: A Play* (1982), about **Langston Hughes**. In 1992, Davis produced his first **novel,** *Just Like Martin,* which explores a father-son relationship in the context of the civil rights movement.

The founder of the Institute of Cinema Artists, a school for young blacks, Davis received a Hall of Fame Award for artistic achievement in 1989 from the **National Association for the Advancement of Colored People** (NAACP). That same year he received the NAACP's Image Award for best performance by a supporting actor for the film *Do the Right Thing*. In the early 1990s Davis appeared on the television series *Evening Shade*.

Further Readings

Black Writers, second edition, Gale, 1994.

Dictionary of Literary Biography, Volume 38: *Afro-American Writers after 1955: Dramatists and Prose Writers,* Gale, 1985.

Funke, Lewis, *The Curtain Rises—The Story of Ossie Davis,* Grosset & Dunlap, 1971.

Thulani Davis
American journalist, poet, and novelist

As a contributor to New York City's *Village Voice,* Davis writes about a variety of aspects of the black experience. In her **poetry** and **novels,** she explores issues such as love, rape, equality, and the power of community.

The poems in Davis's second verse collection, *Playing the Changes* (1985), are written in a city-wise, street-smart manner and address feminist and sexual issues related to growing up as a black female in a large city. Davis's first novel, *1959* (1992), examines the beginnings of the **civil rights movement** from the perspective

of a twelve-year-old girl growing up in a small town. Davis has also written the libretto for *X: The Life and Times of Malcolm X* (1986) and the text for *Malcolm X: The Great Photographs* (1993), a pictorial depiction of the black leader.

Further Readings

Black Writers, second edition, Gale, 1994.

Dawn
Please see "Xenogenesis" Trilogy

Days of Grace: A Memoir
Arthur Ashe
Autobiography, 1993

Arthur Ashe felt compelled to write the fourth of his autobiographical books after a newspaper divulged in 1992 that he had Acquired Immune Deficiency Syndrome or AIDS. He had been infected through a blood transfusion during surgery, performed after his 1979 heart attack. In the memoir, Ashe confesses that he felt guilty about contracting the disease, though he had not used drugs or indulged in unsafe sex. He denies rumors of a homosexual relationship in his past, yet he also defends the rights of gays. In Ashe's evaluation of his life, he castigates himself for waiting until the 1980s to speak out against racism, suggesting that his anti-apartheid activism was perhaps an effort to compensate for his silence in the 1960s during the **civil rights movement**. *Days of Grace* covers Ashe's later achievements, including his Safe Passage Program for inner-city black teens and the Brooklyn Institute for Urban Health that bears his name. Ashe endowed a chair in pediatric AIDS at a research center in Memphis, as well. Some sections of the book comment on what he sees as the failure of blacks in the public eye to be politically forceful, especially sports stars like Gary Player, Earvin Magic Johnson and Michael Jordan. Ashe also offers lighthearted discussion of his rivals Jimmy Connors and John McEnroe, as well as the recollection of a conversation with Jesse Jackson, who accused

Ashe of not being arrogant enough. More general commentary deals with blacks who are prejudiced against Jews and other whites, as well as those who use public assistance when they really have enough money to help themselves. In addition to thoughts on race and **racism**, Ashe examines such topics as politics and sexuality. The last section of *Days of Grace* takes the form of an emotional farewell letter to his daughter, Camera, who was then six years old.

H. G. De Lisser

Jamaican novelist, journalist, and nonfiction writer
Born December 9, 1878.
Died May 18, 1944.

Herbert George De Lisser is remembered as one of the first important novelists of the English-speaking Caribbean, particularly for his books depicting Jamaican political life. Largely self-educated, he began as a proofreader at the *Daily Gleaner* and, after working at other Jamaican newspapers, returned to the *Gleaner* to serve as chief editor from 1904 to 1942.

De Lisser's first and best-known **novel,** published after two books of nonfiction, is ***Jane: A Story of Jamaica*** (1913), better known as *Jane's Career* (1914). In this and other novels he portrays Jamaican history and manners, sometimes with heavy strains of romance and melodrama. He also worked to promote Jamaican arts, science, and industry.

Further Readings

Black Writers, Gale, second edition, 1994.

Dictionary of Literary Biography, Volume 117: *Twentieth-Century Caribbean and Black African Writers,* First Series, Gale, 1992.

Dead Human

Character in *A Beast's Story*

Dead Man

Character in *A Dance of the Forests*

Dead Woman

Character in *A Dance of the Forests*

Death and the King's Horseman

Wole Soyinka
Play, first produced 1976, published 1975

Wole Soyinka's inspiration for *Death and the King's Horseman* was an incident from 1940s Nigeria, concerning a king's ceremonial horseman in Oyo. According to tradition, Elesin is expected to follow his fallen king to the afterlife. He attempts a ritual suicide but is prevented from completing the act by the colonial administrator, Mr. Pilkings, who considers Elesin's plans a needless waste. Dialogue is often written in verse, and the suicide attempt is staged during a costume ball for which the whites are dressed in Yoruban spirit masks. Elesin's son Olunde feels obliged to take his own life to preserve the endangered family honor.

Deconstruction

Deconstruction is a theory about literature that began in the 1970s, in large part as a reaction to **structuralism,** and became the leading school of **literary criticism** in the United States after the Vietnam War. The deconstruction movement is characterized by its concept of textuality, which states that language exists not only on the page, but also in speech, in time, and in culture. The meaning of a word can never be absolute, since every reader brings a different set of cultural and psychological factors to its interpretation—factors that are in turn conditioned by language. A closely related notion is that of intertextuality, which refers to the existence of countless silent cultural and social links between a text and its context. Prominent black critics such as **Henry Louis Gates, Houston A. Baker, Robert Stepto** and **Sunday O. Anozie** frequently make use of deconstructionist concepts in their analyses of black literature.

Miriam DeCosta-Willis

American editor
Born November 1, 1934.

Born in Florence, Alabama, DeCosta-Willis attended Wellesley College and Johns Hopkins University before embarking on a career as a professor of Spanish. *Blacks in Spanish Literature* (1977), which she edited under the name Miriam DeCosta, explores themes of blacks in early Spanish literature as well as in works by today's Latin American and Caribbean authors. DeCosta has coedited several volumes on black writers: *Homespun Images: An Anthology of Black Memphis Writers and Artists* (1989), *Double Stitch: Black Women Write about Mothers and Daughters* (1991), and *Erotique Noire/Black Erotica* (1992). She has also contributed to books on black woman writers, including *Wild Women Don't Wear No Blues* (1993), edited by **Marita Golden**, and has written many articles for scholarly journals.

Further Readings
Black Writers, second edition, Gale, 1994.

Ruby Dee

American actress and writer
Born October 27, 1923(?).

One of America's most prominent black performers, Dee (born Ruby Ann Wallace) began her career in the 1940s at the American Negro Theatre. Meeting fellow artists such as **Sidney Poitier**, she eventually married the group's principal performer, **Ossie Davis**, in 1948. Dee's work on Broadway and in film and television has won her many awards and includes notable performances in *Edge of the City* (film, 1957), *A Raison in the Sun* (stage, 1959; film, 1961), and Davis's satirical play *Purlie Victorious* (1961).

Born in Cleveland, Ohio, Dee wrote the musical *Take It from the Top* (1979, revised as *Twin Bit Gardens*), about an angel who returns to earth to recruit good people to thwart an evil capitalist; and the screenplay *Up Tight* (1968) (in collaboration with Jules Dassin and **Julian Mayfield**), about a black man who betrays his friends after one of them murders a guard during a robbery. She has also written **poetry, short stories,** and **essays.**

Further Readings
Black Writers, first edition, Gale, 1989.

Deighton Boyce

Character in *Brown Girl, Brownstones*

Martin Robinson Delany

American nonfiction writer and novelist
Born May 6, 1812.
Died January 24, 1885.

Delany is acknowledged as the founder of **black nationalism** in the United States. In the books *The Condition, Elevation, Emigration, and Destiny of the Colored People of the United States, Politically Considered* (1852) and *Official Report of the Niger Valley Exploring Party* (1861), and the speech "Political Destiny of the Colored Race on the American Continent" (1854), he argued that blacks could only achieve self-reliance outside the United States. Among Delany's other books is the **novel** *Blake; or the Huts of America* (serialized 1859-1862).

Further Readings
Dictionary of Literary Biography, Volume 50: *Afro-American Writers before the Harlem Renaissance,* Gale, 1986.

Reference Guide to American Literature, St. James Press, third edition, 1994.

Ullman, Victor, *Martin R. Delany: The Beginnings of Black Nationalism,* Beacon Press, 1971.

Samuel R. Delany

American science fiction novelist and short story writer
Born April 1, 1942.

Samuel Ray Delany is one of the **science fiction** genre's most highly respected and popular writers. His fiction frequently focuses on the artist as a social outsider and the problems arising from communication and technology.

The son of a prominent businessman and a clerk with the New York Public Library, Delany was born and raised in Harlem. He began writing fiction while attending a private elementary school and continued as a high school student. In 1961, Delany married Marilyn Hacker, a poet and former classmate who encouraged him to publish his work. In his first **novel,** *Jewels of Aptor* (1962), Delany presents a world that is trying to restore itself following a radioactive fire. This work features elements included in many of Delany's novels: an artist protagonist, an emphasis on **myth**, and an examination of the destructive capabilities of technology.

With *Babel-17* (1966), for which he won his first Nebula Award, Delany began to gain recognition in the science fiction field. This novel examines themes of oppression, guilt, and responsibility in its depiction of intergalactic strife. Delany's subsequent fiction, which includes nearly two dozen novels and collections of short stories, examines many of the same topics and has gained for him the reputation of an author whose works can be enjoyed on many levels.

Delany has also won the Nebula Award for his novel *The Einstein Intersection* (1967), and his **short story** "Aye and Gomorrah" (1967), as well as Nebula and Hugo awards for the novelette *Time Considered as a Helix of Semi-Precious Stones* (1969). Delany's other works include *Dhalgren* (1975), which focuses on a post-holocaust American City, and *Stars in My Pocket Like Grains of Sand* (1984), an erotic science fiction story. He received the Pilgrim Award from the Science Fiction Research Association in 1985.

Further Readings

Black Literature Criticism, Gale, 1992.

Black Writers, second edition, Gale, 1994.

Dictionary of Literary Biography, Volume 33: *Afro-American Fiction Writers after 1955,* Gale, 1984.

William Demby

American novelist
Born December 25, 1922.

Demby has achieved critical acclaim for **novels** centering on protagonists who face situations that require critical moral choices. He is praised for dramatic and insightful analyses of such topics as life, death, and love.

Demby was born in Pittsburgh, Pennsylvania, and spent his youth in Clarksburg, West Virginia. He attended West Virginia State College but left to join the United States Army during World War II. While serving tours of duty in Italy and North Africa, Demby began writing for the military publication *Stars and Stripes*. Following the war, he earned a bachelor's degree from Fisk University. Demby then returned to Italy, where he attended the University of Rome. He spent the next twenty years there as an expatriate writing and translating scripts for television and film. In 1969, Demby began teaching at the College of Staten Island of City University of New York and has subsequently lived in the United States.

While in Italy, Demby wrote his first novel, *Beetlecreek* (1950), about the effects of loneliness and gang violence on three male protagonists living in a small American town. His second novel, *The Catacombs* (1965), is set in Rome and includes Demby as a character. This work makes use of contemporary events, including the Cuban Missile Crisis and the launching of a Russian spaceship, to tell the story of an ill-fated love triangle. Later novels, including *Love Story Black* (1978) and *Blueboy,* (1979) develop similar themes while including elements of **satire** and **autobiography**.

Further Readings

Black Literature Criticism, Gale, 1992.

Black Writers, first edition, Gale, 1989.

Dictionary of Literary Biography, Volume 33: *Afro-American Fiction Writers after 1955,* Gale, 1984.

Della

Character in *Night Song*

Dennis Plunkett

Character in *Omeros*

Tom Dent

American poet and dramatist
Born March 20, 1932.

Born into a prominent New Orleans family, Thomas Covington Dent became socially and politically active after he moved to New York City in 1959. He cofounded the influential Umbra Workshop in 1962 and copublished its **poetry** magazine, *Umbra.* While serving as associate director of the New Orleans Free Southern Theater, Dent wrote the controversial prose narrative *The Ghetto of Desire* (1966), which aired on the television show *Look Up and Live,* and the one-act **plays** *Negro Study No. 34A* (1970) and *Snapshot* (1970). He has written two books of poetry, *Magnolia Street* (1976) and *Blue Lights and River Songs: Poems* (1982). Dent cofounded the literary journal *Callaloo* in 1978.

Further Readings

Black Writers, first edition, Gale, 1989.

Dictionary of Literary Biography, Volume 38: *Afro-American Writers after 1955: Dramatists and Prose Writers,* Gale, 1985.

Denver

Character in *Beloved*

Toi Derricotte

American poet
Born April 12, 1941.

In her poems, Derricotte explores the experiences and victimization of African American women. Born in Detroit, Michigan, Derricotte attended Wayne State University and New York University before pursuing a career teaching and writing. The narrating persona of her first **poetry** collection, *The Empress of the Death House* (1978), lashes out at a world indifferent to or contemptuous of women. Derricotte's second book, *Natural Birth* (1983), weaves her own childhood experiences into an examination of the birth process. Her third volume, *Captivity* (1989), presents images of impoverished neighborhoods and portraits of intercity students. Derricotte's other writings include *Creative Writing: A Manual for Teachers* (1985) and contributions to anthologies and periodicals.

Further Readings

Black Writers, second edition, Gale, 1994.

Dessa

Character in *Dessa Rose*

Dessa Rose

Sherley Anne Williams
Novel, 1986

As **Sherley Anne Williams**'s **novel** begins, Dessa (Odessa Rose) has been sentenced to death for participating in a slave revolt in which several white men were killed. Imprisoned in the sheriff's cellar, awaiting the birth of her child and then execution, Dessa escapes with the help of the sheriff's slaves. The group seeks protection from Ruth Elizabeth Sutton, an aristocrat whose North Carolina farm serves as a haven for escaped slaves. Here, fugitives and farm owner share profits and eventually develop a plan to emigrate to free territory. Ruth poses as a slave owner and sells the "slaves" who escape and reunite, sharing the profits of the sale. They then move on to repeat the scam. The group succeeds in avoiding several dangerous obstacles and eventually settle in free territory in the West.

The Destruction of Black Civilization

Chancellor Williams
History, 1971

In *The Destruction of Black Civilization: Great Issues of a Race from 4500 B.C. to 2000 A.D.*, a panoramic study of Africa's past, **Chancellor Williams** addresses the historical forces which shaped present-day Africa, leaving it "at the bottom of world society." Williams rejects European historical scholarship on Africa, especially that which begins only with the invader's incursion into the continent and that which sets Egypt apart from the rest of Africa. Williams considers repeated invasion from Europe and Asia and massive loss of population, culminating in the final destruction of African civilization in the 17th century, to have been caused by disunity in the face of imperialism. Rejecting capitalism and communism alike as Eurocentric, he calls for a new "Master Plan" for black America based upon traditional African government and black self-reliance. The book received several awards including the Black Academy of Arts and Letters Book Award in 1971 and 1979.

Detective Fiction

Detective fiction is a subgenre of mystery that is one of the most widely read forms of popular literature. The beginnings of this genre are usually traced to Edgar Allan Poe, who established the conventions of detective fiction: A crime (usually murder) is committed; a detective investigates; a number of suspects are considered; the guilty party is discovered and imprisoned, killed, or allowed to escape at the conclusion. In 1932, **Rudolph Fisher** published *The Conjure-Man Dies: A Mystery Tale of Dark Harlem,* the first detective **novel** by an African American. The denouement of the narrative reveals Fisher's medical and scientific knowledge. A quarter of a century later, **Chester Himes** published *For Love of Imabelle* (1957; revised as *A Rage in Harlem,* 1965), the first in his popular series of detective novels. In the 1990s, a series by **Walter Mosley** featuring black detective Ezekiel "Easy" Rawlins earned critical praise.

Alexis Deveaux

American novelist, dramatist, and essayist
Born September 24, 1948.

Deveaux uses her work to address social and political inequities. She portrays the urban experience of many minorities and is especially concerned with issues facing black and Third World women.

Deveaux was born to Richard Hill and Mae Deveaux in New York City. She began teaching English when she was twenty-one and was an instructor in creative writing at Frederick Douglass Creative Arts Center by 1971. She received her B.A. from the State University of New York in 1976 and has supported herself by writing since.

Deveaux has written several **plays,** including "Circles" (1973) and "A Season to Unravel" (1979). In her self-illustrated children's story *Na-ni* (1973), she writes about a poor Harlem child whose dream of a new bicycle goes unfulfilled when the family's welfare check is stolen. The book was praised for the spare, poetic style of its prose as well as the power of the simple line drawings. Deveaux also illustrated her first **novel,** *Spirits in the Streets* (1973), which is set in Harlem. Using a variety of narrative and typographical effects, the novel confronts the consequences of poverty. Deveaux is perhaps best known for her fictional **biography** of Billie Holiday, *Don't Explain: A Song of Billie Holiday* (1980), in which she addresses Holiday's drug addiction and other afflictions. In 1987, Deveaux published another children's book, *An Enchanted Hair Tale,* about a boy whose dreadlocks are enchanted. Deveaux has also served as an essayist for *Essence* magazine since 1981.

Further Readings
Black Writers, first edition, Gale, 1989.

Dhalgren
Samuel R. Delany
Novel, 1975

Dhalgren, **Samuel R. Delany**'s tenth **novel,** is an experimental work centered on a post-holocaust American city called Bellona. The Kid, a nameless artist burdened with psychic stress, arrives at this lawless outpost. The structure of the narrative is displayed through the **poetry** and journal entries of the Kid, who philosophizes ambiguously about the fate of various residents. These fragments of writing also muse upon the role of artists and their art. Meanwhile, the Kid's reflections implicate Bellona as an armed camp gripped by chaos, violence, and obsessive sex. The city is plagued with "scorpions," whom the Kid eventually leads to heroic status. Other positive characters assume mythic proportions. George Harrison is a celebrated black figure, another is Reverend Amy Taylor.

Dialect Poetry

Please see Dialect Prose/Poetry

Dialect Prose/Poetry

The word "dialect" refers to a variety of language associated with a particular group of people, social class, or geographic region. Poems and prose imitating various black dialects have been popular since the late nineteenth century. **Paul Laurence Dunbar**, the first African American poet to gain national fame, built his reputation largely on the southern black dialect poems found in books such as *Lyrics of Lowly Life* (1896), *Li'l Gal* (1904), *A Plantation Portrait* (1905), and *Joggin' erlong* (1906). **Claude McKay** used Jamaican dialect in his **poetry** collections *Songs of Jamaica* (1912) and *Constab Ballads* (1912). More recently, **Derek Walcott** incorporated Caribbean dialects in **plays** such as *Dream on Monkey Mountain* (1967), while writers such as **Sonia Sanchez, Julia Fields**, and **Haki R. Madhubuti** have sought to recreate modern African American dialects in their works.

The height of dialect poetry, however, occurred around the turn of the twentieth century in response to Dunbar's success. The plantation dialect style that he popularized was typically filled with gross misspellings and misuses of English. Most of the black writers who used this style also published works in standard English. Among them is **James Edwin Camp-** **bell**, whose earliest dialect poems actually preceded Dunbar's. Campbell's poems, which reflect the experiences of southern blacks who could still remember slave days, are collected in *Echoes from the Cabin and Elsewhere* (1895). Other poets in this style include **Fenton Johnson**, author of *Visions of the Dusk* (1915) and *Songs of the Soil* (1916), and **Raymond Garfield Dandridge**, nicknamed "The Paul Laurence Dunbar of Cincinnati," whose books include *Penciled Poems* (1917) and *The Poet and Other Poems* (1920).

A Dialogue

James Baldwin and Nikki Giovanni
Commentary, 1973

The book *A Dialogue* arose from a conversation between author **James Baldwin** and poet **Nikki Giovanni**, taped in London, England, on November 4, 1971, for public television station WNET's program *Soul!*, which aired in two segments in December, 1971. For the subsequent book, Giovanni and Baldwin edited a transcribed version of their videotape. The two writers, who differ in age, gender, and philosophical outlook, address concerns common to each, including the situation of blacks in the United States and abroad. Both writers express similar concerns on the direction and outcome of the black freedom movement. Baldwin and Giovanni share personal experiences and pivotal events in their lives while discussing wide-ranging issues, such as race, sexuality, **religion**, emotions, drug abuse, politics, literature, and the state of the black writer in America. While the dialogue sometimes elicits painful memories and confronts difficult truths, both Baldwin and Giovanni ultimately perceive positive effects from the quest for black civil rights and liberties.

Diary

A diary is a personal written record of daily events and thoughts. As private documents, diaries are supposedly not intended for an audience, but some of literary value or historical significance have been made public. Examples of posthumously published diaries include *The Journal of Charlotte L. Forten: A Free Negro in the Slave Era* (1953), which records Forten's firsthand impressions of the abolitionist movement and the Civil War, and *Give Us Each Day: The Diary of Alice Dunbar-Nelson,* edited by **Gloria T. Hull**, 1984, which chronicles the life of one of the first black women to distinguish herself in American letters. **Wole Soyinka**'s *The Man Died: Prison Notes of Wole Soyinka* (1972) is a collection of reflections and anecdotes based on a diary Soyinka kept while in political detention in Nigeria.

Dick

Character in *Song of the City*

Didi

Character in *Motown and Didi: A Love Story*

Die Nigger Die!

H. Rap Brown
Autobiography, 1969

H. Rap Brown, who adopted the name Jamil Abdullah Al-Amin in the 1970s, published *Die Nigger Die!* in 1969, at the height of his fame as a political activist and civil rights leader. The **autobiography** describes his Louisiana childhood and his rise to the chairpersonship of the Student Nonviolent Coordinating Committee (SNCC); it also offers an analysis of racial injustice in America.

Brown believed that force was fundamental to racial oppression, that depriving people of their rights was an intrinsically violent act. In *Die Nigger Die!* he thus rejects the nonviolent methods advocated by **Martin Luther King Jr.** and the **civil rights movement**. In the book he argues that blacks must meet force with force, using guns if necessary. Brown's advocation of violence made the book controversial, especially since it came at a time when riots were sweeping America's poor black neighborhoods.

Birago Diop

Senegalese short story writer
and autobiographer
Born December 11, 1906.
Died November 25, 1989.

Born and raised in Senegal, Birago Ismael Diop travelled to France to study veterinary science. In France, Diop met the leading black writers of the **négritude** movement and was inspired to write his first poems. On his return to Africa in the 1930s, he turned from poems to short stories inspired by West African folktales. *Les Contes d'Amadou Koumba* (1958) won him critical acclaim and the Grand Prix Littéraire de l'Afrique-Occidentale Française. Other collections of stories followed, including *Mother Crocodile: Maman-Caiman* (1981), as well as **plays,** poems, and a five-volume **autobiography**, *Mémoires* (1978-1989). Diop died in Dakar, Senegal, in 1989.

Further Readings
Black Writers, second edition, Gale, 1994.

Cheikh Anta Diop

Senegalese historian
Born in 1923.
Died February 7, 1986.

Diop is probably best remembered for his historical studies of Africa. In 1966, he was honored by the World Festival of Negro Arts as the black intellectual who most influenced the twentieth century. Diop attempted to show that blacks had a larger role in the origin of civilization than was previously recognized. He argued that the ancient Egyptians, who were advanced in science and culture, were black. He also held that the first steps toward civilization began south of the Sahara Desert. He was one of the African historians selected by the United Nations to prepare the history of Africa for the United Nations Economic, Scientific, and Cultural Organization (UNESCO) and he headed Africa's first carbon-14 dating laboratory at the Institut Fondamentale d'Afrique Noire in Senegal. His most famous book is *Nations negres et culture* (1955; *The African Origin of Civilization: Myth or Reality,* 1974). Diop died on February 7, 1986, at his home in Dakar, Senegal. His *Civilization ou barbarie* (*Civilization or Barbarism: An Authentic Anthropology,* 1991) was published posthumously.

Further Readings
Black Writers, second edition, Gale, 1994.

David Mandessi Diop

French poet
Born July 9, 1927.
Died in August, 1960.

Diop was born to African parents in Bordeaux, France. Despite his early **assimilation** to the French way of life, Diop's poems repudiated French culture and lamented the alienation of European Africans. Diop's only published volume, *Coups de pilon: poemes* (1956; *Hammer Blows: Poems,* 1975), established him as an emerging leader of the younger generation of the **négritude** poets. Included were "The Vultures," an anticolonial poem, and "To a Black Child," which was inspired by the lynching of Emmett Till in Mississippi in 1955. In the mid-1950s, Diop returned to Africa to teach. He was killed with his wife in a plane crash near Dakar, Senegal, in August, 1960. His unpublished manuscripts burned in the crash.

Further Readings
Black Writers, second edition, Gale, 1994.

Disappearing Acts

Terry McMillan
Novel, 1989

Terry McMillan's second **novel,** *Disappearing Acts,* is a contemporary story about a two-year relationship between Zora Banks, a college-educated woman from Ohio, and Franklin Swift, a sometimes employed carpenter and construction worker in his thirties who never finished high school. She is a teacher who wants to be a singer; he wants to own his own business.

They meet when she moves into an apartment he is renovating. Because of their past romantic failures, neither wants to become involved. But soon they are living together. The difference in their backgrounds is a major problem. Franklin admires Zora's college education, her steady employment, and her standard English. He speaks a nonstandard English African American dialect.

Franklin has studied for his high school equivalency exam and plans to go to college, but every time he gets a job that pays a decent salary, he is laid off. He becomes depressed, and starts to drink. Zora has to support him financially and psychologically, while trying to keep herself together. Zora blames Franklin's mother for his low self-esteem.

Zora wants Franklin to divorce his wife so they can marry. He refuses, admitting that he cannot afford to. When Zora gets pregnant and has an abortion without telling Franklin, he is hurt. She becomes pregnant again and agrees to keep the child, but Franklin gets depressed and violent, and Zora, concerned for her child, leaves him. Three months later, a changed Franklin visits Zora. He is divorced, has a job, and is no longer drinking. They decide to wait for him to achieve more progress in his own life before trying to live together again. Zora leaves the city for the country to raise their child.

Critics compared McMillan to **Zora Neale Hurston,** for whom she named the novel's heroine.

Discrimination

Discrimination refers to the practice of treating a group or individual unfavorably on the basis of such arbitrary grounds as sex, **religion**, race, or physical handicap. In the United States, the most common form of discrimination historically has been racial. Because of its pervasiveness, discrimination has informed the work of most African American writers in one way or another.

Slavery is one of the severest forms of discrimination. The eradication of slavery at the end of the Civil War altered the legal status of African Americans, but it did not eliminate discrimination. During the **Reconstruction** period just after the war, a string of laws were enacted and three amendments to the Constitution were ratified in an effort to protect the civil rights of blacks; among these were the Thirteenth Amendment (1865), which abolished slavery and involuntary servitude, and the Fourteenth Amendment (1868), which guaranteed citizenship and provided equal protection under the law. Reconstruction legislation, however, eventually produced a wave of anti-African sentiment. White organizations, like the Ku Klux Klan, aimed at intimidating blacks and preventing them from entering society, sprang up throughout the North and the South. In 1883, the U.S. Supreme Court effectively halted the legislative efforts with a ruling on a group of five cases, which became known as the Civil Rights Cases. The court concluded that the Civil Rights Act of 1875 was unconstitutional on the grounds that the Fourteenth Amendment authorized Congress to legislate only against discriminatory state action, and not discrimination by private individuals. Also in the late nineteenth century, a series of laws were passed throughout the South that led to white-imposed **segregation** of the races in all aspects of daily life, including public transportation and schools. It was not until the mid-twentieth century that the federal government began to actively pursue full civil rights for African Americans again.

Countless books by black authors have touched on the theme of racial discrimination. Among notable nonfiction treatments of the subject are *Race, Racism, and American Law* (1973), by **Derrick Albert Bell Jr.** and *Black Life in Corporate America: Swimming in the Mainstream* (1982), by **George B. Davis**. Among autobiographical accounts, ***Manchild in the Promised Land*** (1965), by **Claude Brown**, is considered by many to be the definitive depiction of repressive conditions in an African American ghetto in the mid-twentieth century. A classic fictional portrait of discrimination is **Ralph Ellison**'s **novel *Invisible Man*** (1952), which won a National Book Award for fiction. The acclaimed **play *A Raisin in the Sun*** (1959), by **Lorraine Hansberry**, portrays the experience of a black family buying a house in a white neighborhood.

A second widespread form of discrimination in the United States historically has been based on gender. For African American women, this has presented a double obstacle to equal treatment. In his book ***Sex and Racism in America*** (1965), nonfiction writer **Calvin C. Hernton** argues that sexism and **racism** in the United States are inextricably bound. Another book on the subject is **Gloria T. Hull**'s *All the Women Are White, All the Blacks Are Men, but Some of Us Are Brave: Black Women's Studies* (1982). Among the many novels by African American women that examine the theme of sexual as well as racial oppression are **Alice Walker**'s ***The Color Purple*** (1982) and **Gayl Jones**'s ***Corregidora*** (1975) and *Eva's Man* (1976).

Over the years, discrimination has affected not only what African Americans have written about, but also how readily their writing has been accepted. The first book ever published by an African American was a volume of **poetry** by a young slave named **Phillis Wheatley**. When her book ***Poems on Various Subjects, Religious and Moral*** appeared in London in 1773, her master was required to add a sworn statement of authenticity—such was the disbelief that a black woman could have created such work. In fact, it was not until the **Harlem Renaissance** of the 1920s that black authors received their first widespread critical and popular recognition.

Ditcher
Character in *Black Thunder*

Melvin Dixon
American poet and novelist
Born May 29, 1950.
Died October 26, 1992.

Melvin Winfred Dixon contributed a black perspective to gay and lesbian literature. After attending Wesleyan and Brown Universities, he published the **poetry** volume *Change of Territory* (1983) and two scholarly works. In his **novel** *Trouble the Water* (1989), for which Dixon was awarded the Charles H. and N. Mildred Nilon Award for Excellence in Minority Fiction, a college professor copes with racial and familial upheaval. In *Vanishing Rooms* (1991), Dixon portrays three people affected by the gang rape and murder of a gay white man. Dixon was professor of English at the City University of New York when he died in 1992 of complications from acquired immunodeficiency syndrome (AIDS).

Further Readings
Black Writers, second edition, Gale, 1994.

Do the Right Thing
Spike Lee
Film, 1989

Spike Lee's *Do the Right Thing* is an unflinching story about the racial tensions that divide Bedford-Stuyvesant—a predominantly black neighborhood in New York City—on a hot summer day. Lee, who wrote and directed the film, also plays the main character, Mookie, an easy-going delivery boy for Sal's Famous pizzeria. Throughout the film, individuals of various ages and ethnic backgrounds comically bicker in a good-natured way; however, as the heat intensifies, nerves fray and the arguments become bitter.

The central conflict of *Do the Right Thing* revolves around Sal's Famous, a white-owned pizzeria that features photos of Italian Americans on its "Wall of Fame." Buggin' Out, the most militant member of the community, threatens to boycott Sal's until photos of black people are displayed, too. Shortly before closing for the day, Sal becomes irritated by Buggin' Out's protests and Radio Raheem's deafeningly loud boom box. Sal utters a racial slur, smashes the boom box, and a fight breaks out. When the police arrive, an officer chokes Radio Raheem to death as the neighborhood watches. Although Sal and Mookie are both sympathetic characters, they are polarized by the violence. Mookie throws a garbage can through the glass window at the pizzeria, initiating a riot that destroys Sal's.

Critics have described Lee's *Do the Right Thing* as innovative and provocative. No one—not even Mookie—is portrayed as a hero. At one point, Mookie and other characters of various ethnic backgrounds shout racial insults directly into the movie camera. The film provoked a storm of controversy; some reviewers described it as a brilliant portrait of the mounting irritations that lead to race riots, while others viewed it as a dangerous statement about the inevitability of racial violence. Lee seemed to anticipate differing reactions and concluded his film by juxtaposing two quotes that express conflicting sentiments. The first quote—by **Martin Luther King Jr.**—denounces violence, while the second—by **Malcolm X**—suggests that violence in self-defense is sometimes necessary.

Doaker Charles
Character in *The Piano Lesson*

Doc
Character in *Country Place*

Owen Dodson
American dramatist, poet, and novelist
Born November 28, 1914.
Died June 21, 1983.

Although Owen Vincent Dodson has been recognized for his **poetry, plays,** and fiction, he is perhaps best remembered for the twenty-three years he spent teaching drama at Howard University. In 1974, the Black Repertory Theatre of Washington, DC, paid tribute to his influence on African American drama with a collage of his adapted writings titled *Owen's Song.*

Dodson was born in Brooklyn, New York. His father, a free-lance journalist and director of the National Negro Press Association, introduced Dodson to such leading figures of the day as **Booker T. Washington** and **W. E. B. Du Bois**. Dodson received a bachelor's degree from Bates College in 1936 and a master's from Yale University in 1939. His first plays, "Divine Comedy" (1938) and "The Garden of Time" (1939), were produced while he was still at Yale.

Following brief stints at various colleges and in the U.S. Navy, Dodson wrote and directed "New World A-Coming" (1944), a well-attended pageant commemorating the contribution of black Americans to the war effort. His reputation as a poet was made two years later with the publication of his first volume of verse, *Powerful Long Ladder* (1946). However, he temporarily abandoned poetry for fiction. His first and most acclaimed **novel** was the semi-autobiographical *Boy at the Window* (1951).

In 1947, Dodson began his association with the Howard University Players and began to shape the careers of a whole generation of black artists. In 1949, Dodson led the ensemble on a fourteen-city European tour featuring performances of plays by Henrik Ibsen and DuBose Heyward—the first U.S. State Department sponsored European tour by a black theatre group. After his retirement, he wrote *The Confession Stone* (1970), a series of verse monologues about the life of Jesus, among other works. Dodson died of a heart attack in New York City in 1983.

See also **Poetry of Owen Dodson**

Further Readings
Black Literature Criticism, Gale, 1992.

Black Writers, first edition, Gale, 1989.

Dictionary of Literary Biography, Volume 76: *Afro-American Writers, 1940-1955,* Gale, 1988.

Dom Casmurro
Joaquim Maria Machado de Assis
Novel, 1899

Joaquim Maria Machado de Assis's *Dom Casmurro* centers on a jealous husband who believes his wife been unfaithful and that his best friend is the father of his son. Related by an unreliable narrator, the **novel** is full of deception and ambiguity. The narrator is Bento Santiago, a wealthy and well-educated man often described as a combination of Shakespeare's Othello and Iago. Bento has known both his wife, Capitu, and his best friend, Escobar, since childhood, and though it is impossible to assess Bento's veracity, he appears to be telling his story in an attempt to justify his cruelty toward those closest to him. But the novel avoids certainty, and Machado de Assis seems less interested in establishing guilt or innocence than in exploring the dynamics of one man's perspective of the people around him.

Doopeyduk
Character in *The Free-Lance Pallbearers*

Doot
Character in *Sent for You Yesterday*

Dopefiend, The Story of a Black Junkie
Donald Goines
Novel, 1971

Donald Goines's *Dopefiend, The Story of a Black Junkie* is the graphic story of two young, middle-class blacks who are drawn into the world of drug addiction. Teddy and his girlfriend Terry feed their heroin addiction at a dope house owned by the repulsive dealer, Porky. At the house, Teddy and Terry witness the horrors of heroin addiction as detailed by Goines. They find bloodied, desperate addicts whom Porky is eager to exploit for money and sexual gratification. The **novel** chronicles Teddy's and Terry's attempts to rationalize their choices as they grapple with the intellectual and emotional ramifications of addiction.

Dorcas Manfred

Character in *Jazz*

Dorine Davis

Character in *A Measure of Time*

Doris

Character in *The Catacombs*

Doro

Character in "Patternist Saga"

Frederick Douglass

American autobiographer, editor, and essayist
Born February, 1817(?).
Died February 20, 1895.

Douglass is regarded as one of the most distinguished spokespersons for American blacks in the nineteenth century. An escaped slave, he became the foremost abolitionist of his time, arguing for racial equality in orations and newspaper editorials. His reputation as an influential prose writer rests largely on his **autobiography**, *Narrative of the Life of Frederick Douglass, an American Slave, Written by Himself* (1845).

Douglass was born Frederick Augustus Washington Bailey in Tuckahoe, Maryland, circa February, 1817. His mother was a black slave, and his father was an unidentified, presumably white man. Separated from his mother in infancy, Douglass was nurtured by his mater-

nal grandparents; soon, however, he was put to work on his master's estate. In the mid-1820s, he was sent to a Baltimore, Maryland, household, where the mistress introduced him to reading. Later, the knowledge he acquired through self-education sparked his growing desire for freedom. In 1838, he escaped to New York.

Later that year, Douglass married Anna Murray and moved to New Bedford, Massachusetts, where, because of his fugitive status, he adopted the surname Douglass. In 1841, he joined the Massachusetts Antislavery Society as a lecturer, relating to audiences his experiences as a slave. He eventually published these accounts as *Narrative of the Life of Frederick Douglass*. The book, which Douglass revised several times throughout his life, became an immediate success.

Fearing capture after *Narrative*'s publication, Douglass fled to Great Britain. By the time he returned to the United States in 1847, he had raised enough funds to purchase his freedom and start the *North Star,* a weekly abolitionist newspaper, later renamed *Frederick Douglass' Paper.* In the following years, he continued writing and speaking, and published several of his lectures in book form. He also served as an **Underground Railroad** agent and wrote a novella, *The Heroic Slave* (1853), based on a slave-ship revolt.

During the Civil War, Douglass lobbied for the equitable treatment of black soldiers in the Union ranks, often advising President Abraham Lincoln. After the war, Douglass became increasingly active in politics, serving in posts including marshal of the District of Columbia and minister resident and consul-general to the Republic of Haiti. In 1882, his wife Anna died; two years later, Douglass married Helen Pitts. In 1891, he retired to Anacostia Heights, District of Columbia, where he died from heart failure on February 20, 1895.

Further Readings
Black Literature Criticism, Gale, 1992.

Bontemps, Arna, *Free at Last: The Life of Frederick Douglass,* Dodd, 1971.

Dictionary of Literary Biography, Volume 50: *Afro-American Writers before the Harlem Renaissance,* Gale, 1986.

Huggins, Nathan Irvin, *Slave and Citizen: The Life of Frederick Douglass,* Little, Brown, 1980.

Rita Dove

American poet, novelist, and
short story writer
Born August 28, 1952.

Rita Frances Dove has emerged as one of the most esteemed black poets of the late twentieth century. She was named poet laureate of the United States in 1993, the first black person to hold that title. She also was only the second African American to be awarded a Pulitzer Prize in **poetry,** an honor she received in 1987 for her best-known book, ***Thomas and Beulah*** (1986). Dove has been called a quiet leader—one who does not shy away from complex racial issues, but does not seek them out as the central focus of her work.

Dove was born in Akron, Ohio, on August 28, 1952. Her father, Ray Dove, was one of the first black chemists in the American tire-and-rubber industry, and both of her parents valued education. Dove excelled at Ohio's Miami University, graduating with honors in 1973. The following year, she attended the University of Tübingen on a Fulbright fellowship and completed her M.F.A. at the University of Iowa Writers' Workshop in 1977.

That year also marked the publication of Dove's first chapbook, *Ten Poems* (1977). Her first book-length collection, *The Yellow House on the Corner* (1980), appeared three years later to mixed critical reviews. However, her next work, *Museum* (1983), received a generally favorable response, and she garnered widespread praise for 1986's *Thomas and Beulah.* The latter is a volume of narrative verse that traces Dove's ancestry, beginning with her maternal grandparents. Dove followed *Thomas and Beulah* with the largely autobiographical

Douglass, a powerful orator and prominent abolitionist.

poetry in *Grace Notes* (1989) and a volume of *Selected Poems* (1993). In 1995 she published *Mother Love,* her sixth book of poetry. Written primarily in sonnet form, the verses contemplate motherhood, particularly the often troubled relationships between mothers and daughters.

Although Dove is known primarily as a poet, she has composed fiction and drama as well. Her **novel, *Through the Ivory Gate*** (1992), tells of a talented young black woman who accepts a position as artist-in-residence. Dove's list of publications also includes *Fifth Sunday* (1985), a **short story** collection, and *The Darker Face of the Earth* (1994), a verse drama.

In addition to her work as a writer, Dove has pursued an academic career. Beginning in 1981, she taught at Arizona State University, and in 1989 she became Commonwealth Professor of English at the University of Virginia. Her

Rita Dove in 1992, after the release of her first novel.

Ezekiel Mphahlele's accounting of his life from the age of five to age thirty-eight, at which time he left his country. The book takes its name from a street in Marabastad, a township in Pretoria, South African, where Mphahlele lived with his parents beginning at age thirteen. Through Mphahlele's eyes, readers watch the social and political disintegration that occur around him. This early part of the book is distinguished by the immediacy of the storytelling as well as the vitality of the characters and their struggles to rise above harsh circumstances.

In subsequent chapters, Mphahlele recounts the honors he attained in later life, and the failures, disillusionment, and bitterness he experienced, which ultimately resulted in his voluntary exile to Lagos, Nigeria. Between chapters, Mphahlele includes "interludes" in which he discusses issues of importance to him, such as the dissolution of Marabastad under **apartheid** laws. *Down Second Avenue* is regarded as a classic of South African literature. It is viewed both as a social record of a period in South African history as well as an emotionally profound work about the triumphs and struggles of one man.

husband is the novelist Fred Viebahn. The couple and their daughter live in Charlottesville, Virginia.

See also **Poetry of Rita Dove**

Further Readings
Black Writers, second edition, Gale, 1994.
Dictionary of Literary Biography, Volume 120: *American Poets since World War II,* Third Series, Gale, 1992.

Down Second Avenue
Ezekiel Mphahlele
Autobiography, 1959

Down Second Avenue, which has been translated into eleven languages, represents

Dr. Crookman
Character in *Black No More*

Dr. Dudley Stanton
Character in *The River Niger*

Dr. Ernest Papanek
Character in *Manchild in the Promised Land*

Dr. Gaines
Character in *The Escape; or, A Leap for Freedom*

Dr. Riley
Character in *Youngblood*

Dream on Monkey Mountain

Derek Walcott
Play, first produced 1967, published 1970

In *Dream on Monkey Mountain* (1970), **Derek Walcott** explores the nature of **colonialism** and how West Indian natives who live under Western rule struggle to affirm their own beliefs, leaders, and distant relationship to Africa. The **play**, a stylized, surrealistic, poetic drama set in a West Indian village, centers on the conflict of ethnic identity experienced by the West Indian protagonist, Makak. Makak's crisis stems from his vision that he is descended from ancient African kings and possesses magical powers. The play's dream-like plot is framed with scenes of Makak in prison, where he is confused about his true identity. Here he has his vision, and becomes convinced of his own nobility and healing powers. He travels through the countryside with his companion, Moustique, and becomes known as a savior after healing a dying villager, Joseph. In the epilogue, Makak is released from prison believing he has been touched by God and that he must return to the origins of his people on Monkey Mountain. He also remembers his legal name, Felix Hobain. The play won an Obie Award in 1971.

William J. Drummond

American journalist
Born September 29, 1944.

Born in Oakland, California, and educated at the University of California and Columbia University, William Joe Drummond worked from 1977 until 1983 for the *Los Angeles Times.* At the *Times,* he served as bureau chief in New Delhi and Jerusalem, as a special assistant to the U.S. Department of State, and as a White House associate presss secretary. He covered, among other stories, the **black power** movement on the west coast, the assassination of Senator Robert F. Kennedy in 1968, and the liberation of Bangladesh in 1971. Drummond has also worked as a National Public Radio correspondent from 1979 to 1983 and in 1983 began teaching **journalism** at the University of California at Berkeley.

Further Readings
Black Writers, Gale, first edition, 1989.

David G. Du Bois

American journalist and novelist
Born September, 1925.

David Graham Du Bois, stepson of **W. E. B. Du Bois**, was born in Seattle, Washington, and was the official spokesperson for the Black Panther Party. He attended Columbia University and Peking University before taking degrees from Hunter College and New York University. He has worked for the *Arab Observer* in Cairo, Egypt, as an editor and reporter; as news editor for the *Egyptian Gazette;* as reporter and editor for the Middle East News and Features Agency; as announcer and program writer for Radio Cairo; and in public relations for the Ghana government.

Du Bois was also the editor-in-chief of Black Panther Intercommunal News Service. He has lectured in criminology at the University of California at Berkeley and at Cairo University. He is the author of *And Bid Him Sing* (1975), a **novel** that grew out of his Cairo experiences.

Further Readings
Black Writers, Gale, first edition, 1989.

Shirley Graham Du Bois

American author, dramatist,
and composer
Born November 11, 1896.
Died March 27, 1977.

Born in Indianapolis, Indiana, in 1896, Shirley Graham had established herself long before her marriage in 1951 to **W. E. B. Du**

Bois. Her **epic** opera *Tom-Tom* (1932) guaranteed her reputation as an authority on African American culture. Employed by the Works Progress Administration (WPA) and a student at Yale between 1936 and 1941, Graham wrote several **plays,** including *Little Black Sambo* (1938), *I Gotta Home* (1939), *It's Morning* (1940), and *Dust to Earth* (1941). *Dr. George Washington Carver* (1944) was the first of several biographies she wrote about famous black Americans; other subjects of her study include **Paul Robeson, Phillis Wheatley**, and **Booker T. Washington**. Graham wrote only one **novel,** *Zulu Heart* (1974). She died at eighty in Beijing, China.

Further Readings

Black Writers, first edition, Gale, 1989.

W. E. B. Du Bois

American-born Ghanaian historian
and essayist
Born February 23, 1868.
Died August 27, 1963.

Du Bois was a historian and essayist who shaped both black literature and the campaign for racial justice in America. A controversial figure, he challenged the views of **Booker T. Washington** and changed the study of African American history.

William Edward Burghardt Du Bois was born on February 23, 1868, in Great Barrington, Massachusetts, to Alfred and Mary Burghardt Du Bois. He lived an impoverished existence with his mother—his father abandoned the family early on—yet was fortunate in that his small hometown was not segregated and his intellectual abilities were widely recognized. When his mother died, the community gave him a scholarship to attend Fisk University in Nashville. He graduated in 1888 and won a scholarship to Harvard University, where he earned a second B.A.

in 1890 and an M.A. in 1891. He then spent two years studying at the University of Berlin. In 1896, he became the first African American to receive a Ph.D. from Harvard; his dissertation, *The Suppression of the African Slave-Trade to the United States of America, 1638-1870,* was published that same year.

In Europe, Du Bois had experienced a society free from **racism**, and, after returning to the states, he felt the injustices in America far more keenly; however, he continued to believe that the basis of racism was ignorance and the solution was scientific study. In 1896 the University of Pennsylvania hired him to conduct a study of blacks; *The Philadelphia Negro* (1899) was the first sociological study of a black urban community in America. In 1897, Du Bois was named professor of history and economics at Atlanta University, where he continued his sociological studies of African Americans.

A lynching in Atlanta shattered Du Bois's sense of scholarly detachment about racial issues, and the **essays** collected in *The Souls of Black Folk: Essays and Sketches* (1903) are passionate arguments for social equality. Speaking of the black experience of "twoness" in America, he challenged the views of Washington, who accepted **segregation** and the disenfranchisement of black voters.

In 1909, Du Bois became the only black founding member of the **National Association for the Advancement of Colored People** (NAACP). He was employed by the organization for more than two decades, founding and then editing the periodical *Crisis* until political conflicts forced him to return to Atlanta University in 1934. There he wrote *Black Reconstruction* (1935), submitting the period after the Civil War to a Marxist analysis and arguing for the importance of the role played by African Americans. In 1940, he founded *Phylon,* which quickly became known as the United States's leading journal of African American culture.

Resented by many people both inside and outside the African American community,

Du Bois became an increasingly isolated figure. He was charged with subversion during the McCarthy era and, in 1961, he renounced his American citizenship. Du Bois died two years later in Accra, Ghana, where he is buried.

Further Readings

Black Literature Criticism, Gale, 1992.

Black Writers, first edition, Gale, 1989.

Logan, Rayford W., editor, *W. E. B. Du Bois: A Profile,* Hill & Wang, 1971.

Lewis, David Levering, *W. E. B. Du Bois: Biography of a Race, 1868-1919,* Holt, 1993.

Dude

Character in *Caleb, the Degenerate*

Dulcina

Character in *Where the Hummingbird Flies*

W. E. B. Du Bois was a major force in helping define African American social and political causes.

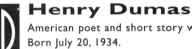

Henry Dumas

American poet and short story writer
Born July 20, 1934.
Died May 23, 1968.

Henry L. Dumas is considered one of the most original African American poets of the 1960s. Born in Sweet Home, Arkansas, Dumas migrated to Harlem at age ten. He entered City College in 1953 but then left for the Air Force, resuming his education at Rutgers University after his discharge in 1957 and becoming increasingly involved in the **civil rights movement**. He supported a wife and two children while writing **poetry, short stories,** and an unfinished **novel,** but lived to see none of his work published in book form. At the age of thirty-four, he was shot and killed by a policeman on a subway platform in what was eventually determined to be a case of mistaken identity.

Dumas's posthumously published work was edited by Hale Chatfield and Eugene Redmond. *Ark of Bones and Other Stories* (1970) consists of pieces ranging from the realistic to the fantastic. The title story describes a mysterious ark that dredges the bones of lynched African Americans from the Mississippi River. Dumas's collection *Poetry for My People* (1970) was reissued as *Play Ebony: Play Ivory* (1974). His poetry has been praised for its spiritual vision and for its authentic rendering of the language of African Americans. Other publications of Dumas's work include *Rope of Wind and Other Stories* (1979) and the unfinished novel *Jonoah and the Green Stone (1976).*

See also **Short Stories of Henry Dumas**

Further Readings

Black Writers, first edition, Gale, 1989.

Dunbar often wrote in African American dialect.

Paul Laurence Dunbar

American poet, short story writer, and novelist
Born June 27, 1872.
Died February 9, 1906.

At the turn of the twentieth century, Dunbar was the most popular black poet in America, admired by figures as diverse as **Booker T. Washington** and **W. E. B. Du Bois**. Dunbar has been faulted for not protesting racial injustice, though scholars have argued that this judgment neglects the realities that faced an African American writing for a largely white audience.

Dunbar was born on June 27, 1872, in Dayton, Ohio, to former slaves. His parents divorced when he was young and his father died soon afterwards; his mother nurtured his love of literature and told him stories about plantation life, which later inspired some of his dialect poems. In high school, Dunbar was an outstanding student; poverty prevented him from going to college. He intended to be a journalist but because of his race no editor offered him a job. He worked as an elevator operator, producing **poetry,** articles, and **short stories** that were published in midwestern newspapers.

An address Dunbar gave to a writer's association in 1892 attracted a broader audience, and in 1893 he privately published *Oak and Ivy.* He also visited Chicago that year, reciting poetry at the World's Columbian Exposition. In 1895 he published ***Majors and Minors*** with the help of white patrons; the volume was reviewed by William Dean Howells, then the most influential literary critic in America, and Dunbar was suddenly famous.

In his review, Howells praised the **dialect poetry** but dismissed the verse in standard English, a verdict that haunted Dunbar throughout his career. Dunbar's ***Lyrics of Lowly Life*** (1896) became a best seller on the basis of the dialect poems, and his other poetry was often rejected by magazines looking for more verses like "The Party," about a gathering of plantation slaves. His dialect poems are generally comic, as are his popular short stories, some of which he published in *Folks from Dixie* (1898).

In 1898, he married Alice Ruth Moore and published his first **novel,** *The Uncalled* (1898), about a white preacher. This novel was commercially and critically unsuccessful, as were the two that followed. His fourth novel, *The Sport of the Gods* (1902) is the only one with a black protagonist—he is unjustly convicted of theft and his family thrown into disarray.

Dunbar fell ill with tuberculosis in 1899 and began drinking heavily soon afterwards. His marriage was largely unhappy and, in 1902, he separated from his wife. He died in Dayton on February 9, 1906.

Further Readings

Black Literature Criticism, Gale, 1992.

Black Writers, first edition, Gale, 1989.

Revell, Peter, *Paul Laurence Dunbar,* Twayne, 1979.

Katherine Dunham
American dancer, anthropologist, and
autobiographer
Born June 22, 1910.

Best known for her contributions to the
world of dance, Dunham is also an anthropologist and autobiographer. As a student, Dunham
was equally attracted to science and art, but she
did not reconcile these interests until 1933,
when she began her anthropology career by
studying ethnic dance. Following her role in *La
Guiablesse,* a ballet based on a West Indian legend, Dunham began researching West Indian
culture. In 1936, she was awarded the Rosenwald grant to travel to the Caribbean. Her experiences there began her lifelong interest in the
culture of the Caribbean, especially Haiti. Dunham's investigation into the origins of West
Indian dance provided her with raw materials
for original choreography and furnished the subject matter for her doctoral thesis, later revised
and published as *Dances of Haiti* (1983).

Dunham's synthesis of old and new dance
movements brought her international acclaim as
a dancer and choreographer. In 1940, she made
her off-Broadway debut in *Tropics and Le Jazz
Hot* and later starred on Broadway and in several Hollywood films, including *Stormy
Weather* (1943) and *Mambo* (1966).

In 1959, Dunham published *A Touch of
Innocence,* a third-person chronicle of her early
life. *Island Possessed* (1969) continues her
story, describing her experiences in Haiti over
twenty-three years. Sometimes under the pseudonym Kaye Dunn, Dunham has also contributed short stories to popular magazines.
Since her retirement from the stage in the 1960s,
Dunham has served as cultural counselor and
director of the Performing Arts Training Center
in East St. Louis, Illinois.

Further Readings
Black Writers, first edition, Gale, 1989.

Dupree Sledge
Character in *Look What They Done to My Song*

Dancer and writer Dunham in 1943.

Dura
Character in *Possessing the Secret of Joy*

 ## *Dust Tracks on a Road*
Zora Neale Hurston
Autobiography, 1942

Dust Tracks on a Road is **Zora Neale
Hurston**'s own story of growing up in Florida.
Considered one of the most controversial figures of the **Harlem Renaissance**, Hurston drew
on her imagination and her anthropological
studies as well as her own experiences to create
a picture of African American life in the Deep
South in the early twentieth century. The book
begins in Eatonville, Florida, where Hurston
spent her childhood, and describes her early life.

ZORA NEALE HURSTON

AUTHOR OF THEIR EYES WERE WATCHING GOD

AN AUTOBIOGRAPHY

DUST TRACKS ON A ROAD

"Warm, witty, imaginative, and down-to-earth by turns, this is a rich and winning book by one of our few genuine, Grade A folk writers."
—*The New Yorker*

Cover for Hurston's memoir of her childhood in Florida.

Especially inspiring is her mother, a former schoolteacher who encourages her daughter to look beyond the limits of her world. When Zora is thirteen, her mother dies. Her father remarries, and Hurston is left without a home or family. She finds work as a maid and discovers a discarded copy of John Milton's complete works in the trash, which helps her decide to return to school. After another job as a maid, she enrolls at Morgan College and then at Howard University in Washington, D.C. Hurston finds friends and patrons who encourage her writing, including the editor **Charles S. Johnson** and the novelist Fanny Hurst. She receives a scholarship

to attend Barnard College and there meets Franz Boas, an anthropologist who encourages her to collect African American **folklore**. With the help of Charlotte Osgood Mason, a wealthy philanthropist and supporter of the arts, Zora begins her work.

Dust Tracks on a Road was sharply criticized by other African American writers for its refusal to attack **segregation**. In one striking example, Hurston records her embarrassment at a black man who insisted on having his hair cut in a barbershop for whites. However, Hurston's lack of sensitivity and apparent obliviousness to her racist environment may derive from her belief in an individual's ability to control her own destiny—a belief she expresses often in *Dust Tracks on a Road.*

Dustland

Please see "Justice" Trilogy

Dutchman

Amiri Baraka
Play, first produced and published 1964

Dutchman, one of **Amiri Baraka**'s best-known **plays**, questions the value of racial integration in America through the interactions of a young, bourgeois black man, Clay, and an attractive, slightly older white woman, Lula, aboard a New York City subway. In the opening scene, Lula initiates a series of sexually charged verbal attacks that arouse mixed feelings of curiosity, desire, and confusion in Clay. She puts her hand on his thigh, only to remove it quickly before offering him an apple and asking that he invite her to a party. Calling attention to his three-piece suit, she suggests that he is dressed as a white man rather than the grandson of a slave. But Clay insists that his grandfather was a night watchman, and when asked if he considers himself a "black nigger," he identifies himself as a poet—a black Baudelaire. Continuing her verbal assault, Lula tells Clay that he is a murderer before insisting that they can both at least pretend to be free of their history.

In the second scene, Lula gains complete control, teasing Clay with promises of sexual pleasure and suggesting that he, as "an escaped nigger," should fear the white passengers boarding the car. After enduring further mockery, Clay finally asserts himself: he slaps Lula and condemns her professed understanding of blackness. The function of African American art and music, he tells her, is to serve as an outlet for black aggression. Clay retreats into the safety of his words, however, warning her never to trust assimilated blacks because they will one day use Western rationalism to justify the murder of whites. As Clay prepares to leave, Lula stabs him twice and commands the other passengers, both black and white, to remove the body at the next stop. As the passengers disembark, a young black man enters the car. After exchanging greetings with the black conductor, who tips his hat to Lula before exiting, he sits down a few seats behind her, implying that the sequence will be repeated.

Typescript page from Baraka's award-winning play.

E-F

I am invisible, understand,

simply because people

refuse to see me.

Invisible Man,
Ralph Ellison, 1952

Eagle

Character in *Night Song* and *The Story of Jumping Mouse*

Earl Davis

Character in *The Past Is the Past*

Easter

Character in *Queen*

Ebony

John H. Johnson, publisher
Magazine, 1945-

According to Johnson's "Publisher's Statement" of November 1, 1990, *Ebony* was created to "celebrate Black excellence and to call our children to new frontiers of excellence."

First published on November 1, 1945, *Ebony*'s first print run of 25,000 copies sold out immediately. Since then, *Ebony* has remained a popular and critical success. The magazine won the CEBA Awards for Communications Excellence to Black Audiences Award of Excellence in 1989, and currently has a circulation rate of almost two million.

Ebony Wood (Bois d'ébène)

Jacques Roumain
Poems, 1945

Written while **Jacques Roumain** was in exile in Europe and published by his widow after his death, *Ebony Wood* consists of three poems that are widely acknowledged to be among Roumain's most militant work. The poem entitled "Ebony Wood" ("Bois d'ébène") is **epic** in scope and describes Roumain's view of the history of the black race and his hope for the future of his people. In "Dirty Blacks" ("Sales Nègres"), Roumain uses forceful lan-

guage to declare that black people must mobilize and revolt against their white oppressors. Finally, in "A New Black Sermon" ("Nouveau Sermon nègre"), Roumain depicts Christ as a black man whose face was whitened by the spit of contemptuous churchgoers. Roumain's activism and attempts to end America's military occupation of Haiti in the 1920s and 1930s are reflected in these poems.

Michael J. C. Echeruo

Nigerian poet and critic
Born March 14, 1937.

Born in Nigeria, Michael Joseph Chukwudalu Echeruo attended Stella Maris College and the University College of Ibadan before earning his Ph.D. from Cornell University in 1965. Echeruo then returned to Nigeria and published *Mortality: Poems* (1968) and *Distanced: New Poems* (1976), whose individual poetic style reflects Echeruo's multicultural influences. He has also written two books of criticism on Joyce Cary, *Joyce Cary and the Novel of Africa* (1973) and *Joyce Cary and the Dimensions of Order* (1979). Echeruo's *The Conditioned Imagination from Shakespeare to Conrad: Studies in the Exo-Cultural Stereotype* (1978), examines racial stereotypes in literature. Beginning in 1981, Echeruo has served as the vice-chancellor of Imo State University in Nigeria.

Further Readings
Black Writers, second edition, Gale, 1994.

Eclair Pockchop

Character in *The Free-Lance Pallbearers*

Ed Grimes

Character in *Jubilee*

Eddie Green

Character in *The Past Is the Past*

Children's advocate Edelman in 1985.

Marian Wright Edelman

American activist and political writer
Born June 6, 1939.

The founder of the Children's Defense Fund, Edelman is considered one of Washington's most effective lobbyists on issues affecting the future of American children.

Born in Bennettsville, South Carolina, on June 6, 1939, Edelman received her B.A. from Spelman College in 1960 and her law degree from Yale University in 1963. She was the first black woman admitted to the Mississippi bar and served as a lawyer on the staff of the **National Association for the Advancement of Colored People** (NAACP) until 1968, when she moved to Washington and began her work on behalf of children. In 1973, she founded the Children's Defense Fund, a nonprofit child advocacy organization that aims to provide

assistance to children while making their needs a matter of public policy.

Edelman continues to promote her cause with facts about poverty and infant mortality, and in 1983 her organization launched a nationwide campaign to reduce teen pregnancies that included multimedia advertising and coalitions in local communities. In her book *Families in Peril: An Agenda for Social Change* (1987), she urges support for poor mothers and children of all races. Edelman has served on a number of national and presidential commissions. In 1980, she became the first black and second woman to chair the Board of Trustees at Spelman College, and in 1985 she was awarded a MacArthur fellowship. Her book *The Measure of Our Success: A Letter to My Children and Yours* was published in 1992.

Further Readings

Black Writers, second edition, Gale, 1994.

Epic Lives, Visible Ink Press, 1993.

S. Randolph Edmonds

American teacher and dramatist
Born April 30, 1900.
Died March 28, 1983.

Sheppard Randolph Edmonds was a driving force behind academic dramatics in African American universities for more than four decades. The speech and drama department he organized at Dillard University in 1935 was the first in a black university. Edmonds's **plays,** which include "Shades and Shadows" (1930) and the collections *Six Plays for a Negro Theatre* (1934) and *The Land of Cotton, and Other Plays* (1942), address issues ranging from civil rights to **slavery**, dramatize the lives of black historical figures, and focus on the daily experiences of blacks. Edmonds also published numerous articles and **essays**.

Further Readings

Black Writers, first edition, Gale, 1989.

Dictionary of Literary Biography, Volume 51: *Afro-American Writers from the Harlem Renaissance to 1940,* Gale, 1987.

Edna Bisnauth

Character in *A Morning in Trinidad*

Education of the Negro prior to 1861

Carter G. Woodson
History, 1915

In *Education of the Negro prior to 1861: A History of the Education of the Colored People of the United States from the Beginning of Slavery to the Civil War,* **Carter G. Woodson** divides the history of black education prior to the Civil War into two periods. During the first period, which ends in 1835, Woodson's research indicates that many slaves were provided some form of educational instruction on the plantations. From 1836 to 1861, however, Woodson reveals that this system of patriarchal education disappeared, primarily due to the growing fear of insurrection following the Nat Turner and Denmark Vesey rebellions. During this second period, slaves received only industrial education.

Junius Edwards

American novelist and short story writer
Born in 1929.

Born in Alexandria, Louisiana, Edwards is known primarily for documenting the dilemmas of the black American soldier. He won first prize in the 1958 *Writer's Digest* Short Story Contest for "Liars Don't Qualify," the story of a black Korean veteran denied permission to register to vote in his Southern town. Edwards's **novel** *If We Must Die* (1961) elaborates on the events of his award-winning story but was less well received than "Mother Dear and Daddy" (1966), about intraracial prejudice, or "Duel with the Clock" (1967), about a young soldier's addiction to drugs. Edwards works in advertising.

Further Readings
Black Writers, second edition, Gale, 1994.

Dictionary of Literary Biography, Volume 33: *Afro-American Fiction Writers after 1955,* Gale, 1984.

Efuru

Character in *Efuru*

Efuru

Flora Nwapa
Novel, 1966

Efuru, **Flora Nwapa**'s first **novel**, is set in the Nigerian village of Oguta, where Nwapa was raised. The novel's protagonist, Efuru, is a beautiful, intelligent woman and a successful trader. Yet she is flawed in the eyes of society because she cannot have a child. In addition, Efuru defies tradition by choosing two husbands without familial approval, and both marriages end disastrously. Although Efuru is unable to fulfill her community's expectations of her as a wife and mother, she is given another role: worshiper of the lake deity. The end of the story questions the importance society places on the role of women as procreators.

Egbo

Character in *The Interpreters*

Cyprian Ekwensi

Nigerian novelist and
short story writer
Born September 26, 1921.

Cyprian Odiatu Duaka Ekwensi is a prolific and popular Nigerian writer whose contributions to African literature are debated. One of the first African authors to write in English, Ekwensi has published nearly thirty books, including *People of the City* (1954), *Jagua Nana* (1961), and *For a Roll of Parchment* (1987). Ekwensi's admirers contend that he is a social realist who raises important issues about urban life in Nigeria. Others have objected to what they consider Ekwensi's lack of skill and obscene portrayals of squalor, decadence, and promiscuity. Ekwensi has worked for the Nigerian government in various media-related capacities since 1951 and became chair of the Federal Nigerian Broadcasting Corporation in 1991.

Further Readings

Black Writers, second edition, Gale, 1994.

Emenyonu, Ernest N., *The Essential Ekwensi: A Literary Celebration of Cyprian Ekwensi's Sixty-Fifth Birthday,* Heinemann, 1987.

Ekweume

Character in *The Concubine*

Lonne Elder III

American dramatist and screenwriter
Born December 26, 1931.

Elder is a dramatist whose **plays** and screenplays document racial tensions and the hardships that prejudice has inflicted on the black community. His works explore the question of black identity by focusing on the resilience of the black family. He is well known for his play *Ceremonies in Dark Old Men* (1965), which explores the options facing a black ghetto family struggling for economic stability and self-fulfillment. The drama received several awards, including a Pulitzer Prize nomination. In *Sounder* (1972), his film adaptation of William H. Armstrong's **novel,** the family's dog becomes identified with the love and determination that hold a family together. Elder received an Academy Award nomination for best screenplay based on material from another medium for the adaptation.

Further Readings

Black Literature Criticism, Gale, 1992.

Black Writers, first edition, Gale, 1989.

Elesin

Character in *Death and the King's Horseman*

Elgar Enders

Character in *The Landlord*

Eli Bolton

Character in *All-Night Visitors*

Elijah Raven

Character in *The Free-Lance Pallbearers*

Eliza

Character in *Mine Boy*

Elizabeth

Character in *A Question of Power*

Elizabeth "Geeder" Perry

Character in *Zeely*

Elizabeth Grimes

Character in *Go Tell It on the Mountain*

Ralph Ellison

American novelist, essayist, and short story writer
Born March 1, 1914.
Died April 16, 1994.

Ralph Waldo Ellison is considered one of the most influential American authors of the twentieth century. He is best known for his **novel** *Invisible Man* (1952), a work that affirms the need for individual self-awareness. Winner of the 1953 National Book Award for fiction, *Invisible Man* is widely regarded as a masterpiece for its treatment of racial repression and betrayal. Shifting between naturalistic, expressionistic, and surrealistic styles, Ellison combined concerns of European and African American literature to chronicle a black youth's quest to discover his identity.

Born on March 1, 1914, in Oklahoma City, Oklahoma, Ellison was raised in an environment that promoted self-fulfillment. His father, who named his son after Ralph Waldo Emerson and hoped to raise him as a poet, died when Ellison was three. Ellison's mother enlisted blacks into the Socialist Party and also was a domestic worker. In the early 1930s, Ellison won a scholarship to Alabama's Tuskegee Institute, where he studied music until 1936. Later, to earn money for his education (after a mix-up regarding his scholarship), he traveled to New York, where he met **Richard Wright** and became involved in the Federal Writers' Project. Encouraged to write a review for *New Challenge,* a publication edited by Wright, Ellison began composing **essays** and stories focusing on the strength of the human spirit and the necessity of racial pride. Two of his most celebrated early short stories—"Flying Home" and "King of the Bingo Game"—foreshadow *Invisible Man* in their portrayal of alienated young protagonists seeking self-understanding.

After serving in the U.S. Merchant Marine during World War II, Ellison envisioned composing a war novel; however, he instead found himself writing *Invisible Man.* The title character is often compared to Voltaire's Candide, who remains optimistic despite having to endure betrayal, manipulation, and disillusionment. Although the work has been faulted by some critics for lacking a stringent militant stance toward civil rights issues, *Invisible Man* received praise upon its publication and continues to generate critical scholarship, with many commentators noting the thematic and stylistic influences of such writers as Ernest Hemingway, James Joyce, and T. S. Eliot.

Throughout his career, Ellison lectured widely throughout the United States and taught at a number of universities, including New York University, where he began teaching in 1970. In addition to *Invisible Man,* he also published two essay collections: *Going to the Territory* (1986), which contains discussions of art and music, fragments of **autobiography**, and tributes to such influences as Wright and Duke Ellington; and *Shadow and Act* (1964), a compilation of reviews, criticism, and interviews concerning art, music, literature, and the influence of the black experience on American culture. This latter volume is often acclaimed for its insights into both *Invisible Man* and an as-yet unpublished second novel, which Ellison left unfinished at the time of his death. Eight excerpts

Ellison, who published *Invisible Man* in 1952.

from the work—which is set in the American South and encompasses the **jazz** age and the **civil rights movement**—have been published in literary journals. Ellison's short stories remain uncollected, although several of them have been published in anthologies, including *A New Southern Harvest* (1957), *The Angry Black* (1962), and *Southwest Fiction* (1980). Ellison, who married Fanny McConnell in 1946, died of pancreatic cancer on April 16, 1994. He is buried in Washington Heights.

Further Readings

Black Literature Criticism, Gale, 1992.

Black Writers, first edition, Gale, 1989.

Dictionary of Literary Biography, Volume 76: *Afro-American Writers, 1940-1955,* Gale, 1988.

Nadel, Alan, *Invisible Criticism: Ralph Ellison and the American Canon,* University of Iowa Press, 1988.

Schor, Edith, *Visible Ellison: A Study of Ralph Ellison's Fiction,* Greenwood Press, 1993.

James A. Emanuel

American poet and essayist
Born January 15, 1921.

James Andrew Emanuel attended Howard University, Northwestern University, and Columbia University. His dissertation on **Langston Hughes** eventually formed the basis of his book *Langston Hughes* (1967). In 1966, he began teaching at the City College of New York (CCNY), where he offered the College's first course in black **poetry.** Emanuel's own poetry, collected in such books as *The Treehouse and Other Poems* (1968), *Black Man Abroad: The Toulouse Poems* (1978), *A Chisel in the Dark: Poems, Selected and New* (1980), and *The Broken Bowl: New and Uncollected Poems* (1983), explores issues relating to black identity. His *Whole Grain: Collected Poems, 1958-1989* was published in 1991. Emanuel has also coedited *Dark Symphony: Negro Literature in America* (1968). His manuscript **autobiography**, *Snowflakes and Steel: My Life as a Poet, 1971-1980,* is housed at Duke University. Emanuel retired from CCNY in 1983 and moved to France.

See also **Poetry of James A. Emanuel**

Further Readings
Black Writers, first edition, Gale, 1989.
Dictionary of Literary Biography, Volume 41: *Afro-American Poets since 1955,* Gale, 1985.

Buchi Emecheta

Nigerian novelist and author of children's literature
Born July 21, 1944.

Emecheta is one of Nigeria's most recognized female writers. Her work is concerned with the subordinate role of women in an agrarian society and the impact of Western values on traditional African cultures. Born in a small village, she entered an arranged marriage at sixteen and later moved with her husband and their children to London; she divorced him after he read and then burned her first **novel.** Several of her books, including *In the Ditch* (1972), *Second-Class Citizen* (1974), and *Head above Water* (1984), are autobiographical. Some of her later novels are historical, including **The Slave Girl** (1977) and *The Rape of Shavi* (1983). *The Joys of Motherhood* (1979), her most critically acclaimed novel, is set during great political and economic changes in Nigeria. Emecheta has also written five children's books.

Further Readings
Black Writers, second edition, Gale, 1994.

Emenike

Character in *The Concubine*

Emergency Exit

Clarence Major
Novel, 1979

The text of **Clarence Major**'s **novel** *Emergency Exit* is composed of epigraphs, poems, paintings, lists, schedules, and other communications from popular culture. In a highly episodic and self-conscious manner, the novel describes the Ingram family of Inlet, Connecticut. Major blurs the line between fiction and reality in this experimental work by such means as having characters talk back to the narrator. Interweaving a traditional love-triangle story with surreal episodes consisting of **fantasy**, anecdotes, dreams, and poems, the novel also includes real incidents from Major's life.

Epic

An epic is a long narrative poem, along the lines of Homer's *Iliad* and *Odyssey,* about the adventures of a hero whose actions are believed to have great historic or cultural importance. The setting is vast and the action is often given cosmic significance through the intervention of **supernatural** forces such as gods, angels, or demons. Epics are typically written in a classical style of grand simplicity with elaborate metaphors and allusions that enhance the symbolic importance of the hero's adventures. In 1877, with the appearance of the epic *Not a Man and Yet a Man,* **Albery Allson Whitman** became the first black American to publish a poem more than 5,000 lines long. His poem tells the story of a slave who eventually escapes to Canada and later fights in the Civil War. *Annie Allen* (1949), for which **Gwendolyn Brooks** received a Pulitzer Prize in 1950, and *Omeros* (1990), by **Derek Walcott**, are examples of twentieth-century epic poems.

Epitaph of a Small Winner
Joaquim Maria Machado de Assis
Novel, 1952

Set in Rio de Janeiro, Brazil, in the late nineteenth century, **Joaquim Maria Machado de Assis**'s *Epitaph of a Small Winner* (*Memórias póstumas de Braz Cubas*) is the post-mortem reminiscences of a man who has just died of pneumonia. Wealthy Braz Cubas is a deceptive and ambiguous narrator as he examines the sixty-five years of his life, describing himself in an unflattering but seemingly unremorseful manner.

As a young man, Cubas is grief-stricken at his mother's death, but he is more affected by the realization that his life, too, will end. He tries his hand at politics and publishing but fails because he lacks the perseverance any kind of success requires. Not finding fulfillment in various romantic and sexual relationships, nor in politics, work, philosophy, and charity, Braz dies childless. He concludes that life amounts to nothing, taking his only consolation in not having inflicted the misery of existence on anyone else.

Olaudah Equiano
African-born British autobiographer
Born about 1745.
Died March 31, 1797.

Equiano was born into the Ibo tribe in what is now Nigeria. At age eleven, he was kidnapped by black slave raiders, sold to British slave traders, and endured transport to America on a slave ship. He was eventually sold to a British sea captain (who renamed him Gustavus Vassa) and began a longtime career as a sailor. With the assistance of several friendly whites, he learned to speak, read, and write English. In the early 1760s he was sold to a Philadelphia merchant. By 1766 he was able to buy his own freedom. He ultimately settled in England and married there.

Equiano traveled as a sailor to many countries and colonies on the North Atlantic and the Mediterranean and even participated in a scientific expedition to the Arctic. In 1789 he published *The Interesting Narrative of the Life of Olaudah Equiano, or Gustavus Vassa, the African, Written by Himself*. This two-volume book, one of the earliest autobiographies by a former slave, was both a remarkable life story and a powerful expose of the horrors of **slavery** and the slave trade. Reprinted several times in the eighteenth and nineteenth centuries, the book has had several new editions since the 1960s.

Further Readings
Black Literature Criticism, Gale, 1992.

Dictionary of Literary Biography, Volume 50: *Afro-American Writers before the Harlem Renaissance,* Gale, 1986.

Ernie
Character in *We Can't Breathe*

The Escape; or, A Leap for Freedom
William Wells Brown
Play, 1858

The milestone publication of *The Escape; or, A Leap for Freedom* in 1858 marked the first time a drama by a black American writer had reached print. Although the work was never staged, **William Wells Brown** often read passages of it at his lectures. Comic in places and poignant in others, *The Escape* centers on two slaves, Glen and Melinda, who secretly marry and escape the abuses of their master, Dr. Gaines, for a life of freedom in Canada.

Many of the themes and plot devices in *The Escape* are drawn from Brown's own life and his familiarity with other abolitionist writers' material. His most scathing commentary in the drama is reserved for a clergyman, Mr. Pinchen, who plans to sell Negro slaves in Natchez to pay his expenses while conducting a camp meeting. Brown also demonstrated that in order to stave off brutality, the slaves were able to appear content and even fond of masters they despised.

Denounced in the twentieth century for its melodrama and oversimplified characterizations, *The Escape* is nonetheless recognized for its ground-breaking exploration of **slavery** by an ex-slave himself. In a preface to the work Brown apologized for the defects in his creation, stating that he had been raised an illiterate slave and thus knew nothing of formal stagecraft. Scholars have noted that this caveat does little to undermine the historical importance of Brown's work.

Escobar
Character in *Dom Casmurro*

Bruno Eseki
Please see Ezekiel Mphahlele

Essay

An essay is a prose composition with a focused subject of discussion. It can be long or short, formal or informal, personal or impersonal. The choice of subject matter is as flexible as the style. Essays by black writers reflect the versatility of the genre, ranging from the abolitionist essays of **Charlotte L. Forten** to **Bill Cosby**'s humorous writings on modern life and from the scholarly writings of **Alain Locke**

to **Eldridge Cleaver**'s fiery denunciations of racial injustice. In the late nineteenth and early twentieth centuries, **Booker T. Washington** and **W. E. B. Du Bois** wrote many influential essays on the African American struggle for freedom. The essays of **Walter White** chronicle the progress of the **civil rights movement** from the 1920s through the 1950s. **James Baldwin**'s *The Fire Next Time* (1963), **Ralph Ellison**'s *Shadow and Act* (1964), and **Eldridge Cleaver**'s *Soul on Ice* (1968), along with these authors' other writings, exposed and denounced the racial injustices of American society and made powerful calls for change. Ellison is also known for his essays on music and art, many of which are collected in *Going to the Territory* (1986). Writers like **Woodie King Jr.,** and **Loften Mitchell** have written extensively on black theater, while scholars such as **Amiri Baraka** and **Henry Louis Gates Jr.** have made important contributions to **literary criticism** and culture studies. Other noted contemporary African American essayists include **Toni Cade Bambara**, **Nikki Giovanni**, **Haki R. Madhubuti**, and **Alice Walker**. Internationally, black leaders and intellectuals such as **Nelson Mandela**, **Frantz Fanon**, and **C. L. R. James** have written influential essays on political, historical, and cultural issues.

Esther
Character in *Cane*

Etta James
Character in *A Short Walk*

Etta Mae Johnson
Character in *The Women of Brewster Place*

Eva Medina Canada
Character in *Eva's Man*

Eva Peace
Character in *Sula*

Eva Turner

Character in *The Women of Brewster Place*

Mari Evans

American poet, essayist, and dramatist
Born July 16, 1923.

Evans attracted the attention of teachers and scholars with her second volume of **poetry,** *I Am a Black Woman* (1970), which demonstrates her strong commitment to the black community. In subsequent years, her work has continued to display a sense of social responsibility and to celebrate African American culture.

Evans, born in Toledo, Ohio, identified her father's encouragement and her discovery of the poetry of **Langston Hughes** as important points in her literary development. She relates this and thoughts about her poetry in an **essay** that appears in *Black Women Writers (1950-1980): A Critical Evaluation* (1984), which she edited.

In 1968, Evans began a five-year stint as producer, writer, and director of *The Black Experience,* a television program for WTTV in Indianapolis. That same year, Evans published her first book, a poetry collection titled *Where Is All the Music?* Evans has continued to explore black culture in poems, essays, **plays,** and children's books. Her poetry collections *Nightstar: 1973-1978* (1981) and *A Dark and Splendid Mass* (1991) are noted for its use of idiom to present authentic black voices. Her works for children include *I Look at Me!* (1973), a personalized preprimer. Her plays include "Eyes" (1979), a musical adapted from **Zora Neale Hurston**'s novel *Their Eyes Were Watching God*. Evans has also taught at several universities since 1969. She received a National Endowment for the Arts Creative Writing Award in 1981.

See also **Poetry of Mari Evans**

Further Readings

Black Writers, first edition, Gale, 1989.

Dictionary of Literary Biography, Volume 41: *Afro-American Poets since 1955,* Gale, 1985.

Eva's Man

Gayl Jones
Novel, 1976

Gayl Jones's *Eva's Man* depicts the violent rebellion of one woman against male domination. Incarcerated in a hospital for the criminally insane, Eva Medina Canada refuses to talk to those around her. Instead, she describes to the reader the people and events that contributed to her present state of mind. Eva remembers Freddy, the neighborhood boy who, by penetrating her with a popsicle stick, provided her sexual initiation; her jealous husband James, who refused to allow her contact with anyone but him; and Alphonse, who secretively took her to bars and propositioned her. Finally Eva tells of another male character, Davis, who imprisoned Eva in his apartment, dehumanized her, and used her as an object to satisfy his sexual desires. Eva, having identified the source of her attacker's power of her, poisoned Davis, bit off his penis, called the police, and waited to be arrested.

An Evening Thought

Jupiter Hammon
Poem, 1760

Jupiter Hammon's first poem, *An Evening Thought: Salvation by Christ, with Penetential Cries,* was also the first work published by a slave in the Western hemisphere. It contains elements of both eighteenth-century devotional songs and later Negro **spirituals**. The word 'salvation' is used twenty-three times as part of the strong religious message communicated by the poem, which was probably written to be read aloud. Hammon's intended message of freedom is subtle, introducing the concept of true salvation, and proclaiming it to be found only in Christ rather than offered by the slave master. Writing partly to a slave audience, Hammon also refutes the notion of blacks as damned, declaring that their souls are "fit for Heaven."

Percival L. Everett

American novelist and short story writer
Born December 22, 1956.

Born in Fort Gordon, Georgia, Everett worked as a **jazz** musician, ranch hand, and high school teacher before making a career as a writer and professor. He has taught at the University of Kentucky, the University of Notre Dame, and the University of California, Riverside, where he became professor of creative writing in 1992.

Everett's first **novel,** *Suder* (1983), chronicles a black baseball player's personal crisis; *Walk Me to the Distance* (1985) tells the story of a Vietnam War veteran; *Zulus* (1989) is a work of **fantasy** fiction. Everett has published a collection of short stories, *The Weather and Women Treat Me Fair* (1989), as well as several other novels, including *God's Country* (1994), about a black tracker and a white cowboy and their search for the latter's wife, who has been abducted.

Further Readings
Black Writers, second edition, Gale, 1994.

Expressionism

Expressionism is an early twentieth-century term, originally used to describe a school of German painting, which soon came to be applied to literature, the theater, and cinema as well. Expressionistic writing is characterized by a focus on emotional states and by an aggressive rejection of both naturalistic depiction and conventional narrative forms. However, its meaning was never clearly defined, and it is often applied to almost any mode of unconventional, highly subjective writing that distorts surface reality. In his classic **novel** *Invisible Man* (1952), **Ralph Ellison** shifts among different literary styles, including expressionism. A similar concept is impressionism, which arose among painters in France. In impressionistic writing, the truth is grasped from fragmentary impressions rather than traditional narrative. In

his acclaimed **short story** collection *Tropic Death* (1926), Eric Walrond uses this style to illustrate the evils of imperialism as he darts from one image to another, depicting cultural impressions more than characters or plot.

Ezeulu

Character in *Arrow of God*

Ezidemili

Character in *Arrow of God*

Sarah Webster Fabio

American poet
Born January 20, 1928.
Died November 7, 1979.

Fabio was born in Nashville, Tennessee, and educated at Fisk University and San Francisco State College. Known as a poet and teacher, Fabio participated in the First World Festival of Negro Art in Dakar, Senegal, in 1966.

Fabio's books include *Race Results: U.S.A.* (1966), *Saga of a Black Man* (1968), *A Mirror* and *A Soul* (published as a two-part volume of poems, 1969), and *Black Talk: Soul, Shield, and Sword* (1973). She also contributed to magazines and edited *Journal of Black Arts Renaissance* and *Phase II.* Fabio also made two sound recordings, "Boss Soul" and "Soul Ain't, Soul Is," for Folkways Records in 1972.

Further Readings
Black Writers, Gale, first edition, 1989.

The Fabulous Miss Marie

Ed Bullins
Play, first produced 1971

Winner of an Obie Award for best Off-Off Broadway drama, *The Fabulous Miss Marie* is the fourth **play** in **Ed Bullins**'s "Twentieth Century Cycle." The drama takes place at the Christmas party of Marie and Bill Horton, a black middle-class couple whose marriage has withstood infidelity on the part of both spouses: Bill has fathered a child by his white lover, while Marie, lusty and pleasure-seeking, chooses and discards lovers on a whim. Marie's independent personality is juxtaposed against that of her niece Wanda, who is sexually exploited and insecure. Steve Benson, a recurring character in the "Twentieth Century Cycle," appears as one of Marie's lovers. As the action unfolds, many of the characters are seen to be self-centered and out of touch with larger social issues; the female characters in particular do not seem willing or able to become parents of a new generation.

Facing Mount Kenya
Jomo Kenyatta
Nonfiction, 1938

In his anthropological study *Facing Mount Kenya: The Tribal Life of the Gikuyu,* **Jomo Kenyatta** reveals much of the life of the Kikuyu (he preferred the "Gikuyu" spelling) people. One of Kenya's most prominent Kikuyus, Kenyatta spent seventeen years in England and travelled widely in Europe, obtaining an education and promoting issues pertinent to black Kenyans. Kenyatta thus brought a racially mixed perspective to his observations about his own people: as a native African, he experienced both the subjugation and repression engendered by British Colonial rule, yet he spent many years immersed in the culture of the European white man. His book, which began as a series of papers, explores in depth many of the cultural characteristics of the Kikuyu. Written in the Western style of sociological analysis, Kenyatta examines politics, tribal practices, religious rituals, government, land ownership, sexual activities, and other Kikuyu rites and customs. Throughout the book he often compares Kikuyu behaviors and conventions to European practices, attempting to justify and rationally explain tribal customs for the white man. In particular, he defends the practice of female circumcision. In general, he attempts to illustrate that the Kikuyu are as worthy a people in their native, indigenous culture as are the whites in Europe.

Ronald L. Fair
American novelist and poet
Born October 27, 1932.

Fair's characteristic use of experimental literary forms has earned him critical respect but little popular recognition. Fair was born in Chicago, Illinois, and began writing as a teenager. After working briefly in the Chicago courts, he wrote his second **novel,** *Hog Butcher* (1966; published as *Cornbread, Earl and Me,* 1975), about judicial injustice, and *World of Nothing* (1970), which deals with religious hypocrisy. In 1971, Fair left the United States to live in Finland. *We Can't Breathe* (1972), about self-destruction and redemption through the creative muse, won the American Library Association's Best Book Award in 1972. Fair has also written two **poetry** collections, *Excerpta* (1975) and *Rufus* (1977).

Further Readings
Black Writers, first edition, Gale, 1989.

Dictionary of Literary Biography, Volume 33: *Afro-American Fiction Writers after 1955,* Gale, 1984.

Families in Peril
Marian Wright Edelman
Nonfiction, 1987

Based on **Marian Wright Edelman**'s Harvard lectures on **W. E. B. Du Bois,** *Families in Peril: An Agenda for Social Change* examines the effects of poverty on American families in the 1980s. As the president of the Children's Defense Fund, Edelman focuses on the plight of children, especially African Americans. She also discusses how whites, like blacks, suffer from illegitimacy, child abuse, unemployment, and crime. Her proposed solutions to poverty-related problems emphasize increased government intervention and include developing an understanding of the facts related to the issues, focusing on manageable portions of problems, and breaking the generational cycle of poverty.

Fanny

Character in *The Landlord* and *The Temple of My Familiar*

Frantz Fanon

French psychologist, activist, and nonfiction writer
Born July 20, 1925.
Died December 6, 1961.

Fanon was a military psychologist whose experiences in French-controlled North Africa led him to write about the evils of **colonialism**. In his best-known and most controversial statement, Fanon recommended violence against an oppressor as both purifying and restorative for the oppressed individual. Although his proposal of using violence to obtain political liberation met with strong criticism, Fanon is nonetheless praised as a humanist and hero.

Born of middle-class parents on the island of Martinique, Fanon learned at an early age that the power structure directing his education discriminated against him because he was black. This lesson was reinforced by his experience with the Free French forces fighting in North Africa and Europe during World War II, and Fanon put his feelings in print in *Peau noire, masques blancs* (1952; *Black Skin, White Masks,* 1967). Following the war Fanon went to France to pursue studies in medicine, became a psychiatrist, and began his service in French-controlled Algeria shortly before armed rebellion broke out. Fanon's sympathies with the rebels caused his expulsion from the hospital in which he worked in 1957.

Fanon was reassigned to Tunisia, where he continued to support Algerian independence and where he began to examine the psychological and material costs of colonization and to propose a different future for colonial peoples. He is chiefly remembered for *Les Damnés de la terre* (1961; *The Damned,* 1963; *The Wretched of the Earth*, 1965), in which he proposes political independence as the precursor to genuine economic and social change. *L'an V de la revolution algerienne* (1959; *Studies in a Dying Colonialism,* 1965; *A Dying Colonialism,* 1967) and *Pour la revolution africaine: Ecrits politiques* (1964; *Toward the African Revolution: Political Essays,* 1967) are collections of **essays** tracing the development of Fanon's thought on **racism** and colonialism.

Further Readings
Black Writers, first edition, Gale, 1989.

Bouvier, Pierre, *Fanon,* Editions Universitaires, 1971.

Caute, David, *Fanon,* Viking, 1970.

Gendzier, Irene L., *Frantz Fanon: A Critical Study,* Pantheon, 1973.

Fantasy/ Supernatural

Fantasy is a literary form, related to **myth, folklore,** and **science fiction,** involving events that transcend the rules of ordinary experience. Fantasy literature is frequently set in nonexistent realms and often features **supernatural** beings and imaginary creatures. In a trilogy of fantasy novels—*Justice and Her Brothers* (1978), *Dustland* (1980), and *The Gathering* (1981)—children's author **Virginia Hamilton** deals with such topics as clairvoyance and time travel. In his **novel** *The Famished Road* (1991), which won the Booker Prize, Nigerian writer **Ben Okri** recounts the story of a child torn between the spirit and the natural world. One popular branch of fantasy literature is the ghost story. **Toni Morrison**'s novel *Tar Baby* (1981) is set on an island that is supposedly haunted by ghosts of African horsemen who escaped enslavement.

The Far Journey of Oudin

Please see The "Guyana" Quartet

Fast Sam, Cool Clyde, and Stuff

Walter Dean Myers
Young adult novel, 1975

Walter Dean Myers's first **novel** for young adults, *Fast Sam, Cool Clyde, and Stuff* is narrated by twelve-year-old Stuff, a young man whose family has just moved to West 116th Street in New York City. There he makes friends with two slightly older boys, Sam and Clyde, and a neighborhood girl, Gloria. Together they deal with an assortment of problems: Clyde's father dies, and his mother begins dating again; a neighborhood boy dies of a drug overdose; Gloria's father abandons her family, which is forced to go on welfare. The young people's mutual friendship proves a source of strength for all of them.

Fatherhood

Bill Cosby
Nonfiction, 1986

Bill Cosby acknowledges at the beginning of *Fatherhood,* his first book, that the entire procreative process seems irrational and inexplicable: it is bizarre, he suggests, that people make and then raise children in spite of all the ensuing aggravations. Written in the sardonic style Cosby uses in his **comedy** sketches, the book follows the phases of paternity from infant expectancy to college graduation. Though he culled the material for the commiserative anecdotes from his role as the father of five children, he never names them or his wife of twenty-two years. Instead, each one is Everychild, and Cosby the father is Everyman. There are passages on sibling squabbles, children's excuses, tough situations where he must punish and forgive, and being the breadwinner without being the boss. *Parenthood* made publishing history by becoming the fastest-selling hardcover.

Jessie Redmon Fauset

American editor and novelist
Born April 27, 1882(?).
Died April 30, 1961.

Fauset was largely responsible for discovering and encouraging many writers during the **Harlem Renaissance,** including **Langston Hughes**, **Countee Cullen**, **Jean Toomer**, and **Claude McKay**. Born in Camden County, New Jersey, Fauset graduated from Cornell University in 1905 and spent the next fourteen years teaching in the public schools of Baltimore and Washington, D.C. In 1919, she moved to New York City to become the literary editor of *Crisis* magazine. In 1920 and 1921, she also edited and did much of the writing for *The Brownies' Book,* a magazine for black children. She hoped to earn her living by writing after leaving *Crisis* in 1926 but ultimately had to return to teaching.

Fauset produced a number of poems, short stories, and **essays** during her long writing career, but her most noted works are her **novels.** *There Is Confusion* (1924) deals with black family life in a world of racial **discrimination**; *Plum Bun: A Novel without a Moral* (1929) is concerned with light-skinned blacks passing as white; *The Chinaberry Tree* (1931) examines miscegenation; and *Comedy, American Style* (1933) centers on a woman who hates being black. Faucet died of heart disease in Philadelphia.

Further Readings
Black Writers, first edition, Gale, 1989.

Dictionary of Literary Biography, Volume 51: *Afro-American Writers from the Harlem Renaissance to 1940,* Gale, 1987.

Sylvander, Carolyn Wedin, *Jessie Redmon Fauset, Black American Writer,* Whitston, 1981.

Elton Clay Fax

American nonfiction writer, essayist, and illustrator
Born October 9, 1909.

An award-winning artist and essayist, Fax is well known for his paintings and children's book illustrations. Born in Baltimore, Maryland, on October 9, 1909, he obtained his B.F.A. from Syracuse University in 1931. His writing in books such as *Contemporary Black Leaders* (1970), *Seventeen Black Artists* (1971), and *Black Artists of the New Generation* (1977) profiles the diversity of black Americans. His **biography** *Garvey* (1972) details the life of **Marcus Garvey**. Fax's travels to East Africa and central Asia inspired *Through Black Eyes: Journeys of a Black Artist in East Africa and Russia* (1974), *Hashar* (1980), *Elychin* (1983), and *Soviet People as I Knew Them* (1988).

Further Readings
Black Writers, second edition, Gale, 1994.

Tom Feelings

American illustrator and autobiographer
Born May 19, 1933.

Thomas Feelings was born May 19, 1933, in Brooklyn, New York, where he also grew up. He studied cartooning before choosing illustration. Distressed at the poor self-image of American blacks and at publishers' lack of interest in positive portrayals of black people and culture, Feelings worked in Ghana from 1964 to 1966. Upon his return to the United States, he began to seek out black authors. The resulting collaborations produced **Julius Lester**'s *To Be a Slave* (1968), and Muriel Feelings's *Moja Means One* (1971) and *Jambo Means Hello* (1974), which was nominated for an American Book Award. Feelings's own writings include his **autobiography** *Black Pilgrimage* (1972) and *Tommy Traveler in the World of Black History* (1991).

Further Readings
Black Writers, first edition, Gale, 1989.
Major Authors and Illustrators for Children and Young Adults, Gale, 1993.

Felice

Character in *Home to Harlem* and *Jazz*

Felix Hobain

Character in *Dream on Monkey Mountain*

Fences

August Wilson
Play, first produced 1985, published 1985

August Wilson's Pulitzer Prize-winning *Fences,* set in 1957, revolves primarily around the family relationships of Troy Maxson, a fifty-three-year-old black garbage collector who at one time entertained thoughts of a career in major league baseball. A fifteen-year term in prison for murder as a much younger man led to the development of his extraordinary skill at baseball. Upon his release, however, he found the major leagues closed to him because of his color. After prison, he married Rose; their son, Cory, a high-school senior as the drama opens, excels at football and has been recruited by a North Carolina college for an athletic scholarship. Troy, however, refuses to discuss his son's college possibilities and angrily questions why Cory is neglecting his part-time job and household chores, which include helping build a fence Rose has requested. Eventually, Troy learns that Cory has been lying about being employed; instead, he is spending more time at football. Infuriated by Cory's deception, Troy demands that the football coach permanently suspend Cory from the team, thereby ruining his chances for a scholarship, a college education, and possible professional career. Finally, Cory leaves home, disgusted with his father's adultery and ongoing mistreatment of Troy's mentally-impaired war-injured younger brother, Gabe. Troy dies in 1965, and Cory returns home, agreeing to attend his father's funeral as his mother points out that despite his actions, his father never intended harm to anyone.

Julia Fields
American poet and author of children's literature
Born January, 1938.

Fields was encouraged early in her career by **Langston Hughes**, who included two of her poems in *New Negro Poets: U.S.A.* (1964). Fields later published *I Heard a Young Man Saying* (1967), *Poems* (1968), *East of Moonlight* (1973), and *A Summoning, A Shining* (1976), which she dedicated to **Robert Hayden**, **Eugene B. Redmond**, and **Clarence Major**. In 1972, Fields was awarded the Seventh Conrad Kent Rivers Memorial Fund Award by *Negro Digest*. *Slow Coins* (1981), which many critics consider to be her best work, contains several poems written in black dialect. In 1988, Fields published a children's book, *The Green Lion of Zion Street*.

See also **Poetry of Julia Fields**

Further Readings
Black Writers, first edition, Gale, 1989.

Dictionary of Literary Biography, Volume 41: *Afro-American Poets since 1955,* Gale, 1985.

Fine Clothes to the Jew
Langston Hughes
Poetry, 1927

Many critics condemned **Langston Hughes**'s second volume of verse, *Fine Clothes to the Jew,* because of its frank treatment of everyday life in Harlem. In poems describing prostitution, gambling, violence, and fundamentalist **religion**, Hughes uses vernacular dialects and common rhythms of everyday speech that were initially excoriated for their apparent vulgarity. However, *Fine Clothes to the Jew* is now widely praised for its vivid portrayal of black urban American folk culture and its poetic innovations: incorporating verbal **realism**, colloquial expression, and blues conventions.

The Fire in the Flint
Walter White
Novel, 1924

A **novel** about race relations and lynching in the South during the years immediately following World War I, **Walter White**'s *The Fire in the Flint* depicts middle-class black Americans and the effects of **racism** on their lives. The novel reflects the extensive research on lynching White conducted on behalf of the **National Association for the Advancement of Colored People** (NAACP).

The protagonist of this story, Dr. Kenneth Harper, is a European-educated black Atlantan. Returning to practice medicine in Georgia, he attempts to rise above prejudice through an optimistic faith in the power of reason, but he is gradually forced to abandon his nonconfrontational attitude and face the brutal realities of racism. In the end, he is lynched by a bloodthirsty mob after he has saved the life of a white child.

The novel attempts to counter the romantic depictions of white Southerners made popular in the early decades of the twentieth century. Although the artistry of *The Fire in the Flint* has been criticized as stilted, archaic, and marred by cliches, the novel offers an accurate depiction of the effects of racism on blacks and whites. The South's double standard of justice, portrayed throughout the novel, is illustrated most effectively by the novel's pessimistic ending, in which a quotation from a newspaper report dismisses Harper as a common hoodlum slain while committing a crime.

The Fire Next Time
James Baldwin
Essays, 1963

James Baldwin's collection of **essays** *The Fire Next Time* is considered one of the most influential books on race relations published during the 1960s. Divided into two sections, the book urges the politicization of both African Americans and European Americans on the issue of **racism**. Baldwin explains that the radicalism and militancy of many prominent African Americans is a reaction to feelings of alienation inspired by traditional American society. Originally published as two separate works—"Letter from a Region in My Mind" in the *New Yorker* and "A Letter to My Nephew" in the *Progressive*—the essays were retitled "Down at the Cross" and "My Dungeon Shook: Letter to My Nephew on the One Hundredth Anniversary of the Emancipation Proclamation" for their appearance in book form. Using rhetorical devices learned in his youth as a Pentecostal preacher and examples from his own life, Baldwin argues for an end to racism.

"Down at the Cross" is an analysis of the limitations of the **Christianity** that Baldwin practiced in childhood. Baldwin traces his personal history from his career as a junior minister and salesman and his exposure to Italian and Jewish cultures in his high school years. He concentrates his perception of the failure of the Christian church to address the problem of racism in general and his sense of alienation in particular. A good portion of "Down at the Cross" is devoted to an analysis of the **Nation of Islam** movement and its leaders Elijah Muhammad and **Malcolm X**. Although Baldwin recognizes that the Black Muslim movement emphasizes separateness and alienation, he values the Nation of Islam for using these feelings to create a sense of community among otherwise alienated African Americans. In "My Dungeon Shook," Baldwin urges his nephew not to base his sense of self-worth on his acceptance by American society but to grow personally so that he can accept society, with all its limitations, within himself.

Rudolph Fisher

American novelist and short story writer
Born May 9, 1897.
Died December 26, 1934.

Respected by a number of notable black writers, Rudolph John Chauncey Fisher helped spark interest in black literature during the **Harlem Renaissance**. Born in Washington, DC, Fisher graduated from Brown University in 1919 and Howard University Medical School in 1924. The following year, he moved to New York, where he began two years of postgraduate medical studies at Columbia University and published his first short stories, including "The City of Refuge."

Fisher began his medical practice in New York in 1927. His first **novel**, *The Walls of Jericho* (1928), attempts to portray all levels of Harlem society, and his second book, *The Conjure Man Dies: A Mystery Tale of Dark Harlem* (1932), is recognized as the first black American detective novel. Fisher also published ten more short stories between 1927 and 1933 (another was published posthumously in 1935), including "Common Meter" (1930), the story of two **jazz** musicians, and "Miss Cynthie" (1933), which centers on a protective black grandmother. Fisher died of a chronic intestinal ailment at the age of thirty-seven.

Further Readings

Black Writers, first edition, Gale, 1989.

Dictionary of Literary Biography, Volume 51: *Afro-American Writers from the Harlem Renaissance to 1940,* Gale, 1987.

Fix Boutan

Character in *A Gathering of Old Men*

The Flagellants (Les Flagellents)

Carlene Hatcher Polite
Novel, 1966

Published in 1966 while **Carlene Hatcher Polite** was living in Paris, *Les Flagellents* was translated in 1967. In the book, Ideal and Jimson meet in Greenwich Village and embark on a mutually painful relationship. They are restricted by the social pressure put on young blacks in the 1960s. The **novel** is written as a series of verbal exchanges in which the two young lovers argue about identity and culture, especially the legacy they have inherited of **slavery** and **apartheid** throughout American history. In a prologue, Ideal reminisces about her upbringing in the South. Her great-grand-mother tells her she must always walk tall and only bend to others' wishes if she pleases. By trying to emulate her great-grandmother, Ideal risks being seen as domineering. Threatened by her assertiveness, Jimson drifts from job to job in an effort to bolster his self-esteem. Eventually he cheats on Ideal, and they bitterly separate.

Flight to Canada

Ishmael Reed
Novel, 1976

A **satire** of **slave narratives, Ishmael Reed**'s *Flight to Canada* is about a slave, Raven Quickskill, who escapes from Virginia and travels to Canada to join other slaves in the abolitionist movement. His owner, Massa Arthur Swille, hires trackers to find him, continuing his efforts to return Quickskill to **slavery** even after the Emancipation Proclamation has been issued. There are a number of unexpected plot twists: Quickskill becomes involved with a Native American princess, and when Swille dies unexpectedly an Uncle Tom-type slave named Uncle Robin, who has written himself into Swille's will, inherits his master's plantation. For Quickskill and the other escaping slaves in the **novel,** Canada is their geographic destination. Yet it becomes increasingly clear that Canada is not the paradise they expect, and the name begins to assume a transcendental significance. "Each man to his own Canada," Quickskill reflects, and all of the black characters ultimately turn to this transcendent vision as their shield against the harsher aspects of reality. In *Flight to Canada* Reed continues the examination of Hoodooism that he began in *Mumbo Jumbo.* Hoodoo becomes a kind of faith that sustains and uplifts without necessarily degrading those who are opposed to it. Reed's main theme is the necessity for African Americans to liberate themselves from the Western myths that have kept them enslaved into the twentieth century.

Flipper Purify

Character in *Jungle Fever*

Folk Tale

Please see Folklore/Folk Tale

Folklore/Folk Tale

Folklore includes the traditions and myths of a culture. Typically, these are passed on by word of mouth or preserved in customs and ceremonies. A folk tale is a story originating in the **oral tradition.** Many writers, among them **Wole Soyinka, Derek Walcott, Amos Tutuola,** and **Louise Bennett,** draw on folktales for inspiration in their stories, poems, and **plays.**

Among the first to identify folklore as a vital component of black culture were **Sterling A. Brown,** and **Zora Neale Hurston,** both of whom began their research in the American South in the 1920s. Subsequently, **Bernard Dadie** published a noted collection of African folktakes in the 1950s, **Jean Price-Mars** wrote several works on Haitian folklore, and **Langston Hughes** and **Arna Bontemps** published *The Book of Negro Folklore* in 1958. More recent collections include *Black Folktales* (1969) and *The Knee-High Man and Other Tales* (1972), by **Julius Lester,** and studies by **Daryl Cumber Dance,** *Shuckin' and Jivin': Folklore from Contemporary Black Americans* (1978) and *Folklore from Contemporary Jamaicans* (1985). Children's books by **Ashley F. Bryan** and **Augusta Baker** retell folktales from many countries.

for colored girls who have considered suicide

Ntozake Shange
Play, first produced 1976, published 1976

A "choreopoem," **Ntozake Shange**'s first piece for theater, *for colored girls who have considered suicide/when the rainbow is enuf,* won the Obie Award in 1977 and was nominated for Tony, Emmy, and Grammy awards. In *for colored girls,* seven black women, each dressed in a different color, recite poetic monologues dealing with their lives and especially with their troubled and painful relationships with black men. The characters, called The Lady in Brown, Yellow, Red, Green, Purple, Blue, and Orange, take turns telling stories. The Lady in Yellow describes losing her virginity on graduation night; the Lady in Brown tells the story of her crush, at age eight, on the Haitian leader Toussaint l'Ouverture, and her attraction for a boy who was also called Toussaint. The women converse and dance together, chanting in unison. Late in the **play**, the Lady in Red recounts the violent and autobiographical tale of Crystal and her lover Beau Willie, an anguished Vietnam veteran. Crystal leaves Beau Willie because of his violence, and tries to raise her children by herself. Willie begs Crystal to marry him, but when she refuses, he drops the two children from her fifth story apartment. Against such violence, the play celebrates the struggles of black women to find their identity, and shows women with different experiences finding unity and solidarity in their storytelling.

For My People
Margaret Walker
Poetry, 1942

For My People was the first book of **poetry** published in America by a black woman in over twenty years, and **Margaret Walker** became the first African American woman to win a prestigious national literary competition when the book earned her the Younger Poet's Award from Yale University.

Echoing the work of earlier black poets such as **Sterling A. Brown**, **Robert Hayden**, and Melvin Tolson, the poems in this collection contemplate the black experience in America. Walker's poetry combines intensity of emotion with realistic portrayals of black life, and the

language of her verses is shaped both by the Biblical phrasing she learned from listening to her father's preaching and by the vocabulary and cadences of the African American folk tradition. In the title poem of the collection Walker speaks of children "in the clay and dust and sand of Alabama / backyards playing baptizing and preaching and doctor," and blacks in both Northern and Southern cities, "lost disinherited dispossessed, and happy / people filling the cabarets... and other people's pockets." She attacks **racism** passionately and demands better treatment, advocating political action and warning of a more violent struggle against racism if nothing else is done. The collection also includes poetry about her African heritage and the beauties of the Southern landscape, as well as a series of poems about types of characters in black **folk tales**.

Calvin Forbes
American poet
Born May 6, 1945.

Forbes developed a distinctive style that is experimental and complex in its use of figurative devices. At the New School for Social Research, Forbes was influenced both by his acquaintance with the poet Jose Garcia Villa and by his reading of authors such as **Langston Hughes** and Philip Larkin. Before he settled into a series of teaching positions, Forbes hitchhiked across the United States, an experience that yielded his first poems. His collections *Blue Monday* (1974) and *From the Book of Shine* (1979) incorporate elements of the **blues** and explore such topics as racial and political identity.

See also **Poetry of Calvin Forbes**

Further Readings
Black Writers, first edition, Gale, 1989.
Dictionary of Literary Biography, Volume 41: *Afro-American Poets since 1955,* Gale, 1985.

Nick Aaron Ford
American nonfiction writer and educator
Born August 4, 1904.
Died July 17, 1982.

Ford was born in Ridgeway, South Carolina, on August 4, 1904. He graduated from Benedict College in 1926 and earned a Ph.D. from the University of Iowa in 1945. He chaired the English Department of Morgan State College from 1945 to 1973, after which he directed the Center for Minority Students at Coppin State College. Ford's first book, *The Contemporary Negro Novel: A Study in Race Relations* appeared in 1936; a collection of his **poetry,** *Songs from the Dark: Original Poems,* was published in 1940. He wrote or edited several books on language and writing and edited two collections of African American literature. His other writings include *Black Studies: Threat or Challenge?* (1973), and *Seeking a Newer World: Memoirs of a Black American Teacher* (1982). Ford died in Baltimore, Maryland, on July 17, 1982.

Further Readings
Black Writers, first edition, Gale, 1989.

Forten chronicled her impressions of the Civil War in her *Journal.*

Leon Forrest
American novelist
Born January 8, 1937.

Forrest was born in Chicago, Illinois, to a family of storytellers and was drawn to creative writing at an early age. His first **novel,** ***There Is a Tree More Ancient Than Eden*** (1973) deals with themes of identity and salvation. The novel's characters reappear in *The Bloodworth Orphans* (1977) and *Two Wings to Veil My Face* (1983). Critics have noted the importance of **oral tradition** in Forrest's work. Forrest became professor of African American studies at Northwestern University in 1984. Among his other writings are the novel *Divine Days* (1992) and the **essay** collection *Relocations of the Spirit* (1994).

Further Readings
Black Writers, second edition, Gale, 1994.
Dictionary of Literary Biography, Volume 33: *Afro-American Fiction Writers after 1955,* Gale, 1984.

Charlotte L. Forten
American diarist, poet, and essayist
Born August 17, 1837(?).
Died July 23, 1914.

Charlotte Lottie Forten is best known for the posthumously published ***The Journal of Charlotte L. Forten: A Free Negro in the Slave Era*** (1953), which records her impressions of issues including **abolitionism** and the Civil War. The author of **poetry** and **essays,** she wrote at times under Miss C. L. F. and Lottie. She assumed the name Charlotte L. Forten Grimké after her 1878 marriage to the Reverend Francis J. Grimké.

Forten was born free in Philadelphia, Pennsylvania, on August 17, 1837 (some sources say 1838), into a prominent family. After her mother's death, she was raised in various households where visiting abolitionists discussed racial issues. She was privately tutored until entering an integrated grammar school in Massachusetts in 1854. She then studied teaching at Salem Normal School, graduating in 1856. Her journals of this period offer appraisals of abolitionists and of literature.

Though often ill with tuberculosis, Forten held several teaching positions and became the first black educator to instruct whites in Massachusetts. Concerned with the education of African Americans, in the early 1860s she participated in South Carolina's Port Royal Experiment, which educated freed blacks.

Forten began writing poetry in 1855; among her works are "A Parting Hymn" (1863) and "The Slave Girl's Prayer" (1860). She became bedridden in 1913 and died of a cerebral embolism on July 23, 1914, in Washington, D.C., where she is buried.

Further Readings

Dictionary of Literary Biography, Volume 50: *Afro-American Writers before the Harlem Renaissance,* Gale, 1986.

Longsworth, Polly, *I, Charlotte Forten, Black and Free,* Crowell, 1970.

Frado

Character in *Our Nig*

Francie Coffin

Character in *Daddy Was a Number Runner*

Francis Herbert

Character in *Where the Hummingbird Flies*

Frank Brown

Character in *The Soul Brothers and Sister Lou*

John Hope Franklin

American historian, biographer, and essayist
Born January 2, 1915.

Franklin is a renowned scholar noted for his investigations into African American history.

He is best known as the author of *George Washington Williams: A Biography* (1985), about the nineteenth-century black historian.

Born in Rentiesville, Oklahoma, Franklin received his A.B. from Fisk University and his Ph.D. in history from Harvard University. He began his teaching career at Fisk and later taught at a number of other institutions, including Howard University, the University of Chicago, and Duke University.

In 1947, Franklin published *From Slavery to Freedom: A History of African Americans*, which is still considered the standard text on African American history. In addition to his editing and contributing to a number of publications, he is also the author of *Reconstruction after the Civil War* (1962), *The Emancipation Proclamation* (1963), and *Racial Equality in America* (1976), which examines the egalitarian principles of America's founding fathers. In 1985, Franklin earned critical praise for *George Washington Williams: A Biography,* which represents forty years of Franklin's research into Williams's life and achievements. More recently, Franklin's *Race and History: Selected Essays, 1938-1988* (1990) and *The Color Line: Legacy for the Twenty-first Century* (1993) have preserved his place as one of America's foremost historians. In the latter volume, Franklin examines the issue of racial equality in the United States, concluding that twentieth-century politicians like Ronald Reagan have impeded race relations by opposing such legislation as affirmative action.

Further Readings

Black Writers, second edition, Gale, 1994.

Franklin Swift

Character in *Disappearing Acts*

Fred Merrit

Character in *The Walls of Jericho*

Freda
Character in *Mama*

Freddy
Character in *Eva's Man*

The Free-Lance Pallbearers
Ishmael Reed
Novel, 1967

Ishmael Reed's first **novel**, *The Free-Lance Pallbearers,* is considered a parody of the confessional narratives that have characterized African American literature since before the Civil War. As in all his works, Reed satirizes European and Christian tradition and Western oppression; he blames whites, called HARRY SAM in the novel, for present world conditions, but he also attacks black leaders.

Reed's parodies of individuals in the black community include characters such as Elijah Raven, a Black Nationalist whose ideas of cultural and racial separation in the United States are exposed as lies; Eclair Pockchop, a minister fronting as an advocate of the people's causes who is later discovered performing sex on SAM; and Doopeyduk, the comic hero of the novel, whose pretensions of being a black intellectual render all of his statements and actions absurd. Reed implies that many such leaders argue against white control by saying that they want to "help the people," but in reality they are only waiting for the chance to betray and exploit poor blacks and to appropriate power. Although Reed reserves his most scathing **satire** for the black leaders who cater to SAM in his palace, his parodies of black leaders caused significant controversy, and many blacks considered the novel's subject matter unrealistic and inappropriate.

Frieda McTeer
Character in *The Bluest Eye*

John Hope Franklin at Howard University in 1956.

From Slavery to Freedom
John Hope Franklin
Nonfiction, 1947

One of the most respected and widely used histories of African Americans, *From Slavery to Freedom: A History of African Americans* traces the story of African Americans from the beginnings of civilization through the present day. It includes extensive information on the history and cultures of Africa and relates the experiences of people of African descent in Latin America, the West Indies, and Canada as well as the United States. In his preface to the first edition, Franklin delineated his approach, which analyzed the position and role of African Americans in American history and culture. A seventh, revised edition, published in 1994 with co-author Alfred A. Moss Jr., extends the book's historical coverage through the early 1990s. Extensive bibliographic notes, maps, photographs, and an appendix of important documents are included.

Charles Fuller

American playwright
Born March 5, 1939.

Charles Henry Fuller Jr. was born in Philadelphia, the son of a prosperous printer. He attended Villanova University from 1956 to 1958 and then spent several years in the United States Army. On his return to Philadelphia, he took courses at La Salle College while holding a variety of jobs.

Fuller's first recognition as a playwright came in 1968 when Princeton University's McCarter Theatre produced *The Village: A Party,* which deals with the problems arising from racial integration. He then moved to New York City, where his **The Brownsville Raid** (1976) was produced. The **play** is based on the 1906 dishonorable discharge of an entire U.S. Army regiment of black soldiers for its alleged involvement in a fatal riot in Brownsville, Texas. Fuller's *Zooman and the Sign* (1980) deals with the killing of a little girl in Philadelphia and *A Soldier's Play* (1981) relates the investigation of the murder of a black army sergeant in Louisiana during World War II. It won the Pulitzer Prize for drama in 1982 and was made into a motion picture, *A Soldier's Story,* in 1984. Fuller has been professor of Afro-American Studies at Temple University since 1988.

Further Readings

Black Literature Criticism, Gale, 1992.

Black Writers, second edition, Gale, 1994.

Dictionary of Literary Biography, Volume 38: *Afro-American Writers after 1955: Dramatists and Prose Writers,* Gale, 1985.

Hoyt Fuller

American editor and author
Born September 10, 1927.
Died May 11, 1981.

Hoyt William Fuller was born September 10, 1927, in Atlanta, Georgia, and graduated from Wayne State University in 1950. After an early career as a reporter, he assumed the editorship of *Black World* (formerly the *Negro Digest*), which under his leadership became a springboard for the **black arts movement** of the 1960s and 1970s. After *Black World* ceased publication in 1976, he joined other black intellectuals in establishing *First World,* which he edited until his death. Fuller's book *Journey to Africa* appeared in 1971. He also contributed articles to mainstream magazines and newspapers, sometimes under the pseudonym William Barrow. He died in Atlanta of a heart attack on May 11, 1981.

Further Readings

Black Writers, first edition, Gale, 1989.

Funnyhouse of a Negro

Adrienne Kennedy
Play, first produced 1962, published 1969

Funnyhouse of a Negro was **Adrienne Kennedy**'s first work for the stage, a one-act **play**, originally staged by Edward Albee, that established her unique voice in black theater and garnered Kennedy an Obie Award in 1964. Primarily written as a portrayal of a young woman whose emotional turmoil is linked to her confusion about her racial ancestry, the play also serves as a metaphor for the collision between African and European cultures. Sarah is a mulatto woman whose confusion over her racial and cultural identity is complicated by the fact that she is living with a Jewish poet named Raymond in a boardinghouse lorded over by an overbearing white woman. Experiencing both alienation from and obsession with white Eurocentric culture, Sarah becomes tormented by violent, overpowering hallucinations that feature such people as her white mother, England's Queen Victoria, Zairian political leader Patrice Lumumba, and a black and powerless Jesus Christ who futilely tries to escape his blackness. The hallucinations appear as Sarah fights to come to an understanding of her own identity, of God, and of love; they allow her to express the intensely personal thoughts and emotions she has not been able to communicate to either Raymond or her parents. However, Sarah's mental fragmentation into multiple personalities is not resolved by the experience. She is driven to commit suicide by the end of the play.

The Future in the Present

C. L. R. James
Essays and fiction, 1977

C. L. R. James's *The Future in the Present* treats numerous topics in its twenty entries. Many of the works originally appeared as chapters of books, as introductions to books, or in periodicals. The **short story** "Triumph," which was first published in the periodical *Trinidad* in 1929, takes place in a Port-of-Spain slum and concerns a voluptuous East Indian black woman who "triumphs" over a neighbor jealous of her sexual relationships by publicly displaying money she received from a disgruntled lover after appeasing his suspicions about other liaisons. The collection also includes treatises on black conditions in Africa, Jamaica, and the United States. Other **essays** encompass such subjects as literature, **biography**, politics, and history.

I believe the poets ... see love and beauty in the blooming of the Black community; power in a people whose only power has been the truth.

Sacred Cows ... and Other Edibles,
Nikki Giovanni, 1988

G.

Character in *In the Castle of My Skin*

Gabe

Character in *Fences*

Gabe Gabriel

Character in *No Place to Be Somebody: A Black-Black Comedy*

Tsegaye Gabre-Medhin

Ethiopian dramatist and teacher
Born August 17, 1936(?).

Tsegaye Kawessa Gabre-Medhin was born in Ambo, Shewa, Ethiopia, in 1935 or 1936. He obtained a law degree from Blackstone School of Law in 1959 and studied experimental theater in London, Paris, and Rome. In 1976 he began teaching theater arts at Addis Ababa University. Gabre-Medhin has written numerous **plays,** most in Amharic. *Oda Oak Oracle* (1964), perhaps his most readily available work in English, is a tragedy in which the village oracle dominates the lives of the play's southern Ethiopian characters. He has also contributed poems to several collections and to periodicals. Gabre-Medhin's work presumes that the artist's responsibility is to tell the truth; he leaves judgment to the audience.

Further Readings
Black Writers, second edition, Gale, 1994.

Gabriel Grimes

Character in *Go Tell It on the Mountain*

Gabriel Prosser

Character in *Black Thunder*

Gaines after the 1993 release of *A Lesson Before Dying.*

Ernest J. Gaines

American novelist and short story writer
Born January 15, 1933.

Best known for *The Autobiography of Miss Jane Pittman* (1971), Gaines is praised for his portrayal of rural Southern black culture. His black protagonists face serious challenges—**racism**, the breakdown of personal relationships, and the loss of tradition—with dignity.

Raised on a Louisiana plantation where he dug potatoes as a child, Gaines later moved with his family to California, where he began to read and write extensively. His first story was published in 1956, while he attended San Francisco State College. Gaines's first **novel,** *Catherine Carmier* (1964), was largely ignored by readers and reviewers. With *Of Love and Dust* (1967), a work condemning the Southern status quo through a tale of forbidden love and the quest for human dignity, Gaines began to receive critical attention. Several **short story** collections followed, including *Bloodline* (1968) and *A Long Day in November* (1971).

In 1971, Gaines finished *The Autobiography of Miss Jane Pittman,* the novel critics consider his masterpiece. Jane's narrative encompasses the African American experience: **slavery**, **Reconstruction**, the **civil rights movement**, and **segregation**. *In My Father's House* (1978) utilizes the theme of alienation that recurs throughout Gaines's fiction.

In 1983, Gaines became professor of English at the University of Southwestern Louisiana and published *A Gathering of Old Men.* This novel presents a group of aging Southern black men who take a stand against injustice by collectively pleading guilty to murder. *A Lesson before Dying* (1993) continues the author's historical depiction of the pride, honor, and manhood that are sustained in a dehumanizing Southern environment.

Further Readings

Black Writers, second edition, Gale, 1994.

Contemporary Literary Criticism, Gale, Volume 3: 1975; Volume 11: 1979; Volume 18: 1981.

Dictionary of Literary Biography, Gale, Volume 2: *American Novelists since World War II,* 1978; Volume 33: *Afro-American Fiction Writers after 1955,* 1984.

Ganja and Hess

Bill Gunn
Film, 1973

In **Bill Gunn**'s film *Ganja and Hess,* originally entitled "The Vampires of Harlem," Hess Green is a rich and sophisticated vampire who drinks blood stored in bloodbanks to satisfy his craving. After Hess's assistant George Meda commits suicide, his beautiful widow Ganja falls in love with Hess, who draws her into the world of the undead. Hess eventually takes his own life. *Ganja and Hess* won critical acclaim and popular success at the Cannes Film Festival in 1973. Gunn's original masterpiece was practically unrecognizable in its American producer's version, but because of screenings at prestigious museums and festivals, the film enjoys a reputation as one of the best films of the 1970s and has an enthusiastic underground following.

Ganja Meda

Character in *Ganja and Hess*

The Garies and Their Friends

Frank J. Webb
Novel, 1857

Frank J. Webb's *The Garies and Their Friends* tells the story of three Southern families and their quest for fortune and happiness in the North. Pretending to be white is a major theme of the **novel**, and some of the characters, like George Winston and Kinch Sanders De Younge, do it in the trickster tradition to dupe unsuspecting white people. The novel is also considered to be the first major work by a black American to include mixed marriages, lynching in a free state, and middle-class values in black communities. Three families, the interracial Garies, the black Ellises, and the white Stevenses, are brought together in a melodramatic plot of bigotry and treachery. Mr. Ellis is maimed after being chased by a mob; Mr. Stevens commits suicide after murdering Mr. Garie. Meanwhile, their sons try to stop the feuding.

Garner

Character in *Beloved*

Marcus Garvey

Jamaican essayist, editor, journalist, and poet
Born August 17, 1887.
Died June 10, 1940.

Marcus Moziah Garvey Jr. founded the "back-to-Africa," or Garveyist, movement among African and West Indian Americans. In his **essays**, poems, and **speeches**, Garvey advocated racial separatism and encouraged people of African heritage to form an independent nation in Africa.

Garvey was born into a poor, working-class family in St. Ann's Bay, Jamaica. He left school at the age of fourteen and found work as a printer's apprentice. He soon involved himself in political **oratory** and labor politics, lobbying white business owners to improve the working conditions of black laborers. He founded the first of his many radical periodicals, *Garvey's Watchman,* in 1910.

Garvey established the Universal Negro Improvement Association (UNIA) in 1914 and later its journalistic organ, the weekly *Negro World* newspaper. In 1916, he went to New York, hoping for a better reception of his ideas. In 1920, the international UNIA convention elected him provisional president of their planned future homeland, the Empire of Africa. Garvey formalized his Pan-Africanist philosophy in essays and manifestos. ***The Philosophy and Opinions of Marcus Garvey; or, Africa for the Africans*** (1923) was his most prominent work during his lifetime. Several additional volumes of his writings were released in the 1980s.

In 1927, Garvey was deported to Jamaica following a jail term for mail fraud. After working unsuccessfully for that country's independence, he moved to England. Garvey's influence steadily decreased until his death in London in 1940; however, his ideas continue to prompt awareness of black culture.

Further Readings
Black Writers, first edition, Gale, 1989.

Martin, Tony, *Race First: The Ideological and Organizational Struggles of Marcus Garvey and the Universal Negro Improvement Association,* Greenwood Press, 1976.

Garveyist Movement
Please see Back-to-Africa Movement

Marcus Garvey, New York City, 1922.

Henry Louis Gates Jr.
American literary critic and editor
Born September 16, 1950.

Gates holds a position of importance and influence in the American academic world. He has become a leader in African American studies and in the effort to promote multiculturalism in schools.

Born on September 16, 1950, in Keyser, West Virginia, Gates grew up in the small town of Piedmont, West Virginia. His father worked as a loader in a paper mill and as a janitor, and his mother was a domestic worker. After a year at a community college, Gates transferred to Yale University in 1969, graduating with highest honors in 1973. That same year he entered Cambridge University and received a master's degree in 1974 and a Ph.D. in 1979. He married Sharon Adams in 1979 and has two daughters.

Gates is a prominent educator, academician, and editor.

the Racial Self (1987) and the American Book Award-winning *The Signifying Monkey: Towards a Theory of Afro-American Literary Criticism* (1988). Both examine the concept of "**signifying**"—a device by which black authors make their points with indirect, often exaggerated, language.

Gates became the John Spencer Bassett Professor of English and Literature at Duke University in 1990. In 1991, he moved to Harvard University as the W. E. B. Du Bois Professor of Humanities, director of the W. E. B. Du Bois Institute for Afro-American Research, and chair of the African American Studies Department.

In 1992, Gates published **Loose Canons: Notes on the Culture Wars**, a collection of his scholarly **essays**. Two years later he released **Colored People** (1994), an autobiographical account of his youth. In addition to contributing to scholarly journals, Gates has written frequently for magazines and newspapers, including the *New York Times*.

Further Readings
Black Writers, second edition, Gale, 1994.
Dictionary of Literary Biography, Volume 67: *Modern American Critics since 1955,* Gale, 1988.

Gates began his teaching career in 1976 at Yale, where he became an associate professor of English and, beginning in 1979, directed the undergraduate program in African American studies. He first received public attention in 1981 upon his receipt of the prestigious MacArthur Foundation Fellowship. About this time he also uncovered a copy of *Our Nig; or, Sketches from the Life of a Free Black*, a rare nineteenth-century **novel,** and proved that the author was a black woman named **Harriet E. Adams Wilson.** Gates's publication of an edition of this novel in 1983 marked the beginning of his subsidiary career as the editor of hitherto little-known works by black writers.

Gates became a professor of African studies and English at Cornell University in 1985, remaining there until 1990. It was during this period that he published two books of **literary criticism**: *Figures in Black: Words, Signs, and*

Gather Together in My Name
Maya Angelou
Autobiography, 1974

Gather Together in My Name, **Maya Angelou**'s second volume of **autobiography**, picks up where *I Know Why the Caged Bird Sings* left off. It tells the story of Angelou's efforts to make her own life in an often hostile world. Although confident at first, she gradually loses control of her life and finds herself becoming dependent on others. In an attempt to impress the father of her son, Angelou takes a job as a Creole cook. Although she has no experience, she learns quickly, but she leaves the job when an affair with a customer ends. Angelou then moves to San Diego, where she becomes a waitress and begins a career as a madam, soliciting for prostitutes. Her work as a nightclub dancer ends when her manager's wife discovers the two of them in a tryst. Angelou tries to enlist in the army, but she is rejected when she lies on the application. Finally, she turns to prostitution, working for a time for a pimp named L. D. Tolbrook. Only the intervention of her brother Bailey keeps her from returning to the whorehouse. Angelou seeks consolation in drugs, but a sordid episode with her lover in a drug house brings her to her senses. She concludes the book by asking forgiveness for this chaotic period of her life.

The Gathering

Please see "Justice" Trilogy

A Gathering of Old Men

Ernest J. Gaines
Novel, 1983

In *A Gathering of Old Men,* **Ernest J. Gaines** depicts life in the rural South, with its remnants of plantation society. Told by fifteen narrators, the story begins with the murder of Beau Boutan, a Cajun farmer, whose body is found lying in the yard of an elderly black man named Mathu. Because Mathu has stood up to whites in the past, many people assume he is responsible for the murder. Quick retribution is expected from the Boutan family, especially the racist patriarch Fix.

Candy Marshall, a wealthy white woman, is determined to protect Mathu, who helped to raise her. She encourages the older men on her plantation to find shotguns and shells like those used to kill Beau, and to meet in a group at Mathu's house. The plan is to have each member of the group—Candy included—individually "confess" to the killing.

As the participants assemble at Mathu's home, they reminisce about life in a racist environment, their lifelong fear of whites, and how they and their forebears suffered. In their final

Typescript page from *A Gathering of Old Men.*

confrontation with the local sheriff and some white thugs who feel they are acting in the Boutans' interests, the elderly black men achieve a measure of courage and dignity they have long felt to be lacking in their lives. At roughly the same time, Fix Boutan discovers that his remaining sons are unwilling to exact lawless revenge for reasons that, though selfish, point to a new era of tolerance in the South.

Violence erupts at Mathu's house nevertheless, and when it subsides, Beau's murderer has been shot as well as a white gang leader. The survivors of the incident are given light sentences, and the black men emerge with a newfound sense of pride and accomplishment.

Published in 1983 to favorable reviews, Gaines's **novel** of rural Louisiana has been adapted for a television movie.

Gator

Character in *Jungle Fever*

Addison Gayle Jr.

American scholar and writer
Born June 2, 1932.

An advocate of the **black aesthetic movement**, Gayle was born in Newport News, Virginia, in 1932. He attended the City University of New York (CUNY) and the University of California at Los Angeles before embarking on an academic career. In 1982 he became a distinguished professor of English at CUNY. Gayle's literary works include *The Black Situation* (1970), *The Way of the New World: The Black Novel in America* (1975), and the autobiographical *Wayward Child: A Personal Odyssey* (1977), in which he describes his rejection of the cultural mainstream of American life and his embracing of his African heritage. He has also written biographies of **Paul Laurence Dunbar, Claude McKay**, and **Richard Wright**. But his best-known work remains *The Black Aesthetic* (1971), a collection of **essays** edited by Gayle and written by prominent black artists who repudiate white aesthetics as a valid basis for judging art.

Further Readings
Black Writers, first edition, Gale, 1989.

Gbenu

Character in *The Dahomean*

General John

Character in *Black Thunder*

Generations: A Memoir

Lucille Clifton
Memoir, 1976

Poet **Lucille Clifton** journeys backward into her family's past in *Generations: A Memoir.* One prominent figure in this prose volume is Clifton's great-great-grandmother, Caroline Donald Sale, who was "born free in Afrika in 1822 [and] died free in America in 1910." In the intervening years, however, young Caroline was kidnapped from her home in Dahomey, West Africa, then brought to America as a slave. Yet Clifton shows how Caroline survived this harsh experience with her dignity and integrity intact, and how she became the matriarch of a family respected by African Americans and European Americans alike.

The saga of Caroline and her descendants is told in memories and vignettes. Clifton recounts, for example, how Caroline walked from New Orleans to Virginia at the age of eight and how Caroline's daughter became the first black woman legally hanged in Virginia after shooting her white lover. Caroline's great-grandson, Samuel Sayles, was Clifton's father. He is pictured as a man "so handsome they called him Mr. Sayles Lord, and when he'd walk down the street women would come out of their houses and say it." Clifton shows how generations connect and communicate with one another, allowing children to take pride in their ancestry and their family name.

George

Character in *We Can't Breathe*

George Andrews

Character in *Mama Day*

George Harrison

Character in *Dhalgren*

George Meda

Character in *Ganja and Hess*

George Waley

Character in *A Morning in Trinidad*

George Washington

Character in *The Life and Loves of Mr. Jiveass Nigger*

George Washington Williams: A Biography

John Hope Franklin
Biography, 1985

African American historian George Washington Williams, who lived from 1849 to 1891, is best known as the author of *History of the Negro Race in America from 1619 to 1880* (1882), one of the first scholarly treatments of the history of African Americans. As a young man Williams served in the Civil War and fought on the side of Mexican revolutionaries who overthrew the Emperor Maximilian in 1867. After serving as the pastor of Baptist congregations in Boston and Cincinnati and briefly editing an African American weekly, *The Commoner,* in 1875 Williams became the first African American elected to the Ohio state legislature. Williams died in England while trying to organize opposition to the brutal Belgian occupation of the Congo. **John Hope Franklin**'s study includes a chronology and a bibliography of Williams's writings.

George Winston

Character in *The Garies and Their Friends*

Geraldine

Character in *The Bluest Eye*

Gezo

Character in *The Dahomean*

Donald B. Gibson

American literary critic
Born July 2, 1933.

Gibson, a literary critic and educator, was born in Kansas City, Missouri, and holds a Ph.D. from Brown University. He has taught at Brown, Wayne State University, Jagiellonian University in Krakow, Poland, and the University of Connecticut. In 1974 he began teaching at Rutgers University.

Gibson's critical works include *The Fiction of Stephen Crane* (1968) and *The Red Badge of Courage: Redefining the Hero* (1988). He has also edited a number of studies, including *Five Black Writers: Essays on Wright, Ellison, Baldwin, Hughes, and LeRoi Jones* (1970), *Black and White: Stories of American Life* (1971), *Modern Black Poets: A Collection of Critical Essays* (1973), and *The Politics of Literary Expression: A Study of Major Black Writers* (1981), and has contributed to literary journals.

Further Readings
Black Writers, first edition, Gale, 1989.

Paula Giddings

American writer
Born in 1948.

A free-lance writer, Giddings was educated at Howard University, with which she has also been affiliated, and has served as Paris bureau chief for Encore America and Worldwide News. She is editor of the *Afro-American Review* and is represented in the anthology *We Speak as Liberators: Young Black Poets* (1970). *When and Where I Enter: The Impact of Black Women on Race and Sex in America* (1984), Giddings's history of the contributions of black women to racial and sexual equality, was widely hailed by feminist critics for its **realism** and clear-sighted interpretation. She also published *In Search of Sisterhood: Delta Sigma Theta and the Challenge of the Black Sorority Movement* and *Regarding Malcolm X,* both in 1994.

Further Readings
Black Writers, first edition, Gale, 1989.

Gikonyo

Character in *A Grain of Wheat*

Beryl Gilroy

Guyanese novelist, poet, and author of
children's literature
Born in 1924.

Gilroy, an educator who became disillusioned with standard readers used by racially mixed students in London, began her literary career by writing children's stories that she felt were more appropriate for this diverse group of children. She chronicles this experience, with others she has had as part of an older generation of blacks in Britain, in the **autobiography** *Black Teacher* (1976). Born in British Guyana, Gilroy attended several universities in England and earned a Ph.D. from Century University before becoming an educator.

Gilroy's other works include the **novel** *Frangipani House* (1990), which grew out of her interest in the elderly and relationships between young and old, and the **poetry** collection *Echoes and Voice* (1991). She has also written *Century* (1991) and *Sunlight and Sweet Water* (1993), among other novels and works of fiction for young adults. In addition, she contributed to *Caribbean Women Writers: Essays from the First International Conference* (1990).

Further Readings

Black Writers, Gale, second edition, 1994.

Giovanni

Character in *Giovanni's Room*

Nikki Giovanni

American poet
Born June 7, 1943.

Giovanni is considered one of the most popular and influential American poets of the late twentieth century. Known for her public appearances and lectures as well as for her verse, she is praised for her insight into the black experience that characterizes her early **poetry** and for the depth and artistry of her later work.

Yolande Cornelia Giovanni Jr. was born in Knoxville, Tennessee, and moved with her family to a suburb of Cincinnati, Ohio, when she was still an infant. Giovanni was an accomplished student and became an avid reader of literature. In 1960 she entered Fisk University in Nashville, Tennessee, but was dismissed in the middle of her first year because of a conflict with the dean of women. Giovanni reentered Fisk in 1964, however, and graduated with high honors in 1967.

Originally a political conservative, Giovanni became involved in the black liberation movement during her college years. Her first three volumes of poetry, *Black Feeling, Black Talk,* (1967) *Black Judgement* (1968), and *Re: Creation* (1970), include examples of Giovanni's black revolutionary rhetoric. However, Giovanni's work and life soon evolved in other directions. She moved to New York City and in 1969 became an associate professor at Rutgers University. Later that year she gave birth to a son, to whom she wrote and dedicated her first volume of children's poetry, *Spin a Soft Black Song* (1971). Giovanni also published a prose work, *Gemini: An Extended Autobiographical Statement on My First Twenty-Five Years of Being a Black Poet,* in 1971; she also released *A Dialogue*, with **James Baldwin** in 1973, and *A Poetic Equation: Conversations with Nikki Giovanni and Margaret Walker* in 1974.

In 1972 Giovanni published *My House,* a volume of poetry that reveals an increased concern with home and family. This collection consists of highly personal autobiographical reminiscences and points toward the introspective tone of her later volumes. *The Women and the Men* (1975) explores complexities in relationships between black women and black men. *Cotton Candy on a Rainy Day* (1978) expresses a sense of the evanescence of life and the futility of most human endeavor. *Those Who Ride the Night Winds* (1983) reflects on the lives of both famous and ordinary people.

In 1978 Giovanni left New York and returned to Cincinnati to live with her parents after her father suffered a stroke. In 1987 she became a professor of English at Virginia Polytechnic Institute and Virginia State University. In *Sacred Cows... and Other Edibles* (1988) she collected some of her previously published **essays**, and in the early 1990s she published such titles as *Racism 101,* the children's poetry collection *Knoxville, Tennessee,* and *Grand Mothers,* all released in 1994.

See also **Poetry of Nikki Giovanni**

Further Readings

Black Literature Criticism, Gale, 1992.

Black Writers, second edition, Gale, 1994.

Dictionary of Literary Biography, Volume 41: *Afro-American Poets since 1955,* Gale, 1985.

Fowler, Virginia C., *Nikki Giovanni,* Twayne, 1992.

Giovanni's Room
James Baldwin
Novel, 1956

Giovanni's Room, **James Baldwin**'s second **novel**, chronicles the protagonist David's quest for sexual identity. A white American, David struggles with his homosexual feelings during and after an affair with a childhood friend, Joey. David is dismayed by his sexual inclinations, which contradict what he considers the traditional role of a male in Western society. He joins the army, hoping to flee his dilemma, but still finds himself unable to accept or overcome his homosexual leanings. He travels to Paris, where he meets Hella Lincoln and proposes to her in another attempt to suppress his homosexuality. Unsure of her feelings, Hella travels to Spain to contemplate her and David's relationship. Alone in Paris, David meets Giovanni, an Italian bartender. Though they begin an affair, David cannot love Giovanni because of his inability to accept himself. Despondent at David's rejection, Giovanni submits to the sexual advances of his employer, Guillaume, but later kills him. Giovanni is brought to trial, convicted, and sentenced to death. Hella, who had returned from Spain and finally accepted David's marriage proposal, learns of David's homosexuality and leaves him. At the end of the

Nikki Giovanni's poems testify to her own evolving awareness and experience.

novel, Giovanni awaits the guillotine and David remains alone.

Gitlow Judson
Character in *Purlie Victorious*

Givens
Character in *Black No More*

Glen
Character in *The Escape; or, A Leap for Freedom*

Gloria
Character in *Fast Sam, Cool Clyde, and Stuff; The Sign in Sidney Brustein's Window; The Young Landlords;* and *Waiting to Exhale.*

Go Tell It on the Mountain

James Baldwin
Novel, 1953

Although a fictional work, this **novel** chronicles two of the most problematic aspects of **James Baldwin**'s existence as a young man: a son's relationship with his stepfather and the impact of fundamentalist **religion** upon the consciousness of a young boy. Set in Harlem in the 1930s, the novel takes place on a single day, the fourteenth birthday of John Grimes. In the first section, fourteen-year-old John begins his journey from childhood to maturity beset with feelings of guilt and ambivalence about his sexuality, his relationship with his mother and father, the nature of their religion, the rebelliousness of his younger brother, Roy, who has his father's love, and his growing hatred of whites. In the second section, the author explores the deadening effects of **racism** on generations of blacks while offering biographical background about the Grimes family, which is presented in a series of flashbacks which reveal the memories of the Grimes's family's older members as they bring their troubles to the Lord in prayer at the Temple of the Fire Baptized. Thus, this section offers insight into John's own character as well as that of his mother, Elizabeth.

Elizabeth became pregnant with John as a result of a love affair with man who committed suicide before John's birth. She then agreed to marry John's stepfather, Gabriel, a storefront preacher whose cruelty to his stepson is symptomatic of his harsh, unloving nature. John, however, is unaware that Gabriel is not his biological father. The third section of the novel concerns John's actual conversion. If he is to escape the pitfalls experienced by his older relatives, he must find his own way on terms different from those of his family. In the end, John seeks redemption through religious ecstasy. As he lies on the floor before the altar of the Temple of the Fire Baptized, he is surrounded with visions of saints and demons, a surrealistic state from which he emerges cleansed, whole, and certain about the direction his life will take.

Baldwin suggests that John is not doomed to repeat a life of failure. As one of the older characters tells Gabriel early in the novel, "[The Lord's] spirit ain't got to work in everybody the same, seems to me."

God Sends Sunday

Arna Bontemps
Novel, 1931

In **Arna Bontemps**'s first **novel**, Little Augie is the most successful jockey in St. Louis during the 1890s, when African American jockeys were commonplace and popular. Augie spends his money as quickly as he wins it, and much of the book takes place in the fancy bars, high-priced brothels, and ballrooms of St. Louis and New Orleans. The novel ends during Augie's poverty-stricken final years. The language of *God Sends Sunday* is highly rhythmic and poetic, and Bontemps won praise for his authentic rendering of African American and Creole speech. Bontemps and **Countee Cullen** later collaborated on a **play** based on this novel. Although this play, *St. Louis Woman,* was never produced, it was later adapted into a successful musical produced in New York City in 1946.

Lucila Alcayaga Godoy

Please see Gabriela Mistral

God's Bits of Wood

Sembène Ousmane
Novel, 1962

Sembène Ousmane's third and most mature **novel**, *God's Bits of Wood* (*Les bouts de bois de Dieu*) was first published in 1960, the year of Senegal's independence from France. Set on the Dakar-Niger railway line during the railworker strikes of 1947 and 1948, the novel describes worker protests against the racist and exploitative working conditions in the French colony and how the violent struggle encroached on the domestic lives of the Senegalese women.

Combining an **epic** scope with intimate character portrayals, *God's Bits of Wood* presents the strike as symbolic of the general struggle for Senegalese nationhood.

God's Trombones: Seven Negro Sermons in Verse

James Weldon Johnson
Poetry, 1927

With the possible exception of his famous hymn "Lift Every Voice and Sing," *God's Trombones* is **James Weldon Johnson**'s most critically acclaimed work. The collection consists of an **essay** and seven poems that retell stories from the Bible, censure sin and sinners, and offer consolation to mourners. Reviewers such as **W. E. B. Du Bois**, **Walter White**, **Countee Cullen**, and **Alain Locke** celebrated the collection for its power and simplicity.

Unlike Johnson's *Fifty Years and Other Poems* (1917), which includes dialect poems in the style of the black poet **Paul Laurence Dunbar**, and Johnson's many dialect songs written for Broadway in conjunction with his brother John Johnson and musician Bob Cole, *God's Trombones* shuns rhyme, meter, and the dialect style. Critics also noted the dignity with which the poet treats his subjects. Johnson, himself an agnostic, used religious themes freely in his earlier **poetry**, but *God's Trombones* evokes black religious fervor using only straightforward African American speech, as in the following excerpt from "Go Down Death—A Funeral Sermon," in which God takes pity on a dying woman in pain: "And God sat back on his throne, / And he commanded that tall, bright angel standing at his right hand: / Call me Death! / And that tall, bright angel cried in a voice / That broke like a clap of thunder: / Call Death!—Call Death! / And the echo sounded down the streets of heaven / Till it reached away back to that shadowy place, / Where death waits with his pale, white horses."

Donald Goines

American novelist
Born December 15, 1937(?).
Died October 21, 1974.

Goines was known for his grim **novels** about prostitutes and drug users in Detroit, Michigan. He was born in Detroit to the proprietors of a dry-cleaning plant. He did well in school, but dropped out in his middle teens to join the U.S. Air Force. He served in Japan during the Korean War, becoming a drug user; when he returned to Detroit in 1955 he was a heroin addict, which he remained for the rest of his life. Crime supported his drug habit: he was arrested fifteen times and served a total of six and a half years during seven prison terms.

Goines began writing while in prison. After several unsuccessful attempts to write western stories and novels, he turned to the more familiar criminal and drug-ridden world within black ghettos. The titles of his first three published novels are self-explanatory: *Dopefiend: The Story of a Black Junkie* (1971); *Whoreson: The Story of A Ghetto Pimp* (1972); and *Black Gangster* (1972). *White Man's Justice, Black Man's Grief* (1973) tells of the injustice a black man suffers in the white-dominated American judicial system.

Goines wrote a total of sixteen novels before his death, some under the pseudonym Al C. Clark All are grimly realistic depictions of criminals in the black ghetto world, written in the street language of that milieu. Goines and his wife were murdered in Highland Park, a suburb of Detroit, in 1974.

Further Readings

Dictionary of Literary Biography, Volume 33: *Afro-American Fiction Writers after 1955,* Gale, 1984.

Stone, Eddie, *Donald Writes No More: A Biography of Donald Goines,* Holloway House, 1974.

Going to Meet the Man

James Baldwin
Short stories, 1965

James Baldwin's first collection of short stories, *Going to Meet the Man,* treats subjects of sexuality, race relations, and the problems of living in America on a uniquely personal basis. Several of the eight stories comprising this volume pursue themes that Baldwin developed more fully in the novels *Another Country* and *Go Tell It on the Mountain*, and the **play** *Blues for Mister Charlie*. In strong and resonant language he describes and interprets his experiences as a homosexual African American in a period of struggle.

"Sonny's Blues" echoes the subject of *Blues for Mister Charlie:* blues music and its relationship to the African American experience. The protagonist, a middle-class algebra teacher, comes to understand his brother, Sonny, a reformed drug addict turned **jazz** pianist, through the music he performs. "The Outing" and "The Rockpile" draw on autobiographical material similar to that in Baldwin's **novel** *Go Tell It on the Mountain*. These stories focus on a young man and his relationship with his stepfather, a Christian fundamentalist preacher, and the rest of his troubled family. In the title story of the collection, "Going to Meet the Man," which mixes images of sex and death, a young southern boy witnesses the brutal lynching of a black man. Years later, as an adult, he is still haunted by his memories of the lynching—so much so that he cannot make love to his wife without threats of violence and racist words. "Come out the Wilderness" tells of a young African American woman whose futile relationship with a white artist leads her to seek the company of a black man. "This Morning, This Evening, So Soon" is the tale of an African American singer who forgets the survival skills he learned in the more racially biased United States while living in Europe.

Marita Golden

American novelist and teacher
Born April 28, 1950.

Golden's writings concern the place of the black woman in the world. Golden was born in Washington, D.C., in 1950. She attended American University and Columbia University, receiving an M.Sc. in 1973, and worked as a teacher before turning to writing full time in 1983. *Migrations of the Heart* (1983), Golden's **autobiography**, met with favorable reviews. Her first **novel,** *A Woman's Place* (1986), describes three black women who meet and become friends at an elite Boston university. *Long Distance Life* (1989) takes the reader into the black streets of Washington, D.C., where Golden was raised. *And Do Remember Me* (1992) charts the struggle of two black women to better themselves. Golden has also edited *Wild Women Don't Wear No Blues* (1993) and *Skin Deep: Black Women and White Women Write about Race* (1995; with Susan Richards Shreve), and written *Saving Our Sons: Raising Black Children in a Turbulent World* (1995).

Further Readings
Black Writers, second edition, Gale, 1994.

The Golden Serpent

Walter Dean Myers
Children's fiction, 1980

Illustrated by Alice and Martin Provensen, **Walter Dean Myers**'s *The Golden Serpent* is set in an unnamed Eastern country. A wise old monk, Pundabi, and his assistant, a young boy named Ali, live in the mountains. One day they are summoned by the king and ordered to solve a mystery or face imprisonment. The catch: they must also determine what the mystery is. Pundabi and Ali trick the king by telling him he has lost his Golden Serpent, and the king joins them on their search through the city. Appalled at the poverty he sees, the king gives up the search and rewards the pair with a bag of gold, which they distribute to the poor.

Jewelle Gomez

American novelist, poet, activist, and teacher
Born September 11, 1948.

Gomez's roots in the African American community and her long involvement in the feminist movement have informed her contributions to gay and lesbian literature. Gomez was born in Boston, Massachusetts, in 1948 and attended Northeastern University and the Columbia University School of Journalism, graduating in 1973. She worked for twenty years in television production and arts administration. Gomez's writings include two volumes of verse, *The Lipstick Papers* (1980) and *Flamingoes and Bears* (1986), and a book of **essays**, *Forty-three Septembers* (1993). *The Gilda Stories* (1991), her first **novel,** combines history, romance, mystery, **science fiction**, and the **supernatural** in a story about a culturally diverse group of vampire healers and activists for social justice.

Further Readings
Black Writers, second edition, Gale, 1994.

lege of Applied Arts and Sciences (now California State University), graduating in 1952. He worked as an actor from 1953 (the year he received an Obie Award for best actor in *Of Mice and Men*) to 1979. Gordone's **play *No Place to Be Somebody: A Black-Black Comedy*** (1967) opened on Broadway in 1969 to rave reviews and in 1970 garnered the Pulitzer Prize for Drama, the Los Angeles Critics Circle Award, and the Drama Desk Award. Gordone's other plays include *Willy Bignigga* and *Chumpanzee* (1970), *Gordone Is a Muthah* (1970), *Baba-Chops* (1975), and *The Last Chord* (1977).

Further Readings
Black Writers, first edition, Gale, 1989.

The Good Fight
Shirley Chisholm
Memoir, 1973

In *The Good Fight,* **Shirley Chisholm**, then U.S. Representative from New York, details her unsuccessful campaign for the Democratic presidential nomination in 1972 and discusses the landslide defeat of the eventual Democratic candidate, George McGovern. Much of her discussion focuses on the challenges of coalition building, particularly as they pertain to the political efforts of minorities and women. Despite her failure to win the nomination, Chisholm assesses her campaign as an important step towards obtaining serious consideration of women and minority candidates for political office. Appendices contain selections from Chisholm's campaign **speeches** and position papers.

Charles Gordone
American playwright, actor, and director
Born October 12, 1925.

Gordone was born in Cleveland, Ohio, in 1925. He attended the Los Angeles State Col-

Lorenz Graham
American author of children's literature
Born January 27, 1902.

A stay in Africa inspired Lorenz Bell Graham's *How God Fix Jonah* (1946), a collection of biblical tales told in Liberian dialect, and *Tales of Momolu* (1946). In the 1950s, Graham adapted classics and biblical stories for *Classics Illustrated* but greater success came with his **novels** for young adults, especially the "Town" series—*South Town* (1958), *North Town* (1965), *Whose Town?* (1965), and *Return to South Town* (1976)—which depicts a black family and their struggles to overcome **racism**. Graham's experiences as a social worker and a probation officer informed his *Carolina Cracker, Detention Center, Runaway,* and *Stolen Car,* which were published in 1972.

Further Readings
Black Writers, first edition, Gale, 1989.
Dictionary of Literary Biography, Volume 76: *Afro-American Writers, 1940-1955,* Gale, 1988.

Shirley Graham
Please see Shirley Graham Du Bois

A Grain of Wheat

Ngugi wa Thiong'o
Novel, 1967

Ngugi wa Thiong'o's *A Grain of Wheat,* written under the name James T. Ngugi, spans the four days preceding Kenyan Independence Day, December 12, 1963. Mugo, Gikonyo, Mumbi, and Karanja, and their guilt-burdened relationships with each other and with resistance leader Kihika, brother of Mumbi, form the basis of the **novel**. Mugo's secret betrayal of Kihika has caused Kihika's execution. Mumbi's husband Gikonyo has been imprisoned for his freedom-fighting efforts, leading to a period of derangement in which he also betrays other revolutionaries. Karanja has turned against his people and allied himself with the British, for which he sustains unceasing guilt. When Gikonyo returns to Mumbi, he finds her the mother of a child by Karanja, and he immediately rejects her. Mugo confesses his involvement in Kihika's death, and Gikonyo in turn scrutinizes his own past behavior, leading him to forgive his wife.

Grant Wiggins

Character in *A Lesson before Dying*

Eloise Greenfield

American author of children's literature
Born May 17, 1929.

Greenfield has written a number of books for children both to teach them about black heritage and to help them celebrate the pleasures of reading. Greenfield was born in North Carolina but has spent most of her life in Washington, D.C. Most of Greenfield's works are aimed at a younger audience. In her easy-to-read biographies, such as *Rosa Parks* (1973), Greenfield informs young readers about the historical contributions of black Americans. Her first **novel,** *Sister* (1974), in which a girl copes with a parent's death, received an Outstanding Book of the Year citation from the *New York Times*. In the picture book *She Come Bringing Me That Little Baby Girl* (1974), a boy must learn to share his parents' love with his new sister. Greenfield and her mother Lessie Little coauthored *Childtimes:*

A Three-Generation Memoir (1979), which describes the childhood memories of Greenfield, her mother, and her maternal grandmother. Greenfield also attempts to relate children to the world around them in her **poetry.** For example, the verses in *Night on Neighborhood Street* (1991) depict children in typical urban situations—attending church, avoiding drugs, and playing games with their families. Greenfield chose the family as the subject of another of her children's books, *William and the Good Old Days* (1993), about how a young boy copes with the illness of his aging grandmother.

Further Readings
Black Writers, second edition, Gale, 1994.

Sam Greenlee

American poet and novelist
Born July 13, 1930.

Greenlee is noted for *The Spook Who Sat by the Door* (1969) and *Baghdad Blues* (1976), **novels** that reflect his personal experience as a foreign service officer with the United States Information Agency during the 1950s and 1960s.

Born in 1930 in Chicago, Illinois, Greenlee earned his B.S. in 1952 at the University of Wisconsin and pursued graduate studies during the 1950s and 1960s at the University of Chicago and the University of Thessaloniki in Greece. Greenlee's first novel, *The Spook Who Sat by the Door* is a futuristic work about the integration of the Central Intelligence Agency and the decision of one of its black recruits to organize urban gangs to fight white oppression. In *Baghdad Blues,* an undercover operative sent to Iraq by the U.S. government to help stabilize that country's monarchy becomes sympathetic to the revolution.

Greenlee has also written the **poetry** collections *Blues for an African Princess* (1971) and *Ammunition!: Poetry and Other Raps* (1975) and has contributed articles and short stories to several periodicals.

Further Readings
Black Writers, first edition, Gale, 1989.

Dick Gregory

American comedian and activist
Born October 12, 1932.

Gregory was one of the first black comedians to perform for white audiences during the 1960s. The popularity of his **comedy** lay in his satirical approach to race relations and his introduction of the non-derogatory racial joke. His appearance at the Playboy Club in Chicago on January 13, 1961, and his subsequent success were highlighted by his use of socially conscious racial humor that proved extremely successful with his audiences.

Gregory's satirical routines reflect his concern with social and political issues. After a childhood of poverty in St. Louis, Missouri, he attended college on a track scholarship and later served two years in the army. Gregory spent several years working as master of ceremonies at Chicago area nightclubs before receiving the spot at the Playboy Club that brought him national attention. He later wrote about his success and his life in *From the Back of the Bus* (1962) and *Nigger: An Autobiography* (1964; with Robert Lipsyte).

As he became an established comedian, Gregory put his convictions into practice by devoting much of his time to the **civil rights movement** of the 1960s. When his concern for America's social problems demanded a greater level of involvement, Gregory entered politics. In 1966, he was a candidate for mayor of Chicago, and he ran for President of the United States in 1968. In such books as *The Shadow That Scares Me* (1968), *No More Lies* (1972), and *Dick Gregory's Political Primer* (1972), Gregory presents his political and social beliefs. Although neither of his electoral campaigns were successful, they drew attention to issues that he felt should be better recognized. Gregory has continued to merge his lifestyle and his beliefs by fasting for world hunger and supporting nonviolence through vegetarianism.

Further Readings

Black Writers, first edition, Gale, 1989.

Dick Gregory is active in the civil rights movement.

Angelina Weld Grimké

American dramatist and poet
Born February 27, 1880.
Died June 10, 1958.

Grimké was a poet and playwright associated with the **Harlem Renaissance**. Admired and frequently anthologized during her lifetime, her work has been neglected since her death, though some scholars still consider Grimké a substantial artist from a critical period in the development of African American literature.

Born in Boston, Grimké came from an intellectual background. Her father was a lawyer, publisher, and writer who served as vice-president of the **National Association for the Advancement of Colored People** (NAACP). Her mother, also a writer, was a white woman who abandoned the family soon after her daughter was born. Grimké attended several prestigious schools, taking summer courses at Harvard University from 1904 to 1910, and spent much of her career teaching English in Washington, D.C.

Grimké suffered extended periods of emotional turmoil, perhaps over her homosexuality, and her literary output seems to have functioned as a therapeutic release. She composed some **poetry** about political subjects but wrote most often about love. Unfulfilled desire is a theme in her poems. In "When the Green Lies Over the Earth" springtime recalls memories of a former loved one, and in the elegiac "To Clarissa Scott Delany" Grimké mourns a dead woman.

In addition to her poetry, Grimké authored one of the earliest American **plays** written for blacks. **Rachel** (1916) offers a bleak perspective on the fate of black children in a racist society. She also wrote a **short story** about the same subject, "The Closing Door" (1919), in which a black woman goes mad and murders her own child soon after it is born.

Further Readings
Black Writers, first edition, Gale, 1989.

Vertamae Grosvenor
American writer
Born April 4, 1938.

Grosvenor was born in Fairfax, South Carolina, in 1938. She attended school in Philadelphia and made her career as a writer. An authority on food and **folklore**, she has written such books as the autobiographical *Vibration Cooking; or, The Traveling Notes of a Geechee Girl* (1970), *Thursday and Every Other Sunday Off: A Domestic Rap* (1972), a volume of **poetry** entitled *Plain Brown Rapper* (1975), and *Black Atlantic Cooking* (1990). Grosvenor's work appears in several anthologies. She has contributed articles and stories to magazines and newspapers and writes a food column for the *Amsterdam News* and a column for the *Chicago Courier.* Grosvenor is heard regularly on National Public Radio (NPR) and

hosts the NPR program "Horizons." Some of her writings have been published under the name Vertamae Smart-Grosvenor.

Further Readings
Black Writers, second edition, Gale, 1994.

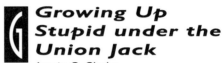

Growing Up Stupid under the Union Jack
Austin C. Clarke
Autobiography, 1980

Austin C. Clarke distilled his memoir *Growing Up Stupid under the Union Jack: A Memoir* from his wartime childhood on the island of Barbados. As an illegitimate black child in a British school, Clarke was alternately insulted, encouraged, and abused. Between 1944 and 1945, he felt the effects of a distant war in terms of rationing and Churchill's **speeches** on the radio. The memoir is an effort to reconcile his rare opportunity for a classical education, paid for by a Panamanian aunt, with his lack of knowledge of his own people and local history.

Guests in the Promised Land
Kristin Hunter
Short stories, 1973

Guests in the Promised Land was **Kristin Hunter**'s first collection of short stories for young readers. It received the *Chicago Tribune Book World* prize for juvenile literature in 1973. The major theme of the collection is acceptance and inclusion in the community, and many of the stories describe how the lack of these has affected young African Americans. In "Debut," for instance, a high school-age girl wants to be accepted by the "hip" group at the regular Friday dance. "Guests in the Promised Land" depicts a group of young men who are welcomed into a posh country club for a day. One of them, named

Robert, takes out his frustrations on the club's property when he is not allowed to play gospel hymns on the club's baby grand piano.

The "Guiana Quartet"

Please see The "Guyana" Quartet

Guillaume

Character in *Giovanni's Room*

Nicolás Guillén

Cuban poet and journalist
Born July 10, 1902.
Died in 1989.

Nicolás Cristobal Guillén y Batista began his career as a newspaper journalist. Considered a master of the so-called Afro-Cuban style, he published his first collection of verse, *Motivos de son* ("Motifs of Sound"), in 1930, after being inspired by a visit to Cuba by **Langston Hughes**. A spate of **poetry** followed, including *Songoro cosongo* (1931), Guillén's masterwork, and his first selection in English, entitled *Cuba Libre* (1948). Forced into exile in the 1950s by the Batista regime, Guillén went to France, where he wrote *La paloma de vuelo popular* ("The Dove of Popular Flight," 1958) and *Elegías* ("Elegies," 1958). His critically acclaimed later work *El gran zoo* (1967) marked a shift in style, as he relied less on strict meter and used spare wording and fractured images. In 1981 Guillén received the Cuban Order of José Martí and became a member of the Cuban Communist Party in his later years. He died in 1989 after a long illness.

See also **Poetry of Nicolás Guillén**

Further Readings
Black Writers, second edition, Gale, 1994.

Guitar

Character in *Song of Solomon*

Bill Gunn

American playwright, actor, and novelist
Born July 15, 1934.

William Harrison Gunn grew up in Philadelphia, but moved to New York in the mid-1950s to pursue a career in acting. Gunn's success on the stage has since engendered parallel careers as a dramatist, novelist, and screenwriter. Much of Gunn's work has been autobiographical; his **play** *Black Picture Show* (1975) depicts the artist's struggle against the taints of commercialism and the politics of success. This theme is reexamined in his Emmy Award-winning teleplay *Johnnas* (1972). Gunn's 1973 film ***Ganja and Hess***, a metaphorical story of vampirism, received high praise at the Cannes Film Festival. Gunn received two Audelco Recognition Awards for *Black Picture Show*.

Further Readings
Black Writers, first edition, Gale, 1989.

Dictionary of Literary Biography, Volume 38: *Afro-American Writers After 1955: Dramatists and Prose Writers,* Gale, 1985.

Guthera

Character in *Matigari ma Njiruungi*

Rosa Guy

Trinidadian-American novelist
Born September 1, 1925(?).

Rosa Cuthbert Guy's family moved from Trinidad to Harlem when she was seven. Guy was born circa 1925 (one source says 1928) and began her career as an actress, playwright and **short story** writer, co-founding the Harlem Writers Guild in the late 1940s. Her first **novel,** *Bird at My Window* (1966) explores the effects of social and domestic forces on its young protagonist. This theme is taken up again in the trilogy *The Friends* (1973), *Ruby* (1976), and *Edith Jackson* (1978). With her adult novel *A Measure of Time* (1983), an ambitious *bildungsroman* set in Alabama and Harlem, Guy addressed a new readership, but she returned to stories about the young with *The Ups and Downs of*

Carl Davis III (1989) and *Billy the Great* (1992), about a interracial friendship between two youngsters.

Further Readings

Contemporary Literary Criticism, Volume 26, Gale 1983.

Dictionary of Literary Biography, Volume 33: *Afro-American Fiction Writers After 1955,* Gale, 1984.

The "Guyana" Quartet
Wilson Harris
Novels, 1960-1963

Wilson Harris's "Guyana" Quartet is made up of the **novels** *Palace of the Peacock, The Far Journey of Oudin, The Whole Armour,* and *The Secret Ladder,* all of which have little in common save their setting—Guyana—and their themes of characters struggling with real and metaphysical dangers in the jungle. *Palace of the Peacock* (1960) describes a surrealistic journey undertaken by a boatload of sailors representing the various races and nationalities living in Guyana. *The Far Journey of Oudin* (1961) focuses on the problems of inheritance as the characters Oudin and Beti flee an unscrupulous employer. In *The Whole Armour* (1962), a prostitute named Magda tries to keep her son away from the police after he is accused of murder. *The Secret Ladder* (1963) is a tale of a scientist's struggle with the necessity of forcibly relocating farmers to improve the local water supply.

Beverly Guy-Sheftall
American educator and writer
Born in 1946.

Guy-Sheftall grew up in Memphis, Tennessee, and earned her B.A. at Spelman College in 1966. She attended Wellesley College before completing her M.A. at Atlanta University in 1968 and her Ph.D. at Emory University. Her dissertation, *Daughters of Sorrow: Attitudes toward Black Women, 1880-1920* was published in 1990. Guy-Sheftall coedited *Sturdy Black Bridges: Visions of Black Women in Literature* (1979), and was a founding coeditor in 1983 of *SAGE: A Scholarly Journal on Black Women.* The founding director of the Women's Research and Resource Center at Spelman College, Guy-Sheftall has served as Anna Julia Professor of English and Women's Studies at Spelman. She is also a consultant to colleges and universities on issues of race, gender, and cultural diversity.

Further Readings

Black Writers, second edition, Gale, 1994.

Gweneth Joseph
Character in *Annie John*

H

I've known rivers:

I've known rivers ancient as

the world and older than

the flow of human blood

in human veins.

My soul has grown deep like

the rivers.

"The Negro Speaks of Rivers,"
Langston Hughes, 1920

189

Hagar

Character in *Song of Solomon*

Hal

Character in *The Temple of My Familiar*

 # Alex Haley

American journalist and novelist
Born August 11, 1921.
Died February 10, 1992.

Haley is the author of two books that have helped shape contemporary African American consciousness: *The Autobiography of Malcolm X* (1965) and the **novel *Roots: The Saga of an American Family*** (1976). The massive popularity of the historical novel and the success of the television mini-series it inspired made Haley a national figure.

Alex Murray Palmer Haley was born on August 11, 1921, to Simon and Bertha Palmer Haley in Ithaca, New York, where both his parents were students. He grew up in Henning, Tennessee, in the midst of an extended family that often exchanged stories about their ancestors. Included in these tales were many about Kunta Kinte, who had been brought over from Africa as a slave; these accounts of Kunta Kinte's life eventually inspired Haley's *Roots*. An indifferent student, Haley attended college only briefly and enlisted in the U.S. Coast Guard in 1939. He began writing out of boredom while at sea and published his first article in a syndicated newspaper supplement. In 1941 he married Nannie Branch, with whom he had two children. Following his divorce, he married Juliette Collins in 1964, with whom he had one daughter. The couple later divorced, and Haley eventually remarried for a third time.

After twenty years of service, Haley retired from the Coast Guard in 1959 and wrote for magazines such as *Reader's Digest* and *Playboy*. In 1965 he reached best-seller status with his first book, *The Autobiography of Malcolm X*, co-written with the leader of the **Nation of Islam**. Although **Malcolm X** initially was suspicious of Haley, the latter eventually earned his trust, and the book went on to sell over five million copies. Critics praised Haley for recreating Malcolm X's emerging political and racial consciousness as well as his commitment to justice.

Two weeks after finishing *Malcolm X,* Haley began research on his ancestry. Writing *Roots* took him twelve years; he conducted extensive research in many countries, working in libraries and archives and even following the approximate course a slave ship would have taken across the Atlantic. Blending fact and fiction, Haley chronicled the life of Kunta Kinte and his descendants in America. Over eight million copies of the book were sold and nearly two million people viewed at least part of the television mini-series based on it.

Roots won numerous awards, including special citations from both the National Book Award and the Pulitzer Prize committees in 1977. Two published authors accused Haley of plagiarism, however, and he eventually settled with one of them for $500,000. In 1979, he helped develop *Roots: The Next Generation,* a sequel to the original television mini-series; another mini-series, *Queen* (1993; with David Stevens), as well as the book *Alex Haley's Queen* (1993; with David Stevens), were based on dictation Haley made about his paternal great-grandmother. He died of cardiac arrest on February 10, 1992, in Seattle, Washington, and is buried on the grounds of the Alex Haley Museum in Henning, Tennessee.

Further Readings
Black Literature Criticism, Gale, 1992.

Black Writers, second edition, Gale, 1994.

Dictionary of Literary Biography, Volume 38: *Afro-American Writers after 1955: Dramatists and Prose Writers,* Gale, 1985.

Hall Montana

Character in *Just Above My Head*

Halle Suggs

Character in *Beloved*

Charles V. Hamilton

American educator
Born October 19, 1929.

Charles Vernon Hamilton's scholarly work addresses social and political issues in the black community. Born in Muskogee, Oklahoma, in 1929, Hamilton joined the political science faculty at Columbia University in 1969, and in 1989 became head of the Metropolitan Applied Research Center (MARC) in New York City. Hamilton's *Black Power: The Politics of Liberation in America* (1967) (in collaboration with **Stokely Carmichael**) presents the philosophy and motivation behind the **black power** movement and is considered a landmark in African American political writing. Hamilton has been a prolific author of scholarly works on black political life, including *The Black Experience in American Politics* (1973) and *Adam Clayton Powell Jr.: The Political Biography of an American Dilemma* (1991).

Further Readings
Black Writers, second edition, Gale, 1994.

Alex Haley, author of *Roots*.

Virginia Hamilton

American author of children's literature
Born March 12, 1936.

Hamilton is a prolific children's author who has received numerous awards for her prose. She is best known for her **novel *M. C. Higgins, the Great*** (1971), the first work to win both the National Book Award and the Newbery Medal.

Hamilton was raised in a small town in Ohio, the descendent of a runaway slave. She studied writing at the New School for Social Research in New York City, where she married poet Arnold Adoff; the couple's honeymoon in Africa would influence her work.

Hamilton's first novel *Zeely* (1967) was praised for its promotion of racial understanding. In 1968, Hamilton published the Edgar Allan Poe Award-winning *The House of Dies Drear*, a mystery centering on the **Underground Railroad**. Family, an important theme in most of Hamilton's books, is the emphasis of *M. C. Higgins, the Great,* which portrays a close-knit family threatened with losing their home. The isolated individual is the focus of ***The Planet of Junior Brown*** (1971), in which lonely people find support in each other.

Hamilton is also noted for mixing **realism**, history, and **folklore**. *The Time-Ago Tales of Jahdu* (1969) contains elements of **fantasy** and mimics traditional folk tales. In the fantasy novels comprising the **"Justice" Trilogy** —*Justice and Her Brothers* (1978), *Dustland* (1980), and *The Gathering* (1981)—she deals with clairvoyance, global disaster, and time travel. Hamilton's recent books include *Bells of Christmas* (1990), *The Dark Way: Stories from the Spirit World* (1990), *Plain City* (1993), and *Jaguarundi* (1994).

Hamilton has also edited numerous publications of the United States Committee for

Award-winning children's author Virginia Hamilton.

Refugees and writes reviews of books related to the history of the American South. She was awarded a MacArthur Foundation grant in 1995.

Further Readings

Black Writers, second edition, Gale, 1994.

Dictionary of Literary Biography, Gale, Volume 33: *Afro-American Fiction Writers after 1955,* 1984; Volume 52: *American Writers for Children since 1960: Fiction,* 1986.

Jupiter Hammon

American preacher, poet, and essayist
Born October 17, 1711.
Died between 1790 and 1806.

Hammon's *An Evening Thought: Salvation by Christ, with Penetential Cries*, composed on December 25, 1760, was the first poem to be published, as a separate work, by a black

person in the United States. Hammon was born and remained all his life a slave on the estate of the Lloyd family, located in Oyster Bay, Long Island, New York. Unlike most slaves, Jupiter learned to read and write and seems to have done clerical tasks, clerked in the community store, and acted as banker for the Lloyds. Following a serious illness in the early 1730s, he began to study the Bible, underwent a religious conversion, and became an evangelical preacher.

During the American Revolution, Hammon moved with the Lloyds to Hartford, Connecticut. There he published a poem (1778) dedicated to another black slave poet, **Phillis Wheatley**; a prose sermon, *A Winter Piece* (1782); and "A Poem for Children with Thoughts on Death" (1782). Following his return to Oyster Bay, Hammon published an **essay**, "An Evening's Improvement" (1783); a poem, "The Kind Master and Dutiful Servant" (1783); and *An Address to the Negroes in the State of New York* (1787). All seven of Hammon's extant writings are religious in content, but they are also subtly phrased protests against **slavery**.

Further Readings

Dictionary of Literary Biography, Volume 50: *Afro-American Writers before the Harlem Renaissance,* Gale, 1986.

O'Neale, Sondra A., *Jupiter Hammon and the Biblical Beginnings of African-American Literature,* Scarecrow Press, 1993.

Hannah

Character in *Sula*

Lorraine Hansberry

American dramatist and essayist
Born May 19, 1930.
Died January 12, 1965.

The literary reputation of Lorraine Vivian Hansberry rests largely on a single **play**, *A Raisin in the Sun* (1959), about a black family buying a house in a white neighborhood. Considered a classic of American theater, it was the first play by a black woman to be produced on Broadway.

A critical event in Hansberry's childhood was precisely such a move to a white neighborhood. She was born in Chicago on May 19, 1930, to Carl and Nannie Perry Hansberry; her father was a realtor who was active in the **National Association for the Advancement of Colored People** (NAACP) and who challenged the city's discriminatory housing covenants in 1938. The family moved into a white area and, while their case moved through the legal system, were at times protected from violent neighbors by armed guards. In 1940, the covenants were struck down by the U.S. Supreme Court.

In 1948, Hansberry entered the University of Wisconsin to study theater, but left in 1950 and moved to New York to pursue a writing career. She became involved in politics, writing for *Freedom* magazine and participating in protests. In 1953, she married Robert Nemiroff, a white man who was also a writer and activist. He provided her with support and she worked at a variety of jobs while developing ideas for several plays.

Hansberry completed *A Raisin in the Sun* in 1957 and read it to a friend, who agreed to produce it. The play earned enthusiastic reviews in tryout productions on the road before it was staged on Broadway, where it enjoyed a successful run; it was later made into a popular movie. In 1959, Hansberry became the first African American to win the New York Drama Critics Circle Award.

Hansberry and Nemiroff divorced in 1964, the same year her next play opened on Broadway. ***The Sign in Sidney Brustein's Window*** about a Jewish intellectual in Greenwich Village who vacillates between social commitment and paralyzing disillusionment, ran to mixed reviews. Hansberry's health had begun to fail before the play went into rehearsal; she died of cancer on January 12, 1965, the same day it closed.

After her death, Nemiroff collected her writings in *To Be Young, Gifted and Black: Lorraine Hansberry in Her Own Words* (1969). He also edited and published three of her plays, including the controversial ***Les Blancs,*** in

Hansberry's play *A Raisin in the Sun* was the first by a black woman to be produced on Broadway.

1972. Hansberry is buried in Croton-on-Hudson, New York.

Further Readings

Black Literature Criticism, Gale, 1992.

Black Writers, first edition, Gale, 1989.

Carter, Steven R., *Hansberry's Drama: Commitment amid Complexity,* University of Illinois Press, 1991.

McKissack, Patricia, *Lorraine Hansberry: Dramatist and Activist,* Delacorte Press, 1994.

Joyce Hansen
American educator and author of children's literature
Born October 18, 1942.

Joyce Viola Hansen grew up in the Bronx neighborhood of New York City. She attended Pace University, completing her B.A.

in 1972, and New York University, earning her M.A. in 1978. A teacher beginning in 1973, Hansen uses her experience with children in her writing. Her first **novel,** *The Gift Giver* (1980), its sequel *Yellow Bird and Me* (1986), and *Home Boy* (1982) concern the lives of contemporary black children in New York. In the extensively researched historical novels *Which Way Freedom?* (1986), which won the Coretta Scott King Award in 1987, and *Out from This Place* (1988) Hansen portrays black children during the Civil War and its aftermath. Her other works include the nonfiction *Between Two Fires: Black Soldiers in the Civil War* (1993), and *The Captive* (1994).

Further Readings

Black Writers, second edition, Gale, 1994.

Twentieth-Century Children's Writers, third edition, St. James Press, 1989.

Happy Ending and Day of Absence
Douglas Turner Ward
Plays, first produced 1965, published 1966

Douglas Turner Ward's two **plays,** produced and published together, are satires of race relations. *Happy Ending* is based on Ward's memories of two of his aunts, who worked as domestics. Nephew Junie derides his aunts Ellie and Vi for their sentimental attachment to the married couple who serve as their employers. His opposition to their behavior changes when he realizes that his aunts have been helping themselves to goods from the white people's house, thus providing him with food and fine clothes. *Day of Absence* is a reverse minstrel show. Black actors play whites, in whiteface. These whites have been left alone in their Southern town without servants, since all the blacks have disappeared. Ward garnered an Obie Award for the plays in 1966.

Vincent Harding
American nonfiction writer and poet
Born July 25, 1931.

Harding, a former civil rights negotiator for various organizations and advisor to **Martin Luther King Jr.**, has written several books on civil rights and the African American struggle against oppression. He has authored *Must Walls Divide?* (1965), ***There Is a River: The Black Struggle for Freedom in America*** (1981), which chronicles the history of black resistance to **slavery,** and *Hope and History: Why We Must Share the Story of the Movement* (1990), a collection of **essays** about the post-World War II African American freedom movement.

Harding holds a Ph.D. from the University of Chicago, for which he wrote a dissertation published as *A Certain Magnificence: Lyman Beecher and the Transformation of American Protestantism, 1775-1863* (1991). He has also worked on a number of television programs about African American history that aired on CBS-TV from 1968 to 1969.

Nathan Hare
American sociologist and nonfiction writer
Born April 9, 1934.

Trained in sociology and psychology, Hare is a controversial academic who argues that the mission of African American scholars is to replace European thought with insights drawn from black heritage. Hare received a Ph.D. in sociology from the University of Chicago and a Ph.D. in psychology from the California School of Professional Psychology. He later taught at several institutions; during the 1960s, he sparked controversy at Howard University by opposing the war in Vietnam and advocating the **black power** movement. His *The Black Anglo-Saxons* (1965) maintains that the African American middle class has shed black values in favor of white cultural standards. In 1968, Hare launched a black studies program at San Francisco State College and received a "Black Is Beautiful" citation from United Black Artists. The following year, he founded *Black Scholar,* a journal of research on African American issues.

In 1974, Hare coedited *Pan-Africanism,* which promotes traditional black communalism in an attempt to chart Africa's future. He has collaborated with his wife, Julia Reed Hare, on *The Endangered Black Family: Coping with the Unisexualization and Coming Extinction of the Black Race* (1984), *Bringing the Black Boy to Manhood: The Passage* (1987), and *The Hare Plan to Overhaul the Public Schools and Educate Every Black Man, Woman, and Child* (1991). In 1977 Hare began a private practice as a psychologist, and in 1984 he began lecturing at San Francisco State University.

Further Readings
Black Writers, second edition, Gale, 1994.

Harlem Renaissance

The Harlem Renaissance is generally considered the first significant movement of black writers and artists in the United States. Centered in the Harlem district of New York City and other urban areas during the 1920s, the movement constituted an unprecedented flowering of cultural activity among African Americans. During this period, new and established black writers published more fiction and **poetry** than ever before, the first influential black literary journals were established, and black authors and artists received their first widespread recognition and serious critical appraisal. Although widely diverse in content and style, works of the Harlem Renaissance were often characterized by heightened racial awareness. Many black writers and artists sought to counteract white racial prejudice as well as to perpetuate African aspects of their cultural heritage. Among the major writers associated with this period are **Claude McKay**, **Jean Toomer**, **Countee**

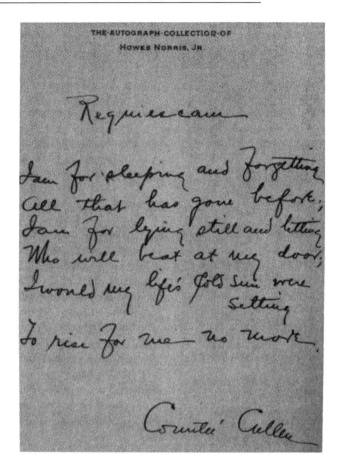

Manuscript of the poem "Requiescam" by Countee Cullen, one of the foremost poets of the Harlem Renaissance.

Cullen, **Langston Hughes**, **Arna Bontemps**, **Nella Larsen**, and **Zora Neale Hurston**.

Between 1890 and 1920, a series of agricultural crises, coupled with a labor shortage in the northern industrial centers, led to the migration of approximately two million black Americans from the rural South to the urban North. Their participation in the urban industrial work force, which resulted in greater racial cohesiveness and economic independence, met with resistance from some conservative whites, provoking a revival of the Ku Klux Klan and an outbreak of racial violence. This period of social upheaval and conflict inspired black intellectuals to reexamine their role in American society and their unique cultural heritage. At the same time, growing interest among white Americans in **jazz** and **blues** music and the discovery of African sculpture by modernist artists broadened the audience for black writing. Some black critics, including **W. E. B. Du Bois** and **Benjamin Brawley**, welcomed the increase in white patronage and stressed the value of literature in fostering racial equality. Others, including **Alain Locke** and **Charles W. Chesnutt**, decried such overt use of literature for propaganda purposes. While few black critics asserted the complete independence of art from social concerns, most believed that literature could best promote racial equality by showing that black writers could produce works rivaling or surpassing those of their white counterparts.

The Harlem Renaissance was formally recognized as a movement in 1925 with the publication of Locke's anthology *The New Negro: An Interpretation*, in which he described the "New Negroes" of the 1920s. The Harlem Renaissance artists sought to chisel out a unique, African-centered culture for blacks and, simultaneously, to improve relations with whites. Their literature was marked by a shift away from moralizing, which had been characteristic of much post-Reconstruction writing. Their self-appointed challenge was to communicate the ills of **racism** with art rather than **essay**. The appearance of African American journals such as Du Bois's *Crisis* and **Charles S. Johnson**'s *Opportunity* made it much easier for black writers to publish in a style that suited their tastes. However, most publishers and readers in the United States were still white, and a controversy developed over the degree to which the perceived expectations of the white establishment should be met. Many African American writers felt that whites, interested only in stereotypical portrayals of blacks as primitive, were unduly fascinated by the more sensational aspects of Harlem life and black sexuality. While this primitivism was rejected by some African American authors as a destructive stereotype, it was actively fostered by others who considered it a continuation of African custom and a defiance of white puritanism.

The body of literature produced during the Harlem Renaissance comprised works of every genre and a wide variety of styles and themes. The most popular and prolific poet of the 1920s was Langston Hughes, whose work delves into the lives of the black working class. Among poets who embraced primitivism was Arna Bontemps, whose poems "The Return" and "Golgotha Is a Mountain" won awards given by *Opportunity* magazine. Another major figure of the period, Countee Cullen, wrote poems exploring the problem of racism and the meaning of Africa for African Americans. Among fiction writers, Claude McKay stands out as author of ***Home to Harlem*** (1928), the first commercially successful **novel** by a black writer. Other notable novels of the era include Nella Larsen's ***Passing*** (1929), which focuses on sophisticated middle class black women who are unable to escape the restrictions of racism; and Jean Toomer's innovative novel ***Cane*** (1923), which demonstrates a strong identification with poor blacks. Essayist **Eric Walrond**, novelist **Walter White**, folklorist Zora Neale Hurston, novelist Rudolph Fisher, and poet **William Waring Cuney** are just some of the other writers associated with the Harlem Renaissance.

The Harlem Renaissance also arrived on the American stage, beginning with the Broadway opening of the black musical *Shuffle Along* in 1921. At the same time, jazz was coming into its own in New York City and Chicago. Historian **Nathan Irvin Huggins** has written about this vibrant period of artistic rebirth in his book *Harlem Renaissance* (1971).

Harlem Shadows: The Poems of Claude McKay

Claude McKay
Poetry, 1922

Harlem Shadows distinguished **Claude McKay** as a new voice in the **Harlem Renais-**

sance. His first collection of **poetry** to be published in the United States, it centers on themes of **racism** and brutality toward blacks in Western society. *Harlem Shadows* contains many of McKay's most famous poems, including "America," "The White City," "The Harlem Dancer," "Outcast," "The Lynching," "Baptism," and "If We Must Die." Many of these pieces, especially "America," "If We Must Die," and "The White City," are hate poems; the latter, in particular, celebrates hatred as a purifying and transfiguring emotion. In "America," McKay compares the oppressive American society to a man-eating tiger, but he also admits his affinity for the culture. "If We Must Die," perhaps McKay's most familiar poem, uses the sonnet form—typically used for love poetry—to call for a militant response to racial violence.

Other poems in the collection are less directly militant. "Harlem Shadows" is about black prostitutes victimized by white civilization, while "The Harlem Dancer" expresses the dignity of a black exotic dancer and singer in contrast to the baseness of the white people who watch her perform. In the remaining poems of the collection, including "The Tropics in New York," McKay turns to the celebration of nature, contrasting his Jamaican youth with his adult, urban life and evoking feelings of displacement and longing: "hungry for the old, familiar ways, / I turned aside and bowed my head and wept."

Harold Lamont

Character in *Rainbow Jordan*

Frances Ellen Watkins Harper

American poet, novelist, short story writer, and orator
Born September 24, 1825.
Died February 22, 1911.

Harper, who also wrote as Effie Afton, was one of the most popular nineteenth-century black American poets. Before the Civil War, her verse focused on abolitionist issues. Two of her most popular works, *Poems on Miscellaneous Subjects* (1854) and *Sketches of Southern Life* (1872), address the problems of blacks in the United States before and after **slavery**. After the war, Harper turned to public speaking, concentrating on equal rights for blacks, women's suffrage, and the Christian crusade against alcohol. Though she was an accomplished orator and writer during her lifetime, her work has not received a significant amount of critical attention since her death.

Harper was born to free parents in the slave state of Maryland. She was raised by her aunt and uncle after the death of her mother and trained as a seamstress at her uncle's school. For a time in the 1850s she taught at the Union Seminary near Columbus, Ohio, where she was an instructor in domestic science. With the publication of *Poems on Miscellaneous Subjects,* however, she gave up teaching and turned to writing and **oratory** for her living. Her collections of **poetry,** which also include *Poems* (1871), *The Sparrow's Fall and Other Poems* (1890), and *Atlanta Offering: Poems* (1895), and her two **novels,** *Moses: A Story of the Nile* (1869) and *Iola Leroy; or, Shadows Uplifted* (1892), were very popular in the nineteenth century. Harper's **short story** "The Two Offers" (1859) is believed to be the first short story by an African American woman to be published in the United States. In recent years three novels by Harper were rediscovered and published as *Minnie's Sacrifice, Sowing and Reaping, Trial and Triumph* (1995). All three of the narratives had originally been serialized in the black periodical the *Christian Recorder.*

See also **Poetry of Frances Ellen Watkins Harper**

Further Readings
Black Literature Criticism, Gale, 1992.

Black Writers, first edition, Gale, 1989.

Dictionary of Literary Biography, Volume 50: *Afro-American Writers before the Harlem Renaissance,* Gale, 1986.

Michael S. Harper

American poet
Born March 18, 1938.

Michael Steven Harper's **poetry** often deals with what he perceives as society's schizophrenia, an opposition between black and white America that contradicts a natural human unity.

Harper was born in Brooklyn, New York, on March 18, 1938. In the early 1950s, Harper's family moved to Los Angeles. Harper studied medicine at Los Angeles State College until a professor claimed that black students could not get into medical school. Harper entered the Iowa Writers Workshop in 1961 and began seriously writing poetry.

Harper's first collection, *Dear John, Dear Coltrane* (1970), was nominated for the National Book Award in 1971, the year Harper became an associate professor at Brown University. In *History Is Your Own Heartbeat: Poems* (1971), *Photographs: Negatives: History as Apple Tree* (1972), and *Song: I Want a Witness* (1972), Harper addresses the need to reestablish familial and historical relations severed by racial discord. In 1973, Harper became a full professor and published *Debridement,* dedicated to his children. His *Images of Kin: New and Selected Poems* (1977) garnered another National Book Award nomination. In 1983, Harper became the I. J. Kapstein Professor of English at Brown and, in 1988, the first Poet Laureate of Rhode Island.

See also **Poetry of Michael S. Harper**

Further Readings

Black Writers, first edition, Gale, 1989.

Dictionary of Literary Biography, Volume 41: *Afro-American Poets since 1955,* Gale, 1985.

Reference Guide to American Literature, St. James Press, third edition, 1994.

Wilson Harris

Guyanese novelist, critic, and poet
Born March 24, 1921.

Theodore Wilson Harris's fiction is noted for its visionary quality and its exploration of the dynamics of language. Born in British Guiana, Harris worked as a land surveyor from 1942 to 1958 before emigrating to London to pursue a writing career. His **poetry,** collected in *Fetish* (1951) and *Eternity to Season* (1954), was written under the pseudonym Kona Waruk. Harris has also written four **novels** known as the **"Guyana" Quartet**: *Palace of the Peacock* (1960), *The Far Journey of Oudin* (1961), *The Whole Armour* (1962), and *The Secret Ladder* (1963). While primarily known for these and the many novels that have followed, Harris's critical **essays**, some of which are collected in *The Womb of Space: The Cross-Cultural Imagination* (1983), have also been well-received. A more recent trilogy—*Carnival* (1985), *The Infinite Rehearsal* (1987), and *The Four Banks of the River of Space* (1990)— has reinforced comparisons with Dante Alighieri, William Blake, and T. S. Eliot.

Further Readings

Black Writers, second edition, Gale, 1994.

Dictionary of Literary Biography, Volume 117: *Twentieth-Century Caribbean and Black African Writers,* First Series, Gale, 1992.

Paul Carter Harrison

American dramatist and critic
Born March 1, 1936.

Harrison was raised in New York and influenced first by Beat **poetry** and later by his studies at Indiana University and the New School for Social Research, where he earned his M.A. in 1962. Attracted by European theater, Harrison began his career in Amsterdam, but returned permanently to the United States in 1967. Harrison's work integrates traditional African **myth** and story with contemporary black American culture. He received an Audelco Recognition Award in 1981 for *Tabernacle* (1969), about the unjust arrest of two black youths, and an Obie Award in 1974 for *The*

Great MacDaddy (1974), about a bootlegger's son's search for wisdom. Harrison has taught at several colleges and universities.

Further Readings

Black Writers, second edition, Gale, 1994.

Dictionary of Literary Biography, Volume 38: *Afro-American Writers after 1955: Dramatists and Prose Writers,* Gale, 1985.

Harry Ames

Character in *The Man Who Cried I Am*

HARRY SAM

Character in *The Free-Lance Pallbearers*

James S. Haskins

American biographer and author of children's literature
Born September 19, 1941.

Haskins has written numerous biographies of important black figures and books about current events and important developments in black history. Born in Montgomery, Alabama, Haskins received a B.A. from Georgetown University, a B.S. from Alabama State University, and an M.A. from the University of New Mexico. He worked for the *New York Daily News* before becoming a teacher in 1966. In 1969, under the name Jim Haskins, he published *Diary of a Harlem Schoolteacher,* which chronicles his experiences teaching in an urban school.

The success of his first publication prompted Haskins to write books intended to help children understand the society in which they live. He produced volumes on the **civil rights movement**, the **black power** movement, the war in Vietnam, and the rise of urban gangs. Haskins also wrote a number of biographies—some intended for a young audience—of figures as wide-ranging as **Langston Hughes, Ralph Bunche, Adam Clayton Powell Jr., Shirley Chisholm, Malcolm X, Barbara Jordan, Martin Luther King Jr., Katherine Dunham,** Hank Aaron, Sugar Ray Leonard, Scott Joplin, Lena Horne, Michael Jackson, Diana Ross, Magic Johnson, Nat King Cole, Scatman Crothers, Colin Powell, Jesse Jackson, and Thurgood Marshall. In 1977 Haskins began teaching English at the University of Florida.

Further Readings

Black Writers, second edition, Gale, 1994.

Robert Hayden

American poet
Born August 4, 1913.
Died February 25, 1980.

Robert Earl Hayden achieved national recognition as a major voice in black literature with the publication of his *Selected Poems* (1966). Hayden's **poetry** combines historical perspective and symbolist method while integrating personal experience, his African American identity, and both traditional and modern poetic forms. The themes in Hayden's work are informed by his adherence to the Bahá'í faith, a prophetic religious movement that espouses human unity.

Born Asa Bundy Sheffey but raised by foster parents Sue Ellen and William Hayden in Detroit, Michigan, Hayden graduated from Detroit City College in 1936. His research into African American history on the Federal Writers' Project from 1936 to 1940 informed the historical basis of his major poems. Hayden also considered his graduate studies with W. H. Auden at the University of Michigan a pivotal element in his development. He earned his graduate degree in 1944 and embarked on an academic career, first at Fisk University in Tennessee and later at the University of Michigan.

Hayden received little critical or public recognition for his early volumes of poetry, *Heart-Shape in the Dust* (1940) and *The Lion and the Archer* (1948). With *A Ballad of*

Poet Robert Hayden.

Remembrance (1962) Hayden began to attract greater critical attention, and the publication of *Selected Poems* sparked public recognition and critical praise.

Amid the racial strife of the 1960s, Hayden was censured by black nationalists for his adherence to an American, rather than a specifically black, literary identity. Even so, his poetry often concerns African American historical experience. In *Words in the Mourning Time* (1970), which was nominated for the National Book Award, Hayden directly addressed contemporary political events. Hayden solidified his burgeoning stature with the publication of *The Night-Blooming Cereus* (1972) and *Angle of Ascent: New and Selected Poems* (1975), his election to the Academy of American Poets in 1975, and his appointment as Consultant in Poetry to the Library of Congress in 1976. In

1979, Hayden received his second National Book Award nomination for *American Journal* (1978). He died of a heart ailment in 1980.

See also **Poetry of Robert Hayden**

Further Readings
Black Writers, first edition, Gale, 1989.

Dictionary of Literary Biography, Volume 76: *Afro-American Writers, 1940-1955,* Gale, 1988.

Fetrow, Fred M., *Robert Hayden,* Twayne, 1984.

Hatcher, John, *From the Auroral Darkness: The Life and Poetry of Robert Hayden,* George Ronald, 1984.

Robert C. Hayden Jr.
American educator and historian
Born August 21, 1937.

Robert Carter Hayden Jr. was born in New Bedford, Massachusetts, and educated at Boston University, where he earned his Ed.M. in 1961. He also attended Harvard University. His active career in education administration—teaching, editing, directing numerous educational programs, and serving on advisory boards—has been matched by his several articles and history books published for young people about the achievements of black American scientists. These include *Seven Black American Scientists* (1970), *Eight Black American Inventors* (1972), and (with Jacqueline Harris) the award-winning *Nine Black American Doctors* (1976). In addition to his administrative work, Hayden has lectured at many universities and has written local history on African American life in Boston.

Further Readings
Black Writers, first edition, Gale, 1989.

Haynes
Character in *Minty Alley*

Bessie Head

South African-born Botswanan novelist
and short story writer
Born July 6, 1937.
Died April 17, 1986.

Bessie Amalia Emery Head explored the effects of oppression and the theme of exile in her works. She was born to racially mixed parents in South Africa but lived and died in Botswana, the subject of much of her writing. Her first **novel,** *When Rain Clouds Gather* (1969), is about an English expatriate and an embittered black South African who try to change traditional agricultural practices in a Botswanan village. *Maru* (1971) is about the problems that arise when two young chiefs fall in love with a newly arrived teacher. Considered her most important work, *A Question of Power* (1973), relates the story of a young woman's mental breakdown. Head also published a **short story** collection and two historical chronicles.

Further Readings

Abrahams, Cecil, editor, *The Tragic Life: Bessie Head and Literature in Southern Africa,* Africa World Press, 1990.

Black Writers, second edition, Gale, 1994.

Nathan C. Heard

American novelist
Born November 7, 1936.

Nathan Cliff Heard was born in Newark, New Jersey, and raised in a ghetto. He dropped out of high school at fifteen and was introduced to literature by a fellow inmate while imprisoned for armed robbery. Heard's semiautobiographical first **novel,** *Howard Street* (1968), depicts ghetto life, portraying pimps, prostitutes, drug addicts, and gang members. The narrative was an immediate success, becoming a bestseller. Three subsequent novels were less popular, but *House of Slammers* (1983) returned Heard to critical favor. Set in a penitentiary, the novel was praised for its stark and vivid account

of the brutality of prison life and for the urgency of its message.

Further Readings

Black Writers, first edition, Gale, 1989.

Dictionary of Literary Biography, Volume 33: *Afro-American Fiction Writers after 1955,* Gale, 1984.

John Hearne

Canadian-born Jamaican novelist
Born February 4, 1926.

Hearne's work is notable for its narrative skill and descriptive style. John Edgar Caulwell Hearne grew up in Jamaica and attended college in Scotland and England before beginning his career as a novelist. Remaining in Europe throughout the 1950s. Hearne wrote a series of **novels,** some under the collaborative pseudonym John Morris, about middle-class life in Cayuna, his fictional counterpart of Jamaica. The first of these novels, *Voices under the Window* (1955), is considered one of his best works. In 1962 Hearne accepted a position at the University of the West Indies. For the next twenty years he devoted less time to fiction but continued to write about Caribbean life and politics. Publication of the historical novel *The Sure Salvation* (1981) renewed Hearne's reputation as a serious novelist.

Further Readings

Black Writers, first edition, Gale, 1989.

The Heart of a Woman

Maya Angelou
Autobiography, 1981

The Heart of a Woman, **Maya Angelou**'s fourth volume of **autobiography,** takes the author's story from 1957 to 1963. In this book, Angelou asserts her intention to become a writer.

She moves to Brooklyn to learn her trade from social activist and author John Killens. Soon she earns acceptance from such established writers as **John Henrik Clarke**, **Paule Marshall**, and **James Baldwin**. She also expands her social conscience, making a commitment to promote civil rights. In cooperation with Godfrey Cambridge, a comedian, she draws on her stage experience to produce a *Cabaret of Freedom* to benefit **Martin Luther King Jr.**'s Southern Christian Leadership Conference.

Angelou also discusses her desertion of her fiancé for a romantic South African named Vusumzi Make. Although in some ways Make expands Angelou's range of experiences—for instance, he encourages her to accept a stage role in Jean Genet's **play** *The Blacks*—in others he betrays her the same way other men in her life have done. Conflicts develop over Make's incessant womanizing and Angelou's refusal to abandon her African American heritage. She finally ends the relationship before a gathering of African diplomats. They approve her decision and promise to welcome her anywhere she decides to go in Africa. The volume ends with Angelou's arrival in Ghana.

Hector
Character in *Omeros*

Helen
Character in *Omeros*

Helen Martin
Character in *Trumbull Park*

Helga Crane
Character in *Quicksand*

Hella Lincoln
Character in *Giovanni's Room*

Essex Hemphill
American editor, poet, and essayist
Born in 1957(?).

Hemphill has become a leading African American voice in the field of gay writing in the United States. He was born circa 1957 and grew up in a working-class neighborhood in Washington, D.C., where he faced both **racism** and homophobia. Starting out as a poet with two self-published collections of verse, *Earth Life* (1985) and *Conditions* (1985), Hemphill has since edited *Brother to Brother* (1991), a controversial collection of writings by thirty-five gay black men, including himself, and addressing such subjects as homophobia, racism, AIDS, and religious intolerance. His *Ceremonies: Prose and Poetry* appeared in 1992 and includes some verses from his earlier collections in addition to new **poetry** and **essays**. Much of Hemphill's work is autobiographical and concerns the development of a black gay identity, while other notable pieces are openly political.

Further Readings
Black Writers, Gale, second edition, 1994.

David Henderson
American poet and prose writer
Born 1942.

Henderson has built his reputation as a mythmaker in the African storytelling tradition. He was born in Harlem and raised there and in the Bronx. While attending college, he helped found alternative publications, including *East Village Other* and *Umbra*.

Henderson wrote his first poem in 1960. He has published three books of **poetry:** *Felix of the Silent Forest* (1967), which merges culture and **myth**; *De Mayor of Harlem* (1970), a collection of **jazz** poetry; and *The Low East* (1980), a celebration of New York.

Henderson's prose writings include the **biography** *Jimi Hendrix: Voodoo Child of the*

Aquarian Age (1978) and the **play** *Ghetto Follies* (1978).

See also **Poetry of David Henderson**

Further Readings
Black Writers, first edition, Gale, 1989.
Dictionary of Literary Biography, Volume 41: *Afro-American Poets since 1955,* Gale, 1985.

George Wylie Henderson
American novelist and short story writer
Born June 14, 1904.

Henderson's writings are a link between the **Harlem Renaissance** of the 1920s and the social protest movement of the 1940s. Noted for their **realism**, his works portray the poor, the ordinary, and the forgotten. Henderson, the son of a minister, was born in Warrior's Stand, Alabama. He learned printing at the Tuskegee Institute before moving to New York to become an apprentice. While still an apprentice, he began to publish short stories.

Henderson's **novels,** *Ollie Miss* (1935) and its sequel *Jule* (1946), relate a rejected pregnant girl's perseverance and her illegitimate son's struggle growing up black and male in America.

Further Readings
Black Writers, first edition, Gale, 1989.
Dictionary of Literary Biography, Volume 51: *Afro-American Writers from the Harlem Renaissance to 1940,* Gale, 1987.

Stephen E. Henderson
American literary critic
Born October 13, 1925.

Henderson, a teacher and literary critic, was born in Key West, Florida, and holds a Ph.D. degree from the University of Wisconsin.

He has taught at Virginia Union University and Morehouse College. Henderson began teaching African American studies at Howard University in 1971 and became director of the Institute for the Arts and the Humanities at Howard in 1973. Henderson coauthored with **Mercer Cook** *The Militant Black Writer in Africa and the United States* (1969) and wrote *Understanding the New Black Poetry: Black Speech and Black Music as Poetic References* (1973). He has contributed articles to *Ebony*, *Black World,* and *New Directions.*

Further Readings
Black Writers, Gale, first edition, 1989.

Henri Christophe
Character in *Toussaint L'Ouverture*

Here I Stand
Paul Robeson
Autobiography, 1958

In *Here I Stand,* **Paul Robeson** shares many of his thoughts and opinions about **racism** and the position of black people in white society. A successful actor and singer, Robeson became associated with the political left in the 1930's. In the McCarthy years, he came under significant public and government attack for suspected communist activities and beliefs. *Here I Stand,* however, does not emphasize the persecution that he endured. Rather, Robeson describes his relationship with his family and his experiences in the United States and abroad, calling for an immediate cessation of racist activities toward blacks, and demands a complete acceptance of black people as full citizens of the United States. Maintaining that white supremacy also harms a certain segment of whites as well as blacks, he believes all Americans would benefit through black liberation and suggests guidelines and methods by which blacks could obtain their civil rights. He sees the success of the black freedom movement dependent upon presenting a united stand, and he recommends specific activities to help achieve accord. *Here I Stand* focuses on the **black power** movement and emphasizes that while blacks need to work with their white allies, it is the responsibility of African Americans to rely on themselves and their own resources in order to ensure liberation.

Calvin C. Hernton

American nonfiction writer, novelist, and poet
Born April 28, 1934.

Calvin Coolidge Hernton's works frequently address the inextricability of sexism and **racism**. Born in Chattanooga, Tennessee, on April 28, 1934, Hernton earned an M.A. in sociology in 1956 and subsequently became a welfare counselor for New York City. His treatise *Sex and Racism in America* (1965) combines personal reflections and case studies to support its central thesis: that racial and sexual polarization are interrelated. *White Papers for White Americans* (1966) considers important African American events of the 1960s, including the **civil rights movement**. From 1965 to 1969, Hernton was a research fellow at the London Institute of Phenomenological Studies. He then became writer in residence at Oberlin College and published *Coming Together: Black Power, White Hatred, and Sexual Hang-ups* (1971). In 1973, Hernton became professor of black studies and creative writing at Oberlin and, in 1974, published the **novel** *Scarecrow*, a psychological study of its characters that Hernton developed while in London. He is also the author of *Medicine Man: Collected Poems* (1976) and *Sexual Mountains and Black Women Writers: Adventure in Sex, Literature, and Real Life* (1987).

Further Readings

Black Writers, first edition, Gale, 1989.

Dictionary of Literary Biography, Volume 38: *Afro-American Writers after 1955: Dramatists and Prose Writers,* Gale, 1985.

A Hero Ain't Nothin' but a Sandwich

Alice Childress
Novel, 1973

Set in the inner city in the late 1960s, **Alice Childress**'s *A Hero Ain't Nothin' but a Sandwich* centers on Benjie Johnson, a thirteen-year-old who becomes addicted to heroin. He responds to the prodding of the neighborhood children, and he takes drugs on a dare just to show he would never be "chicken." Rose Johnson, Benjie's mother, lives with a man named Craig Butler, who is a maintenance worker. Rose has always remarked on Benjie's similarities to his biological father, who abandoned them, so Benjie feels undeserving of his stepfather's care and attention. Rose's mother, Mrs. Ransom Bell, feels marginalized both because she is subject to violence on the street and because her family neglects her. Benjie feels displaced and jealous, and retreats more into drug use. He uses heroin instead of marijuana at the urging of gang members. Then he turns from a user into a drug distributor. Benjie stops paying attention at school, then stops going. The teacher, Nigeria Greene, notifies Benjie's mother so she can get him into a rehabilitation clinic. After trying to prevent Benjie's downward slide into addiction in the name of **black nationalism**, Greene is forced to give up. Benjie takes out his frustrations on Craig, who finally tires of Benjie's stealing from him and leaves for fear of striking out at the boy. But Benjie follows Craig to a boardinghouse and tries to steal from him again. When Craig saves Benjie from a deadly fall from a rooftop, his stepson promises to go back into the clinic out of gratitude. The **novel** ends ambiguously, as Craig waits for Benjie to appear for an appointment at the drug rehabilitation center.

Carolivia Herron

American novelist
Born July 22, 1947.

Herron is best known as the author of the **novel** *Thereafter Johnnie* (1991), a family saga that she wrote over a period of eighteen years and acknowledges to be autobiographical. It explores the effects of **slavery** and miscegenation on modern black-white relations in America, treats the topic of incest, and draws heavily on biblical and legendary language and themes.

Born in Washington, D.C., Herron earned a Ph.D. from the University of Pennsylvania. She taught African American studies and comparative literature at Harvard University from 1986 to 1990 and taught English at Mount Holyoke College in the early 1990s. Herron is also the editor of *Selected Works of Angelina Weld Grimke* (1991).

Further Readings

Black Writers, second edition, Gale, 1994.

Hess Green

Character in *Ganja and Hess*

Leslie Pinckney Hill

American poet, dramatist, and essayist
Born May 14, 1880.
Died February 16, 1960.

Born in Lynchburg, Virginia, Hill was an educator and activist poet who devoted his career and writings to the highest standards of education and equal race relations. He earned bachelor's and master's degrees from Howard University.

Hill's writings and lectures promoted industry, the importance of knowledge, and general goodwill toward all people. His writings differed from those of the protest and black-pride writers of his time. For example, his **poetry** collection ***The Wings of Oppression*** (1921) stresses patience and calm endurance of the black race. Hill's other writings include *Toussaint L'Ouverture: A Dramatic History* (1928), a poetical portrait of the Haitian leader, and *Jethro* (1931), a biblical drama.

Further Readings

Black Writers, first edition, Gale, 1989.

Dictionary of Literary Biography, Volume 51: *Afro-American Writers from the Harlem Renaissance to 1940,* Gale, 1987.

Cover of Childress's popular novel for young adults.

Asa Grant Hilliard III

American educator and historian
Born August 22, 1933.

A psychologist, educator, and African American historian, Hilliard was born in Galveston, Texas, in 1933. He earned degrees in psychology from the University of Denver. Particularly concerned with the development of African American children, much of his work focuses on topics relevant to that group. He contends that young black children dismiss their ability to be achievers or participants in world history when they do not know their people's story, and that these children often revolt in order to draw attention to themselves.

Hilliard has compiled a list of references on the history of African people and has coedited *The Teachings of Ptahhotep: The Oldest Book in the World* (1987).

Further Readings
Black Writers, Gale, second edition, 1994.

David Hilliard
American activist and autobiographer
Born May 15, 1942.

Hilliard became notorious for his involvement with the Black Panther Party, a militant, revolutionary organization founded in 1966 in Oakland, California, by his childhood friend Huey Newton and **Bobby Seale**. Opposing **Martin Luther King Jr.**'s philosophy of peaceful change, the Black Panthers advocated armed struggle as a means for black Americans to gain power. Hilliard served as the group's program administrator from 1966 to 1974 and later became a field representative for a labor union in Oakland. His *This Side of Glory: The Autobiography of David Hilliard and the Story of the Black Panther Party* (1993), as told to Lewis Cole, documents the rise and fall of the Party and the effect it had on Hilliard's life. According to Hilliard, the book was written to correct misinformation circulated by the Federal Bureau of Investigation (FBI).

Further Readings
Black Writers, second edition, Gale, 1994.

Chester Himes
American novelist
Born July 29, 1909.
Died November 12, 1984.

Himes is best known for his series of popular detective **novels** published between 1957

and 1969. Set in Harlem, these works feature formulaic plots, naturalistic prose, and extremely violent protagonists and situations.

Himes was born in Jefferson City, Missouri. He spent much of his childhood moving from city to city before his family settled in Cleveland, Ohio. Dismissed from Ohio State University after one semester, Himes became increasingly involved in crime. After several arrests for burglary he was sentenced at age nineteen to twenty years in prison, where he began to write. After seven years Himes was paroled and hired as a laborer for the Works Progress Administration, then as a researcher on the Ohio Writers' Project. He moved to California in 1942 and began his series of five protest novels, beginning with *If He Hollers Let Him Go* (1945) and ending with *The Primitive* (1955). In these works, Himes depicts the destruction of interracial relationships through race and gender stereotypes. Their protagonists struggle unsuccessfully with environmental and social forces that shape their violent destinies. Himes's other protest novels include *Lonely Crusade* (1947), *Cast the First Stone* (1952), and *The Third Generation* (1954).

During the 1950s, Himes moved to Europe, settling on the Spanish island of Majorca. In 1957, Marcel Duhamel, publisher of the detective story series La Sèrie Noire, convinced Himes to write serial detective novels. Over the next twelve years, Himes wrote a series of novels featuring Harlem detectives Grave Digger Jones and Coffin Ed Johnson. The first of these works, *For Love of Imabelle* (1957) (revised as *A Rage in Harlem* in 1965) received the Grand Prix du Roman Policier in 1957 and established Himes in France as a popular expatriate author. This success was followed by a number of books, including *The Real Cool Killers* (1959), *Cotton Comes to Harlem* (1965), and *Blind Man with a Pistol* (1969). Other works of this period include *A Case of Rape* (1963), *Run Man, Run* (1966), and Himes's **satire** on American racial and sexual mores, *Pinktoes* (1961).

In addition to his novels, Himes published two autobiographical volumes: *The Quality of*

Hurt: The Autobiography of Chester Himes (1972) and My Life of Absurdity: The Autobiography of Chester Himes (1976). Three of his works have been adapted for film. The novel Plan B, which was unfinished when Himes died of Parkinson's disease in 1984, was published posthumously in 1993.

Further Readings

Black Literature Criticism, Gale, 1992.

Black Writers, second edition, Gale, 1994.

Dictionary of Literary Biography, Volume 76: Afro-American Writers, 1940-1955, Gale, 1988.

Milliken, Stephen F. Chester Himes: A Critical Appraisal, University of Missouri Press, 1976.

Popular detective novelist Chester Himes.

The Hippodrome

Cyrus Colter
Novel, 1973

Cyrus Colter's second **novel**, The Hippodrome, follows the degradation of Yeager, a young black writer of religious materials who is manipulated by past events, sexual fears, guilt, accidents, and chance. After murdering his wife and her white lover, Yeager flees, carrying his wife's severed head in a brown bag. He shows it to Bea and Darlene, whom he meets in an all-night cafeteria. Bea offers him refuge because she needs another performer in her sex show staged for white audiences in a big arena-like theater, the hippodrome. The morally stringent Yeager finds himself trapped; he must either participate in the hippodrome activities or he must leave and risk detection and capture.

Everett H. Hoagland III

American poet
Born December 18, 1942.

In his **poetry,** Hoagland stresses the importance of racial pride. During his career, his poetic style has evolved into a fusion of agit-prop, historical narrative, and bebop, which seeks to teach as well as entertain. His best-known collection of poems, Black Velvet (1970), bears the influence of the **black arts movement** and focuses on the unity and shared aesthetic heritage of black people. Hoagland's other books are Ten Poems: A Collection (1968) and Scrimshaw (1976). Though not widely reviewed, his poems and short fiction have appeared in anthologies and literary journals. Hoagland, who was born and raised in Philadelphia, has taught English and humanities at a number of colleges in the United States.

See also **Poetry of Everett H. Hoagland III**

Further Readings

Black Writers, first edition, Gale, 1989.

Dictionary of Literary Biography, Volume 41: Afro-American Poets since 1955, Gale, 1985.

Home
Samm-Art Williams
Play, first produced 1979, published 1980

Samm-Art Williams's *Home* tells the story of Cephus Miles, a young African American born in the rural South. Despite being drafted during the Vietnam War, Cephus refuses to fight and is prosecuted. While in jail he loses the farm he inherited from his grandfather. Later, in a large northern city his past becomes known and he is fired from a job, eventually becoming an alcoholic dependant on welfare. When Cephus learns that his farm has been recovered, he returns to the land, marries a school sweetheart, and begins a new life. *Home* won critical praise for its innovative treatment of the myth of the North as the promised land. In 1980 the **play** won Williams the Audelco Recognition Award.

Home to Harlem
Claude McKay
Novel, 1928

Home to Harlem, **Claude McKay**'s first **novel** and the first commercial bestseller by a black writer, examines conflicts between the unselfconscious black man, represented by the protagonist Jake Brown, and the black man as corrupted by Western society, represented by the Haitian writer Ray—whom some critics believe may represent McKay. The novel opens with Jake's desertion from the army and his return to Harlem. There, Jake encounters a black prostitute named Felice, who secretly returns the money he had paid her. The novel recounts Jake's subsequent search for Felice through the Harlem streets, a quest that paints a picture of the night life of the city. Although Jake enjoys himself in the **jazz** clubs of Harlem, Ray is repressed by his education and distrusts the instincts that allow Jake to survive. Unable to come to terms with his fears, Ray flees to Europe. Jake finally finds Felice and, as the novel ends, departs with her to start a new life in the West.

homegirls & handgrenades
Sonia Sanchez
Poetry, 1984

The winner of the 1985 American Book Award, **Sonia Sanchez**'s *homegirls & handgrenades* examines the pain and alienation of the modern African American experience. In describing a bleak world in which intelligent young women drop out of college and young men suffer from drug addiction, she expresses her sympathy for those who struggle to find love in the midst of suffering. "I am here because I shall not give the / earth up to non-dreamers and earth molesters," she writes, emphasizing her commitment to peace and her condemnation for self-destructive behavior. In "After Saturday Night Comes Sunday," she examines the spiritual and economic suffering a man's drug addiction brings to his children and his wife, whose love cannot save him. Such a tragedy serves as a symptom of what her **poetry** suggests is a more pervasive problem in black America: the absence of self-esteem in a white-dominated society. This theme is also illustrated in the poem "MIAs," which links the detainment of blacks without bail by the South African police, the persecution of villagers by El Salvador's repressive government, and the kidnapping and murder of black children in Atlanta, Georgia. Claiming solidarity with these victims, Sanchez, according to many critics, stands as a compassionate witness to the struggle of oppressed people around the world, offering both a voice of determined resistance to terrorism and the hope for freedom.

Homer Barbee
Character in *Invisible Man*

Bell Hooks
American educator and writer
Born in 1955(?).

A feminist activist and social critic, Hooks is noted for her intellectually challenging and often daring personal examination of African

American culture. In works such as *Ain't I a Woman: Black Women and Feminism* (1981), *Talking Back: Thinking Feminist, Thinking Black* (1988), and *Outlaw Culture, Resisting Representation* (1994), Hooks takes an analytical yet impassioned look at how African American feminism, the **civil rights movement**, capitalism, and critical theory work with and against each other in both society and the individual.

Born as Gloria Watkins circa 1955, Hooks writes under the name of her great-grandmother, Bell Hooks, to pay homage to the unheard voice of black women of past and present. She frequently lowercases her name, to symbolize her skepticism of fame and ego. The search for the voice of black women within current mainstream feminism is the focus of both *Ain't I a Woman* and *Talking Back,* in which Hooks develops the concept of "black feminism" through an examination of the elements of **racism**, sexism, and classism that are unique to African American women. She finds that black and white women alternate between being allies and being at odds. In *Talking Back,* the complex relationship among women of all colors is explored more deeply in a series of **essays** on the black/feminist connection. Writing, teaching, domestic violence, pornography, and racist feminism number among the catalysts that expose this multifaceted association. Hooks's *Art on My Mind* (1995) contains essays on modern art while *Killing Rage* (1995) explores such subjects as the civil rights movement, racism, and anti-Semitism.

Further Readings
Black Writers, second edition, Gale, 1994.

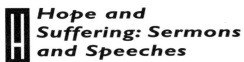

Hope and Suffering: Sermons and Speeches

Desmond Tutu
Nonfiction, 1983

Desmond Tutu's works between 1976 and 1982 are collected in *Hope and Suffering: Sermons and Speeches,* and are divided into four sections. "Introducing South Africa," "Liberation as

a Biblical Theme," "Current Concerns," and "The Divine Intention" are devoted to issues and events considered by Tutu as having helped to preserve the status quo of the **apartheid** system. The first section quotes statistical evidence of racial inequity in the region. The second draws from the books of Exodus and Matthew to show Jesus as a liberator. In the third, Ronald Reagan is criticized for his appeasement of the Afrikaners, and Tutu compares this policy unfavorably to American sanctions erected against Poland once it came under martial law. The last chapter includes Tutu's personal testimony regarding God's will in the trials of South Africa.

Pauline Elizabeth Hopkins

American novelist
Born in 1859.
Died August 13, 1930.

Hopkins was one of the first writers to introduce racial and social themes—notably the advancement of blacks—into nineteenth-century romance **novels**. Born in Portland, Maine, Hopkins spent most of her life in Boston. Her most noted novel, *Contending Forces: A Romance Illustrative of Negro Life North and South* (1900), traces the fortunes of a racially mixed family from 1790 Bermuda to late nineteenth-century Boston. Hopkins used this story to impart her ideas about improving the lives of African Americans, advocating the importance of coupling economic advancement with political power and liberal education. Hopkins also authored serialized novels (some under the name Sarah A. Allen), short stories, and dramas, many of which were published in *Colored American* magazine.

Further Readings
Black Writers, second edition, Gale, 1994.

Horace Xavier

Character in *A Morning in Trinidad*

Frank Horne

American poet, short story writer,
and essayist
Born August 18, 1899.
Died September 7, 1974.

Frank Smith Horne was a minor poet of the **Harlem Renaissance** who wrote about the prejudice and sorrow experienced by blacks. His **poetry** generally is more personal and traditional than that of other writers of the 1920s, focusing on death, infirmity, and the crisis of faith. Born in Brooklyn, Horne practiced optometry before becoming a teacher and, eventually, entering public service.

Horne's reputation derives mainly from *Haverstraw* (1963). Some of the poems in the collection were originally submitted to *Crisis* magazine in the 1920s under the pseudonym Xavier I; the verses revolve around individuals who had an impact on a suicide victim's life. Horne also authored short stories, **essays**, articles, and a pamphlet.

See also **Poetry of Frank S. Horne**

Further Readings

Black Writers, first edition, Gale, 1989.

Dictionary of Literary Biography, Volume 51: *Afro-American Writers from the Harlem Renaissance to 1940,* Gale, 1987.

George Moses Horton

American poet
Born in 1797(?).
Died in 1883(?).

Called the slave bard of North Carolina, Horton was the first professional black writer in the South. Born into **slavery**, he learned to read with his mother's help, but did not learn to write until the publication of his first collection of **poetry**, *The Hope of Liberty,* in 1829. Horton composed and sold love poems and acrostics to initially incredulous, then enthusiastic customers on the state university campus at Chapel Hill.

Horton published two volumes of poetry while a slave. A third appeared in 1865, after which its author, now free, went north to Philadelphia. Horton's poems deal with love, death, **religion**, and slavery.

Further Readings

Dictionary of Literary Biography, Volume 50: *Afro-American Writers before the Harlem Renaissance,* Gale, 1986.

Walser, Richard, *The Black Poet: The Story of George Moses Horton, A North Carolina Slave,* Philosophical Library, 1966.

The House behind the Cedars

Charles W. Chesnutt
Novel, 1900

Charles W. Chesnutt's first **novel**, *The House behind the Cedars,* considers the consequences of miscegenation in post-Civil War America. The protagonist is Rena Walden, a girl of mixed blood born from the relationship between a southern planter and his slave. Rena is light-skinned enough to pass for white, and in the first part of the novel she tries to break into the upper-class society of her small South Carolina town. Her secret is discovered, however, and she is rejected by the man who was to have married her. In the second part of the novel, Rena tries to fit into African American society. Harassed by her lecherous employer and tormented by her former suitor, however, she dies while trying to escape her troubles.

The House of Dies Drear

Virginia Hamilton
Novel, 1968

Virginia Hamilton's second **novel**, *The House of Dies Drear,* winner of the Edgar Allan Poe Award, combines elements of history and mystery when a thirteen-year-old African American boy, Thomas Small, and his father, a history professor, move into a house in Ohio that once served as a station for the **Underground Railroad**. When ghosts begin to appear, a labyrinth of hidden tunnels is revealed, and a treasure discovered, Thomas and his father begin to piece together the mystery with the help of Mr. Pluto, the great-great-grandson of a slave who once found refuge there. At the same time, Thomas gets a lesson in African American heritage.

House of Slammers

Nathan C. Heard
Novel, 1983

House of Slammers, **Nathan C. Heard**'s fifth **novel**, chronicles life in an American penal institution. William "Beans" Butler is an African American who has survived prison life without accepting the sociological crutches and violent ideology that his fellow inmates have adopted in response to their situation. As the time for his parole hearing draws near, Butler risks his chance for freedom by deciding to become involved in a work-stoppage effort, in which he soon assumes a leading role. As the strike grows into a full-scale prison riot, several inmates are killed and the men's hopes for freedom are crushed as the strike is suppressed. Against a backdrop of violence and the brutality of life behind bars, the prison's warden and his chief deputy debate the shortcomings of the penal system.

Vanessa Howard

American poet
Born in 1955.

When she was still a teenager, Howard published her only collection of **poetry,** *A Screaming Whisper* (1972). Praised by critics, *A Screaming Whisper* contains forty-four of Howard's poems, many of which have been reprinted in anthologies such as *Soulscript, Voice of the Children,* and *Tales and Stories.*

Further Readings
Black Writers, second edition, Gale, 1994.

Nathan Irvin Huggins

American historian and editor
Born January 14, 1927.
Died c. January, 1990.

Huggins was best known as the author of books that illuminate important areas in African American history. After earning his doctorate at Harvard University in 1962, the Chicago-born Huggins began teaching at Long Beach State College. He held professorships at Columbia and Harvard universities and served as a consultant to various organizations and broadcast productions.

In his book **Harlem Renaissance** (1971), Huggins examined the flourishing of the arts among blacks during the 1920s, while in *Black Odyssey: The Afro-American Ordeal in Slavery* (1977) he explored the personal impact of **slavery** on the slave. Huggins's *Slave and Citizen: The Life of Frederick Douglass* (1980), a volume in the "Library of American Biography" series, portrays the public aspect of the famed abolitionist. Huggins died of cancer in Cambridge, Massachusetts.

Further Readings
Black Writers, first edition, Gale, 1989.

Hugh

Character in *Lucy*

Langston Hughes

American poet, short story writer, novelist, playwright, autobiographer, and nonfiction writer
Born February 1, 1902.
Died May 22, 1967.

Hughes was one of the seminal figures of the **Harlem Renaissance**; some critics consider him the most significant African American writer of the twentieth century. Hughes inspired and encouraged two generations of black writers, including **Margaret Walker** and **Gwendolyn Brooks**, and later **Ted Joans, Mari Evans,** and **Alice Walker**.

Langston Hughes devoted his versatile and prolific career to portraying the urban experiences of working-class African Americans.

Born in Joplin, Missouri, James Mercer Langston Hughes began his literary career in high school, publishing **poetry** and short fiction in the school magazine. He enrolled at Columbia University in 1921 but left after his freshman year due to racial tensions on campus. From 1923 to 1925 he travelled abroad, visiting West Africa and Europe. His first book, *The Weary Blues* (1926), is a collection of poems that reflects the frenzied atmosphere of Harlem's nightlife. Later that year, Hughes continued his studies, this time at Lincoln University.

Some of Hughes's contemporaries objected to his realistic portrayal of African American culture and values, especially in collections such as *Fine Clothes to the Jew* (1927), *Shakespeare in Harlem* (1942, with Robert Glenn), and *Montage of a Dream Deferred* (1951). Some felt that Hughes fostered racial distrust by emphasizing the seemingly negative traits of black Americans. However, Hughes insisted that his portrayals were realistic and that his characters were common but noble.

In addition to his poetry, Hughes detailed his understanding of African American life in many other genres, including the **novel** *Not without Laughter* (1930), the **autobiography** *The Big Sea: An Autobiography* (1940), the musical *The Sun Do Move* (1942), and short stories such as the **"Simple" Stories,** those involving the character Jesse B. Semple (shortened to Simple). In 1958 he coedited *The Book of Negro Poetry,* a collection of African American and African **folklore**, with **Arna Bontemps**.

Although his peaceful politics eventually conflicted with the militancy of many of the younger black poets, Hughes continued to play a prominent role in black thought throughout the 1960s. In 1960, he was awarded the Spingarn Medal from the **National Association for the Advancement of Colored People** (NAACP). His later works, especially *Ask Your Mama: 12 Moods for Jazz* (1961), *The Panther and the Lash: Poems of Our Times* (1967), and *Black Misery* (1969), address the anger of the decade without endorsing violent action.

Although he died in New York City on May 22, 1968, Hughes's popularity has grown in the years since his death. His works have continued to be anthologized and collected in books such as *Good Morning Revolution: Uncollected Social Protest Writings by Langston Hughes* (1973) and *The Collected Poems of Langston Hughes* (1994).

See also **Poetry of Langston Hughes**

Further Readings

Black Literature Criticism, Gale, 1992.

Black Writers, first edition, Gale, 1989.

Dictionary of Literary Biography, Gale, Volume 4, *American Writers in Paris, 1920-1939,* 1980; Volume 7, *Twentieth-Century American Dramatists,* 1981; Volume 48, *American Poets, 1880-1945,* Second Series, 1986; Volume 51, *Afro-American Writers from the Harlem Renaissance to 1940,* 1987.

Gloria T. Hull

American writer, editor, and poet
Born December 6, 1944.

Born in Shreveport, Louisiana, Gloria Theresa Thompson Hull is an African American studies scholar whose work focuses on African American women and their literature. She has edited and contributed to *All the Women Are White, All the Blacks Are Men, but Some of Us Are Brave: Black Women's Studies* (1982), *Give Us Each Day: The Diary of Alice Dunbar-Nelson* (1984), and *The Works of Alice Dunbar-Nelson* (1988). She also authored *Color, Sex and Poetry: Three Women Writers of the Harlem Renaissance* (1987). Also a poet, Hull has written *Healing Heart, Poems 1973-1988* (1989), which contemplates the influences of experience and culture on the evolution of personal identity.

Further Readings

Black Writers, second edition, Gale, 1994.

Hunter's novels realistically depict African American life in the ghetto.

Kristin Hunter

American novelist and author of children's literature
Born September 12, 1931.

Kristin Eggleston Hunter has influenced many black women writers, and her depictions of black ghetto life have won critical praise for their **realism** as well as their optimism. Born in Philadelphia, Hunter received her B.S. in education from the University of Pennsylvania in 1951. Writing short stories and dramas in her spare time, Hunter worked as a journalist and an advertising copywriter before she won a national competition for her television script *Minority of One* (1955). Beginning her serious writing career shortly afterward, Hunter published her first and most critically acclaimed book, *God Bless the Child* (1964), which tells the story of Rosalie Fleming, a young black girl who tries desperately but unsuccessfully to rise from poverty. Her next work, **The Landlord** (1966), which concerns a wealthy young white man who buys a ghetto apartment building, was her most commercially successful book and was filmed by United Artists in 1970.

Hunter's best-known **novels** were written for young adults. In **The Soul Brothers and Sister Lou** (1968) and its sequel, *Lou in the Limelight* (1981), Hunter describes Louetta Hawkins, who escapes the ghetto by forming a popular singing group. Hunter's novelette *Boss Cat* (1971) was followed by a collection of short stories, **Guests in the Promised Land** (1973).

In 1972, Hunter began teaching creative writing at the University of Pennsylvania. *The Survivors* (1975) describes a friendship between an older black woman and a young boy. In *The Lakestown Rebellion* (1978), the residents of a black neighborhood oppose a planned interstate highway with a series of comical acts of sabotage.

Further Readings

Black Writers, first edition, Gale, 1989.

Dictionary of Literary Biography, Volume 33: *Afro-American Fiction Writers after 1955,* Gale, 1984.

Charlayne Hunter-Gault

American journalist
Born February 27, 1942.

Hunter-Gault is known to television audiences through her reporting and anchor position on WRC-TV in Washington, D.C., and *The MacNeil/Lehrer News Hour* on PBS. She is also known through her work in the print media. In 1963, she took a position as "Talk of the Town" reporter for *The New Yorker* magazine and also served as Harlem bureau chief for *The New York TImes*. Hunter-Gault has won many awards for her work, including Emmys for outstanding coverage of a single breaking news story and for outstanding background/analysis of a single current story, the American Women in Radio and Television Award, the University of Georgia's George Foster Peabody Award for Excellence in Broadcast Journalism, and the Distinguished Urban Reporting Award from the National Urban Coalition. She has been selected Broadcast Personality of the Year by *Good Housekeeping* magazine and was named Journalist of the Year by the National Association of Black Journalists in 1986.

Hunter-Gault was born in Due West, South Carolina, the daughter of a minister and his wife. A gifted student, Hunter-Gault decided in high school that she wanted to be a journalist and applied to a number of colleges. Although she was accepted at Wayne State University in Detroit, civil rights leaders urged her to attend the University of Georgia instead, and she became the first black female student at that school. In her memoir *In My Place* (1992), Hunter-Gault recalls what it was like to be on the front lines of desegregation. The memoir concludes with Hunter-Gault's graduation from college in 1963 but also presents her 1988 commencement speech at the University of Georgia in an addendum.

Further Readings
Black Writers, second edition, Gale, 1994.

Zora Neale Hurston

American novelist and folklorist
Born January 7, 1891.
Died January 28, 1960.

Hurston is recognized as an important writer of the **Harlem Renaissance**. She has influenced such writers as **Ralph Ellison, Toni Morrison, Gayl Jones**, and **Toni Cade Bambara**. The author of four **novels** and a number of short stories, **essays**, and nonfiction works, Hurston is also acknowledged as the first black American to collect and publish African American **folklore**.

Hurston was born and raised in the first incorporated all-black town in America, Eatonville, Florida, which provided the inspiration for most of her fiction. Though she was taken out of school at age thirteen, an employer later arranged for her to complete her primary education. Hurston studied anthropology at Barnard College and Columbia University with the anthropologist Franz Boas—an experience that influenced her work. From 1927 to 1931, Hurston collected African American folklore in Alabama and Florida, working on a private grant.

Hurston drew on this folklore material for her **plays,** musicals, **short stories,** and **novels.** The novel *Jonah's Gourd Vine* (1934) combines her knowledge of folklore with biblical themes. *Mules and Men* (1935) incorporates folktale elements drawn from her hometown's culture. The novel *Their Eyes Were Watching God* (1937), considered Hurston's best work by many critics, tells the story of a woman's quest for fulfillment and liberation. In *Moses, Man of the Mountain* (1939), an allegorical novel of American **slavery**, Hurston used her studies of voodoo in New Orleans. Her **autobiography** *Dust Tracks on a Road* was published in 1942.

By the mid-1940s, Hurston's literary career had largely failed. During the remaining years of her life she worked variously as a newspaper reporter, librarian, and substitute teacher. She suffered a stroke in 1959 and was forced to enter a welfare home in Florida, where she died penniless in 1960. She was buried in an unmarked grave in Fort Pierce's segregated cemetery, the Garden of the Heavenly Rest.

Further Readings

Black Literature Criticism, Gale, 1992.

Black Writers, first edition, Gale, 1989.

Contemporary Literary Criticism, Gale, Volume 7, 1977; Volume 30, 1984.

Dictionary of Literary Biography, Volume 51: *Afro-American Writers from the Harlem Renaissance to 1940,* Gale, 1987.

Earl Ofari Hutchinson

American writer and lecturer
Born October 8, 1945.

Born in Chicago, Illinois, in 1945, Hutchinson attended universities in California, earning a doctorate degree from Pacific Western University. In his writings, Hutchinson focuses on the African American experience, particularly that of males. In *The Assassination of the Black Male Image* (1994), Hutchinson contends that the white-dominated media has perpetuated many of the problems of the black male, while in *The Mugging of Black America* (1991), he deals with the relationship between race and crime. His books *Black Fatherhood: Guide to Male Parenting* (1992) and *Black Fatherhood: Black Women Talk About Their Men* (1994) discuss issues that are related to black males in family situations.

Further Readings

Black Writers, second edition, Gale, 1994.

"I Have a Dream"

Martin Luther King Jr.
Speech, August 28, 1963

On August 28, 1963, in Washington, D.C., **Martin Luther King Jr.** made one of his most

Hunter-Gault as a student at the University of Georgia, 1961.

memorable **speeches**, "I Have a Dream," to a crowd of some 200,000 demonstrators. Noted for its biblical imagery and resounding emotion, the speech has come to symbolize the **civil rights movement**. In the first half of the speech, King catalogued the injustices suffered by African Americans. He reminded listeners that a century after the Emancipation Proclamation many blacks still suffered from **segregation**, **discrimination**, and poverty. King called attention to the country's unfulfilled promises to blacks, criticizing white leaders. He called on blacks to eschew violence in favor of a nonviolent approach to lobbying for equality. Citing the many examples of the harm done by racial prejudice, King argued that the barriers to voting rights should be dissolved and that other segregationist practices should be eliminated. Looking beyond the current challenges to a future in which religious truth triumphs, King then described his vision of an America at peace, insisting that the future must be brighter than the present.

"I Have a Dream" is recognized to be the most momentous and moving speech of King's career. Scholars rank this speech, along with King's *Letter from Birmingham City Jail*, with Abraham Lincoln's Gettysburg Address, Emile Zola's Dreyfus Letter, and John F. Kennedy's Inaugural Address as equals in power and eloquence.

I Know Why the Caged Bird Sings

Maya Angelou
Autobiography, 1970

I Know Why the Caged Bird Sings is the first book in **Maya Angelou**'s multivolume **autobiography**. It tells about her experiences growing up African American and female in the South during the 1930s and 1940s. Angelou—using her birth name of Marguerite Johnson—relates how, when she was about three years old, her parents divorced and she and her older brother Bailey were sent to live with her mother's mother, Annie Henderson, in the town of Stamps, Arkansas. In Stamps, the young girl is exposed to **racism** and **segregation**. Despite the fact that her grandmother owns a significant amount of property in town, she is scorned and humiliated by a white dentist who owes her money. Marguerite views the struggle of local cotton pickers as not very different from the **slavery** their fathers and mothers escaped, and watches relatives receive intimidating threats from white-power groups such as the Ku Klux Klan.

The year she turns eight, Marguerite and Bailey are sent back to her mother, who lives in St. Louis. There Marguerite is neglected by her mother and sexually abused by her mother's boyfriend. When her rapist is found kicked to death, Marguerite retreats into silence, refusing

to speak to anyone except her brother. The two are sent back to Stamps, where Marguerite meets Bertha Flowers, a cultured African American woman who brings her out of her self-imposed silence by introducing her to literature and recitation. After a lynching in Stamps, Annie Henderson sends the two children to join their mother in San Francisco. In California, Marguerite becomes interested in acting and dancing. She becomes more self-reliant after a fight with her father's girlfriend, and later takes a job as the city's first African American female streetcar conductor. The volume ends with Marguerite, secure in the knowledge that she can care for herself, giving birth to her son Guy when she is sixteen years old.

I Speak of Freedom

Kwame Nkrumah
Nonfiction, 1961

It was as the President of Ghana, the first African state to declare independence from colonial rule, that **Kwame Nkrumah** published *I Speak of Freedom: A Statement of African Ideology.* **Speeches** Nkrumah made between 1947 and 1960 served as the basis for a policy statement on political reforms in his country and larger goals regarding pan-African nationalism. The pan-African Conferences of Accra in 1958 and 1960 are referenced, and the President offers himself as a model for emerging national leaders. Contemporary political crises and topics such as travel and education are discussed. Economic development, Ghanaian electoral politics, international relations, and Western fear of communist leanings in African politicians are also addressed.

Ideal

Character in *The Flagellants*

If He Hollers Let Him Go

Chester Himes
Novel, 1945

Chester Himes's *If He Hollers Let Him Go* is a realistic portrayal of several days in the life of a black man fighting to make a living in Los Angeles during World War II. Told in realistic black dialogue, the story of Bob Jones reflects the emotional and psychological state of a man fighting to overcome oppression and gain a sense of autonomy within society. Fleeing Ohio, where jobs were denied him due to his race, Jones gets work in a California shipyard. His efforts are rewarded with a supervisory position that brings him into contact with white Southerner Madge Perkins. After Perkins refuses to assist him on a job, Jones's angry words are reported by Perkins to the department superintendent. Jones is demoted and told that an apology to Perkins would earn him a reinstatement. Angered and humiliated by the situation, Jones forces his way into her apartment, intending to avenge himself by raping her, but when he finds her sexually willing, he leaves. Shortly thereafter, he encounters Perkins in an isolated setting where she attempts to seduce him. When the two are discovered, Perkins, in an effort to protect her reputation, claims she was raped. Jones is arrested, and although the charges are eventually dropped, Jones is forced to join the U.S. Army.

This first volume of Angelou's autobiography chronicles her life up to age sixteen.

If We Must Die

Junius Edwards
Novel, 1961

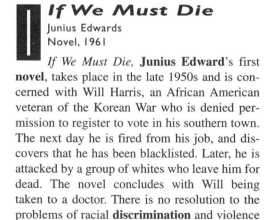

If We Must Die, **Junius Edward**'s first **novel**, takes place in the late 1950s and is concerned with Will Harris, an African American veteran of the Korean War who is denied permission to register to vote in his southern town. The next day he is fired from his job, and discovers that he has been blacklisted. Later, he is attacked by a group of whites who leave him for dead. The novel concludes with Will being taken to a doctor. There is no resolution to the problems of racial **discrimination** and violence that Will has encountered, and little indication that his plight will affect the community. The novel is an extension of Edward's earlier **short story**, "Liars Don't Qualify," which focuses on the initial episode in which Will is denied his right to vote.

Ikem Osodi

Character in *Anthills of the Savannah*

Ilhuoma

Character in *The Concubine*

Imago

Please see "Xenogenesis" Trilogy

In the Castle of My Skin

George Lamming
Novel, 1953

George Lamming's first **novel**, *In the Castle of My Skin,* is a critically acclaimed account of childhood and adolescence on a fictional Caribbean island, San Cristobal. Set against a backdrop of political and social changes and decolonization in the 1930s and 1940s, the novel revolves around the protagonist G. and his development from a nine-year-old to a grown man in Creighton's Village. Autobiographical, the novel reflects Lamming's own childhood and colonial experience in Barbados. He writes in first-person and omniscient narrative about G.'s coming of age in a feudally structured village that is secretly sold by its white landlord, leaving many villagers without homes. Like Lamming, G. eventually leaves his homeland.

In the Fog of the Seasons' End

Alex La Guma
Novel, 1972

Published six years after **Alex La Guma** left South Africa for London, *In the Fog of the Seasons' End* is an autobiographical **novel** that focuses on the resistance and liberation movement against the **apartheid** government of South Africa. Set in the suburbs of Cape Town, the black township of Langa, and briefly in a white township, the story revolves around the

socioeconomic and political circumstances of oppressed South Africans and their segregated environment. The main character, Beukes, takes on the difficult resistance struggle, and his political activities often lead to absences from home and tactics to avoid the brutal security police. The critically acclaimed novel, which has been translated into twenty languages, ends optimistically with the image of a liberated South Africa.

In My Place

Charlayne Hunter-Gault
Autobiography, 1992

Charlayne Hunter-Gault was forced to sue to attend the only university in Georgia with a **journalism** program, and this battle, which she shared with friend and fellow plaintiff Hamilton Holmes, forms the focus of *In My Place.* After a warm description of her childhood in the South, Hunter-Gault discusses her high school interest in journalism. She decided to pursue this dream in college and, despite being accepted to Wayne State University in Detroit, Michigan, Hunter-Gault was encouraged to apply to the University of Georgia. Following a lawsuit which allowed Hunter-Gault and Holmes admission and a violent reaction from white students, the two students were allowed to register. Later Hunter-Gault was a commencement speaker at the University of Georgia, while Holmes had become a member of the University's Board of Advisors.

In New England Winter

Ed Bullins
Play, first produced 1971, published 1969

The second **play** in **Ed Bullins**'s "Twentieth Century Cycle," *In New England Winter* explores the tumultuous relationship between half-brothers Cliff Dawson and Steve Benson. The setting alternates between two places and points in time: an unidentified Southwestern city in 1960 and New England in 1955. In the New England setting, Steve courts a troubled woman while absent without leave from the navy. The other scenes amplify Steve's sibling rivalry and self-hatred as it is revealed that he fathered a child with Cliff's wife. The tension between brothers is amplified by their friends Chuckie and Bummie, whose power struggles drive Steve to murder. The action eventually reveals that despite his callous exterior, Steve is guilty and fearful, and desperately in need of love.

In Spite of the Handicap

James D. Corrothers
Autobiography, 1916

In his **autobiography**, *In Spite of the Handicap,* **James D. Corrothers** recounts his struggles with Northern whites and blacks. He describes being raised by his white grandfather, attending white schools, and his efforts to establish careers in **journalism** and the ministry. He details the racial prejudices of white editors, as well as difficulties with black peers in the ministry. Throughout this work, Corrothers emphasizes the importance of morality, the importance of the assistance he received from whites, and the antipathy he sometimes felt toward other blacks.

In Splendid Error

William Branch
Play, first produced 1954

First titled *Frederick Douglass,* **William Branch**'s three-act **play** *In Splendid Error* is an imaginary recreation of a discussion that took place between abolitionists **Frederick Douglass**

and John Brown at Douglass's home in Rochester, New York, during the 1850s. In the play, Brown, a white man, argues that abolitionists should use guerrilla warfare against the plantation owners. Douglass agrees but later breaks with Brown over the tactic of attacking a federal arsenal at Harpers Ferry, West Virginia, which was not part of the original plan. Branch drew background material from Douglass's **autobiography**, *The Life and Times of Frederick Douglass;* Shirley Graham's *There Was Once A Slave;* and Leonard Ehrlich's *God's Angry Man.*

Indigo Downes

Character in *Mo' Better Blues*

Infants of the Spring

Wallace Thurman
Novel, 1932

Wallace Thurman's second **novel**, *Infants of the Spring,* is a **satire** of the **Harlem Renaissance** and its major and minor figures. It revolves around a young black author, Raymond Taylor, who is attempting to write a serious novel. Raymond resides in a brownstone called the "Niggeratti Manor" along with mainly younger, aspiring literary, artistic, and music artists. He and his friend, Stephen Jorgenson, a graduate student from Copenhagen, Denmark, discuss at length such topics as the residents' decadent actions, black people, their culture, and their struggles for racial equality and artistic integrity. Through Raymond, Thurman suggests that the artists have destroyed their creativity by leading self-destructive lives and listening to patronizing white critics who praise everything they do.

The Ingram Family

Characters in *Emergency Exit*

Innis Brown

Character in *Jubilee*

The Interesting Narrative

Olaudah Equiano
Autobiography, 1789

The Interesting Narrative of the Life of Olaudah Equiano, the first major slave **autobiography** in American literature, tells the story of Equiano, who is sold into **slavery** at age eleven in West Africa in the mid-1750s. After enduring the terrors of crossing the Atlantic in a tightly packed slave ship, he is eventually bought by a British Navy captain in Virginia. He spends ten years working on various Atlantic merchant ships, learns to read, and converts to **Christianity**. He becomes interested in purchasing his freedom, and by 1766 he has saved enough money to do so. He continues to sail as a free man aboard commercial vessels and on scientific expeditions. He eventually settles in England, involves himself in a doomed emigration scheme to Sierra Leone, and writes his autobiography as the English abolitionist movement begins.

The Interpreters

Wole Soyinka
Novel, 1965

Wole Soyinka's first **novel**, *The Interpreters,* portrays life in Lagos and Ibadan, Nigeria, in the early 1960s, shortly after the nation became independent. A social **satire** loosely structured around the discussions of five Nigerian intellectuals, the novel opens with the main characters drinking together at a nightclub in Lagos. Although educated abroad, each of the five men is aware of his African identity and has returned to Nigeria to help shape the country's future. Egbo is torn between his tedious life as a public servant in the Foreign Office and his

desire to lead the traditional society where he was raised. The hard-drinking Sagoe is a journalist and has thus assumed the professional role of commenting upon Nigerian society. Bandele, the most tolerant and kind-hearted of the five, is a university lecturer. Kola is a self-absorbed painter, and Sekoni is a skilled engineer and an artistic genius. *The Interpreters* lacks a formal structure; Soyinka reveals the histories of the five protagonists through the liberal use of flashbacks, dreams, and memories.

In *The Interpreters,* Soyinka satirizes everyone from the ignorant masses to the novel's confused intellectual protagonists. Some of the most humorous scenes center on the Nigerian officials who ape British society. In one scene, a Nigerian surgeon endlessly frets that his English-born wife has neglected to wear gloves to an embassy reception. Throughout the novel, the efforts of the five interpreters are foiled by the corruption and ignorance of Nigerian society. When Sekoni builds a power station in the bush, corrupt officials condemn it. In despair Sekoni destroys his own creation and lapses into madness. When Sekoni is later killed in a car accident, the personal shortcomings of the interpreters are evident. Bandele is the only one of the remaining four interpreters who is self-possessed enough to try to console Sekoni's grieving father. After Sekoni's death, each departs on his own separate course.

Invisible Man

Ralph Ellison
Novel, 1952

Invisible Man, **Ralph Ellison**'s National Book Award-winning **novel**, is written in the traditional style of the novel of education: the young, black narrator moves from a state of innocence to one of experience as he searches for his self-identity. The book relates the narrator's educational journey, the episodes leading to his seclusion in an underground cellar in

Harlem, and his involuntary invisibility, which results from society's inability to see beyond its own racial stereotypes.

The novel establishes themes of betrayal, invisibility, and violence in the opening chapter, known as Ellison's "Battle Royal" scene. The narrator, raised in the American South and named valedictorian of his high school class, is invited to speak before the community's prominent white citizens. After being humiliated by the drunken gathering and forced to fight in a blind boxing match, the protagonist is presented with a college scholarship, leading him to believe that education will help him overcome the racial problems he faces.

The protagonist enrolls at the state college, which resembles **Booker T. Washington**'s Tuskegee Institute and which the youth sees as a paradise. There, he is assigned to chauffeur a white philanthropist, Mr. Norton, and takes him to visit Jim Trueblood, a black sharecropper whom Mr. Norton believes to be a colorful storyteller. Upon hearing Trueblood's account of incest with his daughter, Mr. Norton is both horrified and fascinated by Trueblood's indulgence in moral taboos that he himself has secretly considered transgressing. This scene is significant, according to many critics, because Ellison uses it to refute racial stereotypes. The narrator then drives Mr. Norton to the Golden Day, a crowded saloon filled with black World War I veterans who, after fighting overseas for freedom, have been institutionalized for refusing to conform to **segregation** laws.

Expelled from college because of his ordeal with Mr. Norton, the protagonist goes to Harlem in search of work. He carries sealed letters of reference from Dr. Bledsoe, president of his former college. Though the letters are later revealed to contain character defamations, the narrator is employed by a paint company. As the result of an accident for which he is held responsible, he is hospitalized and given a form of electroshock therapy. The procedure, intended to mimic the effects of a lobotomy, leaves him "desensitized" but able to recall his Southern boyhood. He emerges with a new sense of racial pride.

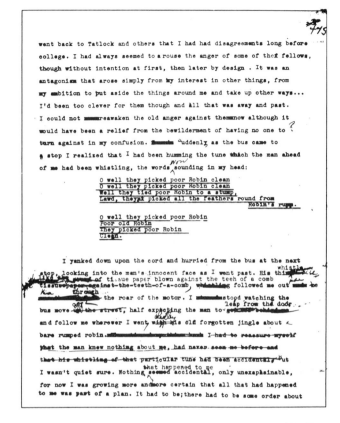

A typescript page from *Invisible Man*.

The protagonist attracts the attention of the Brotherhood, a proto-communist organization, after delivering an impromptu speech on the injustice of an elderly couple's eviction. Though he initially embraces the group's ideals, he later discovers that the organization merely feigns interest in civil rights while it works to repress blacks and deny their individuality. The chaos that ensues in the black community following the exhortations of a fanatic nationalist develops into a hallucinatory treatment of the Harlem race riots of the 1940s. While fleeing the riot's uproar, the narrator falls into a coal cellar that leads to his underground hiding place, which he eventually illuminates with 1,369 light bulbs. In the novel's final section, he meditates upon the meaning of his experiences.

Carole Ione

American poet and memoirist
Born May 28, 1937.

A full-time writer, Ione was born in Washington, D.C., in 1937 and attended Bennington, New York University, New School for Social Research, Helix Institute for Psychotherapy and Healing, and the Chinese Healing Arts Center. She founded *Letters* (now *Live Letters*) in 1974, was a contributing editor to *Essence* in the early 1980s, and has been **poetry** editor at the *Village Voice*. She has received more public recognition, however, for her memoir *Pride of Family: Four Generations of American Women of Color* (1991), selected as a *New York Times* notable book of the year in 1991. *Piramida Negro* (1991) contains a selection of Ione's poems from 1973 to 1991. Her work also appears in magazines and anthologies.

Further Readings
Black Writers, second edition, Gale, 1994.

Irene

Character in *Roots: The Saga of an American Family*

Irene Redfield

Character in *Passing*

Iris

Character in *The Sign in Sidney Brustein's Window*

Iriyise

Character in *Season of Anomy*

Isadora Bailey

Character in *Middle Passage*

That was the question,

   Almeyda,

how we could sustain our love

at a time of cruelty....

It's hard to keep tenderness

when things all around you

   are hard.

Song for Anninho,
Gayl Jones, 1981

J. B.
Character in *Philadelphia Fire*

Jack
Character in *Clara's Old Man*

Jack Carter
Character in *Compromise*

Jackie Falks
Character in *Lonely Crusade*

George Jackson
American political activist and nonfiction writer
Born September 23, 1941.
Died August 21, 1971.

Born in Chicago, George Lester Jackson was a laborer before he became a high-ranking leader in the radical Black Panther party. His books, the first of which won the 1971 Black Academy of Arts and Sciences nonfiction award, are *Soledad Brother: The Prison Letters of George Jackson* (1970) and *Blood in My Eye* (1972). Collections of letters and **essays**, the works recount his life in Soledad and San Quentin prisons from 1961 to 1972 and reveal the influence of his study in revolutionary theory during eight years in solitary confinement.

Imprisoned initially for robbery, Jackson later attracted national attention when he and two other black inmates were charged with the murder of a white guard and became known as the Soledad Brothers. Jackson was shot to death while allegedly trying to escape from San Quentin.

Further Readings
Black Writers, first edition, Gale, 1989.

Jesse Jackson
American author of children's literature
Born January 1, 1908.
Died April 14, 1983.

Jackson wrote primarily for African American adolescents and authored one of the first books for young adults that deals openly with racial prejudice. He was born on January 1, 1908, to Jesse and Mable Rogers Jackson in Columbus, Ohio, where his father worked as a truck driver. Jackson became a probation officer in 1936; his experiences working with youths led him to write young adult **novels.**

Jackson's first novel, ***Call Me Charley*** (1945), is about a black boy who lives in an all-white neighborhood and attends an all-white school. The story of his struggle to gain acceptance and respect, the book was widely praised as a contribution to interracial understanding. Though the novel remains popular, aspects of it appear dated to many critics, particularly the patience with which Charley bears many of the racial insults directed at him. Jackson's later novels include *Tessie* (1968), which describes a young girl from Harlem who wins a scholarship to an all-white private school. In 1974, he published a **biography** of Mahalia Jackson, *Make a Joyful Noise unto the Lord!: The Life of Mahalia Jackson, Queen of Gospel Singers,* which was awarded the Carter G. Woodson Book Award. Jackson was an instructor, a lecturer, and writer-in-residence at Appalachian State University from 1974 until his death in 1983.

Further Readings
Black Writers, first edition, Gale, 1989.

Jacob
Character in *The Slave Girl*

Jacob Brown
Character in *The View from Coyaba*

Jacob Upshur
Character in *This Child's Gonna Live*

Jacoub
Character in *A Black Mass*

Jadine
Character in *Tar Baby*

Jagua
Character in *Jagua Nana*

Award-winning children's author Jesse Jackson.

Jagua Nana
Cyprian Ekwensi
Novel, 1961

Cyprian Ekwensi's second **novel**, *Jagua Nana* is set in post-independence Lagos, Nigeria. The heroine of the novel, a middle-aged prostitute named Jagua, takes her name from the famous British car, the Jaguar, to represent the elegance and magnificence of her physical beauty. As Jagua moves through the nightlife of Lagos and engages in affairs with various partners, the novel reveals the corruption in Nigerian political, social, and economic life, masked by a veneer of glamour and sensuality. The people are exploited, power is abused, public money is embezzled, and public trust is forfeited. The electoral process is shown to be riddled with fraud and violence, including the murder of opponents. But public opinion is muzzled, and the masses suffer in silence. Against this backdrop, Jagua undergoes her own personal fluctuation between innocence and corruption.

Jake Adams
Character in *Corner Boy*

Jake Brown
Character in *Home to Harlem*

Jamal
Character in *Scorpions*

Jahdu
Character in *The Time-Ago Tales of Jahdu*

James
Character in *Eva's Man*

Jake
Character in *We Can't Breathe*

James Bellmont
Character in *Our Nig*

C. L. R. James

Trinidadian historian and critic
Born January 4, 1901.
Died May 31, 1989.

Cyril Lionel Robert James is considered a major thinker and theorist on black freedom and independence in postcolonial times. His works helped shape independence movements in Africa and the West Indies.

The son of a schoolteacher father, James was raised in the Trinidadian capital of Port of Spain in a middle-class black family suffused in British manners and culture. As a result of his upbringing, James retained a lifelong passion for cricket; for a time in the 1920s he performed as a professional cricketer. He also worked as a journalist and helped launch two journals that first published West Indian short fiction during the 1920s.

Despite his middle-class upbringing, James identified strongly with the working classes. His only **novel, *Minty Alley*** (1936), features strong working-class characters and emphasizes the gulf between them and working-class blacks. James later identified with Marxist socialism in *World Revolution, 1917-1936: The Rise and Fall of the Communist International* (1937) (1937) and the Pan-Africanist movement in *A History of Negro Revolt* (1938). He dramatized the revolutionary events in Haiti in his **play Toussaint L'Ouverture** (1936) before completing the major study *The Black Jacobins: Toussaint L'Ouverture and the San Domingo Revolution* (1938), an examination of the early nineteenth-century revolution in Haiti led by **Toussaint L'Ouverture**. Some of James's **essays** are collected in ***The Future in the Present*** (1977), which also contains some fiction; and ***At the Rendezvous of Victory*** (1984), which spans the years from 1931 to 1981.

Further Readings

Black Writers, second edition, Gale, 1994.

Contemporary Literary Criticism, Volume 33, Gale, 1983.

Dictionary of Literary Biography, Volume 125: *Twentieth-Century Caribbean and Black African Writers,* Second Series, Gale, 1993.

James Jackson Jr.

Character in *Queen*

James K. Lewis

Character in *M. C. Higgins, the Great*

James "Obie" Henry

Character in *The Salt Eaters*

Jamestown

Character in *There Is a Tree More Ancient Than Eden*

Jan Erlone

Character in *Native Son*

Jane Burrell

Character in *Jane: A Story of Jamaica*

Jane Pittman

Character in *The Autobiography of Miss Jane Pittman*

Jane Richards

Character in *See How They Run*

Jane: A Story of Jamaica

H. G. De Lisser
Novel, 1913

In **H. G. De Lisser**'s *Jane: A Story of Jamaica* (republished in 1914 as *Jane's Career: A Story of Jamaica*) Jane Burrell, a black country girl, moves from her home in Jamaica to the city of Kingston to seek her fortune. Mrs. Mason is the middle-class mulatto woman who takes Jane in to stay with the family. Race and money separate Jane from her benefactress. The people in the social circle of the Masons are educated and well-mannered, but they are also snobbish and separate themselves as mulattos or "browns" from the blacks in the **novel**. Jane is befriended by Sarah, who used to be the Mason's maid, and Sathyra. The story continues to describe Jane's struggle for independence and equality.

Janie Crawford

Character in *Their Eyes Were Watching God*

Jazz

Jazz is an American form of music with strong connections to black folk music and with roots that extend back into the nineteenth century. This highly original form of musical expression has influenced not only twentieth-century music in particular and culture in general, but also African American literature. The list of black writers who have employed a jazz motif in their work is long and includes such names as **Amiri Baraka**, **Langston Hughes**, **Toni Morrison**, **Sonia Sanchez**, and **Sterling Brown.**

The roots of jazz lie in African American musical forms such as **the blues** and **spirituals** and, before that, in native African musical traditions. However, it was not until the blues came together with ragtime piano playing that jazz was truly born. Though this melding process was taking place in many parts of the United States around 1900, it was in New Orleans that the first fully mature jazz style emerged. New Orleans jazz was based on an intricate style of collective improvisation, in which each instrument in the band had its own specific role. The most influential musician nurtured in New

Orleans was trumpeter Louis Armstrong, the first true virtuoso soloist of jazz. Armstrong later authored an **autobiography**, *Satchmo: My Life in New Orleans* (1954).

In the 1920s, Armstrong and many other New Orleans jazz musicians moved to Chicago and later to New York City. A Chicago style evolved, which emphasized soloists and often added saxophone to the instrumental mix. Meanwhile, jazz piano was coming into its own. Also during this decade, large groups of jazz musicians began to play together, creating the so-called big bands. In the 1930s, bands began playing swing, a type of popular music with a relaxed jazz beat. This style, which flourished into the 1940s, was epitomized by bandleaders such as Count Basie. Basie's autobiography, coauthored with **Albert L. Murray**, was posthumously published in 1985 as *Good Morning Blues: The Autobiography of Count Basie*. Also during the swing era, jazz vocalists such as Billie Holiday came into prominence, and the first large-scale jazz concerts began to be staged.

Bebop, a musical style that employed intricate rhythmic and harmonic elaborations, appeared in the early 1940s. With the advent of 1950s and 1960s came even more radically experimental forms of jazz. In 1958, tenor saxophonist John Coltrane joined trumpeter Miles Davis to introduce modal jazz, a style in which improvisation is based on scales rather than harmonies. Coltrane inspired several black poets, including **Michael S. Harper**, who borrowed titles from some of Coltrane's songs and addressed one volume of poems to the musician; and **Haki R. Madhubuti**, who attempted to replicate Coltrane's sound in his poem "Don't Cry, Scream."

In the late 1960s, fusion jazz, which combines elements of jazz and **soul music**, was born in response to the need to attract a new audience. By the mid-1980s, jazz artists such as trumpeter Wynton Marsalis were once again boasting sizable followings. The evolution of jazz has been documented by numerous authors. One of the most noted efforts is Albert L. Murray's *Stomping the Blues* (1976), which was awarded the Deems Taylor Award for music criticism. In 1958 **Arna Bontemps** and Langston Hughes coedited ***The Book of Negro Folklore***, a collection of essays containing, in part, writings by and about jazz musicians. The impact of jazz on black literature can be seen in the prose of **Toni Cade Bambara**, and is also very much in evidence in the verses of such poets as **Bob Kaufman**, **Jayne Cortez**, **Ted Joans**, and **David Henderson**, who have attempted to adapt the syncopated rhythms and spontaneous inventions of this versatile and vital music form to their work. The topic of jazz music has also interested screenwriters such as **Spike Lee**, whose 1990 film *Mo' Better Blues*, revolves around a modern-day jazz trumpeter.

Jazz

Toni Morrison
Novel, 1992

Jazz, **Toni Morrison**'s sixth **novel**, interweaves themes of self-discovery and individual versus community interests. Two Virginia sharecroppers, Joe and Violet Trace, leave their unhappy country life in 1906 for the promise of a better living in New York City. Both are the product of broken homes: Joe's parents left him to be raised in a foster home by a kindly couple, while Violet's mother committed suicide when Violet's father abandoned her. Joe and Violet discover, however, that the American dream is just as unattainable in their new urban home as it was in the rural South. Although they make some advances in their social positions—Joe rises from fish cleaner to door-to-door salesperson, while Violet works as a beautician—they remain unhappy after twenty years in their new home. Violet finds herself wanting a child and becomes so desperate she almost kidnaps one. Joe seeks solace in an extramarital affair with young Dorcas Manfred, but Dorcas leaves him for the fast life of jazz-age Harlem. In an attempt

to maintain the feeling of being in love again, Joe finds Dorcas and kills her. Violet vents her feelings by mutilating the dead girl's face with a knife. The community, represented by Dorcas's aunt, Alice, forgives the girl's murder, accepts Joe again, and becomes Violet's friend. Violet and Joe draw closer together after Dorcas's friend Felice comes looking for a ring she had loaned to Dorcas on the night she was killed. The Traces come to accept their respective pasts and find comfort in their city lives.

Jeff Williams

Character in *The River Niger*

Lance Jeffers

American poet and novelist
Born November 28, 1919.
Died July 19, 1985.

Jeffers's **poetry** is considered an important expression of contemporary black poetics. Motivated to write by the struggle against racial prejudice, his themes and metaphors reach back to **slavery** and beyond to life in Africa.

Jeffers was born in Fremont, Nebraska, on November 28, 1919. He lived with his grandfather, a medical doctor, in Stromsburg, Nebraska, until his grandfather's death in 1929. He then went to San Francisco to live with his mother and his stepfather, who was a janitor in a predominately white apartment building. The **discrimination** Jeffers endured there contradicted his experiences in Nebraska, and his writings reflect his perceptions concerning black American life.

Jeffers's first two poetry collections, *My Blackness Is the Beauty of This Land* (1970) and *When I Know the Power of My Black Hand* (1974), focus on endurance amidst oppression. While *My Blackness* highlights the courage of blacks when mistreated by whites, *When I Know* expands the scope of oppression to include injustices that other minorities, such as Native Americans, experience. Jeffers's last publication, the **novel** *Witherspoon* (1983), deals with a contemporary minister and the convict he tries to save from execution. Jeffers died on July 19, 1985.

See also **Poetry of Lance Jeffers**

Further Readings
Black Writers, first edition, Gale, 1989.
Dictionary of Literary Biography, Volume 41: *Afro-American Poets since 1955,* Gale, 1985.

Jefferson
Character in *A Lesson before Dying*

Jennie Lee Youngblood
Character in *Youngblood*

Jes Grew
Character in *Mumbo Jumbo*

Jesse B. Semple
Series character in "Simple" Stories

Jesse Robinson
Character in *The Primitive*

Jethro Jackson
Character in *The Soul Brothers and Sister Lou*

Jim
Character in *Jubilee* and *Our Nig*

Jim Lee
Character in *Compromise*

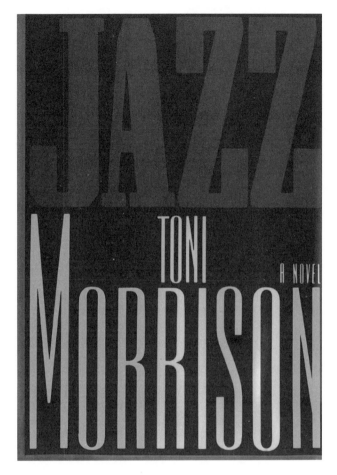

Dust jacket for Morrison's sixth novel.

Jim Monroe
Character in *Cast the First Stone*

Jimmy Aaron
Character in *The Autobiography of Miss Jane Pittman*

Jimson
Character in *The Flagellants*

Jinny Tate
Character in *Zooman and the Sign*

Jinx Jenkins

Character in *The Conjure Man Dies*

Ted Joans

American poet
Born July 4, 1928.

A poet, **jazz** musician, and surrealist painter, Joans was part of the Beat Movement in the 1950s and prominently associated with writers such as Allen Ginsberg and **Amiri Baraka**.

Joans was born on July 4, 1928, in Cairo, Illinois. His father, a musician on Mississippi riverboats, gave him a trumpet and left him in Memphis to fend for himself when he was twelve years old. Joans studied painting and fine arts at Indiana University, receiving his B.F.A. in 1951. He then moved to Greenwich Village in New York, where he painted, wrote **poetry,** and was profiled in magazines such as *Life* and the *New Yorker.*

In 1959, Joans published a collection of poetry entitled *Jazz Poems* but became increasingly disillusioned with the commercialization of the Beat Movement. In 1961, he published a farewell to this stage of his life, *All of Ted Joans and No More.* He left the United States and spent the next decade travelling in Africa and Europe. Joans grew interested in the **black arts movement** during this period and he published *Black Pow-wow: Jazz Poems* (1969). He returned to America and has since published several books, including *Afrodisia: New Poems* (1970) and *The Aardvark-Watcher: Der Erdferkelforscher* (1980), a bilingual volume.

See also **Poetry of Ted Joans**

Further Readings

Black Writers, first edition, Gale, 1989.

Dictionary of Literary Biography, Volume 41: *Afro-American Poets since 1955,* Gale, 1985.

Jodahs

Series character in "Xenogenesis" Trilogy

Joe

Character in *A Brighter Sun*

Joe Brooks

Character in *Teacup Full of Roses*

Joe Lee

Character in *Compromise*

Joe Market

Character in *Lord of the Dark Places*

Joe Pittman

Character in *The Autobiography of Miss Jane Pittman*

Joe Starks

Character in *Their Eyes Were Watching God*

Joe Trace

Character in *Jazz*

Joe Youngblood

Character in *Youngblood*

Joey

Character in *Giovanni's Room*

John

Character in *Mules and Men* and *The Conjure Woman*

John Archer

Character in *The Conjure Man Dies*

John Boy

Character in *Matigari ma Njiruungi*

John Boy Junior

Character in *Matigari ma Njiruungi*

John Dutton

Character in *Jubilee*

John Grimes

Character in *Go Tell It on the Mountain*

John Peck

Character in *Clotel; or, The President's Daughter*

John Power

Character in *Brother Man*

John Strong

Character in *Rachel*

John Washington

Character in *The Chaneysville Incident*

Johnnie Roane

Character in *Country Place*

Johnny Johnson

Character in *Beetlecreek*

Johnny Williams

Character in *No Place to Be Somebody: A Black-Black Comedy*

Charles Johnson

American novelist and short story writer
Born April 23, 1948.

After working as a cartoonist and reporter, Charles Richard Johnson became an assistant professor at the University of Washington, Seattle, in 1976. In 1982, he was named professor of English; he has also served as the director of the creative writing program at the University. He wrote his first, critically praised **novel,** *Faith and the Good Thing* (1974), under the direction of John Gardner. His second novel, *Oxherding Tale* (1982), also received widespread critical acclaim. It details the coming of age of Andrew Hawkins, a young mulatto slave in the pre-Civil War South. *The Sorcerer's Apprentice: Tales and Conjurations* (1988), Johnson's collection of short stories, met with highly favorable reviews and was nominated for the PEN/Faulkner Award for fiction. It includes the story "Popper's Disease," which won the *Callaloo* Creative Writing Award in 1983. Johnson's **Middle Passage** (1990) was awarded the National Book Award and has been compared to Herman Melville's *Moby Dick* and **Ralph Ellison**'s **Invisible Man**. The main character, Rutherford Calhoun, is a newly freed slave who, escaping debtors and an impeding marriage, boards a boat that turns out to be an illegal slave clipper bound for Africa. Calhoun becomes divided in his allegiance to his white American crewmates and his sympathy for the ship's cargo, a group of suffering Allmuseri tribespeople. Johnson is also the author of the **play** *Olly Olly Oxen Free* (1988) and the book *Being and Race: Black Writing since 1970* (1988).

Further Readings

Black Writers, second edition, Gale, 1994.

Dictionary Of Literary Biography, Volume 33: *Afro-American Fiction Writers after 1955,* Gale, 1984.

Reference Guide to American Literature, St. James Press, third edition, 1994.

Charles S. Johnson

American sociologist and editor
Born July 24, 1893.
Died October 27, 1956.

An influential figure in the **Harlem Renaissance**, Charles Spurgeon Johnson was born in Bristol, Virginia, on July 24, 1893, and obtained his Ph.D. from the University of

Chicago in 1918. In 1923, he founded and became the editor of the National Urban League's *Opportunity: A Journal of Negro Life*, which published the work of black writers and scholars. He also sponsored contests designed to showcase and support black literary talent and scholarship. In 1927, Johnson edited Ebony and Topaz, an anthology of work from the magazine. From 1928 to 1947, he headed the sociology department at Fisk University; he was president of the University from 1947 until his death on October 27, 1956.

Further Readings

Black Writers, first edition, Gale, 1989.

Dictionary of Literary Biography, Volume 51: *Afro-American Writers from the Harlem Renaissance to 1940,* Gale, 1987.

Fenton Johnson

American poet
Born May 7, 1888.
Died September 17, 1958.

Johnson is recognized as a minor but significant twentieth-century poet. He is best remembered for his later free verse depictions of urban despair and racial hopelessness.

Johnson was born in Chicago, Illinois, on May 7, 1888, to a wealthy family. His first **poetry** collection, *A Little Dreaming* (1913), explored traditional subjects of love, death, and grief. Johnson's next two poetry volumes, *Visions of the Dusk* (1915) and *Songs of the Soil* (1916), are written in the popular plantation-dialect style, filled with gross misspellings and misuses of English representing black speech.

In the late 1910s, Johnson founded several literary publications, but, due to **racism** and lack of money, they collapsed by 1920. Johnson would have probably been forgotten had he not written a few notable poems. "Tired" (1919) and "The Scarlet Woman" (1922) are considered among his best works; however, his **essay** collection *For the Highest Good* (1920) and the **short story** anthology *Tales of Darkest America*

(1920) added little to his reputation. Johnson spent the last three decades of his life in literary obscurity and died on September 17, 1958.

See also **Poetry of Fenton Johnson**

Further Readings

Black Literature Criticism, Gale, 1992.

Black Writers, first edition, Gale, 1989.

Dictionary of Literary Biography, Gale, Volume 45: *American Poets, 1880-1945,* 1986; Volume 50: *Afro-American Writers before the Harlem Renaissance,* 1986.

Georgia Douglas Johnson

American poet, playwright, and composer
Born September 10, 1886.
Died May 14, 1966.

Johnson was one of the first modern black women to gain recognition as a poet. Often compared to poet Sara Teasdale, Johnson wrote "small verse" reflecting an awareness of the racial concerns of her generation.

Johnson was born in Georgia, where, as a child, she discovered the verse of black poet **William Stanley Braithwaite**. She later attended Howard University and Oberlin Conservatory of Music. Marriage to an attorney brought Johnson to Washington, D.C., where she became active in promoting women's and minority causes.

Johnson's first book of **poetry, *The Heart of a Woman*** (1918), contains short verses descriptive of emotions, including "Sympathy," "Isolation," and "Despair." In *Bronze* (1922), she began to focus on issues of race as well as gender, issuing strong protests against **racism** and prejudice. Following the death of her husband in 1925, Johnson became Commissioner of Conciliation under President Calvin Coolidge. Johnson's *An Autumn Love Cycle* (1928) is similar to her earlier romantic verse in its depiction of various stages of love.

In addition to her poetry, Johnson wrote several **plays** that served as a vehicle for the moral outrage she withheld from her verse. Both *Blue-Eyed Black Boy* (1935) and *Safe* (1936) protest the brutal lynchings of blacks by white mobs. Written for President Franklin Roosevelt's Federal Theater Project, the plays were never performed during Johnson's lifetime because of what producers perceived as a lack of reasonable causes to trigger such lynchings.

See also **Poetry of Georgia Douglas Johnson**

Further Readings
Black Writers, first edition, Gale, 1989.

Dictionary of Literary Biography, Volume 51: *Afro-American Writers from the Harlem Renaissance to 1940,* Gale, 1987.

Helene Johnson
American poet
Born July 7, 1907.

Johnson is best known for a few poems she wrote as one of the youngest members of the **Harlem Renaissance**. Her work began to appear in magazines and anthologies in the mid-1920s, especially *Opportunity: A Journal of Negro Life,* published by the National Urban League. In the magazine's second literary contest, three of Johnson's poems were awarded honorable mention, and her "Summer Matures" took a major prize in the third contest. "Bottled," which appeared in the May 1927 issue of *Vanity Fair,* attracted an even wider notice.

Among Johnson's themes are racial oppression, racial pride and identity, and the beauty of nature. The poems now considered her most important are anthologized in **Countee Cullen**'s *Caroling Dusk: An Anthology of Verse by Negro Poets* (1927).

Further Readings
Dictionary of Literary Biography, Volume 51: *Afro-American Writers from the Harlem Renaissance to 1940,* Gale, 1987.

James Weldon Johnson
American poet, novelist, and editor
Born June 17, 1871.
Died June 26, 1938.

Johnson believed that a wider appreciation for African American writers could be achieved only by transcending what he perceived to be limiting cultural aspects of African American literature, such as the "Negro dialect." He strove to maintain the delicate balance of appealing to the mainstream white audience without betraying African American culture.

Johnson was born in Jacksonville, Florida, on June 17, 1871. His parents provided him with a secure environment in which he was encouraged to excel academically. Johnson graduated from Atlanta University in 1894. After teaching at a grammar school and coediting a newspaper, Johnson set up a private law practice in Florida. He became the United States consul to Puerto Cabello, Venezuela, in 1906, during which time he worked on his only **novel,** ***The Autobiography of an Ex-Coloured Man*** (1912). Published anonymously, *The Autobiography* was widely mistaken for a true account of a light-skinned black man's decision to renounce his race and assimilate into white society. The novel is lauded as an ironic depiction of moral cowardice.

Johnson served as the U.S. consul to Corinto, Nicaragua, from 1909 to 1913 and began writing editorials for the *New York Age* newspaper the next year. His first **poetry** collection, *Fifty Years and Other Poems,* appeared in 1917. The title poem, a commentary on the time that had passed since the Emancipation Proclamation, brought Johnson considerable notoriety but was criticized for its use of dialect, a style Johnson eventually abandoned.

After being appointed the executive secretary of the **National Association for the Advancement of Colored People** (NAACP) in 1920, Johnson published what may be considered his most important contribution to African American literature, *The Book of American Negro Poetry* (1922). The anthology contains

James Weldon Johnson was a major contributor to early twentieth-century African American cultural and literary movements.

Coloured Man. The former title is regarded as a sophisticated reflection on Johnson's public life. *Negro Americans, What Now?* (1934) continues where *Along This Way* leaves off, promoting racial integration and speculating on the future of African Americans.

Johnson died in Wiscasset, Maine, on June 26, 1938, after a train struck his car. Over two thousand mourners attended his Harlem funeral. He is buried in Brooklyn, New York.

Further Readings

Black Literature Criticism, Gale, 1992.

Black Writers, first edition, Gale, 1989.

Dictionary of Literary Biography, Volume 51: *Afro-American Writers from the Harlem Renaissance to 1940,* Gale, 1987.

Levy, Eugene, *James Weldon Johnson: Black Leader, Black Voice,* Chicago University Press, 1973.

the works of thirty-one poets and was the first of its kind ever published.

God's Trombones: Seven Negro Sermons in Verse (1927) is generally considered Johnson's greatest artistic achievement. Combining biblical narratives with the rhythmic speech patterns of the "Negro preacher," Johnson attempted to stylize elements of African American culture to appeal to a universal audience. *Black Manhattan* (1930), Johnson's record of African American contributions to New York's cultural life, was both praised and criticized for its optimism.

Johnson became a professor of creative literature and writing at Fisk University in 1931. He wrote his **autobiography**, *Along This Way* (1933), partly in response to the confusion caused by *The Autobiography of an Ex-*

Lemuel A. Johnson
Nigerian poet, critic, and short story writer
Born December 15, 1941.

Johnson, born in 1941 in Nigeria, was educated at Oberlin College, Pennsylvania State University, and the University of Michigan, where he earned a Ph.D. in 1969. He has also studied at Middlebury College, Université d'Aix-Marseille II, and the University of Paris. He joined the University of Michigan English department as an associate professor in 1972.

Johnson has won scholarly awards for his **poetry** and criticism, including *The Devil, the Gargoyle and the Buffoon: The Negro as Metaphor in Western Literature* (1971). His poetry collections include *Highlife for Caliban* (1973) and *Hand on the Navel* (1978), and his work is represented in anthologies of African literature.

Further Readings

Black Writers, second edition, Gale, 1994.

Gayl Jones

American novelist, poet, and short story writer
Born November 23, 1949.

The gothic **novels** of Jones depict violent interludes in the lives of African Americans. Female protagonists are especially vulnerable in Jones's nightmarish world, and their psychological ordeals unfold in the tradition of black oral storytelling. Although they often emphasize life's torments, Jones's works raise the possibility for more positive interactions between men and women.

Jones was raised in Kentucky, where her mother made up stories to entertain the family. Jones began writing at a young age; while undertaking graduate study at Brown University, she published her first novel, *Corregidora* (1975). Both *Corregidora* and Jones's second novel, *Eva's Man* (1976), present brutal accounts of black women who are sexually and racially exploited. *Corregidora* reveals the torment of a woman whose three generations of female forebears endured a cycle of **slavery**, prostitution, and incest. *Eva's Man* explores the mind of a woman institutionalized for sexually mutilating a male acquaintance. Both novels are written in the first person, resulting in comparisons to **slave narratives** by several critics.

Jones continued to write while she was a member of the English Department at the University of Michigan from 1975-83. Jones's collection of short fiction, *White Rat* (1977), focuses on themes similar to those of her novels. In "Asylum," a young woman is confined to a mental hospital following a series of bizarre incidents signifying her protest against a society that negates personal freedom. While several critics noted structural and plot similarities to her longer works, they observed that Jones's short stories did not allow enough room for needed character development. Jones has also written several collections of **poetry**—including *Song for Anninho* (1981), *The Hermit-Woman* (1983), and *Xarque and Other Poems* (1985)—and a history of the black **oral tradition**, *Liberating Voices: Oral Tradition in African American Literature* (1991).

Jones utilizes the oral storytelling tradition in her novels.

Further Readings

Black Literature Criticism, Gale, 1992.

Black Writers, second edition, Gale, 1994.

Dictionary of Literary Biography, Volume 33: *Afro-American Fiction Writers after 1955*, Gale, 1984.

Jones Higgins

Character in *M. C. Higgins, the Great*

LeRoi Jones

Please see Amiri Baraka

Barbara Jordan

American politician and autobiographer
Born February 21, 1936.

Barbara Charline Jordan first gained widespread attention as a member of the House Judiciary Committee in the United States Con-

In 1972 Barbara Jordan became the first African American Congresswoman from the deep South.

gress when she spoke against President Richard Nixon during a hearing to determine whether he had committed impeachable offenses. Because of the impression her remarks made, Jordan was recognized as one of the nation's most powerful orators.

Jordan was born on February 21, 1936, in Houston, Texas, to Benjamin and Arlyne Patten Jordan. She received her B.A. from Texas Southern University in 1956 and a law degree from Boston University in 1959. Her political career began during the 1960 presidential campaign when she worked as a local organizer for John F. Kennedy. She ran twice for the Texas Senate before winning a seat in 1966, becoming the first black elected to that body since **Reconstruction** . She was elected to Congress in 1972, where she backed proposals to increase the minimum wage, provide free legal services for the indigent, and expand existing programs for the

aged and the ill. Her reputation for inspired **oratory** was confirmed in 1976 when she delivered the keynote address to the Democratic National Convention, the first woman and first African American to do so.

Jordan retired from Congress in 1978. The following year, she published *Barbara Jordan: A Self-Portrait,* cowritten with Shelby Hearon, and accepted a teaching position at the University of Texas at Austin, where she became the Lyndon B. Johnson Centennial Professor of National Policy in 1982. She has also written *Local Government Election Systems* (1984) with Terrell Blodgett.

Further Readings

Black Writers, first edition, Gale, 1989.

Bryant, Ira Babington, *Barbara Charline Jordan: From the Ghetto to the Capitol,* D. Armstrong, 1977.

June Jordan
American poet, novelist, and essayist
Born July 9, 1936.

Distinguished by success in many genres, Jordan's career has been unified by her commitment to African American concerns. Born in Harlem on July 9, 1936, Jordan, who has written under the pseudonym June Meyer, attended Barnard College and the University of Chicago. Her first book, *Who Look at Me* (1969), a poem accompanied by paintings, confronts the nature of racial identification and the relationship between blacks and whites. *Some Changes* (1971), Jordan's first collection of **poetry,** combines both personal and racial issues and addresses both social and aesthetic questions.

Reviewers have praised Jordan for effectively uniting in her works the personal struggle of blacks with themes of their political oppression. In 1971, she published *His Own Where,* a **novel** about rebuilding and reshaping urban neighborhoods, and her second collection of poetry, *New Days: Poems of Exile and Return,* appeared in 1974. She also wrote three books for children during the 1970s, including *Dry*

Victories (1972), an analysis of **Reconstruction** and the **civil rights movement**. Jordan published her collected poetry in *Things That I Do in the Dark* (1977) and her selected prose in *Civil Wars* (1981). Other poetry collections include *Passion: New Poems, 1977-1980* (1980), *Living Room: New Poems, 1980-1984* (1985), *Naming Our Destiny: New and Selected Poems* (1989), and *Harukol/Love Poems* (1994). Since 1989, Jordan has taught African-American Studies and Women's Studies at the University of California, Berkeley.

See also **Poetry of June Jordan**

Further Readings

Black Writers, second edition, Gale, 1994.

Dictionary of Literary Biography, Volume 38: *Afro-American Writers after 1955: Dramatists and Prose Writers,* Gale, 1985.

Joseph

Character in *Dream on Monkey Mountain*

Josephine Lamont

Character in *Rainbow Jordan*

Josephine Rollins

Character in *Youngblood*

E. J. Josey

American editor
Born January 20, 1924.

Elonnie Junius Josey's books focus on the special needs and circumstances facing libraries and librarians. His work addresses various strategies for supporting libraries, including funding and public relations, and he supplements such information with what critics consider sound, practical advice.

Josey was born in 1924 in Norfolk, Virginia, son of Willie and Frances Bailey Josey. He received his A.B. from Howard University in 1949 and his M.A. from Columbia University in 1950. In 1973, he edited *The Black Librarian in*

June Jordan's novels focus on black struggles and political oppression.

America, a volume of **essays** profiling two dozen black librarians whose personal experiences provide an overview of library needs and the limitations on minority librarians. The volume was updated in 1994 as *The Black Librarian in America Revisited.* Josey presented further observations by black librarians in *What Black Librarians Are Saying* (1972). With **Ann Allen Shockley**, Josey co-edited *Handbook of Black Librarianship* (1977), which presents essays discussing resources for African and African American studies and the Black Caucus of the American Library Association. Development of ethnic archives and library programs are examined in *Ethnic Collections in Libraries* (1983), which Josey and Marva L. DeLoach edited. Josey has also addressed the needs of libraries in the face of economic and political difficulties in *Politics and the Support of*

Libraries (1990), a volume edited with Kenneth D. Shearer. Since 1986, Josey has been a professor in the School of Library and Information Science at the University of Pittsburgh.

Further Readings
Black Writers, second edition, Gale, 1994.

Joshua "Shine" Jones
Character in *The Walls of Jericho*

The Journal of Charlotte L. Forten
Charlotte L. Forten
Diary, 1953

Beginning in 1854 and continuing through the Civil War, **Charlotte L. Forten** recorded her activities, aspirations, and observations in a **diary**, which was published nearly a century later as *The Journal of Charlotte L. Forten: A Free Negro in the Slave Era.* The work covers Forten's secondary school and college years in Salem, Massachusetts, where she met or corresponded with many of the prominent abolitionists of the day and persevered at her schoolwork, eager to prove herself as able to excel as any white student. The journal also provides descriptions of Forten's participation in the Port Royal experiment, a Civil War-era federal program that educated and empowered former slaves on islands off the South Carolina coast. Forten's last journal entry was made in April of 1864, while she was still in South Carolina.

Journalism

Journalistic writing refers to the direct presentation of facts or the objective description of events, without any attempt at interpretation. In 1827, *Freedom's Journal,* the first black newspaper, was established to promote **abolitionism**. Since that date, many African American journalists have made their mark in such media as newspaper, magazine, radio, and television. **Ida B. Wells** was the first black woman journalist, beginning her career in the late nineteenth century. In 1910, **Marcus Garvey**, founder of the **back-to-Africa movement**, established the first of his many radical periodicals. In 1973, **Roger Wilkins** shared a special citation from the Pulitzer Prize committee for his reports on Watergate. Wilkins later became the first black chairperson of the National Pulitzer Prize Board. Other nationally recognized journalists include *Washington Post* syndicated columnist **William J. Raspberry**, who was nominated for a Pulitzer Prize in 1982, and syndicated columnist, public affairs commentator, and television panelist **Carl Thomas Rowan**, who has served in the U.S. State Department. Many contemporary print journalists have also achieved success as book authors, including Wilkins, Rowan, **Alex Haley**, **Lerone Bennett Jr.**, and **Ellis Jonathan Cose**.

Until the late 1960s, most serious black journalists worked in print journalism and not in broadcasting—few blacks were allowed on the white-controlled airwaves. It took the riots of the 1960s and a stern warning from a federal commission for the broadcast industry to undertake any concentrated hiring and airing of African Americans. **Ed Bradley**, who was first hired at a New York radio station in 1967, eventually went on to co-host CBS-TV's most successful news show, *60 Minutes.* One of the most visible African American journalists on public television has been *MacNeil/Lehrer News Hour* correspondent **Charlayne Hunter-Gault**, a former *New York Times* reporter who is noted for her in-depth reporting.

Joyce
Series character in "Simple" Stories

Donald Franklin Joyce
American librarian and writer
Born November 4, 1938.

Born in 1938 in Chicago, Illinois, Joyce discovered a passion for books as an undergraduate at Fisk University, developing a particular interest in the literary portrayal of the lives of black people. Becoming a librarian at the Chicago Public Library in 1960, he compiled a catalog of the holdings on African Americans in Chicago libraries. He went on to become an authority on African American publishers, releasing two books in the field, *Gatekeepers of Black Culture: Black-Owned Book Publishing in the United States, 1817-1981* (1983) and *Black Book Publishers in the United States: A Historical Dictionary of the Presses, 1817-1990* (1991). Joyce also published *Blacks in the Humanities, 1750-1984: A Selected Annotated Bibliography* (1986).

Further Readings
Black Writers, second edition, Gale, 1994.

Juanita Wright
Character in *Pinktoes*

Jubilee
Margaret Walker
Novel, 1966

Set in Georgia and Alabama, **Margaret Walker**'s *Jubilee* is divided into three sections: before, during, and after the Civil War. The **novel** tells the story of Vyry Brown, the daughter of a slave, Sis Hetta, and a slave owner, John Dutton. The first section, "Sis Hetta's Child—The Ante-Bellum Years," describes Vyry's childhood and the abuse she suffers from Dutton's wife Salina. Walker also portrays the Duttons' overseer Ed Grimes, who fears the slaves and resents his employer's life of privilege. Vyry asks permission to marry Randall Ware, who was born free, but John Dutton refuses. When Vyry marries Randall in a slave ceremony and tries to escape to him with her two children, she is captured and beaten. The second section of *Jubilee,* "My Eyes Have Seen the Glory," takes place during the Civil War. The men leave to fight and Vyry remains with the family to help them nurse the returning soldiers and care for Lillian Dutton, who has become mentally ill. In the third part of the book, "Forty Years in the Wilderness—Reconstruction and Reaction,"

Vyry is freed from **slavery** and, after finding someone to care for Lillian, she moves to Alabama with her husband Innis Brown, a field hand, and their family. Their search for land and a place to settle is fraught with disaster and hardship; they face floods, exploitation, and the Ku Klux Klan. But, when Vyry helps a white family as a midwife, the grateful family and their neighbors build Vyry and Innis a house. Although Jim, Vyry's son by Randall Ware, argues with his step-father, Randall soon arrives and takes Jim with him to be educated; the two parts of Vyry's family are reconciled.

Jude Greene
Character in *Sula*

Judith Powell
Character in *The Chaneysville Incident*

Julia Miller
Character in *Just Above My Head*

Jumping Mouse
Character in *The Story of Jumping Mouse*

Jungle Fever
Spike Lee
Film, 1991

Spike Lee's fifth film, *Jungle Fever,* is the story of an interracial love affair, of the drug culture in Harlem, and of how myths about skin color affect people. The hero of Lee's *Jungle Fever,* Flipper Purify, is a successful black architect who lives with his wife and daughter in Harlem. When Flipper meets Angie Tucci, an Italian-American secretary from Brooklyn, the two are immediately attracted to each other and soon become romantically involved.

The repercussions of this interracial relationship are profound. Flipper and Angie are violently rejected by their families. Angie is beaten by her father, and Flipper's wife meets with a group of other women in a "war council," in which the women rage against the way that race has affected all their relationships. Flipper's interracial affair is not the only pressure that his family faces. Flipper's crack-addicted brother, Gator, is stealing money and has become a danger to himself and to others. Although Lee was criticized for ignoring the drug problem in his earlier films, drugs are an important theme in *Jungle Fever.*

Although Flipper and Angie flout conventions by briefly living together, they soon break up. Flipper dismisses the relationship by attributing it to "jungle fever," or curiosity about sexual partners of different races that is fueled by cultural myths and stereotypes.

Junior Brown

Character in *The Planet of Junior Brown*

Just Above My Head

James Baldwin
Novel, 1979

Just Above My Head, **James Baldwin**'s last **novel**, is narrated by Hall Montana, a middle-aged African American. He tells the complicated story of his dead brother, Arthur Montana, a homosexual gospel singer struggling to find a place within a society dominated by white heterosexuals. The story opens two years after Arthur's death but quickly flashes back to his childhood days in the early 1950s. As an adolescent, Arthur sings in churches throughout the South and is asked to appear at various freedom rallies. During one of the meetings, Peanut, a close friend of Arthur's, mysteriously disappears and is never heard from again, arousing accusations of abduction and murder by a hostile white mob.

Another of Arthur's young friends, Julia Miller, first appears in the novel as a beautiful eleven-year-old evangelist. Excerpts from her sermons, as well as numerous quotations from gospel hymns, suggest the importance of reli-

gion in African American culture. At the age of fourteen, however, Julia is brutally raped by her father and subsequently loses her religious faith and the desire to preach. Later, after a love affair with Hall and a stint as a prostitute, Julia becomes a successful fashion model in New York. The material rewards brought by her beauty and personality, however, are not enough to satisfy her; she later leaves for North Africa in search of her roots.

Arthur's fame as a singer continues to grow, especially after he begins a love affair with Julia's brother, Jimmy. Their relationship thrives as the two travel the world and live together for several years. Numerous lengthy passages in the novel provide a detailed description of their sexual activities. Despite the depth of his love for Jimmy, Arthur harbors feelings of guilt about his homosexual behavior and begins drinking heavily as a result. While at the height of his fame as a musician, Arthur dies prematurely of a heart attack in a London pub.

Just Give Me a Cool Drink of Water 'fore I Diiie

Maya Angelou
Poetry, 1971

Maya Angelou's *Just Give Me a Cool Drink of Water 'fore I Diiie* was nominated for the Pulitzer Prize in 1972, and illustrates the attention she gives to both individual and communal problems. The first part, "Where Love Is a Scream of Anguish," looks at relations between the sexes on many levels—for example, between a woman and her lover in "No Loser, No Weeper," and between a prostitute and her clients in "They Went Home." In each case, the feelings of love are modified by other feelings of loss, pain, and insecurity. The second part, "Just before the World Ends," looks at issues that affect the world beyond the individual; "Riot: 60's" and "The Calling of Names" explore **racism**; and "On a Bright Day, Next Week" is concerned with nuclear war.

Justice

Series character in "Justice" Trilogy

Justice and Her Brothers

Please see "Justice" Trilogy

"Justice" Trilogy

Virginia Hamilton
Novels, 1978-1981

Virginia Hamilton mixes magic and **realism** in her trilogy, which contains *Justice and Her Brothers* (1978), *Dustland* (1980), and *The Gathering* (1981). The novels chronicle the adventures of eleven-year-old Justice and her thirteen-year-old twin brothers, Thomas and Levi. In the first **novel**, *Justice and Her Brothers,* the evil twin Thomas demonstrates his ability to enter his siblings' minds, which stimulates Justice's own capacity for mind-control, resulting in futuristic time-travel. The second novel, *Dustland,* follows the trio into the post-apocalyptic future where the siblings use extrasensory perception to communicate with strange inhabitants they meet. They also learn how to use their powers for survival. In *The Gathering,* the last book in the trilogy, Justice, Thomas, and Levi realize that the barren landscape of Dustland is the future awaiting mankind, inciting them to combine their powers to fight an evil adversary.

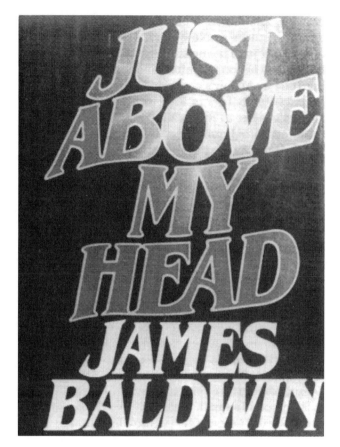

Dust jacket for Baldwin's last novel.

K

. . . recognized as the driving

force of the civil rights

movement in the United

States during the 1960s.

Black Literature Criticism on
Martin Luther King Jr., 1992

Karanja
Character in *A Grain of Wheat*

Kareja
Character in *Petals of Blood*

Karintha
Character in *Cane*

Karolis
Character in *The Toilet*

Katherine Jordan
Character in *Rainbow Jordan*

Bob Kaufman
American poet
Born April 18, 1925.
Died January 12, 1986.

Bob Garnell Kaufman was a poet affiliated with the Beat Generation. He maintained a close association with William Burroughs and Allen Ginsberg for several years and influenced such writers as Jack Kerouac and Lawrence Ferlinghetti. Born in 1925 in New Orleans to a German Orthodox Jewish father and a black Catholic mother from Martinique, Kaufman left home at thirteen and spent twenty years with the Merchant Marine. Taking his inspiration from the solo improvisations of bebop **jazz**, Kaufman pursued an ideal of spontaneous composition, improvising his **poetry** on street corners and rarely bothering to write it down. Many of his publications are the result of transcriptions done by friends. His poetry, particularly the *Abomunist Manifesto* (1959), embodies many of the Beat Generation ideals, including the rejection of belief systems. Under a self-imposed exile from society for much of the last twenty years of his life, Kaufman died from emphysema in 1986.

See also **Poetry of Bob Kaufman**

Further Readings
Black Writers, first edition, Gale, 1989.
Dictionary of Literary Biography, Volume 41: *Afro-American Poets since 1955,* Gale, 1985.

Elizabeth Keckley
American autobiographer
Born in 1818.
Died May 26, 1907.

Born in Virginia in 1818, Keckley was a slave for thirty years before purchasing her and her son's freedom. During Abraham Lincoln's four years as president, Keckley served as Mary Todd Lincoln's seamstress. When Lincoln faced financial hardship following her husband's assassination, Keckley wrote *Behind the Scenes; or, Thirty Years as a Slave and Four Years in the White House* (1868) to help support her. Although Keckley describes her life in Virginia, the book focuses on Mrs. Lincoln and prints several of her letters in the appendix.

Modern critics believe *Behind the Scenes* to be reliable, but Keckley's contemporaries condemned what they considered to be scandalous. Robert Lincoln petitioned the publisher to suppress the book. *Behind the Scenes* was recalled, and its remaining copies were confiscated by Lincoln's supporters. Keckley's dressmaking business began to decline due to the negative publicity, and she died shortly afterward.

Keel Robinson
Character in *Night Song*

William Melvin Kelley
American novelist and short story writer
Born November 1, 1937.

Kelley is an author known for his separatist vision for African Americans. Born in 1937 in New York City, Kelley grew up in a white neighborhood and was educated alongside white students at private schools, including Fieldston and Harvard. As a result, Kelley's early writings espouse nonviolent **assimilation** and focus on the discovery of individual identity that transcends race. Beginning with *A Drop of Patience* (1965), however, he began to examine the ambiguous position of blacks in America. Both the satirical **novel** *dem* (1967) and *Dun-*

fords Travels Everywheres (1970), a novel inspired by James Joyce's *Finnegans Wake* in its literary techniques, are based on a nationalist vision that affirms the worth of African American culture and finds a future for African Americans only in separatism.

Further Readings

Black Writers, first edition, Gale, 1989.

Dictionary of Literary Biography, Volume 33: *Afro-American Fiction Writers after 1955,* Gale, 1984.

Randall Kenan

American fiction writer
Born March 12, 1963.

Randall G. Kenan's writings are noted for their emphasis on the **supernatural**, abundance of detail, and richness of language. Born in Brooklyn, New York, in 1963, Kenan earned a bachelor of arts degree from the University of North Carolina; he has served as a lecturer at Sarah Lawrence College since 1989. Kenan's first two fictional publications bring to life a small African American community in North Carolina called Tims Creek. He fills that community with mythical as well as realistic imagery and complex individuals. *A Visitation of Spirits* (1989) focuses on Thomas Cross, a brilliant student grappling with his homosexuality and his family's history dating from the days of **slavery**. *Let the Dead Bury the Dead and Other Stories* (1992) explores Tims Creek and the larger human condition from a variety of perspectives.

Further Readings

Black Writers, second edition, Gale, 1994.

Adrienne Kennedy

American playwright
Born September 13, 1931.

Kennedy is one of the few modern black dramatists who makes use of **surrealism**. She is best known for controversial, often violent **plays** in which she makes extensive use of symbolism and imagery. While some audiences are uncomfortable with the dark, brutal nature of her work, critics have frequently seen it as poetic.

Kennedy grew up in a middle-class family in Cleveland, Ohio. A gifted child, she could read at age three. Kennedy's memoir, *People Who Led to My Plays* (1987), documents her fascination with film stars and her reverence for the work of Tennessee Williams. Kennedy studied writing at Ohio State University and, at age 29, traveled to West Africa—a trip that inspired her first professionally produced play, *Funnyhouse of a Negro* (1963). This drama explores the psychological problems of a mulatto woman living with a Jewish poet in a boarding house run by a white landlady. The work was produced in New York City by Edward Albee and won an Obie Award in 1964.

A Beast's Story (1966) and *The Owl Answers* (1963), produced together as *Cities in Bezique* (1969), are more elaborate and make greater use of surrealistic techniques than Kennedy's first play. Including composite characters and dreamlike images, the plays were produced by Joseph Papp at the New York Shakespeare Festival. While critical response was mixed, Kennedy's writing was praised for its clarity. In 1971, Kennedy helped found the Women's Theatre Council, a cooperative devoted to providing opportunities for women to direct, act, and have new works produced. In 1980, she was commissioned by the Empire State Youth Theatre Institute to write *A Lancashire Lad,* her first play for children. Kennedy has continued to write plays for young adults and has taught creative writing at major universities in the United States.

Further Readings

Black Writers, second edition, Gale, 1994.

Dictionary of Literary Biography, Volume 38: *Afro-American Writers after 1955; Dramatists and Prose Writers,* Gale, 1985.

Kenneth Harper

Character in *The Fire in the Flint*

Jomo Kenyatta

Kenyan political writer
Born October 20, 1891(?).
Died August 21, 1978.

Kenyatta was the first prime minister of Kenya and the author of several books on African culture and politics. Born Kamau wa Ngengi, he moved to Nairobi as a young man. In 1929 he traveled to London as a representative for the Kikuyu Central Association (KCA), which sought to improve the living conditions of the Kikuyu, Kenya's largest ethnic group. From 1928 to 1930, he also founded and edited KCA's journal *Muigwithania,* the first black journal in Kenya. In addition to his work for KCA in England, Kenyatta studied anthropology at Woodbroke College and at the London School of Economics and Political Science. He later collected a series of his papers on Kikuyu culture in **Facing Mount Kenya: The Tribal Life of the Gikuyu** (1938) and *My People of Kikuyu and the Life of Chief Wangombe* (1942).

Kenyatta returned to Kenya in 1946 and, in 1947, was elected president of Kenya African Union, a prominent political party that supported an ambitious program of land reform and the extension of voting rights for blacks. He was linked, however, with a violent revolutionary movement called the Mau Mau. After being arrested on dubious evidence, Kenyatta was sentenced to prison as a Mau Mau organizer.

Released from detention in 1961, Kenyatta served in several high-level government posts before being elected president in 1964, the year he led Kenya to independence. He later published *Harambee!* (1964), a collection of his political **speeches**, and *Suffering Without Bitterness: The Founding of the Kenya Nation* (1968), an outline of his political philosophy. Kenyatta presided over Kenya until his death in 1978 and, although some have accused him of corruption, many people consider him to have been a pragmatic and innovative leader who encouraged economic growth and independence.

Further Readings
Black Writers, first edition, Gale, 1989.

Kenyatta was the first prime minister of Kenya.

Kharibu
Character in *A Dance of the Forests*

The Kid
Character in *Dhalgren*

Kihika
Character in *A Grain of Wheat*

John Oliver Killens

American novelist
Born January 14, 1916.
Died October 27, 1987.

Killens drew upon his life experiences to produce **novels** revolving around the themes of

John Oliver Killens co-founded the Harlem Writers Guild.

social protest and cultural affirmation, and made creative use of African American **folklore**. He co-founded and served as the chair for the Harlem Writers Guild, which provided a forum for writers—including **Alice Childress**, **Maya Angelou**, and **Ossie Davis**—to read from their works. He served as a writer in residence at several institutions, including Fisk University and Medgar Evers College of the City University of New York.

Killens was born in Macon, Georgia, on January 14, 1916. His parents introduced him to African American literature, but he credited his paternal great-grandmother's stories for his decision to become a writer, a resolution he made during a stint with the U.S. Army in the South Pacific.

Killens's first novel, *Youngblood* (1954), describes a Southern black family's struggle for

survival, and his second, ***And Then We Heard the Thunder*** (1962), traces his experience with **segregation** and **racism** in the military during World War II. A later novel, ***The Cotillion; or, One Good Bull Is Half the Herd*** (1971), satirically treats an annual ball held by an exclusive black women's club in Brooklyn. Killens received Pulitzer Prize nominations for both *And Then We Heard the Thunder* and *The Cotillion.*

Although recognized and praised for his novels, Killens achieved distinction for his essays on the quality of black life in America. His **essay** collection *Black Man's Burden* (1965) espoused a shift toward more militant protest. Killens also wrote **plays,** screenplays, and novelized biographies, including *The Great Black Russian: A Novel on the Life and Times of Alexander Pushkin* (1989), which was one of the first texts to consider the poet's black lineage. Killens died of cancer on October 27, 1987, in Brooklyn.

Further Readings

Black Writers, second edition, Gale, 1994.

Contemporary Literary Criticism, Gale, Volume 10, 1979.

Dictionary of Literary Biography, Volume 33: *Afro-American Fiction Writers after 1955,* Gale, 1984.

Jamaica Kincaid

West Indian-born American essayist, novelist, and short story writer
Born May 25, 1949.

Kincaid is recognized as a major voice in contemporary American literature. She draws on her childhood and her native land, the Caribbean island of Antigua, for the subjects of much of her work. Her strongly autobiographical fiction often concerns the intense emotional bonds between mothers and daughters, while other works examine postcolonial Antigua.

Kincaid was born Elaine Potter Richardson in the British West Indies but left Antigua at age sixteen to become an *au pair* girl in the United States. Although she initially planned to pursue a career in nursing, she instead studied photography at the New York School for Social Research and spent time at Franconia College in New Hampshire. After working briefly as a freelance writer, she was hired for a staff position at the *New Yorker* in 1976. While employed by the magazine, she changed her name to Jamaica Kincaid, choosing a pseudonym symbolic of her native region.

Kincaid's first work, ***At the Bottom of the River*** (1983), is a collection of ten short stories distinguished by her lyrical style and attention to detail. ***Annie John*** (1985), originally published as a series of short stories in the *New Yorker,* focuses on the life of the precocious title character, who struggles to assert her individuality and escape the influence of her domineering and possessive mother. In 1988 Kincaid published a book-length **essay** about the Caribbean, *A Small Place,* in which she described the aftermath of **colonialism** on her native island, particularly the destructive effects on the impoverished society of greed and vice in the government. ***Lucy*** (1990) is a **novel** about a young woman from Antigua who comes to New York to work as an *au pair* girl.

Further Readings

Black Writers, second edition, Gale, 1994.

Contemporary Literary Criticism, Volume 43, Gale, 1987.

Kinch Sanders De Younge

Character in *The Garies and Their Friends*

Kindred

Please see "Patternist Saga"

King Barlo

Character in *Cane*

Kincaid's fiction often focuses on the bond between mothers and daughters.

Coretta Scott King

American autobiographer and editor
Born April 27, 1927.

King is best known for her dedication to her late husband **Martin Luther King Jr.**'s civil rights efforts. After her husband's death in 1968, King founded and chaired both the Martin Luther King Jr. Center for Nonviolent Social Change and the Martin Luther King Jr. Federal Holiday Commission.

King was born in Marion, Alabama, on April 27, 1927. She began a career as a singer in 1948. While studying at the New England Conservatory in Boston, Massachusetts, she met a young Baptist minister, Mr. King, whom she married in 1953. In 1962, King taught music at Morris Brown College in Atlanta, Georgia, and beginning in 1964 she performed "freedom con-

Coretta Scott King addresses an antiwar rally in New York, 1968.

certs" in which she sang, recited **poetry,** and lectured. For the most part, however, she gave up her career plans to join her husband as a civil rights activist.

King's successful **autobiography**, *My Life with Martin Luther King Jr.* (1969), was considered flawed by some critics, who felt she had portrayed her husband as a man without human weaknesses. Others contended, however, that this image was worth preserving.

In addition to her own work, King collected her husband's writings in *The Portable Martin Luther King Jr.: Quotations from the Speeches, Essays, and Lectures of Martin Luther King Jr.* (1992) and *The Words of Martin Luther King Jr.* (1983). She also edited the *Black Americans of Achievement Series.*

King has received numerous awards, including the Wateler Peace Prize (1968) and

honorary doctorates from Boston University (1969) and Princeton University (1970). She has served as a news commentator for the Cable News Network and has been active with a number of organizations, including the National Council of Negro Women.

Further Readings

Black Writers, first edition, Gale, 1989.

Henry, Sondra, and Emily Taitz, *Coretta Scott King: Keeper of the Dream,* Enslow Pubs., 1992.

Patrick, Diane, *Coretta Scott King,* Watts, 1991.

Martin Luther King Jr.

American civil rights leader, orator, and essayist
Born January 15, 1929.
Died April 4, 1968.

King is recognized as the driving force behind the **civil rights movement** in the United States during the 1960s. He chose nonviolence as a method for social reform and encouraged others to fight social injustice with Christian love, kindness, and understanding. King's writings outline and explain the methods he used to lead the movement and the reasons behind his nonviolent approach to social protest. *Stride toward Freedom: The Montgomery Story* (1958) tells of the boycott and desegregation of the Montgomery, Alabama, bus lines, in which King played a leading role.

An eloquent orator, King won national attention through his **speeches** and writings. *Letter from Birmingham City Jail* (1963), a statement of his reasons for fighting against **racism**, and *"I Have a Dream"* (1963), a stirring plea for racial equality, were landmarks in the struggle for civil rights. On January 3, 1964, King was proclaimed "Man of the Year" by *Time* magazine, the first black to be so honored. Later that year he received the Nobel Peace Prize, becoming the twelfth American, the third black, and the youngest—he was thirty-five—person ever to receive the award.

King continued to work for fair treatment and Christian love for all oppressed people through the last years of his life. A campaign against abuses in voter registration in Selma, Alabama, led to the 1965 Voting Rights Act. In *Where Do We Go from Here: Chaos or Community?* (1967), King faulted the **black power** movement as rooted in hatred and separatism. In 1968 King was assassinated in Memphis, Tennessee, where he intended to support a strike among sanitation workers. Some of his last writings, including plans for a protest against the Vietnam War and antipoverty demonstrations in the American North, were posthumously published in *The Trumpet of Conscience* (1968). Almost a decade later he was posthumously awarded the Presidential Medal of Freedom, and in the mid-1980s the U.S. Congress declared a national holiday in his honor.

Further Readings

Black Writers, second edition, Gale, 1994.

King, Coretta Scott, *My Life with Martin Luther King Jr.,* Holt, 1969.

Oates, Stephen B., *Let the Trumpet Sound: The Life of Martin Luther King Jr.,* Harper, 1982.

Martin Luther King Jr. was the most influential nonviolent civil rights activist of the 1960s.

Martin Luther King Sr.

American autobiographer
Born December 19, 1899.
Died November 11, 1984.

Best known as the father of the famous leader, King also played a critical role in the history of the **civil rights movement**.

The son of sharecroppers, King arrived in Atlanta at age sixteen, where he worked by day and attended night school. In 1925, King earned his high school diploma and married Alberta Christine Williams, the daughter of the Reverend A. D. Williams. Impressed with King's oratorical skills, Williams's father-in-law invited King to speak to his congregation at Ebenezer Baptist Church. King became very popular in the community, and upon Williams' death in 1931, King was chosen as his successor.

The congregation grew to several thousand under King's leadership, and he used this audience to address the social issues important to the black community in Atlanta. King soon joined the **National Association for the Advancement of Colored People** (NAACP), the Atlanta Negro Voters League, and the Interracial Council of Atlanta; also, in 1936, he led the first black voting rights march in Atlanta.

The assassination of **Martin Luther King Jr.** in 1968 was only the first in a series of tragic losses for King: his younger son was mysteriously drowned in 1969 and his wife Alberta was shot and killed by a gunman aiming for King. Despite these tragedies, King continued his public service, preaching a policy of nonviolence and exercising his growing political clout. In 1980, King co-authored (with Clayton Riley) *Daddy King: An Autobiography*, in which he

Martin Luther King Sr. speaks at a memorial service for his slain son, 1969.

outlines his four decades involved in the civil rights movement. At the time of his death in 1984, many prominent political and social leaders considered King an important and influential voice in the civil rights movement.

Further Readings
Black Writers, first edition, Gale, 1989.

Woodie King Jr.
American theater producer, essayist, and editor
Born July 27, 1937.

Beginning in the 1960s and 1970s, King set a new direction for African American theater by producing a host of **plays** by African American playwrights. Born in 1937 in Mobile, Alabama, King has been called a renaissance figure in black theater because of his multifaceted work as an actor, director, writer, and producer for the stage and screen. The founder of the non-profit New Federal Theater, King collected his influential writings on the stage in **Black Theatre Present Condition** (1981). A **short story** writer himself, King has also supported the work of other African American writers by editing a number of volumes of **plays, poetry,** and short stories, including *The Forerunners: Black Poets in America* (1975) and *New Plays for the Black Theater* (1989).

Further Readings
Black Writers, second edition, Gale, 1994.

Dictionary of Literary Biography, Volume 38: *Afro-American Writers after 1955: Dramatists and Prose Writers,* Gale, 1985.

"Kiswana"
Character in *The Women of Brewster Place*

Kizzy
Character in *Roots: The Saga of an American Family*

Etheridge Knight
American poet
Born April 19, 1931.
Died March 10, 1991.

Knight was one of the most popular poets of the **black arts movement** in the 1960s. He began writing **poetry** while serving a prison term for armed robbery at Indiana State Prison. In many of his poems, he expressed a desire for freedom and protested the oppression of blacks and the underprivileged. He used graphic language, slang, unconventional punctuation, and simple poetic techniques to make his work accessible to the greatest number of readers. In 1968, he published his first collection, *Poems from Prison; Belly Song and Other Poems* (1973) won nominations for both the Pulitzer

Prize and the National Book Award. Knight's most critically acclaimed work, *Born of a Woman: New and Selected Poems,* was published in 1980. Knight died of lung cancer in Indiana in 1991.

See also **Poetry of Etheridge Knight**

Further Readings
Black Literature Criticism, Gale, 1992.
Black Writers, first edition, Gale, 1989.

Knock on Any Door
Willard Motley
Novel, 1947

Willard Motley's *Knock on Any Door,* a **novel** in the naturalistic tradition, mixes sociology and art. Its main purpose is to expose and criticize society's handling of crime, with flaws in the prison system as its chief target. The plot centers on Nick Romano, an Italian American youth who first gets into trouble when his family is forced to move into poor neighborhoods of Denver and Chicago. In and out of reformatories and jails from age fourteen onward, Nick becomes so regularly exposed to hardened criminals and sadistic officials that his antisocial behavior increases. He is finally executed at the age of twenty-one for the murder of a brutal policeman. Motley conducted extensive research for this first novel, including touring a boys' reformatory and visiting Little Sicily, Chicago's Italian district.

Kojie Anderson
Character in *A Short Walk*

Kola
Character in *The Interpreters*

Konombjo
Character in *Sadhji*

Koomson
Character in *The Beautyful Ones Are Not Yet Born*

Kriss Cummings
Character in *The Primitive*

Kristin Bowers
Character in *South Street*

Johari M. Amini Kunjufu
American poet and educator
Born February 13, 1935.

Kunjufu is an educator and poet active in literary and cultural circles in Chicago, Illinois. She co-founded the Third World Press, the Kuumba Theater, and the Institute of Positive Education there in the late 1960s and early 1970s. The driving themes of Kunjufu's lyric **poetry** *Images in Black* (1967), *Black Essence* (1968), and *Let's Go Some Where* (1970), all published under the name Johari M. Amini, are the centrality of love and the discovery of an authentic black identity. Widely anthologized, Kunjufu's poems have been praised for their imagery and use of African American idiom. Her broadsides *A Folk Fabel [sic] (For My People)* (1969) and *A Hip Tale in the Death Style* (1972) are tales about the dangers of African Americans succumbing to white society's abuses.

See also **Poetry of Johari M. Amini Kunjufu**

Further Readings
Dictionary of Literary Biography, Volume 41: *Afro-American Poets since 1955,* Gale, 1985.

Kunta Kinte
Character in *Roots: The Saga of an American Family*

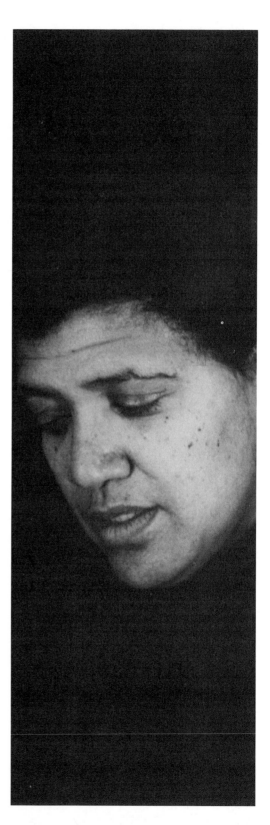

I am Black because I come

from the earth's inside /

now take my word for jewel

in the open light.

Coal, Audre Lorde, 1976

Alex La Guma

South African activist, journalist, novelist, and short story writer
Born February 20, 1925.
Died October 11, 1985.

A lifelong anti-apartheid activist, Justin Alexander La Guma also gave voice to social protest in his **novels.** Born in 1925 in Cape Town, South Africa, La Guma was a left-wing journalist whose political activities led to his occasional imprisonment and constant surveillance by the South African government. While in South Africa as well as after his immigration to London, England, in 1966, La Guma wrote fiction based on real people and events, depicting the devastating effects of racist oppression on communities. Much of his work treats the situations and problems he witnessed in his native Cape Town. His most successful novel, *In the Fog of the Seasons' End* (1972), is his most explicitly autobiographical work and focuses on the anti-apartheid movement.

Further Readings

Abrahams, Cecil A., *Alex La Guma,* Twayne, 1985.

Dictionary of Literary Biography, Volume 117: *Twentieth-Century Caribbean and Black African Writers,* Gale, 1992.

Kartuzov, S. P., *Alex La Guma,* Nauka, 1978.

Joyce A. Ladner

American writer
Born October 12, 1943.

A noted black sociologist, Joyce Ann Ladner was born in 1943 in Waynesboro, Mississippi, and educated at Tougaloo College and Washington University in the 1960s. She has conducted postdoctoral research at the University of Dar es Salaam, Tanzania. She joined the sociology faculty at Hunter College of the City University of New York in 1976.

Ladner's works include *Tomorrow's Tomorrow: The Black Woman* (1971) and *Mixed Families: Adopting Across Racial Boundaries* (1977). She edited *The Death of White Sociology* (1973) and *Adolescence and Poverty: Challenge for the 1990s* (1991) and has contributed to anthologies, newspapers, and periodicals, including *Black Scholar, Essence,* and *Journal of Black Studies and Research.* In 1970 Ladner received the first fellowship from the Black Women's Community Development Foundation for her study "Involvement of Tanzanian Women in Nation Building."

Further Readings

Black Writers, second edition, Gale, 1994.

"Lady in... "

Characters in *for colored girls who have considered suicide*

Lakunle

Character in *The Lion and the Jewel*

George Lamming

Barbadian novelist and essayist
Born June 8, 1927.

Commended for his poetic prose style, George William Lamming has depicted the effects of European colonization on the West Indies and portrayed the West Indian search for a distinct political, economic, and cultural identity. Lamming emigrated to England in 1950; some of his **novels** explore themes of expatriation and the return to Caribbean roots. Acclaimed by critics, *In the Castle of My Skin* (1953) is an account of childhood and adolescence on Lamming's fictional Caribbean island, San Cristobal. *Water with Berries* (1971) and *Natives of My Person* (1972) continue Lamming's exploration of West Indian history.

Further Readings

Black Literature Criticism, Gale, 1992.

Black Writers, second edition, Gale, 1994.

Paquet, Sandra Pouchet, *The Novels of George Lamming,* Heinemann, 1982.

The Landlord

Kristin Hunter
Novel, 1966

Kristin Hunter's second **novel**, *The Landlord* promotes some of the aims of the **civil rights movement** of the 1960s. It shows how interracial harmony, represented by a European American landlord's relationship with his African American tenants, provides benefits for both sides in the racial conflict. The major character is Elgar Enders, a rich young white man, who is psychologically troubled about his relations with his own family. He purchases a run-down apartment building in the ghetto, intending to exploit his renters for his own financial gain. However, as Elgar gets to know his tenants, he becomes fond of them. They include Marge, a former blues singer; "Creole" Du Bois, a closet homosexual; and the beautiful, vivacious Fanny and her family. Rather than exploiting the tenants, Elgar starts to work with them to repair the building. In return, the tenants provide Elgar with the psychological security that was missing from his family life. Elgar enters further into the tenants' community when he begins an affair with Fanny—with the knowledge of her husband. By the end of the novel, he has become like another father to their children.

Pinkie Gordon Lane

American poet and editor
Born January 13, 1923.

First inspired to write **poetry** in her mid-thirties after reading the work of **Gwendolyn Brooks**, Lane has published several volumes of mostly occasional poetry and is widely anthologized. Born in 1923 in Philadelphia, Pennsylvania, Lane was a high school English teacher in Georgia and Florida before moving to Baton Rouge, Louisiana, to become an English professor at Southern University, where she has taught since 1959. Relying primarily on bold but subtle imagery for poetic effect, Lane's work explores and celebrates encounters with the natural world and moments of family life and professional activity. Her second poetry collection, *Mystic Female* (1978), is her most well known and widely praised, receiving a nomination for the Pulitzer Prize. In addition to editing poetry anthologies, she has also written such collections as *Girl at the Window* (1991).

See also **Poetry of Pinkie Gordon Lane**

Further Readings

Dictionary of Literary Biography, Volume 41: *Afro-American Poets since 1955,* Gale, 1985.

Nella Larsen

American novelist
Born April 13, 1891.
Died March 30, 1964.

Although she published only two **novels** and a handful of periodical pieces, Larsen is regarded as an important writer of the **Harlem Renaissance**. Born in Chicago in 1891, Larsen was the child of a West Indian father and a Danish mother. Her father died when she was two years old and her mother remarried a man of her own nationality. Larsen spent her youth among white family members and first experienced an all-black environment when she attended Fisk University in Tennessee for a short time. Larsen worked as a nurse and a librarian in New York before, as the socialite spouse of physicist Elmer S. Imes, she befriended writers and artists taking part in the cultural awakening in Harlem and was encouraged to write.

Larsen's two novels, *Quicksand* (1928) and *Passing* (1929), depict urban middle-class women constrained by society. *Quicksand,* her best-known work, is a semiautobiographical novel that involves a mulatto woman, Helga Crane, who searches in vain for sexual and racial identity. *Quicksand* was awarded a Harmon Foundation prize and received generally enthusiastic reviews. *Passing* is the story of a light-skinned woman, Clare Kendry, who "passes" for white and manages to deceive even her white husband.

In 1930, Larsen became the first African American woman to win a Guggenheim Fellowship and was at the height of her popularity. In the same year, she was accused of plagiarizing her **short story** "Sanctuary." She was eventually exonerated, but the accusation and the scandal haunted her. She then experienced marital problems that resulted in a sensationalized divorce. Larsen withdrew from literary circles and spent the last twenty years of her life working as a nurse in Manhattan hospitals.

Further Readings

Black Literature Criticism, Gale, 1992.

Black Writers, first edition, Gale, 1989.

Dictionary of Literary Biography, Volume 51: *Afro-American Writers from the Harlem Renaissance to 1940,* Gale, 1987.

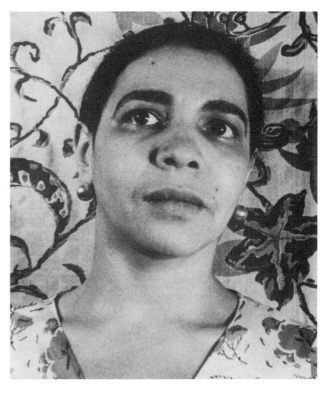

Larsen was an important figure during the Harlem Renaissance movement.

Laura Laballe

Character in *A Morning in Trinidad*

Laurie Lee Youngblood

Character in *Youngblood*

Camara Laye

Guinean novelist
Born January 1, 1928.
Died February 4, 1980.

Widely regarded as Africa's most important novelist to write in French, Laye captured the spirituality and vibrancy of traditional African culture in his books. Born in 1928 in Guinea, Laye was exiled from his home country in 1966 because of his opposition to its government and was forced to live in Senegal until his death in 1980. His first book, the autobiographical *L'Enfant noir* (1953; translated as *The Dark Child*), depicts the traditions of African village life and was written while Laye was an engineering student in Paris. Laye explored similar African themes in his next two **novels,** *Le Regard du roi* (1954; translated as **The Radiance of the King**, 1956) and *Dramouss* (1966; translated as *A Dream of Africa,* 1968). After Laye's wife was imprisoned during a 1970 visit to Guinea, he no longer published overtly political work. His last work, *Le Maître de la parole: Kuoma Lafolo Kuoma* (1978; translated as *The Guardian of the Word,* 1984), is a historical **epic**.

Further Readings

Black Writers, first edition, Gale, 1989.

L The Learning Tree

Gordon Parks
Novel, 1963

The Learning Tree, **Gordon Parks**'s first work of fiction, is a semiautobiographical tale of adolescence in partially integrated Cherokee Flats, Kansas, during the 1920s. Young protagonist Newt Winger has some wild adventures, including losing his virginity after getting lost during a deadly tornado. He cannot, however, escape the racial taunts of neighborhood children. Sarah Winger, Newt's mother, warns her son that there are good things and people in the world but that they can go bad sometimes. She believes that even a small town like the one in which they live can be a learning tree, as she calls it. Newt is in love with a girl, Arcella Jefferson, who turns out to prefer a white boy instead. The boy, Chauncey, impregnates her. Other trouble brews as the town delinquent, Marcus Savage, and his father Booker conspire to frame a drunkard for the murder of a white farmer. Newt, a witness, comes forward at the trial. This leads Booker to commit suicide rather than give himself up to whites, and Marcus later seeks revenge. He steals a gun and tries to kill the grieving Newt. Newt's ambivalence leads him to allow Marcus to flee when the police intervene. He even hopes Marcus will escape, but the renegade is killed in a fall instead. There are many deaths in this story, and Newt eventually becomes inured to their effects. He plans to go to college, but his principal tells him that one of the best students in the town went off to the big city only to wind up a porter. In the end, he leaves town by train, hoping to overcome the racial divisions that hold everywhere in America as strongly as in Cherokee Flats.

Don L. Lee

Please see Haki R. Madhubuti

Lee Edward

Character in *The Time-Ago Tales of Jahdu*

Lee Gordon

Character in *Lonely Crusade*

L Spike Lee

American filmmaker
Born March 20, 1957.

Lee is regarded as one of the premier contemporary American filmmakers. He has attracted international acclaim for his talent as screenwriter, director, producer, actor, and merchandiser of films. The films Lee makes feature non-stereotypical African American characters whose lives and interests are as diverse as the black community itself.

Shelton Jackson Lee was born in Atlanta, Georgia, but his father, a **jazz** musician, moved the family first to Chicago and then to New York when his son was still very young. Lee attended Morehouse College and the New York University Film School, where he won the student director's Academy Award for *Joe's Bed-Stuy Barber Shop: We Cut Heads* (1982). He first attracted critical attention for *She's Gotta Have It* (1986), an examination of black female sexuality. Lee writes about his experiences filming the movie on a shoestring budget in *Spike Lee's "Gotta Have It": Inside Guerilla Filmmaking* (1987).

Lee has also won notoriety within the African American community as a provocateur. *School Daze* (1988) examines factional conflicts, bigotry, and elitism within an all-black college, and some prominent African Americans protested that Lee's depiction reflected unfavorably on black students. ***Do the Right Thing*** (1989) and ***Jungle Fever*** (1991) are both about **racism**; Lee discusses the process of their creation in *"Do the Right Thing": The New Spike Lee Joint* (1989), and *Five for Five: The Films* of *Spike Lee* (1991). When Lee was chosen to direct **Malcolm X** (1992), some black cultural figures feared the filmmaker would corrupt the legacy of the controversial black leader. Lee defended his treatment of the subject in *By Any Means Necessary: The Trials and Tribulations of the Making of "Malcolm X"* (1992). Lee has also released **Mo' Better Blues** (1990), about a self-centered jazz musician; *Crooklyn* (1994), a comedy-drama set in Brooklyn and centering on a middle-class black family; and *Clockers* (1995; with Martin Scorcese), about a murder investigation.

Further Readings

Authors and Artists for Children and Young Adults, Volume 4, Gale, 1990, pp. 165-79.

Black Writers, second edition, Gale, 1994.

Lena

Character in *A Raisin in the Sun*

Filmmaker Spike Lee.

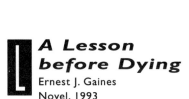

A Lesson before Dying

Ernest J. Gaines
Novel, 1993

An exploration of dignity and bravery in trying circumstances just after World War II, **Ernest J. Gaines**'s *A Lesson before Dying* tells the story of Jefferson, a barely literate young black man who is sentenced to death because he happened to be present when a white man was shot. Jefferson's attorney tries to win a life sentence for him by telling the jury that executing someone so simple would be like putting a hog in the electric chair. The strategy does not work, but it has a profound effect nevertheless. Jefferson's godmother, Miss Emma, finds a teacher to tutor Jefferson, who has taken Grant's words literally, so he will not go to his death thinking he is no better than a hog.

The tutor is Grant Wiggins, a local black man who has earned a college degree. As he struggles to teach the uncooperative Jefferson, Grant must face his own disillusionment—he despairs of the black children he teaches reaping any benefit from schooling, and he is deeply resentful of the humiliations he must endure from members of the white community. He also clashes with the preacher, the Reverend Ambrose, who is seeking to save Jefferson's soul.

Urged on by Miss Emma, Grant commits himself to educating Jefferson, and Jefferson accepts the situation out of respect for his aging godmother. As the men work together, Grant begins to share Jefferson's agony, and Jefferson begins to achieve the dignity and sense of shared endeavor that makes him a man. In due time the law takes its course, and Jefferson is executed. His final actions and thoughts prove inspiring to Grant, who has learned as much from his student as he taught.

Dust jacket for Gaines's novel about a victim of injustice.

A Lesson before Dying was published to favorable reviews and particularly cited for its penetrating character studies. Soon after its release, Gaines was given a "genius" award from the MacArthur Foundation in recognition of his body of work.

Julius Lester

American novelist
Born January 27, 1939.

A musician, political activist, and educator, Julius Bernard Lester writes books for young adults about African American history and heritage. He also publishes fiction and documentaries for adults.

Born in St. Louis, Missouri, in 1939, Lester grew up in the segregated South during the 1940s and 1950s. He graduated from Fisk University in 1960 and became a professor at the University of Massachusetts in 1971, where he still teaches Judaic Studies. Lester became deeply involved in the **civil rights movement** following his graduation from college and served as a member of the Student Non-Violent Coordinating Committee (SNCC). During the 1960s, he also pursued a music career, which led to the publication of his first book, *The 12-String Guitar as Played by Leadbelly: An Instructional Manual* (1965), which he cowrote with folksinger Pete Seeger.

Lester then began writing books about political issues, publishing *The Angry Children of Malcolm X* in 1966. In 1969 Lester wrote his first book for children, *To Be a Slave*. A collection of six short stories developed from oral histories, the book was named as runner-up for the Newbery Medal.

Most of Lester's subjects fall into two categories: those drawn from African American **folklore** and those drawn from black history. *Black Folktales* (1969), Lester's first collection of folk stories, features shrewd animals and cunning people. While some of the characters are taken from African legends and others from American slave tales, they all demonstrate the strength of black resistance to oppression. Lester also deals with white oppression in his second collection of folktales, *The Knee-High Man and Other Tales* (1972). He returned to African American history with ***The Long Journey Home: Stories from Black History*** (1972), a documentary collection of **slave narratives** showcasing ordinary people in adverse circumstances during the post-Civil War **Reconstruction** era. Lester has also continued to write for adults, publishing a **novel,** *Do Lord Remember Me,* in 1985, a collection of writings on **W. E. B. Du Bois** entitled *The Seventh Son* (1971), and two autobiographies.

Further Readings
Black Writers, second edition, Gale, 1994.

Let the Lion Eat Straw

Ellease Southerland
Novel, 1979

Ellease Southerland's autobiographical first **novel**, *Let the Lion Eat Straw,* begins in a tiny rural community of North Carolina, where the child Abeba Torch lives with old Mamma Habblesham. The novel ends about forty years later in New York with the same old beloved midwife, long since dead, ushering Abeba out of life. Through scenes at which she is the center, Abeba perceives the importance of moments in her life involving her husband, Daniel Torch; her fifteen children; and her mother, Angela Williams Lavoisier. The book's title comes from the biblical Isaiah's prophecy of a world of peace. The lion represents Daniel's susceptibility to madness and Angela's ceaseless spitefulness. The prophecy is fulfilled through a spectacular Easter celebration at which the Torch family transforms its own grief and antagonisms, and the sorrows and the deaths of its people, into peace and magnificence.

Lester's books draw on topics related to black folklore and history.

Letter from Birmingham City Jail

Martin Luther King Jr.
Letter, 1963

In spring 1963, **Martin Luther King Jr.** disregarded a court injunction against his organizing a civil rights demonstration in Birmingham, Alabama, and was jailed. While imprisoned, King read a piece jointly submitted by well-known Christian and Jewish leaders to the *Birmingham News,* "Appeal for Law and Order and Common Sense," which decried the mass protests and called King and his Southern Christian Leadership Conference "outside agitators." This criticism prompted a response from King, known as *Letter from Birmingham City Jail,* which has been noted for its power and eloquence and has come to symbolize the struggle for civil rights.

King objected to being termed an outsider, maintaining that no one was an outsider in the human community. He argued that the Birmingham power structure had been unresponsive to blacks and had thus set the stage for demonstrations. King explained the nature of nonviolent protest, stating that an initial determination of whether injustice truly existed was made and that negotiations with community leaders took place to attempt to resolve the issue. After unsuccessfully attempting these steps in Birmingham, King asserted, activists decided that direct action was necessary and learned what action could mean for them, such as possibly spending time in jail. The next stage was a peaceful protest to raise people's consciousness.

Buttressing his arguments with Christian theology, especially that of thirteenth-century saint Thomas Aquinas, King viewed laws as just or unjust in how they corresponded with God's laws. He affirmed his respect for the law but cautioned that history had shown that not all that is legal is just. King called all segregationist statutes unjust because they denied God's view of each individual as unique and precious. King warned the leaders of Christian churches that their communities would become superficial clubs if they did not address social issues and voiced hope that churches would work for social justice. He concluded the letter by apologizing for any exaggerations he might have made and praying for forgiveness if he had not done enough in his efforts to persuade.

Levi

Series character in "Justice" Trilogy

Lewis

Character in *Lucy*

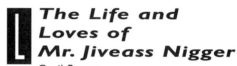

Theophilus Lewis

American writer and drama critic
Born March 4, 1891.
Died September 3, 1974.

A postal worker with a high school education, Lewis came to prominence during the **Harlem Renaissance** as a drama critic and book reviewer. Born in 1891 in Baltimore, Maryland, Lewis began his writing career as a drama critic for the *Messenger* in 1923. He went on to contribute articles to a host of periodicals, including *Commonweal, Ebony and Topaz,* and *Interracial Review.* His most important contribution was his effort to promote serious theater for African American audiences, whose involvement with theater had been limited primarily to light entertainment. He was an ardent supporter of the work of the independent, nonprofit theater com-

panies, as they provided the only venue for serious African American playwrights and actors.

Further Readings
Black Writers, first edition, Gale, 1989.

The Life and Loves of Mr. Jiveass Nigger

Cecil Brown
Novel, 1969

Cecil Brown's first **novel**, a **satire** entitled *The Life and Loves of Mr. Jiveass Nigger* (1969), depicts George Washington, a black student who is stranded in Europe. Looking for help, George contacts an American diplomat, who offers only a window-washing job. After refusing the offer, George makes his way to Copenhagen, where he becomes a gigolo and poses as a literary critic at a tavern. Eventually, George is beaten into a state of unconsciousness in a tavern fight and wakes up in a hospital. There he confronts his loneliness and decides to find an honest way to return to the United States.

Claude M. Lightfoot

American historian, activist, and writer
Born January 19, 1910.
Died July 17, 1991.

Lightfoot dedicated his life to supporting the African American community through his espousal of Marxism. Through his personal experiences of oppression and his scholarship, Lightfoot drew the conclusions that he set forth in the political studies *Ghetto Rebellion to Black Liberation* (1967), *Black America and the World Revolution* (1970), *Racism and Human Survival: Lessons of Nazi Germany for Today's World* (1972), and *Human Rights U.S. Style: From Colonial Times Through the New Deal* (1977).

Lightfoot was born in 1910 in Lake Village, Arkansas, and was educated at Virginia Union University, later receiving his Ph.D. from Rostock University. The founder of the Chicago Young Men's Democratic Organization, Lightfoot became vice president of the American Communist Party in 1959 and remained active in politics throughout his lifetime. Among the awards he received are the outstanding Scholarship Achievement Award from the W. E. B. DuBois Communist Center and the 1979 Salute to Black History Award.

Further Readings
Black Writers, first edition, Gale, 1989.

Sara Lawrence Lightfoot
American writer and biographer
Born in 1944(?).

Lightfoot, a sociologist and a tenured professor at the Harvard Graduate School of Education, examines in her academic works issues of race and class in the American educational system. Among her publications are *Worlds Apart: Relationships between Families and Schools* (1978); *Beyond Bias: Perspectives on Classrooms* (1979), which she coauthored with Jean V. Carew; and *The Good High School: Portraits of Character and Culture* (1983).

Lightfoot was born circa 1944 and attended Swarthmore University. She received a MacArthur prize in 1984. Her first **biography**, the Christopher Award-winning *Balm in Gilead: Journey of a Healer* (1988), tells the story of her mother, a child psychiatrist. In *I've Known Rivers: Lives of Loss and Liberation* (1994), Lightfoot recounts the lives and struggles for identity of six African Americans in their forties and fifties.

Further Readings
Black Writers, second edition, Gale, 1994.

Lilith Iyapo
Series character in "Xenogenesis" Trilogy

Lillian Manning
Character in *The Third Generation*

C. Eric Lincoln
American poet and writer
Born June 23, 1924.

Charles Eric Lincoln is considered a major voice in U.S. race relations and the **civil rights movement**, the development of black protest and **black nationalism**, and the growth and importance of the black church. Born in 1924 in Athens, Alabama, he was educated at LeMoyne College, Fisk University, the University of Chicago Divinity School, and Boston University, where he earned a Ph.D. degree in 1960. He served as professor of **religion** and culture at Duke University from 1976 to 1993.

Lincoln's works include *The Black Muslims in America* (1961, revised, 1982), *The Negro Pilgrimage in America* (1967), *Race, Religion, and the Continuing American Dilemma* (1984), *The Avenue* (1988), and *The Black Church in the African American Experience* (1990). He is editor of the C. Eric Lincoln Series in Black Religion and was founding president of the Black Academy of Arts and Letters. He has also written a volume of **poetry** titled *The Road Since Freedom* (1990).

Further Readings
Black Writers, second edition, Gale, 1994.

Link Williams
Character in *The Narrows*

The Lion and the Jewel
Wole Soyinka
Play, first produced 1959, published 1963

The setting of **Wole Soyinka**'s second **play** is a village named Ilujinle. **Speeches**, mimetic displays, and dance sequences are interspersed with the machinations of the plot. Bale Baroka, a local elder, and a younger man Lakunle, who teaches school, are rivals for the beautiful Sidi. The basic plotline takes the form of a satiric **comedy** of sexual mores, since Lakunle—representing advancing modern civilization—wants to mold the virginal and ignorant Sidi into a proper European lady. Meanwhile, Baroka—preserver of the old order—poses as an impotent old man, in order to seduce Sidi once she believes he is harmless. Baroka already has several wives, though, and the one named Sadiku appears at Sidi's seduction to perform a dance of a sexual predator. Sidi later comments on strangers and their impact on the village in a dance called "The Lost Traveller," which presents the arrival of a foreign photographer from Lagos, an important event in the village's history.

Lisette

Character in *Possessing the Secret of Joy*

Lissie

Character in *The Temple of My Familiar*

Literary Criticism

Criticism is the systematic study and evaluation of literary works, usually based on a specific method or set of principles. The practice of criticism has given rise to numerous theories, such as **structuralism** and **deconstruction,** and schools, such as **modernism, naturalism, realism,** and **romanticism.** This has often produced conflicting, even contradictory, interpretations of literature in general and individual works in particular. For example, the critic **Sunday O. Anozie** has discussed the writing of **Léopold Sédar Senghor** in light of both structuralism and deconstruction.

Until recently, criticism of African American literature tended to emphasize political, his-

torical, and social interpretations. **Black aesthetic movement** writers such as **Amiri Baraka** and **Lawrence P. Neal** exemplify this approach. Some recent critics, most notably **Henry Louis Gates Jr.** and **Houston A. Baker Jr.,** have argued for readings of black literature that explore works in relation to themselves and each other, rather than viewing them as literal reflections of African American history or society. One theory of particular relevance to black writing was developed by Gates and is based on the black vernacular use of **"signifying,"** a rhetorical strategy based on indirection, repetition, reversal, and double meanings.

Little Augie

Character in *God Sends Sunday*

Little Jim Kilgrow

Character in *Youngblood*

The Living Is Easy
Dorothy West
Novel, 1948

Dorothy West's **Harlem Renaissance novel** *The Living Is Easy* examines the situation of black middle and upper class society in Boston just prior to World War I. At age fourteen, the light-skinned Cleo Jericho Judson emigrates from her impoverished family in South Carolina to serve as a spinster's companion in Boston. Cleo has definite intentions of social advancement, and she soon meets and marries the much older Bart Judson, "the Black Banana King," a prosperous Southern immigrant who has built a thriving fruit business. Through his money, Cleo gains entrance into Boston's black upper class. She invites her sisters to live with her, ruining their marriages in the process. In the end, the banana business goes bankrupt, and Bart leaves Boston in search of another job, leaving Cleo in a situation similar to the one she had fled the South to escape.

Alain Locke

American philosopher, writer, and essayist
Born September 13, 1886.
Died June 9, 1954.

An influential figure in the **Harlem Renaissance**, Locke wrote on topics in philosophy, political science, sociology, anthropology, literature, art, music, and African studies. In addition to promoting the development of black culture as a means of moving towards social, political, and economic equality, he urged black American artists and writers to cultivate their African heritage.

Alain Le Roy Locke was born on September 13, 1886, in Philadelphia, Pennsylvania. Both of his parents were schoolteachers. After graduating from Harvard University with honors in 1907, he became the first black Rhodes scholar, earning a degree in literature from Oxford University and studying philosophy for a year at the University of Berlin. In 1911, he spent six months touring the American South, becoming acutely aware of prejudice and **discrimination**. He obtained his Ph.D. from Harvard in 1918.

In 1912, Locke began teaching at Howard University, where he chaired the philosophy department from 1918 to 1953. His anthology *The New Negro: An Interpretation* (1925), A proponent of cultural pluralism, he criticized the practice of **segregation** in schools and urged black educators to develop curricula that would reflect the history and heritage of black Americans. His emphasis on community over the individual sometimes set him at odds with other prominent black thinkers, including **W. E. B. Du Bois** and **Claude McKay**.

Locke died in New York City on June 9, 1954, after a long illness.

Further Readings
Black Writers, first edition, Gale, 1989.

Crane, Clare Bloodgood, *Alain Locke and the Negro Renaissance,* University of California, 1971.

Logan Killicks
Character in *Their Eyes Were Watching God*

Rayford W. Logan

American historian
Born January 7, 1897.
Died November 4, 1982.

Rayford Whittingham Logan is best known for his historical writings. Educated at Williams College and Harvard University, Logan was a professor of history and headed several history departments at various universities, including Virginia Union, Atlanta, and Howard. His writings include *The Negro and the Post-War World: A Primer* (1945) and the two-volume *The Negro in the United States* (1970 and 1971). Logan also coedited *Dictionary of American Negro Biography* (1982), which contains approximately 700 entries and was completed shortly before his death. He is buried in Fort Lincoln Cemetery in Washington, D.C.

Further Readings
Black Writers, first edition, Gale, 1989.

Louis E. Lomax

American journalist and nonfiction writer
Born August 16, 1922.
Died July 30, 1970.

Lomax, the son of teacher and clergyman James Lomax, was born in Valdosta, Georgia. He was educated at Paine College and did graduate study at American University and at Yale University. Lomax was a newspaperman from

1941 to 1958; news commentator on WNTA-TV, New York City (1958-60) and for Metromedia Broadcasting (1964-68); news analyst for KTTV, Los Angeles; news director for WNEW-TV, New York City; news writer for the *Mike Wallace Show;* and host of the television program *Louis Lomax.*

A freelance writer from 1958 until his death, Lomax won the 1961 Anisfield-Wolf Award for the best book concerned with racial problems for *The Reluctant African* (1960). His other books include *The Negro Revolt* (1962), *When the Word is Given: A Report on Elijah Muhammad, Malcolm X, and the Black Muslim World* (1963), *Thailand: The War That Is, The War That Will Be* (1966), and *To Kill a Black Man* (1968). He also contributed to *Life, Look,* and *The Saturday Evening Post* and was a syndicated columnist for the North American Newspaper Alliance.

Lomax was awarded two honorary doctorates and taught philosophy at Georgia State University and humanities and social sciences at Hofstra University. He died in an automobile accident in Santa Rosa, New Mexico.

Further Readings
Black Writers, second edition, Gale, 1994.

Lonely Crusade
Chester Himes
Novel, 1947

Chester Himes's *Lonely Crusade* examines the conflicts of an African American who, after a long period of unemployment, finally gets work, only to find he is being used as a pawn by the white-controlled union to gain the confidence of other blacks. After Lee Gordon accepts a union job at Comstock Aircraft, he is offered a high paying job in the company's personnel department. When his wife becomes angry over her husband's refusal to accept the bribe to sell out the union, Gordon leaves the house. In the company of co-worker Luther McGregor, Gordon is once again offered a bribe; while McGregor accepts, Gordon is

severely beaten for his loyalty to his employer. The Communists, for whom McGregor is possibly a spy, decide that one of their party's members must be sacrificed to satisfy the workers. A white woman named Jackie Falks is expelled from the party, and, despite Gordon's efforts to save her, she is ousted from the union. Gordon's defense of a white woman causes his wife to accuse him of having an affair, leading to further marital discord. After losing control of his job, his work relationships, and his marriage, Gordon is wanted by police who have orders to shoot him on site as the suspected killer of a union agent, orders based on lies told by Falks.

The Long Journey Home
Julius Lester
Children's fiction, 1972

The six stories presented in **Julius Lester**'s *The Long Journey Home: Stories from Black History* are based at least partly on real life **slave narratives**. The opening tale follows a blues singer on his wandering tour of America in the days of sharecropping. Another story focuses on a runaway slave who must continually elude bounty hunters in Ohio. Another features a black cowboy in Texas who is sent to capture a herd of wild mustangs. At first he thinks he would rather run off with them; in the end, he leads them into a corral. He realizes, however, that white handlers will not get to know the horses as well as he did on the range. The book is annotated with explanatory footnotes.

Long Walk to Freedom
Nelson Mandela
Autobiography, 1994

Long Walk to Freedom: The Autobiography of Nelson Mandela chronicles **Nelson Mandela**'s life from his childhood as the son of a

Thembu tribal chief in the village of Qunu to South Africa's most prominent political prisoner and crusader against **apartheid**. He describes his earliest awareness of black oppression and his continuing efforts to educate and liberate black South Africans, even at the expense of his family life. His involvement with the African National Congress (ANC) and other organized civil rights groups led to frequent legal difficulties, including a 1956 arrest for high treason. In 1964 he was sentenced to life imprisonment on maximum-security Robben Island, where he remained until early release on February 10, 1990. Mandela was subsequently elected president of South Africa in April, 1994.

Look What They Done to My Song
John A. McCluskey Jr.
Novel, 1974

Mack is a young musician and follower of **Malcolm X** who is inspired to preach love through his performances. On his way from Santa Fe to Boston, Mack meets a few women for whom he cares but who fail to understand him. The Sledges, a married couple with whom Mack stays for a time, encourage him to be true to himself. Ubangi is a would-be hustler who gets Mack into trouble, and they both wind up traveling to Boston, where Mack finds the woman to support his efforts. Novella Turner brings Mack to Reverend Fuller, who inspires him to realize the black experience in the form of devotional music.

Loose Canons: Notes on the Culture Wars
Henry Louis Gates Jr.
Essays, 1992

In *Loose Canons*, **Henry Louis Gates Jr.** argues that African American literature plays a vital role in shaping the national culture. The collected essays were originally prepared by Gates, a well-known proponent of African American studies, as oral discussions and presentations. Criticizing the Western literary canon for excluding African American literature, Gates insists that this body of work can and should become a part of American letters. Furthermore, Gates argues in the **essay** "Writing, 'Race,' and the Difference It Makes," that critics of black literature need to look to "the black tradition itself" in order to develop relevant theories of criticism. In the book's three sections—"Literature," "The Profession," and "Society"—Gates examines other controversial issues, such as curriculum modification, language bias, and the values of cultural pluralism. Gates emphasizes that African American literature must be integrated into Western canon and conceived of as mainstream literature, not viewed as an intellectual specialty.

Henri Lopes
Zairian statesperson and novelist
Born September 12, 1937.

A former prime minister of the People's Republic of the Congo, Henri Marie-Joseph Lopes has written **novels** and **short stories** that comment on the disparity between developing and traditional Africa. Educated in France during the early 1960s, Lopes returned to Africa to begin a teaching career that led to several high-level government and United Nations positions. His writings include *Tribaliques* (1971; *Tribaliks: Contemporary Congolese Stories,* 1987), which won the 1972 Grand Prix Litteraire de L'Afrique Noire. His satirical novel *Le Pleurer-Rive* (1982; *The Laughing Cry: An African Cock and Bull Story,* 1987) focuses on a mythical African republic and its bullying dictator.

Further Readings
Black Writers, second edition, Gale, 1994.

Lord of the Dark Places

Hal Bennett
Novel, 1970

Lord of the Dark Places, **Hal Bennett**'s third **novel**, is an experimental and satirical work that tells the story of Joe Market, an outrageous southern youth. The novel begins in 1951 with the death of Joe's mother and grandmother in the fictional town of Burnside, Virginia. Joe's grandmother had founded the Church of Stephen Martyr, against which her son Titus had rebelled by founding his own Church of the Naked Disciple. A loyal devotee of his father's church, Joe nominates himself as the lord of dark places and embarks on a series of adventures that take him north. By the close of his odyssey, he is a guilt-driven madman dreaming of black salvation through his own death and redemption. The novel ends with Joe's execution for murder in Trenton, New Jersey, in June 1968.

Audre Lorde

American poet, essayist, autobiographer, and fiction writer
Born February 18, 1934.
Died November 17, 1992.

An author who used her writings to combat racial and sexual injustice, Audre Geraldine Lorde was known as a prominent feminist and gay-rights advocate as well as an award-winning poet popular with mainstream audiences. She also published under the name Rey Domini.

Lorde was born in New York City and grew up in Manhattan, where she wrote her first **poetry** in the eighth grade. She received her bachelor's degree from Hunter College in 1959 and her master's degree in library science from Columbia University in 1961. The following year she married attorney Edwin Ashley Rollins, with whom she had two children; they were divorced in 1970.

Lorde worked as a public librarian until 1968, when she received a National Endowment for the Arts grant and became poet-in-residence at Tougaloo College, beginning a teaching career that would continue until her death. The poems in her first book, *The First Cities* (1968), were praised for their introspective quality and proved a stylistic departure from the more confrontational work of other black writers. Lorde's second book, *Cables to Rage* (1970), was less introspective than its predecessor and began to express a social anger that would find full development in later works. Her collection *From a Land Where Other People Live* (1973) was nominated for a National Book Award. The poetry of *The Black Unicorn* (1978), her seventh book of poetry, draws on West African culture and proclaims a bold racial, political, and sexual liberation.

In 1980, Lorde published *The Cancer Journals,* which describe her struggle with breast cancer. She has written several other works, including the poetry collections *Coal* and *Our Dead behind Us* and the acclaimed **novel** *Zami: A New Spelling of My Name* (1982). Lorde was named poet laureate of the state of New York in 1991. She succumbed to liver cancer at her home in St. Croix in 1992.

See also **Poetry of Audrey Lorde**

Further Readings
Black Writers, first edition, Gale, 1989.
Black Literature Criticism, Gale, 1992.
Dictionary of Literary Biography, Volume 41: *Afro-American Poets since 1955,* Gale, 1985.

Lorraine
Character in *The Women of Brewster Place*

Louetta Hawkins
Character in *The Soul Brothers and Sister Lou*

Louisa
Character in *Cane*

Louvinie
Character in *Meridian*

Love and Marriage

Bill Cosby
Nonfiction, 1989

In *Love and Marriage,* **Bill Cosby** provides comical advice on the topic, recalling his own sexual awakening as an adolescent and drawing on his twenty-five years of marriage. Through anecdotes, he reveals his youthful crushes and dating catastrophes, and dispenses lessons learned from his many years with his wife Camille and their five children. Providing humorous suggestions on such subjects as verbal sparring, conversing, and sexual equality, he focuses on the little annoyances—such as losing the keys, snoring, and getting lost—that plague many happy marriages. He also pays tribute to his parents and their fifty-plus years of marriage, and touches on fatherhood, longing to ask each young man who dates a Cosby daughter, "You're not like *me,* are you?... If you are, then I know what you want and I hope you have the same terrible luck."

Lorde was an award-winning poet and prominent feminist.

Earl Lovelace

Trinidadian novelist and playwright
Born July 13, 1935.

Lovelace chronicles native Trinidadian resistance to the fragmentation of their cultural heritage. His **novels** and **plays** are noted for their use of Caribbean dialect and metaphor and the thematic search for cultural continuity.

Born in Toco, Trinidad, in 1935, Lovelace grew up in Tobago and the Port of Spain. He attended Eastern Caribbean Institute of Agriculture and Forestry before moving to Howard University in the mid-1960s and later to John Hopkins University. He returned to the West Indies in 1977. His 1965 novel, ***While Gods Are Falling***, examines the social effects of decolonization, while *The Wine of Astonishment* (1982) is a historical chronicle of a creole sect banned on Trinidad from 1917 to 1951. Lovelace's play *The New Boss,* produced in

1962, features his characteristic use of folk music and dance, and was followed by other dramas, including *My Name Is Village* (1976) and *Jestina's Calypso* (1978).

Further Readings

Black Writers, second edition, Gale, 1994.

Dictionary of Literary Biography, Volume 125: *Twentieth-Century Caribbean and Black African Writers,* Second Series, Gale, 1993.

Loving Her

Ann Allen Shockley
Novel, 1974

Ann Allen Shockley's first **novel**, *Loving Her,* treats the issue of lesbianism from an interracial perspective. The protagonist, Renay, a divorced, black mother and talented pianist, falls in love with Terry, an affluent white writer. Shockley examines Renay's personal growth as a woman in relation to numerous social factors, including pervasive attitudes toward black women, lesbians, interracial relationships, and children of lesbian women. In addition, the novel chronicles how Renay matures as she sorts through past feelings with her daughter and ex-husband while accepting the true nature of her sexuality. Shockley also presents a cross section of societal views about the women's love affair, depicting those who are repulsed by either the racial or sexual issue, and those who have come to accept the nature of the relationship.

Lt. Robert Samuels

Character in *And Then We Heard the Thunder*

W. F. Lucas

American playwright, editor, and short story writer
Born September 1, 1927.

Wilmer Francis Lucas Jr. has worked variously as a playwright, a correspondent, and a lecturer in comparative Afro-American literature at the New School for Social Research in New York City. Born in Brooklyn, New York, in 1927, Lucas attended New York University in the 1940s. In 1971 he founded the Carpetbag Theatre in Knoxville, Tennessee, which has produced many of his **plays.** *Patent Leather Sunday: And S'More One Act Plays* (1975) contains some of his stage works, and *Bottom Fishing: A Novella and Other Stories,* published in 1974, is a collection of his short stories. Lucas has been affiliated with the University of Tennessee at Knoxville in various capacities since 1970.

Further Readings
Black Writers, first edition, Gale, 1989.

Lucielia Turner

Character in *The Women of Brewster Place*

Lucy

Jamaica Kincaid
Novel, 1990

Jamaica Kincaid's third book follows the life of a young Caribbean immigrant named Lucy. She has run from the limited world of her family, and their expectations that she go to nursing school. After relocating in the United States to work as a nanny for a white couple, Lucy is alienated by the people she encounters. Her employer Mariah, for instance, cannot—despite good intentions—connect with Lucy's view of the world, relationships, and human communication, and a series of unsuccessful social encounters sets Lucy and Mariah apart culturally.

Lucy is gripped by nostalgia for her homeland, yet troubled by memories of rejection by her mother. She befriends Peggy, an Irish girl of whom Mariah disapproves. Both Peggy and Mariah introduce Lucy to male acquaintances with whom, during the course of the **novel**, Lucy has affairs. The first, Hugh, has traveled around the world and understands the pitfalls of cross-cultural interactions. The second, Paul, is an artist.

A relative named Maude Quick visits Lucy, bearing sad news. Since Lucy has been too homesick and ambivalent to read her mother's letters from home, she is not aware that her father has died in poverty. Now, Lucy sends all her money back to the Caribbean, and Mariah sends twice that amount in sympathy. For the first time, Lucy talks about her feelings toward her mother, and later writes her a final letter, giving a false address. Mariah and her husband Lewis have divorced, and Mariah eventually comes to depend heavily on Lucy. Finally, Lucy moves in with Peggy and goes to work for a photographer, Timothy Simon. The novel ends with Lucy's search for self unresolved.

Lucy Josephine Potter

Character in *Lucy*

Lucy Tate

Character in *Sent for You Yesterday*

Lula

Character in *Dutchman*

Luther McGregor

Character in *Lonely Crusade*

Lutie Johnson

Character in *The Street*

Lutiebell Gussie Mae Jenkins

Character in *Purlie Victorious*

Lyrics of Lowly Life

Paul Laurence Dunbar
Poetry, 1896

Lyrics of Lowly Life was **Paul Laurence Dunbar**'s first best seller. It was promoted by the famous American critic William Dean Howells, who reviewed Dunbar's earlier collections *Oak and Ivy* (1893) and *Majors and Minors* (1895) for the magazine *Harper's Weekly*. *Lyrics of Lowly Life* encouraged popular acceptance of Dunbar's work and helped establish him as a major American poet. It also brought him some financial security: the publisher agreed to pay Dunbar a monthly income if he promised to publish his future work with him. The collection includes poems in standard English, such as "Ere Sleep Comes Down to Soothe the Weary Eyes," and in African American dialect, such as "When de Co'n Pone's Hot." These dialect poems, which constitute only about a third of Dunbar's poetic output, attracted the most attention from Dunbar's readers. In his introduction to *Lyrics of Lowly Life,* Howells helped define Dunbar's work by focusing on the dialect poems.

In his dialect poems, Dunbar depicted the folklife and beliefs of late nineteenth-century African Americans. Concentrating largely on humorous situations, Dunbar vividly portrayed the emotions and thoughts of his characters with tenderness and sensitivity. Howells declared that Dunbar's dialect poems were his most original contribution to American **poetry**. The critic recognized in these verses a new and different depiction of rural African American life, drawn with humor and understanding. At the same time, however, by concentrating public attention on these poems, Howells raised expectations about the type of poetry Dunbar could publish and made it hard for the poet to earn acceptance as a writer of more conventional poetry. It became difficult for Dunbar to publish his non-dialect verse—in which he explored his personal pain and suffering—notwithstanding the fact that he was an accomplished prosodist and explored serious philosophical themes with delicately handled imagery.

M

Freeing yourself was one
thing; claiming ownership of
that freed self was another.

Beloved, Toni Morrison, 1987

M. C. Higgins

Character in *M. C. Higgins, the Great*

M. C. Higgins, the Great

Virginia Hamilton
Novel, 1971

The title character of **Virginia Hamilton**'s *M. C. Higgins, the Great* is a thoughtful black teenager who matures as he sorts through conflicting allegiances to his father, his past, and his mother and siblings. Residing with his close-knit family in the Cumberland Mountains, M. C. Higgins wants the clan to move away from an unstable strip-mining heap that is located above their home and which threatens their safety. Though he feels the same attachment to the past as his father, Jones Higgins, M. C. can face the possibility of a different life. He devises a scheme for his mother Banina to sing for James K. Lewis, a stranger who is recording local music, and hopes that she will secure a recording contract and enable the family to move away from the danger. When his scheme falls through, M. C. starts to build a retaining wall that may save his family if the heap slides down the mountain. *M. C. Higgins, the Great* was the first book to be awarded both the National Book Award and the Newbery Medal.

Ma Chess

Character in *Annie John*

Ma Palagada

Character in *The Slave Girl*

Joaquim Maria Machado de Assis

Brazilian novelist and short story writer
Born June 21, 1839.
Died September 29, 1908.

Machado de Assis was considered the foremost Brazilian man of letters at the end of the nineteenth century. Born in Rio de Janeiro to a black house painter and a Portuguese mother, he was trained as a proofreader and typesetter but later became a government bureaucrat. Popular with readers and critics alike—he was already acclaimed in his native country by the time he was twenty-five—Machado de Assis was made president for life of the newly founded Brazilian Academy of Letters in 1897. He continued to write until his death in 1908.

Machado de Assis did not deal with his own mixed heritage in his work. Instead, he concentrated on documenting the foibles of the mostly white Brazilian upper middle class. His most noted works include the **novels** *Memórias póstumas de Braz Cubas* (1881; translated as *Epitaph of a Small Winner*, 1952), the **autobiography** of a dead man, and *Dom Casmurro* (1899), which examines jealousy, hatred, and conceit. Similarly pessimistic in tone, *Quincas Borba* (1891; translated as *Philosopher or Dog?*, 1954) is the story of a philosopher who discovers that his dog's love means more to him than human love or material possessions.

Further Readings
Black Literature Criticism, Gale, 1992.
Contemporary Authors, Volume 107, Gale, 1983.
Twentieth-Century Literary Criticism, Volume 10, Gale, 1983.

Machine Dog

Character in *No Place to Be Somebody: A Black-Black Comedy*

Mack

Character in *Look What They Done to My Song*

William Wellington Mackey

American playwright
Born May 28, 1937.

Mackey's **plays** concern the political struggles of African Americans. He earned a

B.A. from Southern University in 1959 and an M.Ed. from the University of Minnesota in 1964. While working as a physical therapist, Mackey wrote his first play, *Behold! Cometh the Vanderkellans!* (1965), which focuses on the breakdown of a well-established black family. His *A Requiem for Brother X* (1973) was inspired by the death of **Malcolm X** and develops within the context of a family gathering. Mackey received a Rockefeller Foundation Playwright's Grant in 1972 to begin his play *Love Me, Love Me, Daddy, or I Swear I'm Gonna Kill You* (1982).

Further Readings

Black Writers, first edition, Gale, 1989.

Dictionary of Literary Biography, Volume 38: *Afro-American Writers after 1955: Dramatists and Prose Writer,* Gale, 1985.

Macon Dead

Character in *Song of Solomon*

Madame Neilsen

Character in *Les Blancs*

Madge Ann Fishbond

Character in *There Is a Tree More Ancient Than Eden*

Madge Perkins

Character in *If He Hollers Let Him Go*

Naomi Long Madgett

American poet, educator, and publisher
Born July 5, 1923.

Madgett, who has also written as Naomi Cornelia Long and Naomi Long Witherspoon, has been honored both for her **poetry** and for her role in introducing the works of African American writers into school classrooms.

The daughter of a Baptist minister, Madgett was raised in a highly religious household with great respect for the written word. Her first collection of poetry, *Songs to a Phantom Nightingale* (1941), was published before she turned eighteen years of age. After graduating from Virginia State College, marrying, raising a child, and working as a reporter for the African American weekly *Michigan Chronicle,* Madgett began teaching English with an emphasis on black literature at Detroit area high schools in the mid-1950s. From 1968 until her retirement in 1985 she taught English at Eastern Michigan University.

Madgett's collections of poetry include *One and the Many* (1956), *Pink Ladies in the Afternoon* (1972), *Octavia and Other Poems* (1988), and *Remembrance of Spring* (1993). She has also edited anthologies of verse and published nonfiction works for students on literature and creative writing.

See also **Poetry of Naomi Long Madgett**

Further Readings

Black Writers, second edition, Gale, 1994.

Dictionary of Literary Biography, Volume 76: *Afro-American Writers, 1940-1955,* Gale, 1988.

Haki R. Madhubuti

American poet, essayist, and critic
Born February 23, 1942.

One of the most influential contemporary black American poets, Madhubuti has published several collections of verse, including *Think Black* (1967), *Don't Cry, Scream* (1969), and *We Walk the Way of the New World* (1970). His **poetry** made him a leading voice of the **black arts movement**. In a diverse and inventive style that employs black dialect, inventive wordplay, graphic imagery, and structures and rhythms derived from **jazz**, Madhubuti's poetry challenges white **racism** and black passivity and calls for black pride and self-determination.

Madhubuti was born Don Luther Lee in Little Rock, Arkansas, on February 23, 1942. His father abandoned the family soon afterwards, and Madhubuti was raised by his mother in Detroit, Michigan. His mother died when he was sixteen; he completed high school in Chicago, then served in the army from 1960 to 1963. He began writing poetry in the 1960s, while working at a variety of odd jobs in Chicago.

In 1967, Madhubuti founded the Third World Press to publish the work of black writers. Starting in 1968, he also held various teaching and writing positions at American universities. In 1973, he rejected his "slave name" and adopted the name Haki R. Madhubuti, which means "strong" and "precise" in Swahili. While continuing to write and publish poetry, he turned increasingly to the **essay** as a means to promote black culture and to call for the development of black institutions and African-centered education. In essays collected in *Black Men: Obsolete, Single, Dangerous?* (1990), he examines and proposes solutions for dilemmas that confront black American men and undermine black families. He has also edited *Why L.A. Happened: Implications of the '92 Los Angeles Rebellion* (1993) and written the social examination *Claiming Earth: Race, Rape, Ritual, Richness in America and the Search for Enlightened Empowerment* (1994).

See also **Poetry of Haki R. Madhubuti**

Madhubuti was an important figure in the black arts movement.

Further Readings

Black Literature Criticism, Gale, 1992.

Dictionary of Literary Biography, Volume 41: *Afro-American Poets since 1955,* Gale, 1985.

Dictionary of Literary Biography Documentary Series, Volume 8: *The Black Aesthetic Movement,* Gale, 1991.

Melhem, D. H., *Heroism in the New Black Poetry: Introductions and Interviews,* University Press of Kentucky, 1990.

Madume

Character in *The Concubine*

Mag

Character in *Our Nig*

Magda

Series character in *The "Guyana Quartet"*

Magic Frog

Character in *The Story of Jumping Mouse*

 ## Roger Mais

Jamaican novelist and playwright
Born August 11, 1905.
Died June 21, 1955.

A supporter of the Jamaican nationalist movement, Mais is best known for his three **novels** of social protest. Born in 1905 into a middle-class family in Kingston, Jamaica, he grew up and was educated in Jamaica's Blue Mountains; his writings, however, often examine and reveal his empathy with the urban slum

Major is best known for his experimental fiction.

Clarence Major

American novelist and poet
Born December 31, 1936.

Major is considered a pioneer in American experimental fiction. His works—characterized by self-reflexive narratives and authorial intrusions—focus on the nature of fiction and reality, and his innovative use of language has earned him widespread critical attention. He has been credited with charting a new course in American fiction.

Major was born on December 31, 1936, in Atlanta, Georgia, and raised in Chicago, Illinois. An avid reader as a youth, he published his first collection of **poetry,** *The Fires That Burn in Heaven* (1954) at the age of eighteen. A number of poetry collections have followed over the years, and Major has also written nonfiction, including *Dictionary of Afro-American Slang* (1970). In *Fun & Games* (1990), Major's collection of short "fictions," the author continues to bend and twist social **realism** around experimental narratives and prose.

Major's reputation as a writer rests on his **novels.** He published his first, *All-Night Visitors*, in 1969, and followed with *No* in 1979. Most critics, however, consider *Reflex and Bone Structure* (1975) and *Emergency Exit* (1979), two novels about young black men who struggle for self-definition in a hostile society, to be his most accomplished works. Using surreal imagery, Major explores the relationship between author, reader, and text.

Further Readings

Black Literature Criticism, Gale, 1992.

Black Writers, second edition, Gale, 1994.

Dictionary of Literary Biography, Volume 33: *Afro-American Fiction Writers after 1955,* Gale, 1984.

dwellers. Mais began his literary career as a journalist, reviewer, and short-story writer. In 1944, he was imprisoned for attacking English **colonialism** in his **essay** "Now We Know." While in prison, he began his first novel, *The Hills Were Joyful Together,* which was published nine years later in 1953. Mais followed with the novels *Brother Man* (1954), which focuses on the Caribbean religious movement known as Rastafarianism, and *Black Lightning* (1955), a biblical allegory centering on a sculptor. He died of cancer in Kingston in 1955.

Further Readings

Dictionary of Literary Biography, Volume 125: *Twentieth-Century Caribbean and Black African Writers,* Second Series, Gale, 1993.

Maisie

Character in *Mine Boy* and *Minty Alley*

Majors and Minors

Paul Laurence Dunbar
Poetry, 1895

Although it was published by a small printing company in Toledo, Ohio, **Paul Laurence**

William Dean Howells's review of this volume helped launch Dunbar's career.

Dunbar's second collection of **poetry**, *Majors and Minors,* was a major step in establishing the poet's reputation. Henry A. Tobey, a Toledo doctor, and Charles Thatcher, an attorney, sponsored a limited edition of 1000 copies because Dunbar himself was too poor to help pay the costs. In addition, the volume attracted the attention of America's foremost literary critic, William Dean Howells, who reviewed the collection for *Harper's Weekly.* Howells praised Dunbar's work, comparing it to the work of ethnic poets such as Robert Burns and James Russell Lowell.

Drawing some poems from the earlier collection *Oak and Ivy*, *Majors and Minors* provides an overview of Dunbar's poetry. It celebrates both joy and sorrow in poems such as "When Malindy Sings," a celebration of Dunbar's mother, and "The Deserted Plantation," a wistful memory of pre-emancipation days. It is divided into two sections. The sixty-nine "Majors" poems, which Dunbar considered his best work, are written in standard English. Many of them follow the conventions of English nature poetry in the tradition of John Keats and Percy Bysshe Shelley. In them, Dunbar celebrates the seasons, the passing of the days, flowers, birds, and other natural wonders. The other twenty-four poems, the "Minors," are written in African American dialect. One example of this type is "The Party," depicting life on a plantation as joyful and carefree, where churchgoers freely mix with sinners and where the music inspires even "Cripple Joe," stricken with rheumatism, to get up and dance. Although there were fewer of these "Minors" poems in the volume, Howells' review singled them out for praise and established a public expectation for more poetry in this vein from Dunbar. Dunbar found it increasingly difficult to publish serious poetry in the standard English that he preferred.

Makeba, an internationally recognized singer and actor.

Makak

Character in *Dream on Monkey Mountain*

Miriam Makeba

South African musician and autobiographer
Born March 4, 1932.

Zensi Miriam Makeba gained international renown after starring in the anti-apartheid, semi-documentary film *Come Back Africa* in 1959. Although she had been exiled from South Africa when she was very young, she soon secured a reputation as a singer and interpreter of native African folk songs. Makeba became equally known for her anti-apartheid activities, protesting the unfairness of the governmental system that discriminated against black South Africans.

Although she was the daughter of a teacher and a domestic worker and had worked as a domestic servant in South Africa, Makeba was a well-known singer and actor in her native country and toured South Africa, Zimbabwe, and the Congo with a singing group in the mid-1950s before making *Come Back Africa*. Following a screening of the film at the Venice Film Festival, Makeba traveled to London, where she met performer Harry Belafonte. Impressed with her renditions of native African songs, Belafonte became Makeba's promoter and introduced her to American audiences. A guest appearance on *The Steve Allen Show* in November, 1959, marked the beginning of a new career in America for Makeba. Although she became famous for singing African tunes in her Xhosan tribal dialect, Makeba has also sung many other types of music. Her 1965 album *An Evening with Belafonte/Makeba* won a Grammy award for best folk music recording of the year.

Makeba's career took a downturn in the mid-1960s after she married social activist and Black Panther **Stokely Carmichael**. Many of her singing engagements were cancelled in the United States; in order to keep working, Makeba left for Europe. In 1987, she returned to Africa as part of Paul Simon's "Graceland" tour of the continent. She documents her life in her memoir *Makeba: My Story* (1987). Twenty-four songs from her repertoire have been collected in *The World of African Song* (1971).

Further Readings
Black Writers, first edition, Gale, 1989.

Makeba: My Story

Miriam Makeba
Autobiography, 1987

South African singer **Miriam Makeba** wrote her life story with the help of American writer James Hall. At the time Makeba was in her fifties and had achieved international success, but her childhood had been a case study of **apartheid** and violence. *Makeba: My Story* chronicles her life in a poor village on the outskirts of Pretoria where she began singing with her church choir. Harry Belafonte saw Makeba perform in the film *Come Back, Africa* and sponsored her emigration to the United States. Her high-profile personal relationship with Black Panther **Stokely Carmichael** caused her to lose her American residency status.

Makus T'mwarba

Character in *Babel-17*

Malcolm X

American autobiographer and orator
Born May 19, 1925.
Died February 21, 1965.

Malcolm X became famous in the mid-1950s as the foremost spokesperson for the **Nation of Islam**. He opposed the **civil rights movement** and believed that the only response to **racism** was complete withdrawal from Western society. With the help of **Alex Haley**, Malcolm recorded his many dramatic personal and political transformations in ***The Autobiography of Malcolm X*** (1965).

Born Malcolm Little in Omaha, Nebraska, Malcolm was the son of a Baptist minister who supported the views of separatist **Marcus Garvey**. After the family was chased out of Nebraska by the Ku Klux Klan, they settled in Mason, Michigan, where their home was burned and Malcolm's father was murdered. The strain of these events sent Malcolm's mother to a mental institution, and Malcolm and his siblings were placed in foster homes. Malcolm joined one of his half-sisters in Boston and soon drifted into crime. In 1946, he was arrested for robbery and sentenced to ten years in prison. Although incarceration initially heightened his psychological turmoil, Malcolm soon began to educate himself in the prison library. Introduced to the teachings of Elijah Muhammad, leader of the Nation of Islam, Malcolm began a daily correspondence. Upon his release from prison in 1952, Malcolm joined Muhammad in Detroit and took the name Malcolm X to signify the loss of his true African name.

Malcolm X addresses an integration rally in Harlem, 1963.

Malcolm rose quickly in the Nation of Islam. In 1954, he became minister at Harlem's Mosque Number Seven, where he came to national prominence as the spokesperson for many blacks in northern ghettos. Malcolm proved himself extremely effective at proselytizing, and the membership of the church increased greatly after Muhammad made him his first national minister. But Muhammad grew jealous of his minister's fame and Malcolm became increasingly critical of his leader's materialism and sexual excesses. In 1963, their relationship became even more strained after Malcolm violated Muhammad's commandment of silence about the assassination of President John F. Kennedy. Muhammad then ordered Malcolm to be silent for ninety days; though Malcolm complied, increasing disillusionment led him to break with the Nation of Islam.

During this period, Malcolm had begun writing his **autobiography** with Haley. According to Haley, it was only at his urging of Haley that Malcolm agreed not to revise the book into a polemic against his former mentor. Malcolm subsequently made a pilgrimage to Mecca, where he underwent a transformation and began to espouse his belief that American social problems were not entirely based on race. Considered a threat by the Nation of Islam, Malcolm was assassinated in Harlem by members of the organization. *The Autobiography of Malcolm X* was published after his death, as was *Malcolm X Speaks* (1965), a collection of his **speeches**.

Further Readings

Black Literature Criticism, Gale, 1992.

Black Writers, first edition, Gale, 1989.

Goldman, Peter Louis, *Death and Life of Malcolm X,* University of Illinois Press, 1979.

Malcolm X

Spike Lee
Film, 1992

At nearly three-and-a-half hours long, **Spike Lee**'s *Malcolm X* is an **epic biography** of the multifaceted black leader. Lee fought to make this film, arguing that **Malcolm X** should be portrayed by a black director. Once chosen to direct the film, Lee withstood criticism from all sides; some feared Lee's portrayal of Malcolm X would be too radical, while others worried that Lee would depict the **Nation of Islam** in a negative light. Lee also wrangled with Warner Brothers film studio, which assumed financial—but not creative—control of the film after Lee exceeded his budget. Reaction to the completed film was mixed, but most critics acknowledged that presenting Malcolm X's life on screen was a formidable challenge.

In the film's early, most colorful scenes, Malcolm—who is played by Denzel Washington—is shown as a street hustler in Boston and in Harlem. He runs numbers, snorts cocaine, and participates in petty burglaries, before being arrested. In jail Malcolm educates himself and learns about the Nation of Islam. Once Malcolm emerges from jail, he allies himself with the founder of the Nation of Islam, Elijah Muhammad. Malcolm quickly gains a following as an inspiring orator; he preaches that whites are evil and that blacks must become self-sufficient. Lee filmed some of the scenes depicting Malcolm's public appearances in black and white, just as they would have appeared in news footage.

Eventually, Malcolm grows disillusioned with Elijah Muhammad, who is attracted to beautiful women and material possessions. Malcolm distances himself from the Nation of Islam and makes a pilgrimage to Mecca. There, he is embraced by Muslims of different backgrounds and begins to rethink and reject some of his earlier views on race. Just as Malcolm is reaching a new stage in his spiritual development, he is assassinated. Lee ends his film with an image of the endurance of Malcolm X's legacy by showing **Nelson Mandela** as he teaches schoolchildren in South Africa about Malcolm X.

Malcolm X: The Man and His Times

John Henrik Clarke, editor
Essays, 1969

Through **essays** by various authors, **John Henrik Clarke**'s *Malcolm X: The Man and His Times* offers a multifaceted look at the religious and political leader **Malcolm X** at different phases of his life and career. Most of the essays in this book, which Clarke edited, are written by people who knew Malcolm X or were deeply influenced by his **speeches** and the events of his life. Although the vast majority of the contributors admire Malcolm X, a few are critical; for instance, the Reverend Wyatt Tee Walker, a former aide to **Martin Luther King Jr.**, quarrels with Malcolm X's adherence to **black nationalism**. Clarke also includes several of Malcolm X's own speeches in this collection.

Mama

Terry McMillan
Novel, 1987

In 1987 **Terry McMillan** published her first **novel**, *Mama*, which won an American Book Award the following year. *Mama* depicts the struggles of a poverty-stricken black American family from 1964 to 1984. The story is set initially in Point Haven, Michigan, a small, depressed industrial town, where blacks work at the Diamond Crystal Salt Factory or at the Presto-Lite spark plug factory, or as domestics. The action centers on Mildred Peacock, a twenty-seven-year-old mother of five children, whom she strives to support despite her son's drug addiction and eventual imprisonment; her own alcoholism; and her violent-tempered and unfaithful husband, Crook.

Leaving Crook, Mildred attempts to gain financial security for her family, by working at a variety of jobs, including, briefly and reluctantly, as a prostitute. Eventually, she goes on welfare. She also takes in male boarders with questionable pasts, including one that sexually molests her eldest daughter, Freda, aged fourteen. Freda is sensitive to her mother's plight, but disapproves of her methods of dealing with it. The resourceful Mildred finds family and friends more helpful than **religion**. "It ain't that I don't believe in God, I just don't trust his judgment," she says.

Mildred moves in the 1970s to Los Angeles, where a government program enables her to buy a house for her family. In the 1980s, with her children grown up, Mildred returns to Point Haven. She has given up alcohol and cigarettes, reconciled with Freda, and plans to enter a community college and pursue a career.

Mama Day

Gloria Naylor
Novel, 1988

Gloria Naylor's *Mama Day* is set on an all-black rural island called Willow Springs, located off the coasts of Georgia and South Carolina. The settlement was founded by Sapphira Wade, an African slave and sorceress who married and later murdered her owner after forcing him to bequeath his land to his slaves and their offspring. The **novel** focuses on two of Sapphira's descendants—Mama Day, the elderly leader and mystical healer of Willow Springs, and Ophelia "Cocoa" Day, Mama Day's strong-willed grandniece, who lives in New York City but returns to Willow Springs every summer. The book alternates between narratives about Mama Day and stories about Cocoa and her husband George Andrews, a young black man who lives by reason and ritual. Their lives collide when, visiting Mama Day on Willow Springs, Cocoa is secretly poisoned by the evil-spirited Ruby. George is forced to put aside his rational thinking to save her. Ultimately, George saves Cocoa, but only by great personal sacrifice. Meanwhile, Mama Day puts a voodoo curse on Ruby, who dies electrocuted by lightning.

Mama Day

Character in *Mama Day*

Mama Luka

Character in *The Time-Ago Tales of Jahdu*

Mamie Mayson

Character in *Pinktoes*

Mamma Habblesham

Character in *Let the Lion Eat Straw*

"the man"

Character in *The Beautyful Ones Are Not Yet Born*

The Man Died: Prison Notes of Wole Soyinka

Wole Soyinka
Autobiography, 1972

Wole Soyinka's series of autobiographical reflections was originally written in a Nigerian prison, while he was detained without charge during 1967 and 1968. His scribbled notes were eventually collected as *The Man Died.* The title was inspired by a telegram about the beating death of one of the author's colleagues. Soyinka expresses various thoughts about his predicament and the political situation in Nigeria in many formats, including **poetry**, anecdotes, letters, and philosophical musings. More specific discussions of the author's political leanings include an endorsement of a lesser-known group called Third Force. Some stories are immediately personal. At one point Soyinka was sent to a doctor and attempted to make an external contact through the man. Another time he became convinced that his prison cell was no more than a capsule and became hysterically disturbed. Although many of the political and literary references made in passing may be unknown to readers unfamiliar with Nigerian history and culture, much of the material records the mundane details of prison life, which are used as metaphors for withstanding the pressures of injustice. Soyinka reports having a dream about bricklaying, indicative of the growing numbness he feels towards an outside world he cannot see or interact with directly. The entirety of the work Soyinka completed while in prison is arranged in forty-one numbered sections, with a short introduction and several appendices added for publication. The sections appear in loose chronological order. The introduction takes place in Lagos and is followed by coverage of Soyinka's arrest, an interrogation period culminating in the release of a false confession, and a prison transfer to Kaduna. Events leading up to Soyinka's release involve executions of fellow prisoners, a hunger strike, and a false rumor of an impending pardon.

A Man of the People

Chinua Achebe
Novel, 1966

Chinua Achebe's fourth **novel**, *A Man of the People,* reflects events in his native Nigeria. Its publication in January of 1966 came as the Nigerian military was seizing power in the country. The novel examines the loss of political power and stability in postcolonial Africa. It also addresses the question of morality in politics, the meaning and function of national leadership, and the ways that people involved in politics are corrupted. *A Man of the People* takes place in an unnamed African country that has gained independence from its colonial rulers. The narrator of the story is Odili, a university graduate who has lost faith in the ability of his people to govern themselves. His antagonist is Chief Nanga, who exploits the national government as a means for personal gain. Although Nanga is ingratiating, he is mainly concerned with gaining wealth and power rather than in the well-being of his compatriots.

Odili and Nanga confront each other over a variety of issues. Odili encourages an agenda that he believes will benefit the country's citizens. Nanga, however, represents himself as an agent of the people and discourages public trust in Odili by presenting him as an un-African agent of the colonial powers. This attitude allows Nanga and his followers to exploit public funds for personal gain. Thoroughly disgusted with the leadership his people have chosen for themselves, Odili concludes that the strong social and political structures of native African village life have been replaced by anarchy on a national scale. Nanga's misuse of the public's money eventually leads to a national economic crisis and a political scandal. False national election returns further complicate the situation. The military threatens to intervene, and the novel ends with the political situation unresolved.

The Man Who Cried I Am

John A. Williams
Novel, 1967

The Man Who Cried I Am, which brought **John A. Williams** international recognition, is an apocalyptic treatment of the exploitation of blacks by white society. Set in 1963, in the interval between the early successes of the **civil rights movement** and the violent riots that swept American ghettos later in that decade, the **novel** expresses Williams's grand vision of black revolutionary determination and racist white conspiracies.

Max Reddick is a black journalist and novelist living in Amsterdam, where he is slowly dying of colon cancer. He travels to Paris to attend the funeral of a writer named Harry Ames, whom Williams modeled on **Richard Wright**. While there, Reddick discovers that Ames has been murdered, because he uncovered a plot by Western nations to prevent the unification of Africa. Reddick then learns that political figures in the United States are planning a genocidal solution to America's race problem, closely resembling Adolf Hitler's "Final Solution." The plan is code-named "King Alfred," and in his struggle to establish the details and publish the results of his research, Reddick battles with his own internalized **racism**. This impulse is represented by an inner voice called "the Saminone" that attempts to prevent Reddick from asserting himself and protecting not only the collective identity but the very existence of his race.

Manchild in the Promised Land

Claude Brown
Novel, 1965

Manchild in the Promised Land is an autobiographical **novel** that traces **Claude Brown**'s career and transformation from a hard-ened, streetwise young criminal. The protagonist is Sonny, who has been raised by a physically and verbally abusive father and a powerless mother. At the age of eleven, Sonny is a full member of the Buccaneers, a gang of thieves in Harlem. Sonny gets caught and is sent to the Wiltwyck School for emotionally disturbed boys. There he meets the school psychologist, Dr. Ernest Papanek, who makes a strong impression on the young man. However, the lure of the streets proves too strong for Sonny, and he is soon dealing drugs and stealing again.

When he is thirteen, Sonny is shot in the stomach while stealing bedclothes from a neighbor. Soon he ends up in Warwick Reform School, where he spends most of his teenage years. When not in reform school, he sells drugs on the street and runs con games. However, he gradually decides to leave the ghetto. He takes a variety of menial jobs and begins to explore his heritage, developing an interest in **jazz** music and Coptic **Christianity**, a sect with strong roots in African culture and language. Eventually he leaves Harlem to attend college. Sonny's growth is contrasted with the fates of his former friends and his family. His brother Pimp is arrested for armed robbery. His girlfriend Sugar becomes addicted to heroin. However, some of Sonny's friends also escape the streets. His friend Danny breaks his drug habit, marries, and raises two children. His friend Turk enlists in the Air Force and becomes a light heavyweight boxer. Sonny and his friends realize that their ability to face their lives has made their escape possible.

Nelson Mandela

South African political official and civil rights leader
Born in 1918.

A leader in the struggle against **apartheid**, Nelson Rolihlahla Mandela spent twenty-five years in South African prisons, becoming a symbol of resistance and resolve for black South Africans. In 1993 he shared the Nobel Peace

Neslon Mandela votes during South Africa's first all-race election, 1994.

Prize with F. W. de Klerk in recognition of their efforts to establish a multiracial government in South Africa. Mandela was elected South Africa's first black president in April, 1994.

The son of a tribal chief, Mandela was born in 1918 in Umtata, Transkei, South Africa. He received a law degree from the University of South Africa in 1942. Two years later he joined the African National Congress (ANC), becoming a leading proponent of a more confrontational strategy in the struggle against apartheid. In 1958, after divorcing his first wife, he married Nomzamo Winnie Madikileza (**Winnie Mandela**), a social worker and political activist. When the South African government banned the ANC in 1960, Mandela and other ANC leaders were tried on charges of treason but were acquitted. Two years later, Mandela was again arrested for his political activities and sentenced to five years in prison.

In the meantime, in 1961, the ANC had formed an underground paramilitary wing, Umkonto we Sizwe ("Spear of the Nation"), which Mandela commanded. Mandela's role in the organization was revealed in 1963; a year later, he was sentenced to life imprisonment. Following his conviction, possession of his writings was made a criminal offense. Nonetheless, collections of his **speeches** and **essays** were published abroad and widely circulated among South Africans fighting against apartheid. Among these were *No Easy Walk to Freedom* (1965), containing a 1953 address in which he discussed his three political trials, and *The Struggle Is My Life* (1978), which includes four statements from prison. While in prison, Mandela received several awards honoring his human rights accomplishments, was nominated for the Nobel Peace Prize in 1987, and became the focus of an international campaign for his release. He was freed in 1990 by order of South African president F. W. de Klerk.

Despite a bloody power struggle with Inkatha, a Zulu organization, concerning who should represent black South Africans, and the much-disputed implication of Winnie Mandela in a politically motivated murder, Mandela and the ANC managed to force de Klerk's Nationalist Party to end apartheid. South Africa held its first free elections in April, 1994, and Mandela was elected president. His **autobiography**, *Long Walk to Freedom*, appeared the same year.

Further Readings

Benson, Mary, *Nelson Mandela: The Man and the Movement*, Norton, 1986.

Black Writers, second edition, Gale, 1994.

Newsmakers: 1990, Gale, 1990.

Winnie Mandela

South African political activist
Born September, 1936.

Nomzamo Winnie Madikileza Mandela has focused worldwide attention on **apartheid** and issues confronting impoverished South African blacks, particularly women. Although her frequently controversial demands and periodic advocacy of violence to achieve black equality have alienated many apartheid groups, supporters describe her as the "mother of the nation." Her **autobiography**, *Part of My Soul Went with Him* (1985), discusses her political activism and commitment to apartheid as well as the her husband's influence on her life.

Born in Pondoland, South Africa, Mandela moved to Johannesburg in the early 1950's, where she met and later married **Nelson Mandela**. When her husband was convicted of political crimes and sentenced to life imprisonment in 1964, Winnie Mandela became a vocal member of the African National Congress (ANC).

During a thirteen-year period of government-imposed suppression of the ANC, Mandela was detained numerous times, at one time spending seventeen months in prison for illegal involvement with the ANC. In late December, 1976, Mandela was banished to Brandfort in the Orange Free State. After her Brandfort home was firebombed in 1985, the government permitted her to return to Orlando permanently. In Orlando, her association with the Mandela United Football Club, a group of toughs she described as her bodyguards, led to her arrest for kidnapping and assault. The coach of the Football Club was convicted of the murder of a teenager and Mandela stood trial in September, 1990, for related charges in the participation of the kidnapping and assault of three young black men. Although she was acquitted of participation in the beatings, she was found guilty of kidnapping and received a suspended sentence.

Her husband publicly supported her while he was in prison but, following his early release in 1990, he announced their separation. Upon Nelson Mandela's election to the presidency of South Africa, he appointed his estranged wife as to his cabinet despite significant political differences. When her criticisms of the slow pace of reform became too great, however, Nelson Mandela had her removed from his cabinet; still, she remains an elected member of Parliament.

Further Readings
Black Writers, first edition, Gale, 1989.
Contemporary Black Biography, Volume 2, Gale, 1992.

Winnie Mandella has been an activist for racial equality in South Africa since the 1960s.

Manyara
Character in *Mufaro's Beautiful Daughters: An African Tale*

Marching Blacks
Adam Clayton Powell Jr.
Nonfiction, 1945

The book-length **essay** *Marching Blacks: An Interpretive History of the Rise of the Black Common Man* is a result of **Adam Clayton Powell Jr.**'s family history in **slavery** and his own childhood vow to redefine black people as free citizens. While he supports nonviolence, he warns that if white Americans continue to ignore the call of their conscience, another civil war will result. He asserts that the journey out of slavery made a "new Negro," one willing and capable of protesting and resisting exploitation as part of an organized group. Powell recommends the Communist Party for its track record in the case of the Scottsboro brothers in particular and race relations in general. He also criticizes the state of the Christian Church just prior to the U.S. entry into World War II and the existing labor movement as well. Powell declares that the caste system separating light and dark blacks must not be supported by blacks themselves and advises them to move out of the South to avoid its effects. He calls integration the fate of choice for most American blacks and recommends picketing, voting, and boycotting to achieve it. Powell also claims that only when white Americans surrender their fears of intermarriage can blacks feel truly accepted into society.

Marcus Savage

Character in *The Learning Tree*

Margaret Street

Character in *Tar Baby*

Marge

Character in *The Landlord*

Mariah

Character in *Lucy*

Mariah Upshur

Character in *This Child's Gonna Live*

Marie Horton

Character in *The Fabulous Miss Marie*

Marq Dyeth

Character in *Stars in My Pocket Like Grains of Sand*

The Marrow of Tradition
Charles W. Chesnutt
Novel, 1901

The Marrow of Tradition, **Charles W. Chesnutt**'s second **novel**, examines the conflict between two families in Wellington, North Carolina, following the Civil War. Dr. Adam Miller and his wife head a family of mixed blood and progressive ideas. Philip Carteret, who edits the town newspaper, is the patriarch of an influential white family. He advocates racist policies and plots to take over the local government, but his conspiracy leads to violence. A riot occurs, and the Millers's son dies in it. However, Philip is forced to seek Dr. Miller's professional assistance for his own child. At first Dr. Miller refuses, but he soon relents in deference to his responsibilities as the town physician.

Paule Marshall
American novelist and short story writer
Born April 9, 1929.

Recognized as a prominent and innovative voice in contemporary American literature, Marshall has written works that reflect the language and the stories she heard in her mother's kitchen. Marshall's themes include **racism**, the individual's search for personal identity, and the importance of tradition for the African American. She was one of the first authors to explore the psychological trials and concerns of African American women.

Marshall was born in Brooklyn to parents who had emigrated from Barbados after World War I. After receiving her B.A. from Brooklyn College, Marshall worked as a researcher and staff writer for *Our World,* a small magazine that sent her to Brazil and the Caribbean. She would later draw upon these experiences in her fiction. While working for the magazine and attending Hunter College, she began writing her first **novel,** *Brown Girl, Brownstones* (1959). Although the book was largely ignored by readers until it was reprinted in 1981, it received critical praise and prompted Marshall to pursue a literary career. The book is a frank depiction of a young black girl's search for identity and increasing sexual awareness. Marshall's second novel, *The Chosen Place, the Timeless People* (1969), explores the interactions of the oppressed and the oppressor.

Marshall has won several prestigious awards. Her novella collection **Soul Clap Hands and Sing** (1961), which probes emotional and spiritual decline, won the Rosenthal Award, and her novel **Praisesong for the Widow** (1983), which concerns an affluent widow in her sixties who has lost touch with her West Indian/African American roots, received the Before Columbus American Book Award. Marshall began her long affiliation with Yale University as a lecturer in creative writing in 1970.

Further Readings

Black Literature Criticism, Gale, 1992.

Black Writers, second edition, Gale, 1994.

Dictionary of Literary Biography, Volume 33: *Afro-American Fiction Writers after 1955,* Gale, 1984.

Paule Marshall's fiction often explores the psyches of African American women.

Martha

Character in *These Low Grounds*

Tony Martin

Trinidadian historian and editor
Born February 21, 1942.

Martin is known for his works concerning African and African American history, particularly black nationalist leader **Marcus Garvey**. Martin earned a Ph.D. in 1973 and began teaching at various colleges and universities in Trinidad and Tabago and the United States. He has produced a number of books on Garvey, who founded the Universal Negro Improvement Association, including *Race First: The Ideological and Organizational Struggles of Marcus Garvey and the Universal Negro Improvement Association* (1976); *The Poetical Works of Marcus Garvey* (1983), which he edited; and *African*

Fundamentalism: A Literary and Cultural Anthology of Garvey's Harlem Renaissance (1991). Martin was renamed the chair of Wellesley College's Africana Studies department in 1985.

Further Readings

Black Writers, second edition, Gale, 1994.

Mary

Character in *Clotel; or, The President's Daughter*

Mary Bellmont

Character in *Our Nig*

Mary Dalton

Character in *Native Son*

The Masquerade

Please see *Three Plays*

Massa Arthur Swille

Character in *Flight to Canada*

The Master's Mind

Character in *The Salt Eaters*

Mark Mathabane

South African autobiographer and nonfiction writer
Born in 1960.

Born Johannes Mathabane, Mathabane is best known for his memoirs, which focus on his youth in a South African black township and his subsequent life in the United States. Mathabane studied at several American universities before earning a bachelor's degree from Dowling College in 1983. *Kaffir Boy: The True Story of a Black Youth's Coming of Age in Apartheid South Africa* (1986; *Kaffir Boy: Growing out of Apartheid,* 1987) recounts Mathabane's life in the black township of Alexandra, outside of Johannesburg, where he lived in poverty and fear until he received a scholarship to play tennis at an American college. The sequel to *Kaffir Boy, Kaffir Boy in America: An Encounter with Apartheid* (1989), contains Mathabane's reflections on the racial divisions in his adopted country, his own evolution as a writer, and his reunion with his family. The early stages of Mathabane's courtship and marriage to Gail Ernsberger, a white American journalist and writer, are memorialized in *Love in Black and White* (1992), a book they wrote together. Mathabane is also the author of *African Women: Three Generations* (1994), in which he describes the lives of his grandmother, mother, and sister in Africa.

Further Readings
Black Writers, second edition, Gale, 1994.

John F. Matheus

American short story writer
and playwright
Born September 10, 1887.
Died February 19, 1983.

John Frederick Matheus's writings focus on racial oppression and the need for Christian understanding. He received an A.B. in 1910, an A.M. in 1921, and later studied at the Sorbonne and the University of Chicago. Matheus was a professor and head of the Romance languages department at West Virginia State College from 1922 to 1953, when he was named professor emeritus. Although he wrote several **plays,** including *Tambour* (1929) and *Ouanga!* (1939), Matheus is better known for his *A Collection of Short Stories* (1974). His story "Fog" won first prize in a 1925 *Opportunity* contest for short fiction.

Further Readings
Black Writers, first edition, Gale, 1989.

Dictionary of Literary Biography, Volume 51: *Afro-American Writers from the Harlem Renaissance to 1940,* Gale, 1987.

Sharon Bell Mathis

American author of children's literature
Born February 26, 1937.

Mathis has won numerous awards for her children's books that cover a range of realistic themes, including death, drug addiction, alcoholism, and aging. Her works, however, contain a base of hope, pride, and love. Mathis was born in Atlantic City, New Jersey, in 1937 and earned a bachelor's degree in sociology in 1958 and a master's degree in library science in 1975. A teacher and librarian in various Washington, D.C., schools, she wrote her first children's book, *Brooklyn Story,* in 1970; she followed with *Sidewalk Story* (1971), winner of the Council on Interracial Books for Children Prize. Mathis received several awards for **Teacup Full of Roses** (1972) and *The Hundred Penny Box*

(1975). One of her more recent works is *Red Dog, Blue Fly: Football Poems* (1991).

Further Readings

Black Writers, second edition, Gale, 1994.

Dictionary of Literary Biography, Volume 33: *Afro-American Fiction Writers after 1955,* Gale, 1984.

Mathu

Character in *A Gathering of Old Men*

M Matigari ma Njiruungi

Ngugi wa Thiong'o
Novel, 1986

Matigari ma Njiruungi, written in Gikuyu by **Ngugi wa Thiong'o**, tells the allegorical story of Matigari ma Njiruungi's attempt to reclaim his house from colonial homesteaders. After killing Settler Williams and John Boy, the British interlopers who commandeered his home, Matigari learns that his home has been sold to John Boy Junior by Williams's son. A stint in jail for his transgressions momentarily hinders Matigari, but his escape, aided by the prostitute Guthera, permits him to travel Kenya searching for truth and justice. He is captured and sent to a mental institution, but again manages to escape. Eventually deciding that his only recourse lies in killing John Boy Junior for possession of his home, Matigari burns down the house and subsequently sustains serious injury. The **novel** ends with the wounded Matigari being swept away by a river. In 1987 *Matigari* was banned by the Kenyan government.

Matigari ma Njiruungi

Character in *Matigari ma Njiruungi*

Matthew Lovejoy

Character in *The Cotillion*

Mattie Michaels

Character in *The Women of Brewster Place*

Maude Quick

Character in *Lucy*

Mavis

Character in *The Sign in Sidney Brustein's Window*

Max Disher

Character in *Black No More*

Max Reddick

Character in *The Man Who Cried I Am*

M Julian Mayfield

American novelist, playwright, and screenwriter
Born June 6, 1928.
Died October 20, 1984.

Known for his diverse and colorful career, Julian Hudson Mayfield interpreted the black experience through varied media, often using Harlem as his literary vantage point. Born in Greer, South Carolina, in 1928, Mayfield grew up in Washington, D.C., and attended Lincoln University. He first wrote for newspapers, later becoming a scholar, university teacher, and Broadway and Hollywood actor. Mayfield's literary reputation rests on his **novels** *The Hit* (1957), about the numbers game, and *The Long Night* (1958), about a boy's search for his father. His later work conveys his involvement in and concern with the **civil rights movement** in the United States and the movement for freedom from oppression throughout the world.

Further Readings

Black Writers, first edition, Gale, 1989.

Dictionary of Literary Biography, Volume 33: *Afro-American Fiction Writers after 1955,* Gale, 1984.

Benjamin E. Mays

American educator and religious leader
Born August 1, 1894.
Died March 28, 1984.

Benjamin Elijah Mays served as president of Morehouse College, one of the premier black colleges in the United States, during the formative years of many of the country's greatest civil rights leaders. Mays helped establish the college's reputation for academic excellence and directed the college careers of **Martin Luther King Jr.**, Andrew Young, and **Julian Bond**, among others. Mays himself served as a powerful voice for civil rights, calling on both white and black extremists to find common ground and resolve their differences peacefully.

The son of a sharecropper living in South Carolina, Mays graduated from Bates College in 1920 and was ordained a Baptist minister in 1922. He taught at South Carolina State College and served as dean of Howard University's school of **religion** before moving to Atlanta to become president of Morehouse College, a position he held from 1940 until 1967.

Many of Mays' books, including *The Negro's God as Reflected in His Literature* (1938), *Seeking to Be Christian in Race Relations* (1957), and *Lord, the People Have Driven Me On* (1981), reflect his religious background. Mays wrote about his own experiences growing up in the South and helping to lead and inspire the **civil rights movement** in *Born to Rebel: An Autobiography* (1971).

Further Readings
Black Writers, first edition, Gale, 1989.

James A. Mays

American medical writer and novelist
Born May 1, 1939.

Born in Pine Bluff, Arkansas, Mays is a cardiologist who has worked at Los Angeles General Hospital and taught at the Charles R. Drew Medical School in Los Angeles since 1972. He helped found Adopt-a-Family and won

1973-76 and 1974-77 American Medical Association recognition awards.

Mays wrote his **novel** *Mercy Is King* (1975) with the hope that it would be adapted for film and television. It is a story of black and white professionals that he believes presents a more realistic image of blacks than is usually portrayed in the media. His other works include the nonfiction books *Radian* (1981) and *Circle of Five* (1981) and articles published in professional journals. He was associate editor of the *Charles R. Drew Society Newsletter* in 1973 and 1974.

Further Readings
Black Writers, first edition, Gale, 1989.

Ali A. Mazrui

Kenyan essayist
Born February 24, 1933.

Born in Mombasa, Kenya, in 1933 and educated in England and New York, Ali Al'Amin Mazrui is a social scientist noted for his ability to reconcile paradoxes and provoke critical thinking. He is the author of **poetry, short stories, literary criticism**, journal articles, and more than twenty books on contemporary politics. His works address such topics as disunity among African nations, violence and its impact on African society, the problems associated with Africa's multilingualism, the role of the West in African politics, and Africa's place in the modern world. His most recent works include ***The Africans: A Triple Heritage*** (1986), which was adapted for broadcast by the British Broadcasting Corporation, and *Cultural Forces in World Politics* (1990).

Further Readings
Black Writers, second edition, Gale, 1994.
Dictionary of Literary Biography, Volume 125: *Twentieth-Century Caribbean and Black African Writers,* Second Series, Gale, 1993.
Nyang, Sulayman S., *Ali A. Mazrui: The Man and His Work,* Brunswick, 1981.

John S. Mbiti

Kenyan writer, editor, poet, and translator
Born November 30, 1931.

An Anglican priest and a professor in New Testament and African religions and philosophy, John Samuel Mbiti has focused on the subjects of theology and comparative **religion** in his books. Born in Kitui, Kenya, in 1931, he attended college in Kenya and England, earning his Ph.D. at Cambridge University. His publications include *African Religions and Philosophy* (1969), *Love and Marriage in Africa* (1973), *Death and the Hereafter in the Light of Christianity and African Religion* (1974), *Introduction to African Religion* (1975), and *Christian and Jewish Dialogue on Man* (1980), which he edited. Mbiti also wrote the *English-Kamba Vocabulary* (1959) and *Poems of Nature and Faith* (1969).

Further Readings

Black Writers, first edition, Gale, 1989.

George Marion McClellan

American poet and short story writer
Born September 29, 1860.
Died May 17, 1934.

Born in Belfast, Tennessee, McClellan attended Fisk University and Hartford Theological Seminary. While he worked as an educator and a minister, McClellan wrote **poetry** and short stories that are primarily remembered for their conservatism and their intentional emulation of Western poetic styles. The privately published *Poems* (1895) exemplifies McClellan's mainstream style of sentimental, genteel poetry. Although he addresses concerns of Southern blacks in the **short story** collection *Old Greenbottom Inn and Other Stories* (1906), McClellan models his characters after tragic Greek and Shakespearean heroes. Many of McClellan's poems and short stories were reprinted in *The*

Path of Dreams (1916). McClellan had been planning to write a history of American literature at the time of his death in 1934.

See also **Poetry of George Marion McClellan**

Further Readings

Black Writers, first edition, Gale, 1989.

Dictionary of Literary Biography, Volume 50: *Afro-American Writers before the Harlem Renaissance,* Gale, 1986.

Colleen J. McElroy

American poet and short story writer
Born October 30, 1935.

Colleen Johnson McElroy is a poet, **short story** writer, and artist. She was born in St. Louis, Missouri, in 1935 and attended the University of Maryland, Harris Teachers College, Kansas State University, and the University of Washington. She has worked as a speech clinician and English professor. McElroy has garnered several awards, including the Best of Small Presses award for **poetry** and the Pushcart Book Press award. McElroy's poetry collections include *What Madness Brought Me Here: New and Selected Poems, 1968-1988* (1990). *Jesus and Fat Tuesday and Other Short Stories* (1987) is a collection of her fiction.

Further Readings

Black Writers, second edition, Gale, 1994.

James E. McGirt

American poet and short story writer
Born September, 1874.
Died June 13, 1930.

James Ephraim McGirt's most notable contribution to black literature is generally considered to be his publication *McGirt's Maga-*

zine, a periodical that reprinted the work of major black writers, such as **Paul Laurence Dunbar** and **W.E.B. Du Bois.** McGirt was born in 1874 in Robeson County, North Carolina, and educated in private and public schools. Never receiving the same critical attention or respect as the writers he published in his magazine, McGirt wrote **poetry** in folk dialect and in standard English, in the genteel, sentimental style. After receiving mixed reviews for his first poetry volumes—*Avenging the Maine, A Drunken A.B., and Other Poems* (1899) and *For Your Sweet Sake* (1906)—McGirt shifted to prose and **short stories.**

Further Readings

Black Writers, second edition, Gale, 1994.

Dictionary of Literary Biography, Volume 50: *Afro-American Writers before the Harlem Renaissance,* Gale, 1986.

McGirt's Magazine

James E. McGirt
Magazine, published 1903-1909

The Philadelphia journal *McGirt's Magazine* began as a monthly journal and was later published quarterly. **James E. McGirt** showcased his own work, including short stories, enough of his **poetry** to later fill three volumes, and his serial "Black Hand" as well. In his editorials, McGirt spoke out against the new Jim Crow laws. The magazine also supported groups like **W. E. B. Du Bois**'s **Niagara Movement**, and published Du Bois's own material. The National Afro-American Council was also publicized by the magazine. The official journal of the Constitutional Brotherhood of America, *McGirt's Magazine* reprinted articles by commentators Richard R. Wright Jr., Francis J. Grimke, Benjamin T. Tanner, Mary Church Terrell, and others. The primary aim was to rally black voters to support the Fourteenth and Fifteenth Constitutional Amendments.

Claude McKay

Jamaican-born American poet
and novelist
Born September 15, 1889.
Died May 22, 1948.

McKay was a major writer of the **Harlem Renaissance.** His work, which expresses his anger about the poor economic and social position of blacks in American society, helped establish him as a voice for the **civil rights movement** that fought for racial equality after World War I.

McKay was born Festus Claudius McKay on September 15, 1889, to a family of peasant farmers in Sunny Ville, Jamaica. In 1912, after working as a police constable in the city of Kingston, McKay published his first collections of **poetry**: *Songs of Jamaica,* which drew on his Jamaican peasant background, and *Constab Ballads,* which reflected his experiences in Kingston. The two volumes won him the Jamaican Medal of the Institute of Arts and Sciences. He used the money he received to move to the United States. In 1914, he married Eulalie Imelda Edwards, whom he later divorced.

The United States proved not to be the land of opportunity for which McKay had hoped. Editors of larger publications refused his work because he sympathized with black causes. "If We Must Die" (1919) most clearly stated his belief that even interracial violence was preferable to maintaining the status quo. This poem was collected in **Harlem Shadows** (1922), along with other poems protesting the persecution of blacks in America. McKay also espoused communism and, in 1923, visited the Soviet Union.

Living in Europe between 1923 and 1934, McKay wrote **Home to Harlem** (1928), the first commercially successful **novel** by a black writer. He returned to Harlem himself after 1934 and published his **autobiography**, *A Long Way from Home* (1937), and a collection of **essays**, *Harlem: Negro Metropolis* (1940). Baptized into the Roman Catholic church in 1944, McKay resumed writing poetry, extolling his new faith.

He died of heart failure in Chicago on May 22, 1948, and was buried in Woodside, New York.

Further Readings

Black Literature Criticism, Gale, 1992.

Black Writers, first edition, Gale, 1989.

Dictionary of Literary Biography, Gale, Volume 4: *American Writers in Paris, 1920-1939,* 1980; Volume 45: *American Poets, 1880-1945,* First Series, 1986; Volume 51: *Afro-American Writers from the Harlem Renaissance to 1940,* 1987.

Gayle, Addison Jr., *Claude McKay: The Black Poet at War,* Broadside, 1972.

Patricia C. McKissack

American educator and author of children's literature
Born August 9, 1944.

Patricia L'Ann Carwell McKissack, who also writes as L'Ann Carwell, is a prolific children's author. Born in 1944 in Nashville, Tennessee, McKissack was a junior high school English teacher before moving to the University of Missouri, where she began teaching in 1978. Her books for children focus on a wide range of topics, including religious stories, biographies of black historical figures, and folktales. *Flossie and the Fox* (1986), for instance, is based on a folktale McKissack's grandfather told her when she was a child. In *Abram, Abram, Where Are We Going?* (1984), which won the C. S. Lewis Silver Medal, McKissack teamed up with her husband Fredrick in retelling the biblical stories about Abraham in his role as father to many nations.

Many of McKissack's works feature notable African Americans or significant events in black history. Among these are *Jesse Jackson: A Biography* (1989), about the black American religious and political leader; *James Weldon Johnson: "Lift Every Voice and Sing"* (1990), about the man who wrote the hymn that came to symbolize the civil rights struggle; *A Long Hard Journey: The Story of the Pullman Porter* (1990), for which McKissack and her husband shared the Coretta Scott King Award in 1990; and *Black Diamond: The Story of the Negro Baseball Leagues* (1994), also written with her husband.

Further Readings

Black Writers, second edition, Gale, 1994.

Major Authors and Illustrators for Children and Young Adults, Volume 4, Gale, 1993.

Terry McMillan

American novelist
Born October 18, 1951.

Terry L. McMillan's **novels** have met with increasing financial and critical success. Her writings have proven popular with African American women in particular, and her feisty black women heroines have been compared to the characters of such authors as **Alice Walker**.

McMillan was born on October 18, 1951, in Port Huron, Michigan, and developed an interest in books as a teenager. She studied African American literature at a Los Angeles community college before completing her B.S. at the University of California at Berkeley and her M.F.A. at Columbia University in 1979.

In 1987, McMillan published her first novel, *Mama*, depicting the struggles of a poverty-stricken black American family. McMillan promoted the book on her own and, six weeks after its publication, Mama went into a third printing. In 1988, it garnered an American Book Award.

McMillan's next novel, *Disappearing Acts* (1989), is about the relationship between a college-educated woman and a laborer who never finished high school. McMillan herself was involved with a man—Leonard Welch, the father of their son—who held the same occupation and educational level as the novel's character. In 1990, Welch filed a defamation suit against McMillan and her publishers; the petition was defeated in 1991.

McMillan also explored relationships in her 1992 novel *Waiting to Exhale.* Revolving around four professional black women, the novel was well received by the public and earned $2.64

Novelist Terry McMillan won an American Book Award in 1988 for *Mama*.

million for its paperback rights. McMillan co-wrote the screenplay for the novel, which was released in 1995 and starred Whitney Houston. McMillan has also edited *Breaking Ice: An Anthology of Contemporary African-American Fiction* (1990).

Further Readings

Black Writers, second edition, Gale, 1994.

Contemporary Literary Criticism, Gale, Volume 50, 1988, Volume 61, 1991.

James Alan McPherson
American short story writer
Born September 16, 1943.

McPherson is considered one of the most gifted **short story** writers to come into promi-

nence during the 1960s. Born in Savannah, Georgia, McPherson received a law degree from Harvard University and a master's degree in creative writing from the University of Iowa. His stories usually portray working-class people confronting common human problems. McPherson has published two collections, *Hue and Cry: Short Stories* (1969) and *Elbow Room: Stories* (1977), for which he was awarded the Pulitzer Prize in 1978. McPherson has held teaching positions at institutions such as the University of California and the University of Iowa, where he has taught since 1981, the year he received a MacArthur Foundation award.

See also **Short Stories of James Alan McPherson**

Further Readings

Black Writers, first edition, Gale, 1989.

Dictionary of Literary Biography, Volume 38: *Afro-American Writers after 1955: Dramatists and Prose Writers,* Gale, 1985.

McTeers
Character in *The Bluest Eye*

The Measure of Our Success
Marian Wright Edelman
Nonfiction, 1992

As an active political figure and president of the Children's Defense Fund, **Marian Wright Edelman** wrote *The Measure of Our Success: A Letter to My Children and Yours* to convey her principles to her sons and to youths in general, and "out of fear and concern for America's future." The book consists of a foreword by her son Jonah Martin Edelman, a short **autobiography** of the author, a personal letter written by Edelman to her sons regarding the racial challenges they must face, and a series of "lessons for life" in which Edelman outlines her personal and political philosophies.

A Measure of Time

Rosa Guy
Novel, 1983

Rosa Guy's *A Measure of Time* examines the life of Dorine Davis, who supports her family by shoplifting. Attracted to a Harlem hustler who exploits her for money's sake and ultimately causes her arrest, Dorine reconsiders her experiences with men and money, but becomes involved with Tom Rumley anyway. Tom gets her out of jail and introduces her to his gang of shoplifters, with whom she travels the country, using Harlem as a base. Worries about her family, for whom she is sole support, take Dorine temporarily to Alabama. During a later visit there, her consciousness is raised by a racial incident, though this has little effect on her lifestyle.

Dorine continues her pursuit of easy money in Harlem. Released from another prison term, she continues to help her Alabama family and her Harlem associates. Discouraged by Harlem's deterioration, Dorine becomes curious about the early **civil rights movement**.

Tsegaye Gabre Medhin

Please see Tsegaye Gabre-Medhin

Meditations in Limbo

Taban lo Liyong
Novel, 1970

The **novel** *Meditations in Limbo* was written by Taban lo Liyong, a writer who was born circa 1938 in either Uganda or the Sudan. His narrative contains three "characters": Taban himself, his father, and the philosopher Plato. Written in the form of an anti-novel, the book comprises a series of fragmented observations and reflections, supporting one of Liyong's views that life constitutes both complexity and chaos, and that to impose order on events and situations opposes natural confusion. In *Meditations in Limbo,* Liyong uses both his father and Plato as sounding boards for his theories and feelings; topics focus on his father's expectations for Liyong in areas such as tribal responsibilities, arranged marriages, and higher education. In addition, the author challenges Plato's concept of form as constant and enduring, believing rather that form changes and mutates.

Melanie Browne

Character in *The Women of Brewster Place*

Melinda

Character in *The Escape; or, A Leap for Freedom*

Melody Moss

Character in *Blood on the Forge*

Melvin Peterson

Character in *A Soldier's Play*

Meridian

Alice Walker
Novel, 1976

Alice Walker's second **novel**, *Meridian,* is based in part on experiences the author had while living for a time in New York's Lower East Side. Meridian Hill is a civil rights activist who has conducted an on-off relationship with a fellow worker named Truman Held. When he tracks her down in the South, where she is campaigning, ugly memories surface from her past. As a pregnant teen, Meridian enters into a loveless marriage with a womanizer. After she gives birth to a son, she comes to realize that her marriage is over. Because her mother refuses to take the child in, she gives him up for adoption. Later, when she sleeps with Truman, she becomes pregnant again and feels she must have an abortion. Then she has herself sterilized. But Meridian's life leads her back to an acceptance of motherhood when she finds herself at an all-black college, caring for a thirteen-year-old rape victim. The girl, known only as The Wild Child, is pregnant and abandoned by the surrounding community. A story about a slave and associated with a magnolia tree on the college grounds precipitates a healing crisis in Meridian's thinking. According to the story, the slave woman, Louvinie, had her tongue cut out because the stories she told scared the master's son to death. Meridian finally summons the strength to accept her heritage and take her place in a tradition of black womanhood.

Meridian Hill

Character in *Meridian*

Louise Meriwether

American novelist, biographer, and short story writer
Born May 8, 1923.

Best known as a writer of juvenile biographies of noted black figures, Meriwether also wrote the acclaimed **Daddy Was a Number Runner** (1970).

Meriwether spent her childhood living in poverty in Harlem. She later studied English at New York University and **journalism** at the University of California at Los Angeles. She held several jobs in California, working as a reporter, story analyst, and writing instructor; some of her book reviews were published in the *Los Angeles Times* and the *Los Angeles Sentinel*.

Meriwether began writing fiction in the late 1960's, when she joined the Watts Writers' Workshop. Her **novel** *Daddy Was a Number Runner* took nearly five years to complete. Set in Depression-era Harlem, the semi-autobiographical story tells of a young black girl and the effects of poverty on her family. *Daddy Was*

a Number Runner was well-received by critics, and was praised by such noted black authors as **James Baldwin**.

Hoping to offset the relative omission of blacks in American history classes, Meriwether's next four books were juvenile biographies of blacks important to American history: *The Freedom Ship of Robert Small* (1971), *The Heart Man: The Story of Daniel Hale Williams* (1972), *Don't Ride the Bus on Monday: The Rosa Parks Story* (1973), and *Fragments of the Ark* (1994), about the escape of Confederate slave Peter Mango.

Meriwether has also been active in organized black causes. She and **John Hendrik Clarke** formed the anti-Apartheid group Black Concern, she joined the Harlem Writers Guild, and she taught the fiction workshop at the Frederick Douglass Creative Arts Center.

Further Readings
Black Writers, first edition, Gale, 1989.
Dictionary of Literary Biography, *Volume 33:* Afro-American Fiction Writers after 1955, *Gale, 1984.*

Mervyn Herrick

Character in *Where the Hummingbird Flies*

Michael Bowers

Character in *South Street*

Oscar Micheaux

American novelist and filmmaker
Born January 2, 1884.
Died March 26, 1951.

Using melodramatic plots, Micheaux wrote stories that often involved his leading characters in personal and financial struggles for success that mirrored experiences in his own life. Micheaux was born in 1884 into a farming family living near Metropolis, Illinois. His first **novel,** *The Conquest: The Story of a Negro Pioneer, by the Pioneer* (1913), relates his experience as a homesteader in South Dakota. His rewrite of the story, *The Homesteader* (1917), caught the attention of a company that produced movies starring blacks for black audiences. Unable to agree on a contract with the organization, Micheaux formed his own company and wrote, produced, and directed films the rest of his life. He returned to fiction writing in the 1940s, and died in 1951 in Charlotte, North Carolina, while on a promotional tour.

Further Readings

Dictionary of Literary Biography, Volume 50: *Afro-American Writers before the Harlem Renaissance,* Gale, 1986.

Middle Passage

Charles Johnson
Novel, 1990

Charles Johnson's *Middle Passage,* narrated by protagonist Rutherford Calhoun, takes place primarily on an illegal American slave ship in 1830. A twenty-one-year-old freed slave and habitual thief, Calhoun stows away on the *Republic* in order to avoid both a forced marriage to Boston teacher Isadora Bailey and the debts he owes racketeer Papa Zeringue. Somewhat of a contradiction himself, Calhoun was educated in the classics when he was enslaved, which contrasts with his reputation as a liar and cheat. During the voyage, Calhoun discovers that the evil Captain Falcon has stolen African icons and observes him engaging in cruelty to the Allmuseri slaves. A freak wind during the return trip causes the ship to list wildly, sending many of the women and children plunging into the sea. When Calhoun learns that Falcon's secret trunk contains the sacred god of the Allmuseri, he steals the key to the prisoners' chains in an attempt to guarantee security for himself by associating with any faction who may sooner or later hold the power on the *Republic.* Eventually the Allmuseri take over the ship, wreaking violence and destruction in their revolt. When the ship circles aimlessly in the ocean due to ill-

ness among the surviving sailors and captives, Calhoun consoles and reassures those in misery. Ultimately rescued by a ship containing Papa Zeringue and Isadora Bailey as passengers, Calhoun recognizes the mystical hand of fate and marries Isadora.

Mildred Peacock

Character in *Mama*

Milkman Dead

Character in *Song of Solomon*

E. Ethelbert Miller

American poet, editor, and critic
Born November 20, 1950.

Born in New York City, Eugene Ethelbert Miller developed his **poetry** while attending Howard University. In 1974, Miller became director of the University's Afro-American Resource Center. His poetry, collected in *Andromeda* (1974), *The Land of Smiles and the Land of No Smiles* (1974), *Migrant Worker* (1978), and *Season of Hunger/Cry of Rain, Poems, 1975-1980* (1982), reflects his desire to make poetry more accessible. Miller's *Voice of a Native Son: The Poetics of Richard Wright* was published in 1990.

As an editor and critic, Miller also shapes contemporary American poetry by encouraging young talent. In 1977, he edited a collection of poetry by women, *Women Surviving Massacres and Men.* He also organizes the *Ascension* series, which enables beginning poets to read their work to a public audience.

See also **Poetry of E. Ethelbert Miller**

Further Readings

Black Writers, second edition, Gale, 1994.

Dictionary of Literary Biography, Volume 41: *Afro-American Poets since 1955,* Gale, 1985.

Kelly Miller

American educator, journalist, and pamphleteer
Born July 18, 1863.
Died December 29, 1939.

Miller was a major spokesperson for African Americans and a prominent figure at Howard University from 1890 to 1934. He graduated from Howard in 1886, and later became a professor, department head, and eventually a dean at Howard. He earned a national reputation as a writer and lecturer by positioning himself politically between radicals affiliated with the **Niagara Movement** and the conservative views of **Booker T. Washington**. In the 1920s and 1930s Kelly wrote a weekly column which appeared in more than one hundred newspapers, including the *Washington Post* and the *New York Times*. With the publication of *As to the Leopard's Spots: An Open Letter to Thomas Dixon* (1905), Kelly became a successful pamphleteer. His work is collected in *Race Adjustment* (1908) and *The Everlasting Stain* (1924).

Further Readings

Logan, Rayford W. and Winston, Michael R., eds., *Dictionary of American Negro Biography,* W. W. Norton, and Company, 1982.

May Miller

American poet and playwright
Born January 26, 1899.

Acknowledged as one of the first black playwrights to depict African Americans on stage realistically, Miller used her **plays** as a vehicle for teaching black history and portraying such black historical figures as Sojourner Truth and Haitian king Henry Christophe. Miller was born in 1899 in Washington, D.C., the daughter of scholars. She joined a theater group while a student at Howard University, leading her to become a playwright, producer, and drama teacher. Some of her plays are collected in *Negro History in Thirteen Plays* (1935), which she edited. Miller married and retired in 1943 and became a full-time poet; she subsequently wrote nine volumes of **poetry,** including *Into the Clearing* (1959) and *The Ransomed Wait* (1983). Her collected poetry was published in 1989.

Further Readings

Black Writers, second edition, Gale, 1994.
Dictionary of Literary Biography, Volume 41: *Afro-American Poets Since 1955,* Gale, 1985.

Millie Bedford Saunders

Character in *And Then We Heard the Thunder*

Ron Milner

American dramatist
Born May 29, 1938.

In his work, Ronald Milner seeks to reaffirm traditional family values and self-determination, and his dramas often involve individuals struggling to maintain their moral beliefs while confronted by crime, drugs, and **racism**. Though many consider his **plays** moralistic, Milner has garnered praise for the stark **realism** of his settings and for his authentic recreation of urban dialogue and idioms. Milner is best known for *What the Wine Sellers Buy* (1973), in which a seventeen-year-old youth is tempted by a pimp and hustler. The black middle class was the subject of his plays during the 1980s; *Don't Get God Started* (1987) depicts affluent blacks who, plagued by drug addiction and marital infidelity, find solace in **religion**.

Further Readings

Black Literature Criticism, Gale, 1992.
Black Writers, first edition, Gale, 1989.

Mind of My Mind

Please see "Patternist Saga"

Mine Boy

Peter Abrahams
Novel, 1946

Peter Abrahams's second **novel**, *Mine Boy,* describes a South Africa where blacks experience poverty and oppression in the context of the country's politics and history. Critics have claimed that Abrahams provides a convincing reality that challenges the myths perpetuated in the works of the white South African writers of his time. The deplorable conditions are revealed through the novel's secondary characters, including Eliza, whose inability to rise above poverty leads to emotional instability; the alcoholic Daddy, who once led the fight against oppression; and the proletarian Maisie. The main character, Xuma, a migrant laborer, finds success in the industrial, urban setting, learns first-hand about class exploitation and struggle, and prepares for leadership in the inevitable revolution.

Minette

Character in *Brother Man*

Mingo

Character in *Black Thunder*

Mingo Saunders

Character in *The Brownsville Raid*

Minnie Ranson

Character in *The Salt Eaters*

Minty Alley

C. L. R. James
Novel, 1936

The story of a young middle-class black, **C. L. R. James**'s *Minty Alley* examines social ambivalence and class structure in Trinidad in the 1920s. Forced by financial troubles to live among the lower class, the book's protagonist,

Haynes, observes the everyday existence of working class characters, such as Maisie. James depicts the racial prejudices of both the upper and lower classes and explores Maisie's desire to escape poor working conditions and seek a better standard of living in America.

The Mis-Education of the Negro

Carter G. Woodson
Nonfiction, 1933

Carter G. Woodson argues in *The Mis-Education of the Negro* that African Americans have not been taught to value and respect themselves. He condemns both the lack of racial pride among African Americans and the quality of education that they receive. To address these issues, Woodson suggests a reconstruction of the United States education system that would allow for a curriculum focusing on black history and dealing with the unique problems faced by African American students.

Miss Emma

Character in *A Lesson before Dying*

Miss Janie

Character in *The Taking of Miss Janie*

Miss Sophie

Character in *The Piano Lesson*

Gabriela Mistral

Chilean poet and educator
Born April 7, 1889.
Died January 10, 1957.

Mistral, born Lucila Godoy Alcayaga in 1889 in Vicuna, Chile, initially pursued a career in education but is best known for her lyrical **poetry.** Arriving on the literary scene in 1914 with *Sonetos de la muerte* ("Sonnets on Death"), Mistral went on to become one of Latin America's most gifted poets. Her writings in *Desolación* ("Desolation," 1922), *Ternura* ("Tenderness," 1924), *Tala* ("Felling," 1938), and her last collection, *Lagar* ("Wine Press," 1954), center on themes of love, death, childhood, maternity, and **religion**. Mistral received the Nobel Prize in literature in 1945, and her work has been widely anthologized. She died in Hempstead, New York, in 1957.

Further Readings
Black Writers, second edition, Gale, 1994.

Castleman, William J., *Beauty and the Mission of the Teacher: The Life of Gabriela Mistral of Chile,* Exposition, 1982.

Loften Mitchell
American playwright and essayist
Born April 15, 1919.

Mitchell is one of the chief historians of the black theater. In ***Black Drama: The Story of the American Negro in the Theatre*** (1967), he traces black theater in the United States from 1769 through 1964. Born in 1919 in Columbus, North Carolina, Mitchell began writing and acting in theater while still a high school student in Harlem. Later, as a playwright, he focused on themes involving the contributions and struggles of black people in America, the evils of **racism**, and the potential of black artists to enrich American theater. Among Mitchell's best-known **plays** are the drama *A Land Beyond the River* (1957) and the musical *Bubbling Brown Sugar* (1975). In 1975 he published *Voices of the Black Theatre,* containing stories by contemporary black theater figures.

Further Readings
Black Writers, first edition, Gale, 1989.

Dictionary of Literary Biography, Volume 38: *Afro-American Writers after 1955: Dramatists and Prose Writers,* Gale, 1985.

Edgar Mittelhölzer

Guyanese novelist
Born December 16, 1909.
Died May 5, 1965.

Edgar Austin Mittelhölzer was the first professional English-speaking novelist in the Caribbean. Because most of his works, which share the theme of breaking free of bourgeois social conventions, are set in Caribbean locations, Mittelhölzer's **novels** offer insights into a broad cross-section of Caribbean society. Mittelhölzer was born in British Guiana (now Guyana) to upper-class parents of mixed descent. His school years were marked by incidents of idealism and rebellion, and by the time he reached adulthood Mittelhölzer was known for his passion in confronting prejudice and oppression. A prolific writer, he published at least a novel a year during the 1950s and early 1960s. Mittelhölzer is perhaps best known for *A Morning in Trinidad* (1950; *A Morning at the Office,* 1950). He committed suicide in 1965.

Further Readings
Black Writers, first edition, Gale, 1989.

Dictionary of Literary Biography, Volume 117: *Twentieth-Century Caribbean and Black African Writers,* First Series, Gale, 1992.

M'Lissa
Character in *Possessing the Secret of Joy*

Mo' Better Blues
Spike Lee
Film, 1990

In *Mo' Better Blues,* **Spike Lee** examines the life of a successful **jazz** trumpet player, Bleek Gilliam, and the conflicting interests posed by Bleek's career and love life. The film also depicts the camaraderie and rivalries of the music world. Bleek, dedicated to his jazz quintet, is insensitive to the people closest to him, especially the two women whom he is dating— a schoolteacher named Indigo Downes and a jazz singer, Clarke Bentancourt, whom Bleek eventually loses to the band's saxophone player, Shadow Henderson.

Bleek's commitment to his art is explained through flashbacks to his childhood in Brooklyn and scenes of his mother forcing a young Bleek to practice scales while the other boys played baseball.

Despite Bleek's moderate success, his career is damaged by his manager's compulsive gambling. His musical career is finally terminated when he is injured in a fight and can no longer play the trumpet. After a period of soul-searching, Bleek is now ready to commit to Indigo and to the domestic life that he once shunned. The final scenes of the film compress eight years of marital life into a final, few moments of screen time and parallel the earlier flashback by showing Bleek's son practicing the trumpet.

Modernism

Modernism refers to the principles of a literary school that lasted from roughly the beginning of the twentieth century until the end of World War II. This school is defined by its rejection of the literary conventions of the nineteenth century and its opposition to traditional morality, taste, and economic values. One African American poet associated with modernism was **Robert Hayden**, who was eventually appointed Consultant in Poetry to the Library of Congress. As a young man, Hayden studied with British poet W. H. Auden, a leading figure in the modernist movement. Another black writer who was strongly influenced by modernist poets such as T. S. Eliot was **Christopher Okigbo**, author of such **poetry** collections as *Heavensgate* (1962), *Limits* (1964), and *Labyrinths, with Path of Thunder* (1971).

Modingo

Character in *Les Blancs*

Barbara Jean Molette

American playwright
Born January 31, 1940.

Born in Los Angeles, California, in 1940, Molette has been active in the dramatic arts as an instructor, makeup artist and designer, costume designer, drama coordinator, and author of the syndicated column "Upstage/Downstage." Since her 1969 graduation from Florida State University with a master of fine arts, she has adapted **William Wells Brown**'s **play** *The Escape; or, A Leap to Freedom* (1976), and co-authored the plays *Rosalee Pritchett* (1972), *Booji Wooji* (1971), and others with her husband, **Carlton W. Molette II**. They also wrote *Black Theatre: Premise and Presentation* (1986), compiled *Afro-American Theatre: A Bibliography* (1972), and co-authored the filmstrip *Stage Makeup for Black Authors*.

Further Readings
Black Writers, first edition, Gale, 1989.

Carlton W. Molette II

American playwright
Born August 23, 1939.

The recipient of degrees from Morehouse College, the University of Iowa, and Florida State University, Carlton Woodard Molette II has been a professor of speech and drama, postsecondary administrator, director, and theater consultant to colleges, festivals, and organizations. He was born in 1939 in Pine Bluff, Arkansas, the son of a college professor, and has co-authored several **plays,** including *Rosalee Pritchett* (1972) and *Booji Wooji* (1971), and the filmstrip *Stage Makeup for Black Actors,* with his wife, **Barbara Jean Molette**. They also wrote *Black Theatre: Premise and Presentation* (1986) and compiled *Afro-American Theatre: A Bibliography* (1972).

Further Readings
Black Writers, first edition, Gale, 1989.

Monk

Character in *Corner Boy*

Monty

Character in *The Taking of Miss Janie*

Anne Moody

American autobiographer and short story writer
Born September 15, 1940.

An activist and author, Moody was born in 1940 in Wilkerson County, Mississippi, attended Natchez Junior College, and graduated from Tougaloo College with a bachelor's degree in 1964. She has said that she thought of herself first not as a writer but as a civil rights activist in her state, though she became frustrated with the movement's pace there and moved north. Gradually she became disillusioned with the **civil rights movement** entirely because she felt it had become factional and narrowly nationalistic.

Moody's **autobiography**, *Coming of Age in Mississippi* (1969), chronicles not only her youth but also the poverty and brutality that characterized the experience of most blacks in the South when she was growing up there. Published when she was twenty-eight, the account ends with the events of 1964, before the passage of the Voting Rights Act the following year. *Coming of Age in Mississippi* was favorably reviewed and won both the Brotherhood Award from the National Council of Christians and Jews and the Best Book of the Year Award from the National Library Association.

Moody has also contributed short stories and **essays** to *Ms.* and *Mademoiselle,* the latter of which awarded her its silver medal in 1970 for her article "New Hopes for the Seventies." Four of Moody's stories are collected in her second book, *Mr. Death* (1975).

During her involvement with the civil rights movement, Moody worked with the Congress of Racial Equality (CORE) as an organizer and fund-raiser in the 1960s and was a civil rights project coordinator at Cornell University.

She was counsel for New York City's poverty program in 1967.

Further Readings
Black Writers, first edition, Gale, 1989.

Mookie

Character in *Do the Right Thing*

A Morning in Trinidad

Edgar Mittelhölzer
Novel, 1950

Edgar Mittelhölzer's *A Morning in Trinidad* (published in England as *A Morning at the Office*) provides a detailed sketch of the personalities inhabiting the office of Essential Products Limited, Port of Spain, Trinidad, during one morning. Mittelhölzer presents a cross-section of Caribbean nationalities through characters of varying backgrounds and races. The office staff includes Horace Xavier, the African office boy; George Waley, the British manager; Edna Bisnauth and Mr. Jagabir, both of Indian descent; Olga Ten Yip, who is Chinese; and Laura Laballe, a Creole. Many of the characters' lives suggest circumstances and situations peculiar to the history of the West Indies; their attitudes and actions reflect differing socio-economic and racial backgrounds. Mittelhölzer uses interactions between the characters to examine both the apparent social and financial success of whites over non-white races and the Caribbean awareness of racial disparity.

Toni Morrison

American novelist
Born February 18, 1931.

In 1993, Morrison became the first African American woman to win the Nobel Prize for literature. Her works, noted for their poetic language, provocative themes, and powerful storytelling, explore gender and racial conflicts and the many ways that people express their identities.

Morrison was born Chloe Anthony Wofford in Lorain, Ohio, on February 18, 1931. She attended Howard University—where she changed her name to Toni because Chloe was hard to pronounce—and received a master's degree from Cornell University in 1955. Two years later, she returned to Howard to teach English and there met Harold Morrison, a Jamaican architect she married in 1958. After they divorced six years later, Morrison worked as an editor for a textbook subsidiary of Random House. She was working there when she started her first **novel, *The Bluest Eye*** (1969).

Drawing on elements of Morrison's own experience, *The Bluest Eye* portrays a dysfunctional black family, the Breedloves, and a healthy, loving black family, the McTeers, modelled after Morrison's own family. *Sula* (1973), which also looks at the question of identity, focuses on two black women who have chosen different directions for their lives. ***Song of Solomon*** (1977) follows a black man's quest for identity and his search for his ancestry. It won both the National Book Critics' Circle Award and the American Academy and Institute of Arts and Letters Award in 1977.

In 1980, President Jimmy Carter appointed Morrison to the National Council on the Arts. The following year she won admission to the American Academy and Institute of Arts and Letters and published ***Tar Baby***, which is set in the Caribbean and has been described as an allegory of **colonialism**. ***Beloved*** (1987), about an ex-slave's attempt to deal with her past, won the 1988 Pulitzer Prize. Morrison's sixth novel, ***Jazz*** (1992), concerns a middle-aged couple who migrated from the South to Harlem in the early 1900s.

In addition to writing, Morrison has taught at several universities, including Howard, Yale, Cambridge, Harvard, and Princeton. She has also written a **play,** *Dreaming Emmett* (1986), and she continues to edit for Random House, helping to publish works by authors such as **Toni Cade Bambara** and **Gayl Jones**.

Morrison was the first African American woman to win the Nobel Prize for literature.

Further Readings

Black Literature Criticism, Gale, 1992.

Contemporary Literary Criticism, Gale, Volume 4, 1975, Volume 10, 1979, Volume 22, 1982, Volume 55, 1989.

Dictionary of Literary Biography, Gale, Volume 6: *American Novelists since World War II, Second Series,* 1980; Volume 33: *Afro-American Fiction Writers after 1955,* 1984.

Dictionary of Literary Biography Yearbook: 1981, Gale, 1982.

Gates, Henry Louis Jr., and K. A. Appiah, editors, *Toni Morrison: Critical Perspectives, Past and Present,* Amistad, 1993.

McKay, Nellie, editor, G. K. Hall, *Critical Perspectives on Toni Morrison,* 1988.

Moses Washington

Character in *The Chaneysville Incident*

Walter Mosley

American novelist
Born in 1952.

Mosley is the widely praised author of a series of detective **novels** set in Los Angeles and centered around the black detective Ezekiel "Easy" Rawlins. After quitting his job as a computer programmer, Mosley wrote his first novel, *Devil in a Blue Dress* (1990), in which Easy, a World War II veteran, loses his job in the aircraft industry and becomes a private detective. The novel, which is set in 1948, received the Private Eye Writers of America's Shamus Award and was nominated for the Mystery Writers of America's Edgar Award. *A Red Death* (1991) relates the trouble Easy has gotten into with the Internal Revenue Service (IRS) in 1953. To escape prosecution, Easy must spy on a union organizer for the Federal Bureau of Investigation (FBI). Rawlins is married and has a new baby in *White Butterfly* (1992), set in 1956. He is hired by the police to investigate a series of murders. Mosley's fourth Rawlins mystery, *Black Betty* (1994) takes place during 1961; in the book, Rawlins, separated from his wife and daughter and living with two "adopted" children, is hired to find an old acquaintance. Mosley has indicated that he intends to continue the series, bringing Rawlins into the 1980s.

Further Readings

Black Writers, second edition, Gale, 1994.

Willard Motley

American novelist
Born July 14, 1912.
Died March 4, 1965.

Willard Francis Motley is known for his naturalistic portrayal of the lives and struggles of working-class Americans. Born into a middle-class Chicago family, Motley began writing after years of hitchhiking across America, living in flophouses, and working odd jobs—all experiences he drew upon in his fiction. In his **novels,** he explored political corruption, substance abuse, the U.S. exploitation of Mexico, and the prison system. His 1947 novel *Knock on Any Door* relates a ghetto boy's degeneration from a church helper to a hardened killer who eventually faces execution. Motley's *Let No Man Write My Epitaph* (1958) was filmed in 1960.

Further Readings

Black Writers, first edition, Gale, 1989.
Dictionary of Literary Biography, Volume 76: *Afro-American Writers, 1940-1955,* Gale, 1988.

Motown

Character in *Motown and Didi: A Love Story*

Motown and Didi: A Love Story

Walter Dean Myers
Young adult novel, 1984

In **Walter Dean Myers**'s *Motown and Didi,* Motown is a young man who is raised in Harlem by indifferent foster parents. He lives in an abandoned building, survives on money earned from odd jobs, and keeps to himself. Another young Harlem resident, Didi, dreams of a college scholarship despite her poverty, her mother's mental instability, and her brother's heroin addiction. When Didi reports a group of drug dealers to the police, gang members attack her in the street; Motown comes to her defense, and soon they are both targeted by the drug dealers. Their strength of character and their growing love for each other helps them survive in dangerous and tragic circumstances.

Moustique

Character in *Dream on Monkey Mountain*

Ezekiel Mphahlele

South African novelist, autobiographer, and critic
Born December 17, 1919.

Mphahlele was born in a black South African township and his writing contains a humanistic vision shaped by the alienation he experienced during his youth there and during the twenty years he lived in self-imposed exile. In **Down Second Avenue** (1959), he recounts his life from age five until he left his country in 1957. He recounts his later experiences in other autobiographical works, including *The Wanderers* (1971), an acclaimed **novel** about South African blacks and whites in their country and in exile. Mphahlele returned to South Africa in 1977 and published *Chirundu* (1981), in which a man is torn between African traditions and English law. Also well known as a literary critic, Mphahlele has written numerous works about African fiction and **poetry.** He sometimes writes as either Es'kia Mphahlele or Bruno Eseki.

Further Readings

Barnett, Ursula A., *Ezekiel Mphahlele,* Twayne, 1976.
Black Literature Criticism, Gale, 1992.
Black Writers, second edition, Gale, 1994.

Es'kia Mphahlele

Please see Ezekiel Mphahlele

Mr. Ellis

Character in *The Garies and Their Friends*

Mr. Garie

Character in *The Garies and Their Friends*

Mr. Harley

Character in *The Young Landlords*

Mr. Jagabir

Character in *A Morning in Trinidad*

Mr. Pilkings

Character in *Death and the King's Horseman*

Mr. Pinchen

Character in *The Escape; or, A Leap for Freedom*

Mr. Pluto

Character in *The House of Dies Drear*

Mr. Pool

Character in *The Planet of Junior Brown*

Mr. Stevens

Character in *The Garies and Their Friends*

Mrabo

Character in *Sadhji*

Mrs. Bellmont

Character in *Our Nig*

Mrs. Gramby

Character in *Country Place*

Mrs. Mason

Character in *Jane: A Story of Jamaica*

Mrs. Moore

Character in *Our Nig*

Mrs. Ransom Bell

Character in *A Hero Ain't Nothin' but a Sandwich*

Mufaro

Character in *Mufaro's Beautiful Daughters: An African Tale*

Cover of Hurston's collection of folktales and Hoodoo stories.

Mufaro's Beautiful Daughters: An African Tale

John Steptoe
Juvenile, 1987

Written and illustrated by **John Steptoe,** *Mufaro's Beautiful Daughters* reworks a traditional African folktale. Set in Zimbabwe, the story depicts two lovely yet temperamentally different daughters. Nyasha's nature is sweet and gentle, while her sister Manyara is petulant and sullen. When a king announces his wish to marry, Mufaro decides his daughters should vie for the king's consideration. Manyara secretly leaves the night before the planned journey and treats the strangers she meets with contempt; Nyasha, however, shows the same strangers kindness and generosity along the way. When they reach the king's city, the king tells them that he had magically taken the shape of the strangers to test the sisters. He marries Nyasha for her beauty and thoughtfulness, while the ill-tempered Manyara becomes a servant in the king's household; kindness is rewarded and cruelty is punished.

Mugo

Character in *A Grain of Wheat*

Mules and Men

Zora Neale Hurston
Folklore, 1935

Zora Neale Hurston's *Mules and Men* bridges the gap between her career as a creative writer and her profession as an anthropologist, a collector of African American **folk tales** and traditional stories. The book is divided into two parts. The first section deals with material she collected from her home state of Florida. This material is mostly about racial tensions and competition in the days before the Civil War. Some of the stories use talking animals to make points about race relations. In "What the Rabbit Learned," for example, Brer Rabbit shows that he has learned to beware of Brer Dog, despite the latter's assertion that dogs and rabbits are now friends. "The Talking Mule" tells the story of Bill, who one day simply refuses to finish the plowing for his owner, startling the man so much that he runs away. A recurring human character in other stories is John, a slave who always outsmarts Ole Massa, a white plantation owner. "Member Youse a Nigger" is about a bargain John makes with Ole Massa: John agrees to bring in a bumper crop if Ole Massa will in turn give John his freedom. Ole Massa agrees and keeps his promise. As John walks away, however, Ole Massa continually reminds him of his status. John responds each time, but he does not stop walking until he reaches Canada and safety.

The second part of the book contains material collected in and around New Orleans and gives an account of Hoodoo, an accumulation of folk beliefs drawn partly from native African religions. Rather than stories, the second part contains sketches of the characters who practice Hoodoo. Portraying herself as a student, Hurston carefully describes the rituals and beliefs that the different Hoodoo doctors use to drive people away, to bring them back, and in some cases to kill them.

Mumbi

Character in *A Grain of Wheat*

Mumbo Jumbo

Ishmael Reed
Novel, 1972

Set in New Orleans and New York during the 1920s and structured as a mystery **novel**, **Ishmael Reed**'s *Mumbo Jumbo* is a treatise on writing and the African American aesthetic. The basis of this aesthetic is "neo-Hoodooism," a theory Reed describes as the resurgence of the Osirian animistic **religion** that had been suppressed by both Judaism and **Christianity**.

The first chapter of *Mumbo Jumbo* presents the details of the highly complex plot in synopsis or news-flash form. The detective in the story is PaPa LaBas (representing the Hoodoo god Legba), who intends to reconstruct the black aesthetic and sets out to find the original Hoodoo text so he can liberate its mysteries and allow its followers, known as the Jes Grew, to openly practice its tenets. He is opposed by a group called the Atonists dedicated to the preservation of Western civilization. Reed challenges the conventional sense of time in the narrative, introducing a sense of simultaneity to the text and encouraging his readers to feel that all of the actions are thematically and rhetorically related. At the close of the novel the Hoodoo text is burned and Jes Grew withers, but LaBas announces that Jes Grew will reappear some day

Typescript page from *Mumbo Jumbo*.

to make its own text: "A future generation of young artists will accomplish this." He is referring to the writers, painters, politicians, and musicians of the 1960s.

Munira

Character in *Petals of Blood*

Albert L. Murray

American essayist and novelist
Born June 12, 1916.

Murray is best known for his exploration of **the Blues** and his incorporation of a Blues aesthetic in his **novels.** Born in Alabama, Murray received his B.S. degree from the Tuskegee

Institute in 1939 and served as an instructor there until he enlisted in the Air Force in 1943. Murray returned to Tuskegee after World War II and retired from the Air Force in 1962. His **essay** collection *The Omni-Americans: New Perspectives on Black Experience and American Culture* (1970) suggests that African Americans have developed a heroic and distinct culture. Murray contends that one powerful black medium of expression is the Blues, a subject he explores in *The Hero and the Blues* (1973) and *Stomping the Blues* (1976), the latter of which was awarded the Deems Taylor Award for music criticism in 1977. According to Murray, the Blues idiom recognizes the ever-shifting contradictions involved in human existence; with the Blues, blacks are able to affirm a positive attitude while meeting life on its own terms. Murray's novel **Train Whistle Guitar** (1974), in which a Southern black man named Scooter copes with life in 1920s Alabama, reflects this Blues aesthetic. *The Spyglass Tree* (1992), Murray's second novel, further chronicles Scooter's story, this time as a college student at the Tuskegee Institute.

Further Readings
Black Writers, second edition, Gale, 1994.

Dictionary of Literary Biography, Volume 38: *Afro-American Writers after 1955: Dramatists and Prose Writers,* Gale, 1985.

Pauli Murray
American nonfiction wrier and poet
Born November 20, 1910.
Died July 1, 1985.

Challenging governmental and social **discrimination** against blacks and women, Anna Pauline Murray was active in the struggle for racial and sexual equality. Her mulatto background prevented her from totally embracing her African heritage and excluded her from white society. Through writing, Murray revealed her cultural roots. In 1977, she became the first black woman ordained as an Episcopal priest. She published several law books, a collection of **poetry,** and the critically acclaimed personal

histories **Proud Shoes: The Story of An American Family** (1956) and *Song in a Weary Throat: An American Pilgrimage* (1987).

Further Readings
Black Writers, second edition, Gale, 1994.

Dictionary of Literary Biography, Volume 41: *Afro-American Poets since 1955,* Gale, 1985.

Mutt
Character in *Corregidora*

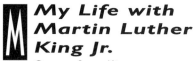

My Life with Martin Luther King Jr.
Coretta Scott King
Autobiography, 1969

In *My Life with Martin Luther King Jr.* **Coretta Scott King** interweaves her personal story with the nonviolent movement led by her husband, **Martin Luther King Jr.** She details her rural Alabama roots, her plans to become a musician, and how her life altered when she fell in love with Martin while they were both students in Boston. She put aside her disappointment that Martin was to be minister and her reluctance to go back to the South and **segregation**. During most of Martin's campaigns for voting and civil rights, Coretta remained at home, which put a strain on the family, but did not keep her from having a sharp perspective of the movement. She covers significant events in the movement until Martin's assassination in 1968 and also provides insight into the **Black Power** movement.

Walter Dean Myers
American novelist, short story writer, nonfiction writer, and author of children's literature
Born August 12, 1937.

Myers is best known for his works for children and young adults. His books span a range of genres, including picture books, fairy tales, and realistic young adult **novels.** Two of the latter, *The Young Landlords* (1979) and *Motown and Didi: A Love Story* (1984), have won the prestigious Coretta Scott King Award, as has his history *Now Is Your Time! The African-American Struggle for Freedom* (1991). Myers has also received a Newbery Honor Award for another young adult novel, *Scorpions* (1988).

Myers was born into an impoverished family in Martinsburg, West Virginia. At age three he was adopted by Herbert and Florence Dean, who settled in New York City's Harlem district. Myers's young adult novels draw on his first-hand experience of black urban and ghetto life. *Fast Sam, Cool Clyde, and Stuff* (1975), for instance, tells the story of three preteen black youths growing up in New York City. *Scorpions* is about a seventh grader who accepts a gun from an older teen.

Myers's picture books cover a wider variety of topics. In *Where Does the Day Go?* (1969), which won the Council on Interracial Books for Children Award, an ethnically diverse group of children talk about night and day with a sensitive and wise black father during a long walk. *The Golden Serpent* (1980) is a fairy tale set in India. In all his works, Myers encourages self-reliance and personal growth in his young readers.

Further Readings
Black Literature Criticism, Gale, 1992.

Black Writers, second edition, Gale, 1994.

Dictionary of Literary Biography, Volume 33: *Afro-American Fiction Writers after 1955,* Gale, 1984.

Mystery Fiction

The mystery is a genre of popular fiction that deals with the solution of a mysterious crime or puzzle. The elements of terror and suspense, along with frightening and strange adventures, often surface as components. A widely read subcategory of mystery fiction is **detective fiction**. American novelist **Walter Mosley** has found success in this latter genre with his series featuring black detective Ezekiel "Easy" Rawlins. **Virginia Hamilton** won an Edgar Allan Poe Award for *The House of Dies Drear* (1968), a mystery for children centering around an old **Underground Railroad** station. **Ishmael Reed** parodies the conventions of mystery writing in his **novels** *Mumbo Jumbo* (1972), which involves a search for original Hoodoo text, and *The Last Days of Louisiana Red* (1974), which features voodoo detective PaPa LaBas. Playwright **Charles Fuller** found success in 1976 with the drama *The Brownsville Raid*, a true story based on the mystery surrounding the discharging of an entire black regiment around the turn of the twentieth century.

Myth

A myth is an anonymous tale emerging from the traditional beliefs of a culture. Myths provide **supernatural** explanations for natural phenomena, and they may also explain cosmic issues like creation and death. African creation myths are among the most varied and imaginative in the world. Black writers have incorporated myths into their work in many ways. For example, Kenyan author **Grace Ogot** has retold a popular Luo village myth in her book *Miaha* (1983; *The Strange Bride,* 1989), while Nigerian poet **Christopher Okigbo** has included elements of myth and ritual in his poems collected in *Heavensgate* (1962) and *Limits* (1964). Dramatist **Paul Carter Harrison** has tried to link traditional African myth with contemporary American culture in his **plays** and **literary criticism**. Other writers who make extensive use of mythology in their writings include **Audre Lorde**, **Rita Dove**, **Kofi Awoonor**, and **Derek Walcott**.

N-O

[I]t is only when people are politically free that other races can give them the respect that is due to them. It is impossible to talk of equality of races in any other terms.

The Autobiography of Kwame Nkrumah,
Kwame Nkrumah, 1957

NAACP

Please see National Association for the Advancement of Colored People

John Nagenda

Ugandan fiction writer and author of children's literature
Born in 1938.

Nagenda is a poet, **short story** writer, playwright, and scholar. Among his works are the children's book *Mukasa* (1973) and *The Seasons of Thomas Tebo* (1986), both of which focus on the author's homeland. While his books are published in English, Nagenda has spoken out in favor of publication in native African languages. Born in 1938 in Gahini, Uganda, Nagenda received his B.A. from Kampala's Makerere University, where he edited the journal *Penpoint* and published the works of many new African writers. Nagenda was also a member of Uganda's national cricket team.

Further Readings

Black Writers, second edition, Gale, 1994.

Na-ni

Alexis Deveaux
Novel, 1973

Na-ni, a children's story written and illustrated by **Alexis Deveaux,** tells the story of a young Harlem girl whose dream of a new bicycle is shattered when the family's welfare check is stolen. Na-ni and her friend sit on the curb and wait for the mailman. While they wait, Na-ni fantasizes about the bicycle she has been promised. The mail is delivered, but before Na-ni's mother can pick up the check, it is stolen from the mail box. Na-ni witnesses the theft, and writes a poem about the experience in her **diary**.

Nanny Crawford

Character in *Their Eyes Were Watching God*

Napoléon Bonaparte

Character in *Toussaint L'Ouverture*

Narrative of the Life of Frederick Douglass

Frederick Douglass
Autobiography, 1845

First published as a small, simple, 125-page volume, *Narrative of the Life of Frederick Douglass, An American Slave, Written by Himself* helped establish **Frederick Douglass** as a political presence while simultaneously denouncing the evils of **slavery**. Drawing material from his orations, Douglass described how he was born into slavery on a Maryland farm, separated from his mother, and severely mistreated as a child. He recounted how he was sent to Baltimore in 1826 to serve as an errand boy and companion to a white child his age. It was there that he learned how to read and write, largely by teaching himsel

Douglass also described the brutal treatment he received as a slave and recounted how he finally escaped to New York City, where abolitionists helped him and his new wife settle in New Bedford, Massachusetts. Douglass's desire to work for the abolitionist cause was dampened somewhat by his fear of being discovered and sent back south to his slavemaster. Nevertheless, he began to speak and write about his experiences as a slave, most notably in his autobiography. Soon after his *Narrative* was published he became so fearful of recapture that he sailed for England. Friends in that

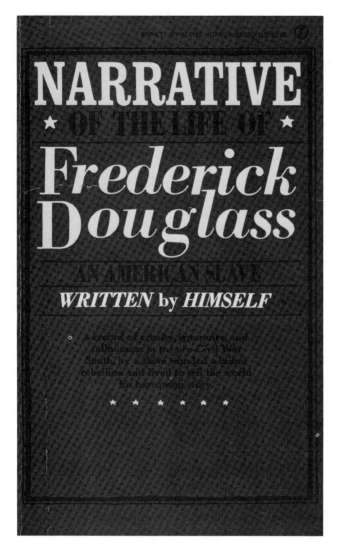

In this book Douglass described the brutality of life as a slave.

The Narrows
Ann Petry
Novel, 1953

Ann Petry's *The Narrows* deals with the tragic affair between a young, well-educated black man and a rich white girl. Set in the black section of a small Connecticut town, the narrative revolves around Link Williams, a black man with great athletic and academic ability, but a weak and indecisive character. The latter trait is perhaps due to his unstable childhood, revealed through a series of flashbacks. Upon returning from Dartmouth to tend bar in his hometown, Link falls hopelessly in love with Camilo Treadway, daughter of the town's leading white family and heiress to an industrial fortune. Only later does Link discover Camilo's real marital status and identity, which leads to violent consequences. The **novel** is distinguished in part by Petry's stylistic experimentation as well as her memorable minor characters, such as Weak Knees, Cat Jimmy, and Bug Eyes.

Nat Turner

Please see *Six Plays for a Negro Theatre*

Nathaniel Turner Witherspoon

Character in *There Is a Tree More Ancient Than Eden*

Nation of Islam

The Nation of Islam is an African American religious movement with black nationalist underpinnings. This distinctive form of Islam, which developed in the United States in the early twentieth century, originally held that the white person is the embodiment of the Devil, who enslaves all nonwhites. Therefore, all nonwhite races should establish a single separate nation within the United States. The Nation of Islam has attracted a number of

country helped him purchase his freedom in 1847. By that time, Douglass's *Narrative* had become a best-seller in America and had been translated into both French and German. He revised the book several times over the course of his life, adding new material that reflected his philosophy and political goals. The last revision was finished in 1892, just three years before his death.

important black writers and speakers over the years, including **Malcolm X** and **Sonia Sanchez**.

The Nation of Islam evolved from two earlier black self-improvement groups: the Universal Negro Improvement Association, founded in 1914 to advance **Marcus Garvey**'s **back-to-Africa movement**, and the Moorish Science Temple of America, founded in 1913 as the first of various new forms of black Islam. One member of the Moorish Science Temple, W. D. Fard, later started a temple that was the beginning of the Nation of Islam. When Fard disappeared under mysterious circumstances in 1934, Elijah Muhammad assumed control. The movement grew under his guidance, especially in the 1950s and 1960s. Members began to be unofficially known as Black Muslims after the publication of **C. Eric Lincoln**'s book *The Black Muslims in America* (1961). This growth in the ranks of adherents was due partly to the charismatic leadership of Muhammad's principal lieutenant, Malcolm X. However, a rift between the two men eventually led Malcolm X to challenge Muhammad's supremacy. As a result, Malcolm X was suspended from the movement in 1963, which marked the first major split in the Nation of Islam.

Around this time, Malcolm X began to dictate his **autobiography** to **Alex Haley**. In 1965, Malcolm X was shot to death by fellow Black Muslims. Both *The Autobiography of Malcolm X* (1965) and *Malcolm X Speaks* (1965), his collected **speeches**, were published posthumously that year. In the 1970s, the new leader of what was renamed the American Muslim Mission rejected color-consciousness, de-emphasized **black nationalism**, and advocated adherence to Islamic practices. However, a dissident Nation of Islam faction formed by Louis Farrakhan in 1978 reasserted the philosophy of black separatism.

Islam has proved to be more popular among black men than women due to its very conservative stance on gender issues. Poet Sonia Sanchez, for example, joined the movement in 1972, but left just three years later because of the conflict between Islamic beliefs and her own emerging feminist views. However, her **poetry** collections *A Blues Book for Blue Black Magical Women* (1973) and *Love Poems* (1973) reflect many ideals of the faith, such as respect for the family. Over the years, the Nation of Islam has affected the lives of numerous African Americans by maintaining schools, running businesses, and establishing rehabilitation programs for convicts and substance abuse victims. The group has also published a weekly newspaper, *Muslim World News* (formerly *Muhammad Speaks*).

National Association for the Advancement of Colored People

The oldest and largest civil rights organization in the United States, the National Association for the Advancement of Colored People (NAACP) was founded in New York City in 1909, when it was called the National Negro Committee. Since that time the NAACP has worked toward its stated goal of eliminating barriers to economic, educational, political, and social equality. Over the years, the group has stressed legal action to promote civil rights in such areas as education, employment, housing, and voting. It also lobbies for antidiscrimination laws and conducts voter registration drives and educational campaigns. Among the noted writers who have played prominent roles in the NAACP are **W. E. B. Du Bois**, **James Weldon Johnson**, **Roy Wilkins**, and **Walter White**.

In 1905, a group of black intellectuals led by Du Bois had banded together to form the **Niagara Movement**, a group that urged African Americans to demand their full civil rights. Three years later, bitter race riots in Springfield, Illinois, Abraham Lincoln's hometown, prompted Niagara Movement leaders to join forces with white liberals. A coalition of sixty people met on Lincoln's birthday in 1909 to discuss a new organization. In 1910, the association adopted its present name and incorporated in New York state. By 1914, it had established some fifty branches throughout the United States. Ironically, Du Bois was the only founding member of the NAACP who was black. He was employed by the association for more than twenty years, editing *Crisis* magazine, the group's principal publication. With Du Bois at the helm, the magazine became the most influential black periodical in the United States. Although it first printed only one thousand copies, by 1920 its circulation had grown a hundredfold.

Since its inception, the NAACP has attempted to better the condition of African Americans through litigation, legislation, and education. In 1915, it organized a boycott of *Birth of a Nation,* a motion picture that depicted black people in a demeaning light. The group also waged a successful campaign to erase the so-called grandfather clause that existed in the voting laws of some southern states. This clause, which stated that only those individuals whose grandfathers had voted could vote themselves, effectively disenfranchised African Americans whose grandfathers had been slaves without voting rights. Perhaps the single greatest victory for the NAACP came in 1954, when the historic *Brown v. Board of Education of Topeka* case threw out the "separate but equal" doctrine established by the Supreme Court in 1896. Thus, racial **segregation** in public schools was declared to be unconstitutional. Several cases leading up to this historic decision had been argued in the courts by the NAACP's legal arm, the Legal Defense and Education Fund, which is now independent of the NAACP.

During the **civil rights movement** of the 1950s and 1960s, the NAACP cooperated with such groups as the Southern Christian Leadership Conference, the Student Nonviolent Coordinating Committee (SNCC), and the Congress of Racial Equality (CORE) on a number of projects. The NAACP contributed to efforts that resulted in the passage of the Civil Rights Acts of 1957 and 1964, the Voting Rights Act of 1965, and the Fair Housing Act of 1968. More recently, it has broadened its traditional mission to encompass such problems within the African American community as teenage pregnancy, poor school performance, drug and substance abuse, and violence against blacks.

Among the black writers with close ties to the NAACP were poet James Weldon Johnson and novelist and essayist Walter White, both of whom served for a time as secretary. Roy Wilkins, who succeeded Du Bois as editor of *Crisis,* went on to become executive secretary and then director of the association. **Derrick Albert Bell Jr.**, a lawyer who worked for the NAACP, has written extensively on the subject of civil rights law. His books include *Race, Racism, and American Law* (1973) and *Shades of Brown: New Perspectives on School Desegregation* (1980).

Native Son

Richard Wright
Novel, 1940

Native Son is considered by most critics to be **Richard Wright**'s best work. Divided into three sections—"Fear," "Flight," and "Fate"—the **novel** examines topics such as black consciousness, racial dynamics, and freedom and determinism.

Native Son's central character is Bigger Thomas, a young black man living in Chicago. In "Fear," Bigger is hired as a chauffeur for a prominent white family, the Daltons. One night, he takes the Dalton's daughter Mary and her boyfriend Jan Erlone to a political speech. Mary and Jan are communists and attempt to befriend Bigger and treat him as an equal, which makes Bigger uncomfortable. When Bigger drives Mary home that night, she is intoxicated and needs Bigger's help to reach her room. While Bigger is putting Mary to bed, blind Mrs. Dalton enters and calls for her daughter. Terrified that he will be discovered in the bedroom and accused of impropriety, Bigger covers Mary's head with a pillow to keep her from answering. In doing so, he accidentally suffocates her. Attempting to conceal the crime, Bigger burns her body in the furnace.

In "Flight," Bigger responds to the murder. Although he implicates Jan to the police, Bigger begins to rationalize his actions. He thinks that he symbolically rejected white oppression and asserted his own identity by killing Mary: "he had murdered and created a new life for himself." When the Daltons discover Mary's charred bones in the furnace, Bigger and his lover Bessie flee. Considering Bessie a hinderance, Bigger murders her and hides in the ghetto until the authorities finally apprehend him.

In "Fate," Wright explicitly develops the debate between free will and determinism. Neither Jan nor Bigger's lawyer Boris A. Max condemn Bigger. They believe that, oppressed by a racist society, he had no choice but to murder. However, Bigger will not concede that his actions were predestined. In fact, the moment that defines Bigger as a free man is the murder itself; he discovers that his actions have liberated him from his passive acceptance of fate. Bigger admits killing Mary and is sentenced to death.

Naturalism

Naturalism is a literary movement of the late nineteenth and early twentieth centuries whose proponents envisioned a type of fiction that would examine human life with the objectivity of scientific inquiry. The naturalists typically portrayed characters as helpless victims, subject to hereditary and environmental forces beyond their control and comprehension. In their works, the naturalists often focused on such subjects as poverty, alcoholism, prostitution, insanity, and disease. One African American novelist who was known for his naturalistic depiction of working-class people was **Willard Motley**. Another naturalist writer was **Chester Himes**, author of a series of popular detective novels including *Cotton Comes to Harlem* (1965). **Ralph Ellison** shifted among several styles, including naturalism, in his **novel** *Invisible Man* (1952), which is widely regarded as a masterpiece of African American literature.

Gloria Naylor

Linden Hills

PENGUIN BOOKS

Naylor's second novel examines women's roles in contemporary America.

Gloria Naylor

American novelist
Born January 25, 1950.

Naylor's **novel** *The Women of Brewster Place* (1982) won the American Book Award for best first fiction in 1983. Since then, Naylor has continued to explore the black female experience in her novels.

Naylor was born in New York City and educated at Brooklyn College and Yale University, where she received an M.A. in Afro-American Studies. Her most celebrated novel, *The Women of Brewster Place,* is noted for its thorough characterizations of black women exploring their relationships and searching for self-identity. In *Linden Hills* (1985), she portrays two black poets' exploration of the world around them and examines women's traditional roles. In **Mama Day** (1988) and *Bailey's Cafe* (1992), Naylor focuses on African American women and their connections to their community and ancestry. Within her fictional worlds, Naylor's characters are free to determine the course of their lives, building upon the self-actualizing tradition embodied by writers of the **Harlem Renaissance**.

Since *The Women of Brewster Place,* Naylor's popularity has grown steadily. Its television adaptation in 1989 introduced her to a wider audience as she continues to explore issues fundamental to the lives of African American women.

Further Readings
Black Writers, second edition, Gale, 1994.

Larry Neal
American playwright and editor
Born September 5, 1937.
Died January 6, 1981.

Neal was deeply interested in the **black arts movement**. Born in Atlanta, Georgia, Lawrence P. Neal soon moved with his family to Philadelphia, where he was raised. After earning a degree from the University of Pennsylvania in 1963, Neal taught at various colleges while continuing to write. Along with **LeRoi Jones**, he edited **Black Fire: An Anthology of Afro-American Writing** (1968), a collection of **essays**, poems, stories, and **plays** by contemporary African American writers that helped define and broaden the black aesthetic. His play *The Glorious Monster in the Bell of the Horn,* staged off-Broadway in 1979, explores the conscious

and subconscious attitudes of blacks from different social classes.

Further Readings
Black Writers, first edition, Gale, 1989.

Dictionary of Literary Biography, Volume 38: *Afro-American Writers after 1955: Dramatists and Prose Writers,* Gale, 1985.

Ned Douglass
Character in *The Autobiography of Miss Jane Pittman*

Negritude

Negritude is a French-language literary movement based on the concept of a shared cultural bond on the part of black Africans and their descendants, wherever they may be in the world. It traces its origins to the former French colonies of Africa and the Caribbean. Negritude poets, novelists, and essayists generally stress four points in their writings. First, black alienation from traditional African culture can lead to feelings of inferiority. Second, European **colonialism** and Western education should be resisted. Third, black Africans should seek to affirm and define their own identity. Fourth, African culture can and should be reclaimed. Many Negritude writers also suggest that blacks can make unique contributions to the world, based on a heightened appreciation of nature, rhythm, and human emotions—aspects of life they say are not so highly valued in the materialistic and rationalistic Western cultures.

Most scholars agree that the 1933 publication of the journal *L'étudiant noir* marked the official birth of the negritude movement. The journal was edited by **Aimé Césaire,** Léon-Gontran Damas, and **Léopold Sédar Senghor,** three black students from Martinique, French Guiana, and French West Africa who were studying in Paris. In this publication, contributors proposed socialist solutions for the problems of exploited peoples. They criticized the arrogance of the West and formulated a new world view for blacks. Their philosophy became very influential among French-speaking intellectuals worldwide. The term "negritude" itself was coined in 1939, when it appeared in Césaire's poem *Cahier d'un retour au pays natal* (1939; *Return to My Native Land*, 1968).

Negritude attracted widespread attention after World War II with the appearance in 1947 of *Présence africaine,* a journal committed to the promotion of negritude concepts, and the publication of *Anthologie de la nouvelle poésie nègre et malgache de langue française* (1948; *Anthology of the New Negro and Malagasy Poetry in French*), an anthology of negritude **poetry** edited by Senghor. After most African colonies achieved independence in the early 1960s, negritude waned as an organized movement. It also came under intense criticism from the next generation of English- and French-speaking African writers, who denounced it as racist and as irrelevant to the problems of post-colonial Africa. Nevertheless, the negritude movement is seen as an important forerunner of newer literary trends.

Of the negritude writers, Senghor achieved the greatest renown, first as a poet and later as the president of the Republic of Senegal. His highly esteemed body of verse has received numerous honors, including consideration for a Nobel Prize in literature. In exalting black culture and values, Senghor emphasized what he perceived as differences between the races. He portrayed blacks as artistic geniuses less gifted in the area of scientific thought. Europe was seen as alien, dehumanized, and dying, while Africa was perceived as vital, nurturing, and thriving. The poems in Senghor's second collection, *Hosties noires* (1948; *Black Sacrifices*), explore his sense of unity with other blacks who share a common experience as an exploited race. His important political writings include *Liberté I: Négritude et humanisme* (1964; *Freedom I: Negritude and Humanism,* 1974). One of the most highly regarded novelists of the negritude movement is **Mongo Beti**, whose *Le pauvre Christ de Bomba* (1956; *The Poor Christ of Bomba*, 1971) explores the situation of educated Africans in the French colonies.

The Negro in Art

Alain Locke, editor
Nonfiction, 1940

Alain Locke's *The Negro in Art: A Pictorial Record of the Negro Artist and of the Negro Theme in Art* combines brief critical and historical **essays**, biographical and critical information, and some two hundred reproductions of works of art. The editor states that his primary objective is to reveal the extent of black contributions to the fine arts. The first section of the book examines the work of black artists from the seventeenth century through the 1930s in Europe and the United States, emphasizing the work of African American artists. Locke suggests that art produced by African American artists was beginning to gain broad critical and public acceptance in the early decades of the twentieth century. He credits the Federal Arts Projects with making it possible for African American artists to continue their work during the Depression, and calls for continued aid and support. Illustrations include works by seventeenth-century Spanish painter Sebastian Gomez and numerous twentieth-century artists, including Henry Ossawa Tanner, Malvin Gray Johnson, and Hale A. Woodruff. A second section discusses what Locke terms the "Negro theme" in art and proposes that the depiction of blacks in European and American art constitutes valuable direct evidence of changing social and cultural attitudes towards people of African descent. A third section looks at the art of Africa and summarizes the characteristics of the art of various regions. Citing the enormous influence of African art in the Modernist art movement, Locke urges African American artists to study the art of their ancestors and to assimilate its principles.

Negro History in Thirteen Plays

May Miller, editor
Plays, 1935

Urged by **Carter Woodson** to dramatize the lives of African heroes and heroines, **May Miller** and dramatist **Willis Richardson** wrote and edited the black history **plays** that comprise *Negro History in Thirteen Plays.* Miller contributed *Christophe's Daughters,* the story of two Haitian princesses; *Harriet Tubman; Samory,* about the legendary leader of the African Sudan; and *Sojourner Truth.* Richardson provided *Antonio Maceo; Attucks, the Martyr; In Menelik's Court; Near Calvary;* and *The Elder Dumas.* Richardson's first four plays emphasize the bravery of blacks, but the fifth unflatteringly depicts French author Alexandre Dumas.

Nel Wright

Character in *Sula*

N Alice Moore Dunbar Nelson

American poet, essayist, and
short story writer
Born July 19, 1875.
Died September 18, 1935.

An active supporter of racial equality, Nelson was one of the first black women to distinguish herself in American literature. She is considered important both for her literary achievements and her sociopolitical contributions.

Alice Ruth Moore was born in New Orleans, Louisiana, on July 19, 1875. She excelled scholastically and entered Straight University at the age of fifteen to study education. Her experiences inspired her first work, **Violets, and Other Tales** (1895), which focuses on the melancholic aspects of love and life.

In 1896, Nelson moved to Massachusetts and began corresponding with **Paul Laurence Dunbar,** whom she married in 1898. One year later, Nelson completed *The Goodness of St. Rocque, and Other Stories,* fourteen tales of Creole life in New Orleans. In 1902, the Dunbars separated, and Nelson moved to Delaware to teach. She married Robert J. Nelson in 1916.

In 1918, Nelson wrote the poem "I Sit and Sew," condemning the rejection of women's contributions during World War I. She became involved politically, serving on organizations including the Circle of Negro War Relief and the Women's Commission on the Council of Defense.

While politically active, Nelson was a columnist for the *Pittsburgh Courier* and the *Washington Eagle* and published poems and stories. She wrote steadily until the end of the 1920s. She died in 1935, in Philadelphia, Pennsylvania. Her **diary** was published in 1984 as *Give Us Each Day: The Diary of Alice Dunbar-Nelson,* edited by **Gloria T. Hull**.

Further Readings
Black Writers, first edition, Gale, 1989.

Dictionary of Literary Biography, Volume 50: *Afro-American Writers before the Harlem Renaissance,* Gale, 1986.

Nettie

Character in *The Color Purple* and *The Temple of My Familiar*

N *The New Negro: An Interpretation*

Alain Locke, editor
Anthology, 1925

An influential anthology of black writing, *The New Negro* was assembled by philosopher **Alain Locke,** who also provides an important introductory **essay**. *The New Negro* is an expanded version of the magazine *The Survey Graphic,* which celebrated black cultural life, especially in the urban north after the Great Migration. Many of the thirty-eight contributors, including **Zora Neale Hurston, Langston Hughes,** and **Countee Cullen,** were later associated with the **Harlem Renaissance**. Other important contributors are **W. E. B. Du Bois,** novelists **Jessie Fauset** and **Jean Toomer,** and Arthur A. Schomburg.

Locke divided *The New Negro* into two parts: "The Negro Renaissance," featuring literary work by contemporary black writers, and "The New Negro in a New World," containing essays on black sociology and politics. The first part begins with four important essays that provide an ideological framework for the collection, and includes **Langston Hughes**'s "The Negro Artist and the Racial Mountain." Also included in the first part are works of fiction, **poetry**, and music—both **spirituals** and urban **jazz**. The second part of *The New Negro* contains essays by notable sociologists and political writers, including **James Weldon Johnson** of the **National Association for the Advancement of Colored People** (NAACP) and **Charles S. Johnson** of the National Urban League. Robert Russa Morton, principal of the Tuskegee Institute, and **Kelly Miller**, a Howard University sociologist, provide essays on the black academy. A compendium of black culture in the mid-twenties, *The New Negro* also features an extensive bibliography on early black literature; black **folklore** in the United States, the West Indies and Africa; black poetry and drama; **slave narratives**; black **biography** and **autobiography**; and music.

The New Window

Please see *Six Plays for a Negro Theatre*

Newt Winger

Character in *The Learning Tree*

N'Gana Frimbo

Character in *The Conjure Man Dies*

Ngongo

Character in *Anthills of the Savannah*

Ngugi wa Thiong'o
Kenyan novelist, dramatist, and critic
Born January 5, 1938.

Ngugi wa Thiong'o, who has also written as James T. Ngugi, is widely regarded as the most significant writer in East Africa. His works show his concern for the inhabitants of his native Kenya, who have been oppressed and exploited by **colonialism** and **Christianity**. In *Weep Not, Child* (1964), his first **novel,** Ngugi attacked colonialism in Kenya. In his 1967 novel, *A Grain of Wheat*, he outlined the history of Kenyan resistance to colonial rule. Ngugi wrote *Caitaani mutharaba-ini* (1980; *Devil on the Cross,* 1982) in his native Gikuyu; it is the first modern novel in the language.

Ngugi was born to the third wife of a small tenant farmer and received his primary education at a missionary school. In 1948, however, he was placed in a school run by Kenyan nationalists, and he maintained a nationalist perspective throughout many of his works. He received a B.A. in 1963 and taught at the University of Nairobi for ten years, eventually becoming chair of the literature department.

Ngugi shows his sympathy for his country's poor in the **play** *Ngaahika Ndeenda: Ithaako ria Ngerekano* (1977; *I Will Marry When I Want,* 1982). This work, and the novel *Petals of Blood* (1977), criticized the Kenyan government and resulted in Ngugi being imprisoned for a year. A later work, *Matigari ma Njiruungi* (1986), was banned by the government. Fearing further reprisals, Ngugi left Kenya in 1982, but he continues to write about oppression and freedom in such works as *Decolonising the Mind* (1986) and *Moving the Centre* (1993).

Further Readings
Bailey, Diana, *Ngugi wa Thiong'o: The River Between, a Critical View,* edited by Yolande Cantu, Collins, 1986.

Dictionary of Literary Biography, Volume 125: *Twentieth-Century Caribbean and Black African Writers,* Second Series, Gale, 1993.

Niagara Movement

The Niagara Movement marked a turning point in African American history. From July 11 to July 13, 1905, a group of twenty-nine black intellectuals and activists from fourteen states met near Niagara Falls. Led by noted historian and essayist **W. E. B. Du Bois**, they rejected the accommodationist philosophy of **Booker T. Washington**, another prominent black thinker of the early twentieth century who believed that blacks should not demand social equality but should instead strive for their own economic improvement. In contrast, the members of the Niagara Movement encouraged African Americans to press for immediate civil rights without compromise. They specifically denounced Washington's policies of conciliation as a means of advancing social reform and of manual and industrial training for blacks as a means of gaining economic security. Among the other specific planks in the Niagara platform were ending racial **discrimination** in the United States and restoring voting rights for blacks.

For the next few years, Niagara Movement participants continued to meet and work through various committees. The Education Committee suggested publishing a report on the schooling of blacks in the South, while the Health Committee oversaw a nationwide campaign directed against tuberculosis in African Americans. However, the movement was hampered by inadequate funding and a policy that restricted membership to black intellectuals. In addition, Washington used his considerable influence to impede the movement's agenda whenever possible. In 1909, the Niagara Movement was succeeded by a new organization, which later became the **National Association for the Advancement of Colored People** (NAACP).

Du Bois's view that an educated black elite should lead African Americans to liberation is presented in *The Souls of Black Folk: Essays and Sketches* (1903), an eloquent plea for social equality. Washington's opposing viewpoints can be found in such books as *The Future of the American Negro* (1899). In 1907, Washington and Du Bois produced a book together titled *The Negro in the South: His Economic Progress in Relation to His Moral and Religious Development.*

Nick Romano

Character in *Knock on Any Door*

Nigeria Greene

Character in *A Hero Ain't Nothin' but a Sandwich*

Nigger: An Autobiography

Dick Gregory with Robert Lipsyte
Autobiography, 1964

The comedian and political activist **Dick Gregory** details his experiences growing up "not poor, just broke" in St. Louis, Missouri. He discusses his early struggles as an entertainer, his eventual success, and his active involvement in the **civil rights movement**. Gregory writes at length about his feelings towards his rarely present father and towards his mother, who raised six children while working as a domestic for wealthy white families. He tells of hustling for small change, washing dishes in return for food, and lying about his age to get a night job in a factory. In high school Gregory excelled in track, winning an athletic scholarship to Southern Illinois University. In 1959 he married Lillian Smith, and for the next two years Gregory, his wife, and their baby daughter lived hand-to-mouth as he hustled for engagements and honed his comic technique, distinguished by a satirical approach to racial issues. His big break came in 1961, when a one-night engagement at Chicago's Playboy Club led to a three-year contract. The final section of Gregory's story deals with his experiences in the early 1960s as a highly visible participant in civil rights demonstrations and rallies, including his several arrests. He ends with an expression of conviction that racial equality will one day be achieved.

Night of My Blood
Kofi Awoonor
Poetry, 1971

Kofi Awoonor's *Night of My Blood* contains poems from his 1964 **poetry** collection, *Rediscovery, and Other Poems*, as well as new verse. Many of the poems address the history of Ghana and its people, which also in a poetic sense symbolize the history of Africa. Awoonor's poems often appear in dirge form, lamenting the circumstances of the black individual concerning independence, lost innocence, and **religion**. In composition, the poems function in layers, as Awoonor weaves several themes into his work. Reflecting numerous motifs, the verse examines **myth** and rituals. Additionally, the verse incorporates elements of euphony in its rhythmic cadence, evoking images of traditional African music and dance.

Night Song
John A. Williams
Novel, 1961

Winner of the Prix de Rome in 1962 (later rescinded without explanation), **John A. Williams**'s *Night Song* portrays the relationship between three people involved in the New York **jazz** scene. David Hillary, a white skid row alcoholic and former English professor, meets jazz legend Richie Stokes (called Eagle), and they go on a drinking spree together. Keel Robinson, operator of a musician's hangout and Eagle's "protector," reluctantly helps the musician restore David's health. David wins acceptance later by rescuing Eagle from a drug overdose. Keel and Eagle lead David toward a spiritual

awakening and a return to his teaching position, but when Eagle and David accidentally fail to meet in David's college town, David betrays Eagle, who eventually dies of an unexplained overdose. The **novel** ends as Keel and his white girlfriend Della make a commitment to each other.

Itabari Njeri
American journalist and memoirist

Itabari Lord Njeri, born Jill Stacey Moreland in Brooklyn, New York, studied voice in New York City and received a B.S. from Boston University School and an M.S. from Columbia University Graduate School of Journalism. Originally a professional singer and actress, Njeri joined National Public Radio in Boston in the early 1970s as a reporter, producer, and host. She has been a feature writer, reporter, and critic for the *Greenville News,* the *Miami Herald,* and the *Los Angeles Times,* winning a 1990 National Association of Black Journalists Award for the year-long *Los Angeles Times* series "The Challenge of Diversity." Her *Every Good-bye Ain't Gone: Family Portraits and Personal Escapades* (1990), a memoir, won the American Book Award. Njeri is also the author of *The Last Plantation* and *Sushi and Grits: The Challenge of Diversity,* both published in 1993.

Further Readings
Black Writers, second edition, Gale, 1994.

Lewis Nkosi
South African novelist, dramatist, and short story writer
Born December 5, 1936.

Nkosi's writing deals with African literature and social concerns. His works include the **play** *The Rhythm of Violence,* (1963), *Tasks and Masks: Themes and Styles of African Literature* (1981), and the **novel** *Mating Birds* (1983).

Nkosi was born in 1936 in Natal, South Africa, where he joined the staff of *Drum* magazine in 1956. In 1960 he left South Africa to attend Harvard University, then moved to England where he taught, wrote, and published his first novel, *Mating Birds,* an allegorical study of **apartheid** and **colonialism**. *Mating Birds* concerns a black man's obsession with a white woman who discreetly encourages his attention. When the couple are discovered together, the woman accuses the man of rape, and he is sentenced to death without understanding the nature of his crime.

Further Readings

Black Literature Criticism, Gale, 1992.

Black Writers, first edition, Gale, 1989.

Kwame Nkrumah

Ghanaian politician, statesperson, and nonfiction writer
Born September 21, 1909.
Died April 27, 1972.

Ghanaian independence leader Kwame Nkrumah rose from humble roots to international prominence. As the leader of the first sub-Saharan colonial territory to achieve political independence, Nkrumah enjoyed immense prestige during the early years of his term in office. It was hoped that his government would serve as a model for democratic self-government in the emerging African states. A sadly powerless figure in his final years, Nkrumah is still honored as a brilliant and inspiring independence leader who helped awaken national pride and political confidence throughout the African continent.

Born the son of a goldsmith and a market trader in British West Africa in 1909, Nkrumah received his early education from Catholic missionaries. In 1935 he traveled to the United States to further his education and was introduced to socialist literature and **pan-Africanism**. After World War II he returned to his native land and formed a left-leaning political party of his own. In the 1951 elections, he won such a large percentage of the votes cast that he became leader of government business, a position equivalent to prime minister. Nkrumah led the Gold Coast, now named Ghana, to complete independence in March, 1957. He discussed the independence movement in his widely read **autobiography** *Ghana* (1957).

Nkrumah never abandoned his pan-African vision. He supported the idea of a Union of African States without arbitrarily defined borders fixed by former colonial powers. This view is articulated in his books *I Speak of Freedom: A Statement of African Ideology* (1961), *Africa Must Unite* (1963), and *Consciencism: Philosophy and Ideology of Decolonization and Development with Particular Reference to the African Revolution* (1964). His reliance on personal rule and persecution of political enemies, however, led to his ouster by a military coup in 1966. He took refuge in Guinea, where he lived in exile for most of his remaining years and penned *Dark Days in Ghana* (1968), a bitter diatribe against his political enemies. He died of cancer in 1972.

Further Readings

Black Writers, second edition, Gale, 1994.

Bretton, Henry L., *Rise and Fall of Kwame Nkrumah: A Study of Personal Rule in Africa,* Praeger, 1966.

McKown, Robin, *Nkrumah: A Biography,* Doubleday, 1973.

Omari, Thompson Peter, *Kwame Nkrumah: The Anatomy of an African Dictatorship,* C. Hurst & Co., 1970.

No Day of Triumph

Saunders Redding
Nonfiction, 1942

Having received a Rockefeller Foundation Fellowship in 1939, **Saunders Redding** was directed to travel through the South, observing and describing what he found there. *No Day* *of Triumph* is the partly autobiographical account this research. The style of the work is simultaneously travelogue, **novel**, history, and research. *No Day of Triumph* is divided into four sections, each bearing the name of a Negro spiritual. The first section chronicles Redding's ancestry and youth. The second and third sections describe the condition of individuals and of black families in the South, with Redding focusing on the hardships of **segregation**. The final section reveals Redding's hope for racial equality. In 1944, Redding received the Mayflower Cup Award, an award given annually in North Carolina, for *No Day of Triumph*.

No Easy Walk to Freedom

Nelson Mandela
Articles, speeches, and trial addresses, 1965

As one of the leaders of the African National Congress (ANC), **Nelson Mandela** was imprisoned for sabotage and treason and sentenced to life at the Robben Island fortress for political prisoners in 1964. At this time, Mandela and eight other ANC leaders were prohibited from publishing articles, giving public interviews, and discussing politics with visitors. Additionally, all of Mandela's **speeches** and published works were banned; possessing his writings was a criminal offense. Despite such restrictions, Mandela's political statements were collected and published in *No Easy Walk to Freedom* and *The Struggle is My Life* (1978).

In *No Easy Walk to Freedom,* Mandela discusses how Africans have struggled against and been affected by **apartheid**. This volume contains Mandela's 1953 presidential address to the Transvall province ANC, his speech at the 1961 All-In African Conference, and excerpts from his testimony at his three political trials. Mandela offers his views on education, poverty, and white supremacy, and he discusses his

Kwame Nkrumah led Ghana to independence in 1957.

desire for equal political rights in South Africa. He points out that the poverty of Africans is encouraged by legislation passed by whites. Stating his opposition to both white domination of blacks and black domination of whites, his closing words focus on the goal of a democratic and free society.

No Longer at Ease

Chinua Achebe
Novel, 1960

No Longer at Ease, **Chinua Achebe**'s second **novel**, serves as a sequel to his first novel, ***Things Fall Apart***. While the first book examines the initial impact of **colonialism** on a

This novel continues the story begun in *Things Fall Apart*.

native African culture, *No Longer at Ease* portrays the situation of Africans just before the colonies gain their independence. It also depicts the collapse of native African values—the ways in which things have fallen apart since the time of the first novel.

The main character of *No Longer at Ease,* Obi Okonkwo, is the grandson of Okonkwo, the protagonist of *Things Fall Apart.* Obi Okonkwo's fall from grace parallels that of modern Nigerian society. The village of Umuofia had sent Obi to England to receive a university education. Obi returns to Nigeria after four years in England, having lost his sense of self and place in the world. He is determined to end govern-

mental corruption and accepts a position with the ministry of education as scholarship secretary. He also falls in love with Clara, a nurse whom he meets during his return voyage. Obi initially upholds his moral standards, resisting an attempt at bribery. However, circumstances place him in debt, and he begins to accept money in return for consideration in awarding scholarships. In addition, he discovers that his tribe will not accept Clara; she is descended from hereditary slaves and by tradition cannot live with freeborn members of the tribe. As Obi's standards slip, he relinquishes control over other aspects of his life: he loses his temper before the Umuofia Progressive Society, Clara breaks her engagement and returns his ring, and he sacrifices the last of his ethics and morality. He is arrested for corruption and brought to trial. The novel ends with Obi's conviction.

No Place to Be Somebody: A Black-Black Comedy

Charles Gordone
Play, first produced 1967, published 1969

Charles Gordone's first **play** as sole author, *No Place to Be Somebody* won the Pulitzer Prize for Drama, the Los Angeles Critics Circle Award, and the Drama Desk Award. The play depicts two main characters, both in absurd positions as black men in a white world. Johnny Williams is a pimp and saloon keeper whose bar is a front for petty crimes. Johnny has various white people working for him—a few prostitutes and bar personnel—and his resentment toward whites is expressed in his interactions with them. The other main character, Gabe Gabriel is an actor who is unemployed because he is considered too light-skinned to play black roles. Gabe continually comments on the action of the play. The denouement is provided when Gabe's imaginary black militant colleague Machine Dog orders Gabe to kill Johnny.

N No Sweetness Here

Ama Ata Aidoo
Short stories, 1970

In *No Sweetness Here,* a collection of eleven short stories, **Ama Ata Aidoo** blends African and Western literary forms to portray the cultural clash of Ghanaian rural tradition and Western urban society. The stories brim with pathos and echo the hopelessness of the title piece, in which a couple divorces and their only child dies. Written over a four- or five-year period, the pieces demonstrate several overarching concerns. "Everything Counts," "In the Cutting of a Drink," "For Whom Things Did Not Change," "Certain Winds from the South," "Something to Talk about on the Way to the Funeral," and "Two Sisters" deal with the impact of modernization on women. "The Late Bud" is a story of sexism and womanhood, while triumph over degradation is the topic of "No Sweetness Here," "A Gift from Somewhere," "The Message," and "Other Versions."

N Nobody Knows My Name

James Baldwin
Essays, 1961

In *Nobody Knows My Name: More Notes of a Native Son,* **James Baldwin** continues his exploration of identity and race relations in the United States that he began in *Notes of a Native Son.* The title **essay**, for instance, contrasts the experience of Baldwin, an African American raised in the North before the Civil Rights era, with that of an African American who has lived his entire life in the segregated South. Baldwin writes that he became acutely aware of the true meaning of **segregation** and second-class citizenship while boarding a bus in Atlanta, Georgia, when he met a man who had lived with these pressures all his life. Another piece examines the problems of integration through the story of a

In this volume Baldwin explores issues of identity and race relations.

mother who makes great sacrifices to see that her son receives a quality education. "East River, Downtown" recreates a demonstration by African Americans at the United Nations after the assassination in 1961 of Patrice Lumumba, prime minister of the Republic of the Congo.

In other essays, Baldwin relates how he was influenced by various artists and public figures. "The Male Prison" is an examination of homosexuality and French writer André Gide. "The Northern Protestant" analyzes the work of Swedish filmmaker Ingmar Bergman. "Faulkner and Segregation" takes issue with William Faulkner's views on segregation, which, Baldwin believes, constitute an apology for the South's behavior toward blacks. A longer essay, "Alas, Poor Richard," dwells on the issue of author **Richard Wright**'s self-imposed exile from the perspective of their former friendship. In "The Black Boy Looks at the White Boy," Baldwin discusses how Norman Mailer's political convictions influenced his writing and possibly damaged his life.

ing with French colonial Africans that occurred when Baldwin was living in Paris. "A Question of Identity" gives a sense of perspective to students who were raised in one culture but who have chosen to live in another. "Equal in Paris" and "Stranger in the Village" examine the role of the black man in post-World War II Europe. In both essays, Baldwin's experiences illuminate his own past and his identity as an African American.

Notes of a Native Son

James Baldwin
Essays, 1955

Notes of a Native Son, **James Baldwin**'s second book and first collection of essays, is widely considered a milestone in African American literature. Not only did it establish Baldwin as a prominent writer, it departed from the topic of race relations addressed by many African American essayists. "Everybody's Protest Novel," the first **essay** in the collection, comments upon the way Harriet Beecher Stowe and **Richard Wright** reinforce images of white superiority in *Uncle Tom's Cabin; or, Life among the Lowly* and *Native Son*, respectively. The second essay, "Many Thousands Gone," also discusses the defects Baldwin perceives in *Native Son*. Publication of the two essays caused a rift between Baldwin and Wright, leading to an estrangement that was never resolved. The third essay is a review of *Carmen Jones,* Oscar Hammerstein's adaptation of Bizet's opera *Carmen* with a black cast.

Other essays in the volume examine life from Baldwin's personal perspective. "The Harlem Ghetto," for instance, is an analysis of Harlem in the years immediately following World War II. Baldwin finds it little different from the Depression-era city where he grew up. In "Notes of a Native Son," Baldwin reflects on his many-layered relationship with his stepfather, a fundamentalist Christian preacher, years after the man has died. "Encounter on the Seine: Black Meets Brown" is a recollection of a meet-

Novel

A novel is a long fictional narrative written in prose, usually organized around a plot or theme with a focus on character development and action. The novel developed from the novella and other early forms of narrative and emerged as a fully evolved literary form around the mid-eighteenth century. The first black novelist was **William Wells Brown**, who published *Clotel; or, The President's Daughter: A Narrative of Slave Life in the United States* in England in 1853. Six years later **Harriet E. Adams Wilson** became the first black woman to publish a novel, releasing *Our Nig; or, Sketches from the Life of a Free Black, In a Two-Story White House, North, Showing That Slavery's Shadows Fall Even There. Our Nig* was also the first novel published in the United States by a black man or woman. Other nineteenth-century novelists include **Pauline Elizabeth Hopkins**, **Frank J. Webb**, and **Frances Ellen Watkins Harper**. Twentieth-century novels by African American authors include **Alice Walker**'s *The Color Purple* (1982) and **Toni Morrison**'s *Beloved* (1987), both of which won Pulitzer Prizes, and **Ralph Ellison**'s *Invisible Man* (1952) and **Charles Johnson**'s *Middle Passage* (1990), both of which received National Book Awards. **Virginia Hamilton**'s novel for children entitled **M. C. Higgins, the Great** (1971) was the first work to be honored with both a National Book Award and the Newbery Medal. Other twentieth-century novelists include **Terry McMillan**, **Toni Cade Bambara**, and **James Baldwin**.

Novella Turner
Character in *Look What They Done to My Song*

Now Is Your Time!
Walter Dean Myers
Nonfiction, 1991

Written for young adult readers, **Walter Dean Myers**'s *Now Is Your Time! The African-American Struggle for Freedom* traces the history of African Americans from colonial times through the modern **civil rights movement**. Sections of chronological narrative are interspersed with anecdotal material and biographical sketches that portray the struggles of individual African Americans within the context of a broader historical picture. Drawing on letters and diaries, the biographical sections of this book relate stories of the Civil War's 54th Regiment of Massachusetts Volunteers and of such notable African Americans as journalist **Ida B. Wells**, inventor George Latimore, and artist Meta Warrick Fuller, as well as many lesser-known figures. Sources are not fully documented, but a select bibliography is provided. *Now Is Your Time!* received a Coretta Scott King Award.

Ntali
Character in *Les Blancs*

Richard Bruce Nugent
American short story writer
Born July 2, 1906.

Nugent was one of the most individualistic figures to emerge during the **Harlem Renaissance** movement. Primarily an artist, Nugent broke social conventions with a sense of humor and intelligence that endeared him to many in the New York literary circles of the 1920s. Along with **Langston Hughes** and **Zora**

Ellison's National Book Award-winning novel.

Neale Hurston, Nugent worked on the short-lived periodical *Fire!* in 1926. He has published several literary works in anthologies and periodicals, including the **short story "Sadhji"** (1925), which was produced as an "African ballet" in 1932. Nugent founded the Harlem Cultural Council in the mid-1960s and appeared in the 1984 film *Before Stonewall*.

Further Readings
Black Writers, first edition, Gale, 1989.

Dictionary of Literary Biography, Volume 51: *Afro-American Writers from the Harlem Renaissance to 1940,* Gale, 1987.

Numbo

Character in *Sadhji*

Nwaka

Character in *Arrow of God*

Flora Nwapa

Nigerian novelist and short
story writer
Born January 13, 1931.

One of the first African woman novelists
to publish in English, Nwapa writes of the
changes taking place in Nigeria. Whether educating children about Igbo spiritual beliefs in
Mammywater (1979) or depicting female self-
actualization in *Women Are Different* (1986),
Nwapa grounds her works in Igbo life and culture. Her first **novel,** *Efuru* (1966), questions
traditional gender roles. The central focus of
Nwapa's work is personal transformation; her
women characters move beyond the traditional
Igbo role of wife and mother in fulfilling their
social, economic, and spiritual needs. In *One Is
Enough* (1981) and *Women Are Different,*
Nwapa celebrates the strength and imagination
of women gaining economic and spiritual independence in Nigeria's modern cities.

Further Readings
Black Writers, second edition, Gale, 1994.

Dictionary of Literary Biography, Volume 125: *Twentieth-Century Caribbean and Black African Writers,*
Second Series, Gale, 1993.

Nyasanu

Character in *The Dahomean*

Nyasha

Character in *Mufaro's Beautiful Daughters: An
African Tale*

Julius K. Nyerere

Tanzanian political leader and nonfiction
writer
Born March, 1922.

A prominent African leader of the 1960s
and 1970s, Julius Kambarage Nyerere was born
in March, 1922, in Butiama-Musoma, Tanganyika (now Tanzania). After earning a
teacher's diploma from Makerere University in
1945 and an M.A. from Edinburgh University in
1952, he entered politics, becoming a leading
spokesperson for his country's independence.
When Tanganyika became independent in 1961
after decades of foreign rule, Nyerere was its
first prime minister. After the 1964 union of
Tanganyika and Zanzibar under the name Tanzania, Nyerere governed the new country as
well, winning re-election to the presidency four
times before resigning in 1985. Committed to
creating an egalitarian society based on socialist
principles, Nyerere was unable to pull his country out of the ranks of the world's poorest
nations, but his reforms did produce improvements in health, a higher rate of literacy, and
greater political stability.

Nyerere's numerous **speeches, essays,**
and other writings detail his policies and viewpoints, emphasizing respect for human rights,
national self-determination, racial equality, and
African unity. Collections of his writings
include *Freedom and Unity—Uhuru na Umoja:
A Selection from Writings and Speeches, 1952-
1965* (1967), *Freedom and Socialism—Uhuru
na Ujama: A Selection from Writings and
Speeches, 1965-1967* (1968), and *Freedom and
Development—Uhuru na Maendeleo: A Selection from Writings and Speeches, 1968-1973*
(1973).

Further Readings
Black Writers, second edition, Gale, 1994.

Hatch, John, *Two African Statesmen: Kaunda of Zam-
bia and Nyerere of Tanzania,* Regnery, 1976.

Obi Okonkwo

Character in *No Longer at Ease*

Obika

Character in *Arrow of God*

Marita Bonner Occomy

American playwright and
short story writer
Born June 16, 1899(?).
Died December 6, 1971.

Marita Odette Bonner Occomy's literary career spanned the **Harlem Renaissance** of the 1920s through the 1940s. Her **essays**, including "On Being Young—a Woman—and Colored" and **plays** like *Exit—An Illusion* (1923) and *The Pot-Maker* (1927) explore interracial prejudice, familial conflict, and romantic intrigue.

Born in Boston circa 1899, Occomy graduated from Radcliffe College in 1922, publishing many short stories after her marriage in 1930. "On the Altar" depicts black women encountering communal stress and interracial violence, while "One True Love" shows their struggles for independence. Her collected works were published as *Frye Street and Environs* in 1987.

Further Readings

Black Writers, second edition, Gale, 1994.

Dictionary of Literary Biography, Volume 51: *Afro-American Writers from the Harlem Renaissance to 1940,* Gale, 1987.

Therman B. O'Daniel

American educator and editor
Born July 9, 1908.
Died in 1986.

In addition to his numerous academic activities, Therman Benjamin O'Daniel edited several books of criticism on African American literary figures, including *Langston Hughes, Black Genius: A Critical Evaluation* (1971) and *James Baldwin: A Critical Evaluation* (1981).

Born in Wilson, North Carolina, O'Daniel received his M.A. from the University of Pennsylvania and attended graduate-level courses at several colleges, including Harvard University. He went on to teach in the English departments of Allen University, Dillard University, and Morgan State University. In 1972, O'Daniel was honored by the Black Academy of Arts and Letters for editing the *College Language Association Journal,* an academic publication of which he was also the cofounder.

Further Readings

Black Writers, first edition, Gale, 1989.

Odessa Rose

Character in *Dessa Rose*

Odili

Character in *A Man of the People*

Ofeyi

Character in *Season of Anomy*

Carl Offord

Trinidadian novelist
Born April 10, 1910.

Carl Ruthven Offord is known for *The White Face* (1943), a **novel** about the northern migration of southern blacks. He has also written several short stories and worked as a newspaper editor and publisher. Offord founded the weekly periodical *Black American* in 1961, and in 1977 directed the first Black American Film Festival.

Born in Trinidad, West Indies, in 1910, Offord moved to New York City at age nineteen, attending the School for Social Research. *The White Face* revolves around a black couple who leave Georgia for New York, where fascist agitators are fomenting hatred of Jews. Taken with the ideas of a charismatic black fascist, the husband beats a Jewish boy and is arrested; his wife cannot prevent his tragic end.

Further Readings

Black Writers, second edition, Gale, 1994.

Dictionary of Literary Biography, Volume 76: *Afro-American Writers, 1940-1955,* Gale, 1988.

Ogbanje Ojebeta

Character in *The Slave Girl*

Grace Ogot

Kenyan short story writer and novelist
Born May 15, 1930.

Ogot has become one of her country's few well-known women writers. Although informed by the changes sweeping African society, her work reflects a strong appreciation for tradition. Ogot was born Grace Emily Akinyi in Butere, Central Nyanza, Kenya, on May 15, 1930. Her writings include a **novel,** *The Promised Land* (1966); the story collections *Land without Thunder* (1968), *The Other Woman* (1976), and *The Island of Tears* (1980); and *Miaha* (1983; *The Strange Bride,* 1989), her version of a popular Luo village **myth**. Ogot has also published stories for children. Elected to the Kenyan parliament in 1983, she resigned in protest two years later but remains active in Kenyan political affairs.

See also **Short Stories of Grace Ogot**

Further Readings

Black Writers, second edition, Gale, 1994.

Dictionary of Literary Biography, Volume 125: *Twentieth-Century Caribbean and Black African Writers,* Second Series, Gale, 1993.

Gabriel Okara

Nigerian poet and novelist
Born April 24(?), 1921.

Gabriel Imomotimi Gbaingbain Okara, who was born in Bumoundi, Nigeria, was an important figure in the development of postcolonial African literature, in which questions of language and identity were persistent themes. Using native Nigerian experience and the English language of his country's colonizers, Okara synthesized a literary style and a new idiom. His **novel** *The Voice* (1964) combines formal experiment with a critique of the Westernization and corruption of newly independent Nigeria. Okara's reputation as a poet rests on the collection *The Fisherman's Invocation* (1978), for which he won the Commonwealth Joint **Poetry** Award in 1979. After the Biafran secessionist conflict, in which many of his manuscripts were destroyed, Okara worked in broadcasting and with the Council for Arts and Culture in Port Harcourt.

See also **Poetry of Gabriel Okara**

Further Readings

Black Writers, first edition, Gale, 1989.

Dictionary of Literary Biography, Volume 125: *Twentieth-Century Caribbean and Black African Writers,* Second Series, Gale, 1993.

Christopher Okigbo

Nigerian poet
Born August 16, 1930.
Died August, 1967.

In his life and writing, Christopher Ifenayichukwu Okigbo combined traditional elements of African culture with **Christianity** and Western poetic techniques. In the collections *Heavensgate* (1962) and *Limits* (1964), Okigbo used myths, rituals, and dense, challenging symbolism. Most readers consider Okigbo's posthumous collection, *Labyrinths, with Path of Thunder* (1971), more mature, in part because the poems are more political. Shortly before his death in 1967, Okigbo co-founded a small, Nigerian-based publishing house with **Chinua Achebe**. Okigbo was killed while fighting as a volunteer for the Biafran army and was posthumously awarded the Biafran National Order of Merit.

Further Readings

Black Literature Criticism, Gale, 1992.

Black Writers, first edition, Gale, 1989.

Dictionary of Literary Biography, Volume 125: *Twentieth-Century Caribbean and Black African Writers,* Second Series, Gale, 1993.

Okolo

Character in *The Voice*

Okonkwo

Character in *Things Fall Apart*

Ben Okri

Nigerian novelist and short story writer
Born in 1959.

Okri was born in Minna, Nigeria, and was educated at Urhobo College, Warri, Nigeria, and the University of Essex, England. In his **novels** and the **short story** collections *Incidents at the Shrine* (1986) and *Stars of the New Curfew* (1988), Okri blends real and **supernatural** imagery to present a portrait of life in postcolonial Nigeria, which has not had a stable government for nearly thirty years. Okri's work has been compared to that of the magical realists, a group that includes Jorge Luis Borges. His fictional compositions have received international acclaim: Okri was awarded the Aga Khan prize for fiction by the *Paris Review* and his most celebrated novel, *The Famished Road* (1991), won the Booker Prize. *The Famished Road*'s main character, Azaro, is an *abiku* child torn between the spirit and natural world. His struggle to free himself from the spirit realm is paralleled by his father's immersion into politics to fight the oppression of the poor. By the novel's end, Azaro recognizes the similarities between the nation and the *abiku;* each is forced to make sacrifices to reach maturity and a new state of being. *The Famished Road*'s sequel, *Songs of Enchantment* (1993), continues to explore the links between Nigeria's popular myths and its political life. Okri is also the author of the novels *Flowers and Shadows* (1980) and *The Landscapes Within* (1981).

Further Readings

Black Writers, second edition, Gale, 1994.

Ol' Cap'n Cotchipee

Character in *Purlie Victorious*

Old Ben Woodfolk

Character in *Black Thunder*

Old Man Pete

Please see *Six Plays for a Negro Theatre*

Ole Massa

Character in *Mules and Men*

Olga Ten Yip

Character in *A Morning in Trinidad*

Oliver Cary

Character in *Comedy, American Style*

Olivia

Character in *Caleb, the Degenerate;* and *Possessing the Secret of Joy*

Olivia Cary

Character in *Comedy, American Style*

Ollie Miss

George Wylie Henderson
Novel, 1935

In *Ollie Miss*, **George Wylie Henderson** tells the tale of a strong young black woman in a rural southern town. The protagonist, Ollie, works on her Uncle Alex's farm. She projects a proud, almost feminist attitude as she labors alongside the male hands, ignoring the taunts of the other workers. One night Ollie discovers that her lover, Jule, has been with another woman. When she confronts Jule's other lover, the knife-wielding woman wounds Ollie. While recovering, Ollie realizes she is pregnant. The news gives her courage; she refuses Jule's attempts at reconciliation and decides to build a life for herself.

Olunde

Character in *Death and the King's Horseman*

O Omeros

Derek Walcott
Poem, 1990

In the poem *Omeros,* (the title is the modern Greek word for Homer) **Derek Walcott** uses **myth** to explore such issues as race, identity, and **colonialism**. Alluding to Greek **epic** poetry such as Homer's *Odyssey* throughout *Omeros,* and to Dante's *Divine Comedy* near the end of the poem, Walcott tells the story of Helen, a West Indian house maid; Achille and Hector, two fishermen who vie for her attention; and Philoctete, another fisherman. Tormented by his love for Helen and by his anger at the commercialism taking over his home, Achille sets off in his boat for the ocean. While at sea, he has a vision in which he is introduced to his African heritage. A major part of the poem traces the journey of Achille and Philoctete to their ancestral land, the coast of West Africa. The poem is also concerned with another character, Dennis Plunkett, a former British officer who is plagued with historical guilt. The work combines the style and theme of Greek epic **poetry** with the realities of modern West Indian life.

O On Being Negro in America

Saunders Redding
Nonfiction, 1951

Combining self-psychoanalysis, personal recollection, and commentary, **Saunders Redding** discusses the plight of African Americans in America. His main theme is the problem caused by the duality of the African American experience. Redding contends that African Americans feel that they must think of themselves not as men and women, but in terms of color and that this self-perception affects their psychological balance. This theory reflects **W. E. B. Du Bois**'s theory of "double consciousness." Redding also discusses integration, the ignorance of races

about each other that yields destructive stereotypes, and the harmful results of **racism** on children. He discusses the failures of attempts at educational and legal equality, touches on the hope **religion** offers when it draws people together, and surveys social and political advancements made by African Americans have made through the efforts of the **National Association for the Advancement of Colored People** (NAACP), the Student Non-Violent Coordinating Committee (SNCC), and **Martin Luther King Jr.**, among others, but feels that race problems are incurable. Redding concludes that the cure for these social ills will require something greater than individual reflection.

O "On the Pulse of Morning"

Maya Angelou
Poem, 1993

Maya Angelou read her poem "On the Pulse of Morning," composed for the occasion, at the inauguration of President Bill Clinton in Washington, D. C., on January 20, 1993. She thus became the first woman and the first African American to be invited to read her **poetry** at a presidential inauguration. Angelou's free-verse poem is dominated by three images announced in its opening line—"A Rock, A River, A Tree"—images Angelou later said had been borrowed from African American **spirituals**. While evoking the horrors of war, exploitation, and oppression, the poem celebrates the diverse ethnic and religious groups that make up the American and the world communities and calls on them to shape a better future. The final stanza emphasizes hope for a new beginning.

Ondine Childs

Character in *Tar Baby*

One Man, One Machet

T. M. Aluko
Novel, 1964

T. M. Aluko's *One Man, One Machet* treats the difficulties encountered by Udo Akpan, a Nigerian district officer responsible for administering tax and agricultural affairs, as he attempts to educate the local citizens in new government policies. Much of the action in the book, set in the 1950s, revolves around Akpan's efforts to overcome political and traditional attitudes while moving forward with the duties of his office. One of his main detractors, Benja-Benja, manages through deception and manipulation to turn local village leaders against Akpan and his strategies. When the new government changes its position on the treatment of cocoa disease affecting crops, the turnabout confuses villagers and causes them to question the ultimate motives of Akpan's government. Overall, Aluko's plot illustrates the complexities involved when colonial government converges with local politics.

Ophelia "Cocoa" Day

Character in *Mama Day*

Opportunity: A Journal of Negro Life

Charles S. Johnson
Magazine, 1923-1927

The house organ of the Urban League of Chicago which **Charles S. Johnson** launched upon joining the organization, *Opportunity* was intended as a vehicle for new black writers and as a competitor with the activist journal *Crisis*. The new publication focused on sociological studies of working and housing conditions in black areas. African art, Gullah culture, Caribbean communities, and other folk subjects were treated in depth. *Opportunity* also became a magnet for **Harlem Renaissance** writers with its prizes and sponsored activities. Encouraging rejection letters were a standard policy. In 1927 Johnson collected various **essays** and illustrations published over the years in the anthology *Ebony and Topaz.*

Oral Literature

Please see Oral Tradition/Literature

Oral Tradition/ Literature

Oral tradition refers to reliance on word of mouth to pass information from individual to individual and from generation to generation. An oral tradition may encompass **folklore,** history, songs, religious beliefs, and other material. Oral transmission has been known to preserve material over many generations, although often with variations. In Africa, there is a particularly rich tradition of orally transmitted **poetry** and narrative. Most tribes have creation myths, and the courts of chiefs often have professional bards who function as tribal historians. Additional forms of oral literature include **trickster tales,** other **folk tales** and myths, proverbs, and riddles. The tradition of black storytelling has influenced many modern writers, including novelists **Gayl Jones** and **Leon Forrest**, poets **Cheryl Clarke** and **Kofi Awoonor,** and **short story** writer **J. California Cooper.** *Anowa* (1970), by Ghanaian dramatist **Ama Ata Aidoo**, is an example of a **play** based on African oral literature.

One salient feature of the African oral tradition is its close link to music. Poetry is almost always chanted or sung. Among tribes with tonal languages, where the meaning of words depends on the pitch at which each syllable is spoken, poetry is also presented on the "talking drum," where the melody rises and falls in conformity with the spoken word. More recent music forms, such as **jazz** and the **blues,** have continued to be intimately connected with the course of black literature. Another characteristic of the African oral tradition is its didactic function, helping to set social norms and teach sophisticated language skills. A discussion of Africa's oral literature with respect to its history and culture can be found in Awoonor's *The Breast of the Earth: A Survey of the History, Culture, and Literature of Africa South of the Sahara* (1975).

Oratory/ Speeches

A speech is a spoken communication to an audience, while an oration is a long speech, particularly for a ceremonial occasion, which is delivered in a formal and dignified manner. Great black orators from **Frederick Douglass** to **Martin Luther King Jr.**, have changed the course of history with their spoken words. One of the most famous speeches of our time is King's 1963 "**I Have a Dream**" speech. Some memorable passages from King's speeches are recorded in *The Portable Martin Luther King Jr.: Quotations from the Speeches, Essays, and Lectures of Martin Luther King Jr.* (1992), edited by **Coretta Scott King**. Other black activists and politicians whose speeches have been collected in book form include **Nelson Mandela, Desmond Tutu, Malcolm X, Angela Davis, Stokely Carmichael**, and **Adam Clayton Powell Jr.**

An Ordinary Woman

Lucille Clifton
Poetry, 1974

Lucille Clifton's third and most popular **poetry** collection is *An Ordinary Woman*. In the title poem of this volume, the author, in her thirty-eighth year, takes time out for self-assessment and finds herself "an ordinary woman."

She reflects on the common experience of unfulfilled expectations. Ordinary in this context does not imply trivial, however. Another image of womanhood found in the book is that of Clifton's mother, Thelma Moore Sayles. The poet remembers her mother as a dedicated wife who, though she failed to have a satisfying marriage, taught her children important lessons about caring for a family. In the collection, Clifton also contemplates her own role as a writer. In "The Poet," she describes the compulsion to create, while in "Love Poem," she denies that she had a choice in becoming a poet and claims that a demon of inspiration has fostered her poetic imagination.

Oscar Jefferson

Character in *Youngblood*

Roi Ottley

American journalist and social historian
Born August 2, 1906.
Died October 1, 1960.

Born in Harlem in 1906, Roi Vincent Ottley became the first black war correspondent to work for a national publication when he accepted assignments with *PM* and *Liberty Magazine* in 1944. He began his career on the *Amsterdam Star News* in 1930, later attending Columbia University and New York University. Ottley's best seller about Harlem, *New World A-Coming: Inside Black America* (1943) inspired a tone poem of the same name by Duke Ellington and became an award-winning radio series. From 1945 until his death in 1960 Ottley was a columnist for the *Chicago Tribune*. He wrote several books of social history about black America, including *The Negro in New York: An Informal Social History, 1926-1940* (1969). He is buried in Burr Oak Cemetery, Chicago.

Further Readings
Black Writers, second edition, Gale, 1994.

Oudin

Series character in The "Guyana" Quartet

Our Nig

Harriet Wilson
Novel, 1859

Set in Massachusetts and New Hampshire, *Our Nig; or, Sketches from the Life of a Free Black*, the first **novel** by a black woman in the United States, is **Harriet Wilson**'s autobiographical story of Frado, a mulatto woman whose experiences of servitude and hardship oppose the myth that Southern blacks were emancipated in the North. The novel begins before Frado's birth with the story of her orphaned white mother Mag and Mag's subsequent marriage to Frado's father Jim, a "kindhearted African." After Jim's untimely death, Mag abandons Frado at the house of the Bellmont family. Frado thus becomes an indentured servant at the age of seven to the tyrannical and abusive social climber Mrs. Bellmont. Mrs. Bellmont's kind-hearted husband is powerless to stop the abuse meted out by his wife and their daughter Mary, and although the two Bellmont sons intervene to protect Frado, they cannot stop their mother and sister. With the death of the eldest son James, Frado's staunchest protector, the beating worsens. Only after years of suffering, when Frado finally confronts Mrs. Bellmont, does the abuse stop. At eighteen, Frado leaves the Bellmonts and lives happily with a woman named Mrs. Moore. However, Frado soon marries Samuel, a charlatan orator who pretends to be a former slave. When Frado becomes pregnant, Samuel abandons her. Frado gives birth to her son in a poorhouse and must put him in a foster home. The novel ends with Wilson's addressing the reader, expressing her hope that royalties received from the sale of her novel will enable her to retrieve her son from foster care.

OUR NIG;

OR,

Sketches from the Life of a Free Black,

IN A TWO-STORY WHITE HOUSE, NORTH.

SHOWING THAT SLAVERY'S SHADOWS FALL EVEN THERE.

BY "OUR NIG."

"I know
That care has iron crowns for many brows;
That Calvaries are everywhere, whereon
Virtue is crucified, and nails and spears
Draw guiltless blood; that sorrow sits and drinks
At sweetest hearts, till all their life is dry;
That gentle spirits on the rack of pain
Grow faint or fierce, and pray and curse by turns;
That hell's temptations, clad in heavenly guise
And armed with might, lie evermore in wait
Along life's path, giving assault to all." — HOLLAND.

BOSTON:
PRINTED BY GEO. C. RAND & AVERY.
1859.

Title page from Wilson's autobiographical slave narrative.

Sembène Ousmane

Senegalese novelist and screenwriter
Born January 8, 1923.

Ousmane is renowned for his **novels** and films that address social wrongs in post-colonial Africa. Most of his works are about underprivileged groups or individuals facing opposition from a corrupt, bureaucratic system.

Born in Senegal, Ousmane was drafted by the colonial French and served in World War II. He was later a docker and union organizer in Marseilles, France, an experience that informed his first novel, *Le Docker noir* (1956; *The Black Docker*, 1987). His second and more widely read novel, *Oh Pays, mon beau peuple!* (1957; title means "Oh My Country, My Beautiful People"), portrays a Senegalese farmer who is rejected by both the black and white communities due to his

interracial marriage and his attempts to modern-
ize the community's farming system. Drawing
on his experiences as a union leader, Ousmane
also wrote *Les Bouts de bois de Dieu* (1960;
God's Bits of Wood, 1962), which recounts the
railworker strikes of 1947 and 1948 on the
Dakar-Niger line. Later, Ousmane became
involved in films. *Le Noire de...* (1966; *Black
Girl,* 1969), which he wrote and directed, was
based on a newspaper article about the suicide
of a black maid in France. The **comedy** *Mand-
abi* (1968; *The Money Order,* 1969) was the first
film written and directed by an African to be
commercially released in Senegal and is often
considered the first African film to reach an
international audience. Garnering rave reviews,
the movie *Xala* (1974; title means "Impotence")
satirized a corrupt African bureaucrat.

Further Readings

Black Literature Criticism, Gale, 1992.
Black Writers, first edition, Gale, 1989.

The Owl Answers

Adrienne Kennedy
Play, 1963

Adrienne Kennedy's *The Owl Answers,*
a surreal exploration of black identity, is set
within a subway that is transformed into the
Tower of London, the study of a black Southern
preacher, and St. Paul's Cathedral. Such transformations support the nonlinear time/space
relationship of the drama. The main character,
"She who Is," is the illegitimate daughter of a
wealthy white man and his black cook. Her
mixed heritage results in feelings of alienation
from both black and white culture. When She
who Is visits London following the death of her
stepfather, Reverend Passmore, she becomes
imprisoned in the Tower of London with a chorus of figures from British history. Continued
symbolic and mythic transformations occur
until She who Is becomes an owl.

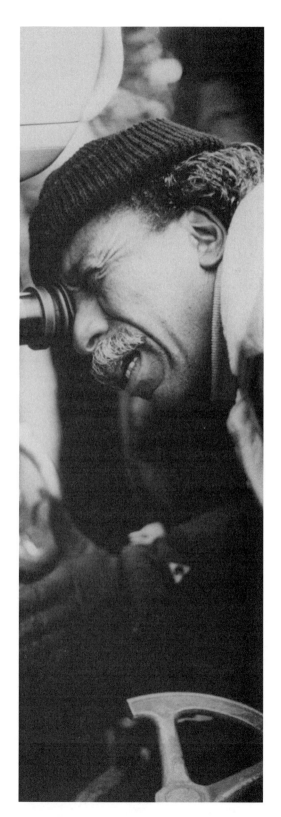

What I want

What I am

What you force me to be

is what you are

For I am you, staring back

from a mirror of poverty

and despair, of revolt and

freedom. Look at me and

know that to destroy me is

to destroy yourself.

Born Black,
Gordon Parks, 1971

Nell Irvin Painter

American educator and historian
Born August 2, 1942.

A university professor of history, Painter was born in 1942 in Houston, Texas, receiving her B.A. and M.A. from the University of California during the 1960s, and her Ph.D. from Harvard University in 1974. Her *Exodusters: Black Migration to Kansas After Reconstruction* (1977) reveals the causes of the exodus of 1879. Characterized by rigorous research, her work encompasses the particular and the global: *The Narrative of Hosea Hudson: His Life as a Negro Communist in the South* (1979), for example, makes exhaustive use of oral sources to provide a detailed historical close-up, while her study *Standing at Armageddon: The United States, 1877-1919* (1987) presents a national overview of a historical period. She has also coedited *Teaching American Indian History* (1993).

Further Readings
Black Writers, first edition, Gale, 1989.

Palace of the Peacock

Please see The "Guyana" Quartet

The Palm-Wine Drinkard

Amos Tutuola
Novel, 1952

Amos Tutuola's first **novel**, *The Palm-Wine Drinkard and His Dead Palm-Wine Tapster in the Deads' Town,* recounts the journey of an expert and devoted palm wine drinker through a fantasy land of magic, marvels, and monsters. When his tapster falls from a tree and dies, the drinker sets out to find him in Deads' Town. During the journey the drinker displays extraordinary cleverness and unusual powers that enable him to circumvent or survive numerous misadventures. Though the drinker finds his tapster in Deads' Town, the latter refuses to re-enter the world of the "alives." Consequently, the drinker returns home, finding that a bitter quarrel between Heaven and Land has resulted in drought and famine. He feeds the remaining multitudes, settles the cosmic dispute, ends the drought and famine, and restores the world to its normal order.

Pan-Africanism

Pan-Africanism is a movement aimed at creating greater unity and cooperation among African states. The movement dates from 1900, when the First Pan-African Congress convened in London. Over the next twenty-seven years, four additional congresses, composed primarily of delegates from the West Indies and the United States, convened to discuss ways to promote African cooperation and unity and protest colonization. One early proponent of Pan-Africanism was Jamaican essayist **Marcus Garvey**, founder of the **back-to-Africa movement**. Garvey outlined his philosophy in **essays** and manifestos. His best-known book during his lifetime was *The Philosophy and Opinions of Marcus Garvey; or, Africa for the Africans* (1923).

Although Pan-Africanism fell out of favor in the 1930s, there was a resurgence of interest in 1944, when several black organizations founded the Pan-African Federation. The next year, the Sixth Pan-African Congress was held. In the 1950s, Africans, who now comprised the majority of federation members, supported political independence. New African nations began to establish various economic and political associations. The most important of these was the Organization of African Unity, founded in 1963. Its purpose is to promote unity among African nations; stop **colonialism** in Africa; promote international cooperation; improve living conditions; protect the autonomy and territory of member nations; and coordinate various policies involving the economy, politics, science, defense, and medicine. The organization is based in Addis Ababa, Ethiopia.

Since Garvey's day, Pan-Africanism has captured the imagination of many black nationalist leaders. Trinidadian historian and critic **C. L. R. James** discusses the movement in *A History of the Negro Revolt* (1938). A later historical analysis can be found in *Pan-Africanism* (1974), coedited by American sociologist **Nathan Hare**. During the height of the **black power** movement in the United States, many activists such as **Stokely Carmichael** embraced Pan-Africanism. A sampling of Carmichael's **speeches** and essays on the topic can be found in *Stokely Speaks: Black Power Back to Pan-Africanism* (1971).

PaPa LaBas
Character in *Mumbo Jumbo*

Papa Zeringue
Character in *Middle Passage*

Parks has achieved success as a writer, photographer, and film director.

Pat Parker
American poet
Born January 20, 1944.
Died June 4, 1989.

A black feminist lesbian mother, Parker addressed in her **poetry** the radical politics of race, class, and gender, but she also wrote love poems. Born in Houston, Texas, Parker was educated in California and held a variety of jobs, working as a radical activist on community issues while publishing such poetry collections as *Child of Myself* (1972) and the retrospective anthology *Movement in Black* (1978). Parker became director of the Feminist Women's Health Center in Oakland, California, in 1978, a position she held until her death from cancer in 1989.

Further Readings
Black Writers, second edition, Gale, 1994.

Moraga, Cherrie, and Gloria Anzaldua, *This Bridge Called My Back: Writings by Radical Women of Color,* Women of Color Press, 1981.

Gordon Parks
American autobiographer, novelist, and photographer
Born November 30, 1912.

In addition to writing both fiction and nonfiction, Gordon Alexander Buchanan Parks has been a photographer, a composer, and a film director and producer. He was born the youngest of fifteen children in Fort Scott, Kansas, to Andrew and Sarah Ross Parks. After his mother died when he was sixteen, he went to live with his sister in St. Paul, Minnesota, but was thrown out after an argument. He worked a series of odd jobs until he decided to become a photographer in the mid-1930s, attracting attention with his documentary pictures detailing the everyday lives of blacks. In 1948, he became a staff photographer for *Life,* the first black to work at the magazine.

Parks wrote a book on a photography in the 1940s and, though he vowed never to write another book, published his first work of fiction, *The Learning Tree*, in 1963. The **novel,** based on his youth, is the story of a black family living in 1920s Kansas. The narrative focuses on the family's adolescent son and his struggles with love, grief, and the other challenges of adulthood. When this book was made into a movie in 1968, Parks produced and directed it, and also wrote the score.

In 1966, Parks published the first of three autobiographies, *A Choice of Weapons*, which begins with his mother's death and ends in 1944, when Parks moved to Harlem. *To Smile in Autumn: A Memoir* (1979) spans the years between 1944 and 1978, his most productive period. *Voices in the Mirror: An Autobiography* (1990) records his impressions of his childhood, as well as the **civil rights movement** and the **black power** struggles of the 1960s. Parks has also published a book of articles and **essays,** *Born Black* (1971), and the novel *Shannon* (1981).

Further Readings

Black Literature Criticism, Gale, 1992.

Black Writers, second edition, Gale, 1994.

Harnan, Terry, *Gordon Parks: Black Photographer and Film Maker,* Garrard, 1972.

Turk, Midge, *Gordon Parks,* Crowell, 1971.

Part of My Soul Went with Him
Winnie Mandela
Autobiography, 1985

Describing her life both with and without her husband **Nelson Mandela,** *Part of My Soul Went with Him* is comprised of interviews with **Winnie Mandela,** conversations with friends and colleagues, and letters from Nelson Mandela. In the **autobiography,** Mandela recounts the early realization that her husband would always give priority to South Africa and the

black struggle for equality. She chronicles arrests and imprisonments, government interventions and restrictions—especially her 1977 banishment from Soweto as punishment for her alleged involvement in the 1976 uprising. Despite legal orders barring her from meeting with more than one person at a time and despite nearly continuous government persecution since her husband's imprisonment in 1964, Mandela writes of challenging her oppressors by disregarding traditional Afrikaner racial customs, and of assuming her husband's crusade for black rights during his incarceration.

Passing
Nella Larsen
Novel, 1929

Passing, the second and last of **Nella Larsen**'s published **novels,** is regarded as one of the notable books to emerge from the **Harlem Renaissance**. A psychological study of middle-class black women, the work depicts sophisticated, urban women who, though possessing carefully cultivated mannerisms and enjoying comfortable lifestyles, can neither escape the restrictions of **racism,** nor erase the consciousness of their heritage. The narrative revolves around Clare Kendry, a beautiful, light-skinned black woman who escapes likely poverty by marrying a wealthy white man, who assumes she is also white. Clare successfully passes into white culture, until a yearning for the company of other blacks leads her to renew ties with Irene Redfield, a childhood friend who has married a prominent black physician in New York City. Soon Clare and Irene's husband discover a mutual attraction, and Irene is alarmed by the perceived threat to her material comfort and social standing. At the novel's conclusion, which has been criticized as unrealistic and ambiguous, Clare either falls, jumps, or is pushed from an open window at a Harlem party, just as her irate husband arrives to confront her about her racial identity.

The Past Is the Past

Richard Wesley

Play, first produced 1974, published 1974

What has been called **Richard Wesley**'s finest short **play** focuses on mutual acceptance between a father and son. Eddie Green, the illegitimate son abandoned by Earl Davis, recognizes his father and confronts him in a pool hall. Realizing who Eddie is, Earl answers the boy's questions with painful honesty. Abandoned by his own father, Earl tells Eddie that the cycle need not continue—Eddie can break it by building a good relationship with his own children. Earl and Eddie go their separate ways, unclear about whether they will ever meet again, but knowing that this confrontation has been significant.

"Patternist Saga"

Octavia E. Butler

Novels, 1977-1980

The five **science fiction** novels that comprise **Octavia E. Butler**'s *Patternist Saga* focus on a **supernatural** character named Doro, a four-thousand-year-old Nubian who survives by killing humans and living in their bodies. He and his descendants have psychic powers, which Doro plans to use to take humankind to the next phase of evolution. Throughout this series, Doro is transformed into men and women of various races and ages. Similarly, his descendants represent diverse social groups. As a result, Butler's *Patternist Saga* explores socially differences from a variety of perspectives.

In the first **novel**, *Patternmaster* (1976), Butler portrays a hierarchical, agrarian society reminiscent of the ancient past. In *Mind of My Mind* (1977), Doro visits one of his families in a futuristic suburb of Los Angeles. He assists his daughter in the maturing process; she eventually changes the direction of the Pattern. The protagonist of the third novel, *Survivor* (1978), confronts the inherent racial and religious prejudices of two warring tribes on another planet. In *Kindred* (1979), a young black California woman travels back in time to an antebellum plantation. The final work of this series, *Wild Seed* (1980), details the romance of Doro and Anyanwu, an eternal priestess. This novel showcases Anyanwu's capacity to be both compassionate and powerful as a feminist leader.

Patternmaster

Please see "Patternist Saga"

Lindsay Patterson

American editor and writer

Born July 22, 1942.

Born in Bastrop, Louisiana, in 1942, Patterson received a B.A. from Virginia State College, before working as a feature writer and columnist for Associated Negro Press and later as an editorial assistant for writer **Langston Hughes**. He has also lectured and co-hosted broadcast programs. The compiler of numerous anthologies of black works in a variety of disciplines, Patterson edited the *Anthology of the American Negro in the Theatre: A Critical Approach* (1968), *An Introduction to Black Literature in America: From 1746 to the Present* (1968), *Black Films and Film-Makers: A Comprehensive Anthology from Stereotype to Superhero* (1973), as well as other publications. He wrote *The Afro-American in Music and Art* (1970).

Further Readings
Black Writers, first edition, Gale, 1989.

Orlando Patterson

Jamaican-born American novelist and sociologist

Born June 5, 1940.

Born in Jamaica in 1940 and immigrating to the United States in 1970, Horace Orlando Lloyd Patterson draws on his West Indian background for his **novels** and scholarly work. Receiving his B.Sc. from the University of the West Indies in 1962, his M.A. from Harvard University in 1971, and his Ph.D. from the London School of Economics in 1965, Patterson began teaching sociology at Harvard in 1971. Patterson's historical novels *The Children of Sisyphus* (1964) and *Die the Long Day* (1972) are set in his native Caribbean and explore the effects of **slavery** upon individuals. In *The Sociology of Slavery: An Analysis of the Origins, Development, and Structure of Negro Slave Society in Jamaica* (1967) and the award-winning *Slavery and Social Death: A Comparative Study* (1982) Patterson's interdisciplinary approach combines historical research and sociological analysis. In 1991 he published *Freedom, Volume 1: Freedom in the Making of Western Culture* (1991).

Further Readings
Black Writers, first edition, Gale, 1989.

Paul
Character in *Lucy*

Paul Brooks
Character in *Teacup Full of Roses*

Paul Cummings
Character in *!Click Song*

Paul D.
Character in *Beloved*

Paul Williams
Character in *The Young Landlords*

Pauline Breedlove
Character in *The Bluest Eye*

Peanut
Character in *Just Above My Head*

Pecola Breedlove
Character in *The Bluest Eye*

Peggy
Character in *Lucy and Pinktoes*

Gayle Pemberton
American educator
Born June 29, 1948.

Born in 1948 into a middle-class Episcopalian family in St. Paul, Minnesota, Gayle Renee Pemberton received her B.A. from the University of Michigan in 1969 and her Ph.D. from Harvard University in 1981. She has taught at several colleges and universities and is the author of *On Teaching the Minority Student: Problems and Strategies* (1988). She has served as associate director of African American studies at Princeton University and addresses in her scholarly work the dominant white structures—linguistic and imaginary—which have defined and determined African American experience. In her memoir *The Hottest Water in Chicago: On Family, Race, Time, and American Culture* (1992; published in 1993 as *The Hottest Water in Chicago: Notes of a Native Daughter*) Pemberton uses **autobiography** as social critique, exploring the dilemmas of the black middle class through personal anecdote.

Further Readings
Black Writers, second edition, Gale, 1994.

Perry Dart
Character in *The Conjure Man Dies*

Margaret Perry
American writer and editor
Born November 15, 1933.

Born in 1933 in Cincinnati, Ohio, Perry attended Western Michigan University, the University of Paris, and Catholic University of America, where she received a master of library science degree. Focusing primarily on Afro-American literature in her published work, she has written *A Bio-Bibliography of Countee P. Cullen, 1903-1946* (1971), *Silence to the Drums: A Survey of the Literature of the Harlem Renaissance* (1976), and *The Harlem Renaissance: An Annotated Bibliography and Commentary* (1982). She has edited *The Short Fiction of Rudolph Fisher* (1987) and contributed to *What Black Librarians Are Saying* (1973). A librarian, professor, and professional speaker, Perry has also contributed articles, stories, and reviews to history, library science, and literary journals.

Further Readings
Black Writers, first edition, Gale, 1989.

Petals of Blood
Ngugi wa Thiong'o
Novel, 1977

Petals of Blood, written by **Ngugi wa Thiong'o**, takes place in the fictional village of Ilmorog over the twelve years after Kenya gained its independence. The **novel** opens with the arrests of Munira, Wanja, Kareja, and Abdulla for the murders of three company directors. The intertwined lives of the suspects, the victims, and the history of postcolonial Ilmorog itself form the basis of the narrative. Earlier, Wanja had been seduced and abandoned by one of the company executives. She moved to Ilmorog, where she started a successful business based on brewing an herbal beverage from the flowers which have "petals of blood." Over time, she has relationships with Munira, Kareja, and Abdulla respectively, and eventually loses

her business to capitalists. Intensely embittered by her financial ruin, she winds up as the madam of the brothel in which the company directors are murdered.

Peter John "Old Jack" Crawley
Character in *The Chaneysville Incident*

Ann Petry
American novelist and short story writer
Born October 12, 1908.

Ann Lane Petry grew up in the only African American family in the town of Old Saybrook, Connecticut. During her youth, she was isolated from the strife many African Americans faced. Petry briefly pursued a career as a pharmacist in her family's business but moved to New York after marrying George D. Petry in 1938. In New York, she worked as an advertising sales representative, reporter, and editor, and witnessed the exploitation and socioeconomic deprivation of urban African Americans for the first time. Petry's experiences in the inner city and her New England upbringing shape her fiction. Some of her characters achieve almost heroic stature as they lead ordinary lives. In her short fiction, irony, humor, and **supernatural** occurrences link her to fellow New England writers.

Known for her intricate plots and vivid characterizations, Petry is a forerunner of a long line of successful black female writers. With the publication of **The Street** (1946), she became the first black female author to address the problems African American women face as they cope with life in the slums. She also became the first black woman in America to have book sales of more than a million copies.

Building her stories around the basic themes of adultery, cruelty, violence, and evil instead of specific African American problems, Petry transcends racial and geographic boundaries. Her **novels Country Place** (1947) and **The**

Ann Petry influenced many black women writers following World War II.

Narrows (1953) both take place in a small, middle-class New England town (Petry had returned to Old Saybrook in 1948). The former was one of the few literary works written by an African American writer using white characters. Petry is also the author of a number of children's books, among them *The Drugstore Cat* (1949), *Tituba of Salem Village* (1964), and *Miss Muriel and Other Stories* (1971).

Further Readings

Black Writers, first edition, Gale, 1989.

Children's Literature Review, Volume 12, Gale, 1987.

Contemporary Literary Criticism, Gale, Volume 1, 1973, Volume 7, 1977, Volume 18, 1981.

Ervin, Hazel Arnett, *Ann Petry: A Bio-Bibliography,* G. K. Hall, 1993.

Reference Guide to American Literature, St. James Press, third edition, 1994.

Pharaoh
Character in *Black Thunder*

Robert Deane Pharr
American novelist
Born July 5, 1916.

Strongly influenced by Sinclair Lewis's *Babbitt,* Pharr's **novels** expose in vivid detail the hidden and marginal aspects of black American life. Born in Richmond, Virginia, Pharr received his B.A. from Virginia Union University in 1939. He was working as a waiter at Columbia University's Faculty Club when his first novel *The Book of Numbers* (1969), was published to popular and critical acclaim. In *S.R.O.* (1971), his long, partly autobiographical novel set in a single-room occupancy hotel, and again in *Giveadamn Brown* (1978), Pharr reveals with humor and empathy the struggles and frustrations of life in Harlem.

Further Readings

Black Writers, first edition, Gale, 1989.

Dictionary of Literary Biography, Volume 33: *Afro-American Fiction Writers after 1955,* Gale, 1984.

Pheoby
Character in *Their Eyes Were Watching God*

Philadelphia Fire
John Edgar Wideman
Novel, 1990

The second **novel** for which **John Edgar Wideman** received the prestigious PEN/Faulkner Award, *Philadelphia Fire* is a complex, nontraditional narrative based on the author's reaction to a real-life event—the fire-bombing of a militant black commune in Philadelphia in 1985. In the novel, which combines fact with fiction, the narrator Cudjoe returns from a self-imposed exile on a Greek island to his native Philadelphia to confront both the tragedy and his own demons. His ruminations blend with those of Wideman himself—whose own son was sentenced to life imprisonment for murder—and later with a mysterious and tormented character named J. B. A meditation on holocaust, the idealism of the 1960s, and the suffering of black Americans, Wideman's novel is meant to be a literary tribute to the people killed in Philadelphia in 1985, an effort to keep the incident from being forgotten.

Philip Bowers

Character in *South Street*

Philip Carteret

Character in *The Marrow of Tradition*

Philoctete

Character in *Omeros*

The Philosophy and Opinions of Marcus Garvey

Marcus Garvey
Essays and manifestos, 1923-1925

Founder of the **back-to-Africa movement** and an advocate of racial separatism, **Marcus Garvey** expresses his Pan-Africanist philosophy in the **essays** collected in two volumes of *The Philosophy and Opinions of Marcus Garvey; or, Africa for the Africans*. The first volume contains Garvey's views on racial problems and his proposal for a solution. This volume, published as Garvey was being charged with federal mail fraud, formed the ideological basis for his defense and reveals his conviction that he was betrayed by his colleagues. The second volume's largest section emphasizes Garvey's political agenda, and a second section comments on his trial, conviction, appeal, and imprisonment. The third section contains documents dealing with his back-to-African campaign. Both volumes of *The Philosophy and Opinions of Marcus Garvey* were edited and produced by Garvey's second wife, Amy Jacques-Garvey.

The racial separation Garvey advocates in this work differs radically from the social, political, and financial equality sought in the **civil rights movement**. Garvey argues that integration would only lead blacks to the status of an underclass and that no race should give up power by accepting such a position. He condemns African American intellectuals as elitist, and maintained that creating a separate, free, and powerful African state was the only way to secure and protect the rights of blacks living outside of Africa.

Garvey also calls for the development of a black theology and aesthetic. He argues that institutionalized **racism** has forced blacks to accept the idea of a white God, and that the same forces have ignored the important achievements of blacks throughout history. While claiming that blacks should develop their own African ideals of physical and artistic beauty, he finds the **Harlem Renaissance** movement in the arts to be elitist.

A Photograph: Lovers in Motion (play)

Please see *Three Pieces*

Phylon (journal)

Please see W. E. B. Du Bois

The Piano Lesson

August Wilson
Play, first produced 1987, published 1990

Winner of a Pulitzer Prize, **August Wilson**'s *The Piano Lesson* takes place in mid-1930s Pittsburgh. Set in the Doaker Charles house, the **play** centers on the conflict between his nephew

Boy Willie Charles, who wants to sell the family's heirloom piano to obtain money to purchase land in the South, and his niece Berniece, Boy Willie's sister, who refuses to sell the piano. A descendant of the white owners who once owned the Charles family is willing to sell Boy Willie the last one hundred acres of the farm, and Boy Willie needs the proceeds from the sale of the piano to finance the purchase. Berniece, however, will not consider selling the piano. Years earlier, Doaker's grandmother and father were traded to another family for the piano, which their owner, Robert Sutter, wished to present to his wife, Miss Sophie, as a gift. Doaker's grandfather, mourning the loss of his family, carved intricately stylized images of his wife and son into the legs of the piano. Over time, the piano legs became a pictorial chronicle of the Doaker family as other images and events were added. Following Miss Sophie's death, Doaker's father retrieved the piano for his family, but at the cost of his life. The tragic events leading to the Doaker family's ultimate possession of the piano coupled with its rich historical symbolism compel Berniece to keep the piano, and eventually Boy Willie agrees and returns south empty-handed. Wilson also wrote the script for the 1995 televised version of *The Piano Lesson,* the first of his plays to be adapted as a movie.

Pierre

Character in *Possessing the Secret of Joy*

Pilate

Character in *Song of Solomon*

Pimp

Character in *Manchild in the Promised Land*

Darryl Pinckney

American critic, essayist and novelist
Born 1953.

Pinckney has contributed stories and **essays** to major newspapers and periodicals, but his major literary achievement has been his first **novel,** *High Cotton* (1992), winner of the Art Seidenbaum Award from the *Los Angeles Times* for first fiction.

Pinckney was born in Indianapolis, Indiana, in 1953. After attending Columbia University he became a Hodder Fellow at Princeton University, and then won a Guggenheim Fellowship. Pinckney is a member of the fourth generation of his family to attend college.

High Cotton's nameless protagonist, like Pinckney, is from an educated Indianapolis family; for this reason the novel has been considered an autobiographical work. The novel describes the protagonist's feeling of alienation from history as well as concurrent racial conflicts. It has been lauded for its examination of these issues.

Further Readings
Black Writers, second edition, Gale, 1994.
Contemporary Literary Criticism, Volume 76, Gale, 1993.

Pinktoes

Chester Himes
Novel, 1961

Chester Himes's *Pinktoes* is a stylized **satire** of the racial and sexual mores at work in "integrated" high society. Mamie Mayson, a Harlem hostess with lofty social ambitions, plans a series of parties to which she invites an assortment of white and African American professors, wealthy philanthropists, and other high ranking members of society. While purporting to be enjoined in an effort to improve relations between the races, partygoers are more concerned with contriving sexual liaisons with members of the opposite race, climbing the social ladder, and trying to ruin the social standing of others. Juanita Wright, a black woman, refuses to attend the festivities, forcing her husband, Wallace, who is fair enough to pass for white, to attend alone. To get even with Juanita for snubbing her, Mamie gossips that Juanita's husband is leaving his wife to live with his mistress, a white woman named Peggy. When Juanita eventually discovers the couple together, she seeks solace into the arms of a white man. Mamie's revenge backfires when the community polarizes along lines of race in response to the Wright's situation. Eventually, however, Mamie convinces Peggy to give up Wallace, who returns to his wife. The social community is reintegrated and Mamie continues her efforts to aid race relations.

The Planet of Junior Brown
Virginia Hamilton
Novel, 1971

Two troubled adolescent boys find hope in friendship and an escape from their societal oppressors in **Virginia Hamilton**'s *The Planet of Junior Brown*. Junior Brown is a 300-hundred pound eighth grader who is also a musical prodigy. He and his friend, homeless orphan Buddy Clark, skip school and attend math and astronomy classes taught by Mr. Pool, a former teacher turned janitor, in the school's basement. When Junior suffers a mental breakdown, Buddy and Mr. Pool scurry him away to Buddy's "planet," a commune of homeless boys living in an abandoned building. There Junior begins a new life.

Plantation Tradition

The plantation tradition refers to a group of white southern nineteenth-century writers who romanticized antebellum **slavery** in their work. Examples include William Gilmore Simms and John Esten Cooke. The desire to refute this vision of slavery and dramatize its immorality motivated a number of black writers both before and after the Civil War. Prior to emancipation, the abolitionist literature written by former slaves such as **Frederick Douglass** and **William Wells Brown** can be considered, in part, a reaction against plantation tradition writing. In the post-war period, the short stories of African American author **Charles W. Chesnutt** contained implicit denunciations of slavery, yet still appealed to white readers of the kind of fiction that waxed nostalgic for the Old South.

Plato
Character in *Meditations in Limbo*

Play

A play is a literary work designed to be presented by actors on a stage. It can take a variety of forms, including **comedy,** tragedy, drama, and melodrama. In 1823, West Indian playwright Henry Brown's play *The Drama of King Shotaway,* the story of an insurrection on the island of St. Vincent, became the first play by a black writer to be produced in the United States. The oldest surviving play written by an African American is **William Wells Brown**'s *The Escape; or, A Leap for Freedom*, published in 1858. Popular and critical acceptance of works by black playwrights was slow in coming. **Angelina Weld Grimké**'s *Rachel*, produced in 1916, was one of the first popularly successful plays written by an African American and presented by African American actors. In 1923, *Chip Woman's Fortune,* a one-act play by **Willis Richardson**, became the first non-musical play by an African American author to open on Broadway; the first Broadway hit by an African American writer was *Mulatto,* by **Langston Hughes**, which ran from 1935 through 1937. Among the black playwrights who have won major awards in the second half of the twentieth century are the American playwrights **Lorraine Hansberry, Ntozake Shange Charles Gordone, August Wilson,** and **Ed Bullins**, Nigerian writer **Wole Soyinka**, and Caribbean author **Derek Walcott.**

Plays of Ted Shine

Ted Shine's drama offers sardonic observations of black life in the South, presenting memorable characters in vivid and often symbolic settings. *Morning, Noon and Night* (1964), for example, features a strong controlling older woman, Gussie Black. A characteristic figure in Shine's work, Black is a pseudoreligious figure who manipulates the other characters for her own gain. A sequel, *Comeback after the Fire* (1969) further develops the character of Sister Sue Willie, an itinerant female evangelist. Among Shine's many one-act **plays**, *Shoes* (1969), *Idabel's Fortune* (1969), *Flora's Kisses* (1969), and the popular *Contribution* (1969) are the most noteworthy.

Plum Bun: A Novel Without a Moral
Jessie Redmon Fauset
Novel, 1929

Jessie Redmon Fauset's *Plum Bun* depicts one African American's efforts to avoid racial prejudice by passing for white. Angela Murray is a young mulatto woman who desires to rise above the drab existence of her parents by crossing the color line and living as a white woman. She is convinced that the only way to accomplish her goal is to marry a rich white man. When her parents die, moves to New York City to study art. She is sure that in this field, she will be able her to surround herself with a wealthy class of people. From among her new circle of white friends she meets wealthy young Roger Fielding, whom Angela determines would be a suitable prospect for a husband. Angela disregards her own attraction to a fellow art student named Anthony Cross in order to pursue Roger. However, Roger has other plans than to marry a poor girl; he makes Angela his mistress and eventually rejects her. Meanwhile, Angela's estranged sister, Virginia, has moved to Harlem and found a loving husband and a successful career teaching music to young black

children. Angela eventually realizes the detrimental effects of turning her back on her family and friends and comes to appreciate the lesson of her sister, who has given of herself and gained happiness in return.

Sterling D. Plumpp
American poet and essayist
Born January 30, 1940.

Sterling Dominic Plumpp is known for works of **poetry** that depict oppression of both the individual African American and the black community. In verse that eschews heavily politicized black vernacular in favor of a more complex, blues-based, and distinctive poetic voice, Plumpp speaks to improving the quality of life for Americans of all races.

Born in Clinton, Mississippi, in 1940, Plumpp moved to Chicago, where he graduated from Roosevelt University in 1968. His experiences with institutionalized oppression inspired much of his verse. His poetry volumes include *Clinton* (1976), *The Mojo Hands Call, I Must Go* (1982), and *Blues: The Story Always Untold* (1989). Plumpp is also the author of *Black Rituals,* a nonfiction study of the social psychology of oppression. He joined the faculty of the University of Illinois in 1971 and became associate professor of black studies in 1984.

Further Readings
Black Writers, first edition, Gale, 1989.

Dictionary of Literary Biography, Volume 41: *Afro-American Poets since 1955,* Gale, 1985.

Poems on Various Subjects
Phillis Wheatley
Poetry, 1773

Poems on Various Subjects, Religious and Moral is the only collection of **Phillis Wheatley**'s **poetry** published during her lifetime.

Printed when Wheatley, a slave owned by John Wheatley of Boston, was in her late teens or early twenties, the book was the first ever published by an African American. Because of this, the London reading public of 1773 was less interested in the content of *Poems on Various Subjects* than in Wheatley herself. The London publisher required John Wheatley, who sponsored the volume's publication, to add a sworn statement of authenticity to indicate that Phillis was the true author of all the poems. Witnesses to the testimony included the royal governor of Massachusetts, Thomas Hutchinson, and the Boston merchant John Hancock.

The poems in the volume show the effects of Phillis's education, beliefs, and upbringing. Almost half the poems in the collection are elegies, written in praise of people who have died, such as the pastor of the Old South Meeting House in Boston, or occasional poems written to commemorate important events. Many of them show the influences of Phillis's models, John Milton and Alexander Pope, in her use of heroic couplets, classical language and construction, and Christian metaphors. The poems also display her devout **Christianity**, based on the Puritan tradition in which she was raised, through their subjects: Bible stories and reflections on the consoling benefits of faith when a loved one dies. Wheatley demonstrates an awareness of her African heritage in poems such as "On Being Brought from Africa to America" and her address to the Earl of Dartmouth, which contains an indictment against **slavery**.

P O E M S

O N

VARIOUS SUBJECTS,

RELIGIOUS AND MORAL.

B Y

PHILLIS WHEATLEY,

NEGRO SERVANT to Mr. JOHN WHEATLEY, of BOSTON, in NEW ENGLAND.

L O N D O N:

Printed for A. BELL, Bookseller, Aldgate; and sold by Messrs. COX and BERRY, King-Street, BOSTON.

M DCC LXXIII.

Frontispiece from Wheatley's poetry volume, composed largely of neoclassical elegiac verse.

A Poetic Equation
Nikki Giovanni and Margaret Walker
Conversations, 1974

A Poetic Equation: Conversations with Nikki Giovanni and Margaret Walker is made up of tape-recorded conversations between **Nikki Giovanni** and **Margaret Walker** that took place during 1972 and 1973. The preface presents biographical information on the two writers: While Walker is from a generation of intellectual Southern blacks who came of age during the Great Depression, World War II, and the development of an American Communist party, Giovanni is an urban child of the sixties and seventies during which open rebellion erupted. From these varied backgrounds, Giovanni and Walker discuss such social and political topics as the black family and the role of women, the black liberation movement, **literary criticism**, and the future of blacks in America. The two writers also comment on each other's creative activities.

An excerpt from an early poem in Phillis Wheatley's hand.

The Poetical Works of James Madison Bell

James Madison Bell
Poetry, 1901

A collection of the best-known poems of the Civil War-era poet, *The Poetical Works of James Madison Bell* offers one black American's response to the Emancipation Proclamation, the death of Lincoln, and the triumph of the Union Army. **James Madison Bell**'s volume includes "The Day and the War" (1864), a narrative poem that takes the reader from the days of **slavery** through the Civil War to Emancipation, with special honor paid to abolitionist John Brown. "The Triumph of Liberty" (1870), also included, reviews four years of war and peace beginning in 1862, offers an elegy for Lincoln, and includes optimistic hopes for the newly freed Americans. *The Poetical Works* also includes one of Bell's religious poems, "Creation Light," a study of the events in the Book of Genesis.

Poetry

In its broadest sense, poetry is writing that evokes feelings or presents ideas through artificial language, as opposed to the everyday language of prose. Poetry exploits the sound, rhythm, and connotations of words as well as their literal meanings. It sometimes, but not always, makes use of meter and rhyme, and it may make a strong appeal to the senses through imagery. The first black American poet is generally considered to be **Lucy Terry**, a slave, who wrote her only known poem, "Bars Fight," in 1746. In 1760, **Jupiter Hammon** became the first black to publish a poem as a separate work, composing *An Evening Thought: Salvation by Christ, with Penetential Cries*, and more than a decade later, **Phillis Wheatley** became the first African American to publish a volume of poetry. **Paul Laurence Dunbar** was the first African American poet to gain national fame, enjoying popularity in the late nineteenth and early twentieth centuries. **Langston Hughes** emerged as one of the most significant black poets of the **Harlem Renaissance**, publishing such collections as *Fine Clothes to the Jew* (1927). **Countee Cullen** was also recognized as one of the most prominent poets of that period. In the mid-twentieth century, **Gwendolyn Brooks** became the first black poet to win a Pulitzer Prize, an honor she received for her collection *Annie Allen* (1949). **Maya Angelou** made history in 1993, reading her poetry at Bill Clinton's presidential inauguration; her poem was published as *On the Pulse of Morning* soon after the ceremony. Another poet, Pulitzer Prize-winner **Rita Dove**, made history that same year as well, becoming the first black person to be named poet laureate of the United States. Other notable poets include **Sonia Sanchez**, **Etheridge Knight**, **Haki R. Madhubuti**, **Nikki Giovanni**, and **Ishmael Reed**.

Poetry of Samuel W. Allen

Much of **Samuel W. Allen**'s **poetry** attempts to relate African and African American cultures. In "There Are No Tears," for example, he contrasts the "tall and cold" skyscraper, representing urban life and modern civilization in America, with "the dark uncertainties" of Africa. Another important theme in Allen's work is **religion**, especially the brand of **Christianity** practiced by Southern blacks. Some of his most powerful poems include cross-cultural biblical and historical allusions. For example, in "Jason Who Was Rent," the title character, who has been "nailed on the northern cross," manages to rise, Christ-like, thus symbolizing the ability of black people to transcend violence and oppression.

The poems collected in *Paul Vesey's Ledger* (1975) build upon Allen's interest in black history. The eighteen untitled poems, organized by chronology and theme, depict the shameful history of American **racism** dating back to colonial times. A number deal with the slave era. For example, "I did not climb the apple trees in Sussex" portrays **slavery** in Mississippi. Other poems in the volume draw on more recent historical events. "As the names of the martyrs mount" pays tribute to such heroes as Nat Turner, Harriet Tubman, **Martin Luther King Jr.**, and **Malcolm X**.

Poetry of Maya Angelou

In January, 1993, on the occasion of Bill Clinton's inauguration, **Maya Angelou** became the first woman and the first African American to read her **poetry** at a presidential inauguration. *"On the Pulse of Morning"* shares characteristics with much of her other poetry. It deals with the struggle to bring order and understanding to individual experience by relating it to the experience of the community. Angelou addresses these problems, as well as others that deal specifically with the condition of African Americans, in collections such as *Just Give Me a Cool Drink of Water 'fore I Diiie* (1971), *Oh Pray My*

Wings Are Gonna Fit Me Well (1975), *And Still I Rise* (1978), *Shaker, Why Don't You Sing?* (1983), *Now Sheba Sings the Song* (1987), and *I Shall Not Be Moved* (1990).

Like her autobiographical works, Angelou's poetry reflects aspects of her personal history. In *Oh Pray My Wings Are Gonna Fit Me Well* and *And Still I Rise,* the poet moves from issues such as love and romance to social and sexual problems such as inadequate support of the poor and the underprivileged, sexual abuse of women, and abusive relationships in general. She then looks at the history and current state of the African American community. In each case, Angelou finds patterns and order in the midst of chaos at all levels, from her own life to the life of her community. *Shaker, Why Don't You Sing?* and *Now Sheba Sings the Song* both deal with feminism and female sexuality as well as individual problems such as depression and insomnia. *I Shall Not Be Moved* directly addresses the lives and problems of African American women and offers multiculturalism as a solution to society's difficulties.

Poetry of Russell Atkins

The **avant-garde** poems of **Russell Atkins** are known for both their stark subject matter and their stylistic innovation. Among the recurring themes are drug addiction, sexual aberration, necrophilia, and abortion. For example, *The Abortionist* (1954) is a controversial poem arranged as a **play** and relates the story of Dr. Drassakar, who performs a violent abortion on the daughter of a hated colleague. Among the stylistic hallmarks of Atkins's work are frequent contractions and grammatical transformations. He also employed the embedding of words within words in such poems as "Lisbon." In addition, poems including Atkins's "Nocturne and Prelude" are among the earliest examples of concrete **poetry** in the United States.

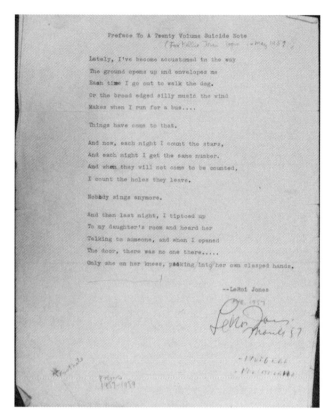

Typescript page from Baraka's *Preface to a Twenty Volume Suicide Note.*

to "lecture" on the horrors of American reality.

With his involvement with **black nationalism**, Baraka articulated a more militant poetic vision. In "Black Art," for instance, he calls for poems that are not merely academic exercises but powerful political expressions of real-world concerns. In "Poem for HalfWhite College Students," he warns black students of the dangers of succumbing to the values of the white academic world, and in "Ka'Ba" he suggests that the African tradition—accessed through black nationalism—can serve as a bastion of self-affirmation, meaning, and order in an oppressive land.

As black nationalism became more confining for Baraka, he adopted a Marxist-Leninist perspective that generated a new aesthetic vision. In such poems as "The Dictatorship of the Proletariat" and "Das Kapital," he serves as a mouthpiece for socialist ideology. In a series of poems entitled *Why's/Wise,* however, he offers a tribute to African American culture, arguing that it represents the only true break from Europe. While maintaining his Marxist stance, he suggests that the only truly American culture can be found in the artistic expressions of African Americans.

Poetry of Amiri Baraka

The development of **Amiri Baraka**'s poetry corresponds to radical personal, philosophical, and political changes. Many of his early poems published in *Preface to a Twenty Volume Suicide Note* (1961) reflect his concerns as a prominent member of the Beat movement. Wishing to free himself from what he considered to be stale, bourgeois academic forms of the Western classical tradition, he turned for inspiration to his own experience and popular American culture. At this point in his career, Baraka's **poetry** reflects his alienation from Africa. In his next volume, *The Dead Lecturer* (1964), Baraka—having left Greenwich Village and his white wife—continues with his rejection of the white aesthetic as he struggles to find the voice

Poetry of Louise Bennett

In her **dialect poetry**, collected in *Jamaica Labrish* (1966) and her *Selected Poems* (1982), **Louise Bennett** blends traditional English verse forms with the **oral tradition** and Creole dialect of her native Jamaica. While the subjects of her poems range from **folklore** to international events, Bennett consistently exhibits pride in her gender and race, and women play prominent roles in her **poetry**. Bennett's often humorous verse is a vehicle for subtle criticism and even defiance of the white male culture that dominates Jamaican society. For example, in "Strike Day," women symbolically grasp the steering wheel: "We drive pon tram car free of cos' / Dis like is fe we own, / An wen we tiad o' de drive / We block de line wid stone."

Poetry of Arna Bontemps

Twenty-three of **Arna Bontemps**'s poems written during the 1920s were later collected in a book titled *Personals* (1963). Characterized by emotional intensity and the spirit of self-discovery, these verses are an artistic record of a young man's creative response to the vibrant milieu of the **Harlem Renaissance**.

One of the poems, "The Return," had won *Opportunity* magazine's Alexander Pushkin Poetry Prize in 1927. Like much of Bontemps's work, it combines personal emotion with racial memory: "Darkness brings the jungle to our room: / the throb of rain is the throb of muffled drums.... / This is a night of love / retained from those lost nights our fathers slept / in huts." In its longing for an earlier, simpler place and time, shown by the repeated phrase "let us go back," it establishes a recurring theme in Bontemps's writing. These strains of primitivism are also heard in "Golgotha Is a Mountain," which won the *Opportunity* poetry prize for 1926. Reflections on **Christianity** are central to "Nocturne at Bethesda," one of the most frequently anthologized of these poems. Another widely read poem, "A Black Man Talks of Reaping," explores unrewarded labor.

Poetry of William Stanley Braithwaite

William Stanley Braithwaite was fascinated by the English romantic tradition, and many of his lyrics reflect this fascination. His poems are technically precise, written in traditional forms, are often motivated by melancholy and mysticism, and frequently refer to dream or trancelike states. Many are dedicated to specific people. For example, in "White Magic: An Ode Read at the Centenary Celebration of the Birth of John Greenleaf Whittier at Faneuil Hall, December 17, 1907," Braithwaite lauds Whittier

for sacrificing art to write about brotherhood. In "Keats Was an Unbeliever," however, Braithwaite praises Keats for making beauty concrete.

Poetry of Gwendolyn Brooks

The poetic achievements of **Gwendolyn Brooks** began with *A Street in Bronzeville* (1945), depicting a street tour of a black Chicago district. This was followed by the Pulitzer Prize winner *Annie Allen* (1949), a verse narrative chronicling in part the development of a young black woman from childhood to maturity. In 1956 Brooks published *Bronzeville Boys and Girls,* a book of verse for children. *The Beaneaters* (1960) deals with the negative feelings of inner city blacks and marks a shift in subject matter from that centered in Brooks's personal experiences to broader social concerns. This trend continues in the new poems included in *Selected Poems* (1963).

Brooks discarded traditional forms and adopted free verse in the black vernacular for *In the Mecca* (1968). Set in a tenement where Brooks once lived, the long title poem about a woman's search for her murdered daughter is followed by material concerned with the new black consciousness of the 1960s. Using black publishers, Brooks released *Riot* (1969), about anger and uprisings among blacks, and *Family Pictures* (1970), dealing with assassinated leaders like **Malcolm X** and exploring the social unrest of the late 1960s. Selections from these two books, along with those from *Aloneness* (1971) and *Beckonings,* (1975) are collected in *To Disembark* (1981). While the material in *Riot* and *Family Pictures* is generally optimistic, the poems in *Aloneness* and *Beckonings* express disillusionment with opportunities for blacks. The prophetic voice in the five new poems of *To Disembark,* in a section entitled "To the Diaspora," concerns itself with the spiritual qualities of black women and prisoners and points the way toward victory and health.

Mayor Harold Washington and Chicago, the I will *City* (1983) contains two long poems that honor Chicago and explore the social changes that led to election of a black mayor. Brooks has also published *The Near-Johannesburg Boy, and Other Poems* (1986), *Gottschalk and the Grande Tarantelle* (1988), and *Winnie* (1988).

hope and celebrates human endurance. "Strong Men," "Remembering Nat Turner," and "Strange Legacies" all speak of inspirational figures, either found in real life or presented as fictional composites. Brown has also written a volume of poetry entitled *The Last Ride of Wild Bill and Eleven Narrative Poems* (1975).

Poetry of Sterling A. Brown

While never using stereotypical dialects, **Sterling A. Brown** evokes the regional cadences of black speech in his **poetry**. Much of his subject matter concerns themes of romance and social isolation found in classic blues tunes. Some titles refer more overtly to the **jazz** aesthetic, like "Ma Rainey," "Tin Roof Blues," and "Riverbank Blues." One poem, "Long Track Blues," was recorded by Brown, with a piano score to back up his performance. His rhyme schemes vary from those of children's songs to structures borrowed from folk ballads. Brown's stanzas portray the broken or at least greatly strained relations between former slaves and former masters in either humorous **satire** or impassive pathos. His most popular comic figure, Slim Greer, appears in five ballads in *The Collected Poems of Sterling A. Brown* (1980). Slim finds himself in a series of difficult situations in intimidating places such as Atlanta, where blacks are not allowed to laugh aloud in public, and Arkansas, where he is mistaken for a Frenchman at a whites-only dance. The tone of other pieces is less lighthearted. The title poem from his debut collection *Southern Road* (1932; revised edition, 1974) is a downbeat, call-and-response roundelay modeled after a worksong. "Sam Smiley" impressionistically records a lynching, while the less graphic "Tornado Blues" bemoans Destruction, Death, and Sorrow chasing the Negro. Brown also articulates a homesteader's aspirations in "After Winter" and the shame of a pilfering housekeeper in "Ruminations of Luke Johnson." Some of Brown's poetry expresses

Poetry of Dennis Brutus

Dennis Brutus synthesizes Western and non-Western literary forms and his experiences as a political prisoner and exile in crafting poems that protest **apartheid** in his native South Africa and oppression elsewhere in the world. Adopting the persona of the troubadour throughout his corpus, Brutus travels the world fighting for racial equality while attempting to voice the concerns of those silenced by injustice. In *Sirens, Knuckles, Boots* (1963), he draws from romantic ideals of chivalry and love in expressing his condemnation of South Africa's racial policies. Forbidden from writing **poetry** in prison, Brutus presented his next volume of poems, *Letters to Martha, and Other Poems from a South African Prison* (1968), in a series of letters to his sister-in-law describing the inhumanity and fear associated with his prison life. *Thoughts Abroad* (1970), published under the pseudonym John Bruin, underscores themes of exile and alienation, while *A Simple Lust* (1973), written during his exile in the United States, contrasts concerns for his compatriots still living under oppression with his own life as a free person. In *Stubborn Hope* (1978), Brutus expands his political focus to a global scale, taking on the role of spokesperson for all people suffering from racial oppression and emphasizing the values of endurance and stoicism. Partaking extensively of the African **oral tradition** of blame-and-praise poetry, Brutus has continued to educate the world about apartheid in such works as *Salutes and Censures* (1984) and *Airs and Tributes* (1989).

Poetry of Margaret Taylor Burroughs

The first major appearance of **Margaret Taylor Burroughs**'s poetry was the inclusion of her poem "Brother Freedom" (1967) in *For Malcolm: Poems on the Life and Death of Malcolm X,* an anthology edited by Burroughs and **Dudley Randall**. In 1968, Burroughs published her first volume of **poetry**, *What Shall I Tell My Children Who Are Black?* The poems express pride in the accomplishments of blacks while evoking the reality of black oppression. Burroughs's second volume of poetry, *Africa, My Africa* (1970), was inspired largely by her 1968 trip to Ghana, and chronicles an African American's journey to Africa through a series of eighteen interrelated poems. The dominant themes in her poetry include the heroic nature of the African American experience, the achievements of African and African American culture, and the long tradition of African and African American freedom fighting.

Poetry of Martin Carter

Martin Carter's work reflects the political and social turmoil in his native Guyana. His early **poetry** is infused with a radical sensibility that voices the need for self-determination among his people. In poetry collections such as *Poems of Resistance from British Guiana* (1954) and *Jail Me Quickly* (1963), he expresses the righteous indignation of an oppressed people and celebrates the revolutionary spirit that led to violence in Guyana in the 1950s. The poet's later works, *Poems of Succession* (1977) and *Poems of Affinity, 1978-1980* (1980), reveal his increasing disillusionment and despair over the failure of the revolutionary generation to bring improvements to the Guyanese government. Throughout his career, Carter has sought to capture the anger and hopelessness of the Guyanese people without resorting to sentimentality or polemics.

Poetry of Lucille Clifton

Lucille Clifton's poems explore such themes as the importance of the family, adversity and triumph in a ghetto community, and the role of the poet. Much of her writing is characterized by the ironic, yet cautiously optimistic, stance exhibited in the title of her first collection, *Good Times: Poems* (1969). The short, simple, free verse in this volume sketches realistic character portraits of inner city dwellers. The book's title poem admonishes readers to reflect upon the "good times." This strong, practical approach to life typifies the predominant tone of Clifton's work.

Clifton's poems present authentic-seeming images of tragedy and heroism. "Lane is the Pretty One," for example, tells the story of the prettiest black girl in town, whose beauty only leads her to suffer abuse and keeps her from fully developing her human potential. The negative images are balanced by reminders about the value of the community, no matter what its socioeconomic circumstances.

The more political poems in Clifton's second collection, *Good News about the Earth: New Poems* (1972), expand upon the theme that the African American community has always produced its share of heroes, despite trying conditions. Among those singled out for mention are **Eldridge Cleaver** and **Malcolm X**. Clifton's third volume of **poetry**, *An Ordinary Woman* (1974), is her most popular.

The poems in Clifton's later book *Two-Headed Woman* (1980) delve further into religious and philosophical themes, revealing that just as there is no physical or spiritual rest for some churchgoers, there also is no respite for those facing life. "To Joan," in the same volume, is a tribute to the saint Joan of Arc.

Poetry of Sam Cornish

Using simple, direct terminology, **Sam Cornish** explores several themes in his **poetry**, often reflecting his anger over the treatment of

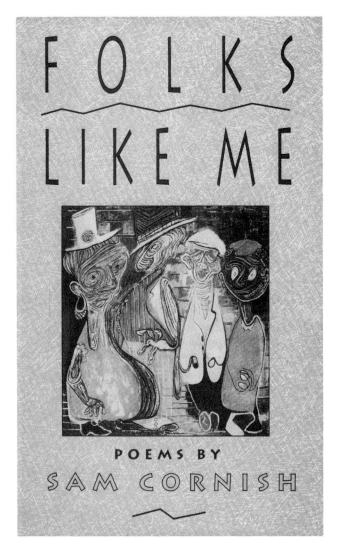

Cornish's poems celebrate black experience through direct, frank language.

Mary McLeod Bethune and Sojourner Truth, while still others celebrate the breadth and strength of the black experience. His later poetry volumes, including *Winters* (1968), *Sometimes* (1973), and *Sam's World* (1978), treat similar issues. His *Folks Like Me* (1993) revolves around the northern migration of black southerners during the twentieth century.

Poetry of Jayne Cortez

Jayne Cortez's **poetry**, modeled after **jazz**, uses improvisational fragments that recall trumpet solos and harness call-and-response patterns. Many poems either mention or are dedicated to famous black jazz artists. More violent works are devoted to themes of exploitation and urban life. *Coagulations: New and Selected Poems* (1982) arranges text diagrammatically in printed form, but Cortez has continued to design poems meant for oral presentation. The collections *Festivals and Funerals* (1971) and *Mouth on Paper* (1977), as well as individual poems like "I Am New York City" employ recombinant imagery. Descriptions repeated in various ways evoke surrealist motifs of potent sexuality and animism. Cortez's other collections include *Pisstained Stairs and the Monkey Man's Wares* (1969), *Scarifications* (1973), and *Poetic Magnetic* (1991).

blacks in American society, beginning in the days of **slavery**. He deals with the suffering of the individual, from contemporary civil rights figures, to historical black heroes, to average persons in the streets. His first poetry collection, *Generations* (1964), presents his ongoing observations of human life in its myriad forms. Some of his poems address tragedy, as in the deaths of **Malcolm X** and **Martin Luther King Jr.**, others deal with such pivotal civil rights figures as

Poetry of Victor Hernández Cruz

Victor Hernández Cruz is considered a Neorican (or Nurican or Nuyorican) poet—a Puerto Rican writer born or raised in the United States whose work exhibits influences of Black English and Spanish as well as cultural influences from Africa and Spain. Born in Puerto Rico and raised in New York City's Spanish

Harlem, Cruz reflected his perceptions of life in the barrio in his early **poetry**. He wrote his first book of verse, *Papo Got His Gun! and Other Poems*, in 1966 while still a high school student. Cruz's *Snaps* (1969) broadens the themes of anger, street life, and heroism explored in *Papo Got His Gun!*, while *Mainland* (1973) reveals a still more expansive multicultural view of life beyond the barrio. *Tropicalization* (1976) turns from the American barrio to more sensual, relaxed Latin American imagery. Cruz collected poetry as well as prose in *By Lingual Wholes* (1982), a volume written in English, Spanish, and "Spanglish," a hybrid language.

Poetry of Countee Cullen

Countee Cullen's major **poetry**, written primarily during the 1920s, came to be closely associated with the **Harlem Renaissance**. His first book, *Color* (1925), which contains some of the poet's most enduring writing, focuses on the theme of race. "Yet Do I Marvel," which uses the sonnet form for which Cullen is best known, explores race in conjunction with another common theme: spirituality. In the poem, the speaker wonders about God's motivation for making a black poet in a world that is hostile to black creativity: "Yet do I marvel at this curious thing: / To make a poet black, and bid him sing!"

Most of Cullen's racial poems express anger or sorrow at the plight of African Americans. "Incident" depicts a boy's first experience with **racism**. "A Brown Girl Dead" comments ironically on the dressing of a dead black girl in the color of her white oppressors. "Heritage" is Cullen's longest and most fully developed treatment of another frequent theme in his work: Africa and its meaning for African Americans. The speaker in this poem yearns for ancestral Africa, yet ultimately sees that it is unattainable from modern America. The poet's ambivalence toward his African heritage is also evident in the conflict between paganism and **Christianity**.

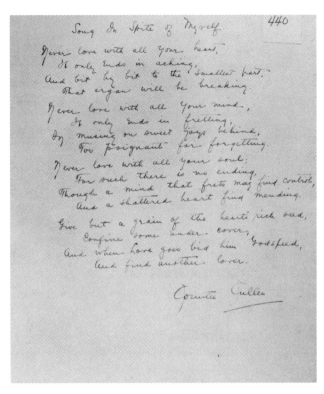

Manuscript of a poem published in *Harper's*, December, 1928.

Cullen's second collection, *Copper Sun* (1927), includes "From the Dark Tower," one of his most influential sonnets. It portrays black people as the planters of American civilization who have as yet failed to reap the bounty of their labors. "Threnody for a Brown Girl" explores society's role in the death of the girl. The narrative title work of *The Black Christ and Other Poems* (1929) deals with a lynching and the inner struggle between Christian faith and the disbelief that the event inspires.

Poetry of William Waring Cuney

William Waring Cuney's best known poem is "No Images," which is considered representative of many concerns of the **Harlem**

Renaissance. Its theme is the desirability and vulnerability of black pride and creativity in a hostile society. The central character is an African American woman who possesses beauty and glory but whose acculturation into a white society and economic poverty have caused her to lose awareness of her merit and to denigrate herself. **Religion** and human relationships are frequent themes in Cuney's other free verse poems. Many make use of folk speech and rhythms. In addition, Cuney, who studied music, incorporated black musical forms into poems such as "Hard-time Blues."

Poetry of Margaret Danner

Africa is the thematic focus of many of **Margaret Danner**'s strongest poems. Her most widely anthologized work is "Far from Africa," a series of four poems. Another poem, "This Is an African Worm," illustrates Danner's use of an African image as a symbol of protest. The worm in the title, representative of black Americans, can only "crawl and wait" rather than face up to its oppressors. Some of Danner's other writings are more celebratory of black people than critical of their plight. "In a Bone White Frame" exemplifies this approach. In this poem, the artist must not waste time acquainting herself with the alien hues of "ming blue, peach, pastel, white." Rather, she should focus on "this huge mahogony oil" that "occupies [her] through every cell."

Poetry of Frank Marshall Davis

Frank Marshall Davis wrote free verse in which the dominant mood is often cynical and bitter. His protest poems are known for their fierce social consciousness, race pride, and strong declamatory voice. "Chicago's Congo (Sonata for an Orchestra)" was written in response to Carl Sandburg's classic "Chicago" (1914). Davis's

version states that "Chicago's blood is kaleidoscopic." "Ebony Under Granite" is the title given to sections in two of Davis's books, *Black Man's Verse* (1935) and *I Am the American Negro* (1937). In these sections, dead African Americans lie under granite headstones and pass judgment on their lives. Here, in "Frank Marshall Davis: Writer," the poet penned a fitting epitaph for himself as "a weaver of jagged words."

Poetry of Owen Dodson

Owen Dodson's four books of **poetry** span the period between the **Harlem Renaissance** and the black activist voices of the 1960s and 1970s. *Powerful Long Ladder* (1946), perhaps the most critically acclaimed of his collections, addresses the plight of blacks, including subservience and exploitation, in a segregated society. The title suggests the protracted struggle necessary for blacks to overcome the impediments to an autonomous existence imposed on them by white society. Comprised of five sections, the book focuses, sometimes autobiographically, on obstructions regularly encountered by black people in everyday life. Dodson examines the problem of racial disparity and finds particular irony in the black liberation from **slavery** only to endure further humiliation and exploitation by whites. Dodson's other poetry collections include *Cages* (1953), *The Confession Stone* (1968; revised in 1970 as *The Confession Stone: Song Cycles*), and *The Harlem Book of the Dead* (1978).

Poetry of Rita Dove

Rita Dove is widely recognized for her skill as a storyteller and as a poetic chronicler of small, precisely observed moments. In her best-known collection of **poetry**, **Thomas and Beulah** (1986), Dove uses the personal histories of her maternal grandparents as a launching point for envisioning the separate but entwined stories of a married couple. When Dove won the Pulitzer Prize for *Thomas and Beulah* in 1987, she was only the second African American woman ever to receive the award.

In her first collection of poetry, *The Yellow House on the Corner* (1980), Dove demonstrates an imaginative sympathy with the world of history and of nature. In "Nexus," Dove compares herself to both a praying mantis and a brontosaurus; like the praying mantis that persists in trying to enter her window, Dove is stubborn in her pursuit of her art. Even Dove's autobiographical poems gather power from allusions to history, to cultural myths, and to religious sources. In *Museum* (1983), her second collection of poetry, Dove examines both her personal history and world history in terms of incidents that seem trivial but prove momentous. For instance, in "Parsley" Dove recounts the tale of Rafael Trujillo, the despotic president of the Dominican Republic who senselessly slaughtered twenty thousand black people because they could not correctly pronounce the Spanish word for parsley.

After the well-received and ambitious *Thomas and Beulah*, Dove's *Grace Notes* (1989) represents a return to lyric poetry. Most of the forty-eight poems in *Grace Notes* are characterized by a musical rhythm and by an attention to the senses, especially touch, sight, and hearing. Dove also takes a witty look at her own role as a writer and creator in a poem entitled "Ars Poetica." Although she also authored a collection of short stories, *Fifth Sunday* (1985), and a **novel**, ***Through the Ivory Gate*** (1992), Dove is best known for her poetry. In 1993 Dove was the first African American ever to be named poet laureate of the United States.

Poetry of James A. Emanuel

In his poetry, **James A. Emanuel** examines the difficulties of African Americans in the United States. Much of his work focuses on events and emotions in his personal relation-

ships. Another key theme involves the unique struggle of the African American poet who tries to establish an individual identity amidst the expectations of his literary peers. Emanuel also uses his writing to analyze racial oppression from a historical perspective, based on specific occurrences of hatred and violence. Emanuel's **poetry** varies from lyrical to dramatic and often reflects the struggle to balance bitterness with hope and resentment with resilience.

Poetry of Mari Evans

In her **poetry**, **Mari Evans** is committed to examining the social concerns of black Americans, and many of her writings celebrate the strengths of the African American community and African American women in particular. In her domestic poems, such as "7:25 Trolley" and "BeAtrice Does the Dinner," Evans has created familiar characters and settings. However, the domestic scene is not the only critical component in cultural vitality. The figure of the hero is another, and Evans has paid tribute to black heroes in poems such as "El Hajj Malik Shabazz," which honors **Malcolm X**. In "once again the poets," Evans outlines four primary responsibilities of poets committed to social **realism**: to listen, watch, warn, and tell.

Poetry of Julia Fields

In the poem "East of Moonlight," **Julia Fields** writes of her desire to "tell some stories to the young" and to "make vivid again the memory / of the old." Fields is indeed a poet who tells stories that capture the folk spirit. "Testimonials" is a highly regarded poetic narrative that explores the strict rituals of rural southern black life. Another critically acclaimed poem, "High on the Hog," demonstrates Fields's deft use of irony to couch critical comment. The

poetry and prose poems in the book *Slow Coins* (1981) are often singled out as among Fields's best. In "Shooting the Big Hookey," for example, Fields uses the cadences and idioms of black dialect to grapple with complex issues of old age and death. In "How Black," she humorously explores some common myths about black skin color.

Poetry of Calvin Forbes

Calvin Forbes began writing **poetry** his early twenties, during the late 1960s, inspired by his travels throughout the United States and Mexico and by other experiences. During his travels he completed his first volume of poems, *Poetry* (1968). His subjects are frequently universal and explore parenthood and growing up in hostile urban surroundings. Yet Forbes offers unconventional treatments of such ideas, as in the poem "Outside the City," in which he renders pastoral settings alien and estranged, recalling the places in which slaves were set to work. In his collections *Blue Monday* (1974) and *From the Book of Shine* (1979), he uses traditional blues meter and rhyme schemes to invoke despair and explore racial and political themes. Forbes was awarded a Fulbright Grant in 1974 and a National Endowment for the Arts Fellowship in 1982-83.

Poetry of Nikki Giovanni

Nikki Giovanni premiered with a trio of verse collections: *Black Feeling, Black Talk* (1967), *Black Judgement* (1968) and *Re: Creation* (1970). In these works she reflected in conversational and emotive language on her experiences with the black liberation movement, gave credit to the blacks who influenced her, and immersed herself in black culture. She also responded to the many violent acts perpetrated

against civil rights leaders and depicted her journey toward becoming a revolutionary.

Giovanni dedicated *Spin a Soft Black Song: Poems for Children* (1971) to her son Tommy. The more than two dozen poems that make up this collection re-create the world of childhood, yet reflect Giovanni's adult concerns. Other works for children include *Ego-Tripping and Other Poems for Young People,* (1973) previously published poems, and *Vacation Time: Poems for Children,* (1980) a light-hearted and ideologically free enjoyment of childhood pleasures.

My House, published in 1971, marked a further departure from Giovanni's revolutionary verse. With a less strident, more lyrical voice, Giovanni drew on her own life, expressing her thoughts and feelings about relationships, primarily using monologues. While she focusing on domestic pleasures and personal relationships, Giovanni also dealt with the struggles of individuals outside the home. Giovanni continued to record her growth as an individual and artist in *The Women and the Men,* published in 1975. The poems of the first section, "The Women," celebrate creativity and ponder the contradictions inherent in life; the second section, "The Men," celebrates the joy of man-woman relationships; and a final section re-assesses some of Giovanni's revolutionary ideas. *Cotton Candy on a Rainy Day* (1978) is a lyrical and introspective collection of reflections on life—its anxieties, realities, responsibilities—and the loneliness and disillusionment of her own life. Giovanni took a new tack in *Those Who Ride the Night Winds* (1983), with prose poem meditations in which she liberally used ellipses to give the impression of spontaneous creation.

Poetry of Nicolás Guillén

Nicolás Guillén was one of the first poets to affirm the black Cuban experience. His poems show a strong Marxist influence and document the turbulent social and political history of Cuba. Major themes addressed include the perceived injustices of capitalism, imperialism, and **racism**.

The poems in Guillén's first collection, *Motivos de son* (1930), are rhythmically structured like the *son,* a sensual African Cuban dance. This book, which became closely identified with the African Caribbean **poetry** movement that began in the mid-1920s, blends Cuban black dialect with Yoruba African words to create an idiosyncratic language that relies as much on sound and rhythm as on word sense to communicate its meaning. One frequently used stylistic device is onomatopoeia. Even the title of Guillén's next collection, *Songoro cosongo* (1931), has no meaning other than what it suggests through rhythm and association. This influential book of "mulatto poetry" tries to reflect Cuba's background and racial makeup.

The underlying social consciousness in these books becomes overt social protest in *West Indies Ltd.: Poemas* (1934). These somber, often satirical, poems depict the history of **slavery** and **colonialism** Cuba. The poems in *La paloma de vuelo popular* (1959) are concerned with revolution, and praise leaders such as Fidel Castro. Similarly, *Tengo,* Guillén's 1964 verse collection, celebrates revolutionary victory. *El gran zoo* (1967) expands upon the theme of social liberation in poems that approach free verse in their deviation from rhyme schemes and metrical patterns associated with African Cuban style.

Poetry of Frances Ellen Watkins Harper

Frances Ellen Watkins Harper's poetry proved very popular with both African and European American audiences through the last half of the nineteenth century. Appealing to a broad audience, Harper's simply stated, highly rhythmic verse is considered the first example of African American protest **poetry**. Although her style was somewhat conservative—Harper used the form of the sentimental ballads of the period—her work introduced many political and social themes that are important to contemporary African American writers. "Eliza Harris," from *Poems on Miscellaneous Subjects* (1854), reflects Harper's strong concern about the condition of African American women. Her collection *Poems* (1871) contains one of her strongest statements against **slavery**, "Bury Me in a Free Land." *Sketches of Southern Life* (1872) relates the stories of former slaves who recall important moments in their lives, such as Aunt Chloe's experiences while "Learning to Read." *Sketches of Southern Life* avoided the black dialect affected by many other nineteenth-century authors writing about the South; instead, Watkins's characters speak in a less stylized, everyday manner. In *The Sparrow's Fall and Other Poems* (1890), "Double Standard" examines sexual **discrimination** against women from a feminist perspective. "The Martyr of Alabama," from *Atlanta Offering: Poems* (1895), condemns the racially motivated murder of a boy who refuses to dance for the entertainment of white men.

Poetry of Michael S. Harper

Michael S. Harper's work emphasizes his dual role as American poet and black poet. Although his poems are personal and historical reflections on the suffering of black Americans, they offer messages of healing rather than despair. Many of his poems draw on the rhythms of **jazz**, **the blues**, and **spirituals**. A number of pieces also celebrate black musicians, as evidenced by the title of Harper's first collection, *Dear John, Dear Coltrane* (1970). The seventy-two poems in that volume revolve around the theme of redemption. For example, "Reuben, Reuben," a poem about Harper's losing a son, centers on his attempt to transcend pain through creativity.

The importance of family appears in the title of another of Harper's collections, *Images of Kin: New and Selected Poems* (1977). One section, titled "Healing Songs," contains poems that typify Harper's search for unity and harmony rather than divisiveness and discord. These poems serve as the wellspring for his later book *Healing Song for the Inner Ear: Poems* (1984). A section called "Uplift from a Dark Tower," examines the ideas of three great African American thinkers of the past—**Frederick Douglass**, **Booker T. Washington**, and **W. E. B. Du Bois** —within the context of white **racism**.

Poetry of Robert Hayden

Drawing from such various influences as the **Harlem Renaissance**, the Baha'i faith, American history, and **poetry** both modern and ancient, **Robert Hayden** wrote complex poems about the black experience, the middle passage, **slavery**, **discrimination**, popular entertainment, personal experiences, and historical figures. Among the first black poets to master the techniques of modernist verse, he adamantly refused to distinguish between black literature and American literature, and thus incurred criticism from the **black arts movement**.

Hayden's best-known poems include "Middle Passage" (1966), a poem inspired by the uprising of slaves aboard the slave ship *Armistad,* "Runagate, Runagate" (1949), a meditation on freedom and the **Underground Railroad**, and "El-Hajj Malik El-Shabazz" (1970), a summation of the life of **Malcolm X**. Hayden is also recognized for his poem "A Ballad of Remembrance" (1948), a complicated and strident work based on an experience the author had at a poetry reading in New Orleans in the 1940s.

Although Hayden was criticized in the 1960s by a younger generation of poets who called for a black aesthetic, he steadfastly defended his intention to write American poetry, unlimited in its scope. While his poetry confronted social issues, it also reflected his religious background with its particular emphasis on the unity of humankind.

Poetry of David Henderson

David Henderson's **poetry** draws on personal experience, popular culture, and Western mythology. In the title poem of his first book, *Felix of the Silent Forest* (1967), Henderson depicts a discarded cartoon cat, no longer immune to superstitions about his blackness, who wanders the city aimlessly. In "Saga of the Audubon Murder," the poet mythically links the birth of George Washington and the assassination of **Malcolm X**. Henderson's second book, *De Mayor of Harlem* (1970), also contains a number of **jazz** poems, which attempt to recreate the syncopated rhythms of jazz, and "documentaries," which report contemporary events such as the 1964 Harlem riots. In addition, Henderson's later work includes some prose poems, such as "Charlie at the Vanguard."

Poetry of Everett H. Hoagland III

Everett H. Hoagland III's **poetry** incorporates musical influences from Bach to Otis Redding , which are either parodied or extended rhythmically to carry across refrains. Without endorsing any specific political stance, Hoagland also affirms the most universal influences of African culture. His first collection, *Black Velvet*, is dedicated to black women everywhere. The poems celebrate a range of themes from procreative sex to the African landscape and lampoon the false iconography European cultures have derived from real African women. Hoagland's championing of the real over the metaphoric is continued in his second major volume, entitled *Scrimshaw* (1976). Individual poems focus on such issues as the cotton gin, Senegal, and strength in a unified diasporic culture. The story of the scrimshaw is told in "The Path of Bones."

Poetry of Frank Horne

Frank Horne reached the height of his literary success in 1925, when his "Letters Found Near a Suicide" received second prize in a **poetry** contest sponsored by *Crisis* magazine. Submitted under the pseudonym Xavier I, the letters in the title are short poems to individuals who played significant roles in a suicide victim's life. Originally, there were eleven letters; seven more were added by 1930, all of which were published as the first section of Horne's 1963 collection, *Haverstraw*. Included in the collection is what has perhaps become Horne's most widely read poem, "To James." In this piece, Horne, who was coaching a high school track team at the time, compares living a life to running a race. He advises: "finish / with an ecstatic burst." Among his other poems, those such as "On Seeing Two Brown Boys in a Catholic Church" deal with **religion**, while others such as "Symphony" focus on infirmity.

Poetry of Langston Hughes

Often based on blues forms and themes, **Langston Hughes**'s poetry celebrates the humblest voices of the black community and affirms their rightful place in American literature. Hughes's attempt to forge a realist poetic rooted in black dialect often met with critical derision, but because of his reputation as a major and innovative poet, many critics consider him the poet laureate of black America.

One of Hughes's most widely anthologized poems, "The Negro Speaks of Rivers" (1920), appeared in his first collection, *The Weary Blues* (1926), which features blues' themes and structures. Hughes's growing concern for the black masses informs the slight but acutely attuned poems of his second volume,

Fine Clothes to the Jew (1927), which was followed by *Dear Lovely Death* (1931) and *The Dream Keeper and Other Poems* (1932).

Hughes's anguished social protest against the economic and political crises of the Depression years informs "Let America Be America Again" (1935) and is felt strongly in the radical collection *A New Song* (1938). In *Shakespeare in Harlem* (1942), the vibrancy of his early **Harlem Renaissance** poems give way to a bleak vision. The poems of *One-Way Ticket* (1949) feature Alberta K. Johnson, a counterpart in **poetry** to Hughes's prose creation, Jesse B. Semple. The decline of Harlem, however, is the subject of one of Hughes's most celebrated works, *Montage of a Dream Deferred* (1951), a series of verse sketches written to be read aloud with accompaniment. *Jazz* is also at the heart of *Ask Your Mama: Twelve Moods for Jazz* (1961), a work some critics considered Hughes's finest work. Hughes's final work, the posthumously published *The Panther and the Lash: Poems of Our Times* (1967), reflects Hughes's bitterness, anger, and frustration about race relations in America.

Hughes's long and distinguished poetic career and his innovations in style and subject matter have inspired two generations of black writers and have immeasurably affected the shape of contemporary black literature.

Poetry of Lance Jeffers

Many of **Lance Jeffers**'s best-known poems deal with the theme of black endurance in the face of white oppression. Those in his first collection, *My Blackness Is the Beauty of This Land* (1970), focus on heroic grandeur diminished by mean circumstances. In "Black Soul of the Land," for example, the speaker looks at an old black man "bent with humiliation and age" but finds within him "a secret manhood tough and tall." In fact, the "beauty" of the book's title is always presented as the external manifestation of internal character. In Jeffers's second collection, *When I Know the Power of My Black Hand* (1974), the theme of oppression is expanded to include not only American **racism** toward blacks, but also global and historical oppression among Native Americans and in Vietnam, Buchenwald, and Peru. Two hallmarks of Jeffers's early style are the use of paradoxical images and the coinage of compound words, such as "corpse-head" and "bluecool." In addition, there is a heavy reliance on such literary devices as alliteration, anaphora, and litanies, establishing a solid link to black rhetorical tradition.

Jeffers's next collection, *O Africa, Where I Baked My Bread* (1977), shifts the thematic focus from survival to love. These poems place considerable literal and figurative emphasis on sexual anatomy. The imagery and grammar of *O Africa* are more straightforward than in Jeffers's previous work. For example, where parallel grammatical constructions occur, they are more direct than those in his earlier **poetry**. The poems in *Grandsire* (1979) are dramatically elegant. The subject of the book's title poem is Jeffers's grandfather, portrayed in the larger-than-life mold of a "giant... who walked the plains of Nebraska like a fearless god!" Jeffers's new mastery of concise narrative is apparent in poems such as "Woman Giving Out Leaflets," in which a character is sketched, a scenario is described, and a moral lesson is delivered in just twelve lines.

Poetry of Ted Joans

In his **poetry**, former Beat generation writer **Ted Joans** rejects conventional American lifestyles, protests social injustice and sexual repression, and celebrates sex, **jazz**, and African culture. Like many of the Beats, Joans began his career in the counterculture movement of the 1950s. His collection *Jazz Poems* (1959) represents his work during this period. Although he helped organize the movement's work in New York, he became disgusted with it when it became overcommercialized, and he decided to leave the country for Europe. He turned to African American themes, using jazz motifs derived from the work of the bebop musicians. He also drew on his experiences as a surrealist artist, creating a decidedly different poetry. For instance, in his farewell to the Beat generation, the collection *All of Ted Joans and No More* (1961), he combines the Beat distaste for conventional culture with references to the French surrealist poet André Breton. *Black Pow-Wow: Jazz Poems* (1969) demonstrates Joans's growing interest in Africa and the **black arts movement**. Such poems as "Lets Get Violent" and "Revenge" support the **black power** movement of the late 1960s and promote united violence. The publication of *Black Pow-Wow* coincided with Joans's decision to return to the United States; *Afrodisia: New Poems* (1970), written while Joans was in Europe, contains poems that pursue African and sexual themes.

Poetry of Fenton Johnson

Fenton Johnson is recognized as a pioneer of African American free verse. However, the early poems in his first collection, *A Little Dreaming* (1913), demonstrate a mastery of traditional forms as well. "Prelude," the first poem in Johnson's *Visions of the Dusk* (1915) states: "And yet some say to me, 'O Man of dusk, / Give us thy songs in broken Afric tongue,— / The music of the peasant in the peasant in the South— / The native strain alone in **poetry**.'" Indeed, Johnson did employ plantation-dialect style in several poems from this period, including "The Creed of the Slave." Yet it is for the fatalistic vision and free verse style of his later poems that Johnson is primarily remembered. Among these are "Aunt Hannah Jackson," "The Banjo Player," "The Minister," "The Scarlet Woman," and "Tired."

Poetry of Georgia Douglas Johnson

Georgia Douglas Johnson wrote romantic, conventional verse—short lyrics drawn primarily from inner life. Many of her early poems are subtle, abstract evocations of particular emotional states. One piece titled "Despair," for instance, focuses on unfulfilled dreams. However, in later work, Johnson revealed an awareness of social conditions and racial concerns that sets her writing apart from that of similarly genteel contemporaries.

In "Black Woman," Johnson depicts a black mother who refuses to bear a child while a slave. This and related poems, such as "The Mother" and "Shall I Say, 'My Son, You're Branded,'" brought what was then a new perspective to the subject of **slavery**. In "Credo," Johnson declares her fundamental belief that black people will eventually enjoy a better future: "I believe in the ultimate justice of Fate; / That the race of men front the sun in their turn."

"I Want to Die While You Love Me" is often singled out as Johnson's literary trademark. In it, the author states a preference for death over the end of love: "Oh, who would care to live, / 'Til love has nothing more to ask / And nothing more to give." Poet and dramatist **Owen Dodson** read this poem at Johnson's funeral.

Poetry of June Jordan

June Jordan's first book, *Who Look at Me* (1969), a poem accompanied by paintings, discusses the relationships between blacks and whites. *Some Changes* (1971), Jordan's first collection of **poetry**, deals with personal subjects—her parents, her life as a young woman—and with national events of the 1960s. The influence of T. S. Eliot, Emily Dickinson, and Shakespeare is evident.

Jordan's second collection of poetry, *New Days: Poems of Exile and Return* (1974), recounts her feelings of alienation from home experienced during a stay abroad in Rome. It also includes the poem "Getting Down to Get Over," about a daughter's passionately trying to connect with her mother. The final poem, "Things That I Do in the Dark," is also the title of the collection that followed, *Things That I Do in the Dark* (1977), an affirmation and celebration of black life.

Things That I Do in the Dark was edited by **Toni Morrison**, and dedicated to Jordan's parents. Several poems discuss violence and liberation. "Who Look at Me" (1969), the first poem in the collection, highlights Jordan's concerns for herself, her parents, her son, her race, and relations between blacks and whites.

Passion: New Poems, 1977-1980 (1980) identifies Walt Whitman as the father of "New World" poets such as Jordan, and discusses the use of violence in liberation struggles. *Living Room: New Poems, 1980-1984* (1985) expresses Jordan's concern about the international issues of the 1980s in such poems as "The Beirut Jokebook."

In *Naming Our Destiny: New and Selected Poems* (1989), the influence of William Butler Yeats's "Leda and the Swan" and the early black American poet **Phillis Wheatley** is evident.

In *The Voice of the Children* (1970) and *New Life: New Room* (1975), Jordan expresses her dedication to the nurturing and well-being of children. Seven of Jordan's poems are included in the anthology *The Black Poets* (1971). The collection *Harukol/Love Poems* appeared in 1994.

Poetry of Bob Kaufman

As a member of the Beat **poetry** movement of the 1950s and 1960s, **Bob Kaufman** used his poems to express such Beat aspects as insanity, poverty, and primitivism. Three of his long poems, *Abomunist Manifesto, Second April,* and *Does the Secret Mind Whisper?,* were published as broadsides in 1959. All convey an attitude of alienation from conventional society. Among the poems in Kaufman's first book, *Solitudes Crowded with Loneliness* (1965), is "Bagel Shop Jazz," a relatively realistic evocation of bohemian life in San Francisco. Kaufman tried in many of his writings to adapt the harmonic intricacies and spontaneous inventions of **jazz** to poetry.

Shine," which tells the story of an African American worker trapped on board the *Titanic* who escapes the sinking ship by refusing to observe the traditions of white society. In "A Poem for Myself (or Blues for a Mississippi Black Boy)," he makes use of the traditional African American blues form to celebrate his freedom. In "The Stretching of the Belly" and "On the Birth of a Black/Baby/Boy," Knight again uses **the blues** form to welcome his son into the world.

Poetry of Etheridge Knight

Etheridge Knight's poetry is collected in three volumes: *Poems from Prison* (1968), *Belly Song and Other Poems* (1973), and *Born of a Woman: New and Selected Poems* (1980). He also contributed to the collection *Black Voices from Prison* (1970). In his verse, Knight wrote about his personal experiences growing up in the segregated South, his service in the United States army, his wounds suffered during the Korean War, and his addiction to narcotics that led to his arrest and imprisonment in Indiana. Freedom is a frequent theme in his **poetry**, as are issues of African American identity, family history, sex, love, and violence. In his later verse he utilized **jazz** and blues rhythms. His work has been celebrated by other prominent African American writers, including **Gwendolyn Brooks**, who visited Knight in prison, **Dudley Randall**, who originally published *Poems from Prison,* and **Sonia Sanchez**, who married Knight after he was released from prison.

Knight developed his poetic voice from the African American **oral tradition** of "toasting." He learned the art while growing up in Mississippi and refined his grasp of it while in prison. Toasting involves the composition of poems of **epic** length and interaction with members of an audience, who are encouraged to add comments or stanzas of their own invention. Knight's use of the toast is probably best demonstrated in "Dark Prophecy: I Sing of

Poetry of Johari M. Amini Kunjufu

The central theme in many of **Johari M. Amini Kunjufu**'s poems is the importance of love for racial unity and of unity for future power. Some of her writings are sensuous explorations of physical love. Others, such as "Masque," are exhortations to black women to love themselves, their men, and each other. In some of her poems, Kunjufu makes creative use of black idiom. "A Revolutionary Requiem," for example, is a cautionary tale in which a "bruh," high on drugs, "wuz still / out / there. yea. / (spacin / didnt know th sewers / had backed / up."

Poetry of Pinkie Gordon Lane

Most of **Pinkie Gordon Lane**'s **poetry** falls solidly within the lyric tradition. In the course of her writing career, Lane has used both traditional forms, such as the Shakespearean sonnet, and free verse to explore personal, subjective experience. Her topics have ranged from family and work to nature and the environment, and she has examined such universal themes as love, hate, death, and the past. In "The Mystic

Female," the poem's persona states that she is "ghost, spirit, woman / exploring the mirrors of my mind." In "Poems to My Father," the mystic female, trying to cope with her father's death, declares: "I meant to tell you this, Papa / I've divorced myself / from your memory."

Poetry of Audre Lorde

An African American lesbian feminist who has suffered from breast cancer, **Audre Lorde** calls for tolerance of different human perspectives throughout her verse. In contrast to most other black poets of 1960s, Lorde adopted a nonconfrontational tone in her early work, emphasizing themes of love and the pleasures of child rearing in her first two collections, *The First Cities* (1968) and *Cables to Rage* (1970), in which she revealed her homosexuality. In her later work, she adopted a more openly political stance, focusing on global oppression and injustice. *From a Land Where Other People Live* (1973) was nominated for the National Book Award for poetry.

One of Lorde's principal themes in *Coal* (1976), is the affirmation and celebration of her African heritage. Specific references to African mythology also pervade her **poetry**, especially in her most critically acclaimed work, *The Black Unicorn* (1978), which affirms her blackness while addressing themes of female relationships and spiritual renewal. As an outspoken feminist, Lorde is highly critical of societies that devalue and persecute women, treating the welfare lines of New York and the brutality and neglect of El Salvador with equal contempt. In "Diaspora," a poem from *Our Dead behind Us* (1986), she compares the evils of **apartheid** in Johannesburg to the **racism** of Alabama. Lorde's sympathy for victims of injustice evolves into a call for unity among women of color and tolerance on matters of color, politics, and sexual orientation. In *The Black Unicorn,*

she celebrates her feelings of love, describing her lesbian relationships through metaphors of writing.

Poetry of Naomi Long Madgett

Naomi Long Madgett's best-known poem may well be "Midway," in which the black speaker is a voice for all African Americans: "I've prayed and slaved and waited and I've sung my song. / You've bled me and you've starved me but I've still grown strong." An earlier poem dealing with black themes, "Refugee," published in *One and the Many* (1956), was selected by **Langston Hughes** and **Arna Bontemps** for inclusion in their influential anthology, *The Poetry of the Negro: 1746-1949* (1949). However, it is only in the more recent of her seven **poetry** volumes, notably *Exits and Entrances* (1978) and *Octavia and Other Poems* (1988), that Madgett has emphasized her African American roots. Many of her poems are lyrics expressing romantic feelings.

Poetry of Haki R. Madhubuti

Haki R. Madhubuti, a leader in the **black arts movement** of the 1960s, has taken an activist stance in his **poetry**. For Madhubuti, race is the central fact from which all other themes derive, and art cannot be divorced from politics. One way in which he has attempted to reinforce black pride is through an accurate rendering of African American dialect and music. His writing style is energetic and explosive, utilizing such devices as startling metaphors, creative coinages, and staccato repetitions.

One frequent theme in Madhubuti's work is the need for self-determination. In the semi-autobiographical poem "Back Again, Home (confessions of an ex-executive)," for example, he tells of a black junior executive who suddenly quits the conventional corporate world. He finds himself without money or food yet in possession again of his own identity and self-respect.

"Don't Cry, Scream," the title poem from Madhubuti's third collection, exemplifies the poet's verbal inventiveness, as he strives to replicate the virtuoso sounds of **jazz** saxophonist John Coltrane. Wordplay is also evident in "Change Is Not Always Progress," in which the poet entreats Africa to resist Western advances: "don't let them / steel / your body as to put / 100 stories of concrete on you / so that you / arrogantly / scrape / the / sky." Madhubuti's skill at turning a memorable phrase is apparent in the brief poem "The New Integrationist."

The second section of Madhubuti's sixth poetry volume, *Book of Life* (1973), takes a new stylistic direction. This sixty-page prose poem consists of ninety-two numbered stanzas. Each is a saying, written in standard English, that reflects the principles of Muslim life. Gone are the street language and the intentional misspellings, as readers are admonished to eat natural food and respect what is old. Madhubuti has published some poetry under the name Don L. Lee.

Poetry of George Marion McClellan

George Marion McClellan's poems are characterized by extreme conservatism and sentimentality. His themes and images are typical of the popular verse of the early 1920s, dealing primarily with nature, love, or **religion**. Firmly grounded in the genteel tradition, McClellan found love in a rose, hope in a dogwood blossom, and pathos in a maiden's death. McClellan's work was praised for its technical merit, imagery, and descriptions of nature, with the

volume *The Path of Dreams* receiving significant critical attention.

Poetry of E. Ethelbert Miller

Most of **E. Ethelbert Miller**'s **poetry** is contained in five works. The poems of *Andromeda* (1974) explore the persona's emotional responses to love relationships and his search for spiritual meaning. The book-length poem *The Land of Smiles and the Land of No Smiles* (1974) relates the victimization of African people, in enslavement and in the contemporary situation of blacks. *Migrant Worker* (1978) explores the contradictions of contemporary black urban life experienced by a collection of characters, including Bo Willie, a street poet. The poems of *Season of Hunger/Cry of Rain, Poems: 1975-1980* (1982) combine a mature political vision with the concerns of personal relationships, again, sometimes via the voice of Bo Willie. In *Where Are the Love Poems for Dictators,* written in 1986, Miller continues to define his political views as he responds to experiences in Latin America. Miller's 1993 collection, *First Light: New and Selected Poems,* is thematically grouped into eight sections. The longest sections of the work explore such topics as Latin America, love affairs, and the deaths of **W. E. B. Du Bois**, **Malcolm X**, **James Baldwin**, and **C. L. R. James**.

Poetry of Gabriel Okara

Gabriel Okara's work is regarded as the first significant English-language **poetry** written by a black African. His early poems were mystical, romantic lyrics that celebrated the primitivism of African life. In "Piano and

Drums," for instance, native customs are symbolized by jungle drums, while the piano represents continental sophistication. As Okara became more concerned with the philosophy of **negritude**, his poems began to show more modernist and surrealist leanings. In "You Laughed and Laughed and Laughed," for example, the narrator utilizes nature imagery and surrealist imagery to declare that Africa will lift the West out of its cold, mechanical existence.

Poetry of Dudley Randall

Dudley Randall's poems explore racial and historical issues and draw on themes and forms taken from both traditional Western **poetry** and the **Harlem Renaissance** movement. His historical perspective on race is evident in "Memorial Wreath," a tribute to black soldiers who served in the Union Army during the Civil War. Randall also memorialized characters from the lower classes of modern American society in such works as "Jailhouse Blues," "Ghetto Girls," "The Aged Whore," and "Bag Woman." His poems "Ballad of Birmingham," about the bombing of an Alabama church, and "Dressed All in Pink," about the assassination of President John F. Kennedy, became the first two in a series of influential broadsides published by Randall.

Poetry of Sonia Sanchez

Sonia Sanchez's poetry chronicles her personal trials and joys within the larger framework of her commitment to **black nationalism** , the cultural revolution of the 1960s in which many African Americans rejected the values of mainstream white America and celebrated their African ancestry. In *Homecoming* (1969), her first volume of **poetry**, she voices her skepti-

cism of what she identifies as America's focus on materialism. Throughout her corpus, Sanchez compliments her militant political views with African American vernacular and African forms. Her poetry also reflects African American spiritual and secular songs in theme, language, and rhythm. In *We A BaddDD People* (1970), she establishes many of the other prominent themes of her poetry, such as the evils of substance abuse , the importance of black role models, and the intra- and interracial relations between men and women. In her next two volumes of poetry, *A Blues Book for Blue Black Magical Women* (1973) and *Love Poems* (1973), written during her membership in the **Nation of Islam**, Sanchez focuses on family relationships and examines the status of black women within American and African American society. The latter work, written during a period of illness and poverty, demonstrates her experimentation with haiku, which enabled her to compress her personal and political message. In *Blue Black Magical Women,* a long praise poem regarded as one of her more ambitious works, she provides a partly autobiographical account of her spiritual and psychological development as an African American woman. Continuing to draw from her own experiences and observations of black America, she focuses on the pain and alienation that accompany lives crippled by poverty and substance abuse. She offers both compassion and a redemptive vision. In later works, such as *Under a Soprano Sky* (1986) Sanchez adds environmental themes to her list of social and political concerns.

Poetry of Léopold Sédar Senghor

The corpus of the former President of the Republic of Senegal affirms the poet's pride in his African heritage. **Léopold Sédar Senghor**'s first major collection of **poetry**, *Chants d'ombre* (1945), recollects the rhythms of songs from Senghor's village. The poems also recount Senghor's feelings of alienation that he experience when he first moved to Paris. In works such as *Hosties noires* (1948), Senghor recounts his experiences as a prisoner of war while serving in the French Colonial Army during World War II. While offering a critique of French **colonialism**, Senghor voices support of **Pan-Africanism** and **negritude**—a literary movement urging black people to reclaim their African past. In some of his later work, such as *Ethiopiques* (1956) and *Nocturnes* (1961), he tempers his militant stance to allow for more conciliatory themes.

Poetry of Melvin B. Tolson

Melvin B. Tolson is remembered for his complex **poetry** that challenges readers to think about the past achievements of African Americans and to contemplate a future of black accomplishment and racial equality. His first published collection, *Rendezvous with America* (1944), contains his best-known poem, "Dark Symphony," which celebrates the historic contributions of black Americans. Arranged in six "movements," thus reflecting Tolson's interest in the formal structure of music, "Dark Symphony" ends with a confident prediction of black progress.

Tolson's second volume of poetry, *Libretto for the Republic of Liberia* (1953), draws heavily on the modernist tradition. It, too, is structured according to musical principles: divided into eight sections, each named for a note in the ascending diatonic scale. *Libretto* explores the theme of universal brotherhood and argues against the evils of **colonialism**. Included in this extended ode are political and tribal histories and tributes to African achievements in science and literature.

Tolson's last major work, *Harlem Gallery: Book I, The Curator* (1965), was the only completed volume in a planned five-book **epic** that would have traced the history of black Americans. Early in his career, Tolson had written a series of character sketches describing

Harlem residents from a variety of racial and social backgrounds. This collection of poetic portraits remained unpublished until after Tolson's death, when it appeared as *A Gallery of Harlem Portraits* (1979). However, these poems served as the inspiration for Tolson's later *Harlem Gallery,* which is considered a tour de force of modernist writing. This book is both a humorous look at Harlem's colorful citizenry and a serious exploration of African American art. It develops a number of memorable characters, including the Curator, who provides the central point of view; Dr. Obi Nkomo, a Bantu educated in the West; and John Laugert, a half-blind artist.

Poetry of Derek Walcott

Derek Walcott's work addresses the Caribbean poet's dual allegiance to his island home and to the Western cultural tradition. Much of Walcott's **poetry** alludes to British literature and is rooted in classic poetic form, but his work, often autobiographical, deals mostly with life and culture in the West Indies and the United States. Walcott published his first volume of poetry, *Twenty-Five Poems* (1948) at eighteen, and followed this with *Epitaph for the Young: A Poem in XII Cantos* (1949) and *Poems* (1953). In his first major collection *In a Green Night* (1962), Walcott explored his confusion at his mixed racial and cultural heritage. With *The Castaway and Other Poems* (1965) he found an answer to this cultural dilemma in the isolated, island figure of Robinson Crusoe. With *The Gulf, and Other Poems* (1969), Crusoe gives way to Odysseus as an emblem of Walcott's personal struggle to synthesize his island experience and literary tradition. The retrospective tone continues in the long verse **autobiography** *Another Life* (1972). With *Sea Grapes* (1976) and *Star Apple Kingdom* (1977) Walcott takes indigenous plants as images of a Caribbean remembered vividly from afar, finding coherence in memory as he travels to Europe and the

United States. The theme of travel and diasporic removal recurs in *The Fortunate Traveller* (1981) where Walcott's American experience replaces his earlier struggles with the vestiges of British **colonialism**. Walcott's estrangement from classic English literature, which he by now sees as inseparable from British imperialism, and his increasingly ambivalent attitude to America are developed in *Midsummer* (1984). In *The Arkansas Testament* (1987), Walcott addresses the division between the local "here" and the global "there." Walcott again appeals to classical literature in *Omeros* (1990), which revisits Homer's *Odyssey,* in theme and style while changing the setting from the Cyclades to the Caribbean.

Poitier in *Lilies of the Field,* 1963.

Sidney Poitier

American actor, director, and
autobiographer
Born February 20, 1927.

Poitier's acting career includes appearances in more than forty films, an Academy Award nomination for his role in *The Defiant Ones* (1958), and the first Academy Award for best actor ever awarded to an African American for his work in *Lilies of the Field* (1963). He is credited as being the first black actor to break through the color bar. The son of a tomato farmer, Poitier was born on February 20, 1927, in Miami, Florida, but grew up in the Bahamas, where he attended school for only four years. As a teenager he returned to Miami and then moved to New York City, where he subsisted on restaurant jobs until he began acting with the American Negro Theatre.

Poitier landed his first major screen role in *No Way Out* (1950), in which he played a black doctor wrongly accused of murdering a white patient. He went on to play strong, positive black characters in a succession of well-received films and **plays,** including the stage (1959) and film (1961) productions of **Lorraine Hansberry**'s *A Raisin in the Sun*. Poitier's popularity peaked in the late 1960s when he played sophisticated, well-educated characters in films like *To Sir, with Love* (1967), *Guess Who's Coming to Dinner* (1967), and *In the Heat of the Night* (1967). He also wrote the original story for his 1968 film *For the Love of Ivy*. In the 1970s, Poitier began to draw criticism from those who believed his roles did not sufficiently challenge racial disparities and did not accurately reflect the realities of black life and culture. Although his acting career suffered, he quickly made a successful transition to directing with such films as *Uptown Saturday Night* (1974) and *Stir Crazy* (1980). Poitier's long and varied career is chronicled in his **autobiography** *This Life* (1980).

Further Readings

Black Writers, first edition, Gale, 1989.

Contemporary Literary Criticism, Volume 26, Gale, 1983.

Marill, Alvin H., *The Films of Sidney Poitier,* Citadel, 1978.

Carlene Hatcher Polite

American novelist
Born August 28, 1932.

Polite's fiction goes beyond conventional methods of plot and character development. Her two published **novels** rely on monologues and **speeches** that display her pleasure in the beauty of language. Polite worked as a dancer and a political activist before writing her first novel, *Les Flagellents* (1966; *The Flagellants*, 1967), published while she was living in Paris. It is the story of a young black couple whose attempts to build a life together are frustrated by a racist society. In her novel *Sister X and the Victims of Foul Play* (1975), two people recount the life of an exotic black dancer killed in a Parisian nightclub; the only speaking characters in the novel are the dancer's costume designer and her former lover.

Further Readings

Black Writers, first edition, Gale, 1989.

Dictionary of Literary Biography, Volume 33: *Afro-American Fiction Writers after 1955,* Gale, 1984.

The Poor Christ of Bomba

Mongo Beti
Novel, 1971

The Poor Christ of Bomba (*Le Pauvre Christ de Bomba*), **Mongo Beti**'s second **novel**, combines comic farce and bitter **satire** in a critique of European imperialism in Africa. Set in an African bush village in the 1930s, it tells the story of the Reverend Father Superior Drumont, who sets out to convert the villagers and save them from the corrupting influences of greed and temptation. But Father Drumont soon discovers that the Africans only embraced his **religion** in order to learn European secrets of material success. He also learns that the missionary house, where African girls are sent to learn the wifely duties of Christian womanhood, has become a house of prostitution. Faced with the overwhelming failure of his civilizing intentions, Father Drumont returns to Europe in despair.

Porky

Character in *Dopefiend, The Story of a Black Junkie*

Possessing the Secret of Joy

Alice Walker
Novel, 1992

The central character in **Alice Walker**'s *Possessing the Secret of Joy,* foreshadowed in *The Color Purple* and *The Temple of My Familiar*, is a victim of the African rite of female circumcision. Tashi, who watches her sister Dura die soon after the operation, is herself circumcised by the same woman, M'Lissa. M'Lissa is a powerful woman, so at first Tashi can only suffer—mentally as well as physically. She moves to the United States and becomes known as Evelyn. Despite her painful disability, she marries Adam Johnson. Because of Tashi's physical limitations, he engages in a sexual affair with a European woman, Lisette, whom he visits twice a year. Oddly, the child of that union, the bisexual and transatlantic Pierre, comes closest to understanding Tashi's in-between status as a woman who cannot experience love fully. Tashi's own child, the slow and methodical Benny, comes to understand the tragedy that befell his mother as a child. Finally, Tashi realizes that the only way she can avenge the death of her sister and her own living death is by returning to Africa and killing M'Lissa. Ironically, this is the only way in which the issue of female circumcision comes to the attention of the international media. A childhood friend named Olivia tries to defend Tashi at her trial and help ban the ritual.

Post Aesthetic Movement

The post aesthetic movement is an artistic response made by African Americans to the **black aesthetic movement** of the 1960s and early 1970s. Writers since that time have adopted a somewhat different tone in their work, with less emphasis placed on the disparity between black and white in the United States. In the words of post aesthetic authors such as **Toni Morrison**, **John Edgar Wideman**, and **Kristin Hunter**, the themes of self-reflection and healing are evident. African Americans are portrayed as looking inward for answers to their own questions, rather than looking to the outside world.

Since the black aesthetic movement, African American writing has become more legitimized in America and barriers have fallen in various genres. For example, **Octavia E. Butler** and **Samuel R. Delany** have delved into the world of science fiction; **Donald Goines** wrote **detective fiction**. Novels of both folk history and the urban experience have been equally well received, and many artists have found that they can straddle more than one genre—**Alice Walker** and **Gayl Jones** being examples—and have published fiction, **poetry**, **essays**, and children's books.

Black women writers have played a particularly important part in the post aesthetic movement. Morrison, Walker, Jones, **Terry McMillan**, and **Gloria Naylor** are all examples of successful female authors who have become prominent figures in the literary arena. Many of these women wrote in reaction to the black aesthetic movement, protesting the subordinate role in which they had been cast by male-oriented **black nationalism**. **Zora Neale Hurston**'s work was resurrected for inspiration. These women were also supported by the women's liberation movement, allowing their works to reach a wider audience. In this way, the somewhat female-repressive politics of black aesthetics provoked women writers to express themselves. By the 1980s, black women writers were at the leading edge of publishing, in both the quality and the quantity of their work.

The feminist underpinnings of much post aesthetic writing can be seen in two novels by Jones, *Corregidora* (1975) and *Eva's Man* (1976). The former centers on a woman whose three generations of female forebears have endured a brutal cycle of **slavery**, prostitution, and incest. The latter focuses on a woman who has been institutionalized for sexually mutilating a male acquaintance. Another well-known example is Walker's **novel** *The Color Purple* (1982), which won a Pulitzer Prize. The narrative depicts black women overcoming both sexual and racial oppression to become strong, creative individuals. Yet another example is Morrison's *Beloved* (1987), which also received a Pulitzer. This novel is the powerful story of a female ex-slave's attempt to come to grips with her tragic past.

One of the most successful works of the late twentieth century was **Alex Haley**'s *Roots: The Saga of an American Family* (1976). This blend of fact and fiction recounts the tale of several generations of Haley's family. The book brought Haley immediate renown and a host of awards, including a Pulitzer and a National Book Award. The ABC telecast of the story in an eight-part miniseries was one of the most watched television events ever. Following the success of *Roots,* many blacks became interested in their African ancestors.

Ted Poston
American journalist and short story writer
Born July 4, 1906.
Died January 11, 1974.

Born in Hopkinsville, Kentucky, Theodore Roosevelt Augustus Major Poston was a pioneering black journalist, with a talent for putting sources at ease and a conversational, riveting prose style. Poston began his career at the *Amsterdam News* in the late 1920s, then worked at the *New York Post* from 1937 until his retirement in 1972. His reporting on racial **discrimination** in the South—often at great personal risk—earned him numerous awards. Poston also wrote many short stories, many of them autobiographical. The most anthologized of these is "The Revolt of the Evil Fairies" (1942), about intraracial prejudice and **segregation** in a small southern town. His stories are collected in *The Dark Side of Hopkinsville* (1991).

Further Readings

Black Writers, second edition, Gale, 1994.

Dictionary of Literary Biography Volume 51: *Afro-American Writers from the Harlem Renaissance to 1940,* Gale, 1987.

Faith, Baby! (1967). Allegations of corruption and a conviction for contempt of court led the House of Representatives to exclude him from the 90th Congress. Although the Supreme Court later ruled that the House's decision was unconstitutional, Powell was defeated in the 1969 primaries. His *Adam by Adam: The Autobiography of Adam Clayton Powell Jr.* (1971) details his life and political career. Powell died of cancer on April 4, 1972.

Further Readings

Black Literature Criticism, Gale, 1992.

Black Writers, first edition, Gale, 1989.

Adam Clayton Powell Jr.

American politician
Born November 29, 1908.
Died April 4, 1972.

Known primarily as a United States Congressperson from Harlem, Powell was the first black member of the House of Representatives from the East. As a politician and a militant African American leader, he made strong gains in the struggle for racial equality.

Powell was born in Connecticut but in 1923 moved to Harlem, where he learned of the ideas of **Marcus Garvey** and began attending meetings of black nationalist groups. During the Depression, Powell himself became a civil rights leader. In 1941, he was elected to the New York City Council and, after serving four years, was elected to Congress as the representative of central Harlem. In Washington, Powell debated with Southern segregationists, challenged **discrimination** in the armed forces, and authored the Powell Amendment, which denies federal funds to projects that tolerate discrimination and which was later incorporated into the Flanagan School Lunch Bill. He documented his views of American race relations in *Marching Blacks: An Interpretive History of the Rise of the Black Common Man* (1945). He also published a collection of sermons and **speeches**, *Keep the*

Praisesong for the Widow

Paule Marshall
Novel, 1983

Praisesong for the Widow is **Paule Marshall**'s most widely reviewed book and winner of the 1984 Before Columbus American Book Award. The protagonist is Avatar "Avey" Johnson, an affluent widow in her late sixties; in her struggle to succeed in a white world, she has lost touch with her West Indian and African American heritage.

In the **novel**, Johnson takes a luxury cruise through the West Indies, and while on the boat she experiences disturbing dreams about her father's great aunt, whom she had visited every summer on a South Carolina island. Her aunt would take her to spot on the island called Ibo Landing, where it was said that a group of slaves, after landing in America, had turned and walked back across the water to Africa. The dream makes Johnson so uneasy that she decides to leave the cruise. But while waiting in Grenada for a plane to New York, she remembers how much closer she had been to her heritage in the years after she was first married, when she and her husband used to dance to **jazz** records and listen to gospel music. She meets a shopkeeper in

Grenada who urges her to accompany him and others on an excursion to Carriacou, the island of their ancestors. During the island celebration, she undergoes a spiritual rebirth and resolves to tell others of her experience.

Prayer Meeting

Ben Caldwell
Play, first produced 1967, published 1968

Ben Caldwell's most acclaimed **play** is a comedic one-act with only two characters—a minister and a burglar. *Prayer Meeting; or, The First Militant Minister* revolves around a black minister who returns home and prays for God's help in avoiding an angry reaction by his congregation to the death of a black teenager at the hands of the police. The burglar, surprised but undetected in the minister's home, listens to the prayer and speaks to the minister, who mistakes the burglar's voice for God's. The burglar takes advantage of the minister's mistake and commands him to disavow nonviolence and substitute the philosophy of "an eye for an eye."

Prejudice and Your Child

Kenneth B. Clark
Nonfiction, 1955

Having prepared the social science information cited by the U. S. Supreme Court in its ruling on desegregation in education, **Kenneth B. Clark** re-examines the data and interprets it for school personnel, churches, social agencies, and parents. Part I of *Prejudice and Your Child*, "The Problem of Prejudice," focuses on the effects of racial prejudice on the personal development of white and black children. Using psychological studies as evidence, Clark argues that prejudice is rooted in and encouraged by insecurity. In Part II, "A Program for Action," Clark

suggests action that organizations and parents can take to address the issue of prejudice.

Jean Price-Mars

Haitian diplomat and ethnologist
Born October 15, 1875.
Died March 2, 1969.

Born in Grande-Riviere du Nord, Haiti, Price-Mars attended the University of Dakar in French West Africa. He later became professor and rector of the University of Haiti. A scholar of Haiti's ethnology and **folklore** with a particular interest in parapsychology and voodoo, Price-Mars wrote *Formation ethnique: Folklore et culture du peuple haïtien* (1939), *Silhouettes de negres et de negrophiles* (1960), and *Ainsi parla l'oncle* (1973; *So Spoke the Uncle,* 1983). He also founded the Haitian Institute of Ethnology. As a diplomat, he served in France, Germany, the Dominican Republic, the United States, and at the United Nations. He was also a member of the Haitian Senate and became Haiti's minister for foreign affairs before his death in Port-au-Prince.

Further Readings
Black Writers, second edition, Gale, 1994.

The Primitive

Chester Himes
Novel, 1955

Chester Himes's *The Primitive* is a story of the destructive power of racial and sexual stereotypes on two otherwise productive people. Jesse Robinson is a mildly successful African American writer who visits New York City to receive an advance against the publication of a new book. He leaves a job at an upstate New York resort and comes to the city where he stays in a boarding house in the slums. With his advance in his pocket, he calls Kriss Cummings, a white woman whom he has known for several years. She is emotionally drained from a recent breakup and refuses to see Robinson for several days. The two eventually meet at Cummings's apartment and with several other acquaintances have a drunken orgy. Cummings is attracted to Robinson as an exotic black "primitive" with great sexual prowess, and she reduces him to the stereotypic black male. Robinson, also succumbing to racial stereotypes, idealizes Cummings as the epitome of femininity and will do anything to make love to her. At one point, in a state of severe inebriation, Robinson kills Cummings but is unaware of her death until the following day.

Protest Fiction

Protest fiction has as its primary, explicit purpose the protesting of some social injustice, such as **racism** or **discrimination**. One example of the many protest novels by black authors is a series of five novels published by **Chester Himes,** beginning in 1945 with *If He Hollers Let Him Go* and ending in 1955 with *The Primitive*. These works depict the destructive effects of race and gender stereotyping in the context of interracial relationships. Another African American author whose works often revolve around themes of social protest is **John Oliver Killens**. His **novel** *And Then We Heard the Thunder* (1962) portrays the negative impact of **segregation** and racism within a military setting. **James Baldwin**'s **essay** "Everybody's Protest Novel" (1949) generated controversy by attacking the authors of protest fiction.

Proud Shoes: The Story of an American Family

Pauli Murray
Biography, 1956

Proud Shoes: The Story of an American Family is the **biography** of **Pauli Murray**'s

maternal grandparents, Robert and Cornelia Fitzgerald, and the story of her own quest for personal identity. On another level, however, it is also representative of the collective ambition of African Americans to identify the positive meaning in the historical experience of blacks in white America. *Proud Shoes* began as an idea for a children's story designed to teach young members of the Fitzgerald family about their genealogical roots. Its scope enlarged as Murray responded to the political tumult of the early 1950s. The final book is a synthesis of oral and written history and literature, the product of Murray's imagination and four years of research.

Proud Shoes examines Robert Fitzgerald's life as a free black man, a veteran of the Civil War, in the South. Fitzgerald, the son of a mulatto father and a white mother, moved from Delaware to Philadelphia, and then to North Carolina with his family. He then wed Cornelia Smith, the daughter of a slave woman raped by the son of a prominent white family. After detailing this background, *Proud Shoes* examines the social, political, and economic challenges Fitzgerald and his family faced.

Pundabi

Character in *The Golden Serpent*

Purlie Victorious

Ossie Davis
Play, first produced 1961, published 1961

Ossie Davis's *Purlie Victorious* is a comedic critique of **racism**, classism, and violence in American society. Set during the 1950s, it tells the story of a young black preacher, Purlie Victorious Judson, whose dream is to establish an African American church in the old barn called Big Bethel. Purlie's antagonist is Ol' Cap'n Cotchipee, a plantation owner of the Old South, who beat Purlie when he was younger. Also involved in the plot are Purlie's brother Gitlow, who seems to accept the Cotchipee's racism, and Cotchipee's son Charlie, who supports desegregation.

In order to buy Big Bethel, Purlie needs a five-hundred-dollar inheritance that was willed to a relative—Cousin Bee, now dead. Cotchipee has control of the inheritance, but Purlie plans to have Lutiebell Gussie Mae Jenkins impersonate Cousin Bee. In a first encounter, Lutiebell fools Cotchipee, but he seems more impressed with her looks than with the credentials Purlie has created for her. Purlie sarcastically honors Cotchipee with several awards, including naming him the "Great White Father of the Year." Touched, Cotchipee sends for the five hundred dollars. When he asks for a receipt, however, Lutiebell signs it with her own name, not Cousin Bee's. Cotchipee orders the sheriff to arrest Purlie, but he escapes.

In the aftermath of Purlie's escape, Gitlow shows up with a promise from Cotchipee to hand over the money in return for Lutiebell's help with the Sunday dinner. Purlie suspects Cotchipee's intentions; and when Lutiebell returns in disgust at having been kissed and pinched, Purlie storms off, returning with the money and Cotchipee's bullwhip. Cotchipee shows up with the sheriff, but Charlie Cotchipee confesses to having taken the money and given it to Purlie. Charlie also admits that he bought Big Bethel but has put the deed in Purlie's name. He asks Purlie if he can join the congregation. At this news Cotchipee drops dead. The **play** ends with Purlie officiating at Cotchipee's funeral.

Purlie Victorious Judson

Character in *Purlie Victorious*

Benjamin Quarles

American historian
Born January 23, 1904.

Quarles is one of the preeminent modern historians of the black American experience

prior to the twentieth century. Quarles's titles *The Negro in the Civil War* (1953), *The Negro in the American Revolution* (1961), and *Black Abolitionists* (1969), as well as his other works on the roles of blacks in the making of America, helped to extend knowledge of black American history to scholars and general readers alike.

Born in 1904 in Boston, Massachusetts, Quarles earned a doctorate at the University of Wisconsin and spent most of his career teaching at Dillard University in New Orleans and Morgan State University in Baltimore. His first book, *Frederick Douglass* (1948), was regarded by critics as an important contribution to African American history. Through this and other books Quarles sought to create a sense of pride and personal worth in black Americans. Although his work has sometimes been criticized as overly optimistic, it has also been praised for debunking the American myth that "liberty and justice for all" has been applied equally to blacks and whites. Among Quarles's most recent collections of writings is *Black Mosaic: Essays in Afro-American History* (1988).

Further Readings
Black Writers, first edition, Gale, 1989.

Queen

Alex Haley and David Stevens
Novel, 1993

Produced as a television miniseries in 1993, *Queen* was first a screenplay and later a **novel** written by Stevens that he based heavily on **Alex Haley**'s taped dictation. Since Haley died in 1992, before *Queen* was completed, accusations denying its historical accuracy center around Stevens' embellishments.

Purportedly a history of Haley's parental heritage, this **slave narrative** begins in Alabama during the 1840s. The title character Queen is the product of a union between a mulatto slave named Easter and the plantation owner's son,

James Jackson Jr. After Jackson dies in the Civil War, Queen is unwelcome in the main house, so she leaves and bears a child shortly afterward. When her husband falls victim to a lynch mob, Queen fights to retain custody of her child. Eventually Queen settles in Savannah, Tennessee, where she and widower Alec Haley give birth to Alex Haley's father.

A Question of Power

Bessie Head
Novel, 1973

Bessie Head's *A Question of Power* depicts the battle between good and evil and tells of the mental disintegration of a young woman. The main character, Elizabeth, comes from South Africa to Botswana to teach. She is considered an outsider both by virtue of her mixed-race parentage and the fact that she is a stranger, and her isolation ultimately leads to mental instability. She begins to hallucinate, losing her sense of reality and sinking into a nightmare world where the characters of Sello and Dan dominate her dreams. Sello, embodying goodness and caring, introduces her to the evil inherent in weakness, while Dan, his evil counterpart, seduces Elizabeth and forces her to endure manifestations of his Satanic power. Elizabeth is eventually confined to a mental hospital where she learns to recognize evil. Having resisted its seduction, she can now feel a sense of belonging within her small community.

Quicksand

Nella Larsen
Novel, 1928

Considered one of the best novels of the **Harlem Renaissance**, *Quicksand* won the Harmon Foundation prize and has long been admired for its complex treatment of both racial heritage and female sexuality. Largely autobiographical, the **novel** focuses on Helga Crane, who, like **Nella Larsen**, is the daughter of a black man and a Scandinavian woman.

Crane's quest takes her from a teaching position at a small college in the South to the elite social circles of New York City and Copenhagen, but by the end of the novel she is married to an illiterate preacher in backwoods Alabama. While her marriage fulfills her longing for an uncomplicated existence and for sexual gratification, it leaves her mired in poverty and continual pregnancy. The book ends with her pregnant and weakened by childbirth.

Teach them that anywhere

people go they have

experience and that all

experience is art.

Yellow Back Radio Broke-Down,
Ishmael Reed, 1969

Rachel

Angelina Weld Grimké
Play, first produced 1916, published 1920

The first successful **play** written by a black author and staged by black actors, **Angela Weld Grimké**'s *Rachel* is not well known today. The play centers on Rachel and Tom Loving, siblings who live in a tenement apartment in New York City. Both characters become increasingly despondent over the treatment of blacks by white Americans. In Rachel's case, her primary concern is a black child left in her care after he is stoned by whites. She ultimately decides to dedicate her life to caring for black youngsters while never bearing any of her own, and she rejects her suitor, John Strong. The play has been criticized for its painful sense of futility as well as its melodrama, but more recent critical interpretations applaud the author for her authentic observations in the era prior to the **Harlem Renaissance**.

Rachel Loving

Character in *Rachel*

Racism

Racism refers to the theory that inherited physical characteristics, such as skin color, determine a person's intellectual, psychological, or behavioral traits. In practice, racism usually takes the form of one race's claim of innate superiority over another. In the United States, this belief has historically been used to justify white-imposed **discrimination** against blacks and racial **segregation**. African American writers have led the way toward exploring the prejudices that underlie racism. Scholarly analyses of the subject by black writers include **Calvin C. Hernton**'s *Sex and Racism in America* (1965), which contends that a link exists between sexism and racism, and **Whitney M. Young Jr.**'s *Beyond Racism: Building an Open Society* (1969), which received a Christopher Award.

Racism has remained a central thematic concern of African American authors. However, the way in which this theme has typically been developed has varied from one historical period to another. In the decades leading up to the Civil War, abolitionists such as **Frederick Douglass** and **William Wells Brown** produced diatribes against **slavery** that were powerful enough to awaken the conscience of a nation. As the bonds of slavery were loosened, black writers clamored to be heard, but their audience and repertoire were limited. White society still controlled most publishing in America, so African American writing was often filtered and distorted through this lens. As a result, most post-Reconstruction era work was an attempt to prove that blacks could fit into middle-class American society. In fact, much literature from this period was an effort by blacks to appear content with their assigned lot. Still, some writers, such as **Paul Laurence Dunbar** and **Charles W. Chesnutt**, tried to depict black life as it really was, not as society wanted it to be. Thus, at least indirectly, these writers helped to break down prevalent stereotypes. With the coming of the **Harlem Renaissance** in the 1920s, African American writers began once again to make a conscious attempt to increase the awareness of racism.

Although black writers have always addressed the evils of racism in their work, the publication of **Richard Wright**'s **novel** *Native Son* in 1940 ushered in a new era in African American literature. Wright maintained that the period of the Harlem Renaissance, with its motto of art for art's sake, was over. He proposed instead that black writers should adopt as their goal the creation of works directly aimed at ending racism. After World War II, African American writers tackled the problem of racism in the military in such books as **Walter White**'s *A Rising Wind: A Report on the Negro Soldier in the European Theater of War* (1945). Then in the 1950s, two highly influential novels by African American authors appeared. **Ralph Ellison**'s *Invisible Man* (1952), which won a National Book Award, was regarded as a masterful examination of racial repression. **James Baldwin**'s *Go Tell It on the Mountain* (1953) was his first novel and, in the estimation of many critics, his most successful. Baldwin went on to become a leading literary spokesperson for the **civil rights movement** of the 1950s and 1960s. His book *The Fire Next Time* (1963) is a plea for reconciliation between the races. These books set the stage for the more overtly political treatment of racism that typified the **black aesthetic movement** of the 1960s and 1970s. During this period writers such as **H. Rap Brown**, who chronicled his work with the Student Nonviolent Coordinating Committee (SNCC) in *Die Nigger Die!* (1969), as well as poet and playwright **Amiri Baraka** and poet and essayist **Haki R. Madhubuti** reflected the political and separatist philosophies of black nationalist leaders.

In the past several decades, many black writers have recorded their experiences with racism in autobiographical volumes. *I Know Why the Caged Bird Sings* (1970), the first installment of **Maya Angelou**'s **autobiography**, reveals the author's encounters with discrimination, hatred, and humiliation in the South of the 1930s and 1940s. *Days of Grace: A Memoir* (1993), the fourth of **Arthur Ashe**'s autobiographies, reveals its author's regret at not speaking out against racism during the civil rights movement but instead waiting to voice his opposition until the 1980s.

Racism and American Education

Kenneth B. Clark and Elinor L. Gordon, editors
Nonfiction, 1970

Racism and American Education: A Dialogue and Agenda for Action, edited by Elinor L. Gordon and **Kenneth B. Clark,** presents the discussions and recommendations of a conference on racial prejudice and education held on the island of Martha's Vineyard, Massachusetts, in July, 1968. The conference was convened by the President's Commission for the Observance

of Human Rights Year, 1968, established by President Lyndon B. Johnson, and was attended by some twenty experts in related fields. Viewing the prevalence of **racism** in American schools as both an impediment to adequate education and a reflection of the pervasiveness of racism in American society, the participants called for a thorough revision of the American education system, including changes in the curriculum, modified teaching standards and evaluation procedures, and greater state and federal involvement in administration and financing.

The Radiance of the King (Le Regard du roi)

Camara Laye
Novel, 1956

The Radiance of the King, **Camara Laye**'s second book, is concerned with the conflict between African and European culture. Its main character is Clarence, a misplaced white man who must adapt to traditional African society in order to survive. Clarence has no means of earning a living unless he can find the king's court and gain a position there. His often comical search for the king, which forms the basis of the plot, is at the same time a spiritual quest for salvation. On one level, this **novel** can be read as a story about any person's attempt to deal with a world in which other people's behavior is often incomprehensible and one's own perceptions are frequently changing. On another level, it has sometimes been interpreted as an allegory about one's search for God.

Radio Raheem

Character in *Do the Right Thing*

The Raft

Please see *Three Plays*

Rahab

Character in *Caleb, the Degenerate*

Rainbow Jordan

Alice Childress
Young adult novel, 1981

The narrative of this **novel** is modeled after **Alice Childress**'s previous work for young adults. Fourteen-year-old Rainbow lives with her mother Kathie and a foster parent, Josephine Lamont. Seventeen chapters in the book are delivered in the manner of monologues by the young protagonist. As a young black girl living among the urban poor, Rainbow must take on important responsibilities and take care of herself unsupervised. Since Kathie was a teenage mother, she and Rainbow often act like siblings instead of mother and daughter. Kathie makes her living as a go-go dancer and faces difficulties developing a new love relationship, with her job and her child on her mind. When Kathie wanders further afield for employment, Rainbow is shuttled over to her foster mother, with whom she has an awkward relationship. Rainbow has a boyfriend, but she is too knowing to give in to his demands for sex. She does well in school and never caves in to peer pressure; she is a model of psychological resourcefulness. Josephine and Rainbow are suddenly thrown together when Mr. Lamont abandons his wife. Josephine eventually assumes the responsibilities of Rainbow's guardian.

A Raisin in the Sun

Lorraine Hansberry
Play, first produced 1959, published 1959

A domestic drama set in a tenement on the south side of Chicago, **Lorraine Hansberry**'s *A Raisin in the Sun* (whose title comes from **Langston Hughes**'s poem "Harlem") tells the story of the Younger family. Following the death of the family's father and provider Big Walter, who has died from overwork and grief over the death of a child, the Youngers await the payment of Walter's life insurance. For Walter's son Wal-

ter Lee, the money would enable him to open a liquor store and give up his degrading work as a chauffeur for a wealthy white; he also dreams of buying pearls for his wife Ruth and sending his son Travis to the best university. Walter Lee's idealistic sister Beneatha dreams of using the money to attend medical school and work in Africa. The family matriarch Lena realizes that the insurance money cannot fulfill all the family's designs, so she uses some of the money as a down-payment on a house in a white neighborhood. Lena gives the remainder to Walter Lee, but he gives it all to his business partner, who absconds. Destitute, Walter Lee considers accepting money from a group of whites to stay away from their neighborhood. At a crucial moment, Lena tells Walter Lee that he can accept the whites' offer if he is prepared to allow his son to watch the humiliating transaction. Despite his earlier cynicism, Walter Lee resolves to move the family into the new house, to brave the inevitable violence and forego the money, but to keep his family's dignity intact.

Ralph Kabnis

Character in *Cane*

Arnold Rampersad

West Indian biographer and critic
Born November 13, 1941.

Literary historian Rampersad is best known as the author of the definitive **biography** *The Life of Langston Hughes,* a two-volume study which has been praised for its comprehensiveness and readability. The first of the volumes, *I, Too, Sing America* (1986), earned Rampersad the 1988 Clarence L. Holte Prize; the second, *I Dream a World* (1988), received an American Book Award in 1990. Rampersad began his career with the publication of *Melville's Israel Potter: A Pilgrimage and Progress* (1969), an examination of a short narrative by Herman Melville. In *The Art and Imagination of W. E. B. Du Bois* (1976), he presented **W. E. B. Du Bois** as a passionate thinker who wrote persuasively about the oppression of black Americans. Rampersad also helped tennis star **Arthur Ashe** write his **autobiography** *Days of Grace: A Memoir* (1993).

Further Readings
Black Writers, second edition, Gale, 1994.

Dudley Randall

American publisher, editor, and poet
Born January 14, 1914.

Dudley Felker Randall provided a new forum for black writers when he founded Broadside Press in 1963. By publishing a series of paperback books by then-unknown black artists, Randall both gave a generation of poets a voice and offered readers reasonably-priced works of literature. One of Broadside's first publications was the acclaimed collection *For Malcolm: Poems on the Life and Death of Malcolm X,* which Randall edited. Writers such as **Etheridge Knight**, **Sonia Sanchez**, **Nikki Giovanni**, and **Haki R. Madhubuti** all published with Broadside and subsequently saw their works appear in affordable paperback form. Randall detailed his experiences as a publisher in *Broadside Memories: Poets I Have Known* (1975). In 1977, Randall sold Broadside Press but remains on its staff as a consultant. Randall's own **poetry** collections include *More To Remember: Poems of Four Decades* (1971), *After the Killing* (1973), and *A Litany of Friends: New and Selected Poems* (1981), all of which have been acclaimed for their technical excellence. In 1981, Randall was appointed the First Poet Laureate of the City of Detroit.

See also **Poetry of Dudley Randall**

Further Readings
Black Writers, first edition, Gale, 1989.

Dictionary of Literary Biography, Volume 41: *Afro-American Poets since 1955,* Gale, 1985.

Randall Ware

Character in *Jubilee*

A. Philip Randolph

American labor organizer and
civil rights activist
Born April 15, 1889.
Died May 16, 1979.

A socialist and Methodist, Asa Philip Randolph believed firmly in the principle of strength in unity. From 1925 to 1968 he was president of the International Brotherhood of Sleeping Car Porters, becoming in 1955 the first vice president of the American Federation of Labor-Congress of Industrial Organizations (AFL-CIO). During World War II his patient but insistent political bargaining led to the desegregation of the arms industry and the military. His success in nonviolent labor organizing paved the way for the **civil rights movement** of the 1960s, and he organized the 1963 March on Washington for Jobs and Freedom, where **Martin Luther King Jr.** gave his famous "**I Have a Dream**" speech. Randolph's writings include *The Negro Freedom Movement* (1968). In 1942 he received the Spingarn Medal from the **National Association for the Advancement of Colored People** (NAACP), and in 1964 the Presidential Medal of Freedom.

Further Readings
Black Writers, second edition, Gale, 1994.

Davis, Daniel S., *Mr. Black Labor: The Story of A. Philip Randolph, Father of the Civil Rights Movement,* Dutton, 1972.

Randy

Character in *Scorpions*

William J. Raspberry

American newspaper columnist
Born October 12, 1935.

A syndicated columnist at the *Washington Post,* William James Raspberry writes editorials that address important social and political issues. Raspberry was nominated for a Pulitzer

Prize in 1982, and has received a number of awards, including the Capitol Press Club's Journalist of the Year award in 1965 for his coverage of the Los Angeles Watts riots.

Raspberry began his career with the black weekly *Indianapolis Recorder* while he was a college student at Indiana Central College. After serving as a public information officer in the U.S. Army from 1960-62, he took a job as a teletypist at the *Washington Post*. Raspberry worked several jobs at the *Post*—obituary writer, city desk reporter, assistant city editor—until he began writing the "Potomac Watch" column in 1966. Raspberry broadened the scope of the "Potomac Watch" pieces to cover national issues, including education, criminal justice, and drug abuse. Since the mid-1960s two of his three weekly columns have been syndicated nationally. A collection of fifty of his columns were republished in *Looking Backward at Us* (1991).

In addition to writing three columns a week, Raspberry has contributed articles to numerous magazines, has taught **journalism** at Howard University, and has appeared on television in the Washington, D.C. area. He also served on the Pulitzer Prize jury from 1975-79 and the Pulitzer Prize Board from 1980-86.

Further Readings
Black Writers, second edition, Gale, 1994.

Rat Korga

Character in *Stars in My Pocket Like Grains of Sand*

Raven Quickskill

Character in *Flight to Canada*

Ray

Character in *Home to Harlem*

Ray Foots

Character in *The Toilet*

H. Cordelia Ray

American poet and educator
Born in 1849(?).
Died January 5, 1916.

Born into a genteel and erudite family, Henrietta Cordelia Ray received her master's degree in pedagogy in 1891 from New York University and worked as a school teacher for approximately thirty years. Ray first came to public notice with her commemorative ode, *Lincoln: Written for the Occasion of the Unveiling of the Freedmen's Monument in Memory of Abraham Lincoln, April 14, 1876* (1893). Ray's poems were published in two collections: *Sonnets* (1893), which displays her mastery of the traditional poetic form, and the larger, retrospective volume *Poems* (1910), which gathers decorous and sentimental verse, nature poems, encomia to familiar and historical figures, ballads, and other traditional forms.

Further Readings
Black Writers, first edition, Gale, 1989.
Dictionary of Literary Biography, Volume 50: *Afro American Writers before the Harlem Renaissance,* Gale, 1986.

Raymond

Character in *Funnyhouse of a Negro*

Raymond Taylor

Character in *Infants of the Spring*

Realism

Broadly defined, realism is the use of details drawn from everyday experience in writing of any genre. **Ron Milner** is one example of an African American writer noted for his realistic dramas. More specifically, realism is a nineteenth-century European literary movement that developed in reaction against the idealized depictions of life characteristic of the Romantic movement. The realists sought to portray familiar characters, situations, and settings in a true-to-life manner. This was achieved primarily by the use of an objective narrative point of view and through the accumulation of accurate detail. The standard for success of any realist work is how faithfully it transfers common experience into literary form. One classic example of realist writing by an African American author is **Claude Brown**'s *Manchild in the Promised Land* (1965), an autobiographical tale of life in a black ghetto during the 1940s and 1950s. The **poetry** and **plays** of **Langston Hughes,** the poetry of **Gwendolyn Brooks**, and the works of playwright **Lorraine Hansberry** abound with gritty, telling details of urban life. **Alice Childress** and **Walter Dean Myers** are among many African American writers for young adults who are noted for the realism of their works.

Reba Sledge

Character in *Look What They Done to My Song*

Reconstruction

The years immediately following the Civil War are known in United States history as the Reconstruction period. It was a time of great political turmoil. Between 1865 and 1877, violent controversy arose over such issues as the legal status of ex-slaves, called freedmen, and the constitutional power of the federal government to intervene in the affairs of states.

Following the war, Republicans, who controlled the U.S. Congress, took up the cause of the newly freed African Americans. Within a decade, three amendments to the Constitution and a string of civil rights laws had been passed. The Thirteenth Amendment abolished **slavery**, the Fourteenth Amendment guaranteed citizenship to African Americans and provided equal protection under the law, and the Fifteenth Amendment was meant to protect the right of all citizens to vote. Civil rights laws passed between 1866 and 1875 outlined and protected basic rights, including the right to purchase and sell property and the right to gain access to public accommodations. However, all did not progress smoothly. The spate of reforms produced a wave of anti-black sentiment. White supremacist organizations such as the Ku Klux Klan sprang up with the goal of intimidating blacks and preventing them from taking their rightful place in society. By 1877, post-war Republican administrations in the Southern states had given way to Southern Democratic administrations hostile to African American rights. Ruling on a group of five cases in 1883, the U.S. Supreme Court concluded that the 1875 Civil Rights Act was unconstitutional on the grounds that the Fourteenth Amendment authorized Congress to legislate only against discriminatory state action, not against **discrimination** by private individuals. Federal efforts to protect the rights of African Americans came to halt until the mid-twentieth century, when they would resume under the pressure of the **civil rights movement.**

One contemporary author who addressed the problems faced by African Americans during the Reconstruction period was **Frances Ellen Watkins Harper**. Her **poetry** collection *Sketches on Southern Life* (1872) was very popular in its day. In 1935, eminent African American historian **W. E. B. Du Bois** analyzed the events of this tumultuous period in his book *Black Reconstruction.* Other books exploring Reconstruction include **Black Power, U.S.A.: The Human Side of Reconstruction, 1867-1877** (1967), by historian and journalist **Lerone Bennett Jr.**, *Dry Victories* (1972), by poet and children's author **June Jordan**, and the novel *The Autobiography of Miss Jane Pittman* (1971), by **Ernest J. Gaines**.

The Red Girl

Character in *Annie John*

The Red Woman

Character in *At the Bottom of the River*

Saunders Redding

American historian and critic
Born October 13, 1906.
Died March 2, 1988.

Jay Saunders Redding was primarily a social critic who sought to examine the place of blacks in American society. He wrote straightforwardly about race relations at a time when it was risky to do so. Redding earned a master's degree from Brown University in 1932. He wrote his first book, *To Make a Poet Black* (1939), while teaching at Southern University in Baton Rouge, Louisiana. A critical survey of black American literature, *To Make a Poet Black* helped Redding secure a Rockefeller Foundation fellowship in 1939. He used that fellowship to travel through the South in preparation for his partly autobiographical work *No Day of Triumph* (1942).

Redding is best known for books that document the contributions of blacks to American history. *They Came in Chains: Americans from Africa,* (1950) *The Lonesome Road: The Story of the Negro's Part in America* (1958), and *The Negro* (1967) utilize biographical vignettes and original sources to document African American history and chronicle race relations. *On Being Negro in America* (1951) examines the effect of American attitudes about race on the lives of African Americans.

A 1944 Guggenheim fellowship enabled Redding to finish his only **novel,** *Stranger and Alone* (1950). A professor of English at Cornell University, Redding died of heart failure in Ithaca, New York, in 1988.

Further Readings

Black Writers, first edition, Gale, 1989.

Dictionary of Literary Biography, Volume 76: *Afro-American Writers, 1940-1955,* Gale, 1988.

Eugene B. Redmond

American poet and editor
Born December 1, 1937.

A prolific writer, Redmond was part of the **black arts movement** of the 1960s. Born in East St. Louis, he attended Southern Illinois University and Washington University. With Sherman Fowler and **Henry Dumas**, Redmond cofounded the Black River Writers Publishing Company, which has published most of his collections of **poetry,** including *Sentry of the Four Golden Pillars* (1970), *River of Bones and Flesh and Blood* (1971), and *Songs from an Afro/Phone: New Poems* (1972). In 1976, Redmond became the poet laureate of East St. Louis. His *Drumvoices: The Mission of Afro-American Poetry, A Critical History* (1976) is a survey of black American poetry from 1946 to 1976. Redmond is the literary executor of Dumas's estate and has edited many collections of his works. In 1970, Redmond became poet-in-residence and professor of English at California State University at Sacramento.

Further Readings

Black Writers, second edition, Gale, 1994.

Dictionary of Literary Biography, Volume 41: *Afro-American Poets since 1955,* Gale, 1985.

Ishmael Reed

American novelist, essayist, poet, and editor
Born February 22, 1938.

Ishmael Scott Reed has created a distinct niche in American letters with experimental works that often parody the white as well as the black establishment. An innovative poet, he uses phonetic spellings and word play blended with what he calls Neo-Hoodooism, offering an alternate cultural tradition for African Americans. Despite criticism from other African American writers and feminists, he remains committed to his satiric commentaries.

Reed was born on February 22, 1938, in Chattanooga, Tennessee. In 1942 he moved to Buffalo, New York, where he later attended the State University of New York. He married Priscilla Rose in 1960, and after the couple separated in 1963 (they later divorced), Reed settled in New York City. There he helped found an underground newspaper, *East Village Other,* and participated in several cultural organizations, experiences that helped shape his artistic development. By the late 1960s he had published and won critical acclaim for his first **novel,** *The Free-Lance Pallbearers* (1967), a parody of the African American confessional narrative. His second novel is a parody as well—*Yellow Back Radio Broke-Down* (1969) targets western pulp fiction and what Reed sees as the repressiveness of American society. In the work, Reed also introduces Neo-Hoodooism, a blend of Haitian voodoo, west African religious practices, and nonlinear time.

By the late 1960s, Reed had begun teaching at the University of California at Berkeley, and in 1970 he married Carla Blank. In the ensuing decade he helped establish the Before Columbus Foundation and co-founded both Yardbird Publishing and Reed, Cannon & Johnson Communications. During this time he also published his first major work of **poetry,** *Conjure: Selected Poems 1963-1970* (1972), which garnered a Pulitzer Prize nomination. He also produced the mystery parodies *Mumbo Jumbo* (1972), set during the **Harlem Renaissance**, and *The Last Days of Louisiana Red* (1974), featuring the voodoo trickster detective PaPa LaBas. In *Flight to Canada* (1976), Reed parodies the **slave narrative**; the work is considered by some critics to be his most significant novel.

Throughout the 1980s Reed won critical respect more for his poetry, such as *New and Collected Poems* (1988), which blends black dialect with mythic elements, and for his collected **essays**, including *God Made Alaska for the Indians* (1982), rather than for his novels. Among the latter is 1982's *The Terrible Twos,* a **satire** of the Reagan years; its 1989 sequel, *The Terrible Threes;* and 1986's *Reckless Eyeballing,* an attack of literary politics. Reed also produced *Japanese by Spring* in 1992 and has edited, under the pseudonym Emmett Coleman, *The Rise, Fall, and...? of Adam Clayton Powell.* In 1993 he published both a novel, *Japanese by Spring,* a parody of academia; and a nonfiction collection, *Airing Dirty Laundry,* a compilation of writings addressing such subjects as the news media and black anti-Semitism.

Further Readings

Black Literature Criticism, Gale, 1992.
Black Writers, second edition, Gale, 1994.

Reed's works parody both the black and the white establishments.

Boyer, Jay, *Ishmael Reed,* Boise State University, 1993.
Dictionary of Literary Biography, Volume 33: *Afro-American Fiction Writers after 1955,* Gale, 1984.

 ## Reflex and Bone Structure

Clarence Major
Novel, 1975

Reflex and Bone Structure is a parody of the detective **novel** in which **Clarence Major** subverts the conventions of the genre by obscuring a killer's identity. Like many of his best-known works, *Reflex and Bone Structure* blurs the distinction between the worlds of the novel and the reader; at the end, the narrator implies that it was he who killed Cora and her lover Dale. A self-reflexive, experimental work as much about the creative process as about characters and events, the novel frequently introduces surrealistic images into otherwise realistic scenes—for example, a rubber plant drying the dishes—forcing readers to question the representational nature of fiction. Major is interested in challenging his readers about their ideas of truth and reality; he considers this questioning relevant to the alienated status of blacks and other minority groups.

Vic Reid

Jamaican novelist
Born May 1, 1913.
Died August 25, 1987.

Victor Stafford Reid was born in Kingston, Jamaica, on May 1, 1913. His fiction, like the stories his mother narrated to him while he was growing up, focuses on Jamaica and its history, people, and heroes. The events in his books date from the mid-seventeenth century through the mid-twentieth century. A major theme in his works, which include the **novels** *New Day* (1948), *The Leopard* (1958), and *Nanny-Town* (1983), is the harmony between nature and the black man. Before becoming known for his fiction, Reid worked in **journalism**, advertising, farming, and the book trade.

Further Readings

Black Writers, first edition, Gale, 1989.

Dictionary of Literary Biography, Volume 125: *Twentieth-Century Caribbean and Black African Writers,* Second Series, Gale, 1993.

Religion

Religion and spirituality have been important themes in black literature from every era. Some of the most esteemed black authors and orators have been ministers and priests, such as **Martin Luther King Jr.**, and **Desmond Tutu**, or the offspring of ministers, such as **Malcolm X**. Many more have been deeply influenced by religious teachings, including religious writing, such as the Bible; speech, such as sermons; and music, such as **spirituals** and gospel. In the second half of the twentieth century, such religious organizations as the Southern Christian Leadership Conference and the **Nation of Islam** became potent forces for political change, playing central roles in the civil rights and **black power** movements.

Historically, African tribal religions varied widely but shared some common elements: They were steeped in ritual, magic, and devotion to the spirits of the dead. In addition, they placed heavy emphasis on the need for knowledge and appreciation of the past. **Christianity** was first introduced to West Africa by the Portuguese in the sixteenth century. Resistance among Africans to Christianization stemmed, in part, from their association of the religion with the slave trade to the New World. In the Americas, missionaries continued their efforts to convert Africans to Christianity. As far back as 1700, the Quakers sponsored monthly meetings for blacks. But an undercurrent of anxiety among a majority of white settlers curbed the formation of free black churches in colonial America, since many colonists feared that blacks might plot rebellions if allowed to gather at separate churches. By the mid-1700s, however, black membership in both the Baptist and Methodist churches had increased significantly. The first book ever published by an African American was **Phillis Wheatley**'s *Poems on Various Subjects, Religious and Moral* (1773), which is filled with poems that display the author's devout Christianity.

The first independent black congregation was organized in South Carolina in the early 1770s, and others sprang up in the early 1800s, largely as outgrowths of established white churches. In the post-Civil War years, black Baptist and Methodist ministers exerted a profound influence on their congregations, urging peaceful social and political involvement among African Americans. For example, African Methodist Episcopal minister **Albery Allson Whitman**'s **epic** poem *Not a Man and Yet a Man* (1877) espouses the idea of liberty for every individual. However, as **segregation** became a national reality in the late nineteenth century, some black churches and ministers began to advocate decidedly separatist solutions to the religious, political, and economic **discrimination** that existed in the United States. By the early 1900s, churches were functioning to unite African Americans politically. Contemporary black congregations reflect the traditional strength of community ties in their continued devotion to social improvement—evident in their youth programs, anti-drug crusades, parochial schools, and campaigns to provide the needy with food, clothing, and shelter.

African American writers have explored religious themes in every literary genre. For example, *Don't Get God Started* (1987), a **play** by **Ron Milner**, depicts affluent blacks who, plagued by worldly troubles, find comfort in religion. *God's Trombones: Seven Negro Sermons in Verse* (1927), a **poetry** and **essay** collection by **James Weldon Johnson**, retells stories from the Bible. Johnson is also author of the famous hymn "Lift Every Voice and Sing." *Just Above My Head* (1979), a **novel** by **James Baldwin**, addresses religion in the context of a gospel singer's homosexuality. Nonfiction treatments of the topic range from the relatively traditional—for example, *The Negro in the South: His Economic Progress in Relation to His Moral and Religious Development* (1907), by **Booker T. Washington** and **W. E. B. Du Bois**—to the more radical—for example, *African Origins of the Major "Western Religions"* (1970) and *We the Black Jews: Witness to the "White Jewish Race" Myth* (1983), by **Yosef ben-Jochannan**. An analysis of the central role religion has played in the course of African American letters can be found in educator and minister **Benjamin E. Mays**'s book *The Negro's God as Reflected in His Literature* (1938).

Rena Walden
Character in *The House behind the Cedars*

Renay
Character in *Loving Her*

Return to My Native Land
Aimé Césaire
Poem, 1968

Written in French in 1939 as **Aimé Césaire** was leaving Paris for his native Martinique, *Return to My Native Land* urges black readers to reject white, Western society and seek their identities in their African roots. The poem is best known for the first use of the word "**negritude**," and it is considered the original statement of the racial and cultural philosophy known as the negritude movement.

In *Return to My Native Land,* Césaire combines both an encyclopedic vocabulary and surreal metaphors with bits of African and Caribbean history to create a new language of African heritage. The first section of the poem surveys the demoralizing effects of **colonialism** on Martinique; the second chronicles Césaire's struggle to free himself from white culture; and the third celebrates negritude. The poem moves from the debilitating effects of racial and colonial oppression to an optimistic vision of the future.

Reuben Tate
Character in *Zooman and the Sign*

Reverend Ambrose
Character in *A Lesson before Dying*

Reverend Father Superior Drumont
Character in *The Poor Christ of Bomba*

Reverend Fuller
Character in *Look What They Done to My Song*

Reverend Passmore

Character in *The Owl Answers*

Reverend Torvald Neilsen

Character in *Les Blancs*

Trevor D. Rhone

Jamaican playwright and screenwriter
Born in 1940.

A popular writer for stage and screen, Rhone is known for his humor and his faithful ear for Jamaican English dialect. With Perry Henzell, Rhone coauthored Jamaica's first feature film, *The Harder They Come* (1973), which combines the rags-to-riches story of singer-songwriter Jimmy Cliff's career with a portrait of the seedy side of Jamaican life. Popular outside Jamaica, its success led to a film adaptation in 1976 of Rhone's comic stage **play** *Smile Orange* (1970), with Rhone as director. Several of Rhone's plays, including the farce *Two Can Play* (1983), have been staged in London and New York, and his screenplay *Milk and Honey* was produced in Canada in 1988.

Further Readings
Black Writers, first edition, Gale, 1989.

Rhythm and Blues

Rhythm and blues is a genre of African American music that is derived from **the blues** and which became popular in the United States after World War II. As black veterans returned home, they found an exciting blues style being played by small combos: jump blues. With its roots in boogie-woogie and the blues-swing arrangements of artists like Count Basie and Cab Calloway, this new blues style soon acquired an enormous following in black urban communities across the country. Soon many jump blues ensembles began to feature singers versed in a smooth gospel-influenced vocal style. In 1949, the popularity of this style led *Billboard* magazine to change its black pop chart title to rhythm and blues, thus coining a name for the new music. Just as blues, religious **spirituals**, and hymns formed gospel, rhythm and blues drew upon gospel, electric urban blues, and swing **jazz** to create a vibrantly modern sound appealing to the younger generation of postwar blacks.

By the early 1950s, numerous street corner singing groups had set out to establish careers in the black popular music scene. Affected by gospel trends in religious music, these vocal groups performed complex harmonies in a cappella style. As they would for rap artists in decades to come, street corners in urban neighborhoods became training grounds for thousands of aspiring young African American singers. The music of these singers became known as doo-wop. The strong relationship between gospel and rhythm and blues was also evident in the music of more hard-edged artists. For example, Ray Charles's 1958 recording "What I'd Say" is famed for its call-and-response pattern, which closely resembles the music sung at that time in Holiness churches and which traces its roots back through slave spirituals to African music.

The rise of white rock and roll around 1955 served to open the floodgates for thousands of black rhythm and blues artists enthusiastic for a nationwide audience. As black music writers have since noted, rock and roll was actually rhythm and blues rechristened with a less racially identified and, thus, more socially acceptable title.

Like other forms of black music, rhythm and blues has made its mark on the rhythm and language of black literature. Poets, in particular, such as **Michael S. Harper** and **Etheridge Knight** are noted for incorporating musical rhythms in their verses. In his nonfiction account *The Autobiography of LeRoi Jones* (1984), **Amiri Baraka** traced the influence of this musical sound on his life.

Matty Rich

American screenwriter, director, and producer
Born November 26, 1971.

Matthew Satisfield Richardson wrote, produced, and directed his award-winning autobiographical film *Straight out of Brooklyn* (1991) while still a teenager. Born in 1971 in Brooklyn, New York, Rich grew up in a violent neighborhood, witnessing the deaths of many close friends and relatives. He made his film in angry testimony to this experience. Despite its small budget, *Straight out of Brooklyn* met with critical and popular acclaim, winning the Special Jury Prize at the Sundance Film Festival, and for Rich the NOVA Award of the Producer's Guild of America for the most promising director. In 1994 Rich released *The Inkwell,* a coming-of-age film revolving around a teenaged youth and his vacation with his family on Martha's Vineyard.

Further Readings
Black Writers, second edition, Gale, 1994.

Richard Davenport

Character in *A Soldier's Play*

Richard Wendell Myles

Character in *Youngblood*

Beah Richards

American actress and playwright

Richards's acting career has spanned four decades, during which time she has gained many stage, television, and film credits. She is best known for her role as **Sidney Poitier**'s mother in the 1967 film *Guess Who's Coming to Dinner.* She was born in Vicksburg, Mississippi, and studied at both Dillard University and San Diego Community Theatre. Her dramatic works provide a feminist perspective on both the racial issues confronting society and the emancipation of women from the domination of men. The author of several **plays,** Richards won an Emmy Award in 1975 for *A Black Woman Speaks* (1975), a monologue that addresses racial oppression between women of different races.

Further Readings
Black Writers, second edition, Gale, 1994.

Willis Richardson

American playwright
Born November 5, 1889.
Died November 8, 1977.

Richardson was a pioneer in black American drama. His realist **play** *The Chip Woman's Fortune* (1923) was the first nonmusical black play on Broadway. Richardson began his career with a series of one-act plays for children before turning to histories and social commentaries for adults. His 1925 drama ***Compromise,*** for example, revolves around race relations in the 1920s South. Richardson was also a stirring advocate of black national theater; he saw theater as an educational institution that would foster black cultural identity. After years of popular neglect, Richardson was rediscovered in the late 1960s, and his work has since been widely anthologized.

Further Readings
Black Writers, first edition, Gale, 1989.

Dictionary of Literary Biography, Volume 51: *Afro-American Writers from the Harlem Renaissance to 1940,* Gale, 1987.

Richie Stokes

Character in *Night Song*

Rico

Character in *What the Wine Sellers Buy*

Rita

Character in *A Brighter Sun*

Richard Rive

South African novelist and educator
Born March 1, 1931.
Died June 4, 1989.

Notable for its ironic humor, Rive's fiction focuses on the details and heroic efforts of the struggle against **apartheid**. His work was banned in South Africa but was widely translated abroad. Rive's best-known works are the **novels** *Emergency* (1964), about the declaration of a state of emergency in Cape Town, South Africa, and its sequel, *Emergency Continued* (1990); ***Buckingham Palace, District Six***, (1986), a novel dramatizing the oppressive actions of the apartheid government in Cape Town; and *Writing Black* (1981), an autobiographical series of sketches and **essays**. Rive held a master's degree from Columbia University and a doctorate from Oxford University, and he later returned to South Africa to teach English. He was murdered in his Cape Town home in June 1989.

Further Readings

Black Writers, second edition, Gale, 1994.

Dictionary of Literary Biography, Volume 125: *Twentieth-Century Caribbean and Black African Writers,* Second Series, Gale, 1993.

The River Niger

Joseph A. Walker
Play, first produced 1972, published 1973, screenplay 1976

Jeff Williams, the protagonist in **Joseph A. Walker**'s *The River Niger,* becomes rebellious after he realizes that his need for self-love surpasses the dreams his father and his family harbor for him. Jeff has dropped out of air-force navigator's school and returned home to seek new direction for his life. He is pulled in opposite directions by his peers, who want him to join in the "revolution"; by his family, who want him to become an officer in the air force; and by his own desire to become an attorney. An emergence of solidarity of the black community occurs as Jeff interacts with people from a variety of black cultural backgrounds, including Dr. Dudley Stanton (a Jamaican doctor), a black South African girl, and an old Southern woman, each of whom possesses a distinctive accent and who signify the significance of language to the **play**'s **realism**.

Conrad Kent Rivers

American poet and short story writer
Born October 15, 1933.
Died March 24, 1968.

Rivers was born in Atlantic City, New Jersey, and published *Perchance to Dream, Othello* (1959) while still a senior at Wilberforce University in Ohio. He received his bachelor's degree in 1960 and after graduate work taught high school English in Chicago, where he cofounded the Organization of Black American Culture (OBAC). The sad, anguished **poetry** in *Dusk at Selma* (1965) reflects Rivers's feelings about the black American experience. He died at age thirty-four, shortly before the publication in London of *The Still Voice of Harlem* (1968). Rivers's work has been widely anthologized.

Further Readings

Black Writers, first edition, Gale, 1989.

Dictionary of Literary Biography, Volume 41: *Afro-American Poets since 1955,* Gale, 1985.

Robby Youngblood

Character in *Youngblood*

Robert Fitzgerald

Character in *Proud Shoes: The Story of an American Family*

Robert Samson

Character in *The Autobiography of Miss Jane Pittman*

Robert Sutter

Character in *The Piano Lesson*

Paul Robeson

American actor, singer, and autobiographer
Born April 9, 1898.
Died January 23, 1976.

A prominent entertainer, Robeson came under attack during the McCarthy era.

Robeson was one of America's most prominent black performers before his career was destroyed as a result of his controversial political positions. Acclaimed for his singing voice, Robeson made numerous recordings and gave concerts in America and Europe that ranged from black **spirituals** to opera. As the third black student to attend Rutgers College, he distinguished himself academically and athletically, becoming a member of the Phi Beta Kappa honor society and an all-American football player. He earned a law degree from Columbia University but soon became dissatisfied with the legal profession and turned to the theater, where he appeared successfully in productions in New York City and London.

As Robeson visited Europe to give performances, he increasingly identified with its political left. In England he was exposed to socialism by playwright George Bernard Shaw. During the 1930s and early 1940s, Robeson's political outspokenness against racial injustice and his admiration for the Soviet Union did not diminish his popularity. In 1943, for example, he was received enthusiastically by theater audiences as the first black actor to play Othello on Broadway with a white supporting cast. The production's long run set a Broadway record for a Shakespearean **play,** and Robeson garnered a Donaldson Award for his performance.

After the end of World War II, when relations between the U.S. and the Soviet Union broke down, Robeson's political stances proved disastrous for his career. He found few opportunities to perform and lost access to his European audience when the U.S. government barred him from traveling abroad. During this period of ostracism he wrote his **autobiography**, *Here I Stand* (1958), in which he examined his political views and their development. By the late 1950s, Robeson was once again allowed to travel. He soon became ill, however, and spent the rest of his life in virtual seclusion in the United States.

Further Readings

Black Writers, first edition, Gale, 1989.

Gilliam, Dorothy Butler, *Paul Robeson: All American,* New Republic Books, 1976.

Robeson, Susan, *The Whole World in His Hands: A Pictorial Biography of Paul Robeson,* Citadel, 1981.

Robin Stokes

Character in *Waiting to Exhale*

Max Robinson

American journalist
Born May 1, 1939.
Died in 1988.

The first black anchor of a prime-time national network television news program, Max C. Robinson was one of four anchors of ABC's nationally-broadcast *World News Tonight* between 1978 and 1983. Born in Richmond, Virginia, in 1939, Robinson was educated at Oberlin College and Indiana University. He began his career in 1959 as a voice-over announcer and worked as a television news anchor and correspondent in Washington, D.C., until 1978. In 1983 Robinson began an association with Chicago's WMAQ-TV. The recipient of numerous awards for his news analysis and excellence in **journalism**, Robinson has received regional and national Emmy awards and honorary doctorates from Atlanta and Virginia State universities. He died of AIDS in 1988.

Further Readings
Black Writers, first edition, Gale, 1989.

Carolyn M. Rodgers

American poet
Born December 14, 1945.

Carolyn Marie Rodgers is an acclaimed poet known for her frank examination of issues that black women face in an ever-changing America. Once a member of the **black arts movement** of the 1960s, Rodgers has since moved toward an introspective poetry that reflects the day-to-day struggles, victories, and routines of black American women.

Born in 1945 in Chicago, Illinois, Rodgers earned a bachelor's degree from Roosevelt University and began publishing poetry while working as a social worker for a Chicago Y.M.C.A. Her early works, including *Paper Soul* (1968) and *Songs of a Blackbird* (1969), reveal the themes of the black arts movement—revolution, black identity, street life, and love. Later volumes such as the National Book Award-nominated *how i got ovah: New and Selected Poems*

(1975) and *The Heart as Ever Green: Poems* (1978) demonstrate the importance of revolution and **religion** in the writer's ongoing search for sel Rodgers has also published *Finite Forms: Poems* (1985) and her first **novel,** *A Little Lower Than Angels* (1984).

Further Readings
Black Writers, second edition, Gale, 1994.

Evans, Mari, editor, *Black Women Writers (1950-1980): A Critical Evaluation,* Doubleday-Anchor, 1984.

Roger Fielding

Character in *Plum Bun: A Novel Without a Moral*

Joel Rogers

Jamaican-born American historian and journalist
Born September, 1880(?).
Died January, 1966.

Joel Augustus Rogers was the first black war correspondent in the history of the United States. Rogers immigrated to the United States in 1906 and became a naturalized citizen in 1917. Self-educated, Rogers was a pioneer black American historian, a prominent black journalist, and a prolific writer; he published many works on African American history and national **biography**, among them *World's Greatest Men and Women of African Descent* (1935) and the two-volume *World's Great Men of Color* (1946-47).

Further Readings
Black Writers, second edition, Gale, 1994.

Charlemae Hill Rollins

American librarian, educator, and biographer
Born June 20, 1897.
Died February 3, 1979.

Rollins promoted pride in black heritage through her work as a librarian, educator, and writer. Although she began as a schoolteacher in

Oklahoma, her most influential post was in the Chicago Public Library system, where she served as a librarian for thirty-six years, thirty-one of which she worked as a children's librarian at the George C. Hall Branch. Throughout her career, she campaigned to end the stereotyped portrayal of blacks in children's literature.

Born in Yazoo City, Mississippi, in 1897, Rollins graduated from Western University in 1915 and later attended Columbia University and the University of Chicago. Her first book, *We Build Together: A Reader's Guide to Negro Life and Literature for Elementary and High School Use* (1941), combined her interests in education and literature. Rollins pressed for the inclusion of authentic black characters in children's literature through her position as an instructor at Roosevelt University in Chicago from 1949 to 1960. ***Christmas Gif': An Anthology of Christmas Poems, Songs, and Stories, Written by and about Negroes*** (1963) also introduced young readers to more realistic and positive pictures of black life.

Rollins set an example for children's writers in her own work. Books such as *They Showed the Way: Forty American Negro Leaders* (1964), *Famous American Negro Poets* (1965), *Great Negro Poets for Children* (1965), and *Famous Negro Entertainers of Stage, Screen, and TV* (1967) present young readers with positive black role models. Rollins' personal friendship with poet **Langston Hughes**, whom she met at a Works Project Administration writer's project sponsored by her library during the Depression, led to the juvenile **biography** *Black Troubadour: Langston Hughes* (1970), which garnered the Coretta Scott King Award in 1971. Rollins died in Chicago on February 3, 1979.

Further Readings
Black Writers, first edition, Gale, 1989.

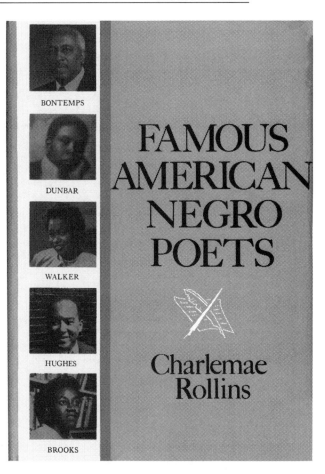

BONTEMPS
DUNBAR
WALKER
HUGHES
BROOKS

FAMOUS AMERICAN NEGRO POETS

Charlemae Rollins

Rollins's 1965 collection of biographies presents young readers with positive role models.

Romanticism

Romanticism refers to a European and American intellectual and artistic movement of the late eighteenth and early nineteenth centuries that sought greater freedom of personal expression than had been allowed by the strict rules of eighteenth-century literary form and logic. The romantics preferred emotional and imaginative expression to rational analysis. They considered the individual to be at the center of all experience and, thus, placed the individual at the center of their art. One African American poet who was strongly influenced by the English romantic tradition was **William Stanley Braithwaite**, who wrote such poems as "Keats Was an Unbeliever." More generally, romanticism can signify any work based on emotional or dreamlike experience and individualistic expression. **Countee Cullen**, **Anne Spencer**, and **Angelina Weld Grimké** were romantic poets in this sense.

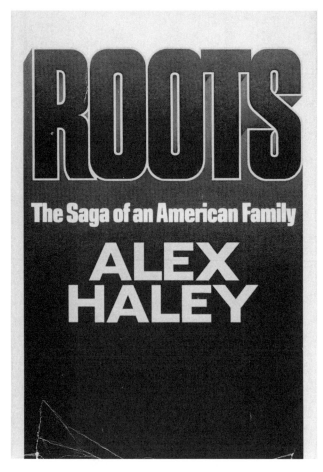

Haley's renowned first novel is based on the history of his mother's family.

work sparked both a renewed interest in African American history and in genealogy.

Roots is the story of Haley's distant ancestor, Kunta Kinte, a West African from what is now Gambia. Kinte is captured by slave traders, loaded on a slaving ship, and taken to the United States. Although he is sold into **slavery** and forced to work on a plantation, Kinte refuses to relinquish his African heritage, ignoring his "slave name," Toby, and responding only to his African name. Kinte dreams of escaping and makes several tries until he loses a foot after the fourth attempt. He marries the plantation cook, Bell, and fathers a child he calls Kizzy, to whom he passes on his story. Kizzy bears a child, fathered by her master, who becomes a cockfighter named Chicken George. One of George's sons, Tom, works as a blacksmith until he is taken away from his wife and sold to a North Carolina tobacco grower. He eventually marries again, this time to Irene, who is part Indian, and the couple have eight children. One of them, Cynthia, is Haley's maternal grandmother; she passes down the family's stories to her daughter and her grandson. Finally, Haley passes on those stories started by Kinte to his own children: William Alexander, Lydia Ann, and Cynthia Gertrude.

Roots: The Saga of an American Family
Alex Haley
Novel, 1976

Roots, **Alex Haley**'s first **novel**, was a popular success in both its print and televised versions. A fictionalized personal history, *Roots* is based on the history of Haley's mother's family. Haley spent over fifteen years researching and writing the book, reconstructing events he could not document, such as the transatlantic crossing from Africa to the United States. The

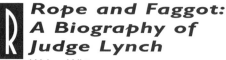

Rope and Faggot: A Biography of Judge Lynch
Walter White
History, 1929

Rope and Faggot: A Biography of Judge Lynch is a sociological and historical study of lynching in the United States. While **Walter White** completed the work during the two years he spent in France on a Guggenheim Fellowship, it is the result of his extensive research on lynching in the American South which he conducted as an investigator for the **National Association for the Advancement of Colored People** (NAACP).

In *Rope and Faggot,* White analyzes the underlying causes of lynching, and he supplements his history with statistical tables correlating racial crimes to locale, population, **religion**, economy, and other factors. While most critics acknowledge the importance of this pioneering study, many have questioned at least some of his methods and conclusions. Perhaps most controversially, White argues that racial violence can be linked to religious beliefs, specifically Methodist and Baptist beliefs. In another chapter, White refutes at length pseudoscientific theories of racial superiority and inferiority that had long been dismissed by serious scholars. For some, these sections threaten the credibility of *Rope and Faggot* as a work of serious research. For others, such as H. L. Mencken and Clarence Darrow, they are crucial to understanding and resolving the problem of mob rule.

Rose

Character in *Fences*

Rose Johnson

Character in *A Hero Ain't Nothin' but a Sandwich*

Jacques Roumain

Haitian poet and fiction writer
Born June 4, 1907.
Died August 18, 1944.

Roumain's writings were closely tied to his political beliefs. A Haitian intellectual who worked on behalf of the oppressed, Roumain brought new attention to the rich native culture of his homeland.

The son of a wealthy mulatto landowner and the grandson of a Haitian president, Roumain was educated in Europe. He returned to Haiti in 1927 and became leader of a pro-nationalist youth movement. Imprisoned and exiled several times for his leftist political activities, Roumain expressed his concerns and frustrations in literary form. In **poetry, short stories,**

and **novels,** most notably *La Proie et l'ombre* (1930; *The Prey and the Darkness*) and *Les Fantoches* (1931; *The Puppets*), Roumain explored a melancholy landscape in which characters exert little control over their destinies. Such other works as *La Montagne ensorcelée* (1931; *The Enchanted Mountain*) and *Gouverneurs de la rosée* (1944; *Masters of the Dew,* 1947) touch on themes of nationalism and communism from the perspective of poor peasants.

Roumain died of a heart attack at age thirty-eight, but his legacy of impassioned literary and political protest left a lasting impact on the people of his native land. In 1945 his widow published *Bois d'ébène* (**Ebony Wood**), a collection containing some of his most militant poems.

Further Readings

Black Writers, first edition, Gale, 1989.

Fowler, Carolyn, *A Knot in the Thread: The Life and Work of Jacques Roumain,* Howard University Press, 1980.

Carl Thomas Rowan

American journalist
Born August 11, 1925.

Rowan is one of the best known black journalists working in the United States. His nationally syndicated column runs three times weekly in various newspapers and he is a frequent lecturer and commentator on public affairs radio and television programs. His other accomplishments include government appointments in the administrations of presidents John F. Kennedy and Lyndon B. Johnson.

Rowan, born in 1925, was raised in a poor family in McMinnville, Tennessee. He was chosen as a candidate for an officer's job in the United States Navy while he was a student at Tennessee State University. Rowan served honorably in the Navy during World War II as a member of a small corps of black naval officers. When he returned, he finished college at Oberlin in Ohio and went on to study **journalism** in

Rowan is a nationally syndicated newspaper columnist.

Minnesota. During the 1950s, he covered the desegregation struggles in the South, including the Montgomery bus boycott and the integration crisis in Little Rock, the Suez Crisis, and the Vietnam War for the *Minneapolis Tribune*. He secured choice assignments in Indonesia and India and formed fast friendships with famous individuals, including **Martin Luther King Jr.** and Eleanor Roosevelt.

Besides his regular reporting job, Rowan also wrote about his experiences in a series of books, including *South of Freedom* (1952), *The Pitiful and the Proud* (1956), and *Go South to Sorrow* (1957). He also wrote the **biography** *Wait Till Next Year: The Life Story of Jackie Robinson* (1960). More recently, his efforts have included *Breaking Barriers: A Memoir* (1991), which details Rowan's own life, including his post in the U.S. State Department under presidents Kennedy and Johnson, his assignment as ambassador to Finland, and his directorship of

the United States Information Agency. Among his most recent work is *Dream Makers, Dream Breakers: The World of Justice Thurgood Marshall* (1994).

Further Readings
Black Writers, second edition, Gale, 1994.

Roy Grimes
Character in *Go Tell It on the Mountain*

Runner Mack

Barry Beckham
Novel, 1972

A stylistically and thematically challenging **novel**, **Barry Beckham**'s *Runner Mack* intertwines naturalistic scenes with daydreams, nightmares, and moments of unexpected chaos. The story follows the progressive disillusionment of Henry Adams, an unskilled worker whose search for opportunity leads only to a noisy and overcrowded ghetto. Henry is drafted into the U.S. Army and finds himself in Alaska, where he meets Runner Mack, a black revolutionary who raises Henry's political consciousness. The two men return to the mainland United States to initiate a revolution by bombing the White House, but both instead meet tragic, untimely deaths.

Russell B. Parker
Character in *Ceremonies in Dark Old Men*

Bayard Rustin
American nonfiction writer
Born March 17, 1910(?).
Died August 24, 1987.

Rustin was a leading civil rights activist who began as an organizer for the Young Communist League and eventually became executive secretary of the pacifist War Resisters' League and a special assistant to **Martin Luther King**

Jr. He later served as president and chair of the A. Philip Randolph Institute, an organization devoted to the promotion of civil rights and the radical restructuring of society and the economy. He authored *Down the Line: The Collected Writings of Bayard Rustin* (1971) and *Strategies for Freedom: The Changing Patterns of Black Protest* (1976).

Rustin was born in West Chester, Pennsylvania. His Quaker upbringing later influenced his search for peaceful means of societal change. During World War II, he was imprisoned as a conscientious objector; after his release, he helped lead many important antiwar and civil rights protest actions, including some of the first freedom rides in the South during the 1940s. Rustin played a pivotal role in organizing the massive 1963 March on Washington for Jobs and Freedom, during which King delivered his "**I Have a Dream**" speech.

Rustin's resistance to black political violence estranged him from the more radical elements of the **civil rights movement**, but he found himself at odds with other activists as well. He opposed the idea of black studies programs in colleges, and in the 1970s he spoke out against racial quotas in employment and education. Over time, his support for Jews, Southeast Asian refugees, and trade unions spurred criticism from some black leaders that Rustin had distanced himself from the civil rights struggle. Rustin responded that he could not expect help unless he gave it himself.

Rustin received many prestigious honors for his efforts, including the Family of Man Award from the National Council of Churches in 1969 and the Lyndon Johnson Award from the Urban League in 1974. He died of a heart attack in New York City in 1987.

Further Readings
Black Writers, first edition, Gale, 1989.

Rustin was a civil rights activist and assistant to Martin Luther King Jr.

Ruth
Character in *A Raisin in the Sun*

Ruth Elizabeth Sutton
Character in *Dessa Rose*

Rutherford Calhoun
Character in *Middle Passage*

Rydra Wong
Character in *Babel-17*

My secret is my eternal
burden—to pierce the
encrustations of soul-
deadening habit, and bare
the mirror of original
nakedness—knowing full
well, it is all futility.

A Dance of the Forests,
Wole Soyinka 1963

Sacred Cows... and Other Edibles

Nikki Giovanni
Essays, 1988

In *Sacred Cows... and Other Edibles,* a collection of **essays** first published in magazines and newspapers, **Nikki Giovanni** addresses a wide range of topics, from the abstract to the mundane. "Reflections on My Profession," "Four Introductions," and "An Answer to Some Questions on How I Write" deal with the art of writing. Giovanni comments in other essays on the role of the black woman today, eschewing the need for special privileges based on race or gender. She comments on the need for role models and reproaches black political leaders for their negative attitudes about the black community. On the lighter side, Giovanni discusses termites, game shows, tennis, national holidays, and describes the adventure of shopping for a car for her mother.

Sadhji

Richard Bruce Nugent
Story, 1925
Play, first produced 1932, published 1927

This story was inspired by a graphic that **Richard Bruce Nugent** submitted to illustrate the anthology *The New Negro* (1925), in which "Sadhji" first appeared. Nugent's story outlines an unrequited love quadrangle involving both heterosexual and homosexual desires. The title character is the beautiful wife of an aging African chieftain, Konombjo. Konombjo is getting on in years, though Sadhji still loves him. Konombjo's son, Mrabo, (who is Sadhji's stepson) secretly hopes to marry Sadhji after Konombjo's death. To further complicate matters, a young man named Numbo is in love with Mrabo, and in an attempt to satisfy Mrabo's desire to marry Sadhji, Numbo murders Konombjo while they are out hunting. Although Numbo's intention is to make Mrabo happy, only misery results. Sadhji commits suicide by throwing herself into the fire of her husband's funeral pyre.

Sadhji

Character in *Sadhji*

Sadiku

Character in *The Lion and the Jewel*

Gabra Madhen Sagaye

Please see Tsegaye Gabre-Medhin

Sagoe

Character in *The Interpreters*

Sal

Character in *Do the Right Thing*

Kalamu ya Salaam

American poet, playwright, essayist, short story writer, and critic
Born March 24, 1947.

A prolific writer, Salaam has received awards for fiction and criticism and founded numerous publications and organizations. Through his activism, **speeches**, and writings, he expresses his pro-African, feminist beliefs.

Born Vallery Ferdinand III in 1947, Salaam has lived his entire life in New Orleans, the city of his birth. He involved himself in the **civil rights movement** during the 1960s and has continued to promote black causes worldwide. His *Iron Flowers: A Poetic Report on a Visit to Haiti* was published in 1979, ten years before America's debate on the plight of Haitian refugees. He has also written *Our Women Keep the Skies from Falling: Six Essays in Support of the Struggle to Smash Sexism and Develop Women* (1980) and *What Is Life?* (1992). His **plays,** each containing a social agenda, have been performed by the Free Southern Theater in

New Orleans. He has also published four volumes of **poetry.**

Further Readings
Black Writers, second edition, Gale, 1994.

Salina Dutton

Character in *Jubilee*

Andrew Salkey

Panamanian poet, novelist, and essayist
Born January 30, 1928.

One of the West Indies' most prolific writers during the 1960s and 1970s, Felix Andrew Alexander Salkey has written numerous **novels** for adults and children, short stories, poems, and **essays.** In addition, he has promoted the writing of fellow West Indians through his editorship of several anthologies.

Born in Panama in 1928, Salkey moved to Jamaica as a small boy, where he was educated in British schools. In 1952 he entered the University of London, graduating in 1955, and remained in England teaching until 1976, when he joined the faculty of Hampshire College in Massachusetts. Many of his novels, including *Escape to an Autumn Pavement* (1960), focus on the effects of exile on West Indians living in London, and their wish to return to the Caribbean.

Further Readings
Black Writers, first edition, Gale, 1989.
Dictionary of Literary Biography, Volume 125: *Twentieth-Century Caribbean and Black African Writers,* Second Series, Gale, 1993.

Sally Hemings

Barbara Chase-Riboud
Novel, 1979

Sally Hemings is a historical **novel** revolving around the relationship Thomas Jefferson is believed to have had with a quadroon slave named Sally Hemings. Although there is little available evidence about Hemings's life and her relationship with Jefferson, **Barbara Chase-Riboud**'s research reaffirmed the suspicion that Jefferson was Hemings's lover and the father of her seven children. The author's findings allowed her to construct a rough outline of Hemings's life, beginning with the slave's employment in Jefferson's Paris household. She then fictionalized her historical findings, trying to recreate the experiences and emotions of Hemings. As an author, Chase-Riboud has long been interested in perspectives that include both black and white experiences, and she presents the Hemings-Jefferson story as a union between the history of both races in America.

Sally Hemings

Character in *Sally Hemings*

The Salt Eaters

Toni Cade Bambara
Novel, 1980

The Salt Eaters, **Toni Cade Bambara**'s first **novel,** focuses on the divisions she perceived in African American and other ethnic communities in the United States during the 1970s. Prior to writing this book, Bambara visited Cuba and Vietnam, and like the novel's heroine, she was a community organizer.

Over the span of two hours, *The Salt Eaters* follows the past, present, and alternative futures of the African American inhabitants of Claybourne, Georgia. Velma Henry, an energetic but disillusioned community organizer, has attempted suicide and has been taken to a local clinic where the staff practices both folk and modern medicine. Velma finds herself surrounded by Minnie Ransom, a faith healer and spiritual force in the community, and a circle of twelve senior citizens known as The Master's Mind—each representing a sign of the zodiac. The story moves in and out of Velma's mind as Minnie uses her powers to attempt to restore her will to live.

Velma and her husband, James "Obie" Henry, who has been unfaithful to her, have been working through the Academy of the Seven Arts community center to bring the factions in the community together. The characters also discuss the need for them to join forces to combat the environmental hazard posed by local nuclear power plant and chemical corporations. Two threats to community health exist in the town: one is caused by the human struggles and clashes among its residents, and the other results from the poisoning of its environment by local corporations. To combat these threats, which are faced by all groups, particularly African Americans and people of the Third World, residents must unite and join with others. Perhaps a restored Velma can help mobilize her community to this end.

Sam

Character in *Anthills of the Savannah* and *We Can't Breathe*

Saminone

Character in *The Man Who Cried I Am*

Stanlake Samkange

Rhodesian novelist and nonfiction writer
Born March 11, 1922.
Died March 6, 1988.

Stanlake John Thompson Samkange (who also wrote as S. J. T. Samkange) was involved for thirty years in the liberation of then-British Rhodesia, and his writings reflect his country's history and struggle. Born in Rhodesia and educated at the University of South Africa and Indiana University, Samkange taught history at U.S. universities for sixteen years, worked for the African People's Union under Joshua Nkomo, and served as a political adviser on the United African National Council from 1977 to 1979.

After Southern Rhodesia became Zimbabwe in 1979, he opened Harare Publishing House there. Among his books are the **novel** *On Trial for My Country* (1966), *Origins of Rhodesia* (1968), and *Oral History: The Zvimba People of Zimbabwe* (1986).

Further Readings
Black Writers, second edition, Gale, 1994.

Henry T. Sampson

American essayist and historian
Born April 22, 1934.

Henry Thomas Sampson has written histories and sourcebooks documenting blacks on stage and film, from the stereotyped minstrels of vaudeville to the development of a black film industry. Born in Jackson, Mississippi, Sampson earned a Ph.D. in nuclear engineering and became director for the Planning and Operations Space Test Program for Aerospace Corporation in 1981. He has also produced documentaries on early black films and filmmakers and has lectured for Pioneer Black Filmmakers. His books include *Blacks in Black and White: A Source Book on Black Films* (1977), *Blacks in Black Face: A Source Book on Early Black Musical Shows* (1980), and *The Ghost Walks: A Chronological History of Blacks in Show Business, 1865-1910* (1988).

Further Readings
Black Writers, second edition, Gale, 1994.

Samuel

Character in *Our Nig* and *The Color Purple*

Sonia Sanchez

American poet, playwright, and essayist
Born September 9, 1934.

Since the 1960s, Sanchez has been recognized as one of the most influential writers and

Sanchez focuses on black experience in America.

proponents of **black nationalism**, the movement to create a distinct cultural identity for black Americans. In her poems, short stories, children's stories, and **plays,** Sanchez often explores themes of alienation and depicts harsh, realistic urban scenes using dialect and word games, such as "the dozens."

Sanchez was born Wilsonia Benita Driver on September 9, 1934, in Birmingham, Alabama. Her mother died when Sanchez was an infant, and when she was nine she moved with her musician father to Harlem. She earned her B.A. from Hunter College in 1955 and, encouraged by a creative writing teacher, began to publish her poems in black periodicals. During the 1960s, Sanchez became active in the black liberation movement and also began her teaching career, championing the first university-level black studies program in the United

States. Late in the 1960s she married **Etheridge Knight**; the couple later divorced.

Homecoming (1969) was Sanchez's first published volume of **poetry,** followed by *We a BaddDDD People* (1970). With these volumes, she established themes she explores in many of her writings: the evils of substance abuse, the importance of positive role models for blacks, and relations between the sexes, both intra- and interracially. From 1972 to 1975, she was a member of the **Nation of Islam**, though ultimately its emphasis on the secondary role of women conflicted with her own emerging feminist views. *A Blues Book for Blue Black Magical Women* (1973) and *Love Poems* (1973) reflect, in part, ideals promoted by the Nation of Islam, including respect for family.

During the 1970s, Sanchez turned to drama and children's books, exploring black feminist themes in her plays *Sister Son/ji* (1969) and *Uh Huh; But How Do It Free Us?* (1974), and fable and **fantasy** in the children's books *It's a New Day* (1971) and *The Adventures of Fathead, Smallhead, and Squarehead* (1973).

The winner of several awards, Sanchez received the 1985 American Book Award for *homegirls & handgrenades* (1984), poems, based on her own experiences, that explore the themes of drug addiction and loneliness. With the collection *Under a Soprano Sky* (1986), she turned to ecological themes. Well-known as a performance artist, Sanchez continues to narrate her works worldwide. She has taught at Temple University since 1979, and most recently published *Wounded in the House of a Friend* (1995).

See also **Poetry of Sonia Sanchez**

Further Readings

Black Literature Criticism, Gale, 1992.

Black Writers, second edition, Gale, 1994.

Dictionary of Literary Biography, Volume 41: *Afro-American Poets since 1955,* Gale, 1985.

Evans, Mari, editor, *Black Women Writers (1950-1980): A Critical Evaluation,* Anchor/Doubleday, 1984.

Poetry Criticism, Volume 9, Gale, 1994.

Sandy Jenkins

Character in *The Black Cat Club*

Sapphira Wade

Character in *Mama Day*

Sarah

Character in *Funnyhouse of a Negro* and *Jane: A Story of Jamaica*

Sarah Winger

Character in *The Learning Tree*

Sathyra

Character in *Jane: A Story of Jamaica*

Satire

Satire refers to a work that uses ridicule, parody, and wit to criticize and provoke change in human nature and institutions. In 1931, **George Samuel Schuyler** published his well-known satirical **novel** *Black No More: Being an Account of the Strange and Wonderful Workings of Science in the Land of the Free*, which involves an imaginary scientific process for turning blacks into whites. Thirty-five years later, **Charles Stevenson Wright** published *The Wig: A Mirror Image* (1966), a satire about a fair-skinned black man who straightens and bleaches his hair and embarks on a quest for power and wealth. **Nanina Alba** wrote a memorable series of satirical short stories featuring a southern white woman named Miss Lucy. Other African American satirists include **Ishmael Reed**, **John Oliver Killens**, **Hal Bennett**, and **Cecil Brown.**

Savannah Jackson

Character in *Waiting to Exhale*

Schoolteacher

Character in *Beloved*

George Samuel Schuyler

American novelist, journalist, and nonfiction writer
Born February 25, 1895.
Died August 31, 1977.

Schuyler was a satirist and journalist whose conservative views on race relations were often at odds with popular opinion. Schuyler was born into a middle-class family in Providence, Rhode Island. After serving in the U.S. Army, he became a journalist. In 1926, he published "The Negro-Art Hokum," a controversial article that recognizes black art in Africa but denies such a distinct black American art. Schuyler is best known for his satirical **novel** *Black No More; Being an Account of the Strange and Wonderful Workings of Science in the Land of the Free* (1931), which revolves around a scientific process that allows blacks to be transformed into whites. In 1931, Schuyler worked as an investigative reporter in Liberia, which led to the publication of a series of newspaper articles about the Liberian slave trade and to his second and final novel, *Slaves Today: A Story of Liberia* (1931). In the ensuing years, Schuyler grew increasingly conservative and anticommunist, as evidenced in his books *The Communist Conspiracy against the Negro* (1947) and *Black and Conservative: The Autobiography of George S. Schuyler* (1966). By the time of his death in 1977, his conservatism had alienated a large part of the black community.

Further Readings

Black Writers, second edition, Gale, 1994.

Dictionary of Literary Biography, Gale, Volume 29: *American Newspaper Journalists, 1926-1950,* 1984; Volume 51: *Afro-American Writers from the Harlem Renaissance to 1940,* 1987.

Philippa Schuyler

American nonfiction writer
Born August 21, 1934.
Died May 7, 1967.

Philippa Duke Schuyler was a concert pianist and composer who began as a child prodigy and toured more than eighty countries. She also worked as a foreign correspondent for United Press Features, *New York Daily Mirror, Manchester Union-Leader,* and Spadea News Syndicate. Born in New York City, Schuyler told her own story in *Adventures in Black and White* (1960). In *Who Killed the Congo?* (1962), she provided a historical and political look at the secession of the Katangan province from the Congo (now Zaire). *Good Men Die* (1969) is a posthumously published account of the Vietnam War. Schuyler was killed in a helicopter accident while she was in South Vietnam for the *Union-Leader* and a concert tour.

Further Readings
Black Writers, first edition, Gale, 1989.

Simone Schwarz-Bart

French West Indian novelist
Born in 1938.

Schwarz-Bart was born in Guadeloupe and chronicles her native country and its inhabitants—former slaves or their descendants—in her critically acclaimed books. She wrote her first two works, *Un Plat de porc aux bananes vertes* (1967; title means "A Dish of Pork with Green Bananas") and *A Woman Named Solitude* (1967), with her husband Andre Schwarz-Bart. She is also the author of *The Bridge of Beyond* (1972) and *Between Two Worlds* (1992). Schwarz-Bart's plots focus on black women struggling with **racism**, superstition, poverty, and the violence of the men with whom they share their lives. Her work has been commended for its depiction of a strongly matrilineal society grounded in an evocative pastoralism.

Further Readings
Black Writers, second edition, Gale, 1994.
Contemporary Literary Criticism, Volume 7, Gale, 1977.

Science Fiction

Science fiction is a type of narrative that is based upon real or imagined scientific theories and technology. It is sometimes, but not always, peopled by alien creatures and set in the future, on other planets, or in different dimensions. Two African American writers who are successful novelists in this popular genre are **Samuel R. Delany** and **Octavia E. Butler**. Delany has received several prestigious awards, for his **novels** *Babel-17* (1966) and *The Einstein Intersection* (1967), his novella *Time Considered as a Helix of Semi-Precious Stones* (1969), and his **short story** "Aye and Gomorrah" (1967). Butler is especially noted for the five-part **"Patternist Saga,"** the **"Xenogenesis" Trilogy,** and her prize-winning novella "Bloodchild."

Scooter

Character in *Train Whistle Guitar*

Scorpions

Walter Dean Myers
Young adult novel, 1988

In *Scorpions* by **Walter Dean Myers**, twelve-year-old Jamal lives in Harlem with his mother and his younger sister. His brother, Randy, who heads up a local gang, the Scorpions, has been jailed for armed robbery. Jamal has always avoided involvement with gangs, and when Randy asks him to take over leadership of the Scorpions, Jamal initially resists. Despite the pleas of his mother and sister and the advice of his best friend, Tito, however, Jamal eventually accepts a gun from his brother's right-hand man and agrees to act as leader. When a power struggle ensues, Jamal abandons his bid for leadership, but a group of gang members tries to kill him. Tito uses the gun to save Jamal's life, but at a devastating emotional cost to himself.

Nathan A. Scott Jr.

American nonfiction writer
Born April 24, 1925.

Nathan Alexander Scott Jr. is known for works that grow out of his interest in **religion** and literature. Born in Cleveland, Ohio, Scott received his Master of Divinity degree from Union Theological Seminary and a Ph.D. from Columbia University. He was ordained as an Episcopal priest in 1960, taught humanities at Howard University from 1948 to 1955 and theology and literature at the University of Chicago Divinity School from 1955 to 1977, and in 1977 became a professor of English and religious studies at the University of Virginia. Scott's works include *Craters of the Spirit: Studies in the Modern Novel* (1968), *The Poetics of Belief: Studies in Coleridge, Arnold, Pater, Santayana, Stevens, and Heidegger* (1985), and *Visions of Presence in Modern American Poetry* (1993).

Further Readings

Black Writers, second edition, Gale, 1994.

Gil Scott-Heron

American musician, novelist, and poet
Born April 1, 1949.

Noted musician Scott-Heron published two **novels** and several volumes of **poetry** while a student during the late 1960s and 1970s. Focusing on revolution as a perceived cure for social problems, these works are a more militant reflection of the themes of injustice, drug abuse, and political corruption that would later manifest themselves in Scott-Heron's music.

The Vulture (1970), Scott-Heron's first novel, recounts a revolutionary group's efforts to rehabilitate a run-down black neighborhood, while 1972's *The Nigger Factory* records the experiences of blacks on a college campus. In both novels, the desire for positive change esca- lates to violence, echoing the author's concerns about injustice and corruption.

Further Readings

Black Writers, first edition, Gale, 1989.
Dictionary of Literary Biography, Volume 41: *Afro-American Poets since 1955,* Gale, 1985.

Sea King

Character in *The Concubine*

Bobby Seale

American political activist and
nonfiction writer
Born October 22, 1936.

A prominent black activist of the 1960s, Robert George Seale was born on October 22, 1936, in Dallas, Texas. After serving three years in the Air Force, he was dishonorably discharged following an altercation with a white colonel. He then enrolled at Merritt College, where he met fellow activist Huey Newton. In 1966, Seale and Newton founded the Black Panther Party, a militant group aiming to obtain equal rights for blacks and to protect ghetto residents from police brutality. Seale outlined the tenets of this organization in *Seize the Time: The Story of the Black Panther Party and Huey P. Newton* (1970), for which he received the Martin Luther King Memorial Prize in 1971.

In 1968, following massive demonstrations at the Democratic National Convention in Chicago, Seale and seven other antiwar activists, dubbed the "Chicago Eight," were charged with crossing state lines for the purpose of inciting a riot. The group's 1969 trial was frequently interrupted by Seale's denunciations of the proceedings and of Judge Julius Hoffman, whom he characterized as a racist. Hoffman eventually had Seale bound and gagged. Convicted on sixteen counts of contempt of court, Seale was sentenced to four years in prison. While in prison, Seale was also charged with ordering the execution of

Seale co-founded the Black Panther Party in 1966.

Alex Rackley, a former Panther who had been accused of disloyalty to the party. Seale's trial on these charges ended in a hung jury in May, 1971, and all charges against him were dropped. Soon thereafter the U.S. government suspended the contempt of court charges against Seale, for which he had already served two years, and he was released from prison in 1972. The same year, he made an unsuccessful bid to be elected mayor of Oakland, California. Seale wrote about his political activism and his prison experiences in *A Lonely Rage: The Autobiography of Bobby Seale* (1978).

Further Readings

Black Writers, first edition, Gale, 1989.

Freed, Donald, *Agony in New Haven: The Trial of Bobby Seale, Ericka Huggins, and the Black Panther Party,* Simon & Schuster, 1973.

Season of Anomy
Wole Soyinka
Novel, 1973

Season of Anomy, **Wole Soyinka**'s second **novel,** offers a pessimistic portrait of Africa's future. The novel opens with an examination of Aiyero, a community that emphasizes justice and the well-being of its people. The images in the first section of the novel pertain to natural processes like farming, the seasons, and vegetation rituals that stand in stark contrast to the scenes of violence that follow. Ofeyi, the novel's idealistic protagonist, believes that Aiyero must spread its ideals of decent living to the whole country. Therefore, he launches a campaign to start a model cocoa plantation within Aiyero and to bring cocoa to every Nigerian. Because the corrupt authorities are selling sawdust flavored with cocoa rather than genuine cocoa, Ofeyi sets out to expose their greed. The ruling power in Nigeria is the Cartel, or a group of cruel dictators backed by military muscle. To retaliate against Ofeyi, one of the dictators abducts Ofeyi's companion, Iriyise.

After Iriyise is abducted, Ofeyi searches for her and his quest closely parallels the **myth** of Orpheus and Eurydice. In the classical myth, the loyal Orpheus ventures to Hades in order to recover his beloved Eurydice from the all-powerful Pluto. While Ofeyi is looking for Iriyise, he witnesses hellish conditions. Soyinka portrays cruelty in *Season of Anomy* as purposeless. Prolonged exposure to genocide and wanton acts of cruelty have transformed human beings into beasts. Ofeyi searches for Iriyise in a mortuary, in a Christian church, and at Temoko, which serves as both a prison camp and a lunatic asylum. When a fight breaks out amongst the lepers of Temoko, Ofeyi seizes his chance to rescue Iriyise. Despite the bleakness of most of the book, the final scenes offer a glimmer of hope. The novel closes as Ofeyi, Iriyise, and a few other refugees walk back towards Aiyero, where they will wait for a chance to change society in the future.

The Secret Ladder
Please see The "Guyana" Quartet

See How They Run

Mary Elizabeth Vroman
Story, 1951

Mary Elizabeth Vroman's *See How They Run* chronicles her experiences as a young third-grade teacher in rural Alabama. The story, written in the stream-of-consciousness technique and published in June, 1951, in *Ladies Home Journal,* addresses her efforts to provide a quality education for her classroom of underprivileged black students. In the story, teacher Jane Richards represents Vroman and demonstrates the daily challenges she faces with forty-three students, who must overcome numerous obstacles in attending school. Some students lack the money to purchase a school lunch, for example; other families cannot afford medical care, while other children must regularly walk long distances to and from school. The title alludes to the "Three Blind Mice" nursery rhyme and reflects Richards's intentions that her students "run away" from their impoverished circumstances to an improved quality of life through education.

Segregation

Segregation is the practice in which members of the same society are separated or isolated because of race, class, or ethnicity. The members of these different groups rarely, if ever, come into contact with one another as equals. In the United States, white-imposed segregation of blacks and whites was the rule up through the first half of the twentieth century. During the years after the Civil War **Reconstruction** period, this informal policy of racial separation was written into law in the southern states. These segregationist statutes of the late nineteenth century came to be known as Jim Crow laws, named after an antebellum minstrel show character. In the intervening decades, African American writers have been on the front lines of the battle to eradicate these laws and enact new ones that protect the civil rights of all Americans.

In 1881, Tennessee passed a law that segregated blacks and whites in railroad cars. Soon similar legislation was enacted throughout the South. In 1896, the U.S. Supreme Court was faced with a case involving the issue of segregation on public transportation. A black man named Homer Adolph Plessy, traveling by train from New Orleans to Covington, Louisiana, refused to ride in the "colored" railway coach and was subsequently arrested. In deciding the case of *Plessy v. Ferguson,* the Supreme Court declared that "separate but equal" public facilities did not violate the Constitution. This ruling paved the way for the segregation of African Americans in all aspects of daily life. By the early twentieth century, blacks were segregated in schools, courtrooms, orphanages, prisons, barber shops, mental asylums, hospitals, and cemeteries. The artificial creation of two separate social spheres—one black, the other white—was maintained through laws that effectively disenfranchised African Americans through devices such as poll taxes, literary tests, and grandfather clauses.

Early in the twentieth century, African American challenges to the system of segregation took two major forms. One approach, represented by historian and essayist **W. E. B. Du Bois**, sought equal treatment for blacks through desegregation. Toward this end, Du Bois was instrumental in founding the **Niagara Movement** and later the **National Association for the Advancement of Colored People** (NAACP). The other approach, led by activist and essayist **Marcus Garvey**, urged the establishment of independent black nations that would be free of white domination. To further this goal, Garvey founded the **back-to-Africa movement**, which was the first mass movement with **black nationalism** as its central theme. These two basic positions resurfaced later in the century as the civil rights and **black power** movements.

The first significant blow against the Jim Crow system came in 1954 with the *Brown v. Board of Education of Topeka, Kansas* case, in which the Supreme Court reversed its earlier "separate but equal" ruling. The court held that compulsory segregation in public schools did not afford black children equal protection under the law. It later directed that desegregated educational facilities be established in a timely manner. In 1979, television journalist **Ed Bradley** reported on the desegregation of public schools in his Emmy Award-winning documentary "Blacks in America: With All Deliberate Speed." Attorney and author **Derrick Albert Bell Jr.** also discussed this historic change of course in his *Shades of Brown: New Perspectives on School Desegregation* (1980). Another milestone in the struggle against segregation came in the mid-1950s when a Montgomery, Alabama, woman named Rosa Parks refused to give up her seat on the bus to a white passenger. Parks later recorded her dedication to issues of justice and peace in the memoir *Quiet Strength: The Faith, the Hope, and the Heart of a Woman Who Changed a Nation* (1995; with Gregory J. Reed). A bus boycott prompted by Parks's arrest catapulted the young **Martin Luther King Jr.** to the forefront of the **civil rights movement** and set the stage for future protests. King detailed these events in *Stride toward Freedom: The Montgomery Story* (1958).

The push for desegregation met with considerable resistance. However, in 1957, the federal government's resolve to enforce the Supreme Court's decision was demonstrated when troops were dispatched to secure the admission of black children into a "white" high school in Little Rock, Arkansas. By the early 1980s, about eighty percent of black students in the South attended integrated schools. Meanwhile, in the North and West, public controversy was escalating over the process of integrating schools by transporting children in school buses long distances from their homes. Busing had arisen because minority populations were often concentrated in inner cities. Later, the Supreme Court virtually barred busing across school-district lines.

Legislation such as the Civil Rights Acts of 1957 and 1964, the Voting Rights Act of 1965, and the Fair Housing Act of 1968 struck at the legal underpinnings of segregation. However, in areas outside the South, segregation was based more on custom and attitudes than on laws. This form of segregation proved difficult to confront, which contributed to frustration and anger among ghetto residents, culminating in a series of riots in the 1960s. Even today, some issues related to segregation remain unsettled, as evidenced by the ongoing debate over the degree to which affirmative action should be used to help members of minority groups gain access to better education and employment.

Segregation has remained a stimulus for many black writers' works. Two major writing movements, the **Harlem Renaissance** and the **black aesthetic movement**, emerged partly in response to the struggle to overcome segregation. In recent years, journalist **Charlayne Hunter-Gault** has provided a personal perspective on desegregation in her memoir *In My Place* (1992). Fictional accounts of experiences with segregation include **John Oliver Killens**'s novels *Youngblood* (1954) and his Pulitzer Prize-nominated *And Then We Heard the Thunder* (1962), as well as **Ernest J. Gaines**'s critically acclaimed **novel *The Autobiography of Miss Jane Pittman*** (1971).

Seize the Time
Bobby Seale
Nonfiction, 1970

Written while **Bobby Seale** was serving a prison term, *Seize the Time: The Story of the Black Panther Party and Huey P. Newton* examines the politics of the Black Panthers. A former national chairperson of the Black Panthers, Seale writes in ghetto vernacular as he discusses the origin of the Black Panther party and the beliefs of its founder, Huey Newton, on the need for African American pride and self-defense. In *Seize the Time*, Seale denounces the authority of black and white policemen, reveals his contempt for the separatism of black nationalists, and calls for an uprising of the underclass. The book includes Seale's accusations against high-level authorities as well as an account of his being bound and gagged at a Chicago trial.

Victor Sejour

American-French poet and playwright
Born June 2, 1817.
Died September, 1874.

Born in New Orleans, Sejour moved to Paris at age nineteen to distinguish himself as a playwright and poet. His work is emotionally and politically charged, and themes of race, nationalism, and social equality figure prominently throughout his prolific literary oeuvre.

Sejour's first published work, the **short story** "Le Mulatre,"(1837) is the tale of a slave who kills his master only to discover that the man was also his father. This story is one of the earliest examples of a black writing against **slavery**. Among Sejour's works for the stage, the **plays** *La chute de sejan* (1849) and *Richard III* (1852) remained popular throughout his lifetime and were staged both in Paris and New Orleans.

Further Readings
Dictionary of Literary Biography, Volume 50: *Afro-American Writers before the Harlem Renaissance,* Gale, 1986.

Sekoni

Character in *The Interpreters*

Selina Boyce

Character in *Brown Girl, Brownstones*

Sello

Character in *A Question of Power*

Sam Selvon

West Indian novelist, playwright, and screenwriter
Born May 20, 1923.

Considered a major figure in the development of West Indian fiction of the 1950s and 1960s, Samuel Dickson Selvon was born and educated in Trinidad but immigrated to England in 1950 and has lived in Canada since 1978. His Trinidadian **novels,** which explore the British influence on Trinidad and racial tensions between black Africans and Indians, include *A Brighter Sun* (1952) and *Turn Again Tiger* (1958). Novels from his London period deal with the problems of unskilled West Indians living there. Among these are *The Lonely Londoners* (1956), *Moses Ascending* (1975), and *Moses Migrating* (1983). Selvon has also written **plays** for the stage, screen, radio, and television, some of which are collected in *Highway in the Sun and Other Plays* (1991).

Further Readings
Dictionary of Literary Biography, Volume 125: *Twentieth-Century Caribbean and Black African Writers,* Second Series, Gale, 1993.

Nasta, Susheila, editor, *Critical Perspectives on Sam Selvon,* Three Continents, 1988.

Ousmane Sembène

Please see Sembène Ousmane

Léopold Sédar Senghor

Senegalese president, poet, essayist, and nonfiction writer
Born October 9, 1906.

Senghor, who also writes under the pseudonyms Silmang Diamano and Patrice Maguilene Kaymor, has achieved international renown both as a poet and a statesperson. He is best known as a leading proponent of **negritude**, a worldwide movement that urged blacks to resist cultural **assimilation** and reclaim their African heritage.

Senghor was born in Joal, Senegal, in what was then French West Africa. He studied at the Sorbonne and conducted his career largely in France until 1960. His first **poetry** collection, *Chants d'ombre* (1945; title means "Songs of Shadow"), was well received in Paris. He served in the French Colonial Army during World War II; most of the poems of *Hosties noires* (1948; title means "Black Sacrifices") were written while Senghor was a prisoner of war. Senghor served as president of the Republic of Senegal for twenty years beginning in 1960, when his country gained its independence from France. Although Senghor continued writing poetry, including *Nocturnes* (1961; *Nocturnes,* 1969) and *Ethiopiques* (1956), he wrote mainly political and critical prose during his presidency, including *Liberté I: Négritude et humanisme* (1964; *Freedom I: Negritude and Humanism,* 1974). Senghor's *Oeuvre Poetique* (1990; *Léopold Sédar Senghor: The Collected Poetry,* 1991) attests to a life that has combined literary and political accomplishment.

See also **Poetry of Léopold Sédar Senghor**

Further Readings
Black Literature Criticism, Gale, 1992.
Black Writers, second edition, Gale, 1994.

John H. Sengstacke

American newspaper editor and publisher
Born November 25, 1912.

Publisher John Herman Henry Sengstacke founded the Negro Newspaper Publishing Association in 1940. Active in politics, he has served on advisory committees for the U.S. Office of War Information and President John F. Kennedy's Committee on Equal Opportunity in the Armed Forces.

Born in Savannah, Georgia, in 1912, Sengstacke graduated from Hampton Institute in 1933. He eventually moved to Chicago to work at the first of several papers, the *Chicago Defender,* as general manager and, eventually, president. Editor of the *Defender* beginning in 1940, Sengstacke served on the board of directors of the *New Pittsburgh Courier, Florida Courier, Michigan Chronicle, Tri-State Defender, Louisville Defender,* and other papers. President and chair of the board of Sengstacke Newspapers, Sengstacke garnered several awards for supporting the black community through his involvement in political and civic activities.

Further Readings
Black Writers, first edition, Gale, 1989.

Sent for You Yesterday

John Edgar Wideman
Novel, 1983

Complex and lyrical and utilizing a range of narrators, **John Edgar Wideman**'s PEN/Faulkner Award-winning **novel** *Sent for You Yesterday* explores the interrelated lives of residents of Pittsburgh's Homewood ghetto. Told mostly from the point of view of Doot, a young man born and raised in the neighborhood, the story also follows the fortunes of Albert Wilkes, a piano player fleeing the police, Brother Tate, an albino with mysterious ways, and the lovers Uncle Carl and Lucy Tate. Praised for its mythological and symbolic links between character and landscape, Wideman's novel also prompted comparisons with the work of William Faulkner. The book was among the first published in an affordable soft-cover first edition for the mass market.

Sethe

Character in *Beloved*

Settler Williams

Character in *Matigari ma Njiruungi*

Severus

Character in *X/Self*

Sex and Racism in America

Calvin C. Hernton
Nonfiction, 1965

Sex and Racism in America employs sociological methodology, interviews, personal reflections, psychology, and anecdotes to dissect the racial and sexual polarization in American society. Divided into four parts—the white woman, the black man, the white man, and the black woman—the work examines the ways in which American society has shaped individual sexual desire and self-image. Among other conclusions, **Calvin C. Hernton** noted that Caucasian standards of beauty and femininity have undermined the self-esteem of black American women and have instilled in black American men both attraction and repulsion at the thought of interracial sexual contact. Praised at the time for its insight and objectivity, *Sex and Racism in America* lays the critical groundwork for much of Hernton's subsequent fiction and **poetry**.

Shadow and Act

Ralph Ellison
Nonfiction, 1964

Ralph Ellison's *Shadow and Act* is a collection of **essays** and personal reminiscences written over a period of twenty-two years. In this work, he integrates his personal beliefs, his racial and national identities, and his theories on literature and music. *Shadow and Act* is divided into three sections. The first of these deals with Ellison's literary theories and personal reminiscences. In the second part, he analyzes the development of **jazz** and **blues** and the role of black artists in creating these musical styles. In the third section, Ellison uses his theories to analyze literature and evaluate other writers. Ellison's writing style in *Shadow and Act* at times takes on existentialist qualities, and he comments on the cultural and political implications for American blacks of various historical events.

Shadow Henderson

Character in *Mo' Better Blues*

The Shadow That Scares Me

Dick Gregory
Nonfiction, 1968

In this collection of **essays**, **Dick Gregory** rails against racial injustice in the North, which he claims is stronger than in the South.

However, he recognizes that Southern blacks have fought hard for the freedoms enjoyed by Northern blacks. He outlines his lifelong policy of nonviolent protest, civil rights, and economic equality. Gregory satirizes whites and blacks alike, castigates organized **religion** but professes strong belief, and endorses the American democratic system. He would rather fight poverty in white and black communities than allow himself to be pigeonholed politically. In one of his anecdotes, he puts aside his vegetarianism to deliver turkeys to needy families in a Mississippi neighborhood.

Ntozake Shange

American dramatist, poet, and novelist
Born October 18, 1948.

Shange is best known for her performance pieces that blend **poetry,** music, and dance. In these and in her **novels** and poetry, she examines what she calls the metaphysical dilemma of being alive, female, and black. A hallmark of Shange's writing is her idiosyncratic, non-traditional use of language and structure.

Shange was born Paulette Williams in Trenton, New Jersey, on October 18, 1948. Despite a rich intellectual environment and a supportive family, she became increasingly sensitive to the limits placed by society on women and blacks. In 1966 she enrolled at Barnard College, where she made the first of what would be several suicide attempts. She graduated in 1970.

It was while in graduate school at the University of California—Los Angeles, where she earned a master's degree in 1973, that she took an African name, Ntozake ("she who comes with her own things") Shange ("who walks like a lion"). Between 1972 and 1975, Shange taught writing and took part in dance performances and poetry readings. She then moved to New York, where her "choreopoem" *for colored girls who have considered suicide/when the rainbow is enuf,* opened on

Shange has won awards for both drama and poetry.

combines narrative, poetry, magic spells, recipes, and letters to tell the stories of three sisters and their relationships with men. *Betsey Brown: A Novel* (1985) is the story of a young girl growing up in St. Louis in the 1950s. *The Love Space Demands: A Continuing Saga* (1991) marked a return to the choreopoem form of *for colored girls.* Shange's third novel, *Liliane: Resurrection of the Daughter* (1994), relates the life of the title character, an artist, from her lovers' perspectives. In 1983, she became associate professor of drama at the University of Houston.

Further Readings

Black Literature Criticism, Gale, 1992.

Black Writers, second edition, Gale, 1994.

Dictionary of Literary Biography, Volume 38: *Afro-American Writers after 1955: Dramatists and Prose Writers,* Gale, 1985.

Broadway in 1976 to immediate success, winning an Obie Award as well as Emmy, Tony, and Grammy Award nominations.

Shange continued to produce **plays** and choreopoems, in addition to teaching drama and creative writing at several universities, including Yale and Howard. In 1981 the dramatic trilogy **Three Pieces** (which includes *Boogie Woogie Landscapes*) was published, winning the *Los Angeles Times* Book Prize for poetry. That year Shange also received an Obie for her adaptation of Bertolt Brecht's *Mother Courage and Her Children.* Shange has also published several collections of poetry, including *Nappy Edges* (1978), fifty poems celebrating the voices of defiantly self-sufficient women, and *From Okra to Greens: Poems* (1984). *Sassafrass, Cypress & Indigo: A Novel* (1982)

Shannon

Gordon Parks
Novel, 1981

Gordon Parks's first adult **novel**, *Shannon,* is a work of historical fiction set in New York at the beginning of the twentieth century. The plot revolves around the Irish O'Farrell family, who rise from humble beginnings when wealthy Shannon Sullivan weds Kevin O'Farrell despite her father's objections. After Kevin inherits a tool company, he builds it into a thriving engineering venture during World War I and becomes a millionaire. In their pursuit of success and prominence, Kevin and Shannon endure a number of personal tragedies: their daughter dies in childbirth, Shannon suffers a mental breakdown, and Kevin is unfaithful to his wife.

She who Is

Character in *The Owl Answers*

Carlotte Watson Sherman

American fiction writer
Born October 14, 1958.

Born in 1958 in Seattle, Washington, Sherman earned a bachelor of arts degree at Seattle University. Her background as a social worker and mental health specialist underlies her examination of psychological wounds, particularly the emotional scars of African Americans. Elements of the sacred also permeate her writing, as do themes involving issues of motherhood and family relationships among women. Many of her characters possess special gifts. Her **short story** collection *Killing Color* (1992), blends elements of mythology, **fantasy**, mystery, and metaphor. She published a **novel,** *One Dark Body,* in 1993.

Further Readings
Black Writers, second edition, Gale, 1994.

Ted Shine

American playwright
Born April 26, 1931.

Shine is noted for his **plays,** which reflect the black consciousness that grew out of the 1960s. They deal with such topics as the black family, **religion**, and the need to belong, and often feature strong-willed, sometimes grotesque, older women. Born in Baton Rouge, Louisiana, Shine graduated from Howard University and earned an M.A. in playwriting at the University of Iowa and a Ph.D. in theater and drama at the University of California. One of his best-known and most frequently produced longer works, *Morning, Noon and Night* (1964), was published in *The Black Teacher and the Dramatic Arts* (1970). He wrote more than sixty scripts for the public television series *Our Street.*

See also **Plays of Ted Shine**

Further Readings
Black Writers, first edition, Gale, 1989.
Dictionary of Literary Biography, Volume 38: *Afro-American Writers after 1955: Dramatists and Prose Writers,* Gale, 1985.

Ann Allen Shockley

American fiction writer and journalist
Born June 21, 1927.

Shockley's fiction portrays the difficulties of the black lesbian experience. Born in Louisville, Kentucky, Shockley was encouraged early to read and write. She was educated at Fisk and Western Reserve (now Case Western Reserve) universities. In 1970, she became a teacher and librarian at Fisk. Homophobia, **racism**, and sexism are the themes of her short stories, some of which are collected in *The Black and White of It* (1980), and the **novels** *Loving Her* (1974)—in which the lesbian relationship is an interracial one—and *Say Jesus and Come to Me* (1982). Shockley has also written articles and cowritten and edited reference works for libraries.

Further Readings
Black Writers, first edition, Gale, 1989.
Dictionary of Literary Biography, Volume 33: *Afro-American Fiction Writers after 1955,* Gale, 1984.

Short Stories of Toni Cade Bambara

Gorilla, My Love (1972), the first collection of **Toni Cade Bambara's short stories,** offers a glimpse into the personal relationships and lives of African Americans, often through the use of first-person narratives. Of the fifteen works in the collection, twelve are stories that Bambara wrote and published between 1959 and 1970 under the name Toni Cade, including her first two published stories: "Sweet Town" (1959) and "Mississippi Ham Rider" (1960). Many of the characters in these stories speak in black dialect. Three original stories are also included in the collection: "Basement," "The Johnson Girls," and "The Survivor." *Gorilla, My Love* won the American Book Award in 1981.

The Sea Birds Are Still Alive (1977), Bambara's second collection of short stories, was influenced by her travels to Cuba and Vietnam. In the title story, a young girl and her mother flee on a boat during the war in Southeast Asia. "The Apprentice," "Broken Field Running," "The Organizer's Wife," and "The Long Night" stress the need for community action.

Two of Bambara's short stories, "Raymond's Run" and "The Three Little Panthers," which she wrote with community activist Geneva Powell, are included in the anthology of short stories *Tales and Stories for Black Folks* (1971). Bambara intended the volume primarily to educate African American secondary and college students about their cultural history. For example, in "The Three Little Panthers," three panthers move back to their neighborhood from the suburbs and reestablish their culture.

Short Stories of Henry Dumas

Henry Dumas's **short story** collections *Ark of Bones and Other Stories* (1970), *Rope of Wind and Other Stories* (1979), and *Goodbye, Sweetwater* (1988) reveal his preoccupation with the plight of poor blacks, his deep explorations of Judeo-Christian religious beliefs, and his devotion to experimental **jazz**, especially the music of Sun Ra. Dumas's short fiction seeks to examine religious and social archetypes in unconventional ways. In "Ark of Bones," for instance, a youngster receives religious initiation on a strange ship that preserves the bones of black lynching victims. "Rope of Wind" concerns another young black man's supernatural but still futile efforts to save a friend from lynching. These and other Dumas stories employ a framework of **myth** to explore the relationship between individual and community and the transcending power of selfless service to others.

Dumas's work also focuses on the place of black children in a predominantly white world. "Rain God" (1968), one of his first published stories, demonstrates how different generations bind together through **folk tales**. In the more sinister work "The Crossing" (1970), a trio of black children take turns scaring each other with a version of Emmett Till's murder that combines both reality and fairy tale. Through symbol, allegory, myth, and **realism**, Dumas seeks to glorify a black community in touch with nature and art as opposed to a white community preoccupied by technology and **racism**.

Short Stories of James Alan McPherson

In the ten stories of **James Alan McPherson**'s collection *Hue and Cry* (1969), a volume named after the ancient legal practice of raising the "hue and cry" against felons, characters not generally successful in their relationships are overwhelmed by a world where the injustices of unfulfilling work, and sexual, class, and racial **discrimination** predominate. Faced with such situations, the characters must battle their own inadequacies as well as frustration, loneliness, mental instability, and impending death. The twelve stories of *Elbow Room* (1977) portray characters who achieve personal integrity as they actively oppose others in situations revealing limits based on sex, race, class, or region. These characters synthesize diverse qualities and acknowledge personal differences and outlooks, as they make "elbow room" for themselves. *Elbow Room* was awarded a Pulitzer Prize in 1978.

Short Stories of Grace Ogot

In the collections *Land without Thunder* (1968), *The Other Woman* (1976), *The Island of Tears* (1980), and *The Strange Bride* (1989), **Grace Ogot** has given poetic voice to the experience of the Luo people in rural Kenya. Many of her stories are based on the day-to-day lives of people she has known or read about; others are adaptations of traditional **folk tales**. One of Ogot's chief themes is the relationship between native and colonial cultures, expressed in tales about traditional healing in an age of science. She has also been praised for her fiction about African family life and the often subordinate role women must take in marriage. Aware of the social and political changes occurring around her in Kenya, Ogot reveals respect and affection for her native culture. She has written in Luo, her native language, in Kiswahili, and in English.

Short Story

A short story is a fictional prose narrative that is shorter and more focused than a **novel.** The short story usually deals with a single episode and sometimes a single character. The author's "tone," or attitude toward the subject matter, generally remains uniform throughout. The first short story published by an African American woman was "The Two Offers," by **Frances Ellen Watkins Harper**, which appeared in 1859. **Jean Toomer**'s anthology *Cane* (1923) includes a number of short stories that have come to be regarded as classics. Other story collections that have met with critical and popular success include **Paul Laurence Dunbar**'s *Folks from Dixie* (1898), **Eric Walrond**'s *Tropic Death* (1926), **Toni Cade Bambara**'s *Gorilla, My Love* (1972), and **Charles Johnson**'s *The Sorcerer's Apprentice: Tales and Conjurations* (1988).

A Short Walk
Alice Childress
Novel, 1979

Alice Childress's second **novel** is geared toward an adult audience. Curie, the main char-

acter, is a southerner who moves north to Harlem. Her trek illuminates certain historical movements of the early part of the twentieth century: **Marcus Garvey**'s **back-to-Africa movement**, lynching, the riots in Harlem during the Depression, and World War II. As an adoptee, Curie has a personal history marked by racial intolerance; she is the offspring of a young black servant and the white youngster from the family who employed her as a domestic. After the death of her mother, Curie is taken in by Bill and Etta James, and she soon becomes Bill's favorite child. Etta returns from her own travels upon the death of her husband and plays matchmaker for Curie and Kojie Anderson. Unfortunately, the marriage is untenable, and Curie escapes to the North once Kojie resorts to beating her. She moves in with a distant relation and takes a job as a card dealer. Curie reunites with her first love, Cecil Green, on the ship Marcus Garvey bought and named the *Frederick Douglass*. Cecil is a reformist and a radical, so Curie must support him and, later, their child as well. Curie becomes sensitive to the oppression keeping Cecil from achieving his goals and watches their daughter grow into an independent young adult.

Shug Avery
Character in *The Color Purple* and *The Temple of My Familiar*

Sidi
Character in *The Lion and the Jewel*

Sidney Brustein
Character in *The Sign in Sidney Brustein's Window*

The Sign in Sidney Brustein's Window
Lorraine Hansberry
Play, first produced 1964, published 1965

Lorraine Hansberry's *The Sign in Sidney Brustein's Window* focuses on a group of

I-I-20

SIDNEY
(Cont.)
And I would rather listen to what they have to talk about than
theatre talk ninety-two hours a day. Yip, yip, yip!, "Sweetie!"

(IRIS has noticed the lay-out
on the coffee table for the
first time)

IRIS
(Picking it up)
So now what? You're going to be an artist? This is awful.

SIDNEY
Put it down. It's not supposed to be a drawing. It's a lay-out for
the —

(He halts, not having meant to
get into it just this way)

IRIS
(Already expecting almost anything)
For what, Sidney.

SIDNEY
(He exhales, heavily and sits)
Harvey Wyatt met some chick—

IRIS
Yes, and—

SIDNEY
—he decided to go live in Majorca. I mean forget the whole scene and just like that
go live in Majorca...

IRIS
(Sitting, one hand
over her lips)
Oh, my God, no...Sidney — no.

SIDNEY
(Shrugging)
So he had to unload the paper.

IRIS
No. God, don't let it be true. Unload it on — whom — Sidney Brustein?
Oh, Sidney, you haven't.

SIDNEY
I know it's hard for you, Iris. To understand what I'm all about—

IRIS
(Slumping where she is)
I don't believe this. I don't believe that you could have come out of
—of that—
(gesturing to the glasses)
—and get into, into something else. Aside from anything else at the moment,
what did you conceivably tell Harvey that you were going to pay him?

SIDNEY
We made an arrangement. Don't worry about it.

IRIS
What kind of arrangement, Sidney?

SIDNEY
An arrangement. That's all. I know what I arranged. I tell you don't
worry about it, that's all.

IRIS
Where in the name of God are you going to get the money pay for a newspaper?

SIDNEY
It's a small newspaper. A weekly.

IRIS
You can't afford to buy a yearly leaflet, Sidney Brustein!

Typescript page from *The Sign in Sidney Brustein's Window.*

intellectuals and political activists in New York's Greenwich Village. Disillusioned with political activism, Sidney Brustein has bought a small newspaper with which he hopes to support the arts. At the play's beginning, he has an idealistic view of his wife Iris and dreams of going with her to the Appalachians. However, Iris begins to change and, challenging Sidney's romantic image of her, finally resolves to leave him. Sidney soon returns to politics, agreeing to place a campaign sign for local politician Wally O'Hara in his window. Just as she is leaving, Iris reveals to Sidney that O'Hara has sold out to organized crime, and in disgust, Sidney becomes depressed. Much of the **play** chronicles a series of arguments and idealistic discussions between Sidney and his relatives, his friends—such as the homosexual playwright

David Ragin, and the Marxist Alton Scales — and his neighbors. Two other important characters are Iris's sisters Gloria, a prostitute, and Mavis, an uncultured middle–class woman whose hopes for a happy married life are dashed by her husband's infidelity. Gloria is refused marriage by Alton Scales—the only major black character—because of his regret over his own family's history of prostitution. After Iris's departure and the revelations about O'Hara, Sidney's idealism collapses, and in act three he joins Gloria and David in a joint complaint against American philistinism, pornography, and materialism. David asks Gloria to take a voyeuristic role in his homosexual affair, but Gloria refuses and commits suicide. Finally, however, Gloria's death makes Sidney see that there is still room for idealism and that he can make the world a better place.

Signifying/ Signifying Monkey

According to a theory developed by prominent literary critic **Henry Louis Gates Jr.**, Signifying, often spelled "signifyin(g)" to distinguish it from the structuralist concept of signification, is a rhetorical device by which black authors make their points with indirect, often exaggerated, language. Included within this is the use of pun, pastiche, repetition, parody, and playing "the dozens" (a verbal game of trading insults) as a method of responding to previous works in their tradition or in the Euro-American literary canon. Gates has constructed his theory around the way the word "signifying" is used in the black vernacular for tricky, indirect language. He notes that the Signifying Monkey is a popular figure in African and African American **trickster tales,** with hundreds of tales about this character documented since the nineteenth century. Gates outlines his ideas in such volumes of **literary criticism** as

Figures in Black: Words, Signs, and the Racial Self (1987) and *The Signifying Monkey: Towards a Theory of Afro-American Literary Criticism* (1988). This departure from a more overtly political reading of black literature has prompted some scholars to read Gates's work as separate from the black experience. Other commentators, however, consider Signifying an insightful theory that highlights the subversive use of language.

Silla Boyce

Character in *Brown Girl, Brownstones*

"Simple" Stories

Langston Hughes
Short Stories, 1943-1965

Langston Hughes's "Simple" stories first appeared in the black newspaper *The Chicago Defender* in 1943. Dialogic in form, they feature the uneducated but wise and sympathetic barfly Jesse B. Semple (Simple for short) and his college-educated ironic foil, Boyd. Simple's common-sense approach to his problems and his hilarious folk wisdom earned the Simple stories a devoted following. Their popularity led to the publication of several anthologies: *Simple Speaks His Mind* (1950), *Simple Takes a Wife* (1953), *Simple Stakes a Claim* (1957), and *Simple's Uncle Sam* (1965). Simple comes originally from Virginia, and his life in New York is divided between work downtown, where he still feels alien, and his home life in Harlem, which offers a refuge from white America. Only in Harlem, and especially on his stool at the Wishing Well bar, does Simple truly flourish. Simple speaks on his favorite topics, race and women (including his girlfriend Zarita and his wife Joyce) and, for the price of a drink, tells stories to Boyd. Simple's opinionated outlook on life provides much of the humor in the stories, but he is in many respects a tragic and lonely figure with no close friends, only sympathetic listeners.

Singin' and Swingin'

Maya Angelou
Autobiography, 1976

Maya Angelou's third volume of **autobiography** covers the years from 1950 to 1955. It begins with her marriage to Tosh Angelos, a white ex-sailor. The match infuriates Angelou's family, especially her mother, who warns Angelou that she can expect nothing but ridicule from her husband's race and suspicion from her own. Soon Angelou is divorced, and she turns to dancing to support herself. She is offered a job at the Purple Onion nightclub and, for the first time in her life, finds acceptance on an equal basis from whites. She turns down the chance to star in a Broadway show in order to tour Europe with a production of *Porgy and Bess*. In time, however, feelings of guilt about deserting her son bring her home to the States.

John Singleton

American screenwriter and film director
Born in 1968(?).

Singleton became one of a number of young black filmmakers who redefined mainstream cinema beginning in the mid-1980s. Born in Los Angeles, California, Singleton developed an interest in film as a youth, and after his high school graduation was accepted to the University of Southern California's film school. Winning several writing awards, Singleton secured a contract with Creative Artists Agency before he graduated in 1990. His first film, *Boyz N the Hood* (1991), garnered him Academy Award nominations for best director (the youngest ever) and best original screenplay. The film chronicles the struggles of three black friends growing up in South Central, a neighborhood of Los Angeles. His second film, *Poetic Justice* (1993), also presents a scenario of life for young blacks and focuses on the experiences of women; the film contains poetry by **Maya**

Angelou. His 1994 film, *Higher Learning,* depicts racial tensions on a university campus.

Further Readings
Black Writers, second edition, Gale, 1994.

Sis Hetta
Character in *Jubilee*

Six Plays for a Negro Theatre
S. Randolph Edmonds
Plays, 1934

S. Randolph Edmond's *Six Plays for a Negro Theatre* features "folk plays," which treat issues common to black **folklore** and superstition; they also dramatize various conditions of the exploitation of African Americans. The collection contains *Bad Man, Old Man Pete, Nat Turner, Breeders, Bleeding Hearts,* and *The New Window.* The **plays**, which often use melodrama to evoke emotional reaction, examine the plight of the black man and woman in various oppressive historical contexts. The dramas are set in diverse locations, from a logging camp to a southern plantation to Harlem to the backwoods of Virginia. The characters range from working men to farmers to slaves to bootleggers. Edmonds illustrates how the conflicts between white domination and the black underclass often lead to tragedy and self-destruction for blacks.

The Slave Girl
Buchi Emecheta
Novel, 1977

Buchi Emecheta's *The Slave Girl* tells the story of Ogbanje Ojebeta, born in 1910 in the small Nigerian village of Ibuza. Orphaned at the age of seven, she is sold by her brother to Ma Palagada, a wealthy cloth merchant and dress-maker. In Ma Palagada's palatial home, Ojebeta is well treated. She attends a Sunday school where she learns to read Ibo. Later she enters a domestic academy, where she learns household skills. When Ma Palagada dies, Ojebeta is released from her servitude and returns to Ibuza. She marries Jacob, a westernized, Christian man, and together they move to Lagos. Some years later, Jacob compensates Ma Palagada's son for the loss of Ojebeta, underscoring the fact that Ojebeta's whole life has been lived at the hands of a succession of masters.

Slave Narrative

American slave narratives are autobiographical accounts by black Americans describing their experiences in **slavery** and often their escape from bondage in the South to freedom in the North. While such narratives appeared in the United States as early as 1703, critics agree that the genre flourished during the heyday of **abolitionism**, from 1831 to the end of the Civil War in 1865. During this period, slave narratives such as **Frederick Douglass**'s *Narrative of the Life of Frederick Douglass, an American Slave, Written by Himself* (1845) and **William Wells Brown**'s *Narrative of William W. Brown, a Fugitive Slave, Written by Himself* (1847) emerged as key documents in the antislavery cause. After 1865 over sixty book-length narratives appeared, notably those of **Booker T. Washington** and George Washington Carver. The largest single group of slave narratives collected were the 2,194 oral histories of elderly ex-slaves gathered in the South in the mid-1930s under the federal government's Work Projects Administration. Other slave narratives include J. W. C. Pennington's *The Fugitive Blacksmith* and John Malvin's *North into Freedom.* As firsthand accounts of enslavement, these narratives exposed the brutality of the chattel system and demonstrated the dignity of black men and women at a time when their very humanity was often questioned by whites.

The slave narratives share several characteristics: a simple, forthright style; vivid characters; and striking dramatic incidents, particularly graphic violence and daring escapes, such as that by Henry Box Brown, who packed himself into a small crate and was shipped north to waiting abolitionists. Because a primary goal of the slave narratives was to obtain the sympathy of white readers, slave narrators were encouraged to adopt conventional literary values, techniques, and language. This has led scholars to question the extent to which white sponsors, abolitionists who supported the publication and distribution of the works, imposed their own voices and styles on the narrations. Critics have suggested that the slave narrators' primary defense against the impositions of white narrators was to subvert white literary forms and language through ironic humor and other devices.

Although slave narratives were widely distributed and extremely popular in the antebellum period, they later lost currency among readers and scholars, who repudiated their historical accuracy and literary worth. A reevaluation beginning in the 1940s, however, reaffirmed the slave narratives' importance as historical records and as rich sources for such fields as anthropology, sociology, **folklore**, linguistics, economics, and political science. In addition, the slave narrative is now recognized as a distinctive literary genre worthy of critical and scholarly attention; beginning in the 1960s, for instance, many scholars have begun to trace the influence of slave narratives on such twentieth-century authors as Charles Chesnutt, **Langston Hughes**, **Richard Wright**, **Ralph Ellison**, **James Baldwin**, and **Alice Walker**. The genre is explored more fully in *The Slave's Narrative* (1985), coedited by **Charles T. Davis** and **Henry Louis Gates Jr.** It was parodied by **Ishmael Reed** in *Flight to Canada* (1976), the **novel** considered by some critics to be his most significant.

Slavery

Slavery is the most absolute and involuntary form of human servitude. In this social institution, slaves are regarded as the property of their masters, and servitude is maintained by force. The modern slave trade began in the fifteenth century, with the exploration of the African coastline and the settling of the Americas. In North America, white colonial landowners, faced with a labor shortage, first began to see African slaves as the solution to their problem in the seventeenth century. The growth of the plantation system in the southern colonies greatly increased the demand for slave laborers. By 1860, there were nearly four million slaves living in the South. Among the many modern books exploring this historical period is **Nathan Irvin Huggins**'s *Black Odyssey: The Afro-American Ordeal in Slavery* (1977).

During this time, **racism** and subjugation became the means to justify the wholesale importation and enslavement of Africans. Slave codes were enacted to control almost every aspect of the slaves' lives, leaving them virtually no rights or freedoms. The brutal conditions led many slaves who could not buy their liberty to risk their lives in escape attempts. Yet the achievements of free black American contemporaries such as eighteenth-century astronomer, mathematician, and almanac author **Benjamin Banneker** stood as sharp repudiation to those who would claim the inferiority of one race to another. So, too, did the works of several African Americans born into slavery who became accomplished creative writers, often through self-education. These included **Phillis Wheatley**, author of *Poems on Various Subjects, Religious and Moral* (1773), who published the first book of **poetry** by a black person in America, and **George Moses Horton**, known as the "slave bard of North Carolina," who became the first black professional writer in the South.

Even as the southern states were becoming more economically dependent upon slavery, many voices in the North were being raised against the institution. Some early antislavery leaders advocated an unhurried end to the practice and supported the return of African Americans to their native land. Both gradualism and repatriation failed to capture much public support, however, and stronger reforms were soon urged. The abolitionist movement, which called for the elimination of slavery, became a potent force in both society in general and literature in particular after 1831. A number of black writers and orators were notable contributors to this movement, including **William Wells Brown**, **Frances Ellen Watkins Harper**, and **Frederick Douglass**, who composed stirring diatribes against slavery. Several classics of black literature dealing with slave life were produced in the mid-1800s. These include Brown's *Clotel; or, The President's Daughter: A Narrative of Slave Life in the United States* (1853), the first **novel** published by an African American author.

In 1865, the end of the Civil War and the adoption of the Thirteenth Amendment to the Constitution spelled the end of slavery in the United States. However, the institution itself and the lives of those who endured it continue to be significant subjects in the writing of twentieth-century black authors. In the late nineteenth century, poets such as **Albery Allson Whitman** and **James Edwin Campbell** addressed slavery in their work. The twentieth century has brought fiction such as **Arna Bontemps**'s *Black Thunder* (1936), a historical novel about a slave rebellion; **Zora Neale Hurston**'s *Moses, Man of the Mountain* (1939), an allegorical novel about American slavery; and **Toni Morrison**'s *Beloved* (1987), the story of an ex-slave's attempt to deal with her past, which won the 1988 Pulitzer Prize. In addition, popular writers such as **Lucille Clifton** and **Alex Haley** have published explorations of their own family histories dating back to slave days. On a broader level, the racism, economic exploitation, and political oppression that have their roots in this practice remain among the prime themes in black literature.

Barbara Smith
American editor and essayist
Born November 16, 1946.

Smith is the first writer to characterize relationships between black women in classic black **novels** as lesbian. Smith startled attendees at the National Conference of Afro-American Writers with a paper that identified relationships between black women in many American novels written between the 1940s and the 1970s as homosexual.

Smith was born in 1946 in Cleveland, Ohio, and earned an M.A. from the University of Pittsburgh in 1971. She has taught at several colleges and universities. In *Home Girls: A Black Feminist Anthology* (1983) , Smith collected writings from black lesbians about what makes their experiences so different from those of other black women, arguing that suppression of such differences would destroy the vitality of black culture. She broadened her scope in her subsequent anthology *Yours in Struggle: Three Feminist Perspectives on Anti-Semitism and Racism,* (1984) which addresses the sexual, religious, and racial stereotyping to which women of color are subjected.

Further Readings
Black Writers, second edition, Gale, 1994.

Jessie Carney Smith
American nonfiction writer and editor
Born September 24, 1930.

Smith has edited several nonfiction works that document the achievements of black Americans, including *Notable Black American Women* (1991) and *Black Firsts* (with Robert Johns and Casper L. Jordan, 1994). In addition, she has written and edited guidebooks to information resources on African American culture, including *Ethnic Genealogy: A Research Guide* (1983).

Smith was born in Greensboro, North Carolina, on September 24, 1930. After earning a Ph.D. from the University of Illinois in 1964, she began a long career as professor of library science and librarian at Fisk University in Nashville, Tennessee. Soon thereafter, she published her first book, *Bibliography for Black Studies Programs* (1969). This was followed by such titles as *Minorities in the United States: Guide to Resources* (1973) and *Black Academic Libraries and Research Collections: An Historical Survey* (1977).

A major focus of Smith's work has been the development and enhancement of black and ethnic librarianship. To this end, she has lectured at several universities, directed research programs, and appeared on radio and television programs. Smith has received many honors for her contributions to African American scholarship, including the Martin Luther King Jr. Black Author's Award in 1982 and the Distinguished Scholars Award from the United Negro College Fund in 1986.

Further Readings
Black Writers, second edition, Gale, 1994.

Soaphead Church

Character in *The Bluest Eye*

A Soldier's Play

Charles Fuller
Play, first produced 1981, published 1982

Charles Fuller's Pulitzer-prize winning drama, *A Soldier's Play,* is set in 1944, at a fictitious army base in Louisiana, and opens with the murder of a black technical sergeant, Vernon Waters. Captain Richard Davenport, a black lawyer, slowly pieces together the character of Waters through interviews with soldiers who knew him. Waters is revealed to be a man whose obsession with gaining approval from his despised white superiors led him to persecute any African American soldier who might justify stereotypical racist perceptions. Waters' main target was C. J. Memphis, a gifted baseball player and blues singer. Waters hounded Memphis continually, had Memphis imprisoned on false charges, and eventually goaded him into suicide. Davenport connects Waters to Memphis' suicide after interviewing the men last seen with Waters—Byrd and Wilcox, two racist officers. They admit that Waters had told them he hated himself, and that he had "killed" for them, alluding to Memphis' suicide which Waters deemed necessary for racial cleansing. While others believe that Byrd and Wilcox are suspects, Davenport remains unconvinced, and finally uncovers the real killer: Melvin Peterson, an African American private who held a grudge against Waters for his unfair treatment of Memphis.

Solly Saunders

Character in *And Then We Heard the Thunder*

Solomon

Character in *Song of Solomon*

Sometimes I Think of Maryland

Joanne M. Braxton
Poetry, 1977

American poet and author Joanne M. Braxton published *Sometimes I Think of Maryland,* a collection of lyrical **poetry**, in 1977 under the pseudonym of Jodi Braxton. In this collection, she reflects on her home in Maryland, her loving family, and other people that she has known. Also included are selections portraying the roles and behaviors of black women and men, and mythical poems that resurrect the mysterious Hoodoo tradition in her family's history. Braxton relies heavily on symbolism, black musical idioms, and sensuous imagery in these works. The collection also projects a motif of loss reflective of family tragedies that Braxton experienced.

Son

Character in *Tar Baby*

Song of the City

Peter Abrahams
Novel, 1945

In his first **novel**, *Song of the City,* **Peter Abrahams** focuses on the political conflicts within South Africa's black and white communities. *Song of the City* opens at the onset of World War II as South Africa's white leaders grapple with the question of whether to join the Allies or remain neutral. In the work, Abrahams provides the full sweep of South African political views from **segregation** and **apartheid** to socialism and pro-Nazism. Dick, the novel's main character, is a domestic servant for a white, liberal professor. Dick longs to rise above his fears in the oppressive society and, after getting in trouble with the laws designed to control blacks in his home village, he moves away to face life in the city.

Song of a Goat

Please see *Three Plays*

Song of Solomon

Toni Morrison
Novel, 1977

Song of Solomon, **Toni Morrison**'s third **novel**, is a story of self-discovery and the search for African American identity. The protagonist, Milkman Dead, travels from his home in Michigan to discover the truth about his family's past. At the same time, he makes a spiritual journey: he must choose between the heartless materialism of his father, Macon Dead, and his Aunt Pilate's sense of history and the importance of family.

In the first part of the novel, Milkman reveals himself to be a young man with no concern for other people. He carries on an affair with his cousin Hagar, Pilate's daughter, exploiting her feelings for him for his own purposes.

Milkman and his friend Guitar try to trace a sack, supposedly filled with gold, that caused a quarrel between Pilate and Macon after the murder of their father and led to their separation. Milkman wants the money for himself but Guitar wants to use it to fund a militant black society, the Seven Days, that carries out racially motivated revenge killings. Pilate has a sack hanging in her living room, but when Guitar and Milkman steal it they discover it contains only rocks and bones.

In the second part of the novel, Milkman continues to look for the sack of gold, retracing his Aunt's flight from her father's murderer. He eventually travels to his ancestral hometown of Shalimar, Virginia—which is named for his great-grandfather Shalimar, or Solomon, who escaped from **slavery** and flew back to Africa on the wind, according to local legend. The journey changes Milkman, awakening in him an understanding of his own past and his values. Milkman brings Pilate to Virginia to help her bury the bones in the sack—the remains of her father— but she is shot by Guitar, who believes that Milkman has betrayed him and kept the gold for himsel The novel ends with Milkman himself taking flight, jumping across a ravine to confront Guitar.

The Soul Brothers and Sister Lou

Kristin Hunter
Young adult novel, 1968

Kristin Hunter's *The Soul Brothers and Sister Lou,* which was awarded the Council on Interracial Books for Children Prize in 1968, is perhaps her best-known and most popular book. It tells the story of fourteen-year-old Louetta Hawkins and her friends—Ulysses McCracken, Frank Brown, David Weldon, and Jethro Jackson— who form a singing group in an attempt to escape from the bleak future awaiting them in the ghetto. However, Jethro is killed by the police in a confrontation at a dance. With the help of former **blues** singer "Blind" Eddie and their high school music teacher, the remaining members of the group compose and record a eulogy for their friend that becomes a popular hit.

Soul Clap Hands and Sing
Paule Marshall
Novella collection, 1961

Soul Clap Hands and Sing is a collection of four novellas, including "Barbados," "Brooklyn," "British Guiana," and "Brazil." As these titles suggest, **Paule Marshall** is concerned with establishing geographical, cultural, and historical contexts for her stories. Each novella centers on blacks in the Americas who share a common heritage in Africa as well as a history of enslavement and colonization. In addition, all focus on men whose relationships with women reveal much about their values and societies. In "Barbados," for example, Watford has devoted himself to making money so that he can live like his British colonial oppressors. However, upon finding a young girl dancing in his coconut grove, Watford sees for the first time the wasteful extravagance of his life.

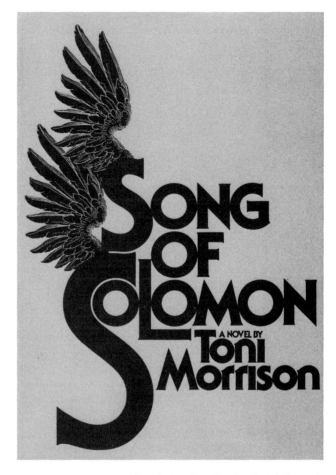

Dust jacket for Morrison's third novel.

Soul on Fire
Eldridge Cleaver
Essays, 1978

Like the earlier *Soul on Ice* (1968), **Eldridge Cleaver**'s *Soul on Fire* traces the development of the author's beliefs. *Soul on Fire* begins in the late 1960s, when Cleaver left the United States after becoming involved in a gunfight with the police. Cleaver was welcomed in socialist countries such as Cuba, Algeria, and Vietnam, and fathered two children. The **essays** recount Cleaver's progressive disillusionment with life abroad. He soon came to think that socialism, as practiced in the countries where he lived, did not function properly. The main focus of the collection is his profound conversion to **Christianity**, which prompted him to return to the United States in 1975 and surrender to the authorities.

Soul on Ice
Eldridge Cleaver
Essays, 1968

Soul on Ice is both an indictment of European American attitudes toward African Americans and **Eldridge Cleaver**'s attempt to understand his own life. In the volume, Cleaver shows how he developed politically into an

African American nationalist. He was inspired by revolutionary writers such as Thomas Paine, Karl Marx, and V. I. Lenin; by black writers such as **Richard Wright** and **James Baldwin**; and by the psychologists Carl Jung and Sigmund Freud, whose works he read in prison. However, the revolutionary and religious leader **Malcolm X** influenced him the most. *Soul on Ice* draws on Malcolm X's ideas about **racism** to refocus the aims of the **civil rights movement** toward radical politics after the assassination of **Martin Luther King Jr.** The book also provided the means for Cleaver's own release from prison, where he was serving a term for drug dealing and rape. After its publication, a group of writers petitioned the government to have him paroled.

In *Soul on Ice,* Cleaver tries to understand the racial polarizations that characterize American society. "On Watts," for instance, interprets the 1965 Los Angeles riots as resulting from the African American community's need to express itself. Using his own story as a model, Cleaver criticizes white America for its racism toward African Americans and other persecuted people. "Initial Reactions on the Assassination of Malcolm X" documents the author's own turn away from racism. Cleaver also looks at the problem of violence within the African American community. "Soul Food" is an indictment of middle-class African Americans, who, Cleaver believes, owe their poor brothers a chance to better themselves. "The Allegory of the Black Eunuchs" and "To All Black Women, from All Black Men" both consider conflicts between the sexes within the community, calling for a unity that transcends gender.

Soul Music

The dominant form of black popular music in the 1960s was the powerful gospel-influenced **rhythm and blues** style known as soul music. Since it paralleled the 1960s civil rights and **black power** movements, soul embodied a sense of racial pride and independence. Songs such as Curtis Mayfield's "People Get Ready," "We're a Winner," and "Choice of Color" bore messages of racial advancement and social change that echoed the themes of contemporary writers such as **James Baldwin** and **Stokely Carmichael**.

Although racial pride played an important role in the rise of soul, one of its main attributes was its relationship to the music of the black church—for there existed, during the 1960s, a distinct pattern among the careers of soul artists. For instance, many African American singers began their careers in gospel, moved to rhythm and blues, and then moved again to soul. Soul singers such as Aretha Franklin cultivated a passionate vocal style filled with gospel-influenced shouts and screams. With the addition of the electric bass, which replaced the acoustic bass featured in most rhythm and blues music of the 1940s and 1950s, artists were provided with a modern, pulsing rhythm that inspired them to reshape the sound of black music. Another singer who achieved great popularity at this time was James Brown. His classic soul numbers include "Out of Sight," "Papa's Got a Brand New Bag," "Cold Sweat," and "I'm Black and I'm Proud." The "James Brown sound" ultimately had a strong impact on the development of fusion **jazz**.

In 1959, Berry Gordy, a Detroit entrepreneur and songwriter, established the Motown Record Corporation, which emerged as one of the largest and most successful African American business enterprises in the United States. Motown soon began producing soul music that was marketed not only to the black community, but to the white middle class as well. The "Motown sound" was considered slicker than the music created by other soul artists, and many Motown acts topped the charts during the 1960s. However, by the end of the decade, the company had fallen into a state of economic decline. In 1969, the Jackson Five became the last major act to join the label before its demise. Biographer and children's author **James S. Haskins** has written biographies of such Motown alumni as Michael Jackson and Diana Ross.

The Souls of Black Folk: Essays and Sketches

W. E. B. Du Bois

Essays, 1903

The Souls of Black Folk: Essays and Sketches is generally considered **W. E. B. Du Bois**'s statement against the then-popular ideology of **Booker T. Washington**. Because it established an influential method of understanding the effects of **slavery** on modern blacks, *The Souls of Black Folk* marks a significant development in black thought.

At the time *The Souls of Black Folk* was published, Washington enjoyed widespread popularity. His **autobiography** *Up from Slavery* (1901) proposed several accommodating courses of action for black Americans: endorsing **segregation,** accepting the denial of voting rights, and undergoing vocational and industrial training instead of pursuing a liberal arts education. Although he condemned slavery, Washington insisted that the institution hurt and benefitted both whites and blacks. He felt that blacks should not be bitter about slavery but should work to succeed in a free America.

In *The Souls of Black Folk,* Du Bois agreed that black Americans should develop themselves, but insisted that Washington's understanding of slavery was anti-historical. Washington had argued that the legacy of slavery was inconsequential to hard-working blacks. For Du Bois, however, slavery was an "emasculating" institution whose influence persisted even after emancipation and **reconstruction.** **Racism** continued detrimental practices and formed the basis of a continuing slavery.

The Souls of Black Folk is not entirely a political treatise, however. Although it discusses Washington's views, the book also contains other types of writing, including a prose elegy on Du Bois's dead son, a **short story**, and a discussion of negro **spirituals**.

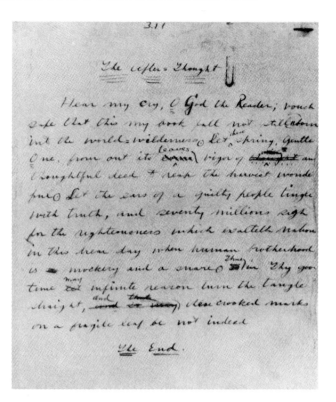

Last page of manuscript from *The Souls of Black Folk.*

South Street

William Gardner Smith

Novel, 1954

In *South Street,* by American writer William Gardner Smith, three brothers are in mourning for their lynched father. However, each of the young men has his own way of reacting to the murder. The eldest of the sons is Claude, who has made a career for himself as a writer. After time spent in Africa and on various civil rights efforts, he retreats from battling racial strife into a mixed marriage with a musician named Kristin. Michael starts the Action Society, a vigilante gang that soon exceeds his control. Philip, despite his aversion to violence, joins this group. After Philip is killed by a white victim in a revenge attack, Claude is forced to leave his wife and reconcile with Michael.

South Town
Lorenz Graham
Novel, 1958

Lorenz Graham's *South Town* is the first in a series of four young adult **novels** that chronicle David Williams and his family, as they face prejudice which at times becomes life-threatening. In *South Town,* the Williams family suffers the consequences of **racism:** David and his sister become the target of school bullies, foreshadowing the more serious troubles the family encounters with firebombings, murder, and harassment. The persecution becomes so severe that the family leaves for the North, where they hope their life will improve. David, looking to fulfill the American dream, vows to become a doctor and return to South Town some day when he is grown. The other volumes in the series are *North Town, Whose Town?,* and *Return to South Town.*

Ellease Southerland
American poet and novelist
Born June 18, 1943.

Though Southerland was first published as a poet and won the 1971 Gwendolyn Brooks Award for Poetry for "Warlock," she came to public attention with the publication of her **novel** *Let the Lion Eat Straw* (1979), which is based on her mother's life and was widely praised by reviewers for its poetic evocation of a black woman's experiences. Southerland was born in Brooklyn and educated at Queens College and Columbia University, where she earned an M.F.A. in 1974. She was a social worker for several years before she began to teach English. Since 1975, she has been poet-in-residence in African literature at Pace University in New York. Some of her **poetry** is collected in *The Magic Sun Spins* (1975).

Further Readings
Black Writers, first edition, Gale, 1989.
Dictionary of Literary Biography, Volume 33: *Afro-American Fiction Writers after 1955,* Gale, 1984.

Thomas Sowell
American economic writer
Born June 30, 1930.

Known for his controversial economic and social views, Sowell supports a laissez-faire economic system and opposes most of the social programs and judicial actions generally favored by black spokespersons. His conclusions on what makes some minority ethnic groups more successful than others are based on extensive research throughout the world and are presented in such books as *Race and Economics* (1975), *Markets and Minorities* (1981), *The Economics and Politics of Race: An International Perspective* (1983), and *Race and Culture: A World View* (1992). Born in Gastonia, North Carolina, Sowell holds a Ph.D. from the University of Chicago. He has taught at several universities and has been a senior fellow of the Hoover Institution at Stanford University since 1980 and a columnist for *Forbes* since 1991.

Further Readings
Black Writers, second edition, Gale, 1994.

Wole Soyinka
Nigerian dramatist, poet, and novelist
Born July 13, 1934.

Soyinka is the first black African to be awarded the Nobel Prize in literature. He is best known in Africa as a spokesperson for individual liberty and human rights, and his understanding of Western intellectual tradition as well as his own Yoruba heritage has won him respect in literary circles throughout the world. His highly stylized works examine themes of individual responsibility, continuity and change, and the corrupting influence of power.

Soyinka was born in Abeokuta, Nigeria. Although his parents represented colonial influences, Soyinka received instruction in Yoruba tribal **folklore** from his grandfather. He completed secondary school in Ibadan and worked briefly as a clerk in Lagos before returning to Ibadan to attend University College. He left

Africa to complete his degree at the University of Leeds in England. In the late 1950s Soyinka worked as a reporter, interviewer, and presenter for the British Broadcasting Corporation (BBC) and also wrote his first **play,** *The Swamp Dwellers* (1958). Throughout his career he has held a succession of academic positions.

Soyinka returned to Nigeria in 1960, shortly after its independence from colonial rule was declared. He began in-depth research into Yoruba folklore and drama and incorporated elements of both into his play *A Dance of the Forests* (1963), a cautionary tale about the perils of attributing all of Nigeria's problems to colonials. *The Lion and the Jewel* (1963), on the other hand, lampoons the indiscriminate embrace of Western modernization.

Soyinka was well established as Nigeria's premier playwright when he published his first **novel,** *The Interpreters* (1965). A sweeping view of Nigerian life in the years immediately following independence, the book met with mixed reviews. That same year Soyinka was arrested on political charges but released after three months for lack of evidence. Two years later he was arrested again during the Biafran crisis and held for twenty-seven months without formal charges. Released in 1969, he left Nigeria soon afterwards. *The Man Died: Prison Notes of Wole Soyinka* (1972), adapted from a **diary** Soyinka kept while in solitary confinement, was universally hailed as a definitive commentary on the Nigerian civil war. The play *Death and the King's Horseman* was written while Soyinka held a fellowship at Churchill College, Cambridge, in 1973 and 1974. He returned to Nigeria only after a change in power in 1975.

After Soyinka's prison term, his work darkened in tone and focused on the consequences of the Biafran war. *Season of Anomy* (1973), his second novel, expresses little hope for Africa's future, while his play *Death and the King's Horseman* (1975) depicts a ceremonial African horseman's attempt to commit suicide after his king dies. Postwar plays such as *Madmen and Specialists* (1970) and *A Play of Giants* (1984) revolve around dark themes as well. In a somewhat lighter mood, *Aké: The Years of*

Soyinka, a prominent Nigerian playwright, won the Nobel Prize for literature in 1986.

Childhood (1981) recounts Soyinka's childhood and brought him acclaim in the United Kingdom and the United States. A sequel, *Isara: A Voyage around Essay,* followed in 1989.

In October, 1986, Soyinka was awarded the Nobel Prize for Literature. Later that year he was named commander of the Federal Republic of Nigeria by General Ibrahim Babangida. In recent years, Soyinka has worked to better Nigerian society in practical ways; for instance, he has campaigned to reduce accidents on Nigerian roads. His writing in such dramatic works as *Before the Deluge* (1991), *A Scourge of Hyacinths* (1991), and *From Zia, with Love* (1992) continues his examination of social issues. In 1994 Soyinka published a revised version of *Art, Dialogue, and Outrage: Essays on Literature and Culture* (first published in Nigeria in 1988). In the pieces collected in the volume he responds to the critical dispute surrounding his work and offers insight into his career as a dramatist.

Further Readings

Black Literature Criticism, Gale, 1992.

Black Writers, second edition, Gale, 1994.

Dictionary of Literary Biography, Volume 125: *Twentieth-Century Caribbean and Black African Writers,* Second Series, Gale, 1993.

Wright, Derek, *Wole Soyinka Revisited,* Twayne, 1993.

Speeches

Please see Oratory/Speeches

Spell #7

Please see *Three Pieces*

Anne Spencer

American poet
Born February 6, 1882.
Died July 27, 1975.

Perhaps because few of her poems were published in her lifetime, Spencer is not widely recognized. Born Annie Bethel Scales Bannister in rural Virginia, Spencer was educated at Virginia Seminary and College. Though she taught briefly and headed an all-black library, her husband provided her with a studio and time to write. **James Weldon Johnson** was instrumental in the publication of her poem "Before the Feast of Shushan" and included it, with four other Spencer poems, in *The Book of American Negro Poetry* (1922). Since then, Spencer's **poetry,** including her protest poem "White Things," has been widely anthologized.

Further Readings

Black Writers, second edition, Gale, 1994.

Dictionary of Literary Biography, Gale, Volume 51: *Afro-American Writers from the Harlem Renaissance to 1940,* 1987; Volume 54: *American Poets, 1880-1945,* Third Series, 1987.

Greene, J. Lee, *Time's Unfading Garden: Anne Spencer's Life and Poetry,* Louisiana State University Press, 1977.

Spirituals

The spiritual is a genre of religious folk song usually based on characters and incidents from the Bible. African American spirituals date back to slave days in the southern states. These emotional songs with strong rhythms are related to white spirituals, which were sung at revival meetings. However, black spirituals also were heavily affected by African traditions. For instance, the spirituals often make use of a call-and-response pattern (i.e., an alternation of solo and chorus) that is typical of African music. The melodies of some spirituals show a direct African influence as well, as does the tendency to accompany the songs with stamping, clapping, and finger-snapping. In turn, spirituals, like other black musical forms, later affected the rhythm and language of African American literature. One of the first critics to identify spirituals as an integral part of the black aesthetic was **Sterling A. Brown**.

Black spirituals, which were frequently used as work songs, served as a means of emotional release for slaves. Some spirituals also contained coded messages in their lyrics and conveyed crucial information to slaves preparing to escape. Well-known examples of spirituals include "Deep River," "Go Down, Moses," "Nobody Knows the Trouble I Seen," "Swing Low, Sweet Chariot," and "Roll, Jordan, Roll." One comprehensive collection of such songs, *The Book of American Negro Spirituals* (1925), was edited by noted poet and anthologist **James Weldon Johnson**. Other volumes of slave spirituals include *Walk Together Children* (1974) and *I'm Going to Sing* (1982), both compiled by folklorist and children's author **Ashley F. Bryan**.

Standing Fast

Roy Wilkins, with Tom Mathews
Autobiography, 1982

Standing Fast: The Autobiography of Roy Wilkins chronicles the history of the **National Association for the Advancement of Colored People** (NAACP) from the late 1920s, when

Roy Wilkins became secretary of the Kansas City chapter. The book recounts Wilkins's tenure as executive secretary with the organization from 1949 to 1977 and his role in striving for equal rights. Wilkins tells of the NAACP's efforts to effect civil rights change through legislation, particularly to outlaw lynchings. In the book, Wilkins also discusses many historical aspects of the fight for the civil liberties of black Americans and the influence of President Lyndon Johnson on the passage of important civil rights laws.

Stars in My Pocket Like Grains of Sand

Samuel R. Delany
Novel, 1984

Samuel R. Delany's *Stars in My Pocket Like Grains of Sand* is an erotic **science fiction** tale that traces the lives of Rat Korga and Marq Dyeth. Korga is a lobotomized slave on Rhyonon, a planet destroyed by a fireball. The only survivor, Korga is rescued by an intergalactic order, the Web. Korga is relocated to Velm, where creatures known as evelm co-exist with humans. Since part of Velm has recently legalized intimate relations between the two races, Korga is paired with Dyeth, an industrial diplomat. They hunt and sing together, but Korga, as the sole survivor of Rhyonon, begins to attract attention. Not only do evelm gather, spaceships which may have been responsible for the destruction of Rhyonon appear. To protect Velm, the Web spirits Korga away.

Stephen Jorgenson

Character in *Infants of the Spring*

Robert B. Stepto

American editor and writer
Born October 28, 1945.

Born in Chicago, Illinois, on October 28, 1945, Robert Burns Stepto received his doctorate from Stanford University. A professor of English and Afro-American studies, Stepto has focused on African American literature in his writings. In *From Behind the Veil: A Study of Afro-American Narrative* (1979), Stepto treats the general adherence to traditional narrative forms in the 1970s, including those first exhibited in **slave narratives**. He edited and contributed to *Afro-American Literature: The Reconstruction of Instruction* (1978) and *Chant of Saints: A Gathering of Afro-American Literature, Art, and Scholarship* (1979). He also co-edited *Afro-American Literature: The Reconstruction of a Literary History* (1981) and *The Collected Papers of Sterling Brown*, Volume I (1981); and edited *Selected Poems by Jay Wright* (1987).

Further Readings

Black Writers, first edition, Gale, 1989.

John Steptoe

American author of children's literature
Born September 14, 1950.
Died August 28, 1989.

John Lewis Steptoe was inspired to embark on his career after realizing the lack of literature to which black children could relate. The illustrator of his own titles, he often addressed issues facing minority children in urban communities. He has won several awards and his work has been widely praised for its optimism and candor.

Steptoe was born on September 14, 1950, in Brooklyn, New York, to John and Elesteen Hill Steptoe. Interested in art from an early age, he attended the New York High School of Art and Design in the mid-1960s. In 1968, he participated in an art program at Vermont Academy and while there wrote and illustrated his first book. Published when he was nineteen, *Stevie* (1969) focuses on a child's experience adapting to his younger brother. The book uses a ghetto setting with black characters and dialogue, but critics considered its appeal universal. It was reprinted in *Life* shortly after its release and brought Steptoe national recognition.

Steptoe in 1969, around the time that his first novel, *Stevie*, was published.

Throughout his career, Steptoe continued to explore the common concerns of children and young adults. *Uptown* (1970) features two boys pondering their lives as adults. *Train Ride* (1971) involves a subway ride two boys take without parental permission and the punishment they subsequently receive. *Daddy Is a Monster... Sometimes* (1980) explores the inherent tensions between children and their parents. *Marcia* (1976), Steptoe's his first young adult **novel,** emphasizes the responsibilities involved in becoming sexually active.

Toward the end of his career, Steptoe became interested in reworking traditional tales. ***The Story of Jumping Mouse: A Native American Legend*** (1984) is based on a folktale about a mouse's transformation into an eagle. ***Mufaro's Beautiful Daughters: An African Tale*** (1987) centers on two very different daughters and makes use of African tribal traditions.

The book won a Coretta Scott King Award and was named a Caldecott Honor Book.

Steptoe died of complications from AIDS in New York City on August 28, 1989.

Further Readings
Black Writers, first edition, Gale, 1989.
Something about the Author, Volume 63, Gale, 1991.

Steve Benson
Character in *In New England Winter* and *The Fabulous Miss Marie*

Steve Carlton
Character in *What the Wine Sellers Buy*

Stevie
John Steptoe
Children's fiction, 1969

John Steptoe created the picture book *Stevie* when he was a teenager. The story involves jealousy and competition between two youngsters. Robert, the narrator, grouses about a younger boy who lives with Robert's family during the week because his mother must work. Using Black English, Robert relates how Little Stevie messes up his room and breaks his toys. Robert also resents that his friends can go off to play without him while he is forced to babysit. When the child's parents move away, however, Robert misses the child. *Stevie* was awarded the Lewis Carroll Shelf Award in 1978. It also received the Society of Illustrators Gold Medal and a citation as an American Library Association Notable Children's Book.

William Still
American abolitionist and writer
Born October 7, 1821.
Died July 14, 1902.

Noted for his involvement in the abolitionist movement and his efforts to aid escaping slaves as part of the **underground railroad** in Philadelphia, Still rose from his roots as the son of a former slave to become an outspoken abolitionist and respected businessperson. His book *The Underground Railroad* (1852) provided an important black perspective balancing the post-Civil War accounts of white abolitionists. *The Underground Railroad* went beyond chronicling the heroic role of white abolitionists to show the bravery of those individuals who risked their lives to attain personal freedom.

Still was born in 1821 near Medford, New Jersey. Though he received little formal schooling, he studied on his own and eventually moved to Philadelphia, where he secured a position with the Pennsylvania Society for the Abolition of Slavery. He continued to work and write on issues supporting the rights of African Americans and founded several organizations to aid black youths.

Further Readings

Khan, Lurey, *One Day, Levin... He Be Free, William Still and the Underground Railroad,* Dutton, 1972.

The Story of Jumping Mouse

John Steptoe
Juvenile, 1984

In *The Story of Jumping Mouse: A Native American Legend*, **John Steptoe** retells a northern Plains Indian story about how the eagle was created. According to the **myth**, Magic Frog transforms a little mouse into a Jumping Mouse to help him complete his travels to a distant land. During his journey, the unselfish Jumping Mouse offers his eyesight to a blind bison and relinquishes his sense of smell to a dying wolf. Nearly helpless, Jumping Mouse realizes his predicament and despairs. However, Magic Frog appears unexpectedly and reminds Jumping Mouse that he still has the power to jump. As Jumping Mouse leaps into the air and begins to soar, Magic Frog tells him his new name will be Eagle; so, Jumping Mouse's charity and kindness are finally rewarded.

Stokely Speaks

Stokely Carmichael
Essays, 1971

A collection of **speeches** made by the militant African American leader between 1966 and 1970, *Stokely Speaks: Black Power Back to Pan-Africanism* documents the development of **Stokely Carmichael**'s ideas during that period. The earlier speeches discuss the building of a basis of "**Black Power**" in the United States through various types of local political and economic activity. The later speeches reveal a more global view, as Carmichael argues that African Americans are a colonized people, calls for international solidarity and unified action among all colonized peoples, advocates an agrarian-based **back-to-Africa movement**, and envisages a strong and united Africa as the key to equality for people of African descent throughout the world.

The Street

Ann Petry
Novel, 1946

Ann Petry's *The Street* revolves around a black woman brutalized by poverty and racial **discrimination**. Raised on Long Island, Lutie Johnson accepts a position as a wealthy Connecticut family's maid, and leaves her son, Bub, in the care of her husband. In Connecticut, she is confronted with her employers' alcoholism and adultery. Lutie then discovers that her husband is supporting another woman on the money Lutie earns; she ends her marriage, quits her job, retrieves her son, and moves to Harlem. Life in Harlem is a ceaseless struggle to protect herself and her son from the predators that surround them. By the novel's end, Lutie has killed a man who was trying to rape her, and Bub has become involved in crime. Lutie ultimately leaves for Chicago, expressing a vague hope of salvaging her life.

A Street in Bronzeville

Gwendolyn Brooks
Poetry, 1945

Gwendolyn Brooks's *A Street in Bronzeville* is organized in two parts, the first containing mostly short poems and a few longer ones describing the hopes and disappointments of residents of Bronzeville (a Chicago neighborhood). Love between black men and women is deromanticized in "The Old-Marrieds," for instance. In the poem, an old couple has grown so familiar with the routine of their lives that their environment has become stifling. Brooks also focuses on **discrimination** among blacks in such poems as "The Ballad of Chocolate Mabbie" and "The Ballad of Pearl May Lee." In the former title, Willie Boone chooses a lighter-skinned girl than Mabbie; in the latter title, Pearl May Lee exacts revenge when a similar situation threatens her. The black women in these poems suffer from poverty and discrimination as the dominant condition of their lives, seen vividly in "Obituary for a Living Lady" and "Sadie and Maude."

Two of the longer narrative poems tell the stories of black men. In "Negro Hero," for example, a black soldier risks his life for white soldiers while making them more aware of their own values. "The Sundays of Satin-Legs Smith" portrays a man who attempts to control a threatening environment with sharp clothes, a hip demeanor, and sexual prowess. In this collection of poems, optimism and pride are tempered by Brooks's realistic portrayal of the squandering of human potential.

The second part, "Gay Chaps at the Bar," contains twelve sonnets that reflect the experiences of black soldiers in World War II in the natural rhythms of everyday speech. The poems reveal the soldiers' thoughts about their lives and relationships as well as the events of the war. In spite of the widespread **racism** portrayed, the reader sees the black men achieve dignity and equality in the heat of battle and in death.

Structuralism

Structuralism is a twentieth-century movement in **literary criticism** that analyzes how literary texts arrive at their meanings, rather than examining the meanings themselves. There are two major types of structural analysis: One looks at the way patterns of linguistic structures unify a specific text and emphasize certain elements of that text, and the other interprets the way literary forms and conventions affect the meaning of language itself. Critics such as **Sunday O. Anozie** argue that a poem, for instance, contains a system of superimposed levels that include the phonological, phonetic, syntactic, prosodic, and semantic. He contends that structuralism provides a means of accounting for such levels and dealing with the internal coherence of the poem. Using this method, Anozie has analyzed the work of writers such as Senegalese poet **Léopold Sédar Senghor.**

The Struggle Is My Life

Nelson Mandela
Speeches, memoirs, prison statements, 1978

Originally published in 1978, *The Struggle Is My Life* was reissued in 1986 and again in 1990 as *Nelson Mandela: The Struggle Is My Life*. The revised 1986 edition contains material from 1944 to 1985, including four statements from **Nelson Mandela** written during his incarceration on Robben Island, and memoirs by two of Mandela's fellow prisoners who had been released. The 1990 edition includes four addresses Mandela gave following his release from prison, a series of photographs of Mandela taken at various times during his life, a biographical introduction, an autobiographical note, and materials Mandela prepared prior to his meetings with former South African president F. W. de Klerk.

Stuff

Character in *Fast Sam, Cool Clyde, and Stuff*

Sugar

Character in *Manchild in the Promised Land*

Sula

Toni Morrison
Novel, 1973

Sula, **Toni Morrison**'s second **novel**, looks at destruction and devastation on several levels: individual, between friends, and within a community. The story purports to tell why the black section of the small town of Medallion, Ohio—known as The Bottom—has been deserted. The agent of the town's destruction is the title character, Sula Peace. Sula comes from an eccentric family; her grandmother, Eva Peace, leaves her children in a neighbor's care for a year and a half after her husband deserts them. She returns missing one of her feet, which she claims to have lost in a railroad accident. Hannah, Sula's mother, burns to death in a yard fire while Sula sits quietly by and does nothing. Nel Wright, Sula's best friend, is with Sula, teasing a young boy named Chicken Little, when he slips from Sula's hands and drowns in the river. Neither of the girls reveals the child's fate; however, as they grow up, their friendship thins.

Sula leaves The Bottom to attend college while Nel marries Jude Greene and becomes a respectable member of the community. When Sula returns home, she brings chaos with her, placing her grandmother in a nursing home and seducing Nel's husband. Although Sula continues to live in The Bottom, she becomes a social outcast, scorned for her refusal to recognize community standards. Sula and Nel have a last encounter at Sula's deathbed, but they quarrel about their respective morals and Nel leaves Sula to die alone. The Bottom community is effectively destroyed shortly after her death when a sudden flood kills most of the residents. At the novel's end, twenty-five years after

Dust jacket for Morrison's second novel.

Sula's death, Nel visits Eva in the nursing home and is shocked when the old woman confuses her with Sula. Nel then visits Sula's grave and realizes how essential her relationship with her dead friend was to her.

Sula Peace

Character in *Sula*

Supernatural

Please see Fantasy/Supernatural

Surrealism

The term surrealism refers to a French literary and artistic movement founded in the 1920s. The surrealists sought to express unconscious thoughts and feelings in their works. The best-known technique for achieving this was automatic writing, the transcription of spontaneous outpourings from the unconscious. With her collection *Firespitter* (1982), **Jayne Cortez** established herself among black surrealist poets. **Adrienne Kennedy** is one of the few black playwrights to make use of surrealistic techniques. Her drama *Cities in Bezique* (1969) employs composite characters and dreamlike images. **Clarence Major** is known for the surreal images found in his **novels *Reflex and Bone Structure*** (1975) and ***Emergency Exit*** (1979). Among other black writers who have incorporated surrealism into their work are the American novelists **Charles Stevenson** and **Ralph Ellison**, Nigerian poet and novelist **Gabriel Okara**, and West Indian poet **Aimé Césaire.**

Survivor

Please see "Patternist Saga"

Efua Sutherland

Ghanaian playwright, poet, and author of children's literature
Born June 27, 1924.

Isolated from the traditional folk culture of her country's rural areas, Sutherland has dedicated her life to conveying Ghanaian traditions and preserving national art forms through her writing. Sutherland incorporates traditional Ghanaian story-telling techniques into her poems, while her **plays** emphasize rhyme, rhythm, music, dance, and audience response. Sutherland writes for children in both English and Akan, a native Ghanaian language, to help promote a bilingual Ghana. Fearing the adoption of English as the official national language, Sutherland urges bilingual education for all children in both elementary and secondary schools.

Further Readings

Black Writers, first edition, Gale, 1989.

Dictionary of Literary Biography, Volume 117: *Twentieth-Century Caribbean and Black African Writers,* First Series, Gale, 1992.

Suwelo

Character in *The Temple of My Familiar*

Sydney Childs

Character in *Tar Baby*

Their voices rise .. the pine

trees are guitars, /

Strumming, pine-needles

fall like sheets of rain .. /

Their voices rise .. the

chorus of the cane /

Is caroling a vesper to the

stars..

"Georgia Dusk," *Cane,*
Jean Toomer, 1923

Taban lo Liyong

Character in *Meditations in Limbo*

The Taking of Miss Janie

Ed Bullins
Play, first produced 1975, published 1981

Perhaps the most controversial of **Ed Bullins**'s plays, *The Taking of Miss Janie* is about the rape of a white woman by a black man. Though the **play** was angrily criticized by both blacks and whites, it won the New York Drama Critics Circle Award in 1975.

Like many of Bullins's plays, *The Taking of Miss Janie* is set at a party—in this case, a gathering of friends who knew each other throughout the 1960s. The characters represent the cultural and political forces that defined that decade and Bullins uses them to deliver a verdict on the period: "We all failed," one of them announces. "... We failed in the test of the times.... We blew it. Blew it completely."

Miss Janie, a white woman, and Monty, a black man, have been involved for thirteen years in an exploitive relationship. Miss Janie has never allowed them to become physically intimate and the sexual tension between them mirrors the tenseness of race relations in America. Emphasizing Miss Janie's symbolic significance is her star-spangled underwear. By the end of the party Monty's frustration reaches a breaking point, and he rapes Miss Janie.

Talking It Over with Roy Wilkins

Roy Wilkins
Anthology, 1977

Roy Wilkins, who served as the Executive Secretary of the **National Association for the Advancement of Colored People** (NAACP) for more than 25 years, comments on the struggles of African Americans in *Talking It Over with Roy Wilkins: Selected Speeches and Writings*, compiled by Helen Solomon and Aminda Wilkins. In the book's **speeches** and **essays**, Roy Wilkins addresses such topics as lynching, busing, and civil rights, and pays tribute to a number of figures—including Willie Mays, Walter P. Reuther, and Harry S. Truman—who contributed to the struggle for racial equality.

Tar Baby

Toni Morrison
Novel, 1981

Tar Baby, **Toni Morrison**'s fourth **novel**, is an allegorical fable about **colonialism**, commitment, and black identity. The fabulous elements are taken from the African American tale of the Rabbit and the Tar Baby. The story takes place in the French West Indies on the fictitious Caribbean Isle des Chevaliers at the estate of Valerian Street, l'Arbe de la Croix. The island is supposedly haunted by the ghosts of African horsemen who escaped enslavement and still roam the local hills, and the island's insects and flowers speak and have feelings.

The Tar Baby of the title is Jadine, the niece of Street's black butler and cook, Sydney and Ondine Childs. Street has sponsored both Jadine's education in France at the Sorbonne and her modelling career. The Rabbit is William Green, better known as Son, who has been running from the law for eight years after having murdered his adulterous wife. Jadine and Son engage in a love affair, but neither of them understands the other. Son believes Jadine is prostituting herself by accepting Street's money, while Jadine thinks Son has a foolishly romantic view of life. The couple distrusts each other's motives as well: Son believes Jadine is trying to force him to accept white culture, while Jadine feels Son is subverting her individuality by forcing her to confront her biological urges. Toward the novel's end, Valerian Street, representing a paternalistic white culture, collapses when he realizes that his wife, Margaret, has been abusing his children, and Sydney and Ondine take over the estate. The jungle begins to overrun l'Arbe de la Croix, erasing the traces of colonialism. Jadine jets off to Paris to become the mistress of a white man and Son escapes into the wilderness of the Isle des Chevaliers to join the ghostly knights that ride there.

Ellen Tarry

American biographer and author
of children's literature
Born in 1906.

Tarry, whose writings are heavily influenced by her involvement in the **civil rights movement**, became one of the first authors to use blacks as main characters in books for children, including *Hezekiah Horton* (1942), which relates the adventures of a small black child growing up in New York. Tarry's several biographies include *Young Jim: The Early Years of James Weldon Johnson* (1967) and *The Third Door: The Autobiography of an American Negro Woman* (1955), the story of her own experiences in Alabama, where she was born, and New York, where she later made her home.

Further Readings
Black Writers, first edition, Gale, 1989.

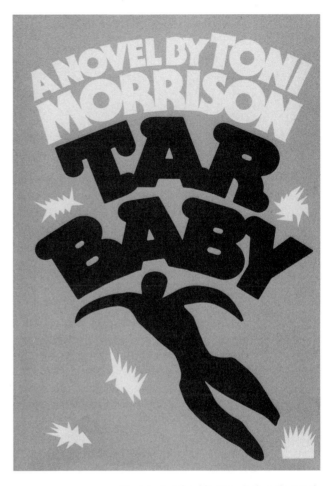

Dust jacket for Morrison's fourth novel.

Tashi Evelyn Johnson

Character in *Possessing the Secret of Joy*

Mildred D. Taylor

American author of children's literature
Born September 13, 1943.

Taylor is known for her Newbery Award-winning *Roll of Thunder, Hear My Cry* (1976), the story of a black Southern Depression family. The Logan family's tale continues in other books, including *Let the Circle Be Unbroken* (1981) and *The Friendship* (1987), both of which won the Coretta Scott King Award. Born in Jackson, Mississippi, Taylor spent most of her youth in Ohio and earned an M.A. degree at the University of Colorado. Although her books deal with the harsh realities of **racism**, they are balanced by her evocation of black family and community strength. In 1990, Taylor won her third Coretta Scott King Award for *The Road to Memphis* (1990).

Further Readings
Black Writers, second edition, Gale, 1994.

Dictionary of Literary Biography, Volume 52: *American Writers for Children since 1960: Fiction,* Gale, 1986.

Something about the Author Autobiography Series, Gale, Volume 5, 1988; Volume 70, 1993.

Tea Cake Woods

Character in *Their Eyes Were Watching God*

Teacup Full of Roses

Sharon Bell Mathis
Young adult novel, 1972

In this **novel** for young people, **Sharon Bell Mathis** depicts a black ghetto family with three sons all looking for a better life—the title's "teacup full of roses." Seventeen-year-old Joe Brooks, the protagonist, decides to give his hard-earned college money to his academically and athletically gifted younger brother, fifteen-year-old Davey. Eldest brother Paul, an artist, wastes his talent on heroin; he eventually dies of an overdose of drugs, which he purchased with the college money he stole from his brothers. When Joe goes after Paul's drug supplier, violence and gunfire erupt, and Davey is accidentally killed in the confrontation. The tragic events lead Joe to a new maturity and appreciation for his own strengths.

Bob Teague

American journalist and author of children's literature
Born October 26, 1929.

Robert Teague has distinguished himself as a sportswriter for the *Milwaukee Journal* and the *New York Times,* as a writer and newscaster for the National Broadcasting Company (NBC), and as a fiction and nonfiction writer for children and adults. Born in Milwaukee, Teague was a star halfback at the University of Wisconsin. In a book for his son Adam, *Letters to a Black Boy* (1968), Teague details growing up in a racist society. He has also written the children's book *Adam in Blunderland* (1971) and *The Flip Side of Soul: Letters to My Son* (1989).

Further Readings

Black Writers, second edition, Gale, 1994.
Something about the Author, Gale, Volume 32, 1983.

Teddy

Character in *Dopefiend, The Story of a Black Junkie*

The Temple of My Familiar

Alice Walker
Novel, 1989

Alice Walker's *The Temple of My Familiar* explores the oral history tradition of storytelling through its diverse characters: Carlotta, Arveyda, Hal, Lissie, Suwelo, and Fanny. Walker also involves characters—Celie, Shug, and Nettie—from her earlier **novel**, ***The Color Purple.*** The book's characters use stories to describe their personal difficulties being blacks and women. Through narrative, Walker also explores several other themes: Africa, women's issues, intergenerational concerns, family relationships, world history, **religion**, Native Americans, and the power of emotions. By creating deceptively simple kitchen conversations among the characters, Walker examines the history of blacks and other oppressed peoples, promoting compassion, understanding, and acceptance.

Teresa Cary

Character in *Comedy, American Style*

Terry

Character in *Dopefiend, The Story of a Black Junkie* and *Loving Her*

Lucy Terry

American poet
Born 1730.
Died 1821.

Terry is often considered the first black American poet. Kidnapped as an infant in Africa, Terry was brought by slave traders to Rhode Island, where she became a slave for Ensign Ebenezer Wells. Her only known poem, "Bars Fight," describes the Indian ambush of

Massachusetts haymakers during King George's War. Although Terry wrote the poem in 1746, it was not published until 1855 in Josiah Gilbert Holland's *History of Western Massachusetts*. Terry obtained her freedom and married Abijah Prince in 1756, and shortly afterward the Prince house became a gathering place for people to listen to Terry's storytelling. Terry is also noted for her sustained but unsuccessful attempt to persuade Williams College to admit her son.

Terry Murray

Character in *Through the Ivory Gate*

Their Eyes Were Watching God

Zora Neale Hurston
Novel, 1937

Zora Neale Hurston's *Their Eyes Were Watching God* depicts an African American woman's struggle to assert herself in rural Florida in the early twentieth century. The protagonist is Janie Crawford, granddaughter of Nanny Crawford, a maid to a white family. Janie is the product of two generations of racial and sexual violence. Nanny gave birth to Janie's mother after being raped by her owner, and Janie's mother bore Janie after being raped by her schoolteacher. The **novel** opens when Nanny, who has kept Janie secluded to prevent more sexual violence, discovers her granddaughter kissing a boy over the fence. Nanny believes that she needs to find Janie a husband quickly. She chooses a local farmer named Logan Killicks, and the two are married. However, Janie quickly becomes bored with Killicks and runs off with Joe Starks, a storekeeper in Eatonville, Florida.

Starks proves to be more complex than Killicks had been, but Janie soon realizes that he regards her as little more than window-dressing for his political ambitions. For about twenty years, Starks dominates Eatonville. He isolates

Cover of Hurston's best-known novel.

his wife, setting her above the rest of the village but also depriving her of her identity. Finally Janie asserts herself. Joe never recovers from this blow, and he dies soon after. Janie inherits the house and the store, and begins living with Tea Cake Woods. For a time the two of them travel through southern Florida, working with migrant laborers. However, Woods is bitten by a dog and contracts rabies. As he sickens, he becomes both violent and paranoid, and he threatens Janie. Finally she is forced to shoot him to save herself. The novel is narrated by Janie after she returns to her home in Eatonville and tells her story to her best friend, Pheoby.

Michael Thelwell

Jamaican novelist and essayist
Born July 25, 1939(?).

Activist and educator Michael Miles Thelwell is best known for his **novel** *The Harder They Come* (1980), and is the author of **essays** and short stories that address civil rights and provide a firsthand perspective on the black experience. He joined the faculty of the University of Massachusetts in 1969.

Thelwell was born circa 1939 in Ulster Spring, Jamaica. His *The Harder They Come* is based on the movie of the same name and details the exploits of "Rhygin," who moves down from the Jamaican hills, discovers the squalor of city life, and turns vigilante. Thelwell's *Duties, Pleasures, and Conflicts: Essays in Struggle* (1987) includes works by other writers published at the height of the **civil rights movement**. In it are works that address black political power and Southern life, a critical essay by **James Baldwin**, and an account of Jesse Jackson's presidential bid.

Further Readings
Black Writers, second edition, Gale, 1994.

Theopolis Parker

Character in *Ceremonies in Dark Old Men*

There Is a River

Vincent Harding
Nonfiction, 1981

The first book in a projected two-volume series on African American history, *There Is a River: The Black Struggle for Freedom in America* covers the period from the beginnings of the European trade in African slaves to the end of the Civil War and the assassination of President Lincoln. The author presents his study as an attempt to combine critical analysis and celebration in examining several centuries of African American resistance and protest. **Vincent Harding** views this struggle as part of a contin-

uous and still developing tradition that is not limited in its implications to the African American community but seeks a redemptive transformation of American society as a whole. Harding discusses numerous cases of group and individual rebellion against the slave system and analyzes the ideas and actions of African American leaders, including Harriet Tubman, Denmark Vesey, Nat Turner, Sojourner Truth, and **Frederick Douglass**. A central area of concern is what the author sees as the ambivalence of African American leaders towards a white American society that while upholding **slavery** also fostered the ideals of freedom, equality, and justice that are cornerstones of the African American struggle.

There Is a Tree More Ancient Than Eden

Leon Forrest
Novel, 1973

A **novel** that makes full use of literary and oral traditions, **Leon Forrest**'s *There Is a Tree More Ancient Than Eden* explores fundamental philosophical questions of identity and salvation, the burden of heritage, and spiritual journey. The book's five sections offer testimony from the protagonist, Nathaniel Turner Witherspoon, his friends Jamestown and Madge Ann Fishbond, and others who have made an impact on Nathan's life. The action takes place while Nathan is sitting in the back of a Cadillac as his mother's funeral procession travels through the South Side of Chicago. The author explores the ways in which personal pain and historical incident interact and the difficult steps the characters must take to achieve spiritual wholeness. **Ralph Ellison** wrote the foreword for the novel, which was rejected by six publishers before being printed in 1973.

Theresa

Character in *The Women of Brewster Place*

The first volume in Heinemann's African Writers Series.

These Low Grounds
Waters Edward Turpin
Novel, 1937

Waters Edward Turpin conceived of *These Low Grounds* as an **epic** covering four generations of a family from the Civil War era to the Great Depression. Martha is a slave freed after the Civil War comes to an end. Her descendants, the Princes, serve as a microcosm for the emancipation of blacks in America. Each family member must overcome sorrow and temptation; they face new social obstacles and take on whatever employment is available to blacks at the time. Members of the Prince family live in different parts of the Northeast as they struggle to unify themselves, despite pressures forcing black men away from their families.

Things Fall Apart
Chinua Achebe
Novel, 1958

Things Fall Apart, **Chinua Achebe**'s first **novel**, is a story about the impact of change on traditional Nigerian Ibo society. Achebe demonstrates how Ibo culture—a strong, independent society, presented with both its good points and its defects—is undermined by Western values. The novel takes place in the village of Umuofia in the late nineteenth century, shortly before

European missionaries reach the village. The protagonist is Okonkwo, an important man in the village and prominent among the counselors of the clan. Okonkwo is embarrassed by his prodigal father, Unoka, known in the village as a weak man. To escape his father's reputation, Okonkwo determines to become the wealthiest and most respected man in the village. However, he lives in fear of failing and becoming weak like his father.

The novel, which is divided into three parts, begins by detailing a year in the life of the village. During the course of this particular year, Okonkwo accidentally shoots a man and is banished to his mother's village of Mbanta for seven years. Part two, set in Mbanta, introduces European missionaries and colonial government. Traditional values begin to crumble under the influence of the Christian church, which gradually attracts converts from the upper levels of Ibo society, a new system of government based on European values, and a new economy based on currency rather than barter. In Part three, Okonkwo returns to Umuofia. After Christians kill a sacred python, villagers respond by burning the Christian church. Okonkwo and some other counselors are summoned by the colonial officer and are imprisoned. Okonkwo can see no way out of this situation other than through violence and kills a messenger the British have sent to the village. When he sees that no one else in the village supports him, he disgraces himself in the eyes of his fellow villagers by committing suicide.

The Third Generation

Chester Himes
Novel, 1954

Chester Himes's *The Third Generation* studies racial strife within a black family. William Taylor, descended from black field-workers is attracted to the aloof nature of a mulatto woman named Lillian Manning, whose ancestors were plantation servants. The two marry but their conflicting backgrounds result in family upheaval. Of the couple's three sons, one leaves home to pursue an education and one is accidentally blinded and lives in a special educational facility. Only Charles, the youngest, remains. The focus of his mother's misguided attentions, Charles is pressured to identify with his white heritage and deny his blackness. As a result of Lillian's intense attention, Charles becomes unnaturally attracted to his mother. When William and Lillian fight, Charles physically attacks his father to protect his mother. Eventually, Lillian's attempts to pamper and groom Charles into a white man destroy all three family members.

This Child's Gonna Live

Sara E. Wright
Novel, 1969

Sara E. Wright's *This Child's Gonna Live* chronicles, in stream-of-consciousness style, the social and economic hardships endured by Mariah Upshur, her husband Jacob, and their extended family during the Depression. Set in a poverty-ridden shore town of eastern Maryland, the **novel** explores Mariah's reactions to her husband's domination as well as to the **racism**, privation, and religious hypocrisy permeating Tangierneck. She sees family members and friends die from disease, malnutrition, and murder, and becomes convinced that only by moving completely away can she escape the futility of her life. She considers suicide when it becomes apparent that she cannot avoid her problems, but her commitment to her family responsibilities prevents her desperate action. Despite the novel's emphasis on death and victimization, it presents a hopeful conclusion, as Mariah affirms her commitment to live.

This Earth, My Brother

Kofi Awoonor
Novel, 1971

Kofi Awoonor has described his **novel** *This Earth, My Brother... An Allegorical Tale of Africa* as a prose poem. As a novel, it operates on two planes: the story itself as narrated by the protagonist Amamu and details the daily social realities which confront and influence him. Amamu's life reveals frustration, futility, and dependence upon the power of others, and serves to illuminate the disparity between Amamu and the upper echelon of citizens who comprise Ghana's lawmakers. On a secondary level, the novel treats the development of Ghana—a land of contrasts, a burgeoning country compromised by inequity and **discrimination**. **Myth** and allegory permeate Awoonor's descriptions of Ghana, and the mermaid appears as a traditional symbol throughout the story.

Philippe Thoby-Marcelin

Haitian poet and novelist
Born December 11, 1904.
Died August 13, 1975.

Thoby-Marcelin was well known in his native Haiti for works of **poetry** and for **novels** he co-wrote with his brother, Pierre Marcelin. Taking as their subject the life and customs of Haitian peasants, the Marcelin brothers' novels were critically acclaimed. Their 1944 work *Canape-Vert* was the first piece of Haitian fiction translated into English, thereby helping to introduce Western readers to Caribbean literature.

Thoby-Marcelin was born in Port-au-Prince. A major figure in the Haitian cultural renaissance of the 1920s, he served in the Ministry of Public Works for several years. Immigrating to the United States in 1949, Thoby-Marcelin embarked on a career as a French translator and continued to write with his brother.

Further Readings
Black Writers, first edition, Gale, 1989.

Thomas

Series character in "Justice" Trilogy; character in *Thomas and Beulah*

Thomas and Beulah

Rita Dove
Poems, 1986

Rita Dove won the 1987 Pulitzer Prize for *Thomas and Beulah,* a collection of narrative poems depicting a marriage. Dove loosely based the characters of Thomas and Beulah on her maternal grandparents. *Thomas and Beulah* consists of two parts: "Mandolin," which is Thomas's story and is told from his perspective, and "Canary in Bloom," which captures Beulah's point of view. Although some of the events in the two halves of the collection overlap, Thomas and Beulah both cherish their unique perceptions. For instance, Thomas experiences lifelong grief and guilt over the drowning death of his best friend, Lem, the subject of the first poem of the collection, "The Event." Beulah is shaped by the domestic realities of her life and by her fantasies of one day traveling to Paris.

In this volume Dove does not attempt to create a seamless narrative; most of her poems concentrate on events of consequence to Thomas or Beulah that might lack significance to other people. At the end, Dove offers a chronology of Thomas and Beulah's shared lives. Although the two obliquely comment on a few important historical events, including World War II and the 1963 March on Washington, the history that concerns them most is idiosyncratic and intensely personal.

Joyce Carol Thomas

American novelist and poet
Born May 25, 1938.

Thomas's works reflect the author's storytelling ability; her 1982 **novel,** *Marked by Fire,* earned praise for its regional dialect and authentic characters and settings. Required reading in many classrooms across the United States, Thomas's young adult novel received several awards.

Thomas was born in Ponca City, Oklahoma, in 1938, and completed her M.A. in 1967 at Stanford. An English professor, she joined the faculty of the University of Tennessee in 1989. *Marked by Fire* chronicles the early life of Abyssinia, a young singer who loses her beautiful voice after being raped. At first Abyssinia questions her faith in God, but support from her close-knit community helps her to gradually recover. The novel's sequel, *Bright Shadow* (1989), continues Abyssinia's story as she grows up and falls in love. Thomas has also written six volumes of **poetry,** including *Brown Honey in Broomwheat Tea* (1993), and several **plays.**

Further Readings

Black Writers, second edition, Gale, 1994.

Lorenzo Thomas

American poet
Born August 31, 1944.

Thomas is known for utilizing vivid imagery in **poetry** that reflects American popular culture and brings to life a personal perspective on his African American heritage. The surrealist movement of the late 1950s helped shape Thomas's early works and continued to influence the verse in such volumes as *Framing the Sunrise* (1975) and *The Bathers* (1981). While noted for their multi-faceted artistry, Thomas's works are grounded in the reality of the Black experience: "The Bathers" concerns demonstrations during the civil rights era in the deep South and contains a social awareness that extends through each of his works.

Further Readings

Black Writers, first edition, Gale, 1989.
Dictionary of Literary Biography, Volume 41: *Afro-American Poets since 1955,* Gale, 1985.

Thomas Small

Character in *The House of Dies Drear*

Three Pieces

Ntozake Shange
Plays, published 1981

The dramatic elements in **Ntozake Shange**'s *Three Pieces*—a collection that includes *A Photograph: Lovers in Motion, Spell #7: geechee jibara quik magic trance manual for technologically stressed third world people (A Theater Piece),* and *Boogie Woogie Landscapes*—defy traditional categorization, stressing **poetry**, music, dance and drama rather than plot. The trilogy won the *Los Angeles Times* Book Prize for Poetry in 1981.

In *A Photograph,* Shange explores the tangle of relationships among Sean David, a photographer, and four other characters: Michael, a dancer; Nevada, an attorney; and Claire, a model who works for Sean. Another attorney, Earl, is also attracted to Sean. Sean has had relationships with each of the women, but he is most attracted to Michael, who wants to bolster his career as a photographer. At the close of the **play** Michael and Sean are together.

Spell #7 begins with a minstrel-show prologue. The play takes place in a bar and features nine friends, all professional artists, who discuss **racism** in America and consider the fate of black artists, complaining that actors in particular are stereotyped and obliged to play degrading roles such as chauffeurs and prostitutes. The piece addresses the condition of blacks, and especially black women, and acknowledges the resilience and fortitude of blacks. Eschewing traditional theatrical forms, *Spell #7* is a choreopoem, using dance and poetry in place of character development.

The experimental, expressionist choreopoem *Boogie Woogie Landscapes* is the most fragmented work in the trilogy, combining dreams, memories, and monologue in one character's "stream of consciousness." Dealing with the experiences of women in America, its protagonist Layla sings and dances with her "nightlife companions," who talk about the oppression of black women. Layla describes the difficulties of her adolescence and her dual identity as both a woman and an African American.

Three Plays
J. P. Clark
Plays, 1964

J. P. Clark's *Three Plays* reprints three of his most popular plays. Written while Clark was still an undergraduate in Nigeria, *Song of a Goat* portrays Ebiere, who is cheating on her husband Zifa with his younger brother, Tonye. When Ebiere and Tonye are discovered, Tonye hangs himself in shame and Zifa drowns himself in the sea. In the **play**'s sequel, *The Masquerade,* Tufa, the illegitimate son of Tonye and Ebiere, lures the innocent Titi into his home. The girl's father follows her and kills the couple in a rage. In *The Raft,* four men—Olotu, Ogro, Kengide, and Ibobo—are adrift at sea. Clark characterizes the people very differently, making them representatives of different segments of society. *Three Plays* thus explores different aspects of human emotion—shame, love, jealousy, and faith—with its strong characterizations and symbolism.

Through the Ivory Gate
Rita Dove
Novel, 1992

At the beginning of Pulitzer Prize-winning poet **Rita Dove**'s first **novel**, *Through the Ivory Gate,* Virginia King returns to her hometown of Akron, Ohio, as an arts consultant in the local elementary school. When she was a child, Virginia's family suddenly moved from Akron to Arizona, but she never understood why their departure was so emotionally charged. During the course of the novel, Virginia becomes reacquainted with her grandmother and her Aunt Carrie. Virginia learns from her Aunt Carrie that her family's move was initiated by Virginia's mother, who found out about an incestuous affair between Carrie and Virginia's father.

As Virginia comes to understand her own past, she encourages her students to express themselves by putting on a puppet show. The puppets reflect Virginia's preoccupation with issues of identity and allow her to express sentiments that she might otherwise have been unable to voice. Virginia also embarks on an ambivalent love affair with Terry Murray, the father of one of her students. Virginia's ambivalence stems from her painful past relationships with men, the histories of which are revealed in dreams and in flashbacks. In the final scenes of the novel, Virginia decides to pursue a stage career in New York City rather than stay with Terry. The novel closes on an optimistic note as Virginia's grandmother explains that painful revelations can lead to future healing.

Howard Thurman
American religious leader and nonfiction writer
Born November 18, 1900.
Died April 10, 1981.

As a pastor, scholar, and writer, Thurman fostered the ideals of racial and social tolerance. Through his advocacy of nonviolence and integration, Thurman helped to lay a foundation for the **civil rights movement** of the 1950s and 1960s, influencing civil rights leaders such as **Martin Luther King Jr.**

Thurman was born on November 8, 1900, in Daytona Beach, Florida. Ordained a Baptist minister in 1925, he served as pastor in Oberlin,

Ohio, from 1926 to 1928. He was a professor of **religion** and an administrator of campus religious life at a number of institutions, including Boston University, where he was the first black member of the full-time faculty.

In more than twenty books, Thurman espoused the ideas of nonviolent resistance developed by Mahatma Gandhi, whom he met on a trip to India in 1935. His writings include works on black **spirituals**, the church community, **Christianity**, and spirituality, and the **autobiography** *With Head and Heart* (1980). Thurman's commitment to an inclusive Christianity led him to cofound the interracial Church for the Fellowship of All Peoples in San Francisco in 1944, where he served as pastor for ten years. In 1953, *Life* magazine named Thurman one of the twelve great preachers of the twentieth century. He received numerous other awards, including honorary degrees from over a dozen colleges and universities.

Further Readings

Black Writers, first edition, Gale, 1989.

Yates, Elizabeth, *Howard Thurman: Portrait of a Practical Dreamer,* John Day, 1964.

Wallace Thurman

American dramatist, novelist, and editor
Born August 16, 1902.
Died December 22, 1934.

Wallace Henry Thurman was a journalist and editor during the **Harlem Renaissance** and one of its severest critics. After holding editorial positions at several literary magazines, he saw his first **play** produced in 1929. *Harlem: A Melodrama of Negro Life in Harlem* opened on Broadway but was condemned by many blacks for its focus on illicit sex, wild parties, and gambling. Thurman's first **novel,** *The Blacker the Berry* (1929), attacks prejudice within the black community. His second novel, *Infants of the Spring* (1932), is about a young black author attempting a serious novel. Here, Thurman satirized the central figures of the Harlem Renaissance, suggesting that they had destroyed their

creativity by leading self-destructive lives and listening to patronizing white critics who praised everything they produced. Thurman died of tuberculosis in New York City.

Further Readings

Black Writers, first edition, Gale, 1989.

Ticey

Character in *The Autobiography of Miss Jane Pittman*

Tiger

Character in *A Brighter Sun*

Ti-Jean

Character in *Ti-Jean and His Brothers*

Ti-Jean and His Brothers

Derek Walcott
Play, first produced 1958, published 1970

In **Derek Walcott**'s allegorical **play** *Ti-Jean and His Brothers,* the devil challenges three brothers to move him to the human emotions of pity and rage. The devil offers anyone who succeeds wealth, but threatens to eat anyone who disappoints him. After his two older brothers fail, Ti-Jean , the humblest of the three, succeeds in making the devil laugh and become angry. The devil allows Ti-Jean to live, but refuses to keep his promise of wealth. Walcott's play blends elements of West Indian **folklore** with a chorus of talking animals to comment on exploitation and **racism**.

Time Flies

Bill Cosby
Nonfiction, 1987

Time Flies is **Bill Cosby**'s response to turning fifty. In wry comments, he recollects and ruminates on such middle-aged traumas as the aggravation of forgetting why one has just entered a room, the embarrassment of losing one's train of thought, and the depressing discovery of love handles around the midsection. A former three-letter college athlete, Cosby reveals that he suffers from hearing loss and hair loss, that his underclothes keep getting tighter, and that his own son can now easily beat him in a track race. Besides treating the universal woes of aging, Cosby ponders the serious social undertones of a culture obsessed with youth.

A Time to Speak, a Time to Act
Julian Bond and Hal Gulliver
Political philosophy, 1972

Written with Hal Gulliver, an Atlanta newspaperman, *A Time to Speak, a Time to Act: The Movement in Politics* collects several **speeches** and statements in which **Julian Bond** outlines his political strategy. Bond believes that blacks can advance political equality by working within the existing democratic framework and by encouraging black solidarity and coalitions with dissenting nonblack groups.

The Time-Ago Tales of Jahdu
Virginia Hamilton
Children's fiction, 1969

Set in Harlem in the late 1960s, **Virginia Hamilton**'s *The Time-Ago Tales of Jahdu* depicts Lee Edward, a youngster who is entertained by his babysitter, Mama Luka. Mama Luka relates to him stories of Jahdu, a black boy who is proud of his heritage. Lee Edward learns from Jahdu that he too can have pride in himself by understanding the history and experience of blacks in America.

Timothy Simon
Character in *Lucy*

Tito
Character in *Scorpions*

Titus Market
Character in *Lord of the Dark Places*

To Be Equal
Whitney M. Young Jr.
Nonfiction, 1964

Whitney M. Young Jr. wrote *To Be Equal* when he was president of the Urban League, and in it he tackled social dilemmas paramount to the peaceful and fruitful coexistence of blacks and whites in modern America. Primarily he considered subsidies for food programs, engineered to counter the serious malnourishment among poor blacks, as an investment rather than a handout. Educating only a minority of blacks, he argued, only widens a gap between the privileged and the masses. He took the issue so seriously that he called upon African Americans to not blind themselves to the reality of black deprivation, a resistance he labeled as a sort of chauvinism. He also asked whites to not be dishonest about the risks involved. Young also advocated an approach to integration built on everyday realities and small courtesies, which might culminate into an unemotional acceptance of people of another race, accomplished without rancor.

To Smile in Autumn: A Memoir
Gordon Parks
Autobiography, 1979

Along with *A Choice of Weapons* (1966) and *Voices in the Mirror: An Autobiography* (1990), *To Smile in Autumn* completes **Gordon Parks**'s three-installment **autobiography**. The book includes new prose pieces, passages from his poems, journals, and letters, and recollections of acquaintances to describe his life from 1944 to 1978. Parks discusses the civil rights turmoil of the 1960s, including poverty in Harlem, Southern **racism**, and the race-riots he witnessed during his years as a photographer for *Life* magazine. Parks also discusses his experiences photographing and interviewing such figures as **Eldridge Cleaver**, **Malcolm X**, and **Stokely Carmichael**, as well as writing, producing and directing the 1968 film version of his **novel** *The Learning Tree* (1963).

The Toilet

Amiri Baraka
Play, first produced and published 1964

Set in the latrine of an urban high school, **Amiri Baraka**'s *The Toilet* examines the ugliness and inhumanity of a social order that prohibits the expression of love between members of different races. At the outset of the **play**, Ray Foots, an intelligent black high school student, finds himself caught between the code of racial separation practiced by the gang that he leads and the politics of racial integration followed by Karolis, a white homosexual student with whom he is developing a friendship. After sending a love letter to Ray, Karolis is beaten by the gang and dragged to the latrine to fight Foots. Although the inwardly sensitive Foots feels pity—and perhaps love—for Karolis, he decides to fight, succumbing to pressure both from the gang, who wish to enforce their racial hatred, and from Karolis himself, who, while in love with Ray's inner beauty, wants to kill the gang leader. All of the gang members join in the beating and leave Karolis in a pool of blood and draped with wet toilet paper. After the others have left, however, a weeping Foots sneaks back, wiping the blood from Karolis's face as he cradles his head in his arms.

Melvin B. Tolson

American poet, journalist, and dramatist
Born February 6, 1898(?).
Died August 29, 1966.

Considered one of America's major black poets, Melvin Beaunorus Tolson asserted an optimistic viewpoint regarding achievements in social and racial equality. He has been praised for his skillful delineation of character and his deft use of language.

Tolson was born in Moberly, Missouri, the son of a Methodist Episcopal minister, and grew up in several small towns in Missouri and Iowa. He attended Fisk University in 1918, later transferring to Lincoln University in Pennsylvania, where he received his degree. Hired in 1924 by Wiley College in Marshall, Texas, Tolson taught English and speech and coached a debate team that was defeated only once in nearly fifteen years.

Tolson obtained a fellowship in 1931 and enrolled in a graduate program in comparative literature at Columbia University. He lived in Harlem and met many of the black artists involved in the **Harlem Renaissance**. During this period, Tolson began writing his first book of **poetry,** the posthumously published *A Gallery of Harlem Portraits* (1979), utilizing Edgar Lee Masters's idea of depicting a community through portraits of its citizens.

In 1937 Tolson started writing a weekly newspaper column on a variety of subjects for the *Washington Tribune* entitled "Caviar and Cabbage." Tolson's poem "Dark Symphony" won the American Negro Exposition National Poetry Contest in 1939. Dealing with historical accomplishments of black Americans and expressing optimism for their future, "Dark Symphony" is included in his collection *Rendezvous with America* (1944), which addresses themes of class unity and the eventual ascent of oppressed peoples.

Tolson moved to Langston University in Oklahoma in 1947 and later that year was named poet laureate of Liberia. For Liberia's centennial celebration he produced *Libretto for the Republic of Liberia* (1953), which extends the themes of racial brotherhood and warns against colonial exploitation. Tolson was elected to the first of four terms as mayor of the all-black city of Langston in 1952. Although he originally planned to write an **epic** poem of five books telling the history of black America, only *Harlem Gallery: Book I, The Curator* (1965)—which includes some reworked poems from *A Gallery of Harlem Portraits*—was completed. In 1966 he received the National Institute and American Academy of Arts and Letters Award in Literature. Following several surgeries for abdominal cancer over a two-year period, Tolson died on August 29, 1966.

See also **Poetry of Melvin B. Tolson**

Further Readings

Black Literature Criticism, Gale 1992.

Black Writers, first edition, Gale, 1989.

Dictionary of Literary Biography, Volume 76: *Afro-American Writers, 1940-1955,* Gale, 1988.

Farnsworth, Robert M., *Melvin B. Tolson, 1898-1966: Plain Talk and Poetic Prophecy,* University of Missouri Press, 1984.

Tom

Character in *Roots: The Saga of an American Family*

Tom Burwell

Character in *Cane*

Tom Loving

Character in *Rachel*

Tom Rumley

Character in *A Measure of Time*

Jean Toomer

American poet, short story writer, dramatist, and essayist
Born December 26, 1894.
Died March 30, 1967.

Toomer achieved literary prominence with *Cane* (1923), a combination of fiction and

Toomer in the mid- to late 1920s.

prose exploring African American culture and spirituality. The child of mixed-race parents, Toomer refused to be classified racially and considered himself representative of the new "American" race encompassing elements of all humanity. This universalist philosophy and his interests in mysticism are reflected in many of his writings. Though he never again achieved the literary acclaim he garnered with *Cane,* he is still considered a seminal figure in African American literature.

Nathan Eugene Toomer was born on December 26, 1894, in Washington, D.C., to a woman of mixed blood and a white Georgia planter. He was raised primarily in the home of his grandfather, Pinckney Benton Stewart Pinchback, who was considered black and had been a powerful Louisiana politician. Toomer lived in white neighborhoods until financial setbacks in 1910 forced the Pinchbacks to move to a less affluent, black area. Having racially mixed experiences and bloodlines, Toomer decided to adopt an identity in which he was neither white nor black, but simply American.

As a young man, Toomer lived a transient lifestyle of work and study, attending several different colleges and universities until deciding in 1919 to become a writer. While serving a literary apprenticeship in Greenwich Village, he met emerging writers such as Edwin Arlington Robinson and Waldo Frank. In the early 1920s, Toomer accepted a post at a rural, black school in Georgia and later toured the South. These experiences enabled him to explore his black roots and provided much of the inspiration for *Cane,* which reveals the strength of the dying black American folk culture.

Toomer continued to explore African American themes in other major works of the time. His one-act **play,** *Balo*—published in the anthology *Plays of Negro Life* (1927)—provides an affirmative view of the black family. Two other works—the **short story** "Withered Skins of Berries," about a young mulatto woman, and the unproduced play *Natalie Mann,* about a middle-class black woman— were not published until 1980, in *The Wayward and the Seeking.* As Toomer gained a reputation as a leader in black letters, he became angered, though, preferring to be regarded simply as an American writer. Ultimately, he distanced himself from his former friends and colleagues and denied his black heritage.

In 1924, disillusioned by the alienation of the modern world, Toomer studied the teachings of Armenian philosopher George Gurdjieff published in *The New Caravan* (1936).

After his first wife, Margery Latimer, died giving birth to a daughter, Toomer married Marjorie Content in 1934 and moved to a farm in Doylestown, Pennsylvania. There, after a dispiriting pilgrimage to India, he converted to Quakerism in 1940 and lived as a recluse and in declining health. Though he continued writing until the mid-1940s, he could not find a publisher—many found his works tedious and

didactic. He died of arteriosclerosis in Doylestown on March 30, 1967. Selections from his many previously unpublished works are contained in the posthumous volume *The Wayward and the Seeking.*

Further Readings

Black Literature Criticism, Gale, 1992.

Dictionary of Literary Biography, Volume 51: *Afro-American Writers from the Harlem Renaissance to 1940,* Gale, 1987.

McKay, Nellie Y., *Jean Toomer: Artist,* University of North Carolina Press, 1984.

Tosh Angelos

Character in *Singin' and Swingin' and Gettin' Merry Like Christmas*

Askia Muhammad Abu Bakr el Toure

American poet, essayist, and artist
Born October 13, 1938.

Born Rolland Snellings in Raleigh, North Carolina, Islamic poet Toure is a noted leader of the **black aesthetic movement**. His work as editor-at-large of *Kitabu Cha Jua* and co-founder of the newspaper *Afro World* in 1985 has strengthened the black liberation movement by documenting racial injustice in America.

Toure's collections *JuJu* (1970) and *Songhai!* (1972) contain visionary **poetry** and prose composed during the height of his involvement in the black aesthetic movement. *JuJu* reflects a black man's search for both national and spiritual identity. *Songhai!* emphasizes Toure's dictum that African American strength lies in a return to the cultural roots of Africa.

Further Readings

Black Writers, second edition, Gale, 1994.

Dictionary of Literary Biography, Volume 41: *Afro-American Poets since 1955,* Gale, 1985.

Toussaint

Character in *for colored girls who have considered suicide*

Toussaint L'Ouverture

C. L. R. James
Play, first produced 1936, revised
and published 1976

An examination of the revolutionary period in Haiti during the late 1800s, *Toussaint L'Ouverture* depicts the strengths and weaknesses of the black leaders of the revolution rather than focusing on the military accomplishments of the slaves involved in the revolt. Most of the major characters in the **play**, including Toussaint, Napoléon Bonaparte, and Henri Christophe, are based on actual historical figures. **C. L. R. James** emphasizes that the winning of Haitian independence did not result in freedom for the Haitian people. Revised and published as *The Black Jacobins* in *A Time... and a Season: 8 Caribbean Plays* in 1976, *Toussaint L'Ouverture* preceded James's major historical study *The Black Jacobins: Toussaint L'Ouverture and the San Domingo Revolution* (1938).

Toward the African Revolution

Franz Fanon
Essays, 1967

Franz Fanon's *Pour la revolution africaine: Ecrits politiques* (1964), translated into English in 1967 as *Toward the African Revolution: Political Essays*, contains chronologically arranged **essays** written between 1952 and 1961, when Fanon was actively involved with the Algerian revolutionary movement, the Front de Libération Nationale (FLN). Some of the book's essays and articles originally appeared in *el Moudjahid,* the publication of the FLN. As a psychologist, Fanon dissects the psychological effects of **colonialism**, explaining the reasons colonized people revolt, the dehu-

manization of the colonized as well as the colonizers, and the relationship between colonialism and **racism**.

Train Whistle Guitar

Albert L. Murray
Novel, 1974

Albert L. Murray's autobiographical **novel** *Train Whistle Guitar* is the story of Scooter, a young black boy growing up in 1920s Gasoline Point, Alabama. Scooter learns about life, death, and sex by exploring his community and observing his elders, but unlike most other protagonists in African American coming-of-age narratives, he never directly experiences the unfairness of **racism**. His tale is told in a style Murray calls "singsongsaying," which in both structure and syntax imitates certain devices of African American music. For example, episodes are linked by brief italicized sections that function much like riffs in **the blues** and **jazz**. The rhythm of the language has been said to echo the strumming of the twelve-bar, twelve-string guitar. At times, the meaning of Murray's words is subordinate to their sound.

Travis

Character in *A Raisin in the Sun*

Trickster Tale

Trickster tales are a type of **folk tale** in which animals are portrayed with the power of speech and the ability to behave like humans. The dominant characteristic of the trickster is his or her ingenuity, which enables the trickster to defeat bigger and stronger animals. A variant of the trickster tale is the escape story, in which the figure must extricate himself from a seemingly impossible situation. Closely linked to the rhetorical practice known as "**sig-**

nifying," trickster tales generally serve satirical or parodic purposes by poking fun at various types of human behavior. In African and African American trickster tales, the trickster figure is often a monkey, a hare, a spider, or a tortoise.

One of the first African American writers to present the trickster figure in literature was **Charles Waddell Chesnutt.** His story "The Goophered Grapevine," which appeared in the *Atlantic Monthly* in 1887, features a white northern couple who move to the South and meet former slave Julius McAdoo, an adept storyteller. McAdoo regales the Northerners with "conjure tales," or **supernatural** folk tales, designed to entertain them and influence decisions they are making. Chesnutt's conjure stories are often tragic, providing indirect commentary on the injustice and cruelty of the **slavery** system.

The trickster figure has been adapted to modern literature by a number of black writers. For example, **Ashley F. Bryan**'s books for children *The Adventures of Aku* (1976) and *The Dancing Granny* (1977) feature Ananse, the spider-trickster. **Louise Bennett** has written several books about the adventures of the same figure, whom she dubs Brer Anancy. **Ishmael Reed** has taken the adaptation a step further in his character PaPa LaBas, the voodoo trickster detective in his mystery parody *The Last Days of Louisiana Red* (1974).

Tropic Death
Eric Walrond
Short stories, 1926

Tropic Death, **Eric Walrond**'s most acclaimed work, consists of ten stories of inhumanity in the American tropics, especially white against black—or imperial power against impoverished native. In "Subjection," for example, a white marine shoots a black canal worker. Walrond also explores the effects of modern technology and exploitation on the Caribbean natural environment; "The Palm Porch" describes the construction of the Panama Canal

in terms of its causing "the gradual death and destruction of the frontier post." Walrond writes in an impressionistic style that quickly shifts from one image to another. He depicts cultural impressions more than characters or plot yet illustrates the disorientation and alienation his characters experience. Considered an example of **avant-garde** writing, *Tropic Death* has been praised by critics such as **W. E. B. DuBois** and **Langston Hughes**.

Quincy Troupe
American poet, editor, and essayist
Born July 23, 1943.

Poet Quincy Thomas Troupe Jr. is noted for the elements of dialect, music, and African American **blues** culture that he brings to his verse. Founder and editor of *Confrontation: A Journal of Third World Literature* and *American Rag,* Troupe has combined his work as a poet with a distinguished academic career that has included positions at Columbia University and the University of California at Berkeley.

Snake-back Solos (1978), Troupe's second volume of **poetry,** recalls images from his childhood in the poems "Today's Subway Ride," "Memory," and "Springtime Ritual." *Snake-back Solos* was followed by *Skulls along the River* (1984) and the prose works *James Baldwin: The Legacy* (1987), which he edited, and *Miles, the Autobiography* (1989), which Troupe coauthored with noted **jazz** musician Miles Davis.

Further Readings
Black Writers, second edition, Gale, 1994.
Dictionary of Literary Biography, Volume 41: *Afro-American Poets since 1955,* Gale, 1985.

Troy Maxson
Character in *Fences*

Truman Held
Character in *Meridian*

Trumbull Park

Frank London Brown
Novel, 1959

Frank London Brown's best-known **novel**, *Trumbull Park,* is a fictionalized account of his family's experiences between 1954 and 1957 as the tenth black family to take up residence in a Chicago housing project. The book elucidates the psychology of blacks who are besieged by anonymous, screaming, bomb-throwing whites and who receive only callous assistance from the police. The police use clanging, smelly paddy wagons to transport the people through the white mobs to and from bus stops, work, the market, and, in the case of expectant mothers, the hospital. While the unrelenting racial tension fosters physical and mental disintegration of some Trumbull Park residents; others emerge as leaders. Protagonist Buggy Martin, for example, is sometimes scared by everything white; his wife, Helen Martin, however, maintains a pragmatic attitude and articulates ways to resist harassment by the white majority.

Gabre-Medhin Tsegaye

Please see Tsegaye Gabre-Medhin

Tshembe Matoseh

Character in *Les Blancs*

Turk

Character in *Manchild in the Promised Land*

Darwin T. Turner

American editor, critic, and poet
Born May 7, 1931.
Died February 11, 1991.

Darwin Theodore Troy Turner was an authority on African American literature. At the age of thirteen, he was admitted to the University of Cincinnati, where he earned his bachelor's and master's degrees within five years. He began teaching English at Clark College in 1949 and earned his doctorate from the University of Chicago in 1956. In 1972, he became chair of African American studies at the University of Iowa, where he continued working until his death.

Turner edited a number of anthologies, including *Black American Literature: Essays, Poetry, Fiction, Drama* (1970), *The Wayward and the Seeking: A Collection of Writings by Jean Toomer* (1980), and *Black Drama in America* (1993). His own works of criticism include *Nathaniel Hawthorne's "The Scarlet Letter"* (1967) and *In a Minor Chord: Three Afro-American Writers and Their Search for Identity* (1971). He contributed to many other works of **literary criticism** and theory and wrote a volume of **poetry,** *Katharsis* (1964). His poetry is also represented in a many anthologies and literary journals. Turner died of a heart attack in Iowa City, Iowa, in 1991.

Further Readings
Black Writers, first edition, Gale, 1989.

Waters Edward Turpin

American novelist and playwright
Born April 9, 1910.
Died November 19, 1968.

One of the first African American writers to chronicle black experiences through several generations, Turpin set a precedent for such writers as **Alex Haley** and his *Roots* saga. *These Low Grounds* (1937) and *O Canaan!* (1939) paint a realistic portrait of black Americans from a historical perspective. *These Low Grounds* follows four generations of the Prince family, from their matriarch's freedom from **slavery** after the Civil War through her descendant's rise in affluence and social standing. Continuing to follow the Prince family, *O*

Canaan! examines the northern migration of blacks to Chicago at the turn of the twentieth century.

Further Readings
Black Writers, first edition, Gale, 1989.

Dictionary of Literary Biography, Volume 51: *Afro-American Writers from the Harlem Renaissance to 1940,* Gale, 1987.

Desmond Tutu
South African orator, sermonist, and essayist
Born October 7, 1931.

Awarded the 1984 Nobel Peace Prize for his role in the struggle against **apartheid**, Archbishop Tutu promoted nonviolent resistance to apartheid and helped place international pressure on the South African government to abandon its racial policies. His activism helped bring about the government's agreement to dismantle the system of apartheid and to hold the country's first "one-person, one-vote" elections in April, 1994.

Desmond Mpilo Tutu was born in the Transvaal town of Klerksdorp on October 7, 1931, and moved with his family to Johannesburg in 1943. Following his graduation from the University of Johannesburg, he taught secondary school. In 1955, he married Leah Nomalizo Shenxane; they would have four children. Two years later, Tutu resigned to protest the institution of state-supervised education in all-black schools. He then began the theological studies that led to his ordination as an Anglican priest in 1961. Over the next fourteen years he served in a variety of Church assignments in England and South Africa. In 1975, he settled in South Africa and dedicated himself to the struggle against apartheid.

As secretary general of the South African Council of Churches from 1978 to 1985, Tutu led that organization's campaign against apartheid. With his 1979 call for Denmark to boycott South African coal, he sparked an international drive for economic sanctions against South Africa. Despite government-imposed restrictions on his right to travel abroad and the constant threat of expulsion or imprisonment, Tutu persisted in his vocal opposition to apartheid. He also rose through the ranks of the Anglican Church, becoming archbishop of Cape Town and Anglican primate of southern Africa in 1986.

Many of Tutu's most influential **speeches** and sermons have been collected in *Crying in the Wilderness: The Struggle for Justice in South Africa* (1982), *Hope and Suffering: Sermons and Speeches* (1983), *The Words of Desmond Tutu* (1989), and *Rainbow People of God* (1994).

Further Readings
Black Literature Criticism, Gale, 1992.

Black Writers, first edition, Gale, 1989.

Tlhagale, Buti, and Itumeleng Mosala, editors, *Hammering Swords into Ploughshares: Essays in Honor of Archbishop Mpilo Desmond Tutu,* Eerdmans, 1987.

Amos Tutuola
Nigerian novelist and short story writer
Born in 1920.

Tutuola was the first Nigerian writer to achieve international recognition. His works draw on traditional **folk tales** and are influenced by his native language, Yoruba. His first published **novel**, *The Palm-Wine Drinkard and His Dead Palm-Wine Tapster in the Deads' Town* (1952), was noted for its unique syntax and its fantastical characters and plots. The novel was admired in the West, but Nigerian critics considered it ungrammatical and unoriginal. Although the language in Tutuola's subsequent work has become more conventional, it maintains its focus on the African **oral tradition**. His later books include *The Witch Herbalist of the Remote Town* (1981) and *The Village Witch Doctor and Other Stories* (1990).

Further Readings
Black Writers, second edition, Gale, 1994.

Ubangi

Character in *Look What They Done to My Song*

Udo Akpan

Character in *One Man, One Machet*

Ulysses McCracken

Character in *The Soul Brothers and Sister Lou*

Unbought and Unbossed

Shirley Chisolm
Autobiography, 1970

In her **autobiography**, *Unbought and Unbossed,* **Shirley Chisolm** remembers her childhood in Brooklyn, describes the events that led to her becoming the first black woman to hold a seat in the U.S. Congress, and discusses her political goals. Although Chisolm began her career as a pre-school teacher, she was involved in local politics before emerging on the state and national scenes. In 1964, she won a seat in the New York State Assembly by a wide margin. During her four-year term, Chisolm particularly supported bills to improve the social conditions of the urban poor. She followed this term with a successful bid for Congress in 1968. *Unbought and Unbossed* is a political manifesto for Chisolm's causes, among them abortion reform, women's rights, voter's rights, and ending the Vietnam War.

Uncle Carl

Character in *Sent for You Yesterday*

Uncle Julius

Character in *The Conjure Woman*

Uncle Robin

Character in *Flight to Canada*

Tutu addressing the United States Congress, 1988.

Underground Railroad

The Underground Railroad was an informal network of antislavery Northerners, mainly blacks, that operated in the United States before the Civil War. The organizers illegally helped fugitive slaves—most of whom were unattached young men with job skills—escape to freedom. The network's operations were described in railroad terms: Guides were called "conductors" and hiding spots were called "stations," while groups of slaves were referred to as "trains." The escape routes typically ran from Virginia and Kentucky across Ohio, or from Maryland across Pennsylvania to New York, New England, and Canada. The clandestine nature of the system has fascinated readers and writers ever since. For example, noted children's author **Virginia Hamilton** centered her award-winning mystery ***The House of Dies Drear*** (1968) on an old Underground Railroad station.

During the 1780s, a group of Quakers organized the first network to help fugitive slaves reach safety. Between 1812 and the Civil War, such organizations became more widespread and effective, aquiring legendary status after the 1830s. From 1830 to 1860, for example, it is estimated that some nine thousand fugitives passed through Philadelphia and some forty thousand through Ohio. The most celebrated black conductor was Harriet Tubman, called the Moses of the blacks, who within a decade made at least ten trips from the North into Southern states and led over two hundred slaves to freedom. Tubman has been the subject of several biographies, including *Harriet Tubman, Conductor on the Underground Railroad* (1955) by **Ann Petry**. Levi Coffin, a Cincinnati Quaker, was another famous rescuer, while other participants in the network included black writers such as **William Wells Brown** and **Frederick Douglass**.

Even greater than the number of slaves helped to safety was the impact of the publicity given the Underground Railroad's activities by antislavery writers and speakers. By graphically demonstrating the determination of blacks and many whites to end **slavery**, such activities made an important contribution to the abolitionist movement. Northerners' flagrant defiance of the Fugitive Slave Act of 1850, which required that runaway slaves be returned to their owners, infuriated many Southerners and added to the growing hostility between the two sections of the country.

Slavery invites comparisons with **Frederick Douglass**'s *My Bondage and My Freedom* and with *The Autobiography of Benjamin Franklin* and *The Education of Henry Adams*. The book has also been described as presenting an unrealistically optimistic picture of black life in post-Civil War America. Unlike Douglass, however, Washington does not focus on the institution of **slavery**, from which he escaped, but on the educational institutions that shaped his life and his work with the Tuskegee Normal and Industrial Institute, which he helped found. Washington begins his story with an explanation of his birth and upbringing, revealing that he was born into slavery in Franklin County, Virginia, but he soon moves on to his learning experiences. Throughout the work he stresses his belief that concrete educational training is of greater value than purely theoretical intellectual accomplishments. For instance, Washington characterizes his delight at being trusted to sweep out a classroom in the home of his white employer: "The sweeping of that room was my college examination, and never did any youth pass an examination for entrance into Harvard or Yale that gave him more genuine satisfaction." On the other hand, Washington considers simple drudgery, like his work in the salt furnaces and coal mines of Malden, West Virginia, of little or no value. *Up from Slavery* follows Washington through his formal education at Hampton Institute in West Virginia through his work in founding and nurturing the Tuskegee Institute. Washington concludes his autobiography in 1896, when he received an honorary degree from Harvard University.

Unoka

Character in *Things Fall Apart*

Up from Slavery

Booker T. Washington with Max Bennett Thrasher
Autobiography, 1901

Booker T. Washington's *Up from Slavery,* which he wrote with Thrasher, a white journalist, is celebrated as a classic American **autobiography**. The story of one man's success, *Up from*

Urmilla

Character in *A Brighter Sun*

Ursa Corregidora

Character in *Corregidora*

Valerian Street

Character in *Tar Baby*

Henry Van Dyke

American novelist
Born October 3, 1928.

Van Dyke's **novels,** which explore race relations across class lines, have been described as offbeat, comical, and sometimes macabre. Born in Allegan, Michigan, Van Dyke moved to Montgomery, Alabama, at the age of four. He later returned to Michigan with his family and earned an A.B and an M.A. from the University of Michigan. In 1958, Van Dyke moved to Manhattan, where he continues to live.

Van Dyke's first novel, *Ladies of the Rachmaninoff Eyes* (1965), was followed by *Blood of Strawberries* (1969). His best known novel, *Dead Piano* (1971), concerns a middle class black family whose quiet life is disrupted by black revolutionaries. Van Dyke has won numerous awards for his writing, including a Guggenheim fellowship in 1971 and an American Academy of Arts and Letters award in 1974.

Further Readings
Black Writers, first edition, Gale, 1989
Dictionary of Literary Biography, Volume 33: *Afro-American Fiction Writers after 1955,* Gale, 1984.

Melvin Van Peebles

American director, playwright, and writer
Born August 21, 1932.

Van Peebles is the director of *Sweet Sweetback's Baadasssss Song* (1971) and *Watermelon Man,* a 1970 film about a white man who becomes black. Much of Van Peebles's later work has been as a playwright: *Ain't Supposed to Die a Natural Death* (1971) was his first U.S.-produced **play.**

Van Peebles was born and raised in Chicago. After producing several film shorts, he moved to Paris and began writing **novels** in self-taught French. His novel *The True American: A Folk Fable* (1976) concerns a black prisoner who is accidentally killed and arrives in Hell, where blacks are treated well because most res-

idents are white and the preferential attention causes them grief. In 1986, he published how-to books on making money in the stock options market; in 1990, he wrote *No Identity Crisis: A Father and Son's Own Story of Working Together*, with his father, Mario Van Peebles .

Further Readings
Black Writers, second edition, Gale, 1994.

Ivan Van Sertima

Guyanese poet and historian
Born January 26, 1935.

Born in Kitty Village, Guyana, and educated at the London School of Oriental and African Studies and Rutgers University, Van Sertima examines African history and its influence on the United States and other countries. One of his best-known works, *They Came before Columbus: The African Presence in Ancient America* (1977), presents anthropological and archeological evidence to show how African people influenced pre-Columbian civilization.

Van Sertima has edited numerous texts about African history, including *Black Women in Antiquity* (1984), *African Presence in Early Europe* (1985), *African Presence in Early America* (1987), *Egypt Revisited* (1985; revised, 1989), and a book of poems, *River and the Wall* (1958). Van Sertima makes his home in New Jersey, where he is an associate professor of African studies at Rutgers.

Further Readings
Black Writers, second edition, Gale, 1994.
Contemporary Poets, St. James Press, 1970.

Iyanla Vanzant

American nonfiction writer
Born September 13, 1952.

Iyanla Rhonda Vanzant has had a widely varied career. After surviving the death of her mother and an abusive childhood and marriage, Vanzant received her B.S. from Medgar Evers College in 1983. She received her J.D. from the City University of New York Law School in 1988 and became a public defender in Philadelphia, where she currently hosts a talk-show. Vanzant has been ordained as a priestess in the ancient African Yoruba tradition. Her writings include *Crowing Glory* (1989), *Tapping the Power Within: A Path to Self-Empowerment for Black Women* (1992), and *Acts of Faith: Daily Meditations for People of Color* (1993).

Further Readings

Black Writers, second edition, Gale, 1994.

Velma Henry

Character in *The Salt Eaters*

Vernon Waters

Character in *A Soldier's Play*

The View from Coyaba

Peter Abrahams
Novel, 1985

In *The View from Coyaba,* **Peter Abrahams**'s objections to Westernism are woven into the story of a family that began with two runaway slaves. Their grandson, Jacob Brown, is the main character. The **novel** follows Jacob's life from the cooperative church settlement he created in the Jamaican Hills to missionary work in Liberia for a black, independent church. Appointed bishop, Jacob marries and eventually is sent to Uganda. After his wife's death, Jacob and his son David, who have been estranged, reconcile. Previously rejecting **Christianity** for **Pan-Africanism**, David decides to follow the teachings of Christ. As the novel closes, an aging Jacob and his son plan to return to Uganda after the tyranny of Idi Amin ends. A doctor, David decides to become a medical missionary.

Violet Trace

Character in *Jazz*

Violets, and Other Tales

Alice Moore Dunbar Nelson
Anthology, 1895

Published before the author met and married poet **Paul Laurence Dunbar**, *Violets, and Other Tales* is a miscellaneous collection of short stories, poems, and **essays** based on her experiences and observations as a young adult. The pieces are sentimental and often melancholy in character, and many of them involve musings on death, including the poem "In Memorium". Pieces such as "Amid the Roses," "Love and the Butterfly," and "At Eventide" evoke the symbolism of natural objects. A recurring image throughout **Alice Moore Dunbar Nelson**'s work are violets, often considered her trademark. In the notable title story of the collection, a young woman sends her beloved a bouquet of violets shortly before she dies. Years later, he happens upon the flowers but cannot remember why he has them, and his unsympathetic wife orders him to throw the withered flowers into the fireplace.

Virginia

Character in *Plum Bun: A Novel Without a Moral*

Virginia King

Character in *Through the Ivory Gate*

The Voice

Gabriel Okara
Novel, 1964

Gabriel Okara's only **novel** tells the story of Okolo, a young man who returns to his hometown after attending school. Okolo's spiritual concerns clash with the materialism of tribal elders, who are happily anticipating the spoils of national independence. The town is predominantly Christian, but its residents suffer from a deficiency of conscience. The most controversial aspect of this book is its experimental use of language. In an effort to retain the flavor of the Ijaw tongue while writing in English, Okara uses such devices as unusual word order and rephrased English sayings.

 ## Voices in the Mirror: An Autobiography

Gordon Parks
Autobiography, 1990

Gordon Parks reviews his long, diverse career in this book, covering the period from 1912 to 1979. Parks was successful not only in the literary field, but in such related arts as photography and film that were previously dominated by whites. Twenty-six chapters tell an episodic tale of the child born in poverty, the young man with a passing interest in petty crime, and the ambitious young photographer. Parks wrote articles to accompany his studies for *Life* magazine, among them a memorable piece on young Harlem gang leader Red Jackson, and covered the civil rights era and the **black power** movement for a predominantly white audience. He eventually directed such feature films as *Shaft* (1971) and *Superfly* (1972). He earned the National Medal of Art from President Ronald Reagan in 1988.

 ## Mary Elizabeth Vroman

American novelist and screenwriter
Born in 1923.
Died April 29, 1967.

Through her work, Mary Elizabeth Gibson Vroman gave insight to a wide audience regarding the plight of impoverished African American children growing up in the segregated South.

Vroman was born in Buffalo, New York, in 1923. She received her bachelor's degree from Alabama State Teachers College and became a teacher. Vroman adapted her **short story "See How They Run"** (1952) into a screenplay for the film *Bright Road* (1953), becoming the first black female member of the Screen Writers Guild.

Vroman's other works include *Esther* (1963), a **novel** about a black woman's struggles to become a nurse, and *Harlem Summer* (1967), a novel for teenagers. Vroman died in 1967 after postsurgical complications.

Further Readings

Black Writers, first edition, Gale, 1989.

Dictionary of Literary Biography, Volume 33: *Afro-American Fiction Writers after 1955,* Gale, 1984.

Vusumzi Make

Character in *The Heart of a Woman*

Vyry Brown

Character in *Jubilee*

W-Z

Kneel to your load,

then balance your

staggering feet /

and walk up that coal ladder

as they do in time, /

one bare foot after the next

in ancestral rhyme.

Omeros,
Derek Walcott, 1990

Gloria Wade-Gayles

American prose writer and poet

Gloria Jean Wade-Gayles's writing focuses on the particular strength and spirituality of the African American woman. Her autobiographical work, *Pushed Back to Strength: A Black Woman's Journey Home* (1993) describes her close-knit family, her experience as a scholarship student at Boston University, and her return to the South to teach at Spelman College, where she was made a professor of English and women's studies in 1989. Born in Memphis, Tennessee, Wade-Gayles has won many awards and honors, among them a United Negro College Fund Mellon Research Grant in 1987 and the DuBois Research Fellowship from Harvard University in 1990. Wade-Gayles's other books include *Anointed to Fly* (1991) and *My Soul Is a Witness: African American Women's Spirituality* (1994).

Further Readings

Black Writers, second edition, Gale, 1994.

Waiting to Exhale

Terry McMillan
Novel, 1992

Terry McMillan's third **novel**, *Waiting to Exhale,* was a *New York Times* best-seller for more than six months and earned $2.64 million for its paperback rights. The book explores the friendships between four middle-class African American women in 1990 in Phoenix, Arizona, and their search for the man of their dreams. McMillan uses both standard English speech and African American dialect to develop the personalities of the characters.

Savannah Jackson drives from Denver, where she's left behind a publicity director position at a major public utility, to Phoenix to take a job with a lower salary. She brings along a guy who turns out to be a freeloader. Robin Stokes, an insurance writer who has just broken up with her boyfriend, is searching for a good-looking man. Her father suffers from Alzheimer's disease, and her mother cares for him.

Dust jacket from McMillan's third novel (1992).

Gloria is concerned about her son, her health, and her hair-salon business, but has not taken steps to improve her future. Bernadine talks about her discontent with her husband and the sacrifice she has made for him, but does nothing to change the situation and is surprised when her husband wants to end their marriage.

The women often get irritated with each other when discussing men, but are more supportive when discussing the other problems in each other's lives. Safe sex is of particular concern to these women, who have a history of multiple sexual partners. The issue takes on more importance when one of Gloria's employees contracts AIDS. Despite their preoccupation with their relationships with men, the women

Walcott won the Nobel Prize for literature in 1992.

know that they will always have their friendships to sustain them.

W Derek Walcott

West Indian poet and dramatist
Born January 23, 1930.

A major voice in West Indian literature, Walcott interweaves Caribbean and European elements in poems and plays that explore racial tensions, the contradictory African and European influences in his West Indian heritage, and the problems of identity inherent to a native culture exploited by **colonialism**. Although English is his second language, Walcott is an acknowledged master of the nuances of his adopted tongue. His **poetry** earned him the Nobel Prize for literature in 1992.

Born in Castries, Saint Lucia, on January 23, 1930, Derek Alton Walcott published his first book of poetry, *25 Poems* (1948), when he was only eighteen. After his first **play,** *Henri Christophe* (1950), was produced, Walcott helped establish the Saint Lucia Arts Guild, where he could cast, direct, and rewrite plays during the production process. After graduating from the University College of West Indies and working briefly as a teacher, he studied theater in New York City in 1957, then moved to Trinidad, where he founded the Little Carib Theater Workshop. In the late 1970s, Walcott began dividing his time between the Caribbean and the United States, where he taught at several universities. In 1985, he joined the staff of Boston University, while continuing to produce and direct plays.

In both content and means of expression, Walcott's plays explore the quest for a Caribbean cultural identity, incorporating Caribbean music, dance, folk traditions, and dialects. *Ti-Jean and His Brothers* (1958) is an allegory containing elements of West Indian **folklore**, while *Dream on Monkey Mountain* (1967), which earned Walcott the 1971 Obie Award, dramatizes the struggle to forge an identity out of a colonized past. *Omeros* (1990) is a West Indian *Odyssey* in which native fisherman, landlords, and prostitutes are cast in Homeric roles.

Walcott also continued to write poetry, publishing his first major collection of verse, *In a Green Night,* in 1962. In contrast to the simple language of his plays, classical allusions, elaborate metaphors, and intricate rhyme schemes are central to his verse, which has been compared to Elizabethan poetry in its complexity. Like his plays, however, his poetry explores problems of origins and identity and the conflict between Caribbean roots, African heritage, and Western influence. His 1972 book-length poem *Another Life* revolves around the West Indian artist, while the poetry gathered in his *Collected Poems* (1984) reflects both the political and cultural transitions within his country and his personal synthesis of West Indian cultural conflicts.

In 1993 Walcott published *Antilles: Fragments of Epic Memory,* his 1992 Nobel Prize address.

See also **Poetry of Derek Walcott**

Further Readings

Black Literature Criticism, Gale, 1992.

Black Writers, second edition, Gale, 1994.

Dictionary of Literary Biography, Volume 117: *Twentieth-Century Caribbean and Black African Writers,* First Series, Gale, 1992.

Hamner, Robert D., *Critical Perspectives on Derek Walcott,* Three Continents, 1993.

Hamner, *Derek Walcott,* revised edition, Twayne, 1993.

Alice Walker

American novelist, essayist, and poet
Born February 9, 1944.

Best known for her Pulitzer Prize-winning **novel** *The Color Purple* (1982), Walker depicts black women struggling for sexual as well as racial equality and emerging as strong, creative individuals. Her negative portraits of black men have been criticized on political and aesthetic grounds, but many have responded by arguing that the drama of women achieving selfhood is an important end in itself.

Walker was born on February 9, 1944, in Eatonton, Georgia, the eighth child of Willie Lee and Minnie Grant Walker. Both her parents were tenant farmers, and as a child she witnessed the severe economic oppression of the sharecropping system as well as violent **racism**. When Walker was eight, her right eye was injured by one of her brothers, resulting in permanent damage to her eye and a facial disfigurement that isolated her as a child. She spent her time reading and writing and carefully observing the people around her. She also formed a close relationship with her mother and her aunts, gaining from them a vision of independent womanhood.

In 1961, Walker entered Spelman College, where she joined the **civil rights movement**; two years later she transferred to Sarah Lawrence College, where she began writing the poems that would eventually appear in *Once*

Pulitzer Prize-winning author Alice Walker in 1993.

(1968). Two years after graduating in 1965, she married Melvyn Leventhal, a Jewish civil rights lawyer; they worked in Mississippi, registering blacks to vote, and would divorce in the mid-1970s.

In 1970, Walker published her first novel, *The Third Life of Grange Copeland,* about the ravages of racism on a black sharecropping family. In *Meridian* (1976), her second novel, she explored a woman's successful efforts to find her place in the civil rights movement. Walker's insistence on attacking sexism in African American relationships was highly controversial because it came at a time when the civil rights movement was struggling to consolidate the gains it had made against racism.

Walker continued, however, to dramatize the oppression of black women. *The Color Purple* is an epistolary novel about Celie, a Southern black woman who is abused by her stepfather and her husband and finally achieves strength through the friendship of other women. Adapted for film in 1985, the novel garnered a National Book Critics Circle Award nomination in 1982 and both the American Book Award and the Pulitzer Prize in 1983.

Walker has published several other volumes of **poetry,** including *Revolutionary Petunias and Other Poems* (1971) and *Her Blue Body Everything We Know* (1991). She has also published collections of short stories as well as books of **essays** on women's issues. In 1974 she released the prose work *A Poetic Equation: Conversations with Nikki Giovanni and Margaret Walker,* and in 1989, she published another novel, *The Temple of My Familiar*, about the reincarnation of an ancient African goddess. Three years later she completed the novel *Possessing the Secret of Joy* (1992), about a young woman who undergoes the African tradition of circumcision.

Further Readings

Black Literature Criticism, Gale, 1992.

Black Writers, second edition, Gale, 1994.

Prenshaw, Peggy W., editor, *Women Writers of the Contemporary South,* University Press of Mississippi, 1984.

David Walker

American abolitionist and essayist
Born September 28, 1785.
Died June 28, 1830.

Walker, a free black and an abolitionist born in Wilmington, North Carolina, became the first African American to publish a pamphlet calling for a slave revolt. The tract, *David Walker's Appeal to the Coloured Citizens of the World* (1829) is credited with inspiring the militant antislavery movement that helped to precipitate the Civil War. *Walker's Appeal* spoke directly to slaves, indicting the evils of the slaveholding system and urging those under its sway to rise in rebellion. Its language was considered strong even by Northern abolitionists; the document created fear and resentment in the South. Circulation of the pamphlet became a crime in the South and a bounty was placed on Walker's

life. He was murdered following the publication of the third edition of *Walker's Appeal.*

Joseph A. Walker

American educator, producer, director, playwright, and actor
Born February 23, 1935.

Born in Washington, D.C., Walker earned a bachelor's degree from Howard University, a master's degree from Catholic University, and a doctorate from New York University. He began working with the Negro Ensemble Company in 1969 as playwright, director, and choreographer. Over the next fifteen years he wrote *The Harangues* (1969), *Ododo* (1970), *Yin Yang* (1973), and *District Line* (1984). Walker's best-known work, the semiautobiographical *The River Niger* (1972), is a realistic portrayal of a struggling African American family in Harlem. The **play** won many awards, including an Obie in 1971 and a Tony in 1973. In 1976 *The River Niger* was adapted for film with a screenplay by Walker.

Further Readings

Black Writers, first edition, Gale 1989.

Contemporary Literary Criticism, Volume 19, Gale, 1981.

Dictionary of Literary Biography, Volume 38: *Afro-American Writers after 1955: Dramatists and Prose Writers,* Gale, 1985.

Margaret Walker

American poet and novelist
Born July 7, 1915.

With the 1942 publication of her first **poetry** collection, *For My People,* Margaret Abigail Walker garnered the Yale University Younger Poet's Award and became the first black American woman honored in a prestigious national competition. She began her literary career in the 1930s and has emerged as a "literary mother" to writers like **Alice Walker** and **Sonia Sanchez.** Walker is known primarily for her long-standing devotion to the heritage of black culture.

Born in Birmingham, Alabama, on July 7, 1915, Walker moved at a young age to New Orleans. She developed an interest in literature, which was nourished by her minister father, who introduced her to the classics. Her mother read verse aloud, and by the age of eleven Walker was reading the **Harlem Renaissance** poets— particularly **Langston Hughes**, whom she later met and who encouraged her to write. Her maternal grandmother told stories about Walker's great-grandmother, a former slave in Georgia, which later inspired Walker's fictional history *Jubilee* (1966).

In the 1930s, Walker attended Northwestern University and became involved with the Works Progress Administration (WPA). Assigned to work with troubled youths, she used the setting of one Italian-black neighborhood for her unpublished **novel** *Goose Island.* In 1936, she was awarded a full-time writing position with WPA and began a friendship with **Richard Wright**, which ended abruptly in 1939. Walker later wrote an account of the novelist's life and works, entitled *Richard Wright, Daemonic Genius: A Portrait of the Man, A Critical Look at His Work* (1988).

In 1939, Walker's work with WPA also ended, and she began graduate studies at the University of Iowa, completing *For My People* for her master's thesis. In the early 1940s, she began teaching at Livingstone College, then at West Virginia State College. She married Firnist James Alexander in 1943 and the first of her four children was born the following year. She resumed work on *Jubilee* and in 1949 began her long affiliation with Jackson State College (now Jackson State University). She finished *Jubilee* in April, 1965, receiving mixed reviews. In 1970 she collected her civil rights poems in *Prophets for a New Day.*

Retiring from Jackson State University in 1979 afforded Walker more time for writing, lecturing, and consulting. In 1988 she released a collection of previously published poetry, *This Is My Century.* She has begun work on a sequel to *Jubilee,* along with an **autobiography**.

Further Readings

Black Literature Criticism, Gale, 1992.

Black Writers, second edition, Gale, 1994.

Margaret Walker won the Younger Poet's Award from Yale in 1942.

Dictionary of Literary Biography, Volume 76: *Afro-American Writers, 1940-1955,* Gale, 1988.

Evans, Mari, editor, *Black Women Writers (1950-1980): A Critical Evaluation,* Anchor/Doubleday, 1984.

Wallace Wright

Character in *Pinktoes*

The Walls of Jericho

Rudolph Fisher

Novel, 1928

The Walls of Jericho, **Rudolph Fisher**'s first **novel**, explores the complex relations between different strata of Harlem society, including the working-class "rats" and the middle-class "dickties," who are usually lighter skinned and better educated than their poorer neighbors. Protagonist Fred Merrit, a mulatto lawyer, buys a house next door to Agatha Cramp, a white liberal who likes to partake of the Harlem nightlife but is alarmed when she realizes that her new neighbor is black. Merrit's house is burned down, not by his white neighbors, as might be expected, but by an African American man who bears him a grudge. Joshua "Shine" Jones and his working-class friends help bring the culprit to justice, proving that humanity and fair play can transcend barriers of complexion and social status.

Wally O'Hara

Character in *The Sign in Sidney Brustein's Window*

Eric Walrond

Guyanese short story writer and journalist
Born in 1898.
Died in 1966.

Walrond is considered an important young writer who came to the public's attention during the **Harlem Renaissance**. Born in 1898 in Georgetown, British Guiana (now Guyana), he immigrated to the United States in 1918 and established himself with his early writings, which are based on the racial bigotry met with in America and which reflect Walrond's indignation and disillusionment.

Walrond's first story published in America was "On Being Black," (1922) which recounts his personal experiences with racial conflict. He also published articles in the early and mid 1920s, including "The Negro Exodus from the South" (1923), in which he explores the effects of the movement of blacks from the rural South to the urban North, and "The Black City" (1924), an **essay** on Harlem. His most noted essay, however, is "The New Negro Faces America" (1923), in which he critiques the philosophies of three major black leaders: **Booker T. Washington**, **W. E. B. Du Bois**, and **Marcus Garvey**.

Walrond's most acclaimed work is his collection of short stories, ***Tropic Death*** (1926),

which focuses on and illuminates the problems faced by migratory blacks of the Caribbean. The book was regarded as an outstanding example of **avant-garde** writing and drew high praise from contemporary critics. Walrond left the United States in 1927 and lived in Europe until his death in 1966.

Further Readings
Black Writers, first edition, Gale, 1989.

Dictionary of Literary Biography, Volume 51: *Afro-American Writers from the Harlem Renaissance to 1940*, Gale, 1987.

Walter Castle

Character in *While Gods Are Falling*

Walter Lee

Character in *A Raisin in the Sun*

Ronald W. Walters

American scholar and writer

Walters earned his undergraduate degree from Fisk University and his master's and doctorate degrees from American University. An activist and scholar, he has been a professor of political science and African American studies and a delegate to foreign countries. Walters's award-winning *Black Presidential Politics in America: A Strategic Approach* (1989) analyzes the role of blacks in presidential elections, in particular in the years 1960, 1968, and 1976, and emphasizes the importance of black support to the success of Democratic nominees. In *Pan Africanism in the African Diaspora: Concepts of Afro-Centricity* (1992), Walters presents a history of the American **black power** movement of the 1960s and 1970s, highlighting American activists and their influence on Brazil, the Caribbean, and West Africa.

Further Readings
Black Writers, second edition, Gale, 1994.

Wanda

Character in *The Fabulous Miss Marie*

Wanja

Character in *Petals of Blood*

Douglas Turner Ward

American actor, producer, director, and writer
Born May 5, 1930.

Ward has been a pioneering force in black theater since 1965, when he co-founded the Negro Ensemble Company, serving as artistic director beginning in 1967. Born in Burnside, Louisiana, in 1930, Ward attended Wilberforce University and the University of Michigan before moving to New York City in 1948. He studied with Paul Mann's Actors Workshop and went on to win Tony, Obie, and Drama Desk awards for acting and directing. His **plays,** which explore **racism** and racial stereotypes with wry humor, include *Happy Ending* and *Day of Absence* (both 1965); *The Reckoning: A Surreal Southern Fable* (1969); *Brotherhood* (1970); and *The Redeemer* (1979).

Further Readings

Black Writers, first edition, Gale, 1989.

Contemporary Literary Criticism, Volume 19, Gale, 1981.

Booker T. Washington

American autobiographer, essayist, and biographer
Born April 5, 1856.
Died November 14, 1915.

A respected educator and cofounder of the Tuskegee Institute, Washington was known as an important social thinker of the early twentieth century. His racial philosophy, which stressed that blacks should not demand social equality but should instead work toward their own economic advancement, prompted criticism from several black intellectuals. Washington's private papers indicate, however, that in spite of his cautious, public stance on racial issues, he used his prominent status to work surreptitiously against **segregation**.

Originally named Booker Taliaferro (he later added the surname Washington), Washington was born into **slavery** on April 5, 1856, at Hale's Farm, near Roanoke, Virginia. His mother was a cook for James Burroughs, a planter; his father was white and possibly related to Burroughs. Freed after the Civil War, Washington and his mother moved to Malden, West Virginia, to join Washington Ferguson, whom his mother had married. The young Washington helped support the family by working in salt furnaces and coal mines. He taught himself the alphabet, studied at night, and in 1872 entered Hampton Institute, a school established for blacks. Three years later he graduated with honors, then taught for a short time in Malden. He returned to Hampton and was recommended by a Hampton administrator for the position of principal of a new normal school for blacks.

When Washington assumed his post at the Tuskegee Normal and Industrial Institute in 1881, he discovered that neither land nor buildings had been purchased for the school, nor were any funds available. Nevertheless, he started classes in a shanty with thirty students, borrowed money for land, and moved the school. In his almost thirty-five years at Tuskegee, he encouraged students to learn industrial skills, believing that economic strength would lead to equality. In addition to working as an educator, he raised money for and publicized the school, and by the time of his death, Tuskegee had an endowment of two million dollars and a staff of two hundred.

Washington also advised several U.S. presidents, including Theodore Roosevelt, on racial issues and was in demand as a lecturer. He delivered his most famous speech, known as the Atlanta Compromise, at the opening of the Cotton States and International Exposition in Sep-

Booker T. Washington's *Up from Slavery* has become a classic American autobiography.

tember, 1895. In it he emphasized his philosophy of "accommodation" by blacks. Many of his **speeches**, as well as his **essays**, were published in book form; among these are *The Future of the American Negro* (1899) and *The Negro in the South: His Economic Progress in Relation to His Moral and Religious Development* (1907; with **W. E. B. Du Bois**). Washington also chronicled his life in several autobiographies, including *The Story of My Life and Work* (1900; with Edgar Webber), which underwent several revisions; the best-selling *Up from Slavery* (1901; with Max Bennett Thrasher); and *Working with the Hands* (1904). He also compiled a **biography** entitled *Frederick Douglass* (1907).

Washington was married three times (in 1882, 1885, and 1893) and had three children. He died of arteriosclerosis and extreme exhaustion on November 14, 1915, in Tuskegee, and is

buried in a tomb overlooking the institute. Thirty years after his death he was elected to the Hall of Fame, New York University, becoming its first black inductee.

Further Readings

Black Writers, first edition, Gale, 1989.

Drinker, Frederick E., *Booker T. Washington: The Master Mind of a Child of Slavery,* National Publishing, 1915.

Harlan, Louis R., *Booker T. Washington: The Wizard of Tuskegee, 1901-1915,* Oxford University Press, 1983.

Mary Helen Washington

American educator, editor, and author
Born January 21, 1941.

Washington is recognized as the editor of anthologies praised for containing unique and sensitive stories describing the life and plight of black women and families. Born in 1941 in Cleveland, Ohio, Washington received her Ph.D. in 1976 from the University of Detroit and is currently an associate professor of English at the University of Massachusetts. She has edited *Black-Eyed Susans: Classic Stories by and about Black Women* (1975), *Midnight Birds: Stories by Contemporary Black Women Writers* (1980), *Invented Lives: Narratives of Black Women, 1860-1960* (1987), and *Memory of Kin: Stories about Family by Black Writers* (1991). These anthologies, with introductions by Washington, address the problems of both **racism** and sexism and contain stories by such noteworthy authors as **Ntozake Shange**, **Alice Walker**, and **Toni Morrison**.

Further Readings

Black Writers, second edition, Gale, 1994.

Watusi

Character in *Who Is Angelina?*

Keenen Ivory Wayans

American comedian, director, and screenwriter
Born in 1958(?).

Beginning his career as a stand-up comedian, Wayans is known for writing, producing, and starring in the popular television show *In Living Color,* which satirized blacks and their culture. He garnered an Emmy Award in 1990 for his work on the program, which he left in 1992.

Born in New York City, Wayans developed his comedic style performing for his large family. After attending college, he took his stand-up routine on the road, first to New York City and then to Los Angeles. The scarcity of good acting roles for blacks in the early 1980s prompted Wayans to work on films like *Hollywood Shuffle* (1987), which he cowrote with Robert Townsend, and eventually led to his first solo effort, the satiric *I'm Gonna Git You Sucka* (1988), which he wrote and directed.

Further Readings
Black Writers, second edition, Gale, 1994.

We Can't Breathe

Ronald L. Fair
Novel, 1972

We Can't Breathe, **Ronald L. Fair**'s fourth **novel**, winner of the American Library Association's Best Book Award, is the author's portrayal of the lives of several African Americans born in the 1930s. Set in Chicago, the novel discusses five African American youths—Ernie, George, Willie, Jake, and Sam—who struggle for survival against the challenges posed by alcohol, drugs, violence, poverty, and **racism**. Throughout their youth, the boys confront tragedy and injustice. The novel, written from the adult perspective of Ernie, offers the narrator the opportunity of self-redemption.

Weak Knees

Character in *The Narrows*

Weasel

Character in *Country Place*

Frank J. Webb

American novelist
Born about 1830.
Died after 1870.

What little is known about Webb comes largely from Harriet Beecher Stowe's preface to his **novel** *The Garies and Their Friends* (1857). Webb was probably born in the late 1820s or 1830s and lived for a time in England, where *The Garies* was published. *The Garies* was one of the first works of fiction to describe the lives and problems of free blacks in the North, including such issues as racially mixed marriage and passing for white. The novel focuses on the interactions of three middle-class families—one white, one black, one racially mixed. Webb also authored two novelettes, *Two Wolves and a Lamb* and *Marvin Hayle,* that were published in periodicals in 1870.

Further Readings
Dictionary of Literary Biography, Volume 50: *Afro-American Writers before the Harlem Renaissance,* Gale, 1986.

Ida B. Wells

American journalist and civil rights activist
Born July 16, 1862.
Died March 25, 1931.

Ida Bell Wells Barnett was a prominent civil rights activist and journalist of the nineteenth century. Born a slave on July 16, 1862, in Holly Springs, Mississippi, she attended Rust College and became a teacher and a journalist.

Wells was a prominent nineteenth-century civil rights activist and journalist.

In 1884, Wells won a suit filed in Memphis against a railroad company after a conductor asked her to move from the ladies' coach to a smoking car. The decision was overturned on appeal but Wells became set on a lifelong course of struggle against racial **discrimination**.

Wells became secretary of the Colored Press Association (later the Afro-American Press Association) and editor of the *Free Speech and Headlight* in 1889. Angered by Wells's editorials about the lynching of blacks, her opponents destroyed the *Free Speech* presses and offices and threatened Wells's life. She then became a columnist for the *New York Age* and began lecturing throughout the Northeast and Great Britain.

Moving to Chicago, she wrote for the *Chicago Conservator,* the city's first black newspaper, and organized Chicago's first civic club for black women. In 1913, she founded the Alpha Suffrage Club of Chicago, the black women's first suffrage organization. In 1930, Wells ran as an independent candidate for the Illinois state senate but was defeated. She died on March 25, 1931, and was buried in Chicago's Oakwood Cemetery.

Further Readings
Epic Lives: One Hundred Black Women Who Made a Difference, Visible Ink Press, 1993.

Frances Cress Welsing
American nonfiction writer
Born March 18, 1935.

Born in Chicago, Illinois, in 1935, Welsing followed in the footsteps of both her father and grandfather by becoming a physician. She graduated from Howard University School of Medicine, where she has also taught, and is a lecturer as well as a general and child psychiatrist. Welsing also has appeared on numerous television and radio shows. The premise of her book *The Cress Theory of Color, Confrontation and Racism (White Supremacy)* (1970), is that white people, fearing white genetic annihilation, dominate and try to eliminate the nonwhite majority. In *The Isis Papers: The Keys to the Colors* (1991), Welsing focused on the concepts of white supremacy and resistance to **racism**.

Further Readings
Black Writers, second edition, Gale, 1994.

Richard Wesley
American playwright
Born July 11, 1945.

Born to working-class parents, Wesley showed an early talent for playwriting. While at Howard University, he studied under **Owen Dodson** and **Ted Shine**. Later, he was playwright-in-residence at the New Lafayette The-atre in Harlem with **Ed Bullins** and J. E. Gaines. His *The Black Terror* (1971) earned him a Drama Desk Award for Outstanding Playwriting. In 1974, Wesley produced what has been referred to as his finest short **play, *The Past Is the Past*,**which focuses on the relationship between a father and son. Wesley has also written screen-plays, including *Uptown Saturday Night* (1974), for which he received the National Association for the Advancement of Colored People's Image Award, and its sequel *Let's Do It Again* (1975). *The Mighty Gents* (1974), about former gang members in a Newark neighborhood, was staged on Broadway in 1978. Wesley has also authored a screen adaptation of **Richard Wright**'s *Native Son* (1986) and the play *The Talented Tenth* (1989), which centers on a group of college-edu-cated, middle-aged blacks.

Further Readings

Black Writers, first edition, Gale, 1989.

Dictionary of Literary Biography, Volume 38: *Afro-American Writers after 1955: Dramatists and Prose Writers,* Gale, 1985.

father was an ex-slave who created a successful business in Massachusetts, and her mother, who was much younger than her father, came from a large Southern family she supported with her husband's money. West's novel *The Living Is Easy* depicts a similar situation, describing a woman who marries an older man for his money and then invites her family to live with her. Exposing the emptiness of some white values adopted by blacks, the novel was well received by critics both when it was first published and when it was reprinted in 1982. In 1995 West published a second novel, *The Wedding,* revolv-ing around black-white relations during a 1950s wedding on Martha's Vineyard.

Further Readings

Black Writers, second edition, Gale, 1994.

Dictionary of Literary Biography, Volume 76: *Afro-American Writers, 1940-1955,* Gale, 1988.

Dorothy West

American novelist, short story writer, and publisher
Born June 2, 1907.

West is best remembered for her role in the **Harlem Renaissance**, founding the journal *Challenge* in the 1930s. *Challenge* highlighted much of the best work of African American writers of the time, including **Langston Hughes** and **Richard Wright**. West is also noted for her **novel *The Living Is Easy*** (1948) and her many short stories, which often feature black urban characters and settings. Her story "The Type-writer," which shared an award with a work by **Zora Neale Hurston**, reflects her fascination with people's hidden motivations.

Some of West's work draws on her own experiences growing up as a middle-class black child in early twentieth-century Boston. Her

What the Wine Sellers Buy

Ron Milner
Play, first produced 1973, published 1974

What the Wine Sellers Buy is a morality **play**, inspired in part by **Ron Milner**'s concern over the glorification of prostitution and drugs in popular culture. The first black-authored play to be staged at Lincoln Center, it became a great critical and popular success in its own right, eventually enjoying a record-breaking nation-wide tour. *Wine Sellers,* which is filled with real-istic detail, depicts the struggles of Steve Carlton, a seventeen-year-old Detroit youth who is tempted to make easy money by turning his own girlfriend into a prostitute. Rico, the pimp who tries to corrupt Steve, also represents an indictment of the American business world. The play leaves the audience with a positive impres-sion, as it focuses on young Steve triumphing over Rico's corruption.

Wheatley was the first African American to publish a volume of poems.

Phillis Wheatley

West African-born American poet
Born in 1753(?).
Died December 5, 1784.

Wheatley was the first African American to publish a volume of poems. Though she was a slave, she was given a thorough education; later she composed neoclassical verse, modelled most closely on the poems of Alexander Pope. She was well known in colonial America and even traveled to England before the Revolutionary War, but she wrote little about her slave status.

Wheatley was born in West Africa, perhaps in what is now known as Senegal, around 1753. She was captured, brought to a Boston, Massachusetts, market as a slave, and sold in 1761 to John Wheatley, who bought her as a companion for his wife. Susanna Wheatley and her daughter, Mary, supervised her education, and contemporary accounts describe Phillis Wheatley as a precocious student. She learned Latin and read classical and continental literature, as well as English **poetry;** she also became a devout Christian, and her Puritan upbringing strongly influenced her poetry.

Her first published poem appears to have been "On Messrs. Hussey and Coffin" in 1767; other early poems include "On Being Brought from Africa to America" and "To the University of Cambridge, in New England." In 1770, she published "An Elegiac Poem, on the Death of That Celebrated Divine, and Eminent Servant of Jesus Christ, the Reverend and Learned George Whitefield." Whitefield had been a leader of the evangelical movement that had swept both England and North America, and Wheatley's poem was reprinted often during the widespread mourning that followed his death. Published in London in 1771, the work attracted the notice of the philanthropist Selina Hastings, Countess of Huntingdon. Wheatley traveled to England in 1773, accompanying the Wheatleys' son Nathan, who had business in London. Sponsored by the Countess of Huntingdon, she visited a variety of political, social, and literary figures before returning to Boston. Later that year, her collection of verse, entitled ***Poems on Various Subjects, Religious and Moral***, was published in London.

Wheatley wrote verse in a form some scholars have called highly stylized and perhaps impersonal; when she was not writing occasional poems to commemorate public events, she wrote elegies on the deaths of people she hardly knew. She often versified the ideals of the American Revolution, celebrating liberty while seldom writing about the institution that held her captive. Her general silence about **slavery** has been the most controversial aspect of her poetic heritage. Her defenders have argued that she had a white, European education and little exposure to other members of her race. Scholars also have pointed to an anti-slavery letter she wrote to a Presbyterian preacher in 1774.

The 1770s marked significant changes in Wheatley's life. She was given her freedom three months before Susanna Wheatley's death on March 3, 1774. Four years later, John Wheatley died; Mary passed away soon thereafter. On April 1, 1778, Wheatley married a free black man named John Peters. Peters proved unable to support her, and she had few skills with which to support herself. In 1779, she attempted to gather subscriptions for another volume of poetry, and though she did not succeed, she continued to publish some poems, including "Liberty and Peace" (1784), about the ending of the Revolutionary War, and *An Elegy, Sacred to the Memory of That Great Divine, the Reverend and Learned Dr. Samuel Cooper* (1784). In 1784, her husband spent time in jail, perhaps for debt, and Wheatley died in Boston on December 5 of that year, while working as a cleaning maid at a boardinghouse.

Further Readings

Black Literature Criticism, Gale, 1992.

Dictionary of Literary Biography, Volume 50: *Afro-American Writers before the Harlem Renaissance,* Gale, 1986.

Robinson, William H., *Phillis Wheatley in the Black American Beginnings,* Broadside Press, 1975.

Where the Hummingbird Flies
Frank Hercules
Novel, 1961

Frank Hercules's first **novel**, *Where the Hummingbird Flies,* draws on his experiences growing up in the colonial West Indies. In this political **satire**, set in colonial Trinidad, Hercules examines many facets of colonial society and explores the implications of change through the novel's three main characters. Mervyn Herrick accepts the idea of independence yet fears its uncertainties; Francis Herbert is a radical who suffers for his views; and Dulcina possesses the beauty and confidence of those capable of acting in their own best interests. Hercules also examines the theme of intraracial

prejudice as a perverse form of self-defense. Hercules's novel was judged as one of the five best novels of the year by *Newsweek* and won the Fletcher Pratt Memorial Fellowship in Prose of the Bread Loaf Writer's Conference.

While Gods Are Falling
Earl Lovelace
Novel, 1965

The manuscript for **Earl Lovelace**'s debut **novel**, *While Gods Are Falling,* garnered a British Petroleum Independence Literary Award in 1964 and was published a year later. The embattled yet idealistic protagonist, Walter Castle, is comparable to the main character of **George Lamming**'s *In the Castle of My Skin* . While living in a poverty-stricken world beset by crime, Walter imagines himself as a castle. In this way he becomes a refuge in which a black Trinidadian may hide from the perils of corruption. The falling gods of the title are the traditional keepers of morality and social order, including teachers, magistrates, and priests. While Lovelace makes Castle the centerpiece of the novel, he does nonetheless concern himself with the problems women have making their way in a manmade world.

White Papers for White Americans
Calvin C. Hernton
Nonfiction, 1966

In *White Papers for White Americans,* a compilation of nonfiction articles, **Calvin C. Hernton** uses an informal, narrative style to reflect on his own identity and analyze the unique dilemmas of Southern blacks. He discusses the rise of black leaders and entertainers in the 1960s and the sociological and political implications of the **Civil Rights Movement**. After examining the relationship between **racism** and the continuing power of the American establishment, Hernton reveals his desire for and reservations about the black revolution that many hoped the Civil Rights Movement would spawn.

Walter White

American essayist, novelist, and nonfiction writer
Born July 1, 1893.
Died March 21, 1955.

Although White published only two **novels,** he is remembered as a significant writer from the **Harlem Renaissance**. He was also a political activist during some of the most powerful years of the **National Association for the Advancement of Colored People** (NAACP). White's first position with the NAACP was to investigate mob violence and lynching in the South; because he had fair skin and blue eyes, he could pose as a white reporter and gather eye-witness accounts. He used this experience to present a unique view of America's racial confrontations during the first decades of the twentieth century.

Walter Francis White was born in Atlanta, Georgia, on July 1, 1893. He began working for the NAACP in 1918 and was serving as its secretary at the time of his death. White's first novel *The Fire in the Flint* (1924) focuses on lynching, while *Flight* (1926) centers on African Americans "passing" as white. While in France under a Guggenheim Fellowship, White wrote *Rope and Faggot: A Biography of Judge Lynch* (1929), an analysis of lynching.

Of historical importance are White's numerous **essays** documenting the successes and failures of the American **civil rights movement** from the early 1920s through the mid-1950s. The collection *A Rising Wind: A Report on the Negro Soldier in the European Theater of War* (1945) examines the worldwide implications of the officially sanctioned **racism** of the American armed forces during World War II. White's final works, *A Man Called White: The Autobiography of Walter White* (1948) and *How Far the Promised Land?* (1955), provide a record of his work with the NAACP and the organization's overall influence on racial policies in America during the first half of the twentieth century. White died on March 21, 1955, in New York City.

Further Readings

Black Writers, first edition, Gale, 1989.

Cannon, Poppy, *A Gentle Knight: My Husband, Walter White,* Rinehart, 1956.

Dictionary of Literary Biography, Volume 51: *Afro-American Writers from the Harlem Renaissance to 1940,* Gale, 1987.

Fraser, Allison, *Walter White, Civil Rights Leader,* Black Americans of Achievement, Chelsea House, 1991.

James Monroe Whitfield

American poet
Born April 10, 1822.
Died April 23, 1871.

A barber who yearned to support himself by writing, Whitfield created a small body of **poetry** dedicated to the plight of the slave and the inequities in the American social system. Whitfield was born to free blacks living in New Hampshire and spent most of his life in Buffalo, New York, where he owned a barber shop. His lone volume of poetry, *America and Other Poems* (1853), examines the topics of history, **slavery**, **religion**, love, ennui, and death. Whitfield was also active in the black separatist movement, vigorously advocating the immigration of blacks to South and Central America. He spent the last decade of his life in the American West and died in San Francisco, California, in 1871.

Further Readings

Dictionary of Literary Biography, Volume 50: *Afro-American Writers before the Harlem Renaissance,* Gale, 1986.

Albery Allson Whitman

American poet
Born May 30, 1851.
Died June 29, 1901.

Light-skinned enough to pass for white, Whitman dedicated much of his **poetry** to an exploration of the evils of **slavery** and imperialism. A largely self-educated man who was born into slavery in 1851, Whitman supported his family by serving as an African Methodist Episcopal minister. His **epic** poem *Not a Man and Yet a Man, with Miscellaneous Poems* (1877) pursues the theme of freedom and its value to every individual. *An Idyl of the South* (1901) contains the poem "The Octoroon," a piece about a doomed love affair between master and slave. Whitman died of pneumonia contracted during a lecture tour in 1901 and was eulogized as one of the most important black poets of the late nineteenth century.

Further Readings

Dictionary of Literary Biography, Volume 50: *Afro-American Writers before the Harlem Renaissance,* Gale, 1986.

White served in a number of positions with the NAACP.

Who Is Angelina?

Al Young
Novel, 1975

Al Young's *Who Is Angelina?* presents a black woman's search for self in the turbulent 1970s. Angelina Green, twenty-six years old, descends into despair when her relationship with her boyfriend ends. Suicidal and distraught, she seeks to dull her pain through the use of alcohol, drugs, and sex. In Mexico on vacation, she becomes romantically involved with Watusi, yet news of her father's serious illness compels her to hurry to his side. A mystical experience while in church with her father allows Angelina to understand that inner peace can be achieved and that she can take control of her life and happiness. Her father urges her to trust her instincts and return to California, where

she recognizes that by eliminating the confusion and disorder characterizing her earlier behavior, she can strengthen her inner self and improve her life.

The Whole Armour

Please see The "Guyana" Quartet

John Edgar Wideman

American novelist
Born June 14, 1941.

Wideman is best known for **novels** and **short stories** that trace the lives of families in and around the black ghetto district of Pittsburgh, Pennsylvania, where he was raised. His major interest is the black individual's quest for self-discovery amidst both personal history and African American heritage.

Wideman studied literature as a Rhodes Scholar at Oxford University and his work reflects both his formal training and his interest in experimenting with narrative technique. His first novel, *A Glance Away* (1967), tells the story of a rehabilitated drug addict who returns home to renew his ties with friends and family while trying to avoid readdiction. In *Hurry Home* (1969), a black law school graduate seeks cultural communion with white society by traveling to Europe and then reaffirms his black heritage in Africa. In **Sent for You Yesterday** (1983), which won the PEN/Faulkner Award, Wideman celebrates the power of the imagination to transcend adversity and restore human bonds. **Philadelphia Fire** (1990) describes the police bombing of a militant, heavily armed black commune and the resulting fire that razed over fifty houses. This novel also won the PEN/Faulkner Award, distinguishing Wideman as the first writer to receive the honor twice. In 1995 Wideman published *Fatheralong: A Meditation on Fathers and Sons, Race and Society.*

Further Readings
Black Literature Criticism, Gale, 1992.

Black Writers, second edition, Gale, 1994.

Dictionary of Literary Biography, Volume 33: *Afro-American Fiction Writers after 1955,* Gale, 1984.

The Wife of His Youth
Charles W. Chesnutt
Short stories, 1899

Charles W. Chesnutt's second collection of short stories, *The Wife of His Youth, and Other Stories of the Color Line,* looks at the issue of miscegenation in post-Civil War America. Many of the stories, including the title story and "A Matter of Principle," are set in the fictional town of Groveland, Ohio. Many of the characters of the collection are based on mixed-blood people Chesnutt knew in Cleveland. Some stories,

including "The Wife of His Youth," depict prejudice within the African American community, while others portray problems faced by newly freed African Americans and people of mixed blood who are trying to find places for themselves in American society.

Wilcox
Character in *A Soldier's Play*

The Wild Child
Character in *Meridian*

Wild Seed
Please see "Patternist Saga"

Roger Wilkins
American lawyer, educator, and journalist
Born March 25, 1932.

Roger Wood Wilkins is noted for his many editorials written for the *Washington Post, New York Times,* and *Nation* magazine. Abandoning a successful career as a lawyer and public servant, Wilkins left the mainstream to serve the African American public, a journey he related in *A Man's Life: An Autobiography* (1982). He has contributed to numerous periodicals and has written a column for *Mother Jones* magazine.

Born in Kansas City, Missouri, Wilkins moved first to Harlem and then to Grand Rapids, Michigan. He earned his law degree in 1956 and practiced in New York City for several years before departing to serve in a variety of governmental jobs. In 1972 he joined the staff of the *Washington Post,* the first of several editorial positions he would hold before leaving **journalism** to work with various political and black organizations.

Further Readings
Black Writers, first edition, Gale, 1989.

Roy Wilkins

American journalist and statesperson
Born August 30, 1901.
Died September 8, 1981.

Wilkins served for more than sixty years as a speaker for racial equality. The grandson of a Mississippi slave, Wilkins grew up in an integrated neighborhood in St. Paul, Minnesota, and later attended the University of Minnesota. While in college he won an **oratory** contest for his speech protesting a lynching in Duluth, but it was not until he became a newspaper reporter in Kansas City, Missouri, that he experienced racial prejudice firsthand. Wilkins began working for the **National Association for the Advancement of Colored People** (NAACP) in 1931; when NAACP executive secretary **Walter White** died in 1955, Wilkins was elected unanimously to the organization's top post. He was director of the NAACP for twenty-two years, during which forced integration of schools, protest marches, boycotts, sit-ins, and urban riots brought attention to America's racial problems.

Wilkins's greatest achievement in the struggle for civil rights was the 1954 Supreme Court decision *Brown v. Board of Education,* which was argued before the Court by NAACP general counsel Thurgood Marshall. Wilkins also worked personally with Presidents John F. Kennedy and Lyndon Johnson toward the passage of civil rights legislation. As racial protests grew more militant during the 1960s, however, Wilkins condemned the violence and warned of the dangers of a separate society.

Wilkins's last years with the NAACP were difficult. The link he shared with the nation's presidency was broken, and he faced challenges to his leadership within the organization. In 1977, at the age of seventy-six, Wilkins retired and Benjamin Hooks was named the new executive director. Wilkins recorded his experiences in *Talking It Over with Roy Wilkins: Selected Speeches and Writings* (1977) and the postumuously published *Standing Fast: The Autobiography of Roy Wilkins* (1982), coauthored with Tom Mathews. Wilkins won many

Wilkins was director of the NAACP from 1955 to 1977.

awards in his long career, including the NAACP's Spingarn Medal in 1964 and the Presidential Medal of Freedom in 1969.

Further Readings

Black Writers, first edition, Gale, 1989.

Brenda Wilkinson

American poet and author of children's literature
Born January 1, 1946.

Wilkinson is best known for her "Ludell" trilogy of books for children, which have received several awards. Praised for their accurate, yet sensitive and compassionate portrayal of rural Southern black life, *Ludell* (1975), *Ludell and Willie* (1976), and *Ludell's New York Time* (1980) follow the life of a poor, young, black child growing up in Waycross, Georgia, from the mid-1950s through the early 1960s. The second volume of the trilogy was nominated for an American Book Award.

Wilkinson was born in Moultrie, Georgia, and moved to New York, where she attended Hunter College. Her books, which reflect her own experiences growing up in the south and moving north, depict the strong bonds that exist within the African American community. Wilkinson is also the author of *Jesse Jackson: Still Fighting for the Dream* (1990) and *Definitely Cool* (1993).

Further Readings
Black Writers, second edition, Gale, 1994.

Will Harris

Character in *If We Must Die*

William "Beans" Butler

Character in *House of Slammers*

William Cato Douglass

Character in *!Click Song*

William Demby

Character in *The Catacombs*

William Green

Character in *Tar Baby*

William Taylor

Character in *The Third Generation*

Chancellor Williams

American historian and novelist
Born December 22, 1905(?).

The son of a slave, Williams grew up in the South, where he learned to question the disparity in opportunity between blacks and whites. Born in Bennettsville, South Carolina, circa 1905, Williams attended Howard University and in 1949 earned a Ph.D. at American University. His best-known work, the controversial *The Destruction of Black Civilization: Great Issues of a Race from 4500 B.C. to 2000 A.D.* (1971), challenges Eurocentric views of African history, offers theories on black American empowerment based on African models, and proposes a "Master Plan" for black unification and development. The work spans six thousand years of African history, revealing common social patterns within the continent's cultures. Among his other nonfiction works is *Problems in African History* (1964); Williams's fiction includes the **novels** *The Raven* (1943), *Have You Been to the River?* (1952), and *The Second Agreement with Hell* (1979).

Further Readings
Black Writers, second edition, Gale, 1994.
Dictionary of Literary Biography, Volume 76: *Afro-American Writers, 1940-1955,* Gale, 1988.

John A. Williams

American novelist, journalist,
and biographer
Born December 5, 1925.

John Alfred Williams is considered one of the outstanding literary talents of his generation. A prolific writer who utilizes a variety of genres, Williams is praised for his storytelling abilities and his focus on sociopolitical issues that offer hope for greater understanding.

Williams was born in Jackson, Mississippi, and raised in Syracuse, New York. He held a succession of jobs in public relations, radio, television, and publishing prior to the publication of his first **novel,** *The Angry Ones,* in 1960. This and Williams's other early novels, *Night Song* (1961) and *Sissie* (1963), offer cautious optimism through the struggles of their black protagonists. In 1962, *Night Song* was awarded the Prix de Rome by the American Academy of Arts and Letters; however, after Williams was interviewed, the prize was rescinded amid speculations of racial prejudice. Williams next three books, ***The Man Who Cried I Am*** (1967), *Sons of Darkness, Sons of Light: A Novel of Some Probability* (1969) and *Captain Blackman* (1972), offer an apocalyptic view of race relations, pitting black revolutionary impulses against white reactionary conspiracies.

A more hopeful viewpoint—based on black solidarity and emerging group values—is evident in Williams's following three novels: *Mothersill and the Foxes* (1975), *The Junior Bachelor Society* (1976), and *!Click Song* (1982), which won the American Book Award. Williams's later novels include *The Berhama Account* (1985) and *Jacob's Ladder* (1987). He has also written biographies of **Martin Luther King Jr.**, **Richard Wright**, and Richard Pryor, and he has published several nonfiction works that expand on many of the issues examined in his novels.

Further Readings
Black Literature Criticism, Gale, 1992.
Black Writers, second edition, Gale, 1994.
Dictionary of Literary Biography, Volume 33: *Afro-American Fiction Writers after 1955,* Gale, 1984.
Muller, Gilbert H., *John A. Williams,* Twayne, 1984.

Juan Williams
Panamanian-born journalist
Born April 10, 1954.

A staff writer for the *Washington Post,* Williams has contributed innumerable columns and lengthy features on African American issues. He has also served as a commentator for *Inside Washington,* a television program originating in the nation's capital. Williams's interest in civil rights led to the publication of *Eyes on the Prize: America's Civil Rights Years, 1954-1965,* a companion volume to the six-part television series of the same name. Both the series and the book provide an overview of a turbulent period in American history, explaining how the **civil rights movement** began and who made it succeed. Williams has also written *Thurgood Marshall* (1992), a book about the late Supreme Court justice.

Further Readings
Black Writers, second edition, Gale, 1994.

Samm-Art Williams
American dramatist
Born January 20, 1946.

Samuel Arthur Williams became a nationally known playwright with the Broadway production of his comedy-drama *Home* (1979), for which he received a Tony Award nomination. The **play** is about a North Carolina farmer who loses his land while in prison for refusing military service during the Vietnam War; he suffers poverty and alcoholism in a large Northern city after his release but redeems himself by sheer strength of character, returning home to reclaim his farm. Often compared to Mark Twain because of his penchant for tall tales and pungent wit, Williams's other plays, including *The Sixteenth Round* (1980) and *Friends* (1983), range from **epic** tragedies and political dramas to domestic farces. In addition to his theater projects, Williams has worked in television as both a writer and an actor.

Further Readings
Black Writers, first edition, Gale, 1989.

Wilson reacts to news of winning the 1990 Pulitzer Prize for drama.

W Sherley Anne Williams

American fiction writer, poet, and critic
Born August 25, 1944.

Williams is best known for the **novel** *Dessa Rose* (1986), which earned enthusiastic reviews for its exploration of the troubles shared by black and white women in the antebellum South. Williams grew up in a housing project and was orphaned while in her teens. Caring teachers encouraged her to follow her literary leanings. A professor at the University of Southern California at San Diego, Williams has also published an **essay** collection, *Give Birth to Brightness: A Thematic Study in Neo-Black Literature* (1972), and a collection of **poetry,** *Some One Sweet Angel Chile* (1982). Her autobio-

graphical collection *The Peacock Poems* (1975) was nominated for the National Book Award for poetry in 1976.

Further Readings
Black Literature Criticism, Gale, 1992.
Black Writers, second edition, Gale, 1994.

Willie

Character in *We Can't Breathe*

W August Wilson

American playwright
Born in 1945.

In the 1980s, Wilson emerged as a major voice in American theater. His dramas, for which he has received such prizes as the Tony Award, the New York Drama Critics Circle Award, and the Pulitzer Prize, are part of a planned play-cycle about black American experience in the twentieth century.

Wilson grew up in Pittsburgh, Pennsylvania. He quit school at the age of sixteen and soon became active in the theater. In 1968, he founded the Black Horizons Theatre Company in St. Paul, Minnesota. There he wrote his first **play,** *Jitney,* set in a Pittsburgh taxi station. It was accepted for production at the O'Neill Theatre Center's National Playwrights Conference in 1982 and was followed by another play, *Fullerton Street.*

Wilson's reputation was established with the production of his third play, *Ma Rainey's Black Bottom* (1981), at the Yale Repertory Theatre under the direction of Yale Drama School's artistic director Lloyd Richards, who became Wilson's mentor and continued to premier the playwright's works at Yale. The play is named after an actual 1920s blues singer and is set in a rehearsal room, where Ma Rainey's musicians recount the difficulties and violence they have experienced in America. The 1984 Broadway production of *Ma Rainey's Black Bottom* was named Best Play of the Year by the New York Drama Critics' Circle.

Wilson's drama *Fences* (1985) is about a former athlete who forbids his son to accept an athletic scholarship; its Broadway production garnered Wilson another New York Drama Critics' Circle best play award, a Tony Award for best play, and the Pulitzer Prize for drama. The 1988 Broadway production of Wilson's *Joe Turner's Come and Gone* (1986), about an ex-convict's efforts to find his wife, was another New York Drama Critics' Circle Award winner. *The Piano Lesson* (1990), which concerns a black family's conflict over the sale of a piano, earned Wilson another New York Drama Critics' Circle best play award and another Pulitzer Prize. Wilson's 1990 play *Two Trains Running,* which was nominated for a Tony Award, appeared on Broadway in 1992. Three years later Wilson adapted *The Piano Lesson* for television.

Further Readings

Black Literature Criticism, Gale, 1992.

Black Writers, second edition, Gale, 1994.

Pereira, Kim, *An African American Odyssey: Self-Authentication in the Plays of August Wilson,* University of Illinois Press, 1994.

Reference Guide to American Literature, St. James Press, third edition, 1994.

Harriet Wilson's *Our Nig* was the first novel by an African American woman.

Harriet Wilson

American novelist
Born circa 1827.
Died after 1863.

Harriet E. Adams Wilson wrote the earliest extant **novel** by an African American woman. Little is known about her life until 1850, the year that begins the decade covered in her autobiographical novel *Our Nig; or, Sketches from the Life of a Free Black, in a Two-Story White House, North, Showing that Slavery's Shadows Fall Even There* (1859).

In 1850, Wilson apparently travelled to Massachusetts, where she suffered from ill health and became the domestic servant of a woman named Walker. She married Thomas Wilson, a fugitive slave, in 1851 and moved with him to New Hampshire. Thomas abandoned his wife shortly before the birth of their son George in 1852. Though he returned for a time, Thomas left again and Wilson was forced to place her son in foster care. Wilson moved to Boston in 1855 and worked as a dressmaker. While in Boston she wrote *Our Nig,* which tells of the **racism** and brutality endured by a black woman indentured in the North. Wilson published the novel hoping to make enough money to retrieve her son, as she explains in a direct appeal to the reader at the end of the text. No documentation of her life after 1863 survives.

Further Readings

Dictionary of Literary Biography, Volume 50: *Afro-American Writers before the Harlem Renaissance,* Gale, 1986.

The Wings of Oppression

Leslie Pinckney Hill
Poetry, 1921

For *The Wings of Oppression,* **Leslie Pinckney Hill** composed a sonnet to commemorate a lynching and blank verse in honor of cultural renewal among blacks despite organized opposition. He wrote about Jim Crow laws and the involvement of blacks in American armed forces during World War I. These poems were designed to advocate self-determination even as they exhorted the reader to rise above hatred and bitterness. Hill's upbeat approach is evident in the subtitles for each of the sections: "Poems of My People," "Poems of the Times," "Poems of Appreciation," "Songs," and "Poems of the Spirit." "To a Caged Canary in a Negro Restaurant" and "Armageddon" develop the theme of countering indignities through pride and hope.

The Women of Brewster Place

Gloria Naylor
Novel, 1982

Gloria Naylor's *The Women of Brewster Place* is woven from individual stories and focuses on the relationships between seven black female residents of Brewster Place—a dilapidated ghetto housing project in an unidentified northern city. As they cope with living in a racist and sexist society, they encounter further abuse from their own husbands, lovers, and chil-

dren. The stories are framed by a prologue entitled "Dawn" and an epilogue called "Dusk." The central character of the **novel** is Mattie Michaels, who, after being seduced by Butch Fuller, bears an illegitimate child and attempts to raise her son alone. He grows up a spoiled delinquent, however, and jumps bail one day, leaving her penniless. So Mattie's friend at Brewster Place, Eva Turner, takes her in. Another story features Etta Mae Johnson, who also helps Mattie when she is betrayed by her son. In Etta Mae's own story, Mattie returns the favor by helping to heal her friend. Mattie also comforts Lucielia Turner in another story, in which Lucielia loses her child to accidental death. In another story, "Kiswana," the adopted name of Melanie Browne, tries to find her roots in Brewster Place rather than in her suburban home. Kiswana experiences a self-revelation when her mother reveals the family's African American heritage. Kiswana, in a following story, tries without success to introduce a welfare mother, Cora Lee, to black high culture. "The Two" involves lesbians Lorraine and Theresa with Ben the janitor. When Lorraine is gang raped by local hood C. C. Baker and his cohorts, she mistakes Ben for a perpetrator and kills him, before dying herself. The final story, "The Block Party," concerns Mattie's dream about tearing down the wall where Lorraine had been gang raped. The novel does not reveal if the wall is really torn down, after all. *The Women of Brewster Place* won an American Book Award in 1983.

Women, Culture, and Politics

Angela Davis
Nonfiction, 1989

For this work, **Angela Davis** adapted **speeches** she had delivered during a five-year period in the mid-1980s. As a professor at San Francisco State University, she felt compelled to point out the ways in which gender, race, and class interact to hold back certain groups in

America. Her arguments in *Women, Culture, and Politics* specifically apply to young black women. One **essay** declares that peace and the military economy in the United States are issues that pose problems that strongly affect African American women. Other sections examine daily life for women in different areas of Africa. In Egypt she interviews black women who believe that her questions about their sexual activities exemplify First World **racism**. Others, she reports, wonder about sexual repression in Egyptian society. Davis also pledges support for artistic endeavors and their potential effect on social mores. In her most crucial argument, however, she portrays the feminist movement as a threat to attempted alliances between labor organizations and African American groups. This she attributes to racism and classism among middle-class white feminists, and she gives examples of a long history of such attitudes going back to early American suffragettes. The only solution to this impasse would be complete socialist reform of the capitalist political structure of the United States.

Woodson founded the *Journal of Negro History* in 1916 and became dean of the School of Liberal Arts at Howard University in 1919. In 1921 he founded Associated Publishers, Inc., which allowed him and his colleagues to disseminate their work at a time when few established publishers were interested in black history, and in 1926 he founded Negro History Week, a precursor of Black History Month. He returned to the subject of education in 1933 with *The Mis-Education of the Negro,* in which he criticized the lack of racial pride among African Americans. In 1937, Woodson founded the *Negro History Bulletin.*

The author of more than fifteen books, Woodson wrote additional scholarly works documenting African American education, the history of black **folklore**, migration, family and work life, and the church, among other topics. Woodson died in Washington, D.C., and was buried in Lincoln Memorial Cemetery in Suitland, Maryland.

Further Readings

Black Writers, second edition, Gale, 1994.

McKissack, Patricia, and Frederick McKissack, *Carter Godwin Woodson: The Father of Black History,* Enslow, 1991.

Carter G. Woodson

American historian
Born December 19, 1875.
Died April 3, 1950.

Carter Godwin Woodson has been called the father of black history. He pioneered the study of black people's contributions to society and culture in the United States.

The child of former slaves, Woodson was born into a large, poor family in New Canton, Virginia, on December 19, 1875. He received bachelor's degrees from Berea College in 1903 and 1907, a master's degree in 1908 from the University of Chicago, and a doctorate from Harvard University in 1912. He established himself as an authority on African American history in 1915 with the publication of his first book, *Education of the Negro Prior to 1861.*

The World of African Song

Miriam Makeba
Music, 1971

Illustrated by Dean Alexander, *The World of African Song* is a collection of twenty-four songs from **Miriam Makeba**'s repertoire. Comments on performances as well as English translations of the lyrics accompany the music, which is arranged for piano and guitar. Traditional and recent South African folk songs as well as songs by contemporary South African musicians are included. The introduction by Solomon Mbabi-Katana provides a brief history of African music and a discussion of indigenous musical instruments.

A World View of Race

Ralph Bunche
Nonfiction, 1936

The result of **Ralph Bunche**'s postdoctoral work in anthropology and colonial policy, *A World View of Race* explores the concept of race and its political function. Bunche argues that race is a mutable concept rather than a scientific fact, and he outlines the role of race in economic and political conflict, imperialism, and the United States' domestic policies. Bunche also addresses contemporary movements to which racial distinctions were integral—the rise of Naziism in Europe and the threat of fascism in the American South.

Wouldn't Take Nothing For My Journey Now

Maya Angelou
Essays, 1993

In twenty-four brief **essays**, **Maya Angelou** offers the lessons she has learned from her life as an African American woman who grew up in Stamps, Arkansas, and went on to read one of her poems at a presidential inauguration. Combining **autobiography** with philosophical meditation, these sermonettes yield what she calls "life lessons" on such topics as tolerance, respect for others, personal charity, virtue, the importance of a personal style, the benefits of living creatively, the challenge of changing directions, death, and renewal. She praises the women whose courage, endurance, faith, and joy have benefitted her. The book is dedicated to Oprah Winfrey.

The Wretched of the Earth

Frantz Fanon
Nonfiction, 1965

Frantz Fanon's best-known work, *The Wretched of the Earth* (originally published as *Les Damnés de la terre,* 1961), is a scathing indictment of **colonialism** and **racism** in Third World countries. It is also a call to arms, for Fanon proposes that those people most oppressed by colonial rule must use violence to gain political independence, a prerequisite for true economic and social improvement. In later sections of the work, Fanon discusses the momentum of such a violent revolution, the likely role of nationalism in a new state, and the nature of post-revolutionary culture. The final section of the work is a collection of psychiatric case studies of mental disorders that Fanon suggests are a result of life under colonial rule.

Charles Stevenson Wright

American novelist
Born June 4, 1932.

Wright is known as a writer whose fiction focuses on how **racism** deprives blacks of financial stability and social status, but who has used humor, sarcasm, and **surrealism** to depict their struggles. His first **novel,** *The Messenger* (1963), is based on his experience trying to earn a living as a writer in New York. Wright turned to **satire** in his second novel, *The Wig: A Mirror Image* (1966), in which a fair-skinned black man straightens his hair and bleaches it blond. Naively confident with his new hairstyle, or "wig," he embarks on a picaresque journey through Manhattan in search of wealth and power. ***Absolutely Nothing to Get Alarmed About*** (1973) is more pessimistic, expressing all the disillusionment and none of the hope of Wright's previous works.

Further Readings

Black Literature Criticism, Gale, 1992.
Black Writers, first edition, Gale, 1989.

Jay Wright

American poet, playwright, and educator
Born May 25, 1935.

Born and raised in the American Southwest, Wright has written **poetry, plays,** and

essays that explore history and **myth** from a multicultural perspective. His allegorical and autobiographical poems often take the form of spiritual journeys or quests for answers to the perplexing questions of the soul. The author of *The Homecoming Singer* (1971), *Soothsayers and Omens* (1976), *The Double Invention of Komo* (1980), *Explications/Interpretations* (1984), and *Selected Poems of Jay Wright*(1987), among others, Wright has lived in Mexico, Scotland, and New England. He is the recipient of numerous grants and awards and was a MacArthur fellow from 1986 until 1991.

Further Readings

Black Writers, second edition, Gale, 1994.

Dictionary of Literary Biography, Volume 41: *Afro-American Poets since 1955,* Gale, 1985.

Richard Wright at work in his home.

 ## Richard Wright

American novelist
Born September 4, 1908.
Died November 28, 1960.

An essential figure in the development of African American literature, influencing such authors as **Ralph Ellison** and **James Baldwin**, Richard Nathaniel Wright has been called one of most powerful writers of the twentieth century. The central characters in his fiction are usually bitter, alienated black men, and his treatment of their experiences provides a vivid portrayal of both the economic and psychological effects of **racism**.

Wright was born in Roxie, Mississippi, on September 4, 1908. His mother was a school-teacher and his father worked as a sharecropper until Wright was three, when the family moved to Memphis, Tennessee. His father deserted them there, and Wright grew up in extreme poverty, shuttling between relatives. His tumultuous childhood was further complicated by his mother's frequent illnesses: she suffered a stroke in 1919, and in 1920 Wright was sent to his grandmother's home in Jackson, where he remained until 1925.

Wright had little formal education. He left school for the last time in the mid-1920s and went to work in Memphis, where he read voraciously. He migrated to Chicago in 1927 at the age of nineteen, finding a job as a postal clerk and continuing to educate himself. He became interested in communism during this period and joined the Communist Party in 1933; he eventually resigned in 1944, however, disillusioned with the party's ideological rigidity.

The ten years Wright spent in Chicago marked his early development as an artist. In 1935, he completed "Cesspool," a **novel** detailing a single day in the life of an angry, black postal worker; the work was not published until after his death, appearing as *Lawd Today* in 1963. He also began composing four novellas about racial oppression in the South; in 1938, these novellas became his first published book, entitled *Uncle Tom's Children.*

Wright had left Chicago for New York in 1937, and in 1939 he was awarded a Guggenheim fellowship, which he used to complete *Native Son* (1940), a novel about a black man who accidently kills a white woman and then murders his mistress. The book sold two hundred thousand copies in less than a month; Wright was compared to Theodore Dreiser and John Steinbeck.

Wright received the Spingarn Medal in the early 1940s, and in 1943 he began writing an autobiographical account of his childhood. *Black Boy: A Record of Childhood and Youth* (1945) chronicles both the cruelty of racial attitudes among Southern whites and what Wright calls the "negative confusions" of the black community. The work was acclaimed by a number of noted individuals, and by March of that year *Black Boy* had sold over four hundred thousand copies.

Wright was married twice, to two white women. His first marriage, to Rose Dhimah Meadman in the late 1930s, ended after the couple separated in 1940. Following his divorce, he remarried in March of 1941, to Ellen Poplar, with whom he had two daughters. The commercial success of his books allowed him to travel to Europe, and in 1947 he immigrated with his family to France, where he remained for the rest of his life.

Living in Paris, Wright read widely in continental philosophies, particularly existentialism. He published three novels during this period, *The Outsider* (1953), *Savage Holiday* (1954), and *The Long Dream* (1958), but none were as well received as his early works. In 1960, he found a publisher for a collection of stories entitled *Eight Men,* which was published posthumously in 1961. Wright died of a heart attack on November 28, 1960, at the age of fifty-two. He is buried in Père Lachaise cemetery, in Paris.

Further Readings
Black Literature Criticism, Gale, 1992.

Black Writers, first edition, Gale, 1989.

Brignano, Russell Carl, *Richard Wright: An Introduction to the Man and His Works,* University of Pittsburgh Press, 1970.

Dictionary of Literary Biography, Volume 76: *Afro-American Writers, 1940-1955,* Gale, 1988.

Webb, Constance, *Richard Wright: A Biography,* Putnam, 1968.

Sara E. Wright
American poet, novelist, and nonfiction writer
Born December 9, 1928.

Born in Wetipquin, Maryland, Sarah Elizabeth Wright attended Howard University, where she was encouraged by **Sterling Brown**, **Owen Dodson**, and **Langston Hughes**. Wright left Howard in 1949 and moved to New York City, where she, Aminata Moseka, **Rosa Guy**, and **Maya Angelou** formed the Cultural Association for Women of African Heritage. Wright later worked as a teacher and at a publishing house in the Philadelphia area, where she cofounded the Philadelphia Writers' Workshop. In 1955, Wright and Lucy Smith published the **poetry** collection *Give Me a Child,* which contains the frequently anthologized "To Some Millions Who Survive Joseph Mander Sr." In 1957, Wright returned to New York, where she joined the Harlem Writers' Guild, whose members included **John Oliver Killens**, **John Henrik Clarke**, **Alice Childress**, and **Paule Marshall**. While there, Wright completed her **novel** *This Child's Gonna Live* (1969), which explores the desperate circumstances of a black family in rural Maryland.

An active member of the Guild until 1972, Wright has since devoted much of her time to teaching at writing workshops. Recently, she wrote *A. Philip Randolph: Integration in the Workplace* (1990), which is part of a series on the history of the **civil rights movement**.

Further Readings
Black Writers, second edition, Gale, 1994.

Dictionary of Literary Biography, Volume 33: *Afro-American Fiction Writers after 1955,* Gale, 1984.

"Xenogenesis" Trilogy
Octavia E. Butler
Novels, 1987-1989

Octavia E. Butler's *Xenogenesis Saga* recounts the adventures of a minority race of humans who must survive as the subjects of a superior extraterrestrial race called the Oankali. These works of **science fiction** focus on the themes of cultural confrontation and accommodation.

In the first **novel** of the saga, *Dawn* (1987), Butler explores the consciousness of Lilith Iyapo, a young black Californian who must learn to tolerate and eventually love the reptilian Oankali who becomes her mate. As Lilith tries to convince other humans to follow her example, she becomes alienated from human society. Lilith's child, Akin, is the protagonist of *Adulthood Rites* (1988). He is kidnapped from his Oankali home and sold to humans who settle with resisters in Phoenix. Akin eventually learns about his own heritage and comes to like humans, and he eventually takes some of his human friends to establish a settlement on Mars. In the final novel of the series, *Imago* (1989), Jodahs and his sibling Aaor have a difficult passage to adulthood as they try to find human mates. At one point, they battle with human resisters, but Jodahs finally wins the trust of their opponents.

X/Self
Edward Kamau Brathwaite
Poetry, 1987

X/Self is the third volume of **Edward Kamau Brathwaite**'s second trilogy of verse. The pieces in the first two volumes, *Mother Poem* (1977) and *Sun Poem* (1982), are set in the Caribbean, while those in *X/Self,* a complex study in centrality and marginality, take place in a mythical "Rome." Severus is the first African to become emperor of Rome, and he brings his marginality with him into the center of Europe. Later, at the edge of the empire, he is defeated and killed, and thus remarginalized. X/Self is the name for the Creole tribes—both loyal and treacherous—who occupy the borders of the empire. *X/Self* examines issues of identity, communication, and miscommunication, using experimental language and "calibanisms," or wordplay.

Xuma
Character in *Mine Boy*

Camille Yarbrough

American poet and fiction writer
Born in 1938.

Yarbrough was a successful dancer and actress before turning to writing. She performed with the **Katherine Dunham** dance troupe and appeared in **plays** and feature films, including *Shaft* in 1973. Yarbrough's writings are directed toward older children and young adults. Her **poetry** collection *Cornrows* (1979) and her **novel** *The Shimmershine Queens* (1989) encourage youngsters to be proud of their African heritage. Yarbrough works in the tradition of West African griot storytellers, using oral history, dance, music, and mime to excite interest in African American culture.

Further Readings
Black Writers, second edition, Gale, 1994.
Children's Literature Review, Volume 29, Gale, 1993.

Yeager
Character in *The Hippodrome*

Frank Yerby
American novelist
Born September 5, 1916.
Died November 29, 1991.

Frank Garvin Yerby was a prolific writer who produced more than 30 novels during his lifetime. His books were primarily adventure stories with colorful language and complex plotlines; several of his works were filmed by major studios. Although many of his novels were best-sellers (over 50 million copies of his books have been sold), Yerby's work was routinely slighted by critics and earmarked as formulaic "pulp" fiction.

The second of four children of a racially mixed couple, Yerby was born in Augusta, Georgia. An excellent student, he attended a private black school and earned a B.A. degree in English from Paine College in 1937 and an M.A. in English from Fisk University in 1938. He began a Ph.D. program in English at the University of Chicago but left after nine months for financial reasons. After teaching at black universities in Florida and Louisiana, Yerby abandoned academia and moved with his first wife to Dearborn, Michigan, to work in a defense plant.

Yerby wrote during this period but was largely unsuccessful until he published the **short story** "Health Card" (1944), which focused on racial injustice and earned Yerby national attention and the O. Henry Memorial Award for the best first story. While his short stories of this period deal with blacks and their environment, the majority of Yerby's novels address racial issues indirectly and focus primarily on white characters.

Yerby's first novel, *The Foxes of Harrow* (1946), was a Southern historical romance. Although critics denounced the novel, it sold millions of copies, was translated into at least twelve languages, and was adapted as a film in 1951. Yerby followed *The Foxes of Harrow* with *The Vixens* (1948), *The Golden Hawk* (1949) and many other publications. Throughout his literary career, Yerby covered such diverse themes as the antebellum South, ancient Greece, early **Christianity**, thirteenth-century crusades, revolution, and prostitution. One of his more critically respected novels, *The Dahomean* (1972), is the story of an African tribal leader in which Yerby directly deals with racial concerns.

From 1955 until his death, Yerby was a resident of Spain, where he married his second wife. An expatriate, Yerby also lived in France

for an extended period. He died of heart failure in Madrid, Spain, and was buried near that city.

Further Readings
Black Writers, first edition, Gale, 1989.
Dictionary of Literary Biography, Volume 76: *Afro-American Writers, 1940-1955,* Gale, 1988.

Yoruba Evelyn Lovejoy
Character in *The Cotillion*

Al Young
American novelist and poet
Born May 31, 1939.

Albert James Young creates highly individualized characters who search for a sense of belonging and seek to come to terms with their lives. He is praised for his rendering of black speech and vernacular. His early career as a **jazz** musician influenced his writing, and his first **novel,** *Snakes* (1970), is the story of the growth of a young musician who moves to New York. The inner journeys of central characters are also explored in the novels *Who Is Angelina?* (1975) and *Sitting Pretty* (1976). In his **poetry,** Young captures both the language of the ghetto and the details of everyday life; his collections include *Dancing* (1969) and *Geography of the Near Past* (1976). His collected poetry was published in 1980.

Further Readings
Black Literature Criticism, Gale, 1992.
Black Writers, second edition, Gale, 1994.

The Young Landlords
Walter Dean Myers
Young adult novel, 1979

Walter Dean Myers's young adult **novel** concerns six ghetto children who become landlords. They buy a rundown tenement from an unscrupulous speculator, Mr. Harley, for a dollar. Paul Williams, who narrates the tale, leads the troupe of reformers—who call themselves the Action Group—in their quest to rehabilitate "The Joint." Paul finds love with a cohort named Gloria, encounters wacky neighbors and exasperating local bureaucrats, and becomes involved in a mystery surrounding stolen stereo equipment. The Action Group discovers that becoming landlords takes more work than they originally expected, but they learn responsibility and community spirit along the way. With the help of a friendly accountant, they keep their heads above water. They also identify the robber. *The Young Landlords* won a Coretta Scott King Award.

Whitney M. Young Jr.

American nonfiction writer
Born July 31, 1921.
Died March 11, 1971.

As director of the National Urban League from 1961 to 1971, Whitney Moore Young Jr. worked for civil rights through his connections to political and business leaders, which often prompted criticism from other blacks. Young considered himself an intermediary between blacks and whites, though critics believed he was compromised by his connections and that he had little influence in the African American community.

Born on July 31, 1921, in Lincoln Ridge, Kentucky, to parents who were active in education, Young earned his B.S. from Kentucky State College in 1941. He then entered the Massachusetts Institute of Technology before receiving an M.A. in social work from the University of Minnesota in 1947. During World War II, he served in an engineering company led by white officers and often helped mediate their disputes with the black enlisted men. In 1944, he married Margaret Buckner; the couple had two children. Three years later he began working for the Urban League in Minnesota and then in

Whitney M. Young Jr. was director of the National Urban League from 1961 to 1971.

Nebraska. In 1961, he left a position at Atlanta University to become executive director of the National Urban League.

During his tenure at the Urban League, Young supervised the opening of thirty-five new chapters, extended operations into urban slums, and increased the budget from $300,000 to almost $35 million. But the overwhelming majority of benefactors to the Urban League were white members of the social and political establishment, and Young often found himself accused of catering to the backers while abandoning the principles of the black movement. Young argued that he was working with the persons—the government and industry leaders—he felt could most directly affect the economic status of blacks.

Young examined racial issues in many of his writings: he published *To Be Equal* in 1964 and, in 1969, released ***Beyond Racism: Building an Open Society***, which received a Christopher Award. Among his other titles are *Status of the Negro Community* (1959) and *Integration: The Role of Labor Education* (1959). In the late 1960s, he hoped to assist the Nixon administration but became disillusioned with its policy on addressing issues facing African Americans. Young died of a heart attack on March 11, 1979, while in Nigeria and is buried in Hartsdale, New York.

Further Readings
Black Writers, first edition, Gale, 1989.

Youngblood
John Oliver Killens
Novel, 1954

Youngblood, **John Oliver Killens**'s first **novel**, examines themes of racial repression, the meaning of manhood, labor relations, and interracial friendship in the early twentieth-century American South. It tells the story of the Youngblood family—Joe and Laurie Lee Youngblood and their two children, Jennie Lee and Robby—and its struggle to overcome the consequences of **segregation** in the small town of Crossroads, Georgia. The Youngbloods are aided in their fight for racial justice by some of their fellow townspeople, including Robby's teacher Richard Wendell Myles and his fiancée, Josephine Rollins; the white laborer Oscar Jefferson, his son, and his black friend Little Jim Kilgrow; and the white physician at a local hospital, Dr. Riley.

Disgusted with the **racism** and poor quality of life in the South, Joe Youngblood wants to move his family north. However, circumstances put this goal out of his reach. He is regularly cheated by the paymaster at his job. His son Robby is arrested by the police for fighting with some white boys and the police force Laurie Lee to punish her son publicly for the incident,

humiliating them both. Joe begins to organize labor unions, hoping to unite both black and white workers. In the process, he is wounded, but both his black and white friends join to help him. A group of black men drives off Ku Klux Klan members who seek to lynch him. Richard Myles persuades his friend Dr. Riley to admit Joe to a whites-only hospital and Oscar Jefferson's son agrees to provide the blood necessary for a transfusion. However, Joe dies as the novel ends, a martyr to the struggle for civil rights. His son Robby makes a vow to continue his father's work in unionizing the workers of Crossroads.

The Younger Family
Characters in *A Raisin in the Sun*

Your Arms Too Short to Box with God
Vinnette Carroll, Alex Bradford, and Micki Grant
Play, first produced 1975

A critically acclaimed two-act musical based on the Gospel of St. Matthew, *Your Arms Too Short to Box with God* features music and lyrics by **Vinnette Carroll,** Alex Bradford, and Micki Grant. Commissioned by the Italian government and directed by Carroll, the **play** was first performed in Spoleto, Italy, at the Festival of Two Worlds in 1975. It was later featured at Ford's Theatre in Washington, D.C., on Broadway, and in a six-month tour that, due to its popularity, was extended to nearly a year and a half. Framed by a church service, the play traces scriptural events from the day Jesus Christ arrives in Jerusalem to the morning of the resurrection.

Zarita
Series character in "Simple" Stories

Zeely

Virginia Hamilton
Novel, 1967

Eleven-year-old Elizabeth "Geeder" Perry visits her uncle's farm for the summer with her brother and develops a fascination for a mysterious and statuesque neighbor girl, Zeely Taber. When Geeder discovers a striking resemblance between Zeely and a photo of a Watusi queen, she fantasizes that Zeely is actually African royalty. Geeder eventually talks to Zeely, who gently teaches her a lesson in reality through a folktale. **Virginia Hamilton**'s first **novel**, noted for its skillful use of language, was chosen as an American Library Association Notable Book, and was also the winner of the Nancy Block Award for racial understanding.

Zeely Taber

Character in *Zeely*

Zooman

Character in *Zooman and the Sign*

Zooman and the Sign

Charles Fuller
Play, first produced 1980, published 1982

The eponymous character of **Charles Fuller**'s drama is a disaffected black youth who accidentally shoots and kills twelve-year-old Jinny Tate as she plays jacks on her front porch. Although neighbors witnessed the murder, fear prevents them from speaking out, much to the frustration of Jinny's parents. As a last resort, Jinny's father Reuben erects a sign on his front porch proclaiming, "The killers of our daughter Jinny are free on the streets because our neighbors will not identify them." Set in a decaying Philadelphia neighborhood over the course of four days, scenes of a family grieving are interspersed with depictions of a remorseless Zooman, who is eventually shot down himself. Although it met with mixed reviews, Fuller's drama was awarded two Obie Awards.

Zoot September

Character in *Buckingham Palace, District Six*

Zora Banks

Character in *Disappearing Acts*

Acknowledgments

The editors wish to thank the copyright holders of the excerpted text included in this volume and the permissions managers of many book and magazine publishing companies for assisting us in securing reprint rights. We are also grateful to the staffs of the Detroit Public Library, the Library of Congress, the University of Detroit Mercy Library, Wayne State University Purdy/Kresge Library Complex, and the University of Michigan Libraries for making their resources available to us. Following is a list of the copyright holders who have granted us permission to reprint material in *The Schomburg Center Guide to Black Literature*. Every effort has been made to trace copyright, but if omissions have been made, please let us know.

Copyrighted Excerpts in *The Schomburg Center Guide to Black Literature* were reprinted from the following books:

Baldwin, James. From *Nobody Knows My Name: More Notes of a Native Son.* Dell Publishing Co., Inc., 1961. Copyright © 1961 by James Baldwin. All rights reserved.—Carmichael, Stokley and Charles V. Hamilton. From *Power: The Politics of Liberation in America.* Random House, 1967. © Copyright, 1967 by Stokley Carmichael and Charles Hamilton. All rights reserved.—Ellison, Ralph. From *Invisible Man.* Vintage Books, 1972. Copyright 1947, 1948, 1952 by Ralph Ellison. All rights reserved.—Giovanni, Nikki. From *Sacred Cows and Other Edibles.* William Morrow and Company, Inc. Copyright © 1988 by Nikki Giovanni. All rights reserved.—Jones, Gayl. From *Song for Anninho.* Lotus Press, 1981. Copyright © 1981 by Gayl Jones. All rights reserved. Reprinted by permission of the publisher.—Lorde, Audre. From *Coal.* W. W. Norton & Company, Inc. Copyright © 1968, 1970, 1976 by Audre Lorde. All rights reserved.—Morrison, Toni. From *Beloved.* Alfred A. Knopf, 1987. Copyright © 1987 by Toni Morrison. All rights reserved.—Nkrumah, Kwame. From *The Autobiography of Kwame Nkrumah.* Thomas Nelson and Sons Ltd., 1957. © Kwame Nkrumah 1957.—Parks, Gordon. From *Born Black.* J. B. Lippincott Company, 1971. Copyright © 1971, 1970, 1968, 1967, 1966, 1965, 1963 by Gordon Parks. All rights reserved.—Reed, Ishmael. From *Yellow Back Radio Broke–Down.* Doubleday & Company, Inc., 1969. Copyright © 1969 by Ishmael Reed. All rights reserved.—Soyinka, Wole. From *Collected Plays.* Oxford University Press, 1973. © Wole Soyinka 1973.—Toomer, Jean. From *Cane.* Liveright, 1923. Copyright 1923 by Boni & Liveright. Renewed 1951 by Jean Toomer. Reprinted by permission of Liveright Publishing Corporation.—Walcott, Derek. From *Omeros.* Farrar Straus Giroux, 1990. Copyright © 1990 by Derek Walcott. All rights reserved.

Photographs and Illustrations appearing in *The Schomburg Center Guide to Black Literature* were received from the following sources:

Cover photographs: Archive Photos; AP/Wide World Photos; © Jerry Bauer.

© Jerry Bauer: **pp. 4, 174, 247, 259, 285, 377, 385, 460, 462;** Jacket of *Anthills of the Savannah,* by Chinua Achebe. Copyright. Used by permission of Doubleday, a division of Bantam Doubleday Dell Publishing Group, Inc.: **p. 16;** Cover of *Arrow of God,* by Chinua

Achebe. Copyright © 1964, 1974 by Paul Bacon. Used by permission of Doubleday, a division of Bantam Doubleday Dell Publishing Group, Inc.: **p. 19;** Cover of *Things Fall Apart,* by Chinua Achebe. Copyright © 1988 by Paul Wearing. Reprinted by permission of Heinemann Educational Books: **p. 441;** Jacket of *No Longer at Ease,* by Chinua Achebe. Copyright. Reprinted by permission of Heinemann Educational Books: **p. 322;** AP/Wide World Photos: **pp. 1, 13, 21, 65, 66, 68, 74, 75, 87, 89, 123, 137, 138, 143, 148, 167, 171, 193, 207, 215, 250, 257, 270, 273, 282, 283, 301, 342, 412, 463, 475, 477, 489;** Cover of *I Know Why the Caged Bird Sings,* by Maya Angelou. Copyright © 1969 by Maya Angelou. Used by permission of Bantam Books, a division of Bantam Doubleday Dell Publishing Group, Inc.: **p. 217;** Archive Photos: **pp. 30, 71, 109, 142, 146, 151, 185, 189, 212, 245, 292, 335, 337, 391, 468;** Photograph by Blackstone-Shelburne, N.Y.: **p. 31;** Camera Press/Archive Photos: **pp. 28, 32, 406;** Jacket of *Nobody Knows My Name,* by James Baldwin. Copyright. Used by permission of Doubleday, a division of Bantam Doubleday Dell Publishing Group, Inc.: **p. 323;** Jacket of *Just above My Head,* by James Baldwin. Copyright. Used by permission of Doubleday, a division of Bantam Doubleday Dell Publishing Group, Inc.: **p. 241;** UPI/Bettmann: pp. **35, 58, 77, 81, 94, 121, 237, 277, 396, 397, 470, 480;** Facsimile of manuscript from *Preface to a Twenty Volume Suicide Note,* by Amiri Baraka. Reprinted by permission of Lilly Library, Indiana University and Amiri Baraka: **p. 350;** Facsimile of manuscript from *Dutchman,* by Amiri Baraka. Reprinted by permission of Lilly Library, Indiana University and Amiri Baraka: **p. 145;** Cover of *A Hero Ain't Nothin' but a Sandwich,* by Alice Childress. Copyright © 1973 by Alice Childress. Reprinted by permission of Avon Books: **p. 205;** Agence France Presse/Archive Photos: **p. 97;** © 1988 Layle Silbert: **p. 98;** Photograph by Ellen Banner: **p. 107;** Title page of *Folks*

Like Me, by Sam Cornish. Copyright © 1993 by Sam Cornish. Reprinted by permission of Zoland Books, Inc.: **p. 354;** The Bettmann Archive: pp. **114, 115, 141, 308, 321, 369, 485;** Facsimile of manuscript from *Requiescam,* by Countee Cullen. Reprinted by permission of the Estate of Countee Cullen and the Amistad Research Center at Tulane University: **p. 195;** Facsimile of manuscript of *Song in Spite of Myself,* by Countee Cullen. Reprinted by permission of the Estate of Countee Cullen and the Amistad Research Center at Tulane University: **p. 355;** Cover of *Narrative of the Life of Frederick Douglass, An American Slave,* by Frederick Douglass. Copyright © 1968 by The New American Library. Used by permission of Dutton Signet, a division of Penguin Books USA Inc.: **p. 310;** Cover of *Invisible Man,* by Ralph Ellison. Copyright © 1947, 1948, 1952 by Ralph Ellison. Copyright © renewed 1980 by Ralph Ellison. Cover design by Janet Odgis & Company. Reprinted by permission of Vintage Books, a division of Random House, Inc.: **p. 325;** Jacket of *Black Women Writers (1950–1980): A Critical Evaluation,* edited by Mari Evans. Copyright. Used by permission of Doubleday, a division of Bantam Doubleday Dell Publishing Group, Inc.: **p. 53;** Jacket of *A Lesson before Dying,* by Ernest J. Gaines. Copyright © 1993 by Ernest J. Gaines. Jacket photograph by Walker Evans; © estate of Walker Evans. Jacket design by Archie Ferguson. Cover design reprinted by permission of Alfred A. Knopf, Inc.: **p. 258;** Cover of *The Autobiography of Miss Jane Pittman,* by Ernest J. Gaines. Copyright © 1971 by Ernest J. Gaines. Used by permission of Bantam books, a division of Bantam Doubleday Dell Publishing Group, Inc.: **p. 26;** UPI/Bettmann Newsphotos: **p. 173, 191, 236;** © Nancy Crampton: **p. 170, 179, 223, 235, 465;** Jacket of *Roots: The Saga of an American Family,* by Alex Haley. Copyright © 1976 by Alex Haley. Used by permission of Doubleday, a division of Bantam Doubleday Dell Publishing Group, Inc.: **p. 394;** Photograph by

Carlo Ontal: **p. 192;** Facsimile of manuscript from *The Sign in Sidney Brustein's Window,* by Lorraine Hansberry. Reprinted by permission of The Estate of Robert Nemiroff: **p. 416;** © Rollie McKenna: **p. 200;** Photograph by John I. Lattony Sr. : **p. 213;** Cover of *Their Eyes Were Watching God,* by Zora Neale Hurston. Copyright © 1937 by J. B. Lippincott Company. Copyright © 1965 by John C. Hurston and Joel Hurston. Reprinted by permission of HarperCollins Publishers, Inc.: **p. 439;** Cover of *Mules and Men,* by Zora Neale Hurston. Cover illustration copyright © 1990 by David Diaz. Cover design by Suzanne Noli. Reprinted by permission of HarperCollins Publishers, Inc.: **p. 304;** Cover of *Dust Tracks on a Road,* by Zora Neale Hurston. Cover illustration © by David Diaz. Cover design by Suzanne Noli. Reprinted by permission of HarperCollins Publishers, Inc.: **p. 144;** Photograph courtesy of Moorland Spingarn Research Center: **p. 234;** Cover of *The Autobiography of an Ex-Colored Man,* by James Weldon Johnson. Introduction and notes copyright © 1990 by William L. Andrews. Used by permission of Viking Penguin, a division of Penguin Books USA Inc. Cover art work reprinted by permission of The Schomburg Center for Research in Black Culture: **p. 24;** Jacket of *Waiting to Exhale,* by Terry McMillan. Copyright 1992 by Terry McMillan. Jacket design by Neil Stuart. Jacket art from the original painting *Ensemble* by Synthia Saint James. Used by permission of Viking Penguin, a division of Penguin Books, USA Inc.: **p. 461;** © Layle Silbert: **pp. 246, 274;** Frank Leonardo/Archive Photos: **p. 248;** Fred W. McDarrah: **pp. 242, 249;** Photograph courtesy of Beinecke Library: **p. 255;** Layle Silbert: **pp. 252, 267;** © Peter Iovino/SAGA All Rights Reserved/Archive Photos: **p. 276;** Jacket of *Sula,* by Toni Morrison. Copyright © 1973 by Toni Morrison. Jacket design by Wendell Minor. Reprinted by permission of Alfred A. Knopf, Inc.: **p. 433;** Jacket of *Song of Solomon,* by Toni Morrison. Copyright © 1977 by Toni Morrison. Jacket design by R. D. Scudellari. Reprinted by permission of Alfred E Knopf, Inc.: **p. 423;** Jacket of *Tar Baby,* by Toni Morrison. Copyright © 1981 by Toni Morrison. Jacket design by R. D. Scudellari. Reprinted by permission of Alfred A. Knopf, Inc.: **p. 437;** Cover of *The Bluest Eye,* by Toni Morrison. Copyright © 1970 by Toni Morrison. Reprinted by permission of Pocket Books, a Division of Simon & Schuster Inc.: **p. 57;** Jacket of *Jazz,* by Toni Morrison. Copyright © 1992 by Toni Morrison. Jacket design by R. D. Scudellari. Reprinted by permission of Alfred A. Knopf, Inc.: **p. 229;** Autographed title page of *Linden Hills,* by Gloria Naylor. Copyright © 1985 by Gloria Naylor. Used by permission of Viking Penguin, a division of Penguin Books USA: **p. 313;** Facsimile of manuscript from *Mumbo Jumbo,* by Ishmael Reed. Reprinted by permission of Ishmael Reed and the University of Delaware Library: **p. 305;** Jacket of *Famous American Negro Poets,* by Charlemae Rollins. Copyright © 1965 by Charlemae Rollins. Reprinted by permission of The Putnam & Grosset Group: **p. 393;** Cover of *A Blues Book for Blue Black Magical Women,* by Sonia Sanchez. Copyright Sonia Sanchez. Reprinted by permission of Broadside Press: **p. 55;** Horst Tappe/ Archive Photos: **pp. 398, 427;** Photograph by Loretta J. Farmer: **p. 430;** Cover of *Cane,* by Jean Toomer. Copyright © 1923 by Boni & Liveright. Copyright © 1951 by Jean Toomer. Cover design by Tim Gaydos. Reprinted by permission of Liveright Publishing Corporation: **p. 80;** Reuters/Bettmann Newsphotos: **p. 455;** Cover of *The Color Purple,* by Alice Walker. Copyright Judith Kazdym Leeds. Reprinted by permission of Judith Kazdym Leeds: **p. 102;** Cover of *Our Nig; or, Sketches from the Life of a Free Black, in a Two-Story White House, North,* by Harriet E. Wilson. Copyright © 1983 by Random House, Inc. Reprinted by permission of Random House, Inc.: **p. 333;** Cover of *Malcolm X,* with the assistance of Alex Haley. Copyright © 1964 by Alex Haley and Malcolm X. Copyright © 1965 by Alex Haley and Betty Shabazz. Cover reprinted by permission of Grove Press, Inc.: **p. 25.**

Index

A

A. Philip Randolph:
  A Biographical Portrait 12
A. Philip Randolph: Integration
  in the Workplace 92, 486
Aaor ("Xenogenesis"
  Trilogy) 487
Aardvark-Watcher: Der
  Erdferkelforscher, The 230
Aaron, Hank 199
Aaron, Jimmy (The Autobiography
  of Miss Jane Pittman) 26
Abdulla (Petals of Blood) 341
Abeba Torch
  (Let the Lion Eat Straw) 259
Abeng 97
Abioseh (Les Blancs) 52
abolitionism 2, 34-5, 39, 40, 70-1,
  131-2, 136, 153-4, 163, 165-6,
  197, 219, 220, 238, 309-10, 345,
  348, 378-9, 418-9, 419-20,
  430-1, 440, 455-6
Abomunist Manifesto 243, 363-4
abortion 132, 455
Abortionist, The 22, 349
Abrahams, Peter 3, 297, 422, 458
Abram, Abram, Where Are We
  Going? 291
Absolutely Nothing to Get
  Alarmed About 3, 484
abuse 101-2, 108, 349, 482
Academy of American Poets 200

Academy Award 150, 369
Accra 216
acculturation 20-1, 355-6
Achebe, Chinua 3-4, 16-17, 19,
  116, 280, 321-2, 328, 441-2
Achille (Omeros) 330
acquired immunodeficiency
  syndrome (AIDS) 20, 106-7,
  124-5, 134, 202, 461-2
activism 12, 57-8, 147, 207,
  247-8, 464
Acts of Faith: Daily Meditations
  for People of Color 457-8
Adam by Adam: The Autobiography
  of Adam Clayton Powell Jr. 372
Adam in Blunderland 438
Adam Clayton Powell Jr. 191
Adam Johnson (Possessing
  the Secret of Joy) 370
Adam Miller (The Marrow
  of Tradition) 284
Adams, Henry (Runner Mack) 396
Adams, Jake (Corner Boy) 107
Address to the Negroes in the
  State of New York, An 4-5, 192
Adele Parker (Ceremonies in
  Dark Old Men) 192
Adenebi (A Dance
  of the Forests) 117-8
Adoff, Arnold 191-2
Adolescence and Poverty:
  Challenge for the 1990s 253
adultery 135, 431
Adulthood Rites 487

Advantage Ashe 20
adventure stories 487-8
Adventures of Aku, The 72, 452
Adventures in Black and
  White 404
Aeneid 14
affirmative action 43, 399, 408
Africa 6, 7, 18, 168, 176, 190,
  288, 355, 356, 362, 365-6, 458
Africa: Mother of "Western
  Civilization" 4, 6, 7
Africa Must Unite 320
Africa, My Africa 5, 75, 353
Africa in Search of Democracy 76
African American life and culture
  47, 211-2, 258, 342, 372-3,
  420-1, 444, 449-50, 477-8
African American history 41-2,
  53, 140-1, 167-8, 176, 182-3,
  191-2, 205-6, 211, 258, 264, 291,
  325, 331-2, 384, 394, 440, 483
African American identity 108-9,
  422, 436-7
African American studies 9, 173-4
African Caribbean movement
  358-9
African Civilizationism 5-6, 7
African Consciousness: Continuity
  and Change in Africa, The 76
African dance 319
African Fundamentalism 285
African heritage 5, 118-9, 168-9,
  328, 346-7, 364, 387, 414-5,
  475-6, 482

Index

M

X

Y

Z

Library of Congress Cataloging-in-Publication Data

The Schomburg Center Guide to black literature from the eighteenth century to the present / editor, Roger M. Valade III, with Denise Kasinec.
    p.   cm.
  Includes biographies of nearly 500 authors and synopses of nearly 500 works.
  Includes bibliographical references and indexes.
  ISBN 0-7876-0289-2
  1. Literature—Black authors—Bio-bibliography. 2. Authors, Black—Biography—Dictionary. 3. Blacks in literature--Bibliography. I. Valade, Roger M. III. II. Kasinec, Denise. III. Schomburg Center for Research in Black Culture. IV. Title.
Z1039.B56V36 1995
[PN841]
809'.8896—dc20
[B]   95-36733
                                                CIP